ENGRAVED BY A. B. WALTER PHILADA

HON. HENRY. A. WISE.
GOVERNOR OF VIRGINIA.

Henry A. Wise
of Virginia.

A BIOGRAPHICAL SKETCH

OF

HENRY A. WISE,

WITH A HISTORY

OF THE

POLITICAL CAMPAIGN IN VIRGINIA IN 1855.

TO WHICH IS ADDED

A REVIEW OF THE POSITION OF PARTIES IN THE UNION, AND A STATEMENT OF THE POLITICAL ISSUES: DISTINGUISHING THEM ON THE EVE OF THE PRESIDENTIAL CAMPAIGN OF **1856.**

BY JAMES P. HAMBLETON, M. D.

J. W. RANDOLPH,
121 MAIN STREET, RICHMOND, VA.
1856.

PRINTED BY JOHN NOWLAN.

TO THE

DEMOCRATIC PRESS OF VIRGINIA,

FOR ITS

POWERFUL INFLUENCE

IN THE

GUBERNATORIAL CAMPAIGN OF 1855,

THIS SKETCH

IS RESPECTFULLY DEDICATED

BY

THE AUTHOR.

PREFACE.

The Gubernatorial Campaign in Virginia, in 1855, will long be remembered as one of unprecedented excitement, of unusual bitterness, and of a character and caste unknown to her States Rights citizens. When all other States had faltered and wavered under the wily and Protean forms of Federalism, the true conservatives of all sections looked, and that not in vain, we are proud to say, to the "Mother of States and Statesmen," to bear aloft, untarnished and untainted, that flag of principles, the strict adherence and unfaltering devotion to which have alike made us the most powerful, the most happy, and the most respected among the States of the Union. The politics of Virginia in 1855, was never, in all her history, in a more critical and alarming condition. Assailed, as she was, on all sides and in all places, by emissaries, tricksters, and all manner of invisible influences, her situation at that time was one of inexplicable delicacy.

The people of Virginia knew their responsibility; and that their course in the contest then pending, would more or less govern the elections of the Southern States. With this knowledge, animated by their love of Democracy, they resolved to preserve the dignity and reputation of their State, and to rise in all their majesty and power, as terrible as an army with banners, and, headed by her noble and gifted son, who knew no defeat, to fight the great political battle, then to come off, of the nation.

It is of him we now offer to give the merest sketch, leaving the interim of his life, with the particulars of his antecedents, which would fill volumes, and his subsequent course, which will doubtless fill more, to be chronicled by one more skilled, more competent, and more practiced, than the subscriber.

James Pinkney Hambleton, M. D.

Pittsylvania C. H., December 1855.

BIOGRAPHICAL SKETCH.

THE BIRTH, PARENTAGE, AND ANCESTRY OF HENRY A. WISE.

Henry Alexander Wise was born December 3d, 1806, at Accomack court-house, called Drummondtown. The house in which his father lived at that time is now (1855) occupied as a tavern-house by William Waddy. His parents were John and Sarah. His father, John Wise, was the son of John Wise, a commissioned colonel of the king, and one of the earliest immigrants to the Eastern Shore of Virginia. He was a man of distinction and consideration in his day. He and his brother Tully, came from the North of England and purchased lands upon the Chesconessex and Deep creeks in Accomack. John Wise, the great grandfather of Henry A., bought 1000 acres of land, upon the Chesconessex, from the Indians, for seven Dutch blankets. Upon a farm of the old original *Dutch blanket tract*, called Clifton, lie the bones of most of the Wise family. After the death of Col. John Wise, this estate descended by primogeniture to John Wise, the father of Henry A., at his death was devised to his two eldest sons, George Douglass and John James Wise. George died unmarried and intestate—and John James took the whole of the manor tract; and his two sons, John James and George Douglass Wise, (nephews) of Henry A., now own it under the original grant. The mother of John Wise was Peggy Douglass, one of the daughters of George Douglass, a Scotch lawyer, who was the first immigrant of this family to this country. His Law books, the old English Reporters, and elementary works, such as a Natura Brevium of the first edition, Coke upon Littleton, printed in 1629—are still in the possession of Governor Wise.

The father of Governor Wise was married twice. His first wife was Mary (called Polly) Henry, daughter of Judge James Henry of Fleet's Bay in Northumberland county, Virginia. By her he had two sons, George Douglass and John James. By his second wife he had four children, William Washington, born in 1800, and died in 1813, Margaret D. P., Henry A., and John C. Wise who is now residing in

Princess Ann county, near Norfolk, and has seven children living, four boys and three girls.

The mother of Governor Wise was Sarah Corbin Cropper, the daughter of General John Cropper of Bowman's Folly in the county of Accomack, on the sea side. Her mother was Margaret, called Peggy, Pettitt. The Croppers were English, the Pettitts Scotch. This cross is called by some genealogists, the "*Bulldog with the Mange*," meaning the English for the *Bull*, and the *Mange* for a certain cutaneous eruption that was at one time common with the Scotch, called the "*Scotch Fiddle.*" Governor Wise's grandfather, Gen. John Cropper, was descended from John Cropper, one of the very earliest immigrants, who came with Sir Edmund Bowman from England and settled at Folly creek. The first John Cropper, the great, great, great grandfather of Governor Wise, was a carpenter by trade. He was familiarly known as the "Little Carpenter." The knight, Sir Edmund Bowman, had three daughters, one married Col. Eyre, one Col. Scarborough (called conjurer) the ancestor of the Hon. George P. Scarborough, the man who put the Broad Arrow of Virginia upon the doorposts of the Quakers near Cambridge, Maryland. The third, and youngest, married the "little carpenter" or John Cropper, against the wishes of the aristocratic Bowman family. After the death of Sir Edmund Bowman, the landed estate upon which he resided, called Bowman's Folly, descended through the "little carpenter" to Colonel John Cropper, from original grant, and remained in his possession until his death in 1821, when it fell into the hands of Thomas R. Joynes.

The life of Col. John Cropper was eminently eventful and patriotic. He was born to wealth, and at the age of eighteen married Peggy Pettitt. At nineteen he was commissioned Captain in the Matthews regiment in February 1776, and that year marched to the Northern campaigns, leaving his wife, 7 months *enciente* with Governor Wise's mother. He fought under Washington at Germantown, Princeton, Monmouth, Trenton, Chadsford, Brandywine, and every where until the war changed its scenes to the South. He returned, after an absence of two years, upon furlough, a Lieut. Col., commissioned upon the grounds of merit by General Marquis de La Fayette, the autograph of which is now in the possession of Governor Wise. On his arrival home, he saw, for the first time, his daughter, then about eighteen months old, whom they called Sarah Corbin Cropper, and who in after life married the father of Henry A. Wise. In 1779 Congress commissioned him full Lieut. Col. of the Virginia Line on Continental establishment. He was wounded in the thigh by a bayonet thrust at the battle of Brandywine, where he fought as Major, his Col. was killed and Lieut. Col. fled; and he brought the ninth Virginia regiment off the field, cut to pieces, under a *Bandanna handkerchief tied to a ramrod.* Afterwards General Knox met him at Chester bridge, when he sprung from his horse and exclaimed to Washington, "*The boy whom we thought lost is found.*" This won for him his spurs. When he returned to Bowman's Folly in the fall of 1778, it was with a furlough of 190 days. But whilst at home within three miles of Accomack court-house, he was aroused in the night by the tories. Kidd, with his "refugees," had landed in barges, surrounded the house and took him out of bed with his wife. They bored the muzzles of their pistols in his temples and denounced him as a d——d rebel, threatened his life, &c. Peggy Pettitt—his wife—of whom he always spoke as a "keen ground razor," procured for him a chance to escape, by stealthily raising the latch of the eastern door of the house, when with a powerful effort, he leaped the heads of the guards, two soldiers with crossed bayonets, and made his way to Thomas Bayly's, who had gone to his goose blind. But there he found a man by the name of William Lilliston, a soldier of the army, who had returned home with him. He and Lilliston procured three old Tower muskets, which they well loaded, and returned to his house. When they got in sight, the whole dwelling appeared illuminated. His wife, with her daughter Sarah Corbin, had been removed to a place of safety, whilst a train of powder was being laid to blow up the old family residence. Just at this critical moment Col. Cropper fired a gun and cried out "come on my brave boys." Lilliston dropped his gun and fled; but Col. Cropper still fired another and another, when the "refugees" took to their heels and their barges!!! Thus he saved his house from flames. When he examined it he found it robbed and riddled. They had broken open and sacked every piece of furniture in the house, smashed all the crockery, and carried off all of his jewelry and family relics, together with his mother's and father's watches. They also had bound and taken to their barges some thirty odd of his slaves. The next day he sent a flag of truce by Lilliston, demanding his property, especially his filial keepsakes, his father's and mother's trinkets. The reply he got was in substance thus: "The property whom you call slaves are liege subjects of his Majesty George the 3d, who don't desire to return to the bondage of a rebel subject. We have no other property of yours except a paper of pins of the manufacture of your d——d allies the French: in lieu of that we send you a paper of *pound pins* of good and liege manufacture, knowing as we do that your women have to go to the thorn-bushes to get the pins to tuck up their smocks." That was all Col. Cropper ever got, except a remarkable death caused by that very paper of *English pound pins.* Thus he was compelled to ask for an extension of his furlough. He rode all the way from Accomack to Valley Forge to get it. The diary of his trip is still in the possession of the family. The result was, his furlough was indefinitely extended, in consideration that he had served through the Northern campaigns, and was not drafted for the Southern under General Greene. He returned, but remained active in service. Governor Nelson commissioned him county Lieut. for Accomack, and as such, he had to bring the cannon out against the tories at Accomack court-house, and fought the battle of Henry's Point, where his life was saved by his body servant George Latchom. He took this command temporarily until he should be again called into the service. As county Lieut. he was in constant correspondence with Governor Nelson, and furnished the army at Yorktown with many supplies, particularly peach brandy, for which the Eastern Shore has long been noted. At last his struggles for independence ended, but not until the very last day of the Revolution. Kidd with his "refugees" had been scouring the whole coast of Maryland and Virginia. The States at that time had their separate fleets of barges. Commodore Barron was in command of the Virginia, and Commodore Whaley of the Maryland fleets. These fleets consisted of barges about eighty feet keel, carrying sixteen oars and a swivel, or gun upon the Long Tom principle, in the bow, upon the Chesapeake bay. Just such had Kidd. The Accomack and Northampton regiment had been cut up and taken prisoners at the battle of Germantown. Among them was Capt. Thomas Parker of Accomack, afterwards Col. Parker. He with Col. Levin Joynes were exchanged and came home. Commodore Whaley with his second Lieut. Levin Handy of Md. came to Accomack C. H. and told Cols. Cropper, Parker and Joynes, that Kidd was coming down the bay, outside of Tangier, with six barges, and that he had five in Watts' island or Pocomoke Sound, and that if he could get another barge from Virginia, he could meet and capture the enemy. Cols. Cropper, Parker and Joynes immediately volunteered and got seventy-five picked men to join them upon condition that Com. Whaley and his second Lieut. Handy was to command them. The condition was accepted, and the barge Victory was then lying in Onancock creek ready. She was hauled up and caulked, equipped and made out into the bay. Kidd and his six barges were in the northwest, about ten miles distant from the mouth of Onancock creek. Robert Handy, first Lieut. and brother of Levin Handy, was about the same distance in the north. Whaley made signal for the Maryland barges to join the Virginia barge Victory. Instead of doing so they turned and fled to the mouth of Pocomoke. This so chagrined Com. Whaley that he begged the Virginians to fight, but declined to command them to do so, as his own barges had so ingloriously fled. His volunteers cheered him into action, and one barge, the Victory, went up into action against six, gunwale to gunwale, and had made three strikes, when alas, her magazine took fire, blew up the barge and all overboard, dashing everything to atoms, and killing every man on board except Cols. Cropper, Parker, and a Scotchman by the name of Gibb. They were picked up out of the water as prisoners of war. Col. Cropper received a sabre cut on his head as he was taken into the barge of Kidd that well nigh cost him his life. Col. Cropper said the last he saw of the gallant Lieut. Handy (a few moments before the blow up) his right arm was hanging by a shred of flesh, and with his left hand he was throwing cold grapeshot at the enemy. This battle was fought the very day the definitive articles of peace were signed at Paris. Maryland has Col. Cropper's report of this bloody action, but has never told it to the world, as we have ever seen or heard of, although her Goldsborough wrote a history of Naval warfare. Her gallant Whaley, the hero of the fight, still lies upon the banks of the Onancock with not a stone to commemorate his patriotic ashes. This was decidedly one of the bloodiest engagements during the Revolution. The three prisoners were exchanged at Accomack C. H., and the friends were dressing the wound of Col. Cropper, when his wife appeared with her infant daughter, Margaret Bayly, (the mother of General Thomas H. Bayly,) sobbing, saying "you deserve it, a Continental army officer, to be leaving your wife and children to fight sailors on the water." Her sobs were hectic, and in pinning her child's dress with one of the *English pound pins* in her mouth, she inhaled it into her lungs and was killed. Washington gave Col. Cropper command of the fourteen lower counties, when about to raise the Provincial army, with a letter of compliment, which I suppose all the wealth of the Indies could not buy away from the pride of the family. He was President of the Cincinnati Society of Virginia, was in the State Senate, made and died a Brigadier General of the Eastern Shore regiment in the month of January 1821, aged 65 years. His mother was Sarah Corbin, the daughter of a Col.

Corbin of a numerous family in the Low Lands. Col. Cropper's first wife was Peggy Pettitt. By her he had two daughters, Sarah Corbin, the mother of Governor Wise, and Margaret Pettitt, the mother of the Hon. Thomas H. Bayly. His second wife was Catharine Bayley, daughter of Thomas Bayly of Accomack. She died in 1854. Her eldest son, Thomas Bayly Cropper, was for some time commander of one of largest San Francisco steamers.

THE POLITICS OF MR. WISE'S ANCESTORS—HIS EDUCATION, PROFESSION AND FIRST MARRIAGE.

The ancestors of Governor Wise on both sides were Virginia Federalists. His father was a man of sound practical mind, charitable and liberal. He acquired considerable fortune by his profession, the law. Prior to 1800 he was Speaker of the House of Delegates, and according to the recollection of Judge Stanard, was a supporter of the celebrated resolutions of '98 and '99. In the hasty arrangement of this sketch, we have not had the opportunity to examine the House Journal of that day. We are inclined to doubt the fact as to Mr. Speaker Wise's supporting those resolutions, because their passage created an epidemic in the ranks of the Federal party and its aliases, from which they have never recovered. At the time of the birth of Governor Wise his father was clerk of the courts of Accomack. He died in 1812.

After the death of Mr. Wise's father, in 1812, and his mother, in 1813, he was taken to Bowman's Folly, the old family seat of his ancestor, the knight, Sir Edmund Bowman. Soon thereafter he was sent to Accomack court-house, and for the first time put under the charge of an old friend of his father, a childless man with a good wife, John Y. Bundick, to commence his education. He was only suffered to remain with Mr. Bundick a very short time, when he was placed under the care of two paternal aunts, at Clifton, on the Chesconessex creek. His elder aunt, Mrs. Outen, taught him his letters and the Lord's prayer. He remained at Clifton two years, and was sent to Margaret academy. This school is said to have been wretchedly conducted. The boys that were sent there learned nothing but mischief, and to murder Greek and Latin. Consequently, the time he spent at Margaret academy was almost squandered. He was sent from there, in his sixteenth year, to Washington college, Pennsylvania. He reached there in 1822, and, with much difficulty, entered the Sophomore class. The college at that time was under the dominion of the Scotch Irish Presbyterians. Dr. Andrew Wylie was the President and the head and front of the institution. It is said he was a gentleman, a philosopher, a linguist, and a metaphysician—a blue stocking who loved gallantry and high game in his pupils. He was also a cavalier who loved virtue for virtue's sake, truth for truth's sake, and his fellow creatures for their own sake. At the time Mr. Wise commenced his collegiate course at Washington, Pennsylvania, there were two most excellent literary societies, the Union and the Washington. He joined the former. It was the custom with these literary societies to contest every spring with each other the palm of debating, of original oration, of essay writing, and of select oratory. In the spring of 1823 Mr. Wise had given such evidences at this early hour of his oratorical powers, that he was selected by his society as the champion to deliver the original oration. Mr. Tomlinson, about twenty years of age, from near Cumberland, Maryland, was the champion of the Washington. The orations were delivered and decided by the judges in favor of Henry A. Wise. Mr. Tomlinson declared from that time eternal hostility to all *beards;* for, said he, "it was the beard upon my face that caused a child to strip me of my honors." Mr. Wise was chosen orator by the Union society three times during his collegiate career, gaining the victory twice, and the third time bringing the judges down to a tie vote.

He graduated in 1825, a short time before he was nineteen; dividing the first honor with a young man by the name of Mitchell, from Maryland. William H. McGuffey (Professor of Moral Philosophy at the University of Virginia) would have taken the same honor without any opponent had he remained the session out. He was tried and suspended for thrashing a fellow student. Mr. Wise volunteered his defence before the faculty. He pleaded guilty. His young *attorney* justified his course, and came well nigh suffering the penalty of his *client.* The standing of Mr. McGuffey was such that the faculty gave him a diploma without examination. He left college before the commencement. This was the first case in which Mr. Wise appeared as a lawyer. How now stand these gentlemen of the same Alma Mater? One adorns the chair of Moral Philosophy in the greatest, best regulated, best conducted and most Republican University in the land; and the other presides over the Commonwealth of Virginia. Mr. Wise left college in 1825, returning through Canada and New York home. He commenced the study of law by reading

Blackstone, in the school of Henry St. George Tucker, in the winter of 1825-26. He remained with Judge Tucker until the fall of 1828, when he returned home and cast his maiden vote for General Andrew Jackson for President in the election of 1828.

In 1827, whilst Mr. Wise was at Winchester, he addressed his first wife, Miss Ann Eliza Jennings, daughter of the Rev. O. Jennings, D. D., of Washington College. He became enamored of this lady whilst at college, and never rested until the marriage rites were celebrated, on the 8th day of October 1828, in the city of Nashville, Tennessee, where her father had been called as pastor of the Presbyterian congregation of that place. Mr. Wise had made his arrangements previously to leaving Virginia to settle in Nashville, which he did. He soon formed a copartnership in the law with Thomas Duncan, Esq., who was soon afterwards accidentally killed in Louisiana. Mr. Wise had some cases in the Supreme Court of the State, and a respectable practice for a young man and a stranger. But still he sighed for the "milk of the ocean," his "own" native Virginia. To gratify his wife, he made every effort to be satisfied in Nashville. But despite all that he could do, he was unhappy outside his native State. There is something peculiar about Virginians in this respect. We rarely if ever find one, no matter how well he may be doing, satisfied for any length of time in any State but his own. Why it is, remains yet to be solved. Finally, to gratify this wish of his heart, he determined, with the consent of his wife, to return to Accomack: which he did in the fall of 1830. When he arrived home, the scenes of his boyhood exhilarated and enlivened a feeble frame which had almost fallen a prey to melancholy. The hallowed associations of youthful days were brought fresh to his recollection, and once more with buoyant spirits and a hopeful heart, he was ready to launch forth into the world to breast all storms, and to meet and grapple with every obstacle. As soon as the spring opened, he entered upon the duties of his profession. He found at the bar, as competitors, George P. Scarburg, Carter M. Braxton, P. P. Mayo, M. W. Fisher, and Vespasian Ellis, now editor of a paper at Washington City called the *Organ*, which professed at one time to be the mouth-piece of the late Know Nothing party, but now shows strong proclivities for being an ally of Horace Greeley. Mr. Wise's abilities and legal proficiencies soon brought him into command of an extensive and lucrative practice, which he continued to hold so long as his mind was drawn from political matters. His great forte as a lawyer is his great power before a jury. He has no superior as a criminal lawyer.

THE COMMENCEMENT OF MR. WISE'S POLITICAL LIFE. HIS FIRST ELECTION TO CONGRESS. DUEL WITH RICHARD COKE. REMOVAL OF THE DEPOSITS. CAPTAIN OF THE AWKWARD SQUAD.

There is no politician who ever lived, who has ever been half as much misrepresented as Henry A. Wise. Born, it is true, like a majority of our early distinguished men, of Federal parents, yet he, as early as 1824, when only eighteen years old, declared himself in favor of Wm. H. Crawford of Georgia, the States Right candidate for President. Owing to indisposition Mr. Crawford was withdrawn from the field, when Mr. Wise declared in favor of General Jackson, and would have voted for him had he been of age. In 1828, John Q. Adams, Henry Clay and General Jackson were candidates for the Presidency. He cast his maiden vote, as we have before mentioned, for General Jackson. He was sent from the York district in 1832 a delegate to the Baltimore National Democratic Convention. In that Convention he supported General Jackson in preference to any man, but when Martin Van Buren received the nomination for the Vice-Presidency, he arose and said, "Mr. President, in the vernacular of the negro's song, 'if I had had not come here, I would not have been here.' I will not not vote for your nominee for Vice-President, my vote shall be cast for Philip P. Barbour of Virginia for that office." Mr. Wise, with many others, voted for Jackson and Barbour. The electoral college of Alabama did the same thing.

In 1832 and '33 the mania of Nullification raged. Mr. Wise espoused the principle expressed in the celebrated resolutions of 1798-99, as reported by James Madison; "that each State for itself is the judge of the infraction and of the mode and manner of redress." Consequently he was opposed on the one hand to the Federal heresies of the Proclamation, Force bill, &c., and on the other hand to the remedies of South Carolina. His views in full upon this subject are set forth in his first address to the York district in 1833.

We will here introduce an extract of a letter, with the comments of Father Ritchie upon the position Mr. Wise occupied at that time.

Extract of a letter, from

"NORFOLK BOROUGH, March 21.

"I was at New Kent Court, this day week, where A. Stevenson delivered an excellent Speech, opposed by Mr. Robertson who also spoke; and from what I could see and hear, Mr. A. Stevenson's Speech was liked much the best. On Monday last I was at York Court, where I heard more speaking. Mr. Henry

A. Wise from Accomack spoke for three hours, and Mr. Richard Coke replied to him, until he gave out, which was until night. Some parts of Mr. W.'s Speech bore very hard upon Mr. Coke. Mr. W. in the first place asked Mr. C. if he was in favor of Nullification. Mr. C. replied in words to this effect; if a State was oppressed, she had a right to nullify. These might not be the exact words; but they amounted to this. Mr. W. then spoke of some letters which Mr. Coke had written to gentlemen on the Eastern Shore, giving them authority to contradict any report about his being a Nullifier—declaring that he was no Nullifier.—Mr. Wise asked, "If you are no Nullifier on the Eastern Shore, where they are opposed to it, and a Nullifier at home, where they are in favor of it, I do not know how you can be both." Mr. Coke then stopped Mr. Wise, and said that he spoke of private letters, and he should consider it as a personal affair, and should treat it as such. Mr. Wise said, "very well, Sir, I am ready for you in any way; but I insist upon it, that these letters were not private, inasmuch as you authorized these gentlemen to circulate what is contained in them; and no matter how disagreeable it is to you at this time, you must bear it." I thought they would have made a personal affair of it, but it turned out differently. Mr. W. also said how many copies of the "Jeffersonian and Virginia Times" had been franked and paid for, and sent to persons in that section who had never ordered it—Mr. W. is opposed to Nullification, and for Virginia State Rights, and in favor of the present Administration. He said he had understood that Mr. Ritchie had declared that he (Mr. R.) did not think he had written his Address—but Mr. W. said that was a small matter, and they could judge of that for themselves. He is a very clever man—about 27 years of age."

☞ Mr. Wise has been misinformed. We have never uttered the idea that he has attributed to us. We have not the pleasure of being personally acquainted with him—but every account that we have heard of him, from those in whose opinions we confide, is of the most favorable character. We understand that he possesses talents of a high order. His Address is a masterly refutation of many of the errors of the day—the doctrines of *Consolidation* as well as of *Nullification*. We had intended to lay copious extracts of it before our readers —but the *long talks* of the Orators at Washington have hitherto prevented it. We disagree with him in what he says of a Bank of the United States; though he does not seem to relish the present Bank. Mr. Wise has been bitterly assailed by the Nullifiers—but he is fully able to defend himself. He asks no quarter from them—and he will give none.—EDITORS.

Upon examination we find that Mr. Wise sustained the administration of General Jackson principally to preserve the Union at that time from the threatening attitude of South Carolina, but still condemned the course of General Jackson, thinking that other and milder means should have been used at that particular crisis. Mr. Wise was as much opposed to the cause that brought about Nullification as John C. Calhoun or any other citizen of South Carolina; but after a high protective bill had passed he thought as Mr. Calhoun did, that the bill was unconstitutional, and could be compromised before the ordinance of South Carolina was passed, as it was afterwards. In sustaining the

Proclamation, therefore, he was only supporting the executive of the nation, and nothing more.

In 1833, Mr. Richard Coke of Williamsburg, the former incumbent of the York district in Congress, was a candidate for re-election. Mr. Coke had represented that district as a Jackson Democrat; but after the appearance of the Proclamation, he turned to be a Nullifier. There was an appeal made from the Western Shore, for a candidate to oppose Mr. Coke on the part of the Jackson party from the Eastern Shore. Several gentlemen were solicited, amongst whom was Mr. Wise, and when all others had refused to accept the nomination, he consented to become a candidate, and announced himself as such at Northumberland court, the second Monday in January 1833. He immediately wrote the address which we have before referred to. This document we consider thoroughly States Right, and Democratic in every particular, with the exception of its sanction and advocacy of a United States Bank. Mr. Madison and the Republican party with Mr. Calhoun at their head, adopted a scheme of this sort soon after the war of 1812, not that they considered it constitutional, but because that party considered it expedient and as a matter of sheer necessity. Mr. Wise, from want of experience in legislation, contended that if a United States Bank was necessary and expedient it was constitutional. This opinion was readily and quickly changed after mature reflection. But to find a contrast of leading politicians of the land upon this much mooted question, we have only to cite the hostility of Henry Clay to a United States Bank at one period of his life, and at a later period being its chief advocate. The speech of Mr. Clay, made whilst opposed to the bank, could never be answered by him or its advocates at any time during the popularity of that great engine and vehicle of political corruption. Who is to be censured most, he that advocates a scheme that is thought to be beneficial and wholesome, but finding it unconstitutional and baneful, turns from it with loathing disgust; or he that supports it, knowing it to be by experience and by the laws of political economy the most dangerous, undermining, unconstitutional and corrupting of all measures either State or Federal? This proposition we consider a clear one; hence it can be easily decided who is the most censurable, Henry Clay or Henry A. Wise.

The contest between Mr. Wise and Mr. Coke was severe and acrimonious. The result was the election of Mr. Wise by four hundred majority and a duel with Mr. Coke. Mr. Wise accused him of great inconsistency, having represented the district four years as a Jackson Democrat, and as soon as Nullification turned up in 1833, denouncing Jackson and going off with Calhoun, and dating his hostility to the administration of the "Old Hero" as far back as the rupture in the cabinet in June 1831. This Mr. Wise considered the grossest inconsistency, when it was a notorious fact that Mr. Coke professed to be a warm supporter of the Jackson administration until the mania of Nullification arose. Upon this point Mr. Coke suffered, and justly, severely. He was so chagrined at his defeat that nothing would atone his grief but blood. Mr. Coke challenged, Mr. Wise accepted. They fought the 25th day of January 1835, over the Eastern branch of the Potomac, on the road leading across the Anacostia bridge, in Maryland, not far from Marlborough. Mr. John Whiting was the second of Mr. Coke, and Mr. John Wray the second of Mr. Wise; both seconds from Hampton, Virginia. Bailie Peyton, Eilbeck Mason and James Love of Kentucky, attended as the friends of Mr. Wise, and Dr. Hall of Washington City, as his surgeon. George Southall attended as the friend, and Dr. Byrd of Gloucester, as the surgeon of Mr. Coke. General Roger Jones of the army attended as the friend of both parties. At one o'clock P. M. they fired, Mr. Wise's ball fracturing the right arm of Mr. Coke, but fortunately not maiming him for life. Thus ended this affair of honor. Mr. Wise was elected to Congress in April 1833, and in the month of October of that year General Jackson removed the public deposits. This act of the executive was looked upon by many of both parties as high-handed and bordering on absolutism. It had the effect of driving from his side a number of his warmest admirers, Nullifiers and Anti-Nullifiers. And amongst these were John C. Calhoun and Henry A. Wise. The excitement following the removal of the deposits was tremendous, long continued, and of a most acrimonious nature. After much discussion and wrangling in the halls of Congress on the subject, seventeen Democrats of the House and several of the Senate filed out of the Jackson ranks. They were called the "Awkward Squad." This was because they could neither go with the administration upon the removal of the deposits, nor with the Federal opposition. This act of General Jackson, although attended at the time with a monetary depression, eventually proved to be one of the best and most judicious moves any public officer ever made.

RE-ELECTION TO CONGRESS IN 1835. REMINISCENCE OF THE DEATH OF JOHN RANDOLPH OF ROANOKE.

In the spring of 1835, Mr. Wise was again a candidate for Congress. He was opposed the second time by his former competitor Mr. Coke. Mr. Coke was only a candidate for a short time, abandoning the canvass at York, and forever afterwards voting at the polls for Mr. Wise.

Mr. Wise has been accused by his enemies of attempting to imitate the eccentric John Randolph of Roanoke. This is a false accusation. He never attempted to ape any pecularity or the eccentricities of any man. He is a man *sui generis*. Mr. Randolph, it is true, was elected to Congress in 1833, but died in the City of Philadelphia before the session opened. Mr. Wise never, in all his life, saw Virginia's distinguished orator and biting satirist. We hazard the assertion that an imitator of John Randolph, in the strict sense of the term, never did and never will exist. What Byron said of Sheridan, we think equally applicable to Mr. Randolph:

> "Sighing that Nature formed but one such man,
> And broke the die—in moulding Sheridan!"

There was one thing that happened to Mr. Randolph that also happened to Mr. Wise, when they took the oath as members of Congress. Mr. Randolph being, it is remembered, elected at the age of 24, had a very feminine and youthful appearance, so much so that the Speaker enquired of him whether he was of the constitutional age, that is, 25. The tart reply was "Ask my constituents, sir." John Y. Mason introduced Mr. Wise to Mr. Speaker Andrew Stevenson, when he enquired, "Where is Mr. Wise?" Mr. Wise then standing before him, whom he took to be one of the pages of the House. Mr. Mason whispered to the Speaker, and told him "that was the gentleman to whom he had just been introduced." The Speaker smiled, and presented the Bible with a pleasant remark about his youthful appearance.

In Mr. Wise's speech upon the removal of the deposits, he quoted a remark of Mr. Randolph, about the "*rara avis*," the "Black Swan," and alluded, episodically, to the fact, that his death had not been announced in that House, saying it was no fault of his. This called out, a few days afterwards, Mr. Randolph's successor, Judge Bouldin, who took the floor and commenced giving the reasons thus: "I will tell my colleague the reason why"—here his head went back, the veins in his temples became corded, his face for a moment was distorted, and he fell back a dead man! What is strange about this whole affair is, that the only allusion to the death of Mr. Randolph ever made in the House of Representatives, caused the death of him who filled his seat!!!

Presidential Campaign of 1836. Pet Bank system. Death of Mrs. Wise. Re-election to Congress in 1837.

The Presidential campaign of 1836, opened with party rancor and animosity, running mountain high. The National Republicans or Federalists, who had gone for John Q. Adams and his bill of abominations, and his light-houses in the skies, in 1828, formed one reserve that wished to elect a President. They held a Convention and nominated Gen. William Henry Harrison of Ohio, for President, and Francis Granger of N. Y. for the Vice Presidency. The regiment that had wheeled out of the Jackson line upon the issues of Nullification and the Removal of the Deposits, formed another reserve. These two reserves at first made an effort to blend themselves into one great party. They for the first time agreed upon a common name, that of "Whig," but still they could not agree upon a common ticket; consequently, the National Republicans, or Federalists, finding there was no chance for an amalgamation, nominated Harrison and Granger. The Nullifiers and those who had been opposed to the removal of the deposits, and had not confidence in the political honesty of General Jackson's "*favorite*," Martin Van Buren, nominated for President Hugh L. White of Tennessee, and John Tyler of Virginia, for Vice-President. The Jackson Democrats put forth for President Martin Van Buren of New York, and Col. Richard M. Johnson of Kentucky, for Vice-President. The unbounded popularity and influence of Gen. Jackson insured the election of his "*favorite.*" Van Buren and Johnson were easily elected. It seems that the leading Southern Democrats in 1836 would not have been as hostile to Mr. Van Buren as they were had they not distrusted him upon two questions that were of vital importance to the South. And those questions were the subject of slavery and the annexation of Texas. As it turned out, Messrs. White, Tyler, Calhoun, Poindexter, McDuffie and Wise were right in manifesting their distrust as to the unfitness and dishonesty of Mr. Van Buren. Although he showed no tangible signs of Abolitionism during his administration, yet he evidently retarded the annexation of Texas, and on his rejection by the people in 1840, he soon showed that he was hostile, and that in the most deadly shape, to the most cherished principles of Southern Democrats. Mr. Van Buren never would have been made President had he not deceived the "Old Hero" upon the Texas question. Gen. Jackson had the annexation of Texas in view as early as 1828; and his "*favorite*" had given him every assurance whilst Secretary of State and Vice-President, that he co-operated with him upon that favorite question. Mr. Van Buren kept the cloven foot of deception concealed from public demonstration until after his defeat. Then it was shown in all its frightful and hideous deformities; and with disastrous consequences to the Democratic party in 1848.

During the spring of 1837, before Mr. Wise reached home from Washington, his dwelling-house with nearly all of his valuable books and papers were consumed by fire. His family were removed to a friend's house in the village of Drummondtown, and that house, in a very mysterious manner, was set on fire also. This so affected the nervous system of his wife, that she never recovered from it, and died in the month of June following. She was the mother of seven children, but left only four living. Mary Elizabeth, wife of Dr. Alexander Y. P. Garnett of Washington City; Obadiah Jennings (the eldest son), who received the appointment of Secretary of Legation to Berlin during the administration of Mr. Pierce; Henry Alexander Wise, Jr., who, at the writing of this sketch, was attending the Theological Seminary at Alexandria, Virginia; and Ann Jennings Wise, the second daughter, is now with her father at Richmond, and who was an infant at the death of her mother.

In 1837 Mr. Wise was a candidate for re-election without opposition. He stood before his district as the advocate of the principles espoused by Hugh Lawson White and John Tyler. That is, opposed to the Pet Bank system, Benton's Sub-treasury, and the reference of Abolition petitions to special or any committee; and the fearless advocate for the annexation of Texas, a tariff for revenue only, &c.

THE GRAVES AND CILLEY DUEL.

Upon no subject has there been so much misunderstanding, misrepresentation, and wilful and unblushing falsehood as upon the unfortunate meeting between Messrs. Graves and Cilley. And upon no subject have there ever been such general excitement and deep-grounded prejudices aroused. It was the peculiar and unavoidable misfortune of Henry A. Wise to be connected with this sad affair. Not that he could not have avoided it, but not as an honorable man, in an honorable way, to an importunate friend. This subject has been a fruitful theme with the enemies and traducers of Mr. Wise, to arouse, excite and prejudice the popular mind. This effort of his foes has to some extent been successful with those who were ignorant of the particulars of this duel, its antecedents, &c. We have used every exertion to get possession of all the facts connected with the affair, which we now submit in as condensed a form as possible:

In 1837 political excitement was greater than was ever known in the Congress of the United States. The House of Representatives was composed of a number of able and fiery debaters, and the issues then before that body frequently brought the talent of the House in collision. The Hon. Jonathan Cilley of Maine took issue on one occasion, upon some subject, with James Watson Webb, editor of the *Courier and Enquirer*, of N. Y., and made what he considered a legitimate attack upon him. Mr. Webb took exceptions to the language used, and demanded satisfaction. He called upon the Hon. Wm. J. Graves, of Ky., to act as his friend. Mr. Graves, without the knowledge, counsel, advice, information, or suspicion of Mr. Wise, carried a letter from Mr. Webb to Mr. Cilley. The letter that was carried has never to this day been seen by Mr. Wise. Mr. Cilley declined to receive the letter, as Mr. Graves alleged, on the ground that he did not choose to be held accountable for words spoken in debate, and would not recognize Mr. Webb's right to call upon him for words spoken of and concerning him on the floor of the House. All this had happened at least a week before Mr. Wise knew a syllable of it. Finally Mr. Graves took exceptions to Mr. Cilley's not receiving the letter of Mr. Webb at his hands, and consulted with Mr. Clay upon that point several days before he mentioned the subject to Mr. Wise. When Mr. Graves came to Mr. Wise for the first time for advice, he said to Mr. Wise that his only anxiety was to do his full duty to his *principal*, and nothing more. Mr. Wise then advised him that Mr. Cilley's ground was perfectly tenable, and could not be excepted to, as he did not choose to be held accountable for a constitutional privilege—for words spoken in debate—because he did not consider that he had assailed the character of James Watson Webb as a gentleman. This explanation satisfied Mr. Graves in that respect; but he said Mr. Cilley had expressed his grounds to him verbally, and then refused to commit them to writing in the *form* which he had inferred from the first interview with him. Mr. Wise then advised Mr. Graves to address Mr. Cilley respectfully, in writing, and request of him to say upon what ground it was he then declined to accept the note at his hands from James Watson Webb. This Mr. Graves did, but not through Mr. Wise. Mr. Cilley's answer was unsatisfactory in this: that it did not admit what Mr. Graves had stated to have passed verbally between them in their first interview. This raised a question, seemingly, of veracity. But still Mr. Wise advised Mr. Graves not to go farther than to demand whether Mr. Cilley meant to assail his statement as untrue. Mr. Graves then saw Mr. Clay as his chief adviser, and after some day or two of delay, came back to Mr. Wise to take his challenge to Mr. Cilley. Mr. Wise declined to do so, and begged him to sleep upon it at least for one night. The next morning he went to Mr. Wise's room, and again urged him to bear Mr. Cilley his challenge. Mr. Wise then discussed the matter, and told him he saw no reason or ground for a challenge save that of a question of *veracity:* that if he called upon that ground, he was sure Mr. Cilley would disclaim all impeachment of his veracity, and there would be an end to the whole affair. And in doing this, Mr. Cilley was still not bound to disclaim imputation upon the character of James Watson Webb:—he could plead his privilege only, without affirming or disclaiming anything as to him. He then, at the instance of Mr. Wise, drew up his challenge, placing it expressly on the ground that Mr. Cilley had assailed his statement as to what occurred when he first carried Webb's note. Mr. Wise again refused to be the bearer of the challenge. Mr. Graves then urged him to go with him to Mr. Clay's room. They went, and submitted each their respective differences of opinion, when Mr. Clay took the challenge which Mr. Graves had written, and pronounced it to be improper, because he had based his call upon the wrong ground—that of veracity. Mr. Clay said that there was but one issue in the case, and that was, that Mr. Cilley had declined to receive Mr. James Watson Webb's note at the hands of Mr. Graves; and unless Mr. Cilley would disclaim imputation upon Mr. Webb as a gentleman, that he, Graves, was bound by the code of honor to step into Webb's shoes, and to challenge directly for that cause. Mr. Clay then threw the challenge aside, as written by Mr. Graves, and drew the form of one, which was afterwards taken by Mr. Cilley, with his own hand and pen. Mr. Graves then copied it again, and proposed to Mr. Wise to be the bearer. He declined again, on the ground that he did not approve the form in which the challenge was written; and, moreover, as the challenge then stood, it was upon a point of punctillio which never could be adjusted in any case without blood.

By this period of the interview, Mr. Menefee of Kentucky had come in, and sided with Mr. Clay against Mr. Wise. Mr. Wise still declined to bear the challenge. Mr. Graves appealed to Messrs. Clay and Menefee to bear witness that on one occasion, in the absence of Mr. Wise from the House of Representatives, he had, without asking the right or the wrong of Mr. Wise's controversy, taken up his personal quarrel, and was ready to fight for him,—that he had more confidence in him than any one else, as his friend, on the ground; and that if he (Wise) suffered him to go upon the field without guarding his life and his honor, and he was brought back a corpse, he desired his wife, his children and his friends to know that he (Wise) had failed to stand by him after he knew he was determined to fight, whether he (Wise) went to the ground with him or not. Is there an honest, courageous and chivalrous heart that beats in the breast of man that could have withstood such an appeal, coming as it did, under such circumstances, and at that particular time?

After this appeal had been made by Mr. Graves, Mr. Wise told him that if nothing else would do him but to fight, and that against his advice, he would consent to guard his life and his honor. Mr. Wise then carried the challenge to Mr. Cilley, copied by Mr. Graves from Mr. Clay's manuscript. Mr. Wise then resolved in his own mind to prevent, if possible, the hostile meeting. After nightfall, General George W. Jones brought an acceptance, and the terms proposed—eighty yards, with rifles. Mr. Wise demurred. Mr. Clay instantly exclaimed: "No Kentuckian can back out from a rifle." Mr. Wise's object still being that of delay, he met Gen. Jones, the next morning and said he must have time to go to Philadelphia for a rifle, as he did not know where else to get one that was reliable. Mr. Jones replied: "Certainly, sir, there must be a gun which can be relied on in the whole District of Columbia!" At this answer Mr. Wise was somewhat vexed, and replied, "if you know of one, sir, I would be glad if you would furnish me with it." Thereupon, the next morning, a rifle, powder flask, bullet moulds, &c., were found upon Mr. Wise's table, with a polite note tendering the rifle, &c., to Mr. Graves. This was no doubt done *bona fide* upon the part of Gen. Jones, but it certainly had the bad effect of hastening the duel. This doubtless would not have happened had General Jones understood the object which Mr. Wise had in view—that of delay. The arrangements being thus far made, there was no time for parleying. Mr. Graves went out the morning previous to the meeting to practice with the rifle. He proved himself to be a very bad shot at a mark. His hand was so huge and clumsy, his fingers so course, that he could not "*taste*" a hair trigger. He would invariably fire before the word was given, and could not hit a barn door at eighty yards. By this time Mr. Wise had procured a fine, large rifle from Mr. John C. Rives of the *Globe*, and filled it with vinegar the night before the duel, for the purpose of cleansing it of rust; and by the appointed time Mr. Wise had Mr. Graves ready and upon the field. He was accompanied by Henry A Wise as his armed second, aided by Hon. John J. Crittenden and Hon. Richard H. Menefee, of Kentucky. Mr. Cilley was accompanied by Hon. George W. Jones, as his armed second, aided by Mr. Schaumburg and Mr. Bynum, and by Dr. Duncan, as surgeon. Before these gentlemen went out, propositions of adjustment were written for the guide of Mr. Graves' second, in case an adjustment should be proposed. Mr. Graves won the position, Mr. Cilley the word. Mr. Graves' second selected the west, because the wind was setting from the northwest, from a knowledge of the fact that Mr. Cilley was a crack shot, thinking that he would not make an allowance for the wind against his ball, the variation of which, from the effects of the wind in the distance of eighty yards, would be six inches. This arrangement, and nothing else, saved the life of Mr. Graves. Mr. Cilley stood east; Mr. Graves west. They fired at one o'clock, P. M., nearly across the rays of the sun; Mr. Graves' face in the light, Mr. Cilley's in the shade. Mr. Graves was ordered not to fire until he had good sight, and at the word "three." At the first fire Mr. Graves obeyed orders coolly, but clearly missed his aim. Mr. Cilley's ball struck the ground about forty yards from the place in which he stood. The loss of his fire evidently made him anxious for another exchange of shots. A second shot being determined on, Mr. Menefee placed the rifle in the hands of Mr. Graves, and upbraided him for being so slow. All being ready, and the combatants appearing cool and collected, at the word "fire," the rifle of Mr. Graves went off, his ball striking the ground about ten paces from his feet. Mr. Cilley raised deliberately and shot with dead aim at about two and a half count. All eyes were then turned to Mr. Graves, who dropped the breach of his rifle as his second ran up to him, thinking he was certainly hit; but it turned out that he had only been pulling at the trigger, when he very calmly blew into the muzzle, exclaiming: "Why, the gun is off." He did not think he had fired. This mortified him. Then came his time for demanding a *third* fire, for the same cause that induced Mr. Cilley to desire a *second* shot. Mr. Graves demanded, and would have a third *fire*. Had Mr. Graves' coat been unbuttoned, the second ball of Mr. Cilley's rifle would have passed through the lapel of his coat. This conclusion was arrived at from the position in which Mr. G. stood and where the ball struck the fence behind him.

As to the propositions of settlement, they were never made, except to enquire what was then to be done. Mr. Cilley yielded nothing; and there was still cause for the duel unmoved, unexplained, unadjusted, and a point of punctillio which can never be explained. Mr. Cilley was obliged to demand a second and Mr. Graves a third fire. Being ready for the fire, they both appeared cool and collected, and there was never a fairer exchange of shots. Mr. Cilley fired a little first, and in one fourth of a second received his mortal wound in front of the left hip, the ball passing entirely through him, severing, no doubt, the aorta. "His rifle fell out of his hands, he beckoned to his second, and died in a few moments, without a struggle or apparently a pang."

After the death of the unfortunate Cilley, the public mind was so excited and indignant by the innumerable falsehoods and slanders emanating from the misinformed, and the enemies of those who were engaged at one time in an attempt at reconciliation and adjustment, that the House of Representatives appointed a committee of investigation, the report of which now stands as a public record. When the committee sat, one of the objects was to throw the *onus* of the whole affair upon Mr. Wise. Mr. Clay heard of the intentions of the committee—told Mr. Wise to tell them to call upon him—that although he had shed tears over the "nine days bubble," yet he was cognizant of all the connected facts, and would take great pleasure, at all times, in setting the misrepresented in their true position.

Mr. James Watson Webb, in 1842, alleged, in the *Courier and Enquirer*, that Mr. Wise had instigated the duel. Such a charge was totally unfounded, unjust and cowardly, from the fact that anything of the sort should emanate from a man like Mr. Webb, who was directly and knowingly connected with the whole affair. Soon after this slanderous and malicious allegation appeared in the *Courier and*

Enquirer, Mr. Wise published the facts of the case in the *Madisonian.* Mr. Clay, finding that explanation might injure him for the Presidency in 1844, or some future time, wrote to Mr. Graves, and got him to say that he (Clay) had no part whatsoever in the advice, counsel, or preparation of the duel. Mr. Clay published that letter in the *National Intelligencer* as true. Whereupon Mr. Wise wrote to him categorical questions, which he placed in the hands of Dr. Linn, of Missouri. Mr. Clay replied, and admitted his whole part in the affair, and generally justified Mr. Wise as well as himself. For this act of injustice, Mr. Wise could never (nor justly) forgive Mr. Clay. How unjust and unkind is it to accuse innocent men of being the instigators of that which is at all times exceedingly offensive to the masses!

Mr. Wise used all possible and honorable means to prevent a hostile meeting between these gentlemen; and never did he consent to accompany Mr. Graves until he told him that he was determined to go upon the field, whether Mr. Wise accompanied him or not.

Mr. Wise once put a challenge into the hands of Hon. S. S. Prentiss, of Mississippi, for Hon. Mr. Gholson, of the same State; but Mr. Prentiss refused to carry it because he said the *onus* was upon Mr. Gholson and not upon Mr. Wise.

Mr. Wise also challenged Hon. Thos. H. Bayly of Acomack, but he refused to accept, upon what grounds we have never heard.

Re-election to Congress in 1839. Presidential Campaign in 1840. Second marriage.

In 1839 Mr. Clay, no doubt, was more anxious to receive the nomination for the Presdency than he was ever before or afterwards. And to make the chances of his nomination more certain, and his election a fixed fact, it was necessary in the opinion of himself and friends, to procure the support and influence of that portion of the Democratic party that had favored the election, in 1836, of Hugh L. White and John Tyler. For this purpose to be secured, Judge White had to be consulted. Mr. Wise being a bosom friend of Judge White, Mr. Clay got him to make the requisite enquiries. In reply to the enquiry whether or not he had any aspirations for the Presidency? he said he had none, and should not have allowed his name to have been placed in that situation in 1836, had it not been to assert his political and personal independence. As for supporting Mr. Van Buren, whom he considered unsound *in toto* upon the questions of Slavery and Texas, he could not think of such a thing. As for Mr. Clay, he held him in the highest personal consideration, but politically, as he understood his policy, they were diametrically opposed to each other, upon the five great cardinal principles that divided the Federal and Republican parties. He could not support Mr. Clay or any other man who advocated a U. States Bank, Protective Tariff, Internal Improvement by the General Government, Distribution, and the right of Congress to abolish slavery in the District of Columbia and the Territories. Mr. Clay authorized Mr. Wise to say to Judge White that he stood thus upon these five cardinal issues:

1. Bank. "He said he had not changed his opinions since 1816. That he had avowed some change in respect to the constitutionality of that measure, which he had always regretted. That he was sorry he had not adhered to the grounds that he had first taken upon that subject. But then, though he believed in the constitutional power of Congress to incorporate a Bank for Treasury purposes, yet such was the force of circumstances and events, existing then in 1839, he was compelled to conclude that a re-charter for many years would be impolitic, unsafe, and inexpedient. It would never be safe to re-charter a U. States Bank whilst there was a popular minority even opposed to its institution. The friends of such an incorporation were bound to await the arbitrament of enlightened public opinion."—"And that he would never again recommend a re-charter of the U. States Bank, unless it should be called for by the popular voice, approaching such unanimity as would increase general confidence and safety."

2. On the Tariff he prided himself as being "its Pacificator, in being the author of the Tariff Compromise of 1832. He considered that the North had obtained its consideration in the first five years of the act, and that it would now be bad faith to deprive the South of the benefits it had bargained for in reduction and in equalization of duties upon protected and unprotected articles alike." He emphatically pledged himself *not* to disturb his own compromise, but to allow it a full and fair operation.

3. Upon Internal Improvements, he said, "the great design of his '*American*' system, as it had been called, was to stimulate the States to enterprises of improvement: that he had never thought that these works could be accomplished as economically and as faithfully by the General Government as by the States, and by private companies and individuals acting under State authority. That he had effectually at-

tained his end. By the appropriations to works, and to surveys already then made, the States had been stimulated to intoxication. That they had run into an enormous debt of 200 millions. He would rather then assuage the fever, and would arrest all farther stimulus until the State debts were paid."

4. Upon the subject of Distribution of the Proceeds of the Public Lands, he said, "He never proposed a distribution of the proceeds, except when there was a large surplus in the treasury. That by his bill in 1832, he had limited the operation to such a time, only five years, as would exhaust the *surplus*. As long as the revenue was required for the payment of the public debt, or for any proper object of expenditure, he would never propose a distribution amongst the States. There was then, 1839, a debt of about forty millions, and likely to be a deficiency of revenue unless the tariff was raised, which could not be done without violating his compromise. It was morally certain, then, that if he was *nominated* and *elected*, there would be no surplus during his term. He would not distribute a deficiency at all."

5. On the subject of Slavery, he admitted that he had advocated the opinion that Congress had power to abolish slavery in the District of Columbia and in the Territories; but further remarked, that he had openly avowed since that time, in the Senate, that he regarded the exercise of that power by Congress, without the consent of the States of Virginia and Maryland, inexpedient and dangerous, and that he would resist the wrong with arms; that he would resist the exercise of the power, as if the power was unconstitutional.

Thus we find Mr. Clay in 1839, although on constitutional grounds opposed to the Democratic party upon every cardinal issue, yet pledging himself to be practically with that party. These pledges being given by Mr. Clay through Mr. Wise to Judge White and his friends, they immediately advocated his nomination in preference to that of Mr. Van Buren. But before the pledges were made, Judge White predicted that Mr. Clay would be shelved by the influence of Mr. Webster, and his influence by what was called the "Triangular Correspondence." This name was given to a correspondence that had sprung up in Rochester, Utica and New York for the purpose of throwing a damper upon the claims of Mr. Clay previous to the meeting of the National Whig Convention at Harrisburg. Judge White was right in his predictions. The name of General Scott was used to defeat Mr. Clay through the Webster influence; William H. Harrison and John Tyler receiving the nomination. But before the Harrisburg Convention met, and after Mr. Clay had made his Anti-Whig pledges to Judge White, he prepared an elaborate speech, the notes of which he showed to Mr. Wise previous to going to the Taylorsville dinner. Mr. Clay delivered this speech with great force, beauty of style, and with the happiest effect. Mr. Wise was invited with Mr. Clay to attend the Taylorsville festival, but it so happened he could not go, but wrote thus to the committee of invitation: That "the Presidency could not add one cubit to his statue, and I wish all the world could be there to hear him." Mr. Wise wrote thus, and wished thus, because he knew what Mr. Clay would say, as he had just made the foregoing pledges and shown him the prepared notes from which he would speak. The policy which he promised to carry out, should he be made President, was, beyond question, practically Democratic. Moreover, there was a desire to get Mr. Clay back into the ranks from which the "Puritan" had enticed him, and with his powerful arm to strike *Nationalism* or Whiggery a crushing blow. This intention was certainly laudable, righteous and patriotic. When the Nationals or Whigs met in Convention at Harrisburg, Pennsylvania, having largely the majority over the anti Van Buren Democrats, they claimed the privilege of placing on the head of their ticket General Harrison. And as John Tyler had been upon the ticket with Judge White in 1836, the anti Van Buren Democrats, knowing that the Senate of the United States was nearly divided upon many issues of momentous importance, claimed the right to nominate a man who, by his casting vote in the Senate, would guard and protect the principles of the States Right party. Consequenty Mr. Tyler was placed upon the ticket for the Vice-Presidency by the anti Van Buren or States Rights Democrats. They could safely do this because the Nationals or Whigs were pledged by their greatest leader, Henry Clay, *against* Bank, Tariff, Internal Improvement, Distribution, Abolition of slavery in the District of Columbia and the Territories by the power of Congress, &c. When the Nationals or Whigs assented that Mr. Tyler should be placed on the ticket for the Vice-Presidency, with General Harrison, it was considered a sure guarantee of the pledges made by Mr. Clay. Mr. Tyler received the nomination as a sort of compromise, independently of Mr. Clay's pledges, through the instrumentality of Mr. Wise. Yet this compromise was not effected without some difficulty by the anti Van Buren Democrats who distrusted the Nationals or Whigs from a knowledge of their antecedents, notwithstanding their pledges. This was arranged by Mr. Wise, very adroitly and justly. William C. Rives had *expunged* Mr. Tyler from the United States Senate, and in turn had become a Conservative late in the day upon the Specie Circular, and appealed to the opposition votes in the Virginia Legislature to send him back to the Senate. The question then arose before that body, "Shall the *victim* or the *instrument* of expunging be sent to the Senate?" But what was strange about the affair was, that Mr. Clay and his friends, favored the return of Mr. Rives to the Senate. At that time Mr. Wise had a few friends in the Virginia Legislature, at the head of whom was John M. Gregory now of Richmond. These friends held the balance of power in that body at that time. The day for an election of United States Senator finally came off, when the ballotings comparatively were almost as numerous as they were for Speaker at the meeting of the 34th Congress, when Richardson, Banks and Fuller were candidates—and for some time with the same effect. The Legislature refusing to elect Mr. Rives, caucuses were held at Washington City and emissaries sent to Richmond; but still no election could be had. Finally it was found out that Mr. Wise and his friends checked their operations, and then an effort was made to bully *him* into subjection and party influence, but to no purpose. The party at Washington then arraigned Mr. Wise in *caucus*, when he defended his position by telling them that "he never intended as long as it was in his power to prevent it, that the *instrument* of expunction should be placed over its *victim* by Whig or anti expunging votes." At last Mr. Wise suggested a compromise; and it was, that his friends would allow Mr. Rives to be elected, if Mr. Clay and his friends would allow Mr. Tyler to be placed on the ticket with General Harrison, to preside over Mr. Rives, and by his casting vote guard the cherished principles of the States Rights Democracy. This proposition was readily assented to, but unavoidably by the Whig party. And but for Mr. Tyler being placed upon the Whig ticket in 1840, Mr. Wise would have remained neutral in that contest. He never would have voted for Harrison and Granger regardless of the pledges of Mr. Clay. He was from the beginning a Tyler advocate, knowing that Mr. Tyler was an undeviating and unflinching defender of States Rights. It was understood that if Mr. Rives was elected to the Senate, that Mr. Tyler should be the nominee for Vice-President. These facts will certainly show to the world that the election of John Tyler to the Presidency, was the overthrow of the United States Bank and many other odious Federal favorites; and will account for Mr. Wise's being the main stay and bulwark of the Tyler administration, which will compare in point of ability to any, Jas. K. Polk's not excepted. Mr. Wise was actuated in the course he took in 1840, through the most strictly Southern Rights conception of the Constitution. And through Mr. Wise, as we have before stated, John Tyler saved the country from Van Burenism, which, like Know Nothingism, is but another name for Abolitionism, or the essence and quintessence of all that is rotten, corrupt and loathsome.

On the 4th of July 1840, Mr. Wise was in the city of Philadelphia, and uttered that sentiment which became so general a watchword of influence, "The Union of the Whigs for the sake of the Union." This was a piece of pure philosophy, as well as a watchword of party. It recommended a union of the Whigs, or those who stood upon the pledges that Mr. Clay had given to Judge White through Mr. Wise, with the National Republican Whigs, *not for themselves* but for the Union. This expression, in fact, was a hint to the Nationals or Whigs, that they were to respect and sustain the principles of the Democratic party. That they were not to use their party for a selfish policy, but to unite with the Democracy to protect the country against the party of Martin Van Buren. The convictions arrived at by Mr. Wise, and that portion of the Democratic party which acted with him, were as true as prophecies, and by his almost superhuman exertions in placing John Tyler upon the Harrisburg ticket, he saved Texas and the Union, and placed the country and the Democratic party in an attitude that insured their success brilliant under the banner of Polk and Dallas in 1844.

In November 1840, Mr. Wise married his second wife, Miss Sarah, third daughter of the Hon. John Sergeant of Philadelphia.

Extra Session of Congress, 1841. Rejection for the Mission to France. Re-election to Congress. Elected Minister to Rio Janeiro. Returns Home in 1847.

The last session of Congress that met under Van Buren was in 1840 and '41. In the spring of 1841 Mr. Wise met with Mr. Clay and Thomas W. Gilmer soon after the election, and was congratulating himself to Mr. Clay thus: Well, sir, said he, "We have fought a good fight in Virginia, sir, and although we did not exactly win the victory, we came off with the honors of war." Mr. Clay replied: "I congratulate myself, sir, that Virginia has gone for the enemy." Why, said

Mr. Wise, "I thought you once said, you would prefer defeat with your mother State for you, to victory with her voice against you." "Sir," said Mr. Clay, "we will no longer be embarrassed by her peculiar opinions." This was the language and sentiment of that great, adroit, astute and disappointed politician Henry Clay. Mr. Clay's interpretation of the whole matter was this: as he had not received the nomination for the Presidency over General Harrison at the Harrisburg Convention, he no longer considered himself bound by his pledges to Judge White. The question now arises, would he have abided those pledges had he been made President? What does the philosophic politician say? For ourselves we shall not hazard an opinion of the man of whom John C. Breckenridge said, "His countrymen had wove for him a laurel wreath, and with common hands had placed it upon his venerable brow and sent him crowned to history." The first thing that was done after the Log Cabin triumph in 1840, was to call an extra session of Congress—so anxious were the successful party to commence the war of extermination, and disvow every pledge to which they had sworn eternal fidelity, and promised a sacred allegiance. Very soon after Mr. Wise reached Washington in the spring of 1841, he saw that it was evidently the intention of the victors, under the leadership of Mr. Clay, to call an extra session. To make all necessary arrangements for this purpose, they assembled in caucus, and gave evident signs by what policy they were dictated and influenced. Mr. Wise not only opposed the extra session, which was gotten up to snatch a bank charter from the arbitrament of enlightened public opinion, which was not be waited for, but to pass harbor and river improvement bills; to distribute a *deficiency* in the Treasury; to revise and increase the Tariff; to violate the Compromise of 1832; to give new life to Protection; and to agitate a Slavery issue; but he opposed the whole Federal scheme from beginning to end, in a speech delivered in the House of Representatives in the month of January previous to the inauguration of General Harrison, and at a time when the Whig party had just swept nearly every State in the Union.

Immediately after the death of President Harrison, Mr. Wise was the first man that rushed to the side of President Tyler and advised him by all means to veto the United States Bank bill, and use every effort to procure the speedy annexation of Texas. Mr. Tyler was denounced as a traitor by a party themselves false and faithless to the most sacred pledges.

Mr. Tyler's political career, which has been eminently States Right and Conservative, stands now upon the public records of the nation for the judgment of posterity.

In 1842 Mr. Wise's name was sent to the United States Senate, through the instrumentality of his friend, Bailie Peyton, for the mission to France. A Whig Senate rejected him. In the spring of 1843 he was a candidate for re-election. Mr. Hill Carter of Shirley, was his opponent, who was induced to run by a Whig clique in the city of Richmond; but although the district had just given Harrison and Tyler 1600 majority, they sustained Mr. Wise against a Whig Senate and triumphantly returned him to Congress by his old majority, 400. On Mr. Wise's return to Congress it was discovered that his physical health was giving away rapidly from the constant excitement of about ten years. Consequently his friends sent his name again to the Senate for the Court of Rio Janeiro. The same influence that had defeated him for the French mission was about to be brought against his name again, with the additional offence he had committed in denouncing the great leader of the Whig party, Henry Clay, in his then recent canvass with Mr. Hill Carter. But before any decision was made in his case, William S. Archer, Senator from Virginia, sought an interview with Mr. Wise, and asked him, why was it he had been so bitter in his late canvass against the apostle of Whiggery, Henry Clay? Mr. Wise then enquired of him "if the French mission, the Brazilian mission and all the rest of the missions belonged to Mr. Clay? And was subserviency to him a necessary qualification for office? Were personal differences, and not public considerations, to govern in selecting foreign ministers? That it was the office of a Senator to enquire, not whether the nomination is fit, is he faithful to the country, but is he a friend of a political favorite who was not in power? In conclusion, he informed Mr. Archer to go back to his friends and tell them that if they would act like men worthy to be called friends of their idol, they would resent his insults, and would do so in their proper persons, and would not do it by abusing their public offices."

Mr. Archer made no report to the caucus, but demanded that Mr. Wise should be sent to Rio Janeiro, which was done.

On the 8th day of February 1844, he resigned his seat in Congress, and sailed from New York for Rio in the month of May following his resignation. His course in Brazil met with the entire approbation of Presidents Tyler and Polk, and their Secretaries of State, Calhoun and Buchanan. He returned home in October 1847.

Retires to private life. State Elector for the State in 1848. Election to the State Convention. Death of his second wife. Elector again for the State in 1852. Third marriage. Personal appearance. Conclusion.

After Mr. Wise returned from Brazil he retired to private life, intending to resume his profession, having been in public life from 1833 to 1847. But the campaign between Cass and Taylor coming on, he was called by the Democratic party of the State to act as one of the electors at large. He immediately buckled on his armor and went boldly to work. In 1850 he was elected to the State Convention which revised the Constitution. His course there is recently known.

During the session of the Convention he received intelligence of the death of his second wife. She was the mother of seven children, leaving at her death only four living; Richard Alsop, Ellen, John Sergeant, and Spencer Wise.

In the month of November 1853, Mr. Wise was married the third time, to Miss Mary Elizabeth Lyons of the city of Richmond, sister of Mr. James Lyons, a distinguished lawyer of that place.

We shall see, in future pages of this volume, under what circumstances and in what manner, he was elected in May 1855, by the people, Governor of the Commonwealth of Virginia for four years, commencing January the 1st, 1856.

Mr. Wise is five feet eleven inches high; his average weight is 130 pounds; he is remarkably lean; was originally fair skinned, but is now swarthy; his hair is a light auburn, and was, when young, almost flaxen, which he generally wears long, and behind his ears; his head is large, with great depth between the temples; his forehead is low, but broad; his eyes large, gray and deep set, arched by a heavy and remarkably expressive brow, which by turns shows all the workings of the inner man; his nose is large and prominent, and is what might be termed a *Virginia nose;* his mouth is capacious; his lips rather thick; his jaws lank and florid; chin broad and prominent, with furrough from the centre downwards; he was originally very strait and active, but begins to stoop a little. Upon the whole he is not a handsome man, but one that will in any assemblage impress the beholder with his manly and defiant features. He is an excessive chewer of tobacco, but never smokes, and rarely drinks anything of an alcoholic character. Mr. Wise is remarkably abstemious and regular in all his habits except chewing tobacco.

Thus we have sketched, in as succinct a manner as possible, the life of one of the most illustrious men ever reared in this commonwealth. Mr. Wise combines qualities that eminently befit him to steer the helm of State through troubled times, especially through this threatening crisis. Thoroughly acquainted and largly experienced in the machinery of government, possessing wide and comprehensive views of the requirements of the nation, firm, decided and inflexible, the fearless tribune of the people, he is competent to the highest duties of State. His course, and triumphant defence of the Democratic faith in the late gubernatorial campaign in this State, entitle him to the highest consisideration and lasting endearment of all who love and wish to perpetuate the Union of the States.

Jefferson has made his memory immortal as the author of the Declaration of Independence and Religious Toleration; Mason as the author of the Bill of Rights; Jackson by severing Bank and Government; and Henry A. Wise by "crushing out," from all law-abiding States, that most detestable, insidious, loathsome, Protean-like, baneful, and contemptible of all isms—Know Nothingism. He is the great benefactor of the people of the nineteenth century. Long may he live to enjoy with his fellow citizens the fruits of his labours. May he wear, with republican simplicity and fidelity, the honors of his country, and preserve unsullied and untarnished those that still await him.

A HISTORY

OF THE

POLITICAL CAMPAIGN

IN VIRGINIA,

IN 1855;

WITH A

BIOGRAPHICAL SKETCH OF

HENRY A. WISE:

BY JAMES P. HAMBLETON, M. D.

J. W. RANDOLPH,
121 MAIN STREET, RICHMOND, VA.
1856.

JOHN NOWLAN, PRINTER.

TO THE

DEMOCRATIC PARTY OF VIRGINIA,

FOR THEIR UNFLINCHING DEVOTION TO THEIR TIME HONORED

PRINCIPLES:

THE CONSTITUTION AND STATES RIGHTS;

AND FOR THEIR UNCOMPROMISING HOSTILITY TO ALL ISMS

OPPOSED TO THE

PURE JEFFERSONIAN DEMOCRACY,

THIS WORK IS RESPECTFULLY INSCRIBED, BY

THE AUTHOR.

INTRODUCTION.

In presenting this work to the public, it is our aim to give a full account of the operations of the secret political society known as the KNOW-NOTHING PARTY, in Virginia, in 1855. In doing this, we hope to present something useful to the living, and which may guard the unthinking in after generations against the machinations of any secret sect, clique or party, that may have for its object a usurpation of the government and its spoils, by other tenure than the popular voice. If we succeed in this we shall have accomplished our chief aim. We shall present the arguments of the ablest men in the land, both as speakers and as writers, against Know-Nothingism, coupled with their defence of the time honored principles of the Democratic party. This work will be compiled principally of such newspaper articles and speeches as were elicited in the war against Know-Nothingism during the gubernatorial canvass of 1855. The newspapers from which we have drawn most copiously, are the Richmond Enquirer, Examiner and Whig. In prefacing these compiled extracts, we have given our opinions succinctly, conscientiously, fearlessly, and unreservedly.

JAMES PINKNEY HAMBLETON, M. D.

Pittsylvania C. H. Va.
December, 1855.

CAMPAIGN OF 1855.

DEMOCRATIC MEETING IN NORFOLK COUNTY IN THE FALL OF 1854.—HON. HENRY A. WISE'S LETTER UPON KNOW-NOTHINGISM.

During the latter part of the summer of 1854, the newspapers of Virginia began to direct their attention to the gubernatorial canvass that was to come off in our state in the next year. Various prominent individuals were spoken of by their respective friends, when, in the early part of September 1854, the citizens of Norfolk county determined to hold a meeting and correspond with these distinguished gentlemen in order to obtain from them an expression of opinion in regard to the new party then said to be organizing in the state, under the cognomen of Know-Nothings. The committee of correspondence appointed by this meeting wrote to the following gentlemen, viz: Ex-Governor William Smith, Lieut. Governor S. F. Leake, Hon. John Letcher, Hon. James A. Seddon, and Hon. Henry A. Wise. All of these gentlemen very promptly answered, and all satisfactorily, with the exception of Ex-Gov. Smith. He answered after a long time, but evasively. Mr. Wise's answer was prompt, plain, satisfactory and elaborate. In his letter to this committee was recognized the true spirit of a southern republican and statesman. There was no document that appeared on the subject which bespoke so truly the sentiments of the Democratic party of Virginia in their utter detestation of *secret political societies and religious intolerance.* We give this masterly production an appropriate insertion in the beginning of this compilation:

ONLY, NEAR ONANCOCK, VIRGINIA,
September 18th, 1854.

To ——— ———:

Dear Sir:—I now proceed to give you the reasons for the opinions I expressed in my letter of the 2nd instant, as fully as my leisure will permit:

I said that I did *not* "think that the present state of affairs in this country is such as to *justify* the formation, by the people, of *any Secret Political* Society."

The laws of the United States—federal and state laws—declare and defend the liberties of our people. They are free in every sense—free in the sense of Magna Charta and beyond Magna Charta; free by the surpassing franchise of *American* Charters, which makes *them Sovereign and their wills the sources of constitutions and laws.*

If the archbishop might say to King John,

"Let every Briton, as his mind, be free;
His person safe; his property secure;
His house as sacred as the fane of Heaven;
Watching, unseen, his ever open door,
Watching the realm, the spirit of the laws;
His fate determined by the rules of right,
His voice enacted in the common voice
And general suffrage of the assembled realm,
No hand invisible to write his doom;
No demon starting at the midnight hour,
To draw his curtain, or to drag him down
To mansions of despair. Wide to the world
Disclose the secrets of the prison walls,
And bid the groanings of the dungeon strike
The public ear—Inviolable preserve
The sacred shield that covers all the land.
The Heaven-conferr'd palladium of the isle,
To Briton's sons, the judgment of their peers,
On these great pillars: freedom of the mind,
Freedom of speech, and freedom of the pen,
Forever changing, yet forever sure,
The base of Briton rests."

—we may say that our American Charters have more than confirmed these laws of the Confessor, and our people have given to them "as free, as full, and as sovereign a consent" as was ever given by John to the bishops and the barons, "at Runnimede, the field of freedom," to which it was said—

"Britain's sons shall come,
Shall tread where heroes and where patriots trod,
To worship as they walk!"

In this country, at this time, does any man think anything? Would he think aloud? Would he speak anything? Would he write anything? His mind is free, his person is safe, his property is secure, his house is his castle, the spirit of the laws is his body-guard and his house-guard; the fate of one is the fate of all measured by the same common rule of right; his voice is heard and felt in the general suffrage of freemen; his trial is in open court, confronted by witnesses and accusers; his prison house has no secrets, and he has the judgment of his peers; and there is nought to make him afraid, so long as he respects the rights of his equals in the eye of the law. Would he propagate Truth?—Truth is free to combat Error. Would he propagate Error?—*Error* itself may stalk abroad and do her mischief and make night itself grow darker, provided Truth is left free to follow, however slowly, with her torches to light up the wreck! Why, then, should any portion of the people desire to retire in secret, and by secret means to propagate a political thought, or word, or deed, by stealth? Why band together, exclusive of others, to do something which all may not know of, towards some political end? If it be good, why not make the good *known*? Why not think it, speak it, write it, act it out openly and aloud? Or, is it evil, which loveth darkness rather than light? When there is no *necessity* to justify a secret association for *political* ends, what else *can* justify it? A caucus may sit in secret to consult on the general policy of a great public party. That may be necessary or convenient; but that even is reprehensible, if carried too far. But here is proposed a great primary, national organization, in its inception—What? *Nobody knows.* To do what? *Nobody knows.* How organized? *Nobody knows.* Governed by whom? *Nobody knows.* How bound? By what rites? By what test oaths? With what limitations and restraints? Nobody, nobody knows!!! All we know is, that persons of *foreign birth* and of *Catholic faith* are proscribed, and so are all others who don't proscribe them at the polls. This is certainly against the spirit of Magna Charta.

Such is our condition of freedom at home, showing no necessity for such a secret organization and its antagonism to the very basis of American rights. And our comparative native and Protestant strength at home repels the plea of such necessity still more. The statistics of immigration show that from 1820 to 1st January, 1853, inclusive, for 32 years and more, 3,204,848 foreigners arrived in the United States, at the average rate of 100,151 per annum; that the number of persons of foreign birth now in the United States is 2,210,839; that the number of natives, whites, is 17,737,578, and of persons whose nativity is "*unknown*," is 39,154. (Quere, by the by:—What will "*Know-Nothings*" do with the "*unknown?*") The number of natives to persons of foreign birth in the United States, is as 8 to 1, and the most of the latter, of course, are *naturalized*. In Virginia the whole number of white natives is 813,891, of persons born out of the State and in the United States, 57,502, making a total of natives of 871,393; and the number of persons born in foreign countries, is 22,953. So that in Virginia the number of natives is to the number of persons born in foreign countries, nearly as 38 to 1.

Again:—the churches of the United States provide accommodations for 14,234,825 votaries; the Roman Catholics for but 667,823; the number of votaries in the Protestant to the number in the Roman Catholic in the United States, as 21 to 1. In Virginia the whole number is 856,436, the Roman Catholics 7,930, or 108 to 1.

The number of churches in the United States is 38,061, of Catholic churches 1,221; more tnan 31 to 1 are Protestant. In Virginia the number of churches is 2,383, of Catholic churches is 17; more than 140 to 1.

The whole value of church property in the United States is $87,328,801, of Catholic church property is $9,256,758, or 9 to 1. In Virginia the whole value of church property is $2,856,076; of Catholic church property, $126,100, or 22 to 1.

In the United States there are four Protestant sects, either of which is larger than the Catholics:

The Baptists provide accommodations for	3,247,029
The Methodists for	4,343,579
The Presbyterians for	2,079,690
The Congregationalists for	801,835
Aggregate of four Protestant sects,	10,472,073
The Catholics for	667,823
Majority of only four Protestant sects,	9,804,250
Add the Episcopalians for	643,598
Majority of only five Protestant sects,	10,447,848

In Virginia there are five Protestant sects, either of which is larger than the number of Catholics in the State.

Baptists,	247,589
Episcopal,	79,684
Lutheran,	18,750
Methodists,	323,708
Presbyterian,	103,625
	773,356
Catholics,	7,930
Majority of free Protestant sects in Virginia,	765,426

Or nearly 98 to 1.

Thus natives are to persons of foreign birth

In the United States, as	8 to 1
In Virginia, as	38 to 1

The Protestant church accommodations are to the Catholic

In the United States, as	21 to 1
In Virginia, as	108 to 1

The number of Protestant churches is to the number of Catholic

In the United States, as	31 to 1
In Virginia, as	140 to 1

The value of Protestant church property in the United States, is to the value of Catholic church property as 9 to 1

In Virginia, as	22 to 1

There are four Protestant sects, each of which is larger than the Catholic, in the United States, and the aggregate of which exceeds the Catholic by a majority of 9,804,250 votaries, and, adding one sect smaller, by a majority of 10,447,848.

In Virginia there are five Protestant sects, each larger than the number of Catholics in the state, and the aggregate of which exceeds the Catholics by a majority of 765,426 votaries.

Now, what has such a *majority* of numbers, and of wealth of natives and of Protestants, to fear from such *minorities* of Catholics and naturalized citizens? What is the necessity for this master majority to resort to *secret organization* against such a minority? I put it fairly: Would they organize at all against the Catholics and naturalized citizens, if the Catholics and naturalized citizens were in the like majority of numbers and of wealth, or if majorities and minorities were reversed? To retire in secret with such a majority, does it not confess to *something* which dares not subject itself to the scrutiny of knowledge, and would have discussion Know-Nothing of its designs and operations and ends? Cannot the Know-Nothings trust to the leading Protestant churches to defend themselves and the souls of all the saints, and sinners too, against the influence of Catholics? Can't they trust to the patriotism and fraternity of natives to guard the land against immigrants? In defence of the reat American Protestant churches, I venture to say in their behalf, that the Pope, and all his priests combined, are not more zealous and watchful in their master's work, or *in the work for the mastery*, than are our Episcopal, Presbyterian, Baptist, Methodist, Lutheran, and Congregational clergy. They are, as a whole church militant, with their armor bright; they are zealous, they are jealous, they are watchful, they are organized, embodied, however divided by sectarianism, yet banded together against Papacy, and learned and active, and politic too as any brotherhood of monks. They need no such political organization to *defend the faith*. Are *they* united in it? Do *they* favor or countenance it among their flocks? To what end? In the name of their religion, I ask them—*Why not rely on God?* And do the Know-Nothings imagine that the pride and love of country are so dead in native hearts, that secret organizations are necessary to beget a new-born patriotism to protect us from foreign influence? Now, in defence of our people, I say for them that no people upon earth are more *possessed* with *nationality* as a strong passion than the freemen of the United States of North America. Nowhere is the filial and domestic tie stronger, nowhere is the tie of kinship more binding, nowhere is there more *amor loci* —the love of *home*, which is the surest foundation of the love of country— nowhere is any country's romance of history more felt, nowhere are the social relations on a better moral foundation, nowhere is there as clear identity of parentage and offspring, nowhere are sons and daughters so "educated to liberty," nowhere have any people such certainty of the knowledge of the reward of vigilance, nowhere have they such freedom of self-government, nowhere is there such trained hatred of kings, lords and aristocracies, nowhere is there more self-independence, or more independence of the Old World or its traditions—in a word, nowhere is there a country whose people have, by birthright, a tithe of what our people have to make them love *that land* which is *their country*, and *that spot* which is *their home!* I am an American, a Virginian! Prouder than ever to have said, "I am a Roman citizen!" So far from Brother Jonathan wanting a national feeling, he is justly suspected abroad of a little too much pride and bigotry of country. The revolution and the last war with Great Britatn, tried us, and the late conquest of Mexico found us not wanting in the sentimentality of *nationalism.* Though so young, we have already a dialect and a mannerism, and our customs and our costume. A city dandy may have his coat cut in Paris, but he would fight a Frenchman in the cloth of his country as quick to-day as a Marion man ever pulled the trigger of a Tower musket against a red-coat Englishman in '76. And peace has tried our patriotism more than war. What people have more reason to love a country from the labor they have bestowed upon its development by the arts of industry? No: as long as the memory of George Washington lives, as long as there shall be a 22d of February and a 4th of July, as long as the everlasting mountains of this continent stand, and our Father of Waters flows, there will be fathers to hand down the stories which make our hearts to glow, and mothers to sing "Hail Columbia" to their babes—and that song is not yet stale. There is no need to revive a sinking patriotism in the hearts of our people. And who would have them be *selfish* in their freedom? Freedom! Liberty! *selfish* and *exclusive!* Never; for it consumeth not in its use, but is like fire in magnifying, by imparting its sparks and its rays of light and of heat. Is there any necessity from abroad for such secret political organizations? Against whom, and against what, is it levelled? Against foreigners by birth.

When we were as weak as *three millions,* we relied largely on foreigners by birth to defend us and aid us in securing independence. Now that we are twenty-two millions strong, how is it we have become so weak in our fears as to apprehend we are to be deprived of our liberties by foreigners? Verily, this seemeth as if Know-Nothings were reversing the order of things, or that there is another and a different feeling from that of the fear arising from a sense of weakness. It comes rather from a proud consciousness of over-weening strength. They wax strong rather, and would kick, like the proud grown fat. It is an *exclusive,* if not an aristocratic feeling in the true sense, which would say to the friends of freedom born abroad: "We had need of you and were glad of your aid when we were weak, but we are now so independent of you that we are not compelled to allow you to enjoy our Republican privileges. We desire the exclusive use of human rights, though to deprive you of their common enjoyment will not enrich us the more and will make you 'poor indeed!'" But not only is it levelled against foreigners by birth, but against the *Pope of Rome.*

There was once a time when the very name of *Papa* frightened us as the children of a nursery. But, now, now! who can be frightened by the temporal or ecclesiastical authority of Pius IX? Has he got back to Rome from his late excursion? Who are his body-guard there? Have the lips of a crowned head kissed his big toe for a century? Are any so poor as to do his Italian crown any reverence? Do not two Catholic powers, France and Austria, hold all his dominions in a detestable dependency? What army, what revenue, what diplomacy, what church domination in even the Catholic countries of the old or the new world has he? Why, the idea of the Pope's influenee at this day is as preposterous as that of a gunpowder plot. I would as soon think of dreading the ghost of Guy Fawkes.

No, there is no necessity, from either oppression or weakness of Protestants or natives. They are both free and strong; and do they now, because they are rich in civil and religious freedom, wish, in turn, to persecute, and exclude the fallen and the down-trodden of the earth?—God forbid!

2d. But there is not only no necessity for this secret political organization, but it is *against the spirit of our laws* and the facts of our history. Some *families* in this Republic render themselves ridiculous, and offensive, too, by the vain pretensions to the exalting accidents of birth. We, in Virginia, are not seldom pointed at for our F. F. V.'s of ancestral arrogance. But, who ever thought that pretension of this sort was so soon to be set up by exclusives for the Republic itself? Some of the ancient European people may boast of their "protoplasts," and of their being themselves "*autochthones*"—that they had fathers and mothers from near Adam, whom they can name as their *first formers*, and that they are of the same unmixed blood, *original inhabitants* of their country. But who were *our protoplasts?* English, Irish, Scotch, German, Dutch, Swedes, French, Swiss, Spanish, Italian, Ethiopian—all people of all nations, tribes, complexions, languages and religions! And who alone are "autochthones" here in North America?—Why, the Indians! *They* are the only true *natives*. One thing we have, and that more distinctly than any other nation: we have our "*eponymas.*" We can name the very hour of our birth as a people. We need recur to no fable of a wolf to whelp us into existence. It may be hard to fix Anno Mundi, or the year of Noah's flood, or the building of Rome. Rome may have her Julian epocha, the Ethiopian their epocha of the Abyssines, the Arabians theirs of the flight of Mahomet, the Persians theirs of the coronation of Jesdegerdis; but ours dates from the Declaration of Independence among the nations of the earth, the 4th day of July, A. D. 1776. As a nation we are but 78 years of age. Many a person is now living who was alive before this nation was born. And the ancestors of this people, about two centuries only ago, were *foreigners*, every one of them coming to the shores of this country, to take it away from the Aborigines, the "autochthones," and to take possession of it by authority, either directly or derivatively, of *Papal Power?* His holiness the Pope was the great grantor of all the new countries of North America. This fiction was a fact of the history of all our first discoveries and settlements. Foreigners, in the name of the Pope and Mother Church, took possession of North America, to have and to hold the same to their heirs against the heathen forever!—and now already their descendants are for excluding foreigners and the Pope's followers from an equal enjoyment of the privileges of this same possession! So strange is human history. Christopher Columbus! Ferdinand and Isabella! What would they have thought of this had they foreseen it when they touched a continent and called it theirs in the name of the Holy Trinity, by authority of the keeper of the keys of heaven, and of the great grantor of the empire and domain of earth? What would have become of our national titles to north-eastern and north-western boundaries, but for the plea of this authority, valid of old among all Christian Powers?

Following the discovery and the possession of the country by foreigners, in virtue of Catholic majesty, came the settlements of the country by force and constraint of *religious intolerance and persecution*. Puritans, Huguenots, Cavaliers, Catholics, Quakers, all came to Western wilds, each in turn persecuted and persecuting for opinion's sake. Oppression of *opinion* was the most odious of the abominations of the Old World's despotism—its only glory and grace is that it made thousands of martyrs. It deluged every country and tainted the air of every clime, and stained the robes of righteousness of every sect *with blood*, with the blood of every human sacrifice, which was honest and earnest in its faith, the hypocrites and hinds of profession alone escaping the swords or the flames of persecution. The colonies were blackened by the burnings of the stake, and were died red with the blood of intolerance.

The American revolution made a new era of liberty to dawn—the era of the *liberty of conscience.* If there is any essence in Americanism, the very salt wherewith it is savored is the freedom of opinion and the liberty of conscience. Is it now proposed that we shall go back to the deeds of the dark ages of despotism? That this broad land, still unoccupied in more than half of its virgin soil, shall no longer be an asylum for the oppressed? That here, as elsewhere, and again, as of old, men shall be burthened by their births and chained for their opinions? I trust that a design of that intent will remain a *secret* buried forever.

I have said this organization was against the spirit of our laws. Our laws sprang from the necessity of the condition of our early settlers. They brought with them from England their Penates, the household gods of an Anglo-Saxon race, the liberties of Magna Charta, the trial by jury, the judgment of the peers, and the other muniments of human dignity and human rights secured by the first English Charta. These, *foreigners* brought with them from Europe. Here they found the virtues to extend these rights and their muniments. The neglect of the mother country left them self-dependent and self-reliant until they were thoroughly taught the lesson of *self-government*—that they could be their own sovereigns—and the very experience of despotism they had once tasted made them hate tyrants, either elective or hereditary. Their destitute and exposed condition trained them to hardy habits and cultivated in them every sterner virtue. They knew privation, fatigue, endurance, self-denial, fortitude, and were made men at arms—cautious, courageous, generous, just and trusting in God. They had to fight Indians, from Philip, on Massachusetts Bay, to Powhatan, on the river of Swans. And they had an unexplored continent to subdue, with its teeming soil, its majestic forests, its towering mountains, and its unequalled rivers. Above all things, they needed population, more fellow-settlers, more *foreigners* to immigrate, and to aid them in the task of founders of empire set before them, to open the forests, to level the hills, and to raise up the valleys of a giant new country. Well, these *foreigners* did their task like men. Such a work! who can exaggerate it? They did it against all odds and in spite of European oppression. They grew and thrived, until they were rich enough to be taxed. They were told taxation was no tyranny. But these foreigners gave the world a new truth of freedom. Taxation without representation was tyranny. The attempt to impose it upon them, the least mite of it, made them resolve, "that they would give millions for defence, but not a cent for tribute." That resolve drove them to the necessity of war, and they, foreigners, Protestants, Catholics and all, took the dire alternative, united as a band of brothers, and declared their dependence upon God alone. And they entered to the world a complaint of grievances —a Declaration of Independence! This was pretty well to show whether foreigners, of any and all religions, just fresh from Europe, could be trusted on the side of America and liberty. One of the first of their complaints was:

"He (George III.) has endeavored to prevent the population of these states, for that purpose obstructing the laws for *naturalization of foreigners,* refusing to pass others to encourage their emigration hither, and raising the conditions of new appropriations of land."

There is the proof that they valued the naturalization of foreigners and the immigration of foreigners hither, and they desired appropriations, new appropriations of land, for immigrants.

Anotheir complaint was, that they had appealed in vain to "British brethren." They said:

"We have appealed to their *native* justice and magnanimity; and we have conjured them, by the ties of our common kindred, to disavow these usurpations, &c. They, too, have been deaf to the voice of justice and consanguinity. We must, therefore, acquiesce in the necessity which denounces our separation, and hold them, as we hold the rest of mankind, enemies in war, in peace friends."

There is proof, too, that Nativism can't always be relied on to help one's own countrymen, and that brethren, and kindred, and consanguinity, will fail a whole people in trouble, just as kinship too often fails families and individuals in the trials of life.

"And," lastly, "for the support of this Declaration, with a firm reliance on the protection of Divine Providence, we mutually pledge to each other our lives, our fortunes, and our sacred honor."

There was tolerance, there was firm reliance on the same one God; there was mutuality of pledge, each to the other, at one altar, and there was a common stake of sacrifice—"lives, fortunes and honor." And who were they? There were Hancock the Puritan, Penn the Quaker, Rutledge the Huguenot, Carroll the Catholic, Lee the Cavalier, Jefferson the Free Thinker. These, representatives of all the signers, and the signers, representatives of all the people of all the colonies.

Oh! my countrymen, did not that "pledge" bind them and bind us, their heirs, forever to faith and hope in God and to charity for each other—to tolerance in religion, and to "mutuality" in political freedom? Down, down with any organization, then, which "denounces" a "separation" between Protestant Virginia and Catholic Maryland—between the children of Catholic Carroll and Protestant George Wythe. Their names stand together among "the signatures," and I will redeem their "mutual" pledges with my "life," my "fortune," and my "sacred honor," "so far as in me lies—so help me, Almighty God!"

I think that here is proof enough that "foreigners" and Catholics both entered as material elements into our Americanism. But before the 4th day of July there were laws passed of the highest authority, to which this secret organization is opposed.

On the 12th of June, '76, the Convention of Virginia passed a "Declaration of Rights." Its 4th section declares: "that no man, or set of men, are entitled to exclusive or separate emoluments or privileges from the community, but in consideration of public services; which not being descendible, neither ought the offices of magistrate, legislator or judge to be hereditary."

Now, does the Know-Nothing organization not claim for the "*native born*" "*set of men*" to be entitled to exclusive privileges from the community as against naturalized and Catholic citizens; and thus, by virtue of birth, to inherit the right of election to the offices of magistrates, legislator or judge, which are not descendible? They set up no such claim for the *individual* person native born, but they do set up a *quality* for *nativity*, to which, and to which alone, they claim, pertains the privileges of eligibility to offices.

Again:—Does this organization not violate the 7th section of this declaration of rights, which forbids "*all* power of *suspending* laws, or the execution of laws, by *any* authority without consent of the representatives of the people, as injurious to their rights, and which ought not to be exercised?" When the laws say, and the representatives of the people say, that Catholics and naturalized citizens *shall* be tolerated and allowed to enjoy the privileges of citizenship, and eligibility to office, have they not organized a secret power to *suspend* these laws and to prevent the execution of them, by their sole authority, without consent of the representatives of the people? This declaration denounces it as injurious to the rights of the people and as a power which ought not to be exercised.

Again:—Does not this organization annul that part of the 8th section of this declaration, which says: "That no man shall be deprived of his liberty, except by the law of the land, or the judgment of his peers?" This don't apply alone to personal liberty, the freedom of the body from prison, but no man shall be deprived of his franchises of any sort, of his liberty in its largest sense, except by the law of the land or the judgment of his peers, the trial by *jury*. Has, then, a private and secret tribunal a right to impose qualifications for office, and to enforce *their* laws by test oaths, so as to deprive any man of his liberty to be elected?

Again:—Is this organization not an Imperium in Imperio against the 14th section of this declaration, which says: "That the people have a right to *uniform* government, and, therefore, that no government separated from or independent of the government of Virginia, ought to be erected or established *within the limits thereof*." It is not a *government*, but does it not, will it not, politically govern the portion of the people belonging to it, differently from what the portion of the people not belonging to it, are governed by the laws of Virginia?

Again:—It does not adhere to the "*justice* and *moderation*" inculcated in the 15th section of the declaration. And lastly, it avowedly opposes the 16th section, which declares, "that *religion*, or the duty which we owe to our Creator, and the manner of discharging it, can be directed only by reason and conviction, not by force or violence; and, therefore, all men are *equally* entitled to the *free exercise* of religion, according to the dictates of *conscience;* and that it is the mutual duty of all to practice Christian forbearance, love and charity towards each other."

But this organization not only contravenes the rules of our Declaration of Independence and Rights, but it is in the face of a positive and perpetual statute, now made a part of our organic law by the new Constitution—the Act of Religious Freedom, passed the 16th of December, 1785. Against this law, this Know-Nothing order attacks the freedom of the mind, by imposing "civil incapacitations;" it "attempts to punish one religion and to propagate another by coercion on both body and mind;" it "sets up its own opinions and modes of thinking as the only true and infallible;" it makes our "civil rights to have a dependence on our religious opinions;" it "deprives citizens of their natural rights, by proscribing them as unworthy the public confidence, by laying upon them an incapacity of being called to offices of trust and emolument, unless they profess or renounce this or that religious opinion;" "it tends to corrupt the principles of that religion it is meant to encourage, by bribing with a monopoly of worldly honors and emoluments, those who will externally profess and conform to it;" it lacks confidence in Truth, which "is great and will prevail," if left to herself; that she is the proper and sufficient antagonist to Error, and has nothing to fear from the conflict, unless by human interposition disarmed of her natural weapons, free argument and debate; it withdraws errors from free argument and debate, and hides them in secret, where they become dangerous, because it is not permitted freely to contradict them.

Let it not be said that this is a restraining statute upon government, and is a prohibition to "legislators and rulers, civil as well as ecclesiastical." If *they* even are restrained by this law, *a fortiori*, every *private* organization, or order, or individual, is restrained. The Know-Nothings will hardly pretend to do what the government itself, and legislators, and rulers, civil as well as ecclesiastical, dare not do. If such be their pretensions they claim to be *above* the law, or to set up a *higher law*—then, *sic volo*, to compel a man to frequent or support any religious worship, and to enforce, restrain, molest, or burthen him, or "to make him suffer" on account of his religious opinions or belief; or to deprive men of their freedom to profess, and by argument to maintain their opinions in matters of religion, and to make the same diminish, enlarge or affect their civil capacities. No, when our Constitutions forbid the legislators to exercise a power, they intend that no such power shall be exercised by any one.

Not only is the law of Virginia thus liberal as to religion, but also as to naturalization.

So far as "Know-Nothingism" opposes our naturalization laws, it is not only against our statute policy, but against Americanism itself. In this it is especially anti-American. One of the best fruits of the American Revolution was to establish, for the first time in the world, the human right of expatriation. Prior to our separate existence as a nation of the earth, the despotisms of the old world had made a law unto themselves, whereby they could hold forever in chains those of mankind who were so unfortunate as to be *born* their subjects. In respect to birthright and the right of expatriation, and the duty of allegiance and protection, and the law of treason, crowned heads held to the ancient dogma: "Once a citizen always a citizen." If a man was so miserable as to be born the slave of a tyrant, he must remain his slave forever. He could never renounce his ill-fated birthright—could never expatriate himself to seek for a better country—and could never forswear the allegiance which bound him to his chains. He might emigrate, might take the wings of the morning and fly to the uttermost parts of the earth, might cross seas and continents, and put oceans, and rivers, and lakes, and mountains between him and the throne in the shadow of which he was born, and he would still "but drag a lengthening chain." Still the despotism might pursue him, find and bind him as a subject slave. If America beckoned to him to fly to her for freedom, and to give her the cunning and the strength of his right arm to help ameliorate her huge proportions and to work out her grand destiny, the tyrant had to be asked for passports and permission to expatriate. But they came—lo! they came! Our laws encouraged them to come. Before '76, Virginia and all the colonies encouraged immigration. It was a necessity as well as a policy of the whole country. Early in the revolution, the king's forces hung some of the best blood of the colonies under the maxim, "Once a citizen, always a citizen." They were traitors if found fighting for us, because they were *once* subjects. Washington was obliged to hold hostages, to prevent the application of this barbarous doctrine of tyranny. At last our struggle ended, and our independence was recognized. George III. was compelled to renounce our allegiance to him, though we *were* born his subjects. But still, when we came to our separate existence, we were called on to recognize the same odious maxim, still adhered to by the despots of Europe: "Once a citizen, always a citizen." Subjects were still told that they should not expatriate themselves, and America was warned that she should not naturalize them without the consent of their monarch masters. Spurning this dogma, and the tyrants who boasted the power to enforce it, the 4th power which the Convention of 1787, that formed our blessed Constitution, enumerated, is: "The Congress shall have power 'to establish an uniform rule of naturalization.'"

The meaning of this was, to say by public law to all Europe and her combined courts, "Your dogma, 'once a citizen always a citizen,' shall cease forever as to the United States of North America. We need population to smooth our rough places, and to make our crooked places straight; but, above and beyond that policy, we are, with the help of God, resolved that this new and giant land shall be one vast asylum for the oppressed of every other land, now and forever!" That is my reading of our law of liberty. Those born in bondage might raise their eyes up in hope of a better country! They might, and should if they would, expatriate themselves, fly from slavery and chains, and *come!*—Ho, every one of them, come to our country and be free with us! They might forswear their allegiance to despots, and should be allowed here to take an oath to liberty and her flag, and her freedom, and they should not be pursued and punished as traitors. When they came and swore that our country should be their country, we would swear to protect them as if in the country born, as if natives—*i. e.*, as naturalized citizens, and they should be *our citizens* and be entitled to *our protection*. And this was in conformity to the only true idea of "Naturalization," which, according to its legal as well as its etymological sense, means, "when one who is an alien is made a natural subject by act of law and consent of the sovereign power of the state." The consent of our sovereign power is written in the Constitution of the United States, and Congress, at an early day after its adoption, passed the acts of naturalization. The leading statute is that of April 14th, 1802. It provided that any alien, being a *free white person*, may be admitted to become a citizen of the United States, or any of them, on the following conditions, and not otherwise:

1st. That he shall have declared on oath or affirmation before the supreme, superior, district or circuit court of some one of the states, or of the territorial districts of the United States, or a circuit or district court of the United States, *three* years (*two* years by act of May 26th, 1824,) at least before his admission, that it was his *bona fide* intention to become a citizen of the United States, and to renounce forever all allegiance and fidelity to any foreign prince, potentate, state or sovereignty, whereof such alien may at the time be a citizen or subject.

2d. That he shall, at the time of his application to be admitted, declare on oath or affirmation before some one of the courts aforesaid, that he will support the Constitution of the United States, and that he doth absolutely and entirely renounce and abjure all allegiance and fidelity to every foreign prince, potentate, state or sovereignty whatever, and particularly, by name, the prince, potentate, state or sovereignty whereof he was before a citizen or subject; which proceedings shall be recorded by the clerk of the court.

3rd. That the court admitting such alien shall be satisfied that he has resided within the United States *five years* at least, and within the state or territory where such court is at the time held, *one year, at least;* and it shall further appear to their satisfaction, that during that time he has *behaved as a man of good moral character*, attached to the principles of the Constitution of the United States, and well disposed to *the good order and happiness of the same;* Provided, That the oath of the applicant shall in no case be allowed to prove his residence.

4th. That in case the alien applying to be admitted to citizenship shall have borne any hereditary title or been of any of the orders of nobility in the kingdom or state from which he came, he shall, in addition to the above requisites, make an express renunciation of his title or order of nobility in the court to which his application shall be made, which renunciation shall be recorded in the said court: Provided, That no alien who shall be a native, citizen, denizen, or subject, of any country, state, or sovereign, with whom the United States shall be at war at the time of his application, shall then be admitted to be a citizen of the United States.

The act has other provisions, and has since been modified from time to time. This statute had not operated a legal life time before Great Britain again asserted the dogma: "*Once* a citizen, always a citizen!" The base and cowardly attack of the Leopard on the Chesapeake, at the mouth of this very bay, in sight of the Virginia shore, was made upon the claim of right to seize British born subjects from on board our man-of-war. The star-spangled banner was struck that day for the last time to the detestable maxim of tyranny:—"Once a citizen, always a citizen." It must not be forgotten that it was upon this doctrine of despots that the *Right of Search* was founded. They arrogated to themselves the prerogative to search our decks on the high seas, and to seize those of our crews who were born in British dominions. In 1812, we declared the last war. For what? For "Free Trade, and Sailors' Rights" That is, for the right of our naturalized-citizen-sailors to sail on the high seas, and to trade abroad free from search and seizure. They had been required to "renounce and abjure," all "allegiance and fidelity" to any other country, state, or sovereignty, and particularly to the country, state, or sovereignty under which they have been natives or citizens, and we had reciprocally undertaken to *protect* them in consideration of their oaths of allegiance and fidelity to the United States. How protect them? By enabling them to fulfil their obligations to us of allegiance and fidelity, by making them free to fight for our flag, and free in every sense, just as if they had been born in our country. Fight for us they did; naturalized, and those not naturalized, were of our crews. They fought in every sea for the flag which threw protection over them, from the first gun of the Constitution frigate to the last gun of the boats on Lake Pontchartrain, in every battle where

"Cannon's mouths were each other greeting,
And yard arm was with yard arm meeting."

That war sealed in the blood of dead and living heroes the eternal, American principle:—"The right of expatriation, the right and duty of naturalization—the right to fly from tyranny to the flag of freedom, and the reciprocal duties of allegiance and protection." And does a party—an order or what not, calling itself an *American* party, now oppose and call upon me to oppose these great American truths, and to put America in the wrong for declaring and fighting the last war of independence against Great Britain? Never! I would as soon go back to wallowing in the mire of European serfdom. I won't do it. I can't do it. No; I will lie down and rise up a Native American, for and not against these imperishable American truths. Nor will any true American, who understands what Americanism is do otherwise. I put a case:

A Prussian born subject came to this country. He complied with our naturalization laws in all respects of notice of intention, residence, oath of allegiance, and proof of good moral character. He remained continuously in the United States the full period of five years. When he had fully filled the measure of his probation and was consummately a naturalized citizen of the United States, he then, and not until then, returned to Prussia to visit an aged father. He was immediately, on his return, seized and forced into the Landwehr, or militia system of Prussia, under the maxim: "Once a citizen, always a citizen!" There he is forced to do service to the king of Prussia at this very hour. He applies for protection to the United States. Would the Know-Nothings interpose in his behalf or not? Look at the principles involved. We, by our laws, encouraged him to come to our country, and here he was allowed to become naturalized, and to that end required to renounce and abjure all allegiance and fidelity to the king of Prussia, and to swear allegiance and fidelity to the United States. The king of Prussia now claims no legal forfeiture from him—he punishes him for no *crime*—he claims of him no *legal debt*—he claims alone that very allegiance and fidelity which we required the man to *abjure* and *renounce*. Not only so, but he hinders the man from *returning* to the United States, and from discharging the allegiance and fidelity we required him to swear to the United States. The king of Prussia says he should do him service for seven years, for this was what he was born to perform; his obligations were due to him first, and his laws were first binding him. The United States say—true, he was born under your laws, but he had a right to expatriate himself; he owed allegiance first to you, but he had a right to forswear it and to swear allegiance to us; your laws first applied, but this is a case of *political* obligation, not of *legal* obligation; it is not for any crime or debt you claim to bind him, but it is for allegiance; and the claim you set up to his services on the ground of his political obligation, his allegiance to you, which we allow him to abjure and renounce, is inconsistent with his political obligation, his allegiance, which we required him to swear to the United States; he has sworn fidelity to us, and we have, by our laws, pledged protection to him.

Such is the issue. Now, with which will the Know-Nothings take sides? With the king of Prussia against our naturalized citizen and against America, or with America and our naturalized citizen? Mark, now, Know-Nothingism is opposed to all foreign influence—against American institutions. The king of Prussia is a pretty potent foreign influence—he was one of the holy alliance of crowned heads. Will they take part with him, and not protect the citizen? Then they *will* aid a foreign influence against our laws! Will they take sides with our naturalized citizen? If so, then upon what grounds? Now, they must have a good cause of interposition to justify us against all the received dogmas of European despotism.

Don't they see, can't they perceive, that they have no other grounds than those I have urged? He is our citizen, *nationalized*, owing us allegiance and we owing him protection. And if we owe him protection *abroad*, because of his sworn allegiance to us as a naturalized citizen, what then can deprive him of his privileges *at home* among us when he returns? If he be a citizen at all, he must be allowed the privileges of citizenship, or he will not be the *equal* of his fellow-citizens. And must not Know-Nothingism strike *at the very equality* of citizenship, or allow him to enjoy all its lawful privileges? If Catholics and naturalized citizens are to be citizens and yet to be proscribed from office, they must be rated as an *inferior* class—an excluded class of citizens. Will it be said that *the law* will not make this distinction? Then are we to understand that Know-Nothings would *not* make them *equal by law?* If not by law, how can they pretend to make them unequal, by their secret order, without law and against law? For them, by secret combination, to make them unequal, to impose a burthen or restriction upon their privileges which the law does not, is to set themselves up above the law, and to supercede by private and secret authority, intangible and irresponsible, the rule of public, political right. Indeed, is this not the very essence of the "Higher Law" doctrine? It cannot be said to be legitimate public sentiment and the action of its authority. Public sentiment, proper, is a concurrence of the common mind in some conclusion, conviction, opinion, taste or action in respect to persons or things subject to its public notice. It will, and it must control the minds and actions of men, by public and conventional opinion. Count Mole said that in France it was stronger than statutes. It is so here. That it is which should decide at the polls of a Republic. But, here is a secret sentiment, which may be so organized as to contradict the public sentiment. Candidate A. may be a native and a Protestant, and may concur with the community, if it be a Know-Nothing community, on every other subject except that of proscribing Catholics and naturalized citizens; and candidate B. may concur with the community on the subject of this proscription alone, and upon no other subject; and yet the Know-Nothings might elect B. by their secret sentiment against the public sentiment. Thus it attacks not only American doctrines of expatriation, allegiance and protection, but the equality of citizenship, and the authority of public sentiment. In the affair of Koszta, how did our blood rush to his rescue? Did the Know-Nothing side with him and Mr. Marcy, or with Hulseman and Austria? If with Koszta, why? Let them ask themselves for the rationale, and see if it can in reason abide with their orders. There is no middle ground in respect to naturalization. We must either have naturalization laws and let foreigners become citizens, on equal terms of capacities and privileges, or we must exclude them altogether. If we abolish naturalization laws, we return to the European dogma: "Once a citizen, always a citizen." If we let foreigners be naturalized and don't extend to them equality of privileges, we set up classes and distinctions of persons wholly opposed to Republicanism. We will, as Rome did, have citizens who may be scourged. The three alternatives are presented—Our present policy, liberal, and just, and tolerant, and equal; or the European policy of holding the noses of native born slaves to the grind-stone of tyranny all their lives; or, odious distinctions of citizenship tending to social and political aristocracy. I am for the present laws of naturalization.

As to religion, the Constitution of the United States, art. 6th, sec. 3, especially provides that no *religious test* shall ever be required as a qualification to any office or public trust under the United States. The state of Virginia has, from her earliest history, passed the most liberal laws, not only towards naturalization, but towards foreigners. But I have said enough to show the spirit of American laws and the true sense of American maxims.

3rd. Know-Nothingism is against the spirit of the Reformation and of Protestantism?

What was there to Reform?

Let the most bigoted Protestant enumerate what he defines to have been the abominations of the church of Rome. What would he say were the worst? The secrets of Jesuitism, of the *Auto da fe*, of the Monasteries and of the Nunneries. The private penalties of the Inquisition's Scavenger's daughter. Proscription, Persecution, Bigotry, Intolerance, Shutting up of the Book of the Word. And do Protestants now mean to out-Jesuit the Jesuits? Do they mean to strike and not be seen? To be felt and not to be heard? To put a shudder upon humanity by the Masks of Mutes? Will they wear the Monkish cowls? Will they inflict penalties at the polls without reasoning together with their fellows at the hustings? Will they proscribe? Persecute? Will they bloat up themselves into that bigotry which would burn non-conformists? Will they not tolerate freedom of conscience, but doom dissenters, in secret conclave, to a forfeiture of civil privileges for a religious difference? Will they not translate the scripture of their faith? Will they visit us with dark lanterns and execute us by signs, and test oaths, and in secresy?

Protestantism! forbid it!

If anything was ever open, fair and free—if anything was ever blatant even—it was the Reformation. To quote from a mighty British pen: "It gave a mighty impulse and increased activity to thought and enquiry, agitated the inert mass of accumulated prejudices throughout Europe. The effect of the concussion was general. but the shock was greatest in this country" (England.) It toppled down the full grown intolerable abuses of centuries at a blow; heaved the ground from under the feet of bigoted faith and slavish obedience; and the roar and dashing of opinions, loosened from their accustomed hold, might be heard like the noise of an angry sea, and has never yet subsided. Germany first broke the spell of misbegotten fear, and gave the watchword; but England joined the shout, and echoed it back, with her island voice, from her thousand cliffs and craggy shores, in a longer and a louder strain. With that cry the genius of Great Britain rose, and threw down the gauntlet to the nations. There was a mighty fermentation; the waters were out; public opinion was in a state of projection; Liberty was held out to all to think and speak the truth; men's brains were busy; their spirits stirring; their hearts full; and their hands not idle. Their eyes were opened to expect the greatest things, and their ears burned with curiosity and zeal to know the truth, that the truth might make them free. The death blow which had been struck at scarlet vice and bloated hypocrisy, loosened tongues, and made the talismans and love tokens of Popish superstitions with which she had beguiled her followers and committed abominations with the people, fall harmless from their necks."

The translation of the Bible was the chief engine in the great work. It threw open, by a secret spring, the rich treasures of religion and morality, which had then been locked up as in a shrine. It revealed the visions of the Prophets, and conveyed the lessons of inspired teachers to the meanest of the people. It gave them a common interest in a common cause. Their hearts burnt within them as they read. It gave a mind to the people, by giving them common subjects of thought and feeling. It cemented their Union of character and sentiment; it created endless diversity and collision of opinion. They found objects to employ their faculties, and a motive in the magnitude of the consequences attached to them, to exert the utmost eagerness in the pursuit of truth, and the most daring intrepidity in maintaining it. Religious controversy sharpens the understanding by the subtlety and remoteness of the topics it discusses, and braces the will by their infinite importance. We perceive in the history of this period a nervous, masculine intellect. No levity, no feebleness, no indifference; or, if there were, it is a relaxation from the intense activity which gives a tone to its general character. But there is a gravity approaching to piety, a seriousness of impression, a conscientious severity of argument, an habitual fervor of enthusiasm in their method of handling almost every subject. The debates of the schoolmen were sharp and subtle enough; but they wanted interest and grandeur, and were besides confined to a few. They did not affect the general mass of the community. But the Bible was thrown open to all ranks and conditions "to own and read," with its wonderful table of contents, from Genesis to the Revelations. Every village in England would present the scene so well described in Burns' "Cotter's Saturday Night." How unlike this agitation, this shock, this angry sea, this fermentation, this shout and its echoes, this impulse and activity, this concussion, this general effect, this blow, this earthquake, this roar and dashing, this longer and louder strain, this public opinion, this liberty to all to think and speak the truth, this stirring of spirits, this opening of eyes, this zeal TO KNOW—not *nothiug*—but the *truth*, that the truth might make them free. How unlike to this is Know-Nothingism, sitting and brooding in secret to proscribe Catholics and naturalized citizens! Protestantism protested against secresy, it protested against shutting out the light of truth, it protested against proscription, bigotry and intolerance. It loosened all tongues and fought the owls and bats of night with the light of meridian day. The argument of Know-Nothings is the argument of silence. The order ignores all knowledge. And its proscription can't arrest itself within the limit of excluding Catholics and naturalized citizens. It must proscribe natives and Protestants both, who will not consent to unite in proscribing Catholics and naturalized citizens. Nor is that all; it must not only apply to birth and religion, it must necessarily extend itself to the business of life as well as to political preferments. The instances have already occurred. Schoolmistresses have been dismissed from schools in Philadelphia, and carpenters from a building in Cincinnati.

4th. It is not only opposed to the Reformation and Protestantism, but it is opposed to the faith, hope and charity of the gospel. Never was any triumph more complete than that of the open conflict of Protestants against the Pope and priestcraft. They did not oppose proscription because it was a policy of Catholics; but they opposed Catholics because they employed proscription. Proscription, not Catholics, was the odium to them. Here, now, is Know-Nothingism combatting proscription and exclusiveness with proscription and exclusiveness, secrecy with secrecy, Jesuitism with Jesuitism. Toleration, by American example, had begun its march throughout the earth. It trusted in the power of truth, had faith in Christian love and charity, and in the certainty that God would decide the contest. Here, now, is an order proposing to destroy the effect of our moral example. The Pope himself would soon be obliged, by our moral suasion, to yield to Protestants in Catholic countries their privileges of worship and rites of burial. But, no, the proposition now is, "to fight the devil with fire," and to proscribe and exclude because they proscribe and exclude. And they take up the weapons of Popery without knowing how to wield them half so cunningly as the Catholics do. The Popish priests are rejoiced to see them giving countenance to their example, and expect to make capital and will make capital out of this step backwards from the progress of the reformation. Protestantism has lost nothing by toleration, but may lose much by proscription.

5th. It is against the peace and purity of the Protestant churches and in aid of priestcraft within their folds, to secretly organize orders for religious combined with political ends. The world—I mean the sinner's world—will be set at war with the sects who unite in this crusade against tolerance and freedom of conscience and of speech. Christ's kingdom is not of this world, and freemen will not submit to have the Protestant any more than the Catholic churches attempt to influence political elections, without a struggle from without. And the churches from within must reach a point when they must struggle among themselves and with each other. *Peace* is the fruit of righteousness, and righteousness and peace must flee away together from a fierce worldly war for secular power. And the churches must be corrupted, too, as evil passions, hatred, and jealousy, and ambition, and envy, and revenge, and strife arise and temptations steal away the hearts of votaries from the humble service of the "meek and lowly Jesus." Protestant priestcraft is cousin germain to Catholic; and where is this to end but in giving to our Protestant priests—the worst of them, I mean—such as will "put on the livery of heaven to serve the devil in"—a control of political power, and thus to bring about the worst union which could be devised, of church and state! The state will prostitute and corrupt any church, and any church will enslave any state. Corrupt our Protestant priests as the Catholics have been, with temporal and political power, and they will be of the same "old leaven"—the same old beast—the same old ox going about with straw in his mouth! And where will the war of sects end? When the Protestant priests have gotten the power, which of their sects is to prevail? The Catholics proscribed, which denomination next is to fall? The Episcopal church, my mother church, is denounced by some as the bastard daughter of the whore of Rome. Is she next to be put upon the list of proscription? And when she is excluded, how are the Predestinarians and Armenians to agree among themselves? Which is to put up the Governor for Virginia or the President for the United States? Which is to have the offices, and how is division to be made of the spoils? Sir, this secret association, founded on proscription and intolerance, must end in nothing short of corruption and persecution of all sects, and in a civil war against the domination of priestcraft, Protestant or Catholic. Indeed, it is so, already, that a real reason for this *secrecy* is that the priests, who have a zeal without knowledge against the Pope, are unwilling to be seen in their union with this dark-lantern movement! Woe, woe, woe! to the hypocrite who leaves the work of his Master, the Prince of Peace, the Great High Priest after the order of Melchisedeck, for a worldly work like this!

6th. It is against free civil government, by instituting a secret oligarchy, beyond the reach of popular and public scrutiny, and supported by blind instruments of tyranny, bound by test oaths. If the oaths and proceedings of induction of members published be true, they bind the noviciates from the start to a passive obedience but to one law, the order of intolerance and proscription. Men are led to them by a burning curiosity to know that they are to *Know-Nothing!* The novelty of admission beguiles them into adherence. They assemble to take oaths and promise to obey. To obey whom? Do the masses, will the masses, is it intended that the masses of their members shall know whom? Where is the central seat of the *Veiled Prophet?* In New York? New England? or Old England? Who knows that Know-Nothingism is not influenced by a cabal abroad—by a foreign influence? Whence passes the sign?—Of course from a common centre somewhere. Is that centre in Virginia, for the orders here? If not, is it not alarming that our people in this state are to be swerved by a sign from somewhere, anywhere else, to go for this or that side of a cause, for this or that candidate for election? Those orders must have degrees; the degrees are higher and lower, of course, and the higher must prescribe the rule to govern. Each degree must have its higher officers, and all the orders must be subject to some one. Now, how many persons constitute the select few of the highest functionaries, nobody knows. Nobody knows who they are, where they are, or how many of them there are. They exist somewhere in the dark. Their blows can't be guarded against, for they strike, not like freemen bold, bravely for rights, but unseen, and to make conquest of rights. Their adherents are sworn to secrecy and to obey. They magnify their numbers and influence by the very mystery of their organization, and the timid and time-serving fly to them for fear of proscription or for hope of reward. They quietly warn friends not to stand in the way of their axe, and friends begin to apprehend that it is time to save themselves by Knowing Nothing. They threaten their enemies, and some of their enemies skulk from fear of offending them. They alarm a nation, and a nation, with its political and church parties, gives them at oncce consideration and respect as a power to be dreaded or courted. Thus, in a night, as it were, has an oligarchy grown up in secret to control our liberties, to dictate to parties, to guide elections, and to pass laws. They are establishing presses, too, but we cannot define from their positions a single principle which we can say Know-Nothings may not disown and disavow. The Prophet of Khorassan never gave out words more cabalistic—words to catch by sounds, and sounding the very opposite of what they really mean. When they have men's fears, curiosity, hopes, the people's voices, the ballot boxes, the press, at their command, how long will our minds be free, or persons safe, or property secure? How long will stand the pillars of freedom of speech and of the pen, when liberty of conscience is gone and birth is made to "make the man?" He is a dastard, indeed, who fears to oppose an oligarchy or secret cabal like this, and loves not human rights well enough to protect them.

7th. It is opposed to our progress as a nation. No new acquisition can ever be made by purchase or conquest, if foreigners or Catholics are in the boundaries of the acquired countries; for, surely we would not seek to take jurisdiction over them; to make them slaves; to raise up a distinct class of persons to be excluded from the privileges of a Republic. If not for their own sakes, for the sake of the Republic we would save ourselves from this example.

As early as 1787, we established a great land ordinance. The most perfect system of eminent domain, of proprietary titles, and of territorial settlements, which the world had ever beheld to bless the homeless children of men. It had the very housewarming of hospitality in it. It wielded the logwood axe, and cleared a continent of forests. It made an exodus in the old world, and dotted the new with log-cabins, around the hearths of which the tears of the aged and the oppressed were wiped away, and cherub children were born to liberty, and sang its songs, and have grown up in its strength and might and majesty. It brought together foreigners of every country and clime—immigrants from Europe of every language and religion, and its most wonderful effect has been to assimilate all races. Irish and German, English and French, Scotch and Spaniard, have met on the western prairies, in the western woods, and have peopled villages and towns and cities—queen cities, rivalling the marts of eastern commerce; and the Teutonic and Celtic and Anglo-Saxon races have in a day mingled into one undistinguishable mass—and that one is American!"—American in every sense and in every feeling, in every instinct, and in every impulse of American patriotism. The raw German's ambition is first to acquire land enough upon which to send word back to the Baron he left behind him, that he does not envy him his principality!

The Irishman no longer hurra's for "my Lord" or "my Lady," but exclaims in his heart of hearts that "this is a free country." The children of all are crossed in blood, in the first generation, so that ethnology can't tell of what parentage they are—they all become brother and sister Jonathans—Jonathans to sow and plant grain—Jonathans to raise and drive stock—Jonathans to organize townships and counties and states of free election—Jonathans to establish schools and colleges and rear orators, sages and statesmen for the Senate—Jonathans to take a true heart aim with the rifle at any foe who dares invade a common country—Jonathans to carry conquest of liberty to other lands, until the whole earth shall be filled with the glory of Americanism! As in the colonies, as in the revolution, as in the last war, so have foreigners and immigrants of every religion and tongue, contributed to build up the temple of American law and liberty, until its spire reaches to heaven, whilst its shadow rests on earth!! If there has been a turnpike road to be beaten out of the rocky metal, or a canal to be dug, foreigners and immigrants have been armed with the mattock and the spade; and, if a battle on sea or land had to be fought, foreigners and immigrants have been armed with the musket and the blade. So have foreigners and immigrants proved that their influence has not impaired the genius, or the grace, or gladness, or glory of American institutions. At no time have they warred upon our religion in the west, and they have been at peace among themselves. The Pope has lost more than he has gained of proselytes by the Catholics coming here. No proscription but one has ever disturbed the religious tolerance of the west, and that one was to drive out the religion of an imposter which struck at every social relation surrounding it. If Know-Nothings may tolerate Mormons, I can't see why they leave *them* to their religious liberty and select the very mother church of Protestantism itself for persecution and proscription. But the west, I repeat, made up of foreigners and immigrants of every religion and tongue, the west is as purely patriotic, as truly American, as genuinely Jonathan, as any people who can claim our nationality. Now, is not here proof in war and in peace that the apprehension of foreign influence, brought here by immigrants, is not only groundless but contradicted by the facts of our settlements and developments? Did a nation ever so grow as we have done under land ordinances and our laws of naturalization? They have not made aristocracies, but sovereigns and sovereignties of the people of the west. They have strengthened the stakes of our dominion and multiplied the sons and daughters of America so that now she can muster an army, and maintain it, too, outnumbering the strength of any invaders, and making "a host of freedom which is the host of God!"

Now, shall all this policy and its proud and happy fruits be cast aside for a contracted and selfish scheme of intolerance and exclusion? Shall the unnumbered sections of our public lands be fenced in against immigrants? Shall hospitality be denied to foreign settlers? Shall no asylum be left open to the poor and the oppressed of Europe? Shall the clearing of our lands be stopped? Shall population be arrested? Shall progress be made to stand still? Are we surfeited with prosperity? Shall no more territory be acquired? Shall Bermuda be left a *mare clausum* of the Gulf of Mexico, and Jamaica, a key of South American conquest and acquisition, in the hands of England; Cuba, a depot of domination over the mouth of the Mississippi, in the hands of Spain, just strong enough to keep it from us for some strong maritime power to seize, whenever they will conquor or force a purchase, Central America, in the gate-way of commerce between our Atlantic and Pacific possessions—lest foreigners be let in among us, and Catholics come to participate in our privileges? Verily, this is a strange way to help American institutions and to promote American progress. No, we have institutions which can embrace a world, all mankind with all their opinions, prejudices and passions, however diverse and clashing, provided we adhere to the law of Christian charity and of free toleration. But the moment we dispense with these laws, the pride, and progress, and glory, and good of American institutions will cease forever, and the memory of them will but goad the affections of their mourners. Selfishness, utter selfishness alone, can enjoy these American blessings, without desiring that all mankind shall participate in their glorious privileges. Nothing, nothing is so dangerous to them, nothing can destroy them so soon and so certainly, as *secret societies*, formed for political and religious ends combined, founded on proscription and intolerance, without necessity, against law, against the spirit of the Christian Reformation, against the whole scope of Protestantism, against the faith, hope, and charity of the Bible, against the peace and purity of the churches; against free government by leading to oligarchy and a union of church and state; against human progress, against national acquisitions, against American hospitality and comity, against American maxims of expatriation, and allegiance and protection, against American settlements and land ordinances, against Americanism in every sense and shape!

Lastly. What are the evils complained of, to make a pretext for these innovations against American policy, as heretofore practised with so much success and such exceeding triumph?

1st. The first cause, most prominent, is that the native and Protestant feeling has been exasperated by the course pursued by both political parties, in the last several Presidential campaigns; they have cajoled and "*honey-fuggled*" with both Catholics and foreigners by birth, naturalized and unnaturalized, *ad nauseam*.

Foreigners and Catholics were not so much to blame for that as both parties. And take these election toys from them, and does any one suppose that they would not resort to some other humbug? Is not another hobby now arising to put down both of these pets of party? Is not the donkey of Know-Nothingism now kicking its heels at the lap-dogs of the "rich Irish brogue" and the "sweet German accent," for the fondlings and pettings of political parties?

2nd. Both parties have violated the election laws and laws of naturalization, in rushing green emigrants, just from on ship-board, up to the polls to vote.

This, again, is the fault of both parties. And this is confined chiefly, if not entirely, to the cities. It don't reach to the ballot boxes of the country at large, and is not a drop in the ocean of our political influence. In New York, Philadelphia, Baltimore, Cincinnati, and New Orleans, the abuse, I venture to say, don't number, in fact, 500 votes. It is nothing everywhere else, in a country of universal suffrage and of twenty millions of free people. And would perjury and fraud in elections be arrested by the attempt to exclude Catholics and foreigners by birth from office?—or, by extending the limitation of time for naturalization?—or, by repealing the naturalization laws? Either of these remedies for the error would mnltiply the perjuries and the frauds and the foreign votes. Then there would be a pretext for obtaining by fraud and force what was denied under law. By making naturalization rather to follow immediately upon the oath of allegiance, and that to depend on the will and the good character of the applicant, fraud and perjury would rather be stripped of their pretexts. The foreigners would be at once exalted in their self-respect and dignity of deportment, right would enable them to exercise the elective franchise in peace, and the country would escape the demoralization resulting from a violation of the laws, and from the means employed to set at nought their force and effect.

3rd. Foreigners have abused the protection of the United States abroad.

If they have, it was a violation of law. They cannot well do it, without the want of care and vigilance in our consular and diplomatic functionaries abroad. Citizens at home abuse our protection, and they are not always punished for their crimes.

4th. Catholics, it is urged, have been combined and obeyed the signs of their bishops and priests in elections, and have been influenced in their votes to a great extent by religious and exclusive considerations.

If they have, that is one of the best reasons why Protestants should not follow their example. It is evil, and the less there is of it the better for all. Let bigotry and proscription belong to any sect rather than to Protestants. When they follow alleged Catholic examples, which they arraign, as dangerous and mischievous, then they themselves become as Catholics, according to their own opinions, dangercus and mischievous.

5th. Catholics and Catholic governments, it is urged, have always excluded Protestants from religious and social privileges in their countries.

And how much have we gained upon them by following the opposite policy? By tolerance we have grown so great as now to make them feel the necessity to respect our title to comity and right to a separate enjoyment of the privileges of Protestants. Our government is interposing in that behalf, and I fear it will not be assisted any in its negotiations by the attempt here to proscribe Catholics and strangers by birth.

6th. It is complained that in some instances, in New York particularly, the Catholics have been arrogant, exclusive and anti-republican in their attempts to control the public schools, and to exclude from them the free and open study of the word of God.

How can this bigotry be subdued by bigotry, which retires itself in secrecy and proscribes all who don't proscribe Catholics? There is no homœpathy in moral disease. Proscription and bigotry and secrecy must not be prescribed for the maladies of proscription, bigotry, and hiding of the word! The diseases would then be epidemics among Protestants, Catholics, and all. The open and lawful and liberal means for either prevention or correction of this evil are simple and efficacious if righteously applied.

7th. It is urged that Catholics recognize the supremacy of the Pope and submission to priestcraft, which might, under circumstances, be destructive of our free government.

Suppose that to be so, there are worse sects among us, whom Know-Nothings pretend not to assail. There are the Mormon polygamists; there are the necromancers of Spiritual Rappings; and there is a sect which aspires not only to destroy free government, but the great globe and all that it inhabit—the millenial Millerites. And, it is about as likely that Millerites will set the world on fire in one day, as that Popery will ever be able to break up or bow down this republic. The prophecies must all fail, and Christ's dominion upon earth must cease, and printing presses and telegraphs and steam must be lost to the arts, and revolutions must go backwards, and the sky must fall and catch Know-Nothings, before the times of Revelations are out, and the Pope catches "Uncle Sam."

No, no, no—there is not a reason in all these complaints, which is not satisfied by our laws as they exist, and not an error, which may not be corrected by the proper application of the lawful authority at our command, without resorting to the extraordinary, extrajudicial, revolutionary, and anti-American plan of a secret society of intolerance and proscription.

I belong to a secret society, but for no political purpose. I am a native Virginian *intus et in cute*, a Virginian; my ancestors on both sides for two hundred years were citizens of this country and this state—half English, half Scotch. I am a Protestant by birth, by baptism, by intellectual belief and by education and by adoption. I am an American, in every fibre and in every feeling an American; yet in every character, in every relation, in every sense, with all my head, and all my heart, and all my might, I protest against this secret organization of native Americans, and of Protestants to proscribe Roman Catholic and naturalized citizens!

Now, will they proscribe me?

That question weighs not a feather with

Your obedient servant,

HENRY A. WISE.

THE FIRST APPEARANCE OF KNOW-NOTHINGISM IN VIRGINIA.

It is unknown to the unitiated at what precise time Know-Nothingism made its entrance into Virginia; but, from the most reliable information we can gather, the first council was organized in the town of Charlottesville, some time in the month of July, 1854, and very soon after another in the city of Richmond. These councils, in pursuance to the Know-Nothing Ritual, were organized by the authority of the Grand Council of Thirteen of the city of New York. From this time until about the latter part of October, we have no newspaper account of operations. But during this interim of nearly three months, it is our impression that the Grand Council of Thirteen was very industriously organizing councils in the various towns and cities of the state. After the state had become well checkered with councils, the Grand Council of Thirteen delegated one Rev. Mr. Evans to establish a state council in the city of Richmond. This state council was empowered by the parent body in New York to grant charters for the establishment of councils in every nook and corner of the state; and the consequence was, that in nearly every secluded grove, retired school-house, and concealed recess, could be found a band of men, veiled in secrecy and under the cover of darkness, administering Jesuitical oaths and teaching cabalistic signs to the thoughtless, indiscreet and unsuspecting noviciates. The citizens of this commonwealth should keep it fresh in their minds, that a portion of her citizens were once engaged in the work of palming upon them a political heresy, through the instrumentality of a Northern emissary, coming under the specious guise and cloak of religion. New York was the hot bed of corruption from which a northern plague was to sweep the home and resting-place of Washington and Jefferson. The Richmond Enquirer noticed, in the following spirited manner, the organization of the state council by the Rev. Evans, of New York:

Know-Nothing Council in Richmond.—It is not generally known, we suspect, that a state council of the Know-Nothing order is to be held in this city to-day. In spite of the severe secrecy of their movements, this fact has transpired; and with it comes the additional intelligence that one Reverend Mr. Evans is present as representative of the "Grand National Council of Thirteen," of which Barker of New York is President. This emissary brings along a redundant supply of the venom of intolerance, wherewith to inoculate the brethren in this region and to corrupt the native generosity of the Virginia character. He imports, also, a copious supply of pass-words and other cabalistic signs, and is in every way equipped for the work of drill-sergeant and hierophant. Is it not a shame that such creatures should come here, and, under cover of darkness, deposit the poison of intolerance and proscription on the soil which Jefferson has consecrated to civil liberty and to freedom of conscience? The movements of the order are directed and controlled by a cabal in New York, and thus, should Know-Nothingism triumph in this state, the government of Virginia will be the creature of the "Council of Thirteen." Esteeming themselves competent to the management of their own affairs, Virginians have been proverbially jealous of foreign influence; nor will they now submit to the usurpation of this conclave of New York Know-Nothings. The sentiment of state-sovereignty and the pride of personal independence are equally outraged by the attempt thus to subjugate us.

Our neighbor of the Dispatch, with commendable forethought, has warned persons attending the Fair against the depredations of the thieves who rifle pockets in the confusion of the crowd. It is our business to admonish all good citizens of the presence of the Know-Nothings, who, adopting the cunning artifice of pick-pockets and burglars, have availed themselves of the confusion and excitement of this occasion, to mature their plot against the security of society.

THE STAUNTON DEMOCRATIC CONVENTION.

After the claims of the various candidates spoken of for Governor had been thoroughly discussed through the public journals, delegates were sent from various counties of the state to meet in Convention at the town of Staunton, November 30th, 1854, for the purpose of making a proper selection of candidates for the office of Governor, Lieut. Governor and Attorney General. This Convention was one of the largest and most talented that ever assembled in the state for a political purpose.

Its proceedings were very animated. Parties soon resolved themselves into two, one of them supporting Mr. Wise, the other Mr. Leake. Its session lasted three days, and Mr. Wise was not nominated until the morning of the third and last day. As its proceedings were marked by great excitement and warmth of feeling, and only an elaborate and detailed rehearsal of them, too voluminous for our space, could do justice to all who participated in the debates and ballotings, we shall confine ourselves to a mere skeleton recital of its leading transactions.

The Convention was organized by the appointment of Oscar M. Crutchfield, Speaker of the House of Delegates, President, and Wm. F. Ritchie, editor of the Enquirer, and Ro. W. Hughes, editor of the Examiner, Secretaries.

The great debate and turning point of everything done by the Convention was upon the original resolution presented by Mr. Shackelford, and upon an amendment which was offered by Mr. Garnett, of Essex, to the same.

Mr. Shackelford's resolution was—

Resolved, That this Convention will not make a nomination for Governor, Lieutenant Governor, or Attorney General, unless the candidate receive votes of this Convention sufficient to represent a majority of the whole Democratic vote of the state.

To this resolution, Mr. Muscoe R. H. Garnett, of the county of Essex, who was the leader of Mr. Wise's friends, offered the following amendment:

Resolved, That it shall require a *majority of the votes cast* to nominate candidates for Governor, Lieutenant Governor and Attorney General.

This amendment was opposed with great ability by many of the leading men of the Convention. The speeches of Messrs. Fauntleroy, Irving, Aylett, James Barbour, N. C. Claiborne, J. W. Massie and W. H. Harman were of great ability and eloquence. It was the most spirited and able off-hand debate that ever transpired in a political convention. The debate was continued into the night of Thursday, the 30th November, 1854, the first day of the session. The vote was then taken, and was scaled on the principle of allowing each county represented a number equal to its Democratic vote in the presidential election of 1852. The process of scaling the vote was so tedious, that the Convention adjourned over until the next morning in order to allow the secretaries time to compute the result.

Friday, Dec. 1.—On the meeting of the Convention this morning, the result of the vote on Garnett's amendment was announced as follows:

For the amendment,	35,212
Against the amendment,	26,194
Majority,	9,018

So decided was the opposition manifested to this result, and to the amendment, that a re-consideration was at once moved, and a long and most animated debate was kept up through the greater portion of the day. Finally, a second vote was taken on the same proposition as at first with the following result:

For the amendment,	32,903
Against it,	29,059
Majority,	3,844

This vote, of course, settled the question, and the Convention decided that the majority of the votes cast in the Convention should nominate a candidate for the party—without reference to thirty unrepresented counties.

The contest on this important proposition was warm and excited from the fact that the adoption of Garnett's amendment was equivalent to the nomination of Mr. Wise; while the adoption of Shackelford's resolution, if not equivalent to the nomination of Mr. Leake, by requiring a vote larger than Mr. Wise's friends could have polled, would have resulted in the nomination of a compromise candidate.

This amendment having been adopted, the Convention proceeded at once to the nomination of a candidate for the office of governor.

Mr. Douglas, of New Kent, put Mr. H. A. Wise in nomination, and Mr. N. C. Claiborne, of Franklin, presented the name of Shelton F. Leake. Prominent among the speakers during the evening were Messrs. Berry of Alexandria, Fauntleroy of Winchester, Skinner of Augusta, Brown of Kanawha, Browne of Stafford, Meade of Petersburg, Kenna of Kanawha, and English of Logan.

All of these speeches were creditable, and many of them eloquent and telling. It cannot be said that they were sermons inculcating doctrines of affection and brotherly love. Although the speakers were personally courteous, yet their political reviews, comments, &c., on public men were the bitterest it is ever one's fortune to listen to. An excited audience, by loud applause and boisterous manifestations of approbation and displeasure, rendered the whole scene one of extraordinary excitement. The large badly lighted hall seemed the theatre of the bitterest and most envenomed feelings during this long and acrimonious debate. Such a scene was never presented in a Democratic Convention before, and we hope never will be presented again. The most violent and pointed assaults upon the prominent men of our own party were the most loudly applauded.

Late on the night of the second day of the session a vote was taken, and the Convention adjourned over until the next morning.

Saturday, Dec. 2.—The first thing done was the announcement of the vote for the nominees for Governor, as follows:

H. A. Wise,	31,416
S. F. Leake,	25,762
Wm. Smith,	2,125
Alex. R. Holladay,	1,236
J. A. Seddon,	2,491
Faulkner,	259
	63,289

Necessary to a choice 31,645.

Wise falling short of a majority 229.

Some further debate took place. Ex-Governor Smith was put in nomination by Mr. Hiner, of Pendleton, and withdrawn. Finally another vote was taken, and the result was—

Wise,	34,034
Leake,	28,009
Seddon,	973
Holladay,	67
Smith,	290
	63,373

Necessary to a choice 31,687.

Majority for Wise 2,347.

And Mr. Wise, was declared to be nominated.

The result of the second ballot was announced on Saturday afternoon, and in consequence of changes in the vote of Halifax and Greenbrier, Mr. Wise was nominated, getting a majority of 2,347. A proposition to make it unanimous failed.

The Convention then proceeded to the nomination of a candidate for the office of Lieut. Governor.

Dr. C. R. Harris of Augusta, A. G. Pendleton of Giles, Henry A. Edmundson of Roanoke, Elisha W. McComas of Kanawha, and Dan'l H. Hoge of Montgomery, were all put in nomination; but all except Dr. Harris and Mr. Pendleton were afterwards withdrawn. After zealous and urgent appeals for the candidates, a vote was taken, and the result was—

Harris,	29,126
Pendleton,	27,859
McComas,	1,121
Edmundson,	2,880
Hoge,	1,015

Necessary to a choice, 31,002.

No election.

The names of Dr. Harris and Mr. Pendleton were withdrawn.

Mr. McComas was again put in nomination, and Col. W. H. Harman was also nominated. A spirited series of eulogies of the nominees ensued, and the vote being taken, was announced, after a recess, as follows:

McComas,	32,520
Harman,	26,447

Mr. McComas was declared duly nominated; and on motion of Col. Harman the nomination was made unanimous.

W. P. Bocock, the then Attorney General, was re-nominated by acclamation.

Mr. McComas being present addressed the Convention.

The following resolution was adopted:

Resolved, That the official career of Franklin Pierce has been marked by a perfect observance of the limitations of the Constitution and an entire fidelity to the principles upon which he came into power; and therefore he is entitled to the confidence of the friends of Constitutional Liberty in every section of the Confederacy.

So the result of the proceedings of the Convention was the following ticket:

For Governor—HENRY A. WISE, of Accomac.

For Lieut. Governor—ELISHA W. McCOMAS, of Kanawha.

For Attorney General—WILLIS P. BOCOCK, of Richmond.

The Convention adjourned *sine die* a little after twelve o'clock at night, the Chairman making a brief valedictory address. The closing scenes were quite uproarious, but not acrimonious as those at an earlier period of the session had been.

COMMENTS OF THE PRESS UPON THE STAUNTON NOMINEES.

These nominations did not give general satisfaction to the Democratic party throughout the state. The principal objection was to Mr. Wise who had voted for the Whig nominees in 1840, and been a very warm opponent of General Jackson in Congress. Although Mr. Wise had been a strict adherent to the party since 1841, and been honored as a public servant by John Tyler and James K. Polk, and performed efficient service on various occasions; yet it was the disposition of many not to give him their support. He was held up to the party as an inconsistent, self-willed, dangerous, and unstable man. The Know-Nothings affected great satisfaction at the result of the Staunton deliberations. No candidate ever went before the people for any office under more discouraging circumstances than Mr. Henry A. Wise. Never was a candidate before so little understood, or so much misrepresented and slandered; but we shall see how gallantly and successfully he surmounted these difficulties:

From the (Rockingham) Valley Democrat.

Our Nominees.—In obedience to the behest of the Democratic Convention held in Staunton last week, we proudly throw our banner to the breeze, inscribed on its ample folds the names of Wise, McComas and Bocock, the chosen standard-bearers of the Democratic party in the coming gubernatorial contest.

We frankly acknowledge the nominations are not our first choice. We preferred others, and endeavored to secure their nomination in Convention. We, however, were disappointed in our wishes, the majority thinking the above ticket the most acceptable one to be recommended to the Democracy of Virginia. We, therefore, surrender our predilections upon the altar of our party, and shall use our utmost exertions to secure the election of the ticket.

It cannot be denied by any that the ticket is composed of men of the highest order of intellect. They are men around whom any party may be proud to rally. Our candidate for governor, Henry A. Wise, the fearless tribune of the people, will sweep the state like an avalanche. As an eminent Southern and fearless advocate of civil and religious liberty we could desire no better leader. His eloquent voice will summon the Democracy to the contest like the red cross of Murdock the sons of Clan-Alpine to the fight. It will arouse the latent energies of the old and excite the enthusiasm of the young—a blaze of enthusiastic fire will burn from every crag and from every cliff, and be reflected from the broad waters of the Ohio to the billowy ocean. Its echoes, like the shrill whistle of Rhoderick Dhu, will arouse the Democracy from the lowlands and the highlands, before whose resistless march the contemptible ism of the day and miserable trumperies of an hour will be scattered like autumnal leaves before the raging whirlwind.

We deem it superfluous to speak of his political character. In the halls of legislation he has won a national reputation, and stands before the country as a brilliant orator and accomplished statesman. Like Portia, his private character is above reproach. The breath of suspicion has not even dared to dim its lustre and brightness.

Our candidate for Lieutenant Governor, E. W. McComas, is a young man of ability and of the strictest integrity. As a member of the late Reform Convention he distinguished himself as an able and eloquent debater, and fearless advocate of the people's rights. He is eminently qualified for the position, and cannot fail to make an excellent presiding officer of the Senate. He has borne the flag of his country on the burning plains of Mexico, and won the distinction of a brave and generous soldier. He will ably sustain the leader of the Democracy in bearing aloft the democratic banner, and is entitled and should receive the cordial support of the democratic party of Virginia.

The name of Willis P. Bocock, our candidate for Attorney General, is familiar to the people of Virginia. He has proven himself to be a sound and able lawyer, pre-eminently qualified for the position to which he has been elevated. We trust the democracy will honor him again with their confidence.

Our candidates are now in the field, and it behooves every lover of democratic principles to buckle on his armor and go forth to battle against the hosts of Federalism and Know-Nothingism. The old flag ship of democracy must be kept on the old democratic platform of Jefferson and Madison. If the democracy do their duty we doubt not the result. With such chivalric spirits as Wise, McComas and Bocock as leaders, the democratic party proudly go forth to the battle, and challange our opponents to marshal their forces under whatever flag they may see proper. We care not whether it be under the banner of Federalism or the contemptible, drooping and cowardly oriflamb of Know-Nothingism; we shall meet them with the same pleasure, confident that our gallant champions will fearlessly and gallantly bear the States-Rights banner triumphantly to victory.

Democrats of the Tenth Legion! sleep not at your posts! If you would fulfil the just expectations of your party, and acquit yourselves with credit, you must prepare for the contest. Let action, ACTION! be your motto—plant the standard of democracy upon every hill-top and in every valley, and rally beneath its broad folds, with unity of feeling and sentiment, for Wise, McComas and Bocock.

Not less emphatic was the endorsement of the Richmond Examiner, which had most earnestly, of all the Democratic journals, remonstrated against the nomination of Mr. Wise. We extract its declaration of adhesion to the Staunton nominations:

From the Richmond Examiner of December 8th, 1854.

We should feel sorry, indeed, if there could be any doubt as to the course we and those who acted with us at Staunton shall pursue in the canvass now commenced. We shall go for the ticket. We have attested the sincerity of our preferences for men, openly, honestly and sufficiently. We have done so without reference to the maxim which modern political ethics have made a cardinal rule of conduct with successful candidates, *that they have friends to reward and enemies to punish;* for we went to Staunton under the conviction that we should not be able to overcome the vote by which our preferences were defeated. The question between men has been decided against us by regular and authoritative adjudication. The only question now is between the ticket of the Republican party of Virginia and that of the opposition to it, of whatever hue, form and creed. There is but one honorable choice; and, whether the opposition comes from the bosom of the Democratic party itself, or the dark caverns of secret conspiracy, or the veteran, scarred ranks of the ancient, open, declared Whig adversary, or from all quarters combined, we shall defend the Staunton nominations.

We have no fulsome eulogy for the distinguished nominees. We are more skilled in the language of censure than of laudation. Panegyric is not our *forte*, nor man-worship our besetting sin. But we will say, that Mr. Wise is eminently worthy of the confidence and support of the Virginia people. His brilliant qualities as a man will reflect lustre upon the office for which he is recommended. He is a man to whom we have never felt but one objection personally, and that was, that though as sound in politics now as the strictest Republican of the Virginia school, his career *had* been inconsistent and his record contradictory in a manner and to a degree which rendered it difficult for the party speakers and writers in this canvass to defend him, according to the old mode of party reasoning. We have said this frequently, and we do not mean to unsay it in the canvass at hand. But of all claims to public office, those of the mere party men are the flimsiest and most wretched. Consistency, in the mere party sense—that of having voted the party ticket blind, on all occasions, wright or wrong, through thick and thin—that of having sworn and argued that a measure was right whenever it was endorsed by party, and wrong whenever not—consistency of this base, cheap, description, is anything but "a jewel." The man who is ever faithful to his own convictions, scorning to submit his judgment to the behests either of party or of any other influence but his own conscience, is a true man, and is very apt to be fit recipient of public trust. The man who holds no opinion of his own, and who boasts to have never differed from his party in any act or thought of his life, is more apt to be a demagogue than a statesman. True consistency lies in fidelity to one's convictions of duty, however changing; and he is the safe politician who boldly avows and bravely adheres to those convictions under all circumstances. It is remarked that all the really great women the world has produced have held peculiar notions on the point of virtue. It is certain that the greatest statesmen of our country have been distinguished for their political inconsistency. Even Jefferson himself repudiated in the writings from Monticello the anti-slavery principles to which the prime of his life had been devoted. Jackson went into the executive office advocating some of the worst measures of the Federalists, proclaimed during his administration the most alarming and arrogant Federal dogmas, and yet laid down the reins of government with the merited reputation of a hero and champion of state rights. Calhoun, the honest politician, the Cato of his day, may be quoted on both sides of almost every great measure of public policy. Honesty, fidelity, capacity—the Jeffersonian tests—these, at last, are the true qualifications for office. Consistency, in the vulgar acceptation, belongs oftener to the demagogue and ignoramus than to the honest politician and the capable statesman. Those high personal qualities which make us love, admire, and trust in men, belong oftener to the rash, impulsive and brave, than to the cautious, calculating, and "consistent." If you judge Mr. Wise by the acts of his life, we admit that, in our opinion, he has few claims to consistency. But if you judge him by the impulses of his nature, and the fidelity and chivalric bravery of his adherence to them, the verdict in his favor is emphatic and beyond question.

The political horizon is filled with admonitions of trouble. The recent elections at the north reveal a state of feeling very portentious to the south. We are upon the eve of times which will try men's souls. Let us have a tried, brave, true southern man in the executive office of Virginia. At a time like this, let us look to the *metal* of our men, rather than to their "records." The Democracy of Virginia have declared at Staunton that they care not for political antecedents or partisan animosities, twenty years gone by, in the presence of the danger now threatening the south. They have resolved that old and obsolete differences, such as used to divide them from their political opponents at home, are not to be remembered against the true southern man in a contest upon that issue above all other issues—northern aggression against southern rights.

There is significance in the nomination of Mr. Wise. The Democracy of of Virginia have resolved, in disregard of past domestic animosities and old differences of opinion, to manifest their stern, uncompromising temper on the sectional issue by the man they mean to place at the head of affairs. When we make Henry A. Wise governor of Virginia, the north will know what we mean.

Mr. McComas is comparatively a young man; but has already distinguished himself by valuable public service. He has fought gallantly and won enviable laurels upon the field of battle. He was a member of the Reform Convention of 1850–51; and served with credit to himself and to the satisfaction of his constituents. He has always been a zealous advocate of the doctrines of State Rights; and, since he was entitled to a vote, has been an active, efficient and consistent Democrat.

Mr. Bocock has already passed the ordeal of the polls; and has proved an industrious, faithful and eminently able officer. The testimony to his efficiency, capacity and industry in the office of Attorney General, is unqualified and conclusive, and is alike creditable to himself and to the party which conferred the office upon bim.

The reasons in favor of rallying to this ticket are conclusive; and we invoke all the Democracy of Virginia to a zealous and active support of it. We repeat our sincere and candid opinions: The party will do its duty:—There is no danger of defeat.

CONFIDENCE OF THE OPPOSITION.

The opposition were so confident that the Staunton state ticket had produced schism and discord in the Democratic ranks, that the Richmond Whig made bold to forewarn the Democracy of their coming fate, in the following language:

"The indications of public sentiment throughout the country, as far as we can gather it, from the tone of the Whig and Democratic press, and from our private correspondence, foreshadow a gloomy prospect for the nominees of the Staunton Convention. In the Whig ranks there is union of sentiment, harmony of action, and resolution of purpose; in the Democratic ranks there is discord, apprehension, and a general and growing mistrust. * * * We can assure our neighbor that the great Whig party is vital in its existence—firmly united—and fully prepared for a successful campaign. At the proper time, and in due form, and with united forces, it will unfold its banner, and we fear nothing for its success."

As soon as it was known in other parts of the Union that the Democracy of Virginia were ready for the conflict, with the hitherto invincible Know-Nothings, all eyes were turned upon the state. It was well known that the Democracy had to contend with a formidable, wily and insidious enemy, flushed with victory. The Democratic party felt its danger and the responsibility of its position. Their brethren of the southern states felt a deep anxiety for the success of the Democracy of a state that had always repudiated and withstood Federalism in all its Protean characters. The Washington Sentinel contained the following article counseling the party against the snares of the enemy, the boasts of the new party, and calling upon Virginia to preserve her escutcheon untarnished:

THE VIRGINIA ELECTIONS.—The state of Virginia is regarded at this time with great interest by all parties. In a few months elections for state officers and members of Congress will be held, and more than ordinary preparations are now being made for the opening canvass. The ancient renown of that venerable commonwealth, her undeviating consistency, and her political influence, attract to her a large share of public attention.

Thoroughly and consistently Democratic, as she has ever been, the Democrats are naturally solicitous that she should maintain that character. When other states have faltered and fallen, she has been true and unflinching, and hence it would be a signal triumph for the opposition if they could gain her. To that triumph they proudly and ambitiously aspire. Already they begin to boast. Months in advance of the election, here in Washington, they begin to claim the victory. They have rolls, lists and records. In imagination they have elected their governor and stricken down several Democratic members of Congress. They give the figures with great precision, and boldly aver, that all arrangements to secure their success have been completely consummated.

It is meet that the free citizens of Virginia should know that grand councils have gravely assembled to decide for whom they shall vote, and that instructions have been issued which they are imperiously required to obey. The time was when they owed allegiance to their state. That time has passed. The time was, when they announced their opinions and their purposes in the open streets and in the public highways. That time, too, has passed. Those mysterious men who sprung up from the gutters of New York and commenced their remarkable career by carrying city elections, have swept with a success almost unparalleled the abolitionized state of Massachusetts, where Democrats were odious, and even Free Soil Whigs were wanting in rankness—these mysterious men have taken the good old state of Virginia under their especial guardianship. In the secret lodges—at the midnight conclaves, in Boston and in New York, in Chicago and Syracuse, they pray and they weep over the proud old commonwealth. They have vowed to win her, and no effort will be spared to execute that vow. We are told that here in Washington plans have been consummated by which the fate of Democracy in Virginia is sealed! Of course we attach no importance to the information. It is but the boast that is designed to discourage Democrats and encourage the opposition.

The opposition! What is it? It is not that old and respectable and avowed Whig opposition that we were wont to encounter, with Bank, Tariff and Distribution inscribed on its banners. It is not that opposition that Clay led and Webster battled for. It is a fusion, an amalgation of isms. For the first time fusion is proposed in Virginia. For the first time an ism has dared to rear its crest in that ancient Dominion.

Those who join this opposition will not do as our opponents of the olden time were accustomed to do. They will not stand up and declare their sentiments like freemen. When these men meet in the open streets and the public highways, they will give mysterious signals—that none but the initiated can understand. They dare not talk out like honest men.

Has the Old Dominion fallen so low that her sons are afraid to proclaim their sentiments? Are those who are wont to interchange their opinions on public affairs, when they met at court greens, at country stores, or at cross roads, struck dumb by a secret and a despotic association that had its origin in a distant state, with different institutions? We devoutly pray that no such degeneracy will curse that good old state, whose greatest fault has been that she uttered her sentiments too boldly.

Yet, it cannot be denied that the opposition to Democracy, in Virginia, has resolved itself into this mysterious organization. Most of those who were Whigs, are Whigs no longer. Without pretending to be convinced of the unsoundness of their principles, they have renounced those principles, and gone over to a party that professes its willingness to support either a Bank or an anti-Bank, a Tariff or anti-Tariff, a Distribution or an anti-Distribution man. Indeed, although nearly the whole of those who belong to this opposition to the Democracy of Virginia are Whigs, they declare, privately and publicly, that they would rather support Democratic than Whig candidates. Two contradictions are involved in this declaration. First, that being Whigs, they should prefer Democrats; and, secondly, that, prefering Democrats, they should oppose the regular Democratic nominees. This contradiction, or rather these contradictions, are explained in this way: They want to get disappointed and disaffected Democrats to run against the regular nominees, in order to relieve themselves of the odium of being a Whig organization, and in order to entice Democrats into that organization.

But we are happy to say that the better sort of Whigs—those who scorn impure alliances, those who love open honesty and manly independence, and who will not agree to be controlled by a secret society that sprang up outside of Virginia and in an anti-slavery state, will not act in conjunction with this opposition. They will do as many of the strongest Whigs of Illinois did in the recent election in that state. They will vote for the Democratic candidates. If they are forced to quit their party, they will rather vote with an open, a manly, and an honest party, than with a secret and a mysterious order that has disbanded and scattered them. A state rights Whig is more a Democrat than a Know-Nothing.

THE CRY OF DISAFFECTION.

A report was industriously circulated throughout the state that many of the most prominent men of the party were not only dissatisfied with the Staunton ticket, but would not give it their support. This had not only a great tendency to dissatisfy a large portion of the masses, but almost threatened a rupture, the very object aimed at by the Know-Nothing party. The report was false. It was true that there were some dissatisfied individuals who had had the confidence of the Democratic party; but these were, for the most part, or had been regarded, to use a popular term, as "fishy." It was these persons, claiming prominence and position in the party, and considering their claims for office and honor overlooked, that exhibited these disloyal proclivities. But the report was wholly untrue in regard to the sound members of the party. The Charlottesville Jeffersonian disposed in the following very effectual manner of the report in regard to several prominent and influential men:

From the Charlottesville Jeffersonian.

One of the many means resorted to by the Whigs, in order to produce disaffection in the Democratic party towards their nominees, is the statement which has been going the rounds of the opposition press, to the effect that five of the Democratic members of Congress from Virginia, (viz:) Messrs. Bayly, Letcher, McMullen, Smith and Powell, would not sustain the nomination of Mr. Wise. Now, for the satisfaction of our Democratic friends, we are authorized to state upon authentic information, that this rumor is a sheer fabrication of the enemies of the Democratic party, and that all the above named gentlemen, together with the entire Virginia delegation in Congress, will support Mr. Wise and the rest of the ticket. We were assured by Mr. Powell himself, in a personal interview with him, that the entire ticket would receive his support. The friends of Mr. Leake should not permit any such influences to induce them to withhold their support from the nominee of our party. We have been assured by Mr. Leake himself, that he, too, would give a zealous support to the nomination of Mr. Wise, and he *urges* that all of his friends should do likewise; since, in refusing to support Mr. Wise, they may lose everything, and cannot by possibility gain anything. They may not only lose the governor, but also their delegates to the Legislature, and their representatives in Congress. Issues of momentous importance depend upon the triumph of the Democracy in the approaching election. The New York Herald and its co-adjutors boast that they have for the present prostrated the administration party in the North, and they urge upon their friends in Virginia by all means to defeat Mr. Wise, or they regard his election as a test of the strength of the administration, and of Democratic States Rights principles in Virginia. They regard Mr. Wise as a champion of the administration in its support of the constitutional guarantees of the South. They know, moreover, that his election would crush out Nnow-Nothingism in this section of the Union, and would present an impassable barrier to the progress of that fusion which in the North has resulted in the election of a majority of anti-Nebraska and anti-Fugitive Slave Law men to Congress. Hence their anxiety to have him defeated. As we intimated above, in the approaching election, not only the supremacy of the Democratic party in the executive department of our state government, but the political complexion of the next Legislature, and of the Virginia representation in both Houses of Congress are involved. Upon the next Legislature will devolve the duty of electing two United States Senators, in the place of Messrs. Mason and Hunter, whose terms will soon expire. We, therefore, regard the success of our county delegations, and of our candidates for Congress, and the consequent ascendancy of the Democracy of Virginia in both branches of the National Legislature, as of paramount importance. For it is evident already, that another great battle must be fought on the floor of Congress, with the anti-Nebraska, Know-Nothing Fusionists of the North, who, 'tis said, have now a majority in the House of Representatives. We would entreat our friends, then, for the sake of the success of our county delegations, and of our faithful and sterling representative in Congress, Hon. Paulus Powell, if from no other consideration, to come up unitedly to the support of the nominees of the party, and present an unbroken phalanx, as in days past, to the common enemies of Democracy.

MR. WISE OPENS THE CANVASS—HIS ANTECEDENTS.

The Hon. Henry A. Wise, after publishing a list of appointments, opened the canvass at Ashland Hall, Norfolk city, January the 5th, 1855, in the manner thus described by the *Argus* newspaper of that city:

The campaign was commenced on Wednesday evening at Ashland Hall by our gallant and glorious nominee for Governor, in an address to a most crowded audience. The room was filled to overflowing by the most eager listeners, whom the eloquence of his words held strictly attentive for over two hours. The address was *his own*—such as he alone can deliver—forcible, well arranged, argumentative; abounding in the most bitter sarcasm and the most soothing appeals. It was one of his noblest efforts. Of its effect, we can say, as our neighbor of the *News*, that "we can only judge by the strict order maintained, the earnest attention with which it was heard, and the frequent bursts of applause that followed his telling, sabre-like flashes of eloquence." His words "were as fire that ran," and thrilled the whole audience.

He reviewed briefly and lucidly his opinions on those principles upheld by the Democratic party for government, both federal and state—the great fundamentals of all republican institutions, and the safety of our own glorious Union. He, in every way, surrounded himself by arguments and illustrations that were unanswerable; and when he burst forth upon the principles that underlie the Know-Nothing question, he portrayed the real views of this secret organization; the fallacy of its positions; its proscription on account of religion; and exposed fully the dangers that were to follow from the success of a secret political party. His views were such as to render conclusive to the mind of any man as to which side he should take in this new sect—that of openly expressing whatever touches on political questions. It would be useless in us to attempt to give even a synopsis of his speech. His manner is so original, his style so peculiarly his own, and the force of his remarks such, that in attempting to give them in synopsis by our own words, would be futile and weak. We may recur again to this subject. One must hear Mr. Wise for himself. With us it is as with Job—our language must be, "Whom I shall see [and hear] for myself, and not for another."

As soon as Mr. Wise thus sounded the note of battle, the Know-Nothing and Whig press commenced an examination of his political antecedents. Their great effort was to prove that he had been an active Whig in the vigor of his life, had been an acknowledged and most distinguished leader of that organization, and that he now proclaimed that he had "no recantations to make." Never was the political history of any man so little understood by the masses as that of Henry A. Wise, during the late canvass in Virginia. We will here introduce Mr. Wise's own explanation as appeared in the Richmond *Enquirer*, April 14, 1843. This explanation is satisfactory to every unprejudiced mind, and did much to allay the prejudices of the "old line Democracy" against him:

MR. WISE IN 1843.

To the Editor of the Enquirer:

NORTHUMBERLAND, APRIL 4, 1843.

Dear Sir:—Yesterday was a great day in old Northumberland. Mr. Wise was here, and the high character he brought with him, acquired in Congress, and from the hustings, drew out an unusually large concourse of persons. I had often heard of his powers before the people; but his efforts on this occasion exceeded my most extravagant calculations. He enchained the attention of his audience for about four hours, in a speech characterised for ability, eloquence, and the most withering sarcasm. He commenced by giving us a history of his political career, begun about ten years ago in the Congress of the United States, and showed, conclusively, that so far as the great principles which at present agitate the country, the Bank, the Tariff, Internal Improvement, Distribution, and Abolition are concerned, *he* has not changed one jot or tittle. The evidence he adduced was irresistible. No candid and unprejudiced mind could have listened to him and not been convinced. He stated, (what I have no doubt was the fact,) that John Tyler was nominated at Harrisburg, because of his States Rights Republican Whig principles, and that there was in that Convention a union of National Republicans and States Rights Whigs, for a common object, (with the understanding that the states rights doctrines were to be carried out, if they succeeded,) and *that object*, the defeat of Mr. Van Buren, to whose re-election Mr. Wise was then opposed—that this same republican portion of the Whig party was that fragment of the old Jackson party that had gone off under the white flag of '36—that as soon would oil and water unite, as the principles of the old Hamiltonian federal party, and those of the republican states rights portion of the Whig party of 1840—and that, upon their ascendancy to power, should they, (the federal portion of the Whig party of 1840,) attempt to carry out the federal doctrines, the states rights portion, who had no sympathy for them in principle, would rebel—and that the party common of 1840, must be dissolved into its original elements. This, Mr. Wise demonstrated, as with a pencil of light, was the relative position of the republican and federal wing of the great Whig army, when General Harrison came into power. In relation to his Hanover letter, to which allusion, in some way by speech, sign, or manner, was made, he explicitly said, before he ever pledged his support in any form to Mr. Clay, he obtained a distinct avowal of his sentiments, and a pledge in regard to *five cardinal points.* Said he, "Mr. Clay, we differ widely upon fundamental principles, which must ever be a gulf between us, unless relinquished by you. How do you stand on the subject of a bank? Virginia is opposed to one." "Why, my dear sir," replied Mr. Clay, "this is a subject, which, whatever may be my theoretical views, the public mind is not now ripe for, and I am perfectly willing to leave it to 'the arbitrament of public opinion." "But, Mr. Clay, on the subject of the Tariff, you are looked upon as the father of this system, and you are so wedded to it, you could hardly be tempted to give it up. I am uncompromisingly opposed to it." "Why," said Mr. Clay, "all I wanted in the first instance, was to give a stimulus to the manufacturing interests of the country. That is already done. I am perfectly willing to abide by the compromise act—however much we differ upon the subject, theoretically, practically, we will be together." "But then, Mr. Clay, on the subject of internal improvement, how are you?" "Why, my dear sir, all I wished was to encourage a spirit of improvement among the states, and this has been carried already too far by the states themselves." "But on the subject of abolition of slavery in the District, Mr. Clay, you admit the power of Congress to act upon the subject, upon the principle of 'exclusive legislation,' " "My dear sir," rejoined Mr. Clay, "while these are my opinions conscientiously formed, I am a son of Virginia, and a slaveholder of Kentucky, and I would suffer the tortures of the inquisition, before I would sign a bill having for its object the abolition of slavery in the District, or in any manner give countenance to the subject." Now, by these professions and tests, how wide were Mr. Clay and Mr. Wise, *practically* apart? and had not Mr. Wise every reason to suppose that Mr. Clay, as a gentleman, would literally fulfil these pledges? Let those who are holding up this Hanover letter in judgment against Mr. Wise, take it in connection with these pledges of Mr. Clay, and Mr. Clay's own Hanover speech, and they are welcome to all the advantage they can derive. Mr. Wise admitted he had undergone more changes with respect to Mr. Clay, as a man, than he had ever done towards any one in his life—that he went to Congress the first time with strong prejudices and no very kind feelings towards him—that it was a long time before he had an introduction to him—and that when political co-operation brought them together, he felt the fascination and power of the charmer. Now, Mr. Wise says, for reasons which he assigned, and which are perfectly satisfactory to every unprejudiced and honest mind, he has no opinion of Henry Clay, either as a *politician* or as a *man*. He has forfeited his respect forever as to both.

But to return to the canvass of 1840, and the events which have succeeded. In 1840, pending the contest of that memorable campaign, whilst Mr. Clay was looking forward to succeed General Harrison, and to be "the power behind the throne, greater than the throne itself,"—in his administration, he was the enthusiastic admirer of Mr. Wise, never meeting him after a separation, however short, but with the utmost cordiality and kindness. After the election, and Virginia had gone against General Harrison, what was his manner on meeting Mr. Wise in Washington? Cordial as before? No, says Mr. Wise, but with the cold salutation: "How do you do, sir? I congratulate myself that Virginia has gone for Mr. Van Buren; we will no longer be embarrassed by her peculiar opinions." Well may this expression have struck Mr. Wise with amazement. The cloven foot was shown—the policy of the Federal Whigs was developed by their leader. "No longer embarrassed by her peculiar opinions," by which he intended contempt and derision of "Virginia abstractions," or of a strict construction of our glorious Federal Constitution. From that hour, Mr. Wise's confidence was gone, and who could blame him for indulging feelings of indignation towards a man who had wormed himself artfully into his confidence, and when he had seen the Whig ticket triumph despite of the opposition of Virginia, turned his back upon his pledges, and disregarded those courtesies and civilities which characterize the intercourse of mutual friends? With such a man, ambition is the vortex which swallows up every kind feeling of the human heart, and leaves scarcely a redeeming quality behind. An extra session of Congress was called, and, though Mr. Clay had agreed *practically* to go along with Mr. Wise, all those measures which had been renounced and given up by Mr. Clay in 1840, were sought in hot haste, through his instrumentality, to be palmed off upon the nation. The bank question, which was to be left to the enlightenment of public opinion, was snatched from the people—a rivalry was begot between Mr. Clay and Mr. Webster, in consequence of General Harrison's preference for the latter; and ere the old chief had been killed by the annoyance of hungry office-seekers, (the Simon Pures of 1840,) and the course of political aspirants for the presidency, Mr. Clay secretly aimed at his administration the artillery of war. All this Mr. Wise proved, and proved satisfactorily. The compromise act was violated, and an odious bankrupt law passed, contrary to every pledge Mr. Clay had made Mr. Wise.

Mr. Wise, in the course of his address, triumphantly vindicated John Tyler against the charges of treachery, Iscariotism, Arnoldism, immorality, fraud, dishonesty, and the thousand and one coarse and malicious epithets which have been heaped upon him by Federal Whiggery, without stint and without measure. He proved, beyond the possibility of a doubt, that Mr. Tyler had always been opposed to the constitutionality of a bank, and that he could not have signed a charter without perjury—that there was no evidence to show that even General Harrison would have signed a bank charter; and he quoted the letter of the General in '22, wherein he states, the Bank of the United States is unconstitutional, it not being necessary to carry out an expressly granted power, and that had he the power, he would issue a *fieri facias*, and revoke the charter—and, also, the Whig address in Richmond in 1840, wherein it is claimed for General Harrison, that he is as much opposed to *the* United States Bank as any man could be, and far sounder upon that subject than Mr. Van Buren. Mr. Wise said he advised freely with Mr. Tyler upon the subject of a bank—that he differed from him as to its constitutionality, but, at the same time, urged him to take that course which his conscience dictated, without regard to whom it might offend or whom please—that if he could do so, as did Mr. Madison, according to the principle of *stare decisis*, to do so, but to take care and sign only a full-blooded animal, no mongrel—only such as would confer most benefit upon the country—but to take his own course in the matter, and not to compromit by his advice, his character, his conscience or his honor. Mr. Wise said he had frequently witnessed the agony of that man upon this very question, and had seen him almost sweat drops of blood, and wished that he could have been in his place, as he believed he had the nerve to look down with scorn and contempt upon his revilers and slanderers, and those reptiles whose business it is to assail private character to subserve party and ambitious ends. Mr. Wise farther said, they had tried every way they could to entrap John Tyler, and that the very bill prepared by Mr. Clay himself contained the same objectionable feature as that of Mr. Ewing, which Mr. Clay had contemptuously denominated "a rickety concern"—that any bill John Tyler could have framed, or any friend of Mr. Webster, would have met his unqualified condemnation—that he wanted the credit himself of preparing the bill, and getting through Congress all the Whig measures, that he might retire to Ashland upon the dignity of these measures, become the idol of the Whig party, and the candidate for the succession. Mr. Wise, in defining his position upon the bank question, said, though he differed from Mr. Tyler, and knew he differed in 1840, he had merged that into questions which he considered of far greater magnitude. Though he believed a United States Bank constitutional, the time had passed for chartering one. The first effect of a bank, he contended, was depletive, and he cited in proof the history of the country from 1816 to 1825. He assimilated the condition of the country now to a patient who was already prostrate from the loss of blood, and asked if, in this state of things, a physician would be found so rash and foolish as to think of taking more blood, and thereby sink the powers of the system beyond the point of reaction. He said the fate of the United States Bank and the Bank of Pennsylvania, which was but a continuation of it; the cries of orphans and widows who had been reduced to penury and want by its explosion; and the fact that Nicholas Biddle, with all his financial knowledge, once standing high in public estimation, had failed to make it a benefit, and himself become a bankrupt in character and person, all admonished us that no such institution could ever again find favor with the people of the United States.

Mr. Wise showed, and showed from the record, the Whig address of 1840, that if all deserters are to be shot, Mr. Tyler and himself should not be selected as the victims, but those who put forth their principles in 1840, and have since abandoned them; and humorously said, that if such were the sentence, and the words "take aim, fire" to be given, you would see no little dipping and doging in the crowd, among the old Hamiltonian National Republican Federalists, who had long cherished and often lauded the doctrines of Hamilton, Pickering and Adams to the stars. He also satisfied all who heard him, that in regard to the Cilley duel, the mountain of odium, which he had borne, should properly have rested upon the shoulders of another. He said that it was a fair duel—but that if censure and odium attached to any one, it should be to Henry Clay, for he was the counseller and adviser, and dictated the terms of the duel—that he (Mr. W.) protested against the rifle and the language of the challenge, which closed the door to an adjustment of the difficulty, but was overruled by Mr. Clay—that he expressed an unwillingness to be the bearer of a challenge so uncompromising in its character, but at length yielded to appeal from Mr. Graves, who reminded him that he had been his friend on a similar occasion.

The development of these facts was made by him, because, when his character was assailed, and assailed unjustly, as Mr. Clay knew, Mr. Wise appealed to him to do him justice, and put this matter right before the nation, Mr. Clay avoided all opportunity to do so, and no alternative was left Mr. Wise but to suffer the odium, or else give the facts to the public.

Mr. Wise, in conclusion, said his private vote was his own, and he should tell no one how or for whom it should be given in the coming presidential election. But he would not hesitate to say for whom it should not be given: that he could never vote for Henry Clay, as constable, or anything else. He said he believed, to the fullest extent, in the right of the people to instruct their representatives; and if the election went before Congress, and his district had voted for Mr. Clay, he should deposit his vote for him. Mr. Wise, upon the whole, made a most favorable impression. As a Virginian, I feel proud of him, and do applaud him for the gallant manner in which he has stood by Mr. Tyler, Virginia's own son, in one of the most trying positions in which man was ever placed, when slander with her thousand tongues was at work, and everything done by a reckless party to destroy the fair fame of an honest and upright man.

THE ISSUES OF THE CANVASS.

Know-Nothingism was introduced in Virginia under the specious guise of a great conservative organization; knowing no North, no South, no East, no West; repudiating all sectionalism, and utterly discarding old party lines and old party issues. It professed to be national, republican, and constitutional in all its tenets and intentions. In the month of December, 1854, the Richmond Whig denied in the most emphatic terms, that the Know-Nothing party would supercede the old Whig party, counselled against the abandonment of a single Whig tenet; but advised, nevertheless, a fusion with Know-Nothingism in a common effort to "expel the Goths and Vandals," who had so long ruled and plundered the state. Whig orators, Whig editors, Whig letter-writers and Whig politicians took up the role thus assigned them, declaring that the Know-Nothing organization was no Whig trick, but a great party of reform, embracing alike Democrats and Whigs. Rather than submit to the victorious Democracy, the Whig and its party preferred to foster, encourage, uphold and advance a Northernism untried upon Southern soil. Thus were presented to the Democracy the old issues of Federalism, coupled with religious intolerance and proscription of foreigners. The Enquirer published the following commentary upon the issues of the canvass, January 8th, 1854:

THE WHIG FLAG IN THE DUST—AMALGAMATION WITH THE KNOW-NOTHINGS.—When, in its issue of the 25th December, the Richmond Whig scornfully repelled the suggestion that the Whig party of Virginia should abandon their organization and submit to the sway of Know-Nothingism, we did not suspect the sincerity of its purpose, nor mistrust the strength of its resolution. Nor for one moment did we entertain the thought that the Whig could be driven from its manly position by the threats of the American Organ, and be forced to accept, with expressions of satisfaction, the very overture which it had just rejected with an air of insulted dignity.

From an article in the Whig of Wednesday, which proposes to indicate the present policy of its party, we select the following extract:

"We remark, then, that our first impressions were in favor of holding a Whig State Convention. But subsequent reflection, and an impartial survey of the whole field, and a calm review of all the circumstances by which we are surrounded, have conducted us to an opposite conclusion. The Whig party, at the last trial of strength, was in a large minority in the state, and while we believe that we might, and probably would succeed alone, considering the elements that might perhaps combine in our favor, yet it is better and safer, in our opinion, not to rely too confidently upon our own unaided strength, but to so act as to gather to our side, men of all parties and persuasions who are sick of misrule and wish for reform. We counsel not the abandonment of a single Whig tenet, but only urge a course which will, first, effectually expel the Goths and Vandals, and ultimately, probably immediately, result in putting Whig measures and Whig policy in the ascendant. We, therefore, respectfully and kindly suggest to such of our friends as entertain a wish for a convention, to abandon it at once—at least for the present. If unforeseen circumstances should hereafter arise to render one necessary, March or April will be early enough to consider the matter."

The contrast between the spirit of its former declaration, and the temper of this paragraph, is sufficiently striking to convict the Whig of a very flagrant inconsistency. But, it is not to this point that we wish to direct the attention of the public. The article in the Whig is not cited for any purpose of controversy, but to exhibit the policy of its party in this important crisis of public affairs. We have here the distinct avowal of its recognised organ that the Whig party of Virginia no longer exists as an independent organization, but is disbanded and merged into Know-Nothingism. And we have moreover the declaration, that the motive of this extraordinary proceeding springs from no higher impulse than an appetite for the spoils of office.

We are reluctant to believe that the Whig party of Virginia will submissively adopt the advice of their organ. The opinion we entertain of their character forbids the inference that they will consent to desert the flag under which they have fought so long and so gallantly, and transfer their principles and their allegiance to the up-start order of Know-Nothings. We may be deceived, but we will not admit the possibility of an absolute and ignominious submission of the Whigs of Virginia to the insolent dictation of the Know-Nothings, until the surrender is ratified by the party. The leaders we know are too often ready to adopt any expedient that may gratify their lust of power, but the honest masses of the Whig party are exempt from the influence of any such motive, and, if we be not mistaken, they will indignantly refuse to play the menial and the lackey to a secret and suspected cabal of bigots and demagogues.

The Whig, anticipating certain success from the coalition with the Know-Nothings, exultingly predicts the speedy ascendancy of Whig measures and Whig policy. If any well-meaning Democrat has been misled by the deceitful promises of Know-Nothingism, this declaration will startle him from his delusion, for it is equivalent to an avowal that the Know-Nothing organization is but a contrivance for the restoration of the Whig party to power.

The article from the Whig is suggestive of much instructive reflection to the people of Virginia, and we propose to resume its consideration to-morrow. Meanwhile, let it be borne in mind that the Richmond Whig recommends a fusion of Whigs and Know-Nothings, for the purpose of effecting an immediate restoration of Whig measures and Whig policy in the government of Virginia.

"We counsel not the abandonment of a single Whig tenet, but only urge a course which will first effectually expel the Goths and Vandals, and ultimately, probably immediately, result in putting Whig measures and Whig policy in the ascendant."—[*Richmond Whig, Jan.* 3.

In the beginning, the Know-Nothing organization was represented as a protest of the people against the selfishness and corruption of politicians, and its ostensible aim was the reform of abuse and the rescue of the government from the despotism of party. Under this specious pretence, Know-Nothingism was introduced into Virginia, with a pledge from its advocates of equal antagonism to the Whig and Democratic parties. Its deceitful promise of neutrality and reform, seduced some Democrats from their party, and imparted strength and impulse to the organization.

We never mistook the character and tendency of Know-Nothingism. From the start, we denounced it as an imposture. We detected the falsity of its pretensions, and exposed the hidden purpose of its authors. We affirmed that it was at bottom a political movement, and foretold that if not arrested it would result in the overthrow of the Democratic party.

Our suspicions were justified, and our prediction fulfilled, in the progress of events. The political aim and party affinity of Know-Nothingism were soon developed in its successes. Every Know-Nothing triumph was achieved in alliance with the Whig party, and was in effect a Democratic defeat.

Still the organs of Know-Nothingism protested its independence of party, and persisted in the endeavor to seduce Democrats into its embrace.

At last an alliance between the Whig party in Virginia and the Know-Nothings, has been concluded, and although its conditions have not been communicated to the world, an organ of one of the high contracting parties has very distinctly foreshadowed its effect. The prodigious boasting of the British journals, after the accession of Austria to the alliance of the Western Powers, is eclipsed by the excessive exultation of the Richmond Whig over the league between the Know-Nothings and the Whig party in Virginia. It will result, exclaims the Whig, in an ecstacy of enthusiam, "in the expulsion of the Goths and Vandals"—that is, the Democrats—from power, and "in the ultimate, if not immediate ascendancy of Whig measures and Whig policy." We thank the Whig for this candid avowal, and we trust that its simplicity and *naivete* will not be corrupted by the associations into which it will be thrown by its alliance with the Know-Nothings.

If the deceptive pretences of Know-Nothingism have seduced any honest Democrat into the order, he will make haste and come out of it, after learning that he is aiding in the ascendancy of Whig measures and Whig policy. If any Democrat who has not yet foresworn allegiance to his party, imagines that there is nothing in the character or probable issue of the present canvass, to incite him to the zealous support of Wise, he will learn, from the declaration of the Richmond Whig, that the defeat of Wise will result in the expulsion of the Goths and Vandals, and the ascendancy of Whig measures and Whig policy; and learning this, he will repress every feeling of disappointment and disaffection, and exhibiting the disinterested devotion of a patriot, will throw himself with all his soul and all his might into a struggle on which depends the triumph or defeat of his party and his principles. The coalition is not animated by an impulse of personal hostility to Henry A. Wise, nor is its object limited to his defeat. It makes war upon him as the champion of the Democratic party, and it contemplates nothing less than the expulsion of the Goths and Vandals, and the ascendancy of Whig measures and Whig policy. The pretence of neutrality and independence of party, by which Know-Nothingism seeks to allure recruits to its standard, is a deception and a snare, and the aim of the organization is the ascendancy of Whig measures and Whig policy.

Again we thank the Whig for its manly, out-spoken candor. Disdaining to practice a deception on the people, the Whig frankly avows what it expects to accomplish by its alliance with the Know-Nothings. Let no man reproach it with indiscretion; it saw the advantage of secrecy and dissimulation, but chose rather than compromise its character, to apprise the Democracy of the aim of the coalition, and to admonish them of the necessity of vigilance and effort in defence of their principles.

THE KNOW-NOTHING RITUAL EXPOSED.

The Know-Nothing party or organization was the first political party in the history of this government that undertook to follow the example of the Jacobin clubs of France. This Know-Nothing party was one of the deepest and most skillfully panned, and most dangerous political movements that was ever concocted in any country. There were many true patriots that were deluded into the organization, some of whom had, and many of whom had not the courage to withdraw; but we trust we shall be pardoned for expressing the decided conviction that the leaders of the order should have their names classed in history with those of Burr and Arnold. This *new party* had a regularly prescribed ritual, to which every man who became a member had to conform. This ritual was composed of oaths, pass-words, signs, and ceremonies of initiation. Many who went through these ceremonies were offended with their puerility, and it is not surprising that some few, shocked at the incendiarism thus inculcated should, from a patriotic conviction of duty, have resolved to lay them before their countrymen. We here introduce the ritual in full, as published in the various Democratic papers of the state; the authenticity of which was repeatedly acknowledged by members of the order. Mr. Wise was the first Democrat in the state that came in possession of the ritual. It was first exposed in the state of Illinois, and as soon as Governor Lybrook procured the ritual he endorsed it to Mr. Wise. Through Mr. Wise it was published simultaneously in the

Richmond Enquirer and Examiner, then copied by Democratic papers throughout the state. After the conclusion of the canvass, Mr. Wise enclosed it to the sender, Governor Lybrook. The Demecracy of Virginia return to Governor Lybrook their sincere thanks for his efficient and timely service so considerately rendered to our gallant standard bearer.

THE KNOW-NOTHING RITUAL OR "CONSTITUTION OF THE GRAND COUNCIL OF THE UNITED STATES OF NORTH AMERICA—ADOPTED UNANIMOUSLY, JUNE 17, 1854—THE ANNIVERSARY OF THE BATTLE OF BUNKER HILL."

ARTICLE I.

This organization shall be known by the name and title of *The Grand Council of the United States of North America*, and its jurisdiction and power shall extend to all the states, districts, and territories of the United States of North America.

ARTICLE II.

A person to become a member of any subordinate council must be twenty-one years of age; he must believe in the existence of a Supreme Being as the Creator and Preserver of the Universe; he must be a native born citizen; a Protestant, born of Protestant parents, reared under Protestant influence, and not united in marriage with a Roman Catholic; Provided, nevertheless, that in this last respect, the state, district, or territorial council shall be authorized to so construct their respective constitutions as shall best promote the interest of the American cause in their several jurisdictions; And provided, moreover, that no member who may have a Roman Catholic wife shall be eligible to any office in this order.

ARTICLE III.

SEC. 1. The object of this organization shall be to resist the insidious policy of the Church of Rome, and other foreign influence against the institutions of our country by placing in all offices in the gift of the people, or by appointment, none but native born Protestant citizens.

SEC. 2. The Grand Council shall hold its annual meeting on the first Tuesday in the month of June, at such place as shall be designated by the Grand Council at the previous annual meeting, and it may adjourn from time to time. Special meetings shall be called by the President on the written request of five delegations representing five State Councils; Provided, that sixty days' notice shall be given to the State Councils previous to said meeting.

SEC. 3. The Grand Council shall be composed of thirteen delegates, from each state, to be chosen by the State Councils; and each district, or territory where a District or Territorial Council shall exist, shall be entitled to send five delegates, to be chosen from said Councils; and when no District or Territorial Council shall exist, such district or territory shall be entitled to send five delegates, if five or more Subordinate Councils shall exist in such district or territory; Provided, that in the nomination of candidates for President and Vice President of the United States, each state shall be entitled to the same number of votes as they shall have members in both houses of Congress. In all sessions of the Grand Council, thirty-two delegates, representing thirteen states, territories, or districts, shall constitute a quorum for the transaction of business.

SEC. 4. The Grand Council shall be vested with the following powers and privileges:

It shall be the head of the organization for the United States of North

America, and shall fix and establish all signs, grips, pass-words, and such other secret work as may seem to it necessary.

It shall have power to decide upon all matters appertaining to national politics.

It shall have the power to exact from the State Councils quarterly or annual statements as to the number of members under their jurisdictions, and in relation to all other matters necessary for its information.

It shall have the power to form state, territorial or district councils, and to grant dispensations for the formation of such bodies when five subordinate councils shall have been put in operation in any state, territory or district, and application made.

It shall have the power to determine upon a mode of punishment in case of any dereliction of duty on the part of its members or officers.

It shall have the power to adopt cabalistic characters for the purpose of writing or telegraphing—said characters to be communicated to the presidents of the State Councils, and by them to the presidents of the Subordinate Councils.

It shall have the power to adopt any and every measure it may deem necessary to secure the success of the organization: provided, that nothing shall be done by the said Grand Council in violation of the Constitution; and provided, further, that in all political matters, its members may be instructed by the State Councils, and if so instructed, shall carry out such instructions of the State Councils which they represent until overruled by a majority of the Grand Council.

ARTICLE IV.

The president shall always preside over the Grand Council when present, and in his absence the vice president shall preside, and in the absence of both, the Grand Council shall appoint a president *pro tempore;* and the presiding officer may at all times call a member to the chair, but such appointment shall not extend beyond one session of the Grand Council.

ARTICLE V.

SEC. 1. The officers of the Grand Council shall be a president, vice president, corresponding secretary, recording secretary, treasurer, two sentinels and such other officers as as the Grand Council may see fit to appoint from time to time, and the secretaries and sentinels may receive such compensations as the Grand Council shall determine.

SEC. 2. The duties of the several officers created by this Constitution shall be such as the work of this organization prescribes.

ARTICLE VI.

SEC. 1. All officers provided for by this Constitution, except the sentinels, shall be elected annually by ballot. The president may appoint sentinels from time to time, or otherwise.

SEC. 2. A majority of all the votes cast shall be requisite to an election to any office.

SEC. 3. All officers and delegates must be full degree members of this organization.

SEC. 4. All vacancies in the elective offices shall be filled by a vote of the Grand Council, and only for the unexpired term of the said vacancy.

ARTICLE VII.

SEC. 1. The Grand Council shall entertain and decide all cases of appeal, and it shall establish a form of appeal.

SEC. 2. The Grand Council shall levy a tax upon the State, District or Territorial Councils, for the support of the Grand Council, to be paid in such manner and at such times as the Grand Council shall determine.

ARTICLE VIII.

The Grand Council may alter or amend this Constitution, at any regular annual meeting, by a two-thirds' vote of the members present; provided such amendment shall be adopted by a two-thirds' vote of the Grand Council at its next succeeding annual meeting.

On page 11 commences the "General Rules and Regulations," which occupy pages, 11, 12 and 13, and are as follows:

GENERAL RULES AND REGULATIONS.

RULE ONE.—Each state, district or territory in which there may exist five or more Subordinate Councils working under dispensations from the Grand Council of the United States of North America, or under regular dispensations from some state, district or territory, are duly empowered to establish themselves into a State, District or Territorial Council, and when so established, to form for themselves constitutions and by-laws for their government, in pursuance of and in consonance with the Constitution of the Grand Council of the United States; provided, however, that all district or territorial constitutions shall be subject to the approval of the Grand Council of the United States.

RULE TWO.—All State, District or Territorial Councils, when established, shall have full power and authority to establish all Subordinate Councils within their respective limits; and the constitutions and by-laws of all such Subordinate Councils must be approved by their respective State, District or Territorial Councils.

RULE THREE.—All State, District or Territorial Councils, when established and until the formation of constitutions, shall work under the Constitution of the Grand Council of the United States.

RULE FOUR.—In all cases where, for the convenience of the organization, two State or Territorial Councils may be established, the two councils together shall be entitled to but thirteen delegates in the Grand Council of the United States—the proportioned number of delegates to depend on the number of members in the organization; provided, that no state shall be allowed to have more than one State Council without the consent of the Grand Council of the United States.

RULE FIVE.—In any state, district or territory, where there may be more than one organization working on the same basis (to wit: "Lodges" and "Councils,") the same shall be required to combine; the officers of each organization shall resign, and new officers be elected; and thereafter these bodies shall be known as State Councils and Subordinate Councils; and new charters shall be granted to them by the Grand Council.

RULE SIX.—It shall be considered a penal offence for any brother not an officer of a Subordinate Council, to make use of the sign or summons adopted for public notification, except by direction of the president; or for the officers of a council to post the same at any other time than from midnight to one hour before daybreak; and this rule shall be incorporated into the by-laws of the State, District and Territorial Councils.

RULE SEVEN.—The determination of the necessity and mode of issuing the posters for public notification shall be entrusted to the judgment of the State, District or Territorial Councils.

RULE EIGHT.—The respective State, District or Territorial Councils shall be required to make statements of the number of members within their respective limits at the next annual meeting of the Grand Council, and annually thereafter at the regular annual meeting.

RULE NINE.—The Grand Council of the United States shall pay from its treasury the necessary expenses of its members in attendance upon its sessions.

RULE TEN.—Each State, District or Territorial Council shall be taxed ten dollars per annum for each Subordinate Council under its jurisdiction, said tax to be paid in semi-annual instalments of five dollars each, payable in the months of June and December.

RULE ELEVEN.—The following shall be the key to determine and ascertain the purport of any communication that may be addressed to the president of a State, District or Territorial Council by the president of the Grand Council, who is hereby instructed to communicate a knowledge of the same to said officers:

* * * * *

* * * * *

RULE TWELVE.—The clause of the article of the constitution relative to belief in the Supreme being is obligatory upon every State and Subordinate Council, as well as upon each individual member.

Pages 15 and 16 treat of "Special Votes," viz:

SPECIAL VOTES.

FIRST.—This Grand Council hereby grants to the state of Virginia two State Councils—the one to be located in Eastern and the other in Western Virginia, the Blue Ridge mountains being the geographical line between the two jurisdictions.

SECOND.—The president shall have power, till the next session of the Grand Council, to grant dispensations for the formation of State, District or Territorial Councils, in form most agreeable to his own discretion, upon application being made.

THIRD.—The delegates from the several states, districts or territories, who were elected for, or in attendance upon, this Grand Council, shall hold their seats for one year; and the State, District or Territorial Councils are hereby authorized to fill up their respective delegations; provided, that when there are two or more organizations in any one state, district or territory, the delegation shall be chosen after the union, as provided for by the Constitution of this Grand Council.

FOURTH.—The next meeting of the Grand Council shall be holden at Cincinnati on the third Wednesday of November, 1854, at 3 o'clock, P. M.

FIFTH.—Messrs. D———, of New Jersey, D——— and S———, of Massachusetts, are appointed a committee to examine, revise, correct, and prepare for publication, the constitution, general rules and regulations, and special votes of the Grand Council, with a list of the officers and members, with their autograph address in full, and the states, districts or territories they represent, and such other necessary matters as may be deemed expedient and judicious to publish, and forward the same to the printer; when issued, to the number of five hundred, a copy to be sent to each member of this Grand Council, and the residue to be placed at the disposal of the president.

RITUAL.

FIRST DEGREE COUNCIL.—OUTSIDE.

Marshal.—Gentlemen: Are you candidates for admission to this organization? [Each answers, "I am."]

Marshal.—Before proceeding further it is necessary that you take an obligation of secrecy.

Are you willing to take such an obligation? ["I am."]

Marshal.—You will now place yourselves in a position to receive it. [*Position.*—Place the right hand on the Holy Bible and Cross.]

Obligation.—You do solemnly swear* upon this Holy Bible and Cross,

*In cases where candidates are known to be conscientious about taking an oath, they may be allowed to make solemn affirmation—this provision to be understood as applying whenever necessary in either obligation.

before Almighty God and these witnesses, that you will not divulge any question now proposed to you, whether you become a member of this organization or not, and that you will never, under any circumstances, mention the name of any person or persons you see present, nor that you know such an organization to be in existence, and that you will true answers make to every question asked you to the best of your knowledge and belief: so help you God. ["I do."]

First Question.—Are you twenty-one years of age? ["I am."]

Second Question.—Do you believe in the existence of a Supreme Being, the Creator and Preserver of the Universe, and that an obligation at this time taken will be binding upon you through life? ["I do."]

Third Question.—Were you born within the limits or under the jurisdiction of the United States of America? ["I was."]

Fourth Question.—In religious belief are you a Roman Chatholic? ["No."]

Fifth Question.—Have you or have you not been reared under Prótestant influence? ["Yes," or "No."]

Sixth Question.—Are, or were, either of your parents Roman Catholic in religious belief? ["No."]

Seventh Question.—If married, is your wife a Roman Catholic? ["No," or "Yes,"—the answer to be valued as the Constitution of the State Council provide.]

Eighth Question.—Are you willing to use your influence and vote only for native born American citizens for all the offices of honor or trust in the gift of the people, to the exclusion of all foreigners and aliens, and of Roman Catholics in particular, and without regard to party predilections? ["I am."]

INSIDE.

Marshal.—Worthy President: I have examined these candidates, and finding them duly qualified, present them for obligation. [*If the examination in the ante-room gave evidence of even partial objection to any candidate the Marshal should state it to the President, before introducing the candidates.*]

President.—My friends: Previous to your uniting with and becoming members of this organization, it will be necessary for you to take upon yourselves a solemn obligation—one which we have all taken and intend sacredly to keep through life. It will not conflict with the duties you owe to yourselves, your families, your country, or your God. With this assurance are you still willing to proceed? [Each answers, "I am."]

Obligation.—You and each of you, of your own free will and accord, in the presence of Almighty God and these witnesses, your right hand resting on this Holy Bible and Cross, and your left hand raised towards Heaven, (or *if it be preferred,* your left hand resting on your breast and your right hand raised towards Heaven,) in token of your sincerity, do solemnly promise and swear* that you will not make known to any person or persons any of the signs, secrets, mysteries, or objects of this organization, unless it be to those whom, after due examination, or lawful information, you shall find to be members of this organization in good standing; that you will not cut, carve, print, paint, stamp, stain, or in any way, directly or indirectly, expose any of the secrets or objects of this order, nor suffer it to be done by others, if in your power to prevent it, unless it be for official instruction; that so long as you are connected with this organization, if not regularly dismissed from it, you will, in all things, political or social, so far as this order is concerned, comply with the will of the majority, when expressed in a lawful manner, though it may conflict with your personal

* See prior note relative to affirmation.

preference, so long as it does not conflict with the Grand, State or Subordinate Constitutions, the Constitution of the United States of America, or that of the State in which you reside; and that you will not, under any circumstances whatever, knowingly, recommend an unworthy person for initiation, nor suffer it to be done, if in your power to prevent it. You furthermore promise and declare that you will not vote, nor give your influence for any man for any office in the gift of the people, unless he be an American born citizen, in favor of Americans born ruling America, nor if he be a Roman Catholic, and that you will not, under any circumstances, expose the name of any member of this order, nor reveal the existence of such an organization. To all the foregoing you bind yourselves, under the no less penalty than that of being expelled from this order, and of having your name posted and circulated throughout all the different councils of the United States as a perjurer and as a traitor to God and your country, as a being unfit to be employed and trusted, countenanced or supported in any business transaction, as a person unworthy the confidence of all good men, and as one at whom the finger of scorn should ever be pointed. So help you God! [Each answers "I do."]

President.—Worthy Marshal: You will now present these brothers to the Secretary that he may record their names and residences; which being done, you will present them to the Instructor for final instruction.

Marshal.—Worthy Instructor: By direction of the Worthy President, I present to you these brothers for final instructions, they having signed the constitution.

Instructor.—Brothers: At the outer door you will make any ordinary alarm. When the wicket is opened, you will ask what is the pass? The outside sentinel will reply, give it—when you will give the term pass, and be admitted to the ante-room. You will then proceed to the inner door and give one rap. When the wicket is opened, give your name, the number of your council, the explanation of the term-pass, and the degree pass-word. If these be found correct, on being reported to the vice-president you will be admitted to the council. You will then proceed to the centre of the room, and address the president with the countersign, which is performed thus—[*Position*—the right hand placed on the heart and quickly withdrawn, the person remaining perfectly erect.] When this salutation is recognised, you will turn to the vice-president and address him in the same manner, who will also reply. You will then quietly take your seat. This sign is peculiar to this degree, and is never to be used outside of the council room. When retiring, you will address the officers in the same manner, and also give the degree pass-word to the inside sentinel.

The *term pass-word* is ———, [*the word to be established by each state council for its respective Subordinates.*] The *explanation of the term pass*, to be used at the inner door, is ———, [*to be established by each state, &c.*] The *degree pass-word* is twenty-one. The *traveling pass-word and explanation*, (which is changed annually by the grand president, and which is used only when the brother is traveling beyond the jurisdiction of his own state, district or territory,) is Yorktown—the place of final victory.

The sign of recognition is by placing the index finger of the right hand in the space between the buttons of the coat, vest or skirt, and elevating the thumb. The answer is given by placing the thumb of the right hand in the same place.

The grip is given in the form of a lady's slight shake of the hand, by bringing the three fingers of the right hand into such a position as to bring the thumb slightly upon the nail of the middle finger, dropping the hand immediately, when the following conversation ensues—the challenging party first saying what time? The answer, time for work. Then the response—are you, followed by the rejoinder, we are.

Public notice for mass meetings is given by means of a right angle triangular piece of paper, [a diagram is here given,] white in color. If information is wanted of the object of the gathering, or of the place, &c., the inquirer will ask of an undoubted brother only, have you seen SAM to-day? The reply will be go to ———, at ——— o'clock. A piece of paper of the same shape, red in color, will signify suspected danger. If the color is red, with an equilateral triangular piece cut out, thus: [a diagram is here given] it will denote actual trouble, which requires that you come prepared to meet it.

Brothers, you are now initiated into and made acquainted with the work and organization of a council of this degree of the order; and here, upon the threshold of our institution, with the remembrance of your solemn obligation fresh upon us all, we extend to you the welcome and the sympathies of honest and patriotic hearts. In becoming members of this order, we do not compel you to act with us against your better judgment; and should you at any time wish to withdraw, from conscientious scruples, it will be our duty to grant you a dismission in good faith.

It has no doubt been long apparent to you, brothers, that foreign influence and Roman Catholicism have been making steady and alarming progress in our country. You cannot have failed to observe the significant transition of the foreign born and Romanist from a character quiet, retiring and even abject, to one bold, threatening, turbulent, and even despotic in its appearance and assumptions. You must have become alarmed at the systematic and rapidly augmenting power of these dangerous and unnatural elements of our national condition. So it is, brothers, with others besides yourselves, in every state of the Union. A sense of danger has struck the great heart of the nation. In every city, town and hamlet the danger has been seen and the alarm sounded. And hence true men have devised this order as a means of disseminating patriotic principles, of keeping alive the fire of national virtue, of fostering the national intelligence, and of advancing America and the American interest on the one side, and on the other of checking the stride of the foreigner or alien, of thwarting the machinations and subverting the deadly plans of the Jesuit and Papist.

SECOND DEGREE COUNCIL.

Marshal.—Worthy President: These brothers having been duly elected to the 2d degree of this order, I present them before you for obligation.

President.—Brothers: You will place your left hand upon your right breast, and extend your right hand towards the flag of our country preparatory to obligation. [*Each Council room should have a neat American flag festooned over the platform of the President.*]

Obligation.—You, and each of you, of your own free will and accord, in the presence of Almighty God and these witnesses, your left hand resting on your right breast, and your right hand extended to the flag of your country, do most solemnly and sincerely swear that you will not, under any circumstances, disclose in any manner, nor suffer it to be done by others if in your power to prevent it, the name, signs, pass-words, or other secrets of this degree; that you will in all things conform to all the rules and regulations of this order, and to the Constitution and By-Laws of this or any other Council to which you may be attached, so long as they do not conflict with the Constitution of the United States, nor that of the state in which you reside; that you will, under all circumstances, if in your power so to do, attend all regular signs and summonses that may be thrown or sent out by a brother of this or any other degree of this order; that you will support in all political matters, for all political offices 2d degree members of this order, providing it be necessary for the American interest; that if it may be done legally, you will, when elected to any office remove all foreigners, aliens or Roman Catholics from office, and that you will in no case appoint such to office. All this you promise and declare on your honor as Americans to sustain and abide by without any hesitation or mental reservation whatever. So help you God, and keep you steadfast! [Each will answer, "I do."]

President.—Brother Marshal: You will now present the brothers to the Instructor for final instruction in this degree of the order.

Marshal.—Brother Instructor: By direction of our worthy President, I present these brothers before you that you may instruct them in the secrets and mysteries of the second degree of the order.

Instructor.—Brothers: In this degree we have an entering-sign and counter-sign. At the outer door proceed the same as in the first degree. At the inner door you will make too distinct raps and proceed as in the first degree, giving the second degree pass-word, which is seventy-six, instead of that of the first degree. If found to be correct, you will then be admitted, and proceed to the centre of the floor, giving the counter-sign, which is made thus: POSITION.—Place the left hand upon the right breast, the right hand extended towards the flag of our country, which should be suspended over the platform of the President. When recognized, you will quietly take your seat.

Brothers, you are now duly initiated into this, the second degree of the order. Renewing the congratulations which we extended to you upon your admission to the first degree, we admonish you by every tie that may move you as patriots to aid us in our efforts to restore the political institutions of our country to their original purity. Begin with the youth of our land. Refresh their minds with the history of our country, the glorious battles and the brilliant acts of patriotism, which is our common inheritance. Point them to the wise sages and the profound statesmen who founded our government. Instil into their bosoms an ardent love for the Union. Above all else, keep alive in their hearts the memory, the maxims and the deathless example of our illustrious Washington.

Brothers, recalling to your minds the solemn obligations which you have severally taken in this and the first degree, I now pronounce you entitled to all the privileges of membership in this organization, and the President—who ALONE is entitled to communicate it,—will inform you of the name of the order.

President.—Brothers: You are members in full fellowship of The Supreme Order of the Star Spangled Banner.

KNOW-NOTHINGISM AN ALIAS OF FEDERALISM.

No charge was more powerfully urged, or made a deeper impression upon the popular mind in Virginia, during the canvass we are delineating, than that the Know-Nothing party was but a new form of the old protean party of Federalists. We shall not undertake to run over the proofs that were adduced in support of this charge. But the identity of the Know-Nothing doctrines, of religious intolerance and proscription of foreigners, with the leading tenets of the original Federal party, is so striking and palpable, that we insert here from the Richmond Examiner of February 20, 1855, republished from its issue of September 12, 1854, that journal's remarks on this subject:

THE PATERNITY OF KNOW-NOTHINGISM—A POLITICAL CHRONICLE.—The Democratic party of this country was first built up by Jefferson and Madison, for the purpose of crushing the Federal or Native American party, of which John Adams was the official head. Native Americanism, in whatever name or under whatever disguise it appears, is no recent thing in this country. It is a hoary and oft punished abomination of the Federal party. Opposition to the foreigner, cruel, intolerant, and lawless, has, at intervals, characterized that party ever since 1787. It is true that the Federal party had no formal existence at that time; but the men who, a few years afterwards, became the leaders of the Federal party manifested their hostility to foreign born citizens during the deliberations of the Convention which framed the Constitution of the United States. The men who shaped and penned the odious alien law, sought to engraft "Nativeism" upon the organic law of the country.

The Madison Papers establish the fact that the leading Federal members of the Convention of 1787, sought every opportunity for excluding the foreigners from the most valued rights of citizenship. Upon the subject of naturalization, a majority of the subsequent leaders of this party were in favor of a prohibitory period of twenty-one years. Governeur Morris, afterwards the Corypheus of Federalism, was the leader of the party hostile to all foreigners seeking a refuge in America; whilst James Madison was the leader of the noble party which proclaimed in the Convention—and that in the broadest sense—the doctrines of equal rights and untrammeled religious and civil liberty, to native and foreign born citizens. That great Virginian, whose principles now form the basis of those of the Democratic party, was thus early enlisted, by all the sympathies of his generous heart, in defence of the poverty-stricken, the oppressed, the persecuted and unfortunate of every clime. The unexampled growth and prosperity of this republic illustrates the wisdom and sagacity of those noble sympathies. He recognized and proclaimed that America was forever to be the home of the victims o European despotism, religious and political, and the Constitution stands as the "Ark and Covenant" of the solemn pledges of our forefathers. The great principles of republicanism taught Jefferson, Madison and Washington the propriety and wise policy of extending to respectable foreign emigrants that protection and those privileges which would bind them by the ties of gratitude and affection to the land of their adoption. This they considered better than having in our midst a class of discontented, restless persons, destitute of all those political privileges which constitute the pride of an American citizen. Evidences of this spirit of Catholic humanity, as well as of statesmanlike sagacity, are everywhere to be found in the debates of the Convention of 1787. Thus, in the Madison Papers, page 1300:

"Mr. Madison wished to maintain the character of liberality which had been professed in all the constitutions and publications of America. He wished to invite foreigners of merit and republican principles among us. That part of America which had encouraged them most, had advanced most rapidly in population, agriculture and the arts."

Contrast this noble and benevolent language with that of a leading Federalist, who, with all the stupidity and bigotry of his party, opposed the protection of all foreign born citizens.

Mr. Morris said, Madison Papers, page 1277:

"As to the citizens of the world (emigrants) he did not wish to see them in our councils. He would not trust them. The men who shake off their attachments to their mother country can never love another."

This is language with which none but a Federalist, disgusted with republicanism, could have insulted a convention of patriots and heroes, who were fresh from battle fields, where the great struggle was to "*shake off*" an unnatural and oppressive mother country. And in this extract we have the sum and substance of that senseless and brutal hostility which the Federal party practiced, under all its names and disguises, from 1787 to 1855. The mere fact of emigration, not the vices of the emigrant, is the crime. The oaths of naturalization and allegiance violate the old English and Federal doctrine of "once a subject, always a subject." If the emigrant has been driven away by the unjust, cruel laws, or lawlessness—as the case may be—of the mother country; if he has been imprisoned, pillaged, and denied the right of worshiping his God in his own way, by the same mother country, it is still a crime for him, in another and more congenial land, to make that oath of allegiance which a heart overwhelming with gratitude dictates. In reply to Mr. Morris' denunciation of foreign citizens, Mr. Madison said:

"He thought any restriction, however, in the Constitution unnecessary and improper; unnecessary because the National Legislature is to have the right of regulating naturalization * * —improper because it will give a tincture of illiberality to the Constitution; because it will put it out of the power of the National Legislature, even by special acts of naturalization, to confer upon meritorious strangers the full rank of citizenship; and because it will discourage the most desirable class of people from emigrating to the United States. Should the proposed Constitution have the intended effect of giving stability and reputation to our government, great numbers of respectable Europeans, MEN WHO LOVED LIBERTY, and wished to partake of its blessings, would be ready to transfer their fortunes hither."—*Madison Papers, page* 1278.

The leaders of the Federal party who labored to convert every foreign emigrant into a sort of Helot, and endeavored to perpetuate his degradation by registering in the organic laws of the United States the act of outlawry, were not disheartened by their defeat in the Convention of 1787. The journals and debates of the first and second Congress after the adoption and ratification of the Federal Constitution, prove that when the naturalization laws were under consideration and discussion, there were attempts made by those who at a subsequent period supported John Adams, to deny all emigrants the privilege of becoming citizens for twenty years after their arrival in this country. Thus, again, did the men who afterwards aided Jefferson and Madison in crushing the alien and sedition laws, prevent the Federal party from inflicting a grievous wrong upon the foreigners who had sought this country to enjoy religious and political liberty. From the baptismal font of the Constitution of the United States to the present day, the Democratic party has never deserted or disregarded the rights of the respectable foreign born citizen.

But the intense hatred of the Federal party to all foreign born citizens triumphed for a brief period during the administration of John Adams. The opposition to foreign born citizens of the United States, manifested by a few leading Federalists during Washington's administration, became the settled policy of that party in 1796. Laws were passed during the administration of John Adams for the oppression and punishment of foreign emigrants. To reach and crush these unhappy people, the Constitution was violated by the passage of the Alien and Sedition Laws. The only object of the law against aliens, and the principal object of the Sedition Law, was to deny resident aliens and foreign born citizens the rights of native born Americans. These laws were aimed especially against German, French, Scotch, Irish and English emigrants. They were genuine native American laws for the persecution of foreign born citizens. The Alien law enabled the President to arrest a man not only without trial, not only without conviction, not only without certain information, but upon mere suspicion; and when arrested, to send him from the country or cast him into prison. It denied the right of trial by jury, the privilege of habeas corpus—in a word, the privileges of trial which we extend to the vilest negro. The other law—that against sedition—was intended to close the mouths of the people, to prevent free discussion, to muzzle the press, to check the constituent from commenting upon the acts of his representatives, and to render the President sacred by penal enactments. The humblest mechanic, or editor, who should express in print his opinion of the President or any member of Congress, charging them with faithlessness in the discharge of their duties, was liable under the Sedition law, to imprisonment and a fine of two thousand dollars. Each single soul within the compass of this Union, native or foreign born, great or small, rich or poor, who uttered, whispered, or declared anything containing a charge against the President, was subject to the penalties of this abominable law.

We have said that both the Alien and the Sedition laws were intended for the oppression of foreign born citizens. The Alien law was intended to bear upon none others than foreigners; the Sedition law, as Adams well knew, would operate expressly against that class. During the administration of John Adams, the brilliant and most uncompromising opponents of his unconstitutional measures, were the political refugees from other countries. These men having suffered from the oppression of monarchical laws at home, were naturally the advocates of a republican form of government. They believed with Thomas Jefferson, in his letter to Mazzei, that under the blighting influence of Federalism,—

"In the place of that noble love of liberty and republican government which carried us through the war, an Anglican monarchical and aristocratic party had sprung up, whose avowed object is to draw over us the substance, as they have already done the powers, of the British government."

And another authority informs us that:

"There were then two hundred papers published in the United States; one hundred and seventy-eight were in favor of the Federal administration; about twenty-two were opposed to the measures then adopted, and a greater portion of these were in the hands of foreigners."—*Williams' Administration of John Adams, p.* 133.

This affords a clue to the secret reasons which governed the Federal party in passing the Sedition law. It was to crush these twenty-two independent presses—to put down all opposition to the monarchical and unconstitutional proceedings of the Executive and a corrupt legislature. The first prosecutions under this act were of four editors, three of whom were foreigners. The treatment of Callender, Cooper, Lyon and Holt, furnish the best commentary upon the Sedition law. Peters, Iredell, Addison, and Chase, were the judicial blood-hounds let loose upon these foreign born Democratic editors. Mr. Lyon, an intelligent Englishman, in a Democratic paper, called "The Time-Piece," spoke of "the ridiculous pomp, idle parade, and selfish avarice" of John Adams.—(Wood's Suppressed History of Adams' Administration, page 164.)—He was arrested, tried and convicted by a packed jury, and Judge Iredell, after commenting upon the heinous crime of ridiculing the President, passed sentence:

"That you be imprisoned four months for the costs of this trial, and fined one thousand dollars."—*Wharton's State Trials of the U. S., page* 337. "This unfortunate man was then conducted out of court and thrown into a dungeon six feet square, where he was left to starve during a rigorous winter."—*Wood's Suppressed History, page* 156.

We might multiply, if it was necessary, the cases of cruel prosecution and persecution practiced by the Federal judges and Federal officers upon our foreign born citizens during the administration of Adams. They were hunted by official blood-hounds, remorseless as Mohawks, convicted by packed juries, and sentenced by judges as corrupt as Jeffries.

These were the blessings, this the protection afforded to foreign born citizens by the Federal Whig administration of John Adams. All the power, all the influence of that administration, were directed against the foreigners who sought refuge in this country after the revolution—for they were Democrats. They took grounds for Thomas Jefferson, and against the Federal party, and they were hunted down for this crime, as if they had been beasts of prey, and unworthy of the protection which the negro now enjoys.

They were torn from their homes at the discretion of the President, and the social rights of freemen, open accusation, *habeas corpus*, and trial by jury, denied. They were incarcerated if they dared to arraign a public officer for political misdeeds.

The Native American party of the days of John Adams was more respectable, both in numbers and measures, than any that has since existed. It had for its leaders nearly all the educated aristocratic members of that Federal party which, during George Washington's eight years' administration, was omnipotent in the United States. It had the prestige of education, wealth, talent, position, office, and members. It is idle to suppose that any subsequent organization of Native Americans, under any name or disguise, will ever equal in strength or influence the Native American organization of 1796. The first had for its executive head a patriot of the revolution, John Adams; the last has for its head the drunken senator in Congress of one of the smallest states in the Union. So odious did Native Americanism become in 1800, that the Democratic party, formally organized only two years before—led on by two great Virginians—crushed the party that originated the Alien and Sedition laws, and elevated Jefferson to the Presidency. The present Democratic party was formed for the purpose of repealing the Alien and Sedition laws. "Justice to the oppressed foreigners," was the cry of the Democratic masses who rallied to the resolutions of 1798-'99. Those resolutions the national Democratic party unanimously endorsed at Baltimore in 1852.

The Old Dominion, God bless her, ever true to the Constitution, was first to raise the battle-cry in defence of persecuted foreigners, who were every where falling victims to the Alien and Sedition laws.

The Virginia resolutions of '98 and '99, and the report of James Madison in their vindication, prove this. The following constitutes the fourth of the series:

"That the General Assembly doth particularly protest against the palpable and alarming infractions of the Constitution in the two late cases of the Alien and Sedition acts, passed at the late session of Congress; the first of which exercises a power delegated to the Federal government, and which, by uniting legislative and judicial powers to those of the Executive, utterly subverts the general principle of a free government as well as the particular organization and positive provisions of the Federal Constitution; and the other of which acts exercises a power not delegated by the Constitution; a power which, more than any other, ought to excite unusual alarm, because it is leveled against that right of freely examining public measures and character, which has ever been justly deemed the only effectual guardian of every other right."

The 8th of the series is not less emphatic. Speaks of the Alien and Sedition laws as

"Acts which assume to create, define, and punish crimes, other than those enumerated in the Constitution, are altogether void and of no force, and that the power to create, define and punish such other crimes, is reserved, and of right appertains solely and exclusively, to the respective states, each within its own territory."

Indeed, so indignant was the Whig Central Committee at Washington with the Democratic party, for having reaffirmed their former anti-Native American resolutions of 1798–'99, that it burst forth during the canvass of 1852 in the following tirade against the fourth and eighth resolutions:

"These resolutions constituted their political Bible, from which they are constantly preaching doctrines utterly subversive of the government, and which would, if entertained by a majority of even one or two states, involve us in the horrors of civil war."

The Democratic party, under the lead of Jefferson, acquired, by advocating a repeal of the Alien and Sedition laws, a popularity in the country which it has never lost. A wise and prevalent change of the policy of the general government towards foreign born emigrants characterized the administration of Thomas Jefferson. In his first annual message he recommended to Congress the adoption of naturalization laws calculated to attract intelligent emigrants from all portions of Europe. The Democratic party, during the first session of Congress after Jefferson's election to the presidency, lost no time in repealing those infamous and unconstitutional Alien and Sedition laws by which the first Native American party in this country oppressed the friendless strangers of every clime.

The liberal, humane and republican policy of Jefferson towards our foreign born citizens was imitated by Madison, and tended greatly to increase the emigration to the United States. Thousands of useful men flocked to this country. The repeal of the original naturalization laws, which required a residence of fourteen years previous to the naturalization, took place during Jefferson's administration.

The war of 1812 was declared and conducted by the Democratic party mainly for the purpose of protecting our foreign born citizens from the British pretence that Englishmen could not get rid of their allegiance. This doctrine was, as we have seen, the popular one with several leading federalists who were members of the Convention of 1787. It was denied by the Democratic party of the United States, and as Great Britain proceeded to practice it, war war the result. This was as usual, the Whigs of that day considered damnable and accursed, and all Native Americans, Yankee cowards and New England parsons denounced the war, Mr. Madison and the foreign born citizens, in the style with which the war with Mexico was abused. The Whig party not only opposed the war for the defence of our English born citizens, but called a convention to abuse and villify the authors of the war and to burn blue lights for the enemy. The convention is pretty generally known as the Hartford Convention, and was composed of a varied assortment of Whigs, Federalists, cowards, traitors, Yankee demagogues, and parsons, every man of whom richly deserved hanging. In this convention, the proceedings of which constitute the most nefarious chapter of our political history, there was again manifested the most settled and deep rooted hostility to the foreign born citizens. The sentiment which blazed in 1787, which was embodied in the Alien and Sedition laws of 1796, and which was crushed in 1800 and 1801, burnt fiercely in 1812.

The following extract, from the proceedings of the Hartford Convention, will be worth the perusal of every Democrat who contemplates resorting to any other political organization than the party of Madison and Jefferson:

"*Seventhly.*—The easy admission of naturalized foreigners, to places of trust, honor or profit, operating as an inducement to the malcontent subjects of the old world to come to these states in quest of executive patronage and to repay it by an abject devotion to executive measures.

"Another amendment, subordinate in importance, but still in a high degree expedient, relates to the exclusion of foreigners hereafter arriving in the United States from the capacity of holding offices of trust, honor or profit.

"That the stock of population already in these states is amply sufficient to render this nation in due time sufficiently great and powerful, is not a controvertible question. Nor will it be seriously pretended, that the national deficiency in wisdom, arts, science, arms, or virtue, needs to be replenished from foreign countries. Still, it is agreed, that a liberal policy should offer the rights of hospitality, and the choice of settlement, to those who are disposed to visit the country. But why admit to a participation in the government aliens who were no parties to the compact—who were ignorant of the nature of our institutions, and have no stake in the welfare of the country but what is recent and transitory? It is surely a privilege sufficient, to admit them, after due probation, to become citizens for all but political purposes. To extend it beyond these limits, is to encourage foreigners to come to these states as candidates for preferment. The convention forbear to express their opinion upon the inauspicious effects which have already resulted to the honor and piece of this nation, from this misplaced and indiscriminate liberality.

"*Sixth.*—No person who shall hereafter be naturalized shall be eligible as a member of the Senate or House of Representatives of the United States, nor capable of holding any civil office under the authority of the United States."

Here we have Know-Nothingism with a vengeance. Neither the Native American party of 1844, nor its nameless offspring of 1854, can boast of much progress since the days of the Hartford Convention of 1812. Every odious feature of the modern creed seems to have been embodied in that of the traitor and cowards, who met at Hartford to plot and conspire against their own country in time of war. Really Native Americanism, although possessing a long pedigree, will hardly venture to boast of its disreputable ancestors. Its blood has certainly coursed through very dirty and unclean channels ever since its birth in the Convention of 1787.

Nativeism is a foul and ugly eruption that has broken out upon the body of the Federal Whig party every twenty or thirty years for the last sixty-odd years. Democracy found a cure for the disease in 1787, in 1800, in 1812 and in 1844, and it will do so in 1855 and 1856. The swilling Senator of Delaware is no match for those who fight for the great principles of Jefferson and Madison. The influence and opinions of two such dead statesmen are ample, in the old Dominion, against the machinations of twenty thousand midnight politicians in disguise and without a name. Temporary defeat—if defeat were possible—in the defence of the largest civil and religious liberty guaranteed to all by the Constitution, would but nerve the Democratic party to a more vigorous and determined struggle. God never intended this fair land to be ruled by people who register their decrees for the destruction of the Constitution in secret and midnight conclaves.

Foreign Born Democratic Martyrs.—The subject of martyrdom, Popish and political, has become a theme of much popular excitement and of great general interest, and we expect soon to have a series of awful revelations from Sam disclosing the existence of Spanish inquisitions in every hamlet of a thousand inhabitants in the land. Mrs. Partington is also said to entertain and to have expressed the opinion that the Jesuits are at the bottom of Know-Nothingism, and that a thumb screw can be found in the breeches-pocket of every member of the second degree of the secret order. There is an interesting chapter of domestic martyrology to which justice has never been done, and when the next edition of Fox's Martyrs appears, we hope to see it incorporated in its far-famed pages. We refer to the foreign born citizens of this country who were, fifty-seven years ago, persecuted by the early Know-Nothings, or Federalists, for exercising liberty of the press and of speech.

For Democracy, in its infancy in this country, had to contend against a Know-Nothing, proscriptive, Native American spirit, more ferocious and intolerant than that which now, in secrecy and at midnight, is seeking to trample the Constitution under foot. From the very commencement of our government, the more intelligent political refugees and foreign emigrants instinctively attached themselves to the old Democratic party. When that party was weak, and in a hopeless minority, our foreign born citizens were loyal and true as they now are. When the Federalists, with aristocratic pomp and splendor, misruled the land, they failed to win the confidence of the emigrants who had fled from monarchy and slavery at home to find liberty and Democracy in this country. The early emigrants to this country were men of education and intelligence. The political disturbances of the latter part of the eighteenth century drove them across the Atlantic by thousands. Jefferson, from his distinguished sympathies for the cause of liberty all over the world, was the object of their especial admiration. Long suffering and tyranny at home having made them familiar with all the odious phases of aristocracy, however skilfully disguised, they saw through the thin and semi-transparent mask of republicanism with which the elder Adams and his party sought to conceal their opinions and purposes. Hence, the peevishness and notorious irascibility of that testy old gentleman were kept constantly at boiling point by the foreign born Democracy.

There were, in 1787, only twenty-two Democratic newspapers in the United States, and of that number twenty were edited by foreigners. Their assaults drove the Federal party almost to madness. Jefferson records in his "*Anas*" how Adams and his political associates writhed under the assaults of these men. The Federal party, however, was then powerful in numbers and resources. Adams had inherited the abundant popularity of his great predecessor, but to lose it by his folly, tyranny and aristocratic proclivities. He was too proud to correct the errors of his administration, and held his Democratic opponents, native and foreign, in too great contempt to attempt to conciliate them. He endeavored to put down Democracy, as Know-Nothingism proposes to crush out Catholicism, by persecution. Forgetting that in a republic, all laws rest upon public opinion, he thought to strangle Democracy by unconstitutional enactments against aliens and the liberty of the press. The attempt was made, and "the blood of the martyrs became the seed of the church." A Federal Congress readily obeyed his wishes and enacted the alien and sedition laws. Armed with those statutes for two years he wreaked his vengeance mainly on Democrats of foreign birth. At the end of that time the Democratic party arose like a young giant, and dashed the whole structure of Federalism to the earth, hurled the old party from power, and inaugurated the great National Democratic party of this country. From that day to this, foreign born citizens have been ever faithful to the Democratic party. The reasons for this lasting friendship are honorable alike to both parties. The only Democratic martyrs of this country were foreign born citizens, and when the Democratic party waxed strong they blotted from our statute books all the unconstitutional laws by which our foreign born citizens were once placed at the mercy of a Federal Executive.

For the express purpose of depriving this class of citizens of their rights and liberties, the following laws were enacted by Congress, July 6th, and 14th, 1798. As the Know-Nothings are endeavoring to manufacture a proscriptive spirit in the United States precisely similar to that of the year

1798, it may be well for the people of Virginia to learn a few timely and instructive lessons from a perusal of the laws in question.

The Sedition Law enacted—

"That if any person shall write, print, utter, or publish, or shall cause or procure to be written, printed, uttered, or published, or shall knowingly and willingly assist, or aid in writing, printing, uttering, or publishing any false, scandalous and malicious writings or writing against the government of the United States, or either house of the Congress of the United States, or the President of the United States, with intent to defame the said government, or either house of the said Congress, or the said President, or to bring them into contempt or disrepute, or to excite against them, or either or any of them, the hatred of the good people of the United States, or to stir up sedition within the United States, * * * * * he shall be punished by a fine not exceeding two thousand dollars, and by imprisonment not exceeding two years.—1 *Peters' Statutes at Large, p.* 598."

The "Alien Act," the provisions of which are too long for insertion in *extenso* in this article, provided—

"That the President of the United States shall be and is hereby authorized, in any event aforesaid, by his proclamation thereof, or other public act, to direct the conduct to be observed on the part of the United States towards aliens * * * * the manner and degree of the restraint to which they shall be subjected, and in what cases and upon what security their residence shall be permitted, and to provide for the removal of those who, not being permitted, to reside in the United States, shall refuse or neglect to depart therefrom.—1 *Peters' Statutes at Large, page* 577."

It is with difficulty that the present generation can be taught to believe that such laws as we have given above once disgraced our statute books, abridging the liberty of speech, and leaving aliens upon our soil completely at the mercy of the President, denying them the right of trial by jury, and of confronting their accusers.

Not only, however, were there such laws, but, as we shall presently see, more than one foreign born Democrat was martyred for his hatred of federalism and love for the principles of Jefferson.

I.—*The Case of Mathew Lyon.*—[American State Trials, pp. 333, 343.] Mathew Lyon was an Irishman by birth, who came to this country uneducated and destitute. By energy and honesty he arose from the position of an apprentice to that of a representative in Congress from the state of Vermont. Whilst a member of Congress he distinguished himself by his patriotic devotion to the cause of Democracy, and his spirited opposition to Adams' administration.

In exercising the privileges of his office as a representative in Congress, he addressed a series of articles to his constituents, commenting upon the character of the administration of John Adams. In consequence of this, on the 5th of October, 1798, he was indicted for a seditious libel, and the indictment set forth the following libellous matter:

"As to the executive, when I shall see the efforts of that power bent on the promotion of the comfort, the happiness, and accommodation of the people, that executive shall have my zealous and uniform support; but whenever I shall, on the part of the executive, see every consideration of the public welfare swallowed up in a continual grasp for power, in an unbounded thirst for ridiculous pomp, foolish adulation and selfish avarice; when I shall behold men of real merit daily turned out of office for no other cause but independency of sentiment; when I shall see men of firmness, merit, years, ability and experience, discarded in their applications for office, for fear they possess that independence, and men of meanness preferred for the ease with which they take up and advocate opinions, the consequence of which they know nothing; when I shall see the sacred name of religion employed as a state engine to make mankind hate and persecute one another, I shall not be their humble advocate."

Although this language was as just as it was proper and legitimate, yet a packed jury of Yankee Federalists found the defendant guilty, and a Federal hack, Judge Patterson, pronounced the following sentence:

"Mathew Lyon, as a member of the federal legislature, you must be well acquainted with the mischiefs which flow from an unlicensed abuse of the government, and of the motives which led to the passage of the act under which this indictment is proved. * * Your position, so far from making the case one which might slip with a nominal fine through the hands of the court, would make impunity conspicuous, should such a fine be imposed. What, however, has tended to mitigate the sentence, which would otherwise have been imposed, is, what I am sorry to hear of, the reduced condition of your estate. The judgment of the court is, that you stand imprisoned four months, pay the cost of prosecution, and a fine of one thousand dollars, and stand committed until this sentence be complied with."

The mildness of early Know-Nothing despotism is here beautifully illustrated. A foreign born Democrat addresses a letter to his constituents, commenting upon the executive department of the government, as was his duty as their representative; he is tried for it by a packed jury and a federal court, found guilty, and assured by the judge that the magnitude of his offence is greatly increased by his being a member of Congress, and that the only regret of the federal Jeffries is, that the smallness of the defendant's fortune forced him to fine him only one thousand dollars.

All of Lyon's sentence was rigourously enforced. He was at first denied the use of pen, ink, paper and books, and confined in a cell sixteen feet wide by twelve long, (see Wharton's State Trials, p. 341,) the common receptacle for horse-thieves, money-forgers, runaway negroes, and other rascals and felons.

A Federal newspaper thus gloated in coarse and inhuman joy over his imprisonment, precisely as a Know-Nothing organ of the present day would do if a foreign born Democrat was to be ejected from office:

"*The Lyon of Vermont.*—To-morrow morning, at 11 o'clock, will be exposed to view the Lyon of Vermont. This singular animal is said to have been caught in the bogs of Hibernia, and when quite a whelp transported to America; curiosity inducing a New Yorker to buy him, and moving to the country, afterwards exchanged him for a yoke of young bulls with a Vermonter. * * His pelt resembles more the wolf, or the tiger, and his gestures bear a remarkable resemblance to the bear; this, however, may be ascribed to his having been in the habit of associating with that species of wild beast on the mountains. He was brought to this place in a waggon.—*Porcupine Gazette, June 6th*, 1797."

But this poor man, whilst languishing in a foul and unwholsome prison during the cold months of a New England winter, the victim of a tyrant whose native American antipathies the Know-Nothings of the present day appear to have adopted, was not forgotten by a faithful constituency. They espoused his cause, and whilst in the clutches of his Federal oppressors, re-elected him to Congress—the records of the day showing the following vote:

Lyon, (Democrat, and in prison,)	3,482
Williams, Federalist,	1,554
Lyon's majority,	1,928

Released from prison amid the tumultous rejoicings of his friends, he repaired to Philadelphia to take his seat in the Congress to which he had been elected whilst in jail.

The insolent Federal majority in the House of Representatives met him with the following resolution:

"Resolved, That Mathew Lyon, a member of this House, having been convicted of being a notorious and seditious person, and of a depraved mind and wicked and diabolical disposition, and of wickedly, deceitfully and maliciously contriving to defame the government of the United States, and of having, with design and intent to defame John Adams, President of the United States * * * be therefore expelled from this House."

The Federalists were all willing to expel this persecuted foreigner; but Mr. Nicholas, *of Virginia*, eloquently defended him, and they could not get a two-thirds' vote. Again the great Federal organ of that day aimed its envenomed darts at poor Lyon's head, February, 1799:

"Lyon looks remarkably well for a gentleman just out of jail. This man's re-election, whilst confined as a criminal, is a new and striking proof of the excellence of universal suffrage. * * * Happy the nation where there is but one step from the dungeon to the Legislature. Well might the pathetic Mr. Murray, (speaking of the old alien law,) express his fears that the influx of foreigners would "contaminate the purity and simplicity of American manners."

This is a very fair specimen of Know-Nothing sentiment fifty-six years ago.

The persecuted Lyon lived, however, to wrest the state of Vermont temporarily from Federal misrule, subsequently removed to the state of Kentucky, represented that state in the House of Representatives from 1803 to 1811, refused the office of commissary for the Western army, which was tendered to him by Thomas Jefferson, and died at the advanced age of seventy-eight. He survived the old Know-Nothing or Federal party more than a quarter of a century, and on the 4th of July, 1840, Congress refunded to his representatives, with interest, the iniquitous fine of one thousand dollars, imposed upon him in 1799.

Next in the list of foreign born citizens who braved fine and imprisonment in defence of Democracy, and by fierce denunciations of Federalism, stands—

II.—*The case of Anthony Hoswell.*—Amer. State Trials, pp. 584, 687.

Anthony Hoswell was born in England in 1763, a gentleman by birth and education, who espoused to cause of freedom, and fought on the side of the colonies during the revolutionary war, and perilled his life at Monmouth.

He subsequently became distinguished as a Democratic editor, and especially by his boldness and talent excited the hatred of the Federal party.

In 1800, at Windsor, in the state of Vermont, he was, under the "Sedition act," indicted for publishing, as the Federalists avered, the following libellous matter:

To the enemies of political persecution in the Western district of Vermont: Your representative (Mathew Lyon) is holden by the oppressive hand of usurped power in a loathsome prison, deprived almost of the right of reason, and suffering all the indignities which can be heaped upon him by a hard-hearted savage, who has, to the disgrace of Federalism, been elevated to a station where he can satiate his barbarity on the misery of his victims. But in spite of Fitch, (the marshal) and to their sorrow, time will pass away, and the month of February will arrive and bring with it the defender of our right? No. Without exertion it will not. ***Eleven hundred dollars must be paid for his ransom, &c.***

Although the prisoner proved the truth of every allegation in the matter charged as libellous, the jury returned a verdict of guilty, and the court sentenced the prisoner to a fine of two hundred dollars and imprisonment for two months.

The indignities with which this noble and bold Democrat was treated after he was arrested was the subject of bitter party feeling for a long time.

He was arrested at night, and notified to prepare for a journey to Rutland early in the morning. Accordingly, at a very early hour, Mr. Hoswell, although in very poor health and totally unaccustomed to riding, was compelled to mount a horse and ride sixty miles through the rain on a cold day in October, to the jail at Rutland. Here he was thrown into a filthy prison at midnight, notwithstanding his entreaties to be permitted to dry his clothes, which were saturated with the rain. Several of the most responsible men in Rutland offered any security the marshal might demand, to induce him to grant these requests, but in vain. The prisoner was thrown into the prison, and never afterwards recovered entirely from the shock thus given his health. His sentence was rigidly carried out, and at the expiration of his term of confinement, an immense concourse of people from the neighboring country assembled to welcome him back to liberty, and to signalize their disapprobation of his imprisonment. He marched forth from his quarters at the jail to the tune of Yankee Doodle, played by a band, while the discharge of cannon signified the general satisfaction at his release. [See Wharton's Criminal Trials, page 687.]

This victim of early Native Americanism was, says a distinguished author, "highly respected, not only by his friends, but by his political opponents. He was distinguished in private life by exemplary conduct in the discharge of his duties, and by his devotion to the moral and religious improvement of society." [Wharton, page 688.]

Mr. Hoswell was a gentleman, a brave revolutionary soldier, wedded to the cause of liberty; but as he was a Democrat, and a foreign born citizen, he was treated like a common felon by the Know-Nothings of 1798. But the list of foreign born Democrats who stood by our party in its infancy, and braved persecution and the torture of cruel imprisonment for their opinions, is a long one.

III.—*The Case of Thomas Cooper.*—[American State Trials, page 677.] The learned and celebrated Thomas Cooper was the next victim sacrificed to gratify John Adams' hatred of foreign born Democrats, whose blows were aimed principally at the accomplished Democratic writers whose pens were driving him to desperation.

Thomas Cooper was an Englishman by birth, and a graduate of Oxford. He was the intimate friend of the celebrated Priestly, and a barrister, an author of distinction, and a chemist of great reputation, He was, at different periods in his life, a professor in Dickinson College, and also in the University of Pennsylvania. He was for several years a presiding judge of one of the districts of Pennsylvania, and filled a professorship in Columbia College, South Carolina, for many years previous to his death. His translation of the "Pandects of Justinian" is regarded as a master piece of admirable and classical scholarship by the legal profession to this day.

He was an ardent Democrat, and one of the earliest and most devoted friends of Thomas Jefferson. Hence his appearance in the catalogue of foreign born Democratic martyrs. In 1800, he was tried for what the Know-Nothings of that day called "*Seditious Libel*," and the libellous matter charged in the indictment was as follows. As in the cases already cited, our readers will perceive that it was dangerous, in the day of the early

Know-Nothings, for a foreigner to say a word against the Federal party and their aristocratic president. But to the libellous matter:

"At that time he (John Adams) had just entered office; he was hardly in the infancy of political mistake: even those who doubted his capacity thought well of his intentions. Nor were we yet saddled with the expense of a permanent navy, or threatened under his auspices with the existence of a standing army. Our credit was not yet reduced so low as to borrow money at eight per cent. in time of peace, while the unnecessary violence of official expressions might justly have provoked a war. Mr. Adams had not yet projected his embassies to Prussia and Russia, nor had he yet interfered as president of the United States to influence the decisions of a court of justice—a stretch of authority which the monarch of Great Britain would have shrunk from—an interference without precedent against law and against mercy. This melancholy case of Jonathan Robbins, a native American, forcibly impressed by the British, and delivered up, with the advice of Mr. Adams, to the mock trial of a British court-martial, had not yet astonished the republican citizens of this free country; a case too little known, but of which the people ought to be fully apprised before the election, and they shall be.—[Amer. State Trials, p. 658."]

As was usual in 1800, when Federal marshals, packed Federal juries, and Federal prosecutors and judges agreed in their interpretation of Federal laws, Mr. Cooper was found guilty, and the infamous Judge Chase, of Callender notoriety, sentenced the defendant "to pay a fine of four hundred dollars, to be imprisoned for six months, and at the end of that period to find surety for himself in a thousand, and two securities in five hundred dollars each."—[Wharton's Criminal Trials, page 679.]

But the length of this article admonishes us to hasten on with our list of foreign born Democrats who were true to our cause when courage was more essential in the defence of our sentiments than at present.

IV.—*Case of William Duane.*—[American State Trials, page 344.]—Wm. Duane was born in this country, but as his parents were Irish emigrants, he spent the early part of his life in Ireland, his mother having returned to that country after the death of her husband. He was the first editor of the celebrated London Times, and the intimate friend of Horne Tooke. He returned to this country in 1795, and became the editor of the leading Democratic organ of that day, the Aurora. Mr. Jefferson always declared that he was indebted to "Duane and the Aurora newspaper for his election to the presidency." The justice and severity of his attacks upon the Federal party rendered him the object of open violence. During Mr. Adams' administration some troops of horse were sent from Philadelphia to Reading, to cut down the liberty poles of the Democratic party in "Old Berks," and to perform other heroic achievements worthy of Adams and his primitive Know-Nothing friends. These body guards of the Federal despot lived very freely and indulged in all the license of an enemy's force in a hostile land.

A letter was published in the Aurora, complaining of their outrages. On their return to Philadelphia, a large party of officers proceeded to the Aurora office, and, placing sentinels over the printers, dragged out the editor of the Aurora, Mr. Duane, and beat him until he was insensible.

Yet this Democratic martyr was a scholar and gentleman, a patriot and a soldier, whose works on education, history, military science, politics, and political economy, are well known to the present generation. His influence and instrumentality in building up the Democratic party, Jefferson and Madison both regarded as great as their own.

To these cases we might add those of Callender, Reynolds, Moore, Cumming, Frothingham, and others, all foreign born Democrats—men of education and talents, who were the victims of Federal lawlessness and cruelty, when, in 1798, the Native American party was sufficiently strong to deprive our foreign born citizens of the right of trial by jury, and of the liberty of speech, and of the press. The cases cited at length in this article illustrate the atrocious tendency of Native Americanism, when clothed with power under the forms of law, to oppress and persecute our foreign born citizens.

The lessons of experience are always the best that can be read to an intelligent people,—nor will they be lost upon the people of Virginia at this time, when, after the lapse of more than half a century, we have a party in our midst plotting in secrecy and at midnight to strip our foreign born citizens of their rights.

No true Democrat, bearing in mind the political devotion of the foreign born citizens of this country to our principles and measures, from the days of their early persecution by the Federalists to the present, can, or will lend his aid to a band of conspirators, seeking, in open disregard of the Constitution, to strip these innocent and faithful citizens of their rights.

ORATORS OF THE CANVASS.

We can safely assert that political excitement never ran higher in any state, than in Virginia in 1855. And we can moreover aver with truth, that there never was so general an interest manifested in the discussion of political issues. This was attributable principally to two things: in the first place to the facts and sound arguments set forth by the talented press of our State; and secondly, to the stirring appeals and impassioned eloquence of our public speakers. They addressed the masses in every section of the State, appealing to the time-honored principles of the Democratic party, dissecting the monstrous ritual of Know Nothingism, and inviting its devotees to meet them in open discussion.

One of the first speeches of the campaign was a most powerful one, from the Hon. Stephen A. Douglass of Illinois, delivered in Richmond in the month of March; but owing to some misunderstanding with the stenographer employed by the editor of the Examiner to report it, it was never written out for publication. The speech produced a most profound impression in Richmond, and evidently exerted a great influence in the State, as he addressed an immense audience, many of whom were residents of the country.

The Examiner contained the following extended notice of the Senator's oration.

JUDGE DOUGLAS IN RICHMOND.—The citizens of Richmond had the pleasure of hearing a speech, Tuesday night, 27th March, from the author of the Nebraska-Kansas act. Nothing but a *verbatim* report would present the address in its real strength and merit; for every sentence was an argument, and the speech possessed the characteristic of a sphere in compacting the greatest quantity of matter within the smallest extent of surface.

His illustration of that great principle—of which himself may be pronounced the living *embodiment*—of the absolute right of the people in each State, and territory, (about to become a State,) to decide upon its own institutions, subject only to the constitution, a principle which is the very corner stone of State Rights politics—was clear, beautiful and conclusive.

His narration of the incident's of the last year's struggle in Illinois, to defeat himself for championing and the Democratic party for endorsing this principle, was interesting in the extreme. He said that this principle was opposed in Illinois by the Fusion, and he explained that to be a combination of Abolitionists, Whigs, Know Nothings and anti-Liquor men, against the great Nebraska principle, and against the Democratic party sustaining it. He declared that the Fusion was thus constituted in every State at the North, except New York, where fortuitous circumstances had operated to qualify the rule in some degree. He admitted that some Democrats had left their own organization and gone into the Know Nothing councils; and while he admitted that many Know Nothings were not Abolitionists, yet he declared that the Abolstionists and Free-soilers had the majority in their councils, and controlled the action of the Order, the minority being *sworn* to co-operate with the majority.

He also admitted the fact, that the Whigs did not all merge with the Abolitionists and the Know Nothings in the Fusion; but that the high-toned and honorable portion of that once glorious party co operated with the Democracy in the elections. He said that the Democracy of Illinois owed their triumph in the State elections by a majority of 3,000 votes, and in Col. W. A. Richardson's district in the success of that gallant and indomitable State Rights man—to Whig votes. He said that ten per cent. of the Whigs of the State had segregated themselves from the mass of their party, and, by rallying to the side of the Democracy, had saved the State ticket and Colonel Richardson. We take pleasure in making prominent this declaration of Judge Douglas, for God forbid that any Southern editor should refuse to acknowledge a fact so dear to the whole South, and so honorable to the Silver Grays of the North. In the same degree that we iterate and reprobate the fact that the Know Nothings of the North, as a party, and the great body of the Whigs of the North, as either Freesoilers or Know Nothings, oppose the great Douglas-Nebraska-State-Rights principle of popular sovereignty—do we rejoice in, exult over and reiterate the fact that an honorable, inflexible fragment of the old Whig party of the North still cling, even unto political martyrdom, to the Constitution of their country.

Declaring that the Know Nothings everywhere at the North co-operated with the FUSION in ostracising and proscribing Nebraska men and warring upon the Nebraska principle, the JUDGE went into a calm and most overwhelming argument against that organization. He assailed it as hostile to that *open, free discussion*, which was essential to the health and vitality of popular government. His argument upon this topic was as clear and convincing as it was striking and original. The Know Nothing Order not only shrank from full and open discussion before the people, but it struck a deadly blow at the principle of representative accountability to the people, by substituting the secret club which nominated the legislator or the executive officer, for the people at large, in whom only is lodged the sovereignty of the State.

He assailed their oaths in a powerful but calm and respectful argument. An oath to obey the dictation of the club was an oath to disregard the dictates of conscience in all cases where the individual's opinion conflicted with the decree of the Order. It substituted, in a government where the individual and the people are sovereign, a conflicting sovereignty and a different and dangerous authority, that of a secret and irresponsible cabal.

He said there were a great many honest men who saw the dilemma in which their Know Nothingism placed them as good citizens, and yet were deterred from leaving the Order from conscientious scruples in regard to the oath they had taken in their initiation. He did not think an oath to violate one's conscience ought to be obeyed, and he cited the passage from ST. MARK, reciting the occurrence between Herod and the daughter of Herodias, as illustrating the fatal consequences of a vicious vow.

"For Herod himself had sent forth and laid hold upon John, and bound him in prison for Herodias' sake, his brother Philip's wife; for he had married her.

For John had said unto Herod, It is not lawful for thee to have thy brother's wife.

Therefore, Herodias had a quarrel against him, and would have killed him, but she could not.

For Herod feared John, knowing that he was a just man and an holy, and observed him; and when he heard him, he did many things, and heard him gladly.

And when a convenient day was come, that Herod, on his birth-day, made a supper to his lords, high captains, and chief estates of Galilee;

And when the daughter of the said Herodias came in, and danced, and pleased Herod and them that sat with him, the King said unto the damsel, ask of me whatsoever thou wilt, and I will give it thee.

And he swore unto her, whatever thou shalt ask of me, I will give it thee, even unto half of my kingdom.

And she went forth, and said unto her mother, what shall I ask? and she said the head of John the Baptist.

And she came in straightway with haste unto the King, and asked, saying, I wish that thou give me, by and by in a charger, the head of John the Baptist.

And the King was exceedingly sorry; yet *for his oath's sake*, and for their sakes which sat with him, he would not reject her."

The distinguished speaker advised the Democracy against an unlawful alliance with the Herodias of Federalism, and against pledging themselves to the damsel Know Nothingism, her daughter, by unlawful oaths and rash stipulations of the favors, contrary to conscience, to old friendship and to duty.

He examined the *tests*, prescribed by the Order for office and suffrage, and was especially able and powerful in his exposition of their unconstitutionality and anti-republicanism.

The first of these tests, was *birth*, a test familiar in England, and in monarchies; but, until now, unknown in these free States, where the great test was *merit*. Birth was a thing over which men had no control and did not enter at all into the republican qualification of *merit*. It did not follow that everybody born on this side of the Atlantic was fit for suffrage and office, any more than that all born on the other side were unfit. Everybody knew that America could produce rogues as well as honest citizens; indeed he was not sure but that she could beat the world in rogues as well as in every other article. She certainly produced a larger proportion of honest citizens than any other country; for here *merit* had been made the test of qualification for office, and furnished an inducement to rectitude. The test of *birth* was arbitrary and aristocratic; the test of *merit* was philosophic, just, and democratic. It was a great democratic test, and true Democrats could not abandon it for the monarchial, accidental and unjust principle, that merit, or qualification, or superiority, was dependent on birth. His allusion to his gallant colleague, General SHIELDS, a soldier who had not shed blood enough for his adopted country to atone for the accident of his birth on Irish soil, was touching and eloquent.

The test of *religious belief* was arbitrary, unjust and oppressive. It was contrary to the Constitution, which expressly forbade that "any *religious test* should *ever* be required as a qualification to any office of public trust under this government." Every Know Nothing who took an oath binding him to try candidates by this *test*, took an oath against the Constitution of the Union. He did not charge them with intentional culpability in this act, which he knew they must have done in thoughtlessness and without due examination, but he warned them against persisting in an oath in direct antagonism to the Constitution of their country.

We have glanced rapidly over, and stated loosely some of the leading topics of Judge DOUGLAS's speech. It is possible that we may succeed in obtaining from the distinguished Senator, a full report of it; but fearing we might not be able to do so, we could not refrain from presenting to our readers the foregoing abstract of an address which will long be remembered in Richmond, and which was as dignified, national, statesmanlike and able as was ever delivered before the people of this city.

As some cynical objections are rife among the opposition to a citizen from a Northern State having thus taken part in our domestic contest, it is due to Mr. DOUGLAS to say that it was with great difficulty he could be induced to speak here, on his rapid transit through the State, as we personally know. If there is a man in the Union in whom such a "crime" would be no crime, it is in the author of the Repeal of the Missouri Proviso.

MR. HUNTER'S SPEECH IN RICHMOND.

The speech of Senator R. M. T. Hunter was one of the most argumentative and unanswerable that was delivered in the whole campaign. This speech was published and extensively circulated, and that with telling effect during the canvass. It is a document which will ever repay an attentive perusal.

Fellow Citizens: I appear before you this evening, not merely to show my appreciation of the courtesy of your invitation to address you, but also because, in the present critical condition of public affairs, I desire to commune with my friends and constituents. I also wish to speak to the people of this good city, who have proved, by their past history, that whenever the safety of the government or the honor of the State demands a service at their hands, the call will not be made upon them in vain. I stand here this evening to appeal to you, in the name of both these high considerations, and if I fail to make good that appeal, it will be owing to my fault, and not because the occasion does not justify it.

Peace has its trials as well as war; and the same spirit which gathered your sons around the flag of the country in the war of 1812, will rally them to the defence of the political banner of their native State, if they see it about to be prostrated and trampled in the dust. I have said that the present is a critical condition of public affairs; and, truly, the signs of the times are such as to warrant me in thus characterizing it. In the world without we have war, and should it continue much longer, or enlarge the field of its operations, it is impossible but that some of its agitations must reach us also. Within, the elements of domestic strife are already maturing in angry discontent, as if in presage of the coming storm. The cloud which for so long has hung in the northeastern quarter of our horizon, grows larger and darker, and is visibly nearing us in the distance. When was it ever before, that a majority of the popular branch of Congress would probably be in favour of abolishing slavery in the District of Columbia; of abolishing what is called the domestic slave trade; of abolishing slavery whereever it may exist in the Territories; and to repeal the fugitive slave law, to say nothing of the restoration of the odious Missouri restriction, now so happily removed? More than one of the Southern States have declared that the execution of some of these measures would present, in their opinion, the "*casus fœderis*" itself; and yet to such extremities will the present House of Representatives be probably willing to drive us at the next session. Such are the trials for which we have already had warning to prepare. For the present, a Democratic President and a Democratic Senate stand, as "the lion in the path," between them and the execution of their measures. But these anti-slavery men boast that they have already secured "the Church, the School and the State," the great natural corporations of all human society, as they have been not inaptly denominated; and that they are thus possessed of all the main avenues through which public sentiment in the North may be concentrated, and poured upon the devoted South. And what are our preparations for this contest? It is evident that we must depend upon Truth, the Constitution, the sacred compact of Federation, and such defences as we may make in their behalf, for our safety and peace. Are we burnishing our armor for the fight? Are we making ready for the contest? These are some of the topics upon which I desire to commune with you this evening.

Fellow citizens, it seems to me there is yet another circumstance which must make us more anxious with regard to the future. It is, that these issues have been precipitated upon us with the assistance of a new and strange party, which has arisen in our midst, which, by some wild freak of taste, or in some fit of reckless levity, has called itself "the Know Nothing party," whose opinions upon many important subjects are unknown, and whose principles in regard to some other subjects, so far as known, would seem to be highly mischievous and dangerous.

I have said that these isms had been precipitated upon us with the assistance of this party in the North. Can there be a doubt of it? They constituted a portion of the "fusionists" who sought to turn out young Dodge of Iowa, who had been so true to the Constitution and just to the South, and to substitute a free-soiler in his place. In Illinois, too, they acted in like manner towards the gallant Shields. In Massachusetts, the Know Nothings constituted a majority of those who sent Wilson to the Senate of the United States, where his declarations have been such as to leave no doubt of his extreme and dangerous opinions upon the subject of slavery. Indeed, I heard Judge Douglass, in a debate in the Senate, declare that, in the non-slaveholding States, this new party, so far as he was acquainted with its history, had invariably cast its vote for the anti-slavery and anti-Nebrasbra candidates, and he challenged an instance to be produced, in which they had voted for a candidate in favor of the Nebraska bill. The case could not be produced, except that Governor Seward mentioned some one man in New York, who had been elected to some office by the vote of the Know Nothings. To which Judge Douglass well replied, that in New York there were two Know Nothing parties, one the "bogus," and the other genuine, so that there might be grave mistakes in referring to their action in New York for an explanation of their principles. Now, all this proves one of two things, either that this party, in the North, is deeply infected with the abolition feeling, or else, that it is so indifferent upon the subject, that it is willing to elect men who would drive the South to any extremity, and expose us to the most severe and dangerous trials. How, then, can we affiliate with men who seem to consider the peace and safety of the South, as the cheap material upon which rash experiments may be tried with impunity? Ought it not to make us anxious to find that the overtures for affiliation, made by such a party, have not been instantly rejected by Southern men with scorn?

It seems to me, that the very apparition of such a party in our midst, is calculated to inspire feelings of distrust and apprehension. When was it ever heard of before, that a party could be organized for political purposes in this State, which deliberated and acted in secret, and veiled the very names of their members in impenetrable mystery! When was it ever before that a party could have existed here, avowing itself to be strong enough to seize upon the administration of public affairs in this great confederacy, and yet refusing to declare its opinions upon all the leading questions which have heretofore characterised our political divisions? When it ought to speak, it is silent, and some of the sentiments it does speak, in my opinion, ought neither to be entertained nor uttered. But what can be the purpose of a secret political society in this country, or what can be its legitimate object? Under the despotic governments of the old world, we have heard of such organizations, but their object was to strike at the ruling power in the State; they concealed not only their deliberations and actions, but also the names of their members, because if either had been known, their rulers would not only have frustrated their purposes, but punished the individuals who entertained them. Under such circumstances, we can see some reason for their secrecy, but what excuse can be offered for a secret political organization in this country? Here the ruling power is that of the people; it is popular sovereignty which governs. Is that the power which this new party strikes at? is it popular government which they wish to subvert? Why conceal themselves and their action from its supervision, unless they fear it; and, why fear it, unless they are opposed to it? What they profess upon this subject we do not know; this may be amongst the secrets of the prison house.

But this we do know that they refuse their sympathies to the people, and strike at the wholesome and legitimate influences of public opinion, by acting secretly and withdrawing from its jurisdiction. Now I say, that the party which strikes at the just influence of public opinion, and refuses to submit its political action to that wholesome jurisdiction, strikes at popular government itself, for it is through the action of the former that the latter becomes practicable or even possible. Why is it that we so often hear it said of such, and such a people, that for them a popular and free form of government is impossible? Because there exists not amongst them a sufficiently free and enlightened state of public opinion to enable the people to direct properly the affairs of their government. But how can public opinion be either purified or enlightened, unless there be free thought, free speech, and a free press; and how can the people think, speak, and print freely, if the proper subjects for such action are concealed from their view? To make a popular government possible, that government must be directed by popular opinion, intelligently formed upon the subjects of its action, and not by chance-sentiment or impromptu emotions. In the one case, law is a rule prescribed by the supreme authority in a State, and government becomes systematic and regular; in the other, law is a mere matter of impulse, and government a succession of shifts and contrivances to avoid anarchy. But how can the people form an opinion with regard to the subject of their political action, unless the deliberations before them be open and public?

The framers of our Constitution felt the necessity for publicity, in regard to political action, so deeply, as to prescribe, that "each House shall keep a journal of its proceedings, and, from time to time, publish the same, excepting such parts as may in their judgment require secrecy; and the yeas and nays of the members of either House on any question, shall, at the desire of one-fifth of those present, be entered upon the journal." This journal was to be kept, and published, in order that the *people* might understand, and criticise, and regulate the proceedings of their servants, who are thus made to act under a constant sense of the supervision of the constituent body. Even so small a minority as one fifth, were authorised to order the yeas and nays, that each member should be held to his individual responsibility, and that the weaker party, when it felt itself aggrieved by the stronger, might appeal to the great bar of public opinion, where probably under the influences of truth, reason, and just feeling, judgment would be pronounced by the supreme authority in the State, a judgment which would always command respect, and, in most instances, carry along with it conviction also. Without the practises corresponding with these provisions in the constitution, representative government would become impossible, and justice a thing no longer to be expected. To satisfy ourselves of the truth of these conclusions, let us suppose, for an instant, that the American Congress, deliberated and acted in secrecy. How long would its representative character endure, and for how long afterwards could it probably be reckoned amongst the free governments of the earth? All individual responsibility would be gone. No man could tell how any member voted. Accordingly as the act was popular or unpopular in his district, he would be entitled to the presumption of having voted for, or against it. The reasons upon which a measure passed could never be given; the propositions made and rejected, would be unknown, and thus a power far more irresponsible than any ever exercised by either Cæsar or Czar, would be wielded by this many-headed monster.

But the old fathers of our state left us still more conclusive evidence of their estimate of the importance of publicity in political proceedings. They were not content with exacting it from the representative, but enforced the principle on the constituent body also. They required each elector to vote, not by the dead letter of the secret ballot, but with the free and manly utterance of the "living voice." And thus it is, by wise and ancient prescription, that the Virginian has ever given his vote in the light of day, and before the world. Preserving the "*os sublime*," and presenting a brow as open to the inspection of his neighbor as his heart is clear to the search of Him who made it, he stands at the polls, proudly conscious that he is there the master, not as the man, and willing himself to meet all his fair responsibilities to public opinion; for that act of power, he justly expects a return of the same generous confidence from his fellow citizens.

But, gentlemen, I have shown you the probable effect of this secrecy upon the representative. Should we mend matters much by transferring it to the constituent body, or rather, to the portion which seeks to rule it? Popular government, to be good, must be the result of public opinion, formed with all the aids of a free interchange of thought and sentiment, but this interchange becomes impossible, when a portion of the people seclude themselves from their fellows, and conceal from them their thoughts and purposes.

Popular government, to be just, must command the assent of a majority, or, as some have thought, of even more than a majority; but here is a scheme of a secret political organization, by which a minority may rule a majority, without the least responsibility to public opinion. In the first place, their very mystery gives them power, and conveys an exaggerated idea of strength to the public mind; for it is the way of the world, to take "*Omni ignotum pro magnifico.*" Next, their organization and discipline may make a minority an over match for the undisciplined majority who act from individual impulse. Lastly, their rules of proceeding seem designed to secure this predominance of the minority. Whatever may have been the individual differences of opinion within the lodge, outside of it they act as one man; so far as the order itself is concerned, there are before the public eye neither majorities nor minorities. The minority must give up their opinion; and thus the order acts by the force of its whole numbers. A measure may have been adopted within the order by a small majority, but before the public it carries with it the weight of the whole mass. The order itself, as compared with the great body of the people, may be in the minority, but by its superior organization it may divide and rule them; and thus a measure may be passed, although a large majority of the people are really opposed to it, if its enemies within and without the order are estimated together. It is no matter then where you establish this secrecy with regard to political action, the effect is the same: you destroy the just influences of public opinion, nay, you make the existence of a public opinion impossible, and thus popular government itself, becomes impracticable.

Fellow-citizens, we have heretofore felicitated ourselves upon the idea, that the power of public opinion in this country was becoming so much greater and more enlighted as to relieve our form of government of some of the subjects of its hitherto necessary jurisdiction, and to increase its capacity for extending over greater areas of territory and larger masses of people. But it seems that we are to renounce these long cherished ideas, and a retrograde march is fast becoming the order of the day. In the name of Heaven from whence do these new lights spring, which are so to uproot the fixed opinions of centuries? He who seeks to destroy the influence of public opinion, or to deprive it of judisdiction, strikes at the moving principle of human progress itself, and raises a fratricidal hand against the best hopes of his race. It is this influence, which has given the greatest impulse to the march of human improvement; and as the mighty sphere of its jurisdiction enlarges with the growth of time, the governments and institutions of man are called up, one by one, to answer at that great bar where reason is free to plead, and truth, when once revealed, pronounces its irreversible decrees.

The Church, the State, and the School all contribute to the stream of thought, which swells the mighty tide of public opinion, and each profits by the modifying influences of the judgments which are pronounced on their ideas at that bar, by way of return. Here, indeed, is the great and conservative tribunal, before which all must in turn appear. It can elevate the weak to the level of the strong, and the most powerful is strengthened by its aid. Through doors of oak, and bolts of iron, it penetrates into the closed council chamber of princes, where its voice, if not obeyed, is at least respected and feared. It whispers the word of warning into the secret ear of the ruler, and through the long watches of the night he tosses in sleepless anxiety to ponder upon its meaning. None are so high as to be above its influence, and he must be poor indeed, who is beneath it. The weakest and humblest of human beings, if he be strong enough to make his moan audible, may summon his oppressor to appear at the bar from whose sentence he can neither appeal, nor escape, no matter what may be his power or his place. It was to public opinion that Martin Luther appealed, when he took issue with the See of Rome, whose power at that day was nearly co-extensive with Christendom, and, before that bar, the poor monk became the peer of pontiffs and Cæsars, and a judgment was pronounced in that cause, which toppled down many a place of strength, in which human authority had dreamed itself to be secure for centuries yet to come. It was to public opinion that John Locke appealed, when, stripped of his living and fellowship for opinion's sake, by the cruel edict of an arbitrary prince, he was sent forth, a wanderer upon the world, a houseless and homeless man, and, as was vainly supposed, crushed alike in fortune and aspiration. But his proud spirit refused to be down, and he spoke the great work in his essay in favor of religious toleration, which could no more be hushed, or silenced, until the test acts, and persecuting ordinances of his native land had fallen before it, and the great doctrine of liberty of conscience had been established, wherever his own English was the vernacular tongue.

A poor Scotch philosopher, whose views when first published, would have been scouted upon "change," now exercises, through the force of public opinion, a larger influence over the laws which regulate the trade of the world, than all the merchant princes and statesmen of his day. Dynasties which have withstood the destroying efforts of a Charles the Great, a Turenne, or a Marlborough, and defied the arts of their political, or strategic skill have fallen before the breath of public opinion, when put into motion by some poor scholar or unheeded philosopher, who spoke from the narrow precincts of his neglected cell, or dreary garret. The ideas of Luther and Locke, and perhaps of Rousseau, have, through the force of public opinion, written more changes upon the face of human institutions and governments, than the arts or the arms of the statesmen and the generals of whom I have just spoken. This jurisdiction of the only earthly tribunal, where the strong and the weak must meet upon equal terms, where reason is free to speak, and truth alone is powerful, is that of all others, which this new party, by some strange perversity of opinion, would seek to destroy. What a sin against human progress, what an outrage upon the best hopes of man for social and political improvement! But why should this party so fear public opinion, unless they believed that it would pronounce against them? If they supposed the contrary, would they not seek its mighty aid by proclaiming their purposes to the world? There can be but two motives for concealing their action upon political affairs, which concern the welfare of all, and these are either the fear of public opinion, or a distrust of the people. Is this a country where we can afford to encourage a party which acts upon such ideas? But, fellow-citizens, there is another reason special to ourselves for regarding secret political associations as mischievous and dangerous.

Mr. Calhoun used to say, that after all, the political issues in every country grew out of the contests of two parties, which belong to all organized human societies—the one, he called the "tax consuming party," and the other, the "tax paying party." The tax consumers are those who receive more money from the Treasury, in the shape of patronage, than they contribute to it in the payment of public dues. They look, therefore, to the government for the means of support, and vote, not as citizens seeking moral benefits, but as individuals in pursuit of personal interests and pecuniary gain. The tax paying party are those who look to government for political good only, and contribute more in money to the Treasury than they receive in return. If the former obtains the chief power in the State, then, sooner or later, there must be an end to free and popular government. The very ends of their organization require them first to increase the taxes as much as possible, in order to swell the fund which is to be converted to their own uses; and next, to appropriate this money unequally, that they may secure themselves the lion's share. In such hands, government is administered for the personal benefit alone, of those who manage it, and not for those for whom it was made, if its original form was popular—a species of tyranny which no people have ever long tolerated, when there were so many to be served. In the downward progress of free institutions, when their doctrine takes this direction, the first symptom is the appearance of factions which look not to the general good of society, but to the particular interests of themselves. Headed by such men as Sylla and Marius, cruel oppression and bloody proscription become the order of the day, until the people, weary of their sufferings, seek protection from them all under a Cæsar, preferring the "dead level of an Oriental despotism," to the unequal exactions and diversified tyranny of this many-headed monster. Now, in this country, the temptations and facilities for the formation of such a party, are so great as to make its appearance a thing to be feared and guarded against. The fund which constitutes the object of plunder is already great and daily growing to be enormous. Forty or fifty millions of annual expenditure, soon to be increased, probably, as our country grows and enlarges, to sixty or seventy millions, constitutes a fund which holds out a great temptation to those who may be disposed to struggle for it as prize money. The facilities too, for forming such a party are by no means small. It may be a combination of two particular interests, to live upon exactions from a third. Such was believed, by some, to be the effect of the old American system, which united the manufacturing and internal improvement interests against the agricultural. Or the combination may consist of two sections against a third. If the taxes are raised and expended unequally, the majority, who control the government, may be interested in swelling the public resources, whose burden falls on a part and whose benefits are mainly appropriated to themselves. Last and worst, the day may arrive when a mere combination of office-holders, by means of their numbers and superior organization, may be strong enough to administer the government for their own particular benefit. Any, or all of these events, which are possible, would destroy our popular institutions. What has been our protection against this danger heretofore? It has consisted in the publicity of political proceedings. Parties were forced to divide upon principles—principles which looked, or professed to look, to the good of the whole, and not of the part. Political issues were thus forced to be broadly taken, and argued upon general and generous views. The one or the other party was wrong, of course, but still the country could not be much injured by either; because, if the good of the whole was really the object of pursuit, their measures, when adopted by the government, would be abandoned, if proved to be injurious. The people, too, are thus saved, as far as it is possible to save them, from the selfish combinations of which I have been speaking. So long as political action is public, they observe the fact, if men of opposite political opinion are suddenly found voting together, and suspecting selfish views, by a sort of instinct of self-preservation, they are sure to strike at the combination. But, destroy all this, convert the public meeting into the secret association for political purposes, and what is to save us from the domination of such a party as that which I have been describing? There is the strongest temptation for such action, and you remove the most efficient restraint. The "fear of Hell," says the poet,

"Is the hangman's whip,
To hold the wretch in order."

The same conservative influence is exercised by the fear of the retributive justice administered by public opinion. Within the secret conclave of this association, there can be no such fear to restrain. The action of an individual and the very fact of his membership, are concealed. Individually, he is responsible to the world for nothing. Before the puble, there is no such thing as individual responsibility, or opinion, within the whole hosts of the Order. All must obey the edict, all must vindicate the opinion, when once it is determined upon. Here the disappointed office seeker may hide his blushes under the shades of secrecy and of night, as he drives the perfect bargain, by which his principles are to be bartered away for renewed hopes of the prize, which he failed to seize before. Here, too, combinations for the most sefish and dangerous purposes may be formed, without the fear of punishment or detection. If they do not exist now, will any man say that they may not be soon expected, with such temptations and facilities for their formation? Permit me, fellow citizens, to expose the dangers of such an association, by an illustration, which I think ought to strike every one. We have seen that the action of the last Congress upon the Nebraska bill, severed the Whig party North and South. For the repeal of the Missouri restriction, not one vote was given by a Northern Whig. The Southern Whigs very properly, refused to act as a party with such confederates. If there are men amongst them, or elsewhere in the South, who prefer office to the peace and safety of their States, and who, feeling that the anti-slavery sentiment is predominant in the free States, which constitute the majority in the government, would be willing to unite with them in order to secure their own personal interests, still, they would not dare to seek such an alliance, whilst political action is open and public.

Such a man would be afraid to do so; he would fear the public opinion of the South, the censures of nearly all, Whig and Democrat, and the scorn of his fellow-citizens, who would regard him as a renegade and traitor. But adopt this contrivance of a secret political association, and how easy may it be for such persons to effect their purposes. The union may be formed, and yet none can know it, except those who are bound to vindicate it. If this association fails in its objects, the world is none the worse for it; if it succeeds, they win the golden prizes of office and power, for which they are willing to risk much more perhaps than they have put in peril. Then, upon this dangerous question of slavery, the South would lose one of its great defences, and lose the power to enforce the united action of her sons. What, after all, has been our chief security in the fierce agitation of this question? Has it not been in the timely warning which was given us, by the publicity of political proceedings? If a dangerous anti-slavery agitation, sprang up at the North, it was open and public. The conservative press of the country took the matter in hand, and an opportunity was given for exchanging sentiment between the different sections; the consequences of such measures could be pointed out, and thus, even in the most excited states of the public mind, an opportunity was afforded for the sober second thought of the people to come to the rescue. But now, large masses may be secretly committed to the most dangerous opinions, and the men may be selected to carry them out, without time for previous warning, or expostulation, so that opposing sections may be suddenly brought into the presence of each other, and precipitated upon the most dangerous issues, when retreat is difficult, and compromise becomes impossible.

But, fellow-citizens, the dangers of these secret associations do not end here. If this one succeeds, others must follow. In self-defence, those who do not belong to this order, will use the same means by which it has acquired power; and the open political action for which this country has been distinguished, will be converted in a warfare of secret associations. Instead of the open, manly, stand-up mode of fighting, so characteristic of the Anglo-Saxon and Anglo-American race, we shall substitute the dark intrigue and stiletto warfare of the Italian. That such a change in our political habits would have the effect of transforming the moral character of our people, is not to be doubted. Is there a man present, who would desire to see such transformation? Fellow citizens, let me beg you to beware of these secret political associations. Beware of the mysterious blandishments of this new seducer. It is said to be but the first step that costs. You may be tampering with a danger of whose whole character you are little aware.

Far up on the Missouri, near to Fort Benton, upon a high cliff, which commands an extensive view of the surrounding country, it is said, that a Blackfoot Indian Chief directed himself to be buried on horseback, with his face turned down the stream, to look out, as he said, for the white man, the destroyer of his race, when he should come up the river. If you would look out for the destroyer of your free institutions, and popular form of government, fix your eye upon the door of the secret political association;—from that door, the worst enemy of all, will come.

But I have not told the whole story against this new Order. As I said before, they have avowed opinions upon certain subjects, which, in my judgment, are highly dangerous and mischievous. They propose to destroy the liberty of conscience itself, by proscribing the members of the Roman Catholic religion from all offices, whether high or low. Thus not only persecuting these men for opinion sake, but introducing a religious test, as a qualification for office. I know it is said, that this proscription from office is no persecution, because it is not accompanied by corporal sufference; but is there not moral degradation, and does not that often carry with it a far keener pang to the sensitive spirit than the most severe physical punishment? You say that the Roman Catholic is unworthy to enjoy the full privileges of a citizen, or to fill the meanest office; that men of all other religions and sects, Mahomedans, Buddhists, even Infidels and Atheists, may be capable of holding office, but he is incapable, because he cannot be trusted as being loyal and patriotic; you fix upon his brow the brand of political inferiority, and, after wounding him thus in the point of honor, you say he has suffered no punishment Is not such moral isolation to a noble and sensitive mind, more than bodily incarceration sometimes?

> "Stone walls do not a prison make,
> Nor iron bars a cage."

You may confine a man's body, and if he enjoys the respect and kindly feelings of his race, who look to him as a martyr in a noble cause, he bears up cheerfully under it all; but not so, if you exclude him from the pale of human sympathy, and expose him to public insult and moral isolation in the midst of his kind. It is vain to say, that this is no punishment for opinion sake. In a country like this, where office has heretofore been open to all, the exclusion would be more keenly felt, than in others, where the privilege was not so extensive. But our glorious old Bill of Rights provided "that religion, or the duty we owe to our Creator, and the manner of discharging it, can be directed only by reason and conscience, not by force or violence; and therefore all men are entitled to a free exercise of religion, according to the dictates of conscience, and that it is the mutual duty of all to practise Christian forbearance, love, and charity, towards each other." The act for the establishment of religious freedom, passed by Virginia in 1786, and upon which Mr. Jefferson prided himself so much as to reckon it, along with the Declaration of Independence, amongst the things for which he ought to be remembered by posterity, declared, "that no man shall be compelled to frequent, or support, any religious worship, place or ministry whatever, nor shall he be enforced, restrained, molested, or burdened in his body, or goods, nor shall he otherwise suffer on account of his religious opinion or belief; but that all men shall be free to profess, and by argument to maintain their opinions in matters of religion; and that the same shall in no wise *diminish*, enlarge, or affect their civil capacities." Such were the ideas of the old fathers of our State, and may the day never come when they shall be treated as obsolete!

But the Federal Constitution has also something to say upon this subject. It expressly declares, "that no religious test shall ever be required as a qualification to any office, or public trust, under the United States." Now, this was manifestly a provision in favor of religious freedom, and it was intended to secure the reality, and not the idea, the thing, and not the name, the substance, and not the shadow.

The thing designed to be secured, was that the offices should be thrown open to persons of all religious persuasions, and that no man's opinion on that subject should incapacitate him for that privilege. Now, we obey this injunction of the Constitution in the letter, when we forbear to pass a law establishing such tests; but do we not violate its spirit if we transfer the deed from the representative to the constituent body, and bind this last by vows and pledges, to vote for no man for office who is himself a Catholic, or who would appoint members of that religion to office? We may preserve the shadow of the constitutional provision, but do we not sacrifice the substance, by such an evasion? or, will it be maintained, that the Constitution binds us only as members of the government, and not as individual citizens? Surely this is a poor view of such a question. We obey the Constitution not as a matter of compulsion, but of choice; not as a thing forced upon us, but because we love it; because we concur in its principles, and sympathise in its spirit. It is the compact of government to which we have agreed, and we are bound not only in our public, but also our private capacities, to execute it in its spirit and truth. The Constitution of the United States, in reference to its objects, may be said to consist of three portions; first, it establishes the machinery of government; next, it distributes the moving power amongst the parts of the machinery; and, thirdly, it provides certain securities for the rights of States, and of individuals. Now, these last are of the very essence of the compact, and constitute the conditions upon which it was formed. All the parties, therefore, who enjoy the benefits of the compact, are bound to carry out the stipulations, whose execution may depend upon their agency. How often have we complained of those Northern States, which evade the obligation in regard to foreign slaves, and, without violating the letter of the Constitution, defeat the spirit of its provisions by interposing obstacles in the way of the recovery of such fugitives? We have said, justly, as it seems to me, that when they take the benefit of all the provisions of the Constitution which interest them, they are bound to carry out in good faith those which concern the other parties to the compact; their obligation is to carry out the object of that provision in its spirit, not merely to abstain from violating its letter. Now, may not the same be said of the provisions of the Constitution in regard to religious freedom? Were they not also of the essence of the compact? Could the Federal Constitution have been ratified in Virginia, if it had been supposed to sanction the idea of the establishment of religious tests, as a qualification for office. As it is, it was received with fierce opposition by many of our most distinguished statesmen; but what would have been said if it had contained an authority for such religious tests as are now proposed as qualifications for office? James Madison was its great advocate and defender, as it now stands; but, in the contingency of which I speak, what would he have said of it, distinguished as he was for large and generous sentiments on the subject of human liberty? And what would old George Mason have said, the author of the declaration in favor of religious freedom, in our Bill of Rights? And, above all, what would he have said, who once exclaimed, "Give me liberty, or give me death," when it was supposed that life and property were imperilled by such a declaration!

Fellow-citizens, I care not in what capacity it be, whether as representatives or constituents, that we violate the spirit and defeat the objects of the Constitution; in either case, we sap and mine the foundations of our government, and disregard our plainest obligations as citizens.

But I object to this proscription of Catholics, on account of their religious opinions, for other reasons, which are yet to be given. It is undoing the work of Martin Luther; it is unprotestantizing Protestantism itself, and returning to the practices of the darkest ages of religious bigotry and persecution.

What was the great object of Luther's mission?—Was it not to establish the right of private judgment in matters of conscience? And what was the great work of Protestantism? Was it not to make good that right and that duty of individuals, and to enter a solemn protest against any human authority, whether of bishops, churches, or governments, to overrule or destroy it? And yet there are men, claiming to be good Protestants, who propose to punish, by proscription from office, all persons whose private judgments lead them to the adoption of the Catholic faith. I have shown how such a proscription may be a punishment of the worst sort; but I go farther, and say that the idea upon which this is justified, if carried out to its logica consequences, must lead us to far greater lengths. In short, there is no middle ground between absolute and perfect toleration on the one hand, or positive persecution on the other. If the Catholics are unfit to hold any office, however small, on account of their faith, they are unfit to vote; for it requires as much patriotic feeling and sound judgment to do the one as the other. If, then, they are incompetent to the discharge of the first duties of citizenship, and are to be treated as aliens, they become dangerous members of the society which thus distrusts them: and the plainest dictates of prudence would seem to require their removal. Louis XIV. therefore, who revoked the edict of Nantes, and drove so many of his Huguenot subjects to bear their industry and their arts to Germany, Holland, England, and even to this country, did but carry out the principles upon which it is now proposed to act, to its inevitable and logical consequences. As I said before, there can be no middle ground, no debatable land, between positive prohibition and perfect toleration. If the right of private judgment in matters of conscience, exists at all, it is absolute and independent of all human authority. Such is the result of the great principle established by Luther, and such the mighty work of Protestant reform. It is now a little more than three centuries, since the city of Worms presented one of the most remarkable scenes which has ever appeared in the course of human affairs. The Emperor Charles, the German Cæsar, had convened there a diet of princely dignitaries. The Archduke, Electors, Landgraves, Margraves, civil and ecclesiastical Princes, Counts of the Empire and belted Knights were there, numbering, in all, more than two hundred persons of regal, or semi-regal estate. That Diet was assembled to consider the case of a poor monk of Wittemburg, who had made an issue with the See of Rome, upon nothing less than the ri ht of private judgment in matters of conscience, and dared to take an appeal to public opinion for its judgment, upon that great controversy. So poor was that monk, that he depended upon the charity of one Prince for the money which was to bear his expenses to Worms, and upon that of another, for the very clothing which he wore; he had neither official place, nor dignity, nor was there one man whose services he could, as a matter of right, command; but he had spoken the word at which whole nations must pause to listen. It was in vain that his friends, and even the more generous of his enemies, dissuaded him from appearing before that Diet. They said, that the German Cæsar, at that day in point of temporal power the foremost man in all the world, was his bitter and implacable foe; that his Spanish cavaliers, at that day the truest representatives of Christian chivalry, were riding about the streets upon their mules, and swearing vengeance against the monk and his friends; that the Church of Rome, whose ecclesiastical censures then fulminated over nearly the whole of Christendom, would be there with its hostile array of learning and power, and that potentates, ecclesiastical and civil, would also be there, thirsting and crying aloud for his blood. But he said he would go, if there were as many devils to meet him in Worms, as there were tiles upon the houses. And he did go, he did appear before that Cæsar, whose frown indeed was terrible, before that Church exulting in its pride of strength, and before those princes who had fixed an evil eye upon him; his face was pale, but with study and not with fear; his body so emaciated with vigils and labor that its every bone could be detected by the least observant eye; in human form, he was not above the average stature, but as a representative man, the representative of the mightiest issue which it had ever fallen to mortal lot to make, he towered in moral majesty to the height of that great argument, by which he was to sustain it. The fire of his eye quenched not in the presence of imperial majesty itself, the tones of his voice rung clear and true as the tempered steel, and he faltered not as he responded to the ensnaring questions of the adversary; his heart quailed not before that great array of hostile power. He spoke, and princes, catching the infection of his noble zeal, crowded about him in the council-chamber, and said to him, "Speak, speak out like a man," fear not them who can kill the body, but cannot harm the soul; wild, warlike soldiers too, were won by the gallant bearing of the lion-hearted priest. "Monk," said a celebrated captain of the times, "take heed to your steps, you are treading a path far more dangerous than any that the rest of us have ever pursued; but if you are in the right road, God will not abandon you." He did speak out, with a fearlessness which not the bravest of those princes could themselves have exhibited, and he did pursue his path with faith far greater than the trust of the old captain, that being in the right road, God would not abandon him. Threats could not appal nor blandishments seduce him, until at last, run out by his perseverance, the Catholic Bishop of Treves said unto him, "Then, tell us, yourself, what we ought to do to settle this controversy."—"I must reply to you," said Luther, "in the words of Gamalial, 'let the thing alone; for if this work be of men it will come to nought, but if it be of God, you cannot overthrow it.'" Brave words these of the old Jewish Doctor of Laws, fit to be spoken by him, and fit to be repeated by Luther. Well might St. Paul be proud to have been bred at the feet of such a man; well did this judgment deserve to be recorded on the imperishable page of Holy Writ, to endure when the reports and decrees of all other lawyers shall have passed away and been f rgotten! They were the first great words ever spoken in favor of religious freedom, spoken by Gamalial, to save the apostles from Jewish persecution, repeated by Luther to defend himself against Catholic persecution, and now let the Catholics, in their turn, use them to protect themselves against Protestant persecution.

But, fellow citizens, I have spoken of this issue in regard to the right of private judgment in matters of conscience, as being the most important which it has ever fallen to mortal lot to make. Human history and experience bear me out in that assertion. For this principle has proved to be the foundation stone of the fabric, not merely of religious, but of civil liberty also. It was a declaration in favor of individual freedom. The individual mind burst loose from the bonds of human authority, and aroused itself from the slumber of ages. A new moving principle within the mind itself, was thus allowed full room for play, and each individual intellect becoming instinct with motion, and quickening into a higher life, human energy seemed to receive a new impulse, and developed itself in greater activity, and under more varied forms, than had ever characterized it before. Our race sprung forward as with a bound, in its march of improvement, and may be said to have achieved more of progress in the last three centuries, under the influence of this mighty reformation, than it had accomplished through the whole period of its authentic history; which preceded the Christian era. And yet, it is this great work of Luther, which we are now called upon to undo. We are to destroy the right of private judgment in matters of conscience, and persecute Catholics for their religious opinion's sake. As I have said, more than once, upon this subject, there is no half-way house, no middle ground.

It may be said, I know, that the early Protestants did not extend their own principles so far; that they themselves kindled the fire of religious persecution. But even the discoverers of great principles do not always carry them out to their logical consequences. The progress of Truth may be certain, but its pace is slow, and yet great principles will work out their ultimate results. John Milton had a glimpse of the truth, that absolute toleration must be the irresistible result of the great principle of Protestant reform, when he said: "Give me the liberty to know, to utter, and argue freely, according to conscience, above all liberties." John Locke took in the whole truth, and proclaimed it in his celebrated essay, and the old fathers of our State, were the disciples of his political school. By their bill of rights, and their celebrated act upon that subject, they did establish, as they supposed, a perfect religious freedom. Has not this experiment worked well so far, both for Church and State? Have they not happily grown side by side in harmony, and not in opposition to each other? Have we experienced any mischief from this absolute toleration of religious opinion? Have we been injured by the fact, that Catholics could vote, and hold offices amongst us? Have not these Catholics divided amongst the great parties of the country, and voted upon political, rather than religious tests? Do Whigs complain that too many of them vote with the Democrats? This is not more a Catholic than a Protestant sin, because more Protestants than Catholics vote with that party? Do the Democrats complain that too many of them vote with the Whigs? Again, it may be replied, that there are more Protestants than Catholics who vote with that party. But can there be any political danger from allowing men of all religious persuasions to vote? By doing so, you certainly widen the basis upon which your government stands, and increase the number of those who bound to it by the ties of sympathy and interest. Where can be the danger, so long as political proceedings are open and public, and representative and constituent can question each other face to face? If a representative is with you on political tests, does it matter, so far as the politician is concerned, what are his opinions upon other subjects? If he is with you on the subjects of trade, currency, and the principles of constitutional construction, when they are in issue, does it matter that he differs from you on the doctrine of transubstantiation? Will not a Catholic who agrees with you on all the political issues, and differs from you in religion, make you a better legislative representative than a Protestant who agrees with you in religion, but differs from you on all matters of political principle? Is it not entirely in our

6

power to ascertain how they stand, when tried by their political tests, so long as political action is open and public? If there be danger from such a toleration, it can only exist when political deliberations and actions are veiled in secrecy. I know that an attempt has been made to except the Catholic from the operation of the great principle of religious toleration, by maintaining that he is proscribed for civil, rather than religious reasons, because he is said to acknowledge the supremacy of the Church over the State, in temporal matters.

Fellow citizens, such a distinction does not in truth exist. The Catholic of the present day, no more admits the supremacy of the Church in temporal matters than the Protestant; their difference is in regard to spiritual concerns. The Protestant maintains the right of private judgment in matters of conscience; the Catholic believes, that in spiritual affairs the decisions of the Church ought to overrule the individual judgment. But Protestants and Catholics, all Christian churches and individuals, believe that the allegiance which they owe to God is higher than any obligation to man; and that in a conflict between human and divine laws, you must serve God rather than man.

But how can such an opinion interfere with the capacity of a citizen to discharge his political duties, unless the civil government undertakes to legislate upon religious subjects, and to draw spiritual matters under a temporal jurisdiction, instead of keeping them apart, as was ordered by Christ, when he said, "Render unto Cæsar the things that are Cæsar's, and unto God the things that are God's," and as has been our practice heretofore in the administration of civil affairs?

But suppose we once commence with this work of proscribing Catholics for their religious opinions—where is it to end? With the Catholics? Trust not so vain a delusion. The jealousy of religious bigotry is a thing which grows with what it feeds upon. Next we shall hear that the Quaker is to be proscribed for civil rather than religious reasons: he will not defend his country in time of war. Then there is much to criticise in the government of this Church, and grave objections to that of another. One is arbitrary, and of a temper unsuited to free institutions; another is aristocratic, and unfitted to the genius of a democratic people. Some, too, may be suspected of an effort to engross the political offices and power of the country, and appropriate them to their own members. If they proscribe others, they must themselves be proscribed; and in this new era of secret political association, there is room given for every suspicion, and opportunities are afforded for the most dangerous combinations. Who does not know the peculiar susceptibilities of sectarian jealousy? Who can fail to see the dangers of the warfare which would thus spring up amongst the different Christian sects? And when men become weary of the agitation of such contests, in which each set of religious opinions is in turn proscribed, will they not say at last to the government, "Tell us what to believe; establish your church; relieve us from this state of uncertainty, and let each man enjoy once more in peace the shade of his own vine and fig tree."

It seems to me, far better to pursue the present practice; tolerate all religions, and have each church free to pursue its mission in its own way, and to select the most appropriate field for its labors. If you then have more churches, you have more Christians also, and if there must be a human tribunal to set upon their differences, let it be that of public opinion. Here is a jurisdiction, which can take charge of matters far too delicate for the positive regulation of government. Questions of morals, of honor, of social and personal propriety, which involve distinctions far too nice, and shades of coloring far too delicate to be defined by positive law, may be satisfactorily adjusted here. Here, too, is a field of battle where none can be injured, where Reason furnishes the only weapons, and Truth must be the gainer, no matter who comes out victor in the contest. On this side we know there will be peace and safety, on the other there must be danger and discord. And we are to run all this risk, for what?

Because, you say, there is a probability that the interests of the church may clash with those of the State, and that, in such a case, the American Catholic might vote not according to his duties as a citizen, but to his feelings as a churchman. Take your own supposition, this is but a remote possibility, a case of mere chance; but if you proscribe the Catholic for his religion, you make that danger certain, of which there was but a chance before. You put him under the ban; you refuse him the equal privileges of a citizen, and stamp upon him the brand of inferiority. His first object then is to remove that stigma. He no longer acts with the great parties of the country, according to his opinions upon political issues which concern all, but his first object is to remove the oppression under which he labors, and he feels justified in voting in any manner to secure that end. The very thing which you dread will assuredly come to pass, and, through your own agency, he will vote not as an American citizen, but as a Catholic; he will no longer come forward, as now, to give your government a ready and cheerful support; that government is no longer bound to him by the ties of interest and sympathy, if it proscribes and oppresses him. He will become indifferent, and perhaps hostile to the government, which has treated him as an alien and as a member of an inferior cast of society. Why estrange one who is so valuable as a friend, and convert him, perhaps, into an enemy?

But, fellow-citizens, I went a little too far, when I said, it was proposed to proscribe Catholics from all offices in this country. There are some offices, which the sons and daughters of that Church are still considered competent to discharge. I mean the offices of Christian charity, of ministration to the sick. The sister of charity may enter yonder pest-house, from whose dread portals the bravest and strongest man quails and shrinks; she may breathe there the breath of the pestilence which walks abroad, in that mansion of misery, in order to minister to disease where it is most loathsome, and to relieve suffering where it is most helpless. There, too, the tones of her voice may be heard mingling with the last accents of human despair, to soothe the fainting soul, as she points through the gloom of the dark valley of the shadow of death to the Cross of Christ, which stands transfigured in celestial light, to bridge the way from Earth to Heaven; and when cholera or yellow fever invades your cities, the Catholic Priest may refuse to take refuge in flight, holding the place of the true Soldier of the Cross, to be by the sick man's bed, even though death pervades the air, because he may there tender the ministrations of his holy office to those who need them most. But, if some of the objects of their care should arise from the bed, which, but for them, would have been the bed of death, and should any such say to them, if he be a Protestant, "I am going forth to proscribe your Church, to put you under the ban, to declare you unworthy of the common privilege of citizens, and to degrade you as a caste, because I am afraid that you, poor priest, and you, gentle sister, will rob me of my rights and deprive me of my liberties?" what would they say to such an address as this? They might not utter the thought, but would it not be the feeling of the least rebellious nature, if it were still human to say, "let him go, like the Pharisee of old, enjoying his greetings in the market place, and his chief place at the feasts, and thank his God that he is not a sinner as this publican." But, what would you say, fellow-citizens, to such a sentiment, if it were uttered in your presence? You would say that it was a sentiment unfit to be either entertained or expressed.

But for what is it that I am pleading, here in Virginia, before an intelligent audience of her sons, and in the year of our Lord, 1855? For Religious Freedom, for Liberty of conscience. I can scarcely realize the idea, I am almost ashamed to confess it, and yet it is even so. If any man had foretold to me, two years ago, that such an heresy could be exhumed from the dead, and that the breath of life could be so breathed into it as to give it vitality enough to become a living issue upon the soil of the Old Dominion, I should have laughed to scorn the prophet and his prophecy. And here is a thing, they tell me, to be feared; and certainly a thing formidable enough to be met. *"Nulla vestigia retrorsum."*—"Let here be no no steps backwards," said John Hampden; a noble maxim certainly as applied to the march of human liberty. Here, though, is not a step backwards, but a retrograde march of centuries, and from light into that darkness again out of which we had once emerged with so much pain and difficulty. If a people so enlightened, as I had fondly believed ours to be, can be induced to make such a retrograde march as this, I shall begin to lose my faith in human progress, and fear that the political reformer rolls the stone of Sisyphus, which can never reach the expected goal. But why does this new party select the Catholic Church as the particular object of its proscriptions? They certainly seem to have begged, borrowed, or in some other way obtained some leading ideas from that Church, and which, in my opinion, constitute its most objectionable features. Old John Milton somewhere reproaches his Protestant brethren for certain persecuting practices, and says they have fallen into the "most Popish of Papist errors." I think the same may be said of this Know-Nothing party. Do they object to the secret Inquisition of that Church, which inquires into spiritual offences?—have *they* not a secret inquisition, which inquires into political offences? Does it not sit upon your character and mine, try us when we cannot be heard, condemn us when we had not been arraigned, and execute its sentence without serving upon the victim a notice of its existence?

The old Vehmic tribunal so terrible for its secret inquisition and visitations, used to take care, at least, that the bowl and the cord should be laid by some invisible hand at the bedside of the victim, to give him warning when he awoke of the fate that awaited him. But here is an inquisition whose sentences are executed without even that premonition. Do the Know Nothings object that the Catholics deny the right of private judgment in matters of conscience? Surely, they do the same thing with regard to the Catholic, when they proscribe and persecute him on account of his religious opinions. They refuse to allow him to worship God according to his own conscience, except under such pains and penalties as they choose to prescribe. Do they object to the Catholics as members of a political community because they believe in the supremacy of the church in spiritual matters? Why, then, do they declare a far more dangerous doctrine, and assert the supremacy of their council in matters temporal and political? A man may believe in the spiritual supremacy of a church, and yet discharge his political duties, according to his individual conscience and conviction; but he who admits the political supremacy of a council, cannot perform his duties as a citizen, according to his own judgment and conscience. When the edict is once pronounced by the council, it can neither be disputed nor disobeyed by the members. After this, there must be neither majorities nor minorities in the Order; but all must move, act and speak together, as if with one will. That greatest of all liberties—as Milton called it—the liberty to know, to argue, and to utter freely according to conscience, is not one of their privileges. With what face, then, can a party, holding such doctrines as these, proscribe men for entertaining far less dangerous opinions? What the practices of these Know-Nothings may be with regard to confession and absolution, I know not, but it is very clear, that if the power to command the moral action of individuals exist, the power to absolve them from the consequences of sin ought to go along with it.

But this party is not content with proscribing Catholics, and treating them as aliens in the bosom of American society. There are about 2,200,000 foreigners amongst us, and these, too, are to be considered as incapable of holding office under the government. Not only are they to be forever disqualified for office, but hereafter the term of probation for naturalization is to be so lengthened as to make the law itself illusory. It is to be observed, that what is proposed to be done, will not diminish much the number of emigrants who hereafter will come to our shores, nor was it probably intended, when this Order originated, that such an effect should be produced, for reasons which I will presently give. The proposed party will deteriorate the quality of the emigration; it will shut out men of fortune and education, because they prefer our institutions and desire to incorporate themselves into the great body of American society, to share its privileges and partake of its destiny; it will cut off those, too, who come here from choice, not from any desire or expectation of office, but who would be unwilling to live where they could never be capable of holding it. But all those who move from necessity, for the means of subsistence, must still come, for even the Know Nothings will give them leave to toil. Then these constitute the great mass of foreign emigrants that come to our shores. The question, then, is, as to their treatment after they reach here. Shall they be denied all political franchises? Shall they be treated as aliens in our midst, and thus made indifferent, or, perhaps, hostile to our government and institutions? Or, shall they be treated as heretofore, by our fathers and ourselves, who have sought to bind them to our country by the ties of sympathy and interest, and for that purpose have held out a reasonable hope, that a place should be made for them in our political society, as soon as they can show by certain evidences, that they are fit for it?

Here is an immense power in our midst. The question is, how shall it be treated? Shall we bind it to us by the kindly ties of affection, and the still stronger bonds of interest, or shall we alienate and estrange it? That, then, is the true issue of principle to which I shall speak. There are minor questions of detail, which I have not time now to discuss. In all the great operations of society, certain evils are incidental, which must be provided for as they arise, not by destroying, but by regulating the system. So, too, the process of assimilating the foreign element into American society, has its incidental evils, which may be met as the special cases arise; for some the police powers of the States are ample, and others may be guarded against by the Federal Government, without disturbing the general features of the process itself. What I maintain is, that this new element ought to be assimilated with the great body of American society, as far as it can be done, and that a place ought to be made for the foreigner in our political society, as soon as a reasonable evidence is given of his being fit for it.

In discussing this issue, I may be permitted, I trust, to enter a little into the history of the question itself. At all times the tide of human emigration seems to have been directed by some law of nature, which thus provides for that fusion and inter-communication of races, which has been proved to be necessary to the general progress of the whole. There is not a great people upon record who did not spring from a mixture of races. The Greek, the Roman, the English and the French, all sprang from a mixture of stocks. The Jewish were more exclusive, but it is also to be remembered that they lost power and empire. The emigrations from which all this resulted in ancient times, were forced or armed emigrations. The stronger and weaker races, when living side by side, owed their proximity to the fact, that the former had brought the latter to their own homes as slaves, or else, seizing the country of the subjugated had settled in it as being more desirable than their own. Thus it was, in ancient times, that the necessity for an interchange of the habits, thoughts and characteristic ideas of the different races was satisfied. Routes through which the forced emigration of the African slave was conducted before the Egyptian pyramids were built, are, some of them, still used for the same purpose. The irruptions of the Goths, the Vandals and Huns, were so many armed immigrations, and the same may be said of the Crusaders. All these seem to have been designed to serve some great purpose in the economy of nature, by mingling different races, and interchanging amongst all, the ideas and thoughts peculiar to each. The discovery of America, which made so many changes in the course of human affairs, seems also to have presented a new law for the direction of the stream of emigration. The great law of trade, the law of demand and supply, now intervened to impel and regulate it. A wilderness was to be opened, and the field was large enough for all who might choose to come. Our forefathers held out every inducement to encourage emigration from abroad. Upon this subject the policy of Virginia was peculiarly liberal, and lands were given to those who would settle amongst us. At the time of the Declaration of Independence, it was made a cause of complaint against the Crown, that obstacles had been interposed in the way of foreign emigration. After the adoption of the present Constitution, and during the administration of Washington, a law was passed allowing a foreigner to be naturalized, after a residence of five years. Under the Federal Administration of John Adams, the period was extended to fourteen years; but the five years term was restored again, when the Republican party came in under Mr. Jefferson. Thus it has stood, with no expression of dissatisfaction, until within a few years past, with the single exception, as I believe, of the Hartford Convention, which sought to revive the fourteen years term.

Under this legislation, the course of emigration has been rapid, and, as was generally supposed, until lately, beneficial to the country. The foreigner settled beside us, to participate in our hopes and cares, to share with us the chances of life, and contribute the resources of his mind and body to the growth and prosperity of American society, in which, for the most part, he felt a common interest with ourselves. It was the boast of the Old Hun, that grass never grew after the tread of his horse's hoof; it was not so with the emigrant who came here; he made two blades of grass grow where one grew before, and helped to gladden the waste places of nature with all the arts of cultivation and civilization. To trace the agency of this foreign element in the various developments of American society, I believe, would be startling enough to those who have not much considered the subject. Certain it is, that our growth would have been much less rapid without it. I think, too, that an examination of the history of this emigration will show, that if nature be left free to pursue her course, there can be no danger that the foreign will overpower the native element in their influences upon our state of society. In looking over a well reasoned analysis of the statistics of emigration, as given by our recent census, which appeared in one of the foreign periodicals, I met with some results for which, I confess, I was not prepared. Its general geographical distribution was not, in some important respects, such as I had expected to find it; of the 2,200,000 foreigners in this country, only about 305,000 are in the slave States, In the northwestern free States, less than one third of these emigrants is to be found, and of 1,900,000 inhabitants of these States not born within them, 1,330,000 are native American. As a consequence of all this, it follows that most of these foreigners are in the Atlantic non-slaveholding States, amongst which New York and Massachusetts share most largely, and nearly six-sevenths of their number are to be found north of the 37th parallel of latitude.

It appears, then, that the mass of these foreigners settled in the old States, where the home influence was strongest, and replacing as many native born citizens, these last took up their line of march to the wilderness to add to the domain of cultivation, to build up another addition to the American Empire, to found new States, and mould and form their institutions. Instead, then, of Europeanising Americans, Europeans were thus Americanized. The American influence predominates everywhere; and notwithstanding the number of these foreigners, they are so distributed as to make the process of their assimilation with American society more rapid and easy. This country, then, has been indeed the true "*officena gentium,*" and not only the workshop in which many nations have toiled, but a grand national manufactory, in which men of various races have received the true American mould. It is estimated, in the article of which I speak, that 400,000 able-bodied laborers of both sexes, are now annually coming to this country from abroad, and if this statement should startle those who have seen that the Custom House returns give only 367,000 as the total number of foreign emigrants, let him remember, that both Chickering and De Bow estimate their returns as being 50 per cent. under the true count. Of these, a very large proportion has been ascertained to be over 10, and under 40 years of age. When the statistics upon this subject are collated and compared, it will be found, I think, that the estimate of 400,000 is, at least, a probable approximation to the true number. Now, whilst most of these laborers settle in the free Atlantic States, to drive the looms of New England, and keep the workshops of New York and Pennsylvania busy, a larger number of native born citizens march annually into the wilderness to add a new belt to the domain of cultivation and civilization. Who can estimate in figures the effects of this double process upon the growth and prosperity of the Confederacy, and particularly of the free States? If you estimate the annual production of each emigrant laborer at only $ 150, you have 60,000,000 for this item alone, to say nothing of the money which many of them bring to pay their passage and establish themselves in the country. Now, does any man suppose that the free States, and Massachusetts especially, where this Know Nothing Order seems to have established its head quarters, can intend to stop the influx of such a stream of wealth as this? Shut off this flood of emigration entirely from our shores, and such a blight would fall upon Massachusetts as she has not seen heretofore in the course of her history. She not only does not intend to produce such a result, but she does not profess even to desire it. On the contrary, it has been her policy to attract the foreign laborer to this country by a double process. Through the restrictive system, she sought to shut out the product of his labor from the American market, if he worked abroad, whilst she proposed to give him the exclusive possession of it, if he would transfer his labor to this country. To attract cheap labor to her soil, has been a great object of her policy; and now that she has substituted the native for the foreign laborer, she proposes to disfranchise the latter—to deny him the privileges of citizenship. And thus, whilst she is so anxious to free the African slave in the South, she is engaged in a scheme to proscribe and degrade; yes, sirs, and to enslave—for there are degrees of slavery—all that portion of her own white laborers who are foreign born. To make such an experiment upon the native-born laborer, would be too dangerous to attempt; but to substitute him with the foreigner, and after filling her workshops with the latter, to disfranchise and proscribe him, would produce the same effect in the end. The laborer would be prostrated at the foot of the capitalist, whose reign would be supreme. The interests of labor are one North and South, foreign and native born, and he who seeks to set one portion against another, is destroying the house by dividing it. Mr. Jefferson said that there was a natural alliance between the Northern laborer and the South. Both are concerned for the interests of labor; and most of the sympathy which the South has found in the North, has grown out of that natural bond. It is this power, then, that has been friendly to us that we are invoked to strike. The power which drives the loom, and makes busy the workshops at the North, is friendly to that which raises the cotton and the corn for their use; and now we are gravely asked to rob it of its fair political weight, and to transfer it to the capitalist, who so far has been against us!

It is to be remembered, that every white inhabitant, whether foreign or alien, is counted in estimating the political power of the States. In the actual and probable state of Massachusetts society, such a policy would throw its whole power into the hands of her capitalists, to be wielded it is likely, as it has been heretofore used, against ourselves. But, it may be said, she can disfranchise the foreigner at home without our assistance; and so she may; but if other

States refuse to follow her example, she cannot persevere in it. If she treats the foreigner much worst than her neighbor, he will go to States that are more liberal; and thus she will lose his labor which is essential to her. At any rate, she is not entitled to any assistance or countenance which the Federal government might give. By way of atonement for the sin which she meditates against her own labor, she would be moral at the expense of others, and turn loose the African slave in the South, our safety, being the cheap material upon which all sorts of experiments may be tried. Now, so far as Virginia is concerned, shall we not say that we adopt neither branch of her policy. The African slave we shall not turn loose, because his present condition is better both for him and for us; and the white laborer we intend to be free—free to enter into an equal competition for all the prizes of life—free to pursue all the avenues to honor or profit, and free to hope and aspire for all that can give dignity to man and happiness to life. If he fails it will be owing to himself, and not because the opportunities of success are denied him by the policy of the government to which he is attached. If he be a native, then, like St. Paul, he was born a Roman citizen; if he be of foreign birth, then, like the Centurian, he shall not be forced to pay a great price for the privilege, but a place shall be opened for him in our political society, as soon as he gives evidence of his fitness for it. Such is the policy which we have heretofore pursued, and, in the main, it has worked well. The serpent is yet to be warmed into life in this country, which would sting the bosom that protected it.

We have thus, not only been able to receive this large foreign element and assimilate it into our system, but also to convert it into the means of a new growth. Instead of being an alien power in the bosom of our society, we have attached it to us by the strong ties of sympathy and interest. If we should offer extraordinary and unnatural inducements to this emigration, it might become mischievous, by pouring in so rapidly as to destroy the homogeneous character of our people. But if we leave nature free to pursue her own course, there can be no danger either of this or of an unwholesome competition between the foreign and native born laborer. So long as a field is open large enough to employ profitably those at home, and those who will come from abroad, the supply will follow the demand. The whole mass of our productions will thus be increased, and it is the interest of every one within the bosom of our society, that this should be as great as possible, for it is the common store from which all must draw. When this labor becomes less profitable, the demand will fall off, and with it the supply; so that the competition of the foreigner will cease just at that point of time when its inconveniences become serious. I have shown how this, which is one of the greatest operations of society, has been heretofore conducted by the laws of trade, so as to secure us as many of its benefits, and as few of its inconveniences, as was, perhaps, possible. That some evils and inconveniences will attend so large an operation, I do not deny, but they are evils, which, for the most part, may be cured by legislation, adapted to the special cases, without making the vain effort to strike down the system. The results of the old feeling we have seen; what would be those of the new I cannot pretend to measure in extent, but something may be said of their nature.

The proscriptive means which are proposed, if the right of suffrage be left to the foreigner, will certainly produce the evil which it is proposed to remedy. The foreigner will vote not as an American citizen, upon the general merits of political issues, but as a foreigner, to remove the ban under which he lies. But if you disfranchise him entirely, then you alienate this immense power in the bosom of your system of society. For it is an immense force now, and will continue to be so, notwithstanding political disabilities, whilst there is so great a demand for the means of subsistence. This is quite a new experiment in the conduct of society, and has not been tried except in those cases where one portion has actually subjugated another. The naturalization laws of old States, already filled with people, and to which the emigration is next to nothing, can afford no precedents to us. Here they still come in great numbers, and it is not even proposed to exclude them. The sole question is as to their treatment after they reach our shores. Shall we make them friends or enemies? It has been our ancient policy to cultivate their friendship. Why not continue to pursue it?

Having thus traced the principles which this new party proposes to some of their most obvious consequences, let me call your attention now to the number of important questions which they refuse to speak of at all. They have nothing to say upon the subjects of the Tariff, the Currency, the Internal Improvement system, upon the questions as to the absolute or limited power of the General Government over the public lands, or as to the great canons of constitutional construction. Shall we be told that these questions are all obsolete? In the endless varieties of human commerce are not cases constantly presenting themselves with new relations, and requiring different applications of the laws of trade? Does not the course of our Federal legislation constantly present us with cases for the application of all the principles involved in the old issues? And yet the very issues and principles which are involved in the daily business of the Government are "ignored," as I believe they call it, by this new party. Why, they "ignore" the subject of slavery itself. Can the South afford to have such a subject as this ignored? Thus, it would seem, that this new party have not only said things that they ought not to have said, but they have left unsaid things which they ought to have said.

But fellow-citizens, is it not worthy of a moment's thought, to see what are to be the moral effects of these new practices upon the character of our people? Who would transform the old Virginian—such as we used to know him—such, as I trust, he still is—into what he must become, if he make this radical change in his habits and feelings?—The old Virginia was frank, manly and generous, and made so by his early training and the character of his political institutions. He had his faults, it is true, but they were, for the most part, the excesses of a brave and manly spirit. Reckless he might be—a little too ready to conceive an insult, or too prone to follow the word with a blow; but he had no secret malice nor mean revenge in his nature. His friendships and his enmities were known, and he scorned to strike a foe without giving him notice beforehand. If he had opinions, the world might know them; and when he acted as a citizen, he was ready to meet all the responsibilities of that action, either at the bar of public opinion or elsewhere. Who would be willing to transform such a man into the secret agitator, muffling his face, and treading the dark alley to the back door of his midnight conventicle, there to determine upon measures involving the welfare of his fellow-citizens, and yet giving them no notice of things that were to affect them so deeply; or sitting, perhaps, in secret judgment upon some unsuspecting neighbor, trying him and condemning him unseen, or unheard, in matters touching his political character and standing, and involving, it may be, the little office which gives bread to his family; and yet, when that man meets him in the morning, and offers him the hand of unsuspecting friendship, he is unable to relieve his heart by saying to him, "You wrong yourself and me by such undeserved friendship and confidence; you are grasping the hand which will strike you a blow where you will feel it most keenly?" It would be some relief to a generous mind to be able to say this much; but, spell-bound by some terrible vow or oath of secrecy, he must walk on in silence and bear the galling load of unmerited confidence. The edict having gone forth, he must obey it; he can express no opinion in opposition to it; he must whisper no dissent; he must breathe no murmur against it. He belongs not to himself, but to his Order.

And this is the Order for which the old parties, are exhorted to disband their organization, and lay down their arms. I regret to say, that there are some symptoms of a determination on the part of the Whigs to take service under this new party. It has been said by some wit, "That next to an old friend, we love an old enemy." I will not pronounce upon that sentiment, but certain it is, that I prefer the old to the new enemy. The old Whigs were a manly party; their issues were open; they might be wrong, but they fought upon principles, and principles which professed to look to the welfare of the whole, and not of a part; they used no secret contrivances to circumvent their adversary, but met him in the open field. If they obtained power you knew what to expect from them. But what a change is here, my countrymen, where this new party appears to take their place in the political arena? It is not, however, for me to give judgment in this case, or to proffer advice to the Whig party, "*non nostrum tantas companere lites.*" But I do protest against disbanding the Democratic party for any such organization. We are told that the principles of this party, and upon which the people have given a favorable verdict, are obsolete. If so, it must be for the reason that they are so firmly fixed in the affection of the people, as not to be shaken hereafter; but if they are thus fixed, it was the Democratic party that achieved the work. Is that just ground for disbanding them? Do we change our physician because he has heretofore cured us, or our preacher because he has convinced us, or our house-joiner because his work has pleased us? But how can it be said, that the great principles of our public policy in regard to commerce and currency, or the great doctrines of constitutional construction, can ever become obsolete? Whilst our government lasts, they must constantly recur, and be applied in its daily legislation. But why disband the Democratic party? For the greater part of a period of more than fifty years, it has administered the affairs of the federal government in such a a manner as to enforce respect abroad, to secure to us at home such peace and harmony as have never been found to exist elsewhere, in connection with the enjoyment of so much liberty, and to develop the moral and material resources of the country to an extent heretofore unparalled in the history of the world. It has shown itself, too, to have been the only party with a spirit broad and comprehensive enough to steer the ship of State safely through the storms of sectional contests. When section was arrayed against section upon the protective policy, it was this party which intervened to adjust matters satisfactorily enough, for peace, at least, by the application of the great principles of free trade. Under the still more fearful agitations of the slavery question, the South has found chiefly within the ranks of this party, the Northern friends who could dare to be just to her and true to the Constitution, without fear of the personal consequences which such a course was sure to involve. During the last Congress, so far as the free States are concerned, that party entitled itself to the lasting respect and gratitude of the South, for removing the odious ban of the Missouri restriction. Throughout the representation of the whole of the non-slaveholding States, no man was to be found, outside of the Democratic party, who sustained the Nebraska bill. And now that they are in difficulties, for so noble a discharge of their duties to the Constitution, is this a time to desert or distrust them?

Fellow citizens, I have spoken of the issues which we are to meet, and of the trials which await us. In view of these, I would ask every man, who has a Southern heart in his bosom, if he would not, instead of the present state of things, restore, if he could, the Democratic party as it was in the last Congress, to its former power in that body? If this could be done, every friend of peace and the Union would breathe freer and easier; there would be no fear of a successful attempt in any branch of the Government to abolish slavery in the District of Columbia, or in the Territories, or the slave trade between the States, or to repeal the fugitive slave law, or to restore the Missouri restriction. If then such a change would be desirable, the next best thing, assuredly, would be to unite the South, as a body, to the conservative men of the North, who are doing battle for the Constitution, and dare to be just to our rights. Let us, in this way, keep together a party strong enough to defend the constitution and the peace of the country, until the sober second thought of the people comes in to the rescue, if, indeed, we are to be rescued at all. What other road is there so probably safe as this? And where are those conservative men to be found, in any strength, in the free States, except in the Democratic party? But why, of all the States in the confederacy, should Virginia be exhorted to desert the Democratic party, and at such an hour as this? Has she lost faith in their principles? Are they not, for the most part, her own principles? Loring, of Massachusetts, in a late eloquent letter, has ascribed the origin of that party mainly to Virginia. It has been said, that all the great religions of the world have issued from the tents of Shem; it may be said, I think, with as much truth, that many of the great principles of the Democratic party, emanated from the log cabin of the Virginia pioneer. The foundations of much of its public policy are to be found in our colonial history; and in the outset of that party, under the Federal Constitution, it was led by Virginians. The very banner which is now waiving over its hosts in the field, is, to a great extent, the work of Virginia hands. How much of its web and its wood were contributed by Jefferson and Madison—how many of its mottoes were inscribed by Virginia intellect—how much of its embellishment is due to Virginia genius? Why, then, should Virginia desert the Democratic party, and at this time? That party has met with a succession of reverses in the free States; the tide of the battle has now rolled to our feet, and the eyes of the whole country are fixed upon us. Are we invited to leave our posts now, because of so many defeats elsewhere? Is it the cry of "*sauve qui peut*" which runs along the line? Are we to desert our friends in extremity to seek for personal safety? or, worse still, to wheel out of line and fire upon them, that we may make our separate peace with the foe? Perish the base thought. Why is it that our friends are in difficulty? Because they did justice to us in the Nebraska bill, and refused to wrong the South. Is this, then, a time to desert and abandon them to the tender mercies of the cruel odds which are against them? In such an event, well might the old Commonwealth hang her head in shame, and bow her neck to the yoke of the oppressor; for how could she hope for the trust of friends or the respect of foes, after such conduct?

Sirs, it seems to me, that no true son of Virginia, no matter what his politics, ought to wish her to change now, to leave the field when such desertion would attach so cruel an attaint to her shield. "If she is to change," we ought to say, "let it be at some other time;" not now, when the eyes of the whole country are so intently fixed upon her, and when the hopes of her Democratic brethren everywhere are concentrated upon her, to redeem the fortunes of the fight. Should we fail them now, they might well say, as Bruce said to his friend at Bannockburn: "Ah, Randolph, there is a rose fallen from your chapter," because his enemy had passed when he kept ward.

But, fellow citizens, may I not say in your name, and in that of the great body of the Virginia Democracy, the enemy shall not pass when we keep ward; we will roll back the tide of battle which has reached our feet, and redeem, as more than once before, the fortunes of this fight. And why not both say and do it? They are the principles of Virginia which are at issue; the principles to which for more than fifty years she has adhered through good and evil report, and which she has ever regarded as constituting the bulwarks of her safety; they are the principles, too, which are associated with the recollection of so many struggles in which she bore a conspicuous part, as to be identified with her name and her glory. The traditions of the past must speak for them; the teachings of our fathers, the maxims of the homestead, will plead for them. "Oh earth, earth, earth!" said the Hebrew prophet, when, wearied out with the perversity of his countrymen, he turned to his native soil, and adjured that, to see if he could not arouse within it some answering spirit.

If such an appeal was made in such a cause to the soil of the Old Dominion, it seems to me that the "genius loci" would spring forth, and trumpet-tongued, sound the call, which, from the topmost height of her mountains to the lowest depth of her vallies, would summon her sons to the rescue.

Fellow citizens, it has been said, "Let Americans rule America." I say, let American principles rule America, and the more that can be rallied to their support the better. In the same sense, I say let Virginians rule Virginia; let Virginia principles rule Virginia. Above all, let us not go to Massachusetts just at this time, to borrow counsel or beg for guidance. Let us not borrow from her any of those "isms" which have made her so fruitful a cause of trouble to her neighbors and unhappiness to herself. Let us not take from her this last of her "isms," or carry her sealed letters and secret cipher. For aught we know, they may prove to be the letters of Bellerophon, and we may become the unconscious bearers of the warrant for our own destruction.

The time has been when Virginia and Massachusetts exchanged presents of sentiment and opinion, but they were sentiments in favour of human freedom, and not declarations against that greatest of all liberties, the liberty of conscience. For myself, I have closed the pages of Massachusetts history, since it became evident that this new party had complete possession of her State government. I have not followed to the conclusions any of their propositions; to translate their old Latin motto into English, because the language is foreign; or to introduce the songs of the Hutchinson family into legislative session, or to exclude from their public schools the study of all languages but the vernacular. Nor have I enquired very curiously into the precise amount of Know Nothing literature which existed, to fill the immense void which would be made by excluding all that was not English. But, I beg pardon, there have been some events in her recent history so startling as to enforce the most unwilling attention. I have seen, with pain and mortification, that a committee of her Legislature, armed with the majesty and power of the State, did, but the other day, make a descent upon some unprotected Catholic ladies, who were conducting a private school, and used, or rather abused, their authority to insult these defenceless females. I have watched, too, with the deepest interest, the case of Loring, to see if the power of that great State is to be used to crush a man, merely because he obeyed the obligations of his oath, of the constitution, and of the law which he was appointed to administer. If that deed be consummated, then I say let her face be turned to the wall; let us endeavor to forget it for awhile, at least until these terrible delusions shall have passed away, which vex the brain, and disturb the brow.

Fellow citizens, if the long cherished principles of Virginia are to fall, let it be at another time, and not now. Let us perish in some open field, in fair and manly fight; but let us not die by the bowstring of the mute. If the good old flag ship of Democracy is to go down, let it be with colors flying, and to the sound of martial music, and firing the last shot in the locker, in token that the Old Guard may die, but cannot surrender. But who talks of failure? These principles will live, and I trust endure for centuries yet to come; that old ship will not go down, but

> "Its flag shall brave a thousand years,
> The battle and the breeze."

Virginia is now aroused to a true sense of the importance of the contest. She understands what principles are in issue, and she will soon be in the field with all her banners waiving, and ready to charge with all her chivalry. In the darkest hour of the revolution, Gen. Washington said, that when all else failed, he would plant his flag in west Augusta, and there defend it to the last. If the Democratic party should be defeated in all other places, let it come to its favorite stronghold in the Old Dominion, and plant its banner there. And let us defend and protect it, until the people come up to its rescue, as come they will, if we preserve the liberty to know, to argue, and to utter freely, according to conscience, and thus afford them the opportunity to understand their interests: Whilst that continues, I will neither bate in heart, nor hope, nor consider all is lost until that too is taken from us.

But, fellow-citizens, I tax your patience much too far. I have been carried on by earnest wish to impress you as deeply with a sense of the importance of the present crisis, as I feel it myself. I have not had the power to do it, as I ought to have known before-hand; yet I struggled on under the hope that some chance arrow might reach its mark. I felt, too, it was my duty to warn you of the danger, which, in my opinion, lies before you. I have shown you the issues which we are to meet; the trials that are not to be avoided. If there be any peaceful solution of these difficulties, I have pointed you to the only direction in which I think it can be found. In this case, I believe it to be not only the path of safety, but that of honor also. You will see, therefore, why I have pressed you so earnestly to take it. I do not say that there is no other peaceful solution of our difficulties, but merely that I do not see it if it exists. Providence sometimes opens up unexpected avenues of escape from peril. My own knowledge, too, even of the past, is very limited; my foreknowledge still more so. There are chances which I do not pretend to estimate. I shall be glad to avail myself of any which may turn up; for, next to the safety and honor of my country, I desire its peace. Yes, sirs, its peace; for sometimes the whole story of national happiness may be written in that one word. I must aver, therefore, that I regard these interests as too vast to be staked upon chance. But let me say now, and once for all, that whatever may betide her, I stand by my State. If troubles should come, I will take my full share, without pausing to inquire what party, or who of her sons, brought them upon her. We are the children of a common mother, and it is our first duty to defend her.

But if these responsibilities are to be met, and I admit my obligation to do so, let me at least have the satisfaction of feeling, that if Virginia goes into the contest with no taint upon her brow, or reproach upon her fidelity to the sacred obligations of friendship, may it never be said of her, that she brought her trouble upon herself by deserting her friends when in peril and difficulty, and may the cry of craven never pursue her as "the pilot that blenched at the helm, when the storm blew the loudest." If all else is lost, let us at least save her honor. To do this, nothing more is necessary than that she should be true to herself; for that much we surely ought to be able to answer.

MR. WISE AT ALEXANDRIA.

Mr. Wise addressed the citizens of Alexandria in one of the ablest speeches he made during the campaign. And fortunately a talented corps of reporters were present, who took down the speech as it was spoken. If mistakes occurred in this report we have never heard of them, either from Mr. Wise or his friends. And as we take for granted that it was the only true and correct report that was ever given of him during the canvass, we shall give it an insertion in this compilation. The speech was delivered on the night of Saturday, the 3d of February, at Liberty Hall, before an immense concourse of citizens and strangers, a very large majority of the members of Congress, and many citizens of Washington, having been attracted by the fame of his oratory.

[Reported for the N. Y. Herald.]

Mr. Wise's Speech at Alexandria.—I appear before you to-night, citizens of Alexandria, not upon my own account, but as the standard bearer of the Democratic party of this State, regularly nominated in accordance with the time-honored usage of the party. I come as endorsed and twice endorsed by the Democratic party, named as I was to be its elector in 1848, and in 1852; elector for the people, and now nominated for the governorship of the state of Virginia. If any Democrat in this assembly recollects that, in times past, I did not always regard regularly organized nominations, and chooses to vote against me on that account, let him so do, provided he will stand where I have ever stood—upon principle, acting *bona fide*, an earnest honest man; let him then, I say, vote against me. When he does it let him remember that he then does the very act for which he is condemning me—vote against the regular nominee. If there be any Whig in this assembly who will vote against me because I am not what he calls consistent, and because I have chosen to use party as a servant and not as a master, I would not ask him for his vote. But I would ask him not to be like me, whom he chooses to deem inconsistent. (Applause.) I ask him, when he comes to the polls, to be true and clear in act and conscience; not carrying before him the dark lantern of a secret association and gripping a Democrat with one hand and a Whig with the other. If he is the jewel of consistency, which he would have me be, let him be himself guiltless. But, gentlemen, though I have come before you a man nominated by a party, the standard bearer of a party, doing battle for its principles, still I come not here to-night to address party. I appear before the people, without distinction of party, to address myself to a republican people charged with the sacred and holy trust of self-government. I come to address myself to a people whose only means of self-government is by election. I come to address myself to the reason, and the conscience, and the judgment, and the will of the people, whose reason, and conscience, and judgment, and will, must be exercised in the election, and let me ask you—every considerate, every couscientious man, every man with a stake in hand, either of capital or of labor—let me ask you what are the considerations which ought to govern a republican people charged with the trust assigned to you of worthily bestowing on a man the highest office in the gift of the people? Gentlemen, you have great, momentous, deeply interesting topics of domestic policy for your consideration. There is your public credit, your public works, your commerce, your agriculture, your mining and manufacturing, and the great subject of popular instruction. At this moment causes are operating, not only affecting your national credit, your state credit, but touching the nerves, the tender nerves of your private purses. All Europe is in arms, and the labor of Europe is abstracted from the world of commerce. The most powerful sovereigns of the earth are in battle array. Each crowned head of Europe is calling for gold—incessantly demanding gold, in quantities which Australia and California, and Siberia cannot supply. And this demand for gold affects your national credit, your state credit, and your private credit. I mean not to create any alarm; I mean not to cause any excitement or distrust in your minds in relation to the condition of your credit; but I mean to say that, at no moment of my life have I seen the time when there was more necessity than there is at present for prudence in government, and prudence in private affairs. But there is a salvo, thank God! We live on a continent long enough and broad enough to feed the world. We have wheat, we have corn, we have pork and beef. One little port, which has grown up like Jonah's gourd in a single night, on the lakes, can send more wheat to market than any four ports of Russia; and that city which is called the Queen City of the West, is haunted by the ghosts of slaughtered swine. (Laughter.) One single power of Europe now at war, has held up in London the thermometer of exchange for all the world; still, we have the producing power of provisions and munitions of war. (Cheers.) While they are fighting, thank God, we can be feeding. (Laughter.) This, this is the salvo. Where the almighty dollar is made so much of, human food has, by the adventitious aid of causes now existing, advanced in value; wheat has doubled its price. I make these remarks in order to bring your attention to the subject of the public credit of the state of Virginia, whose bonds have already touched eighty-five cents in the dollar. How long that war may last, what accidents may happen from it, what collisions may be produced by it, no human foresight can now see. But let us be prepared, and then come what may, I pledge myself—if elected Governor of Virginia—that, though direst necessity may come, come what will, at all hazards, the public credit of the state of Virginia shall be preserved. (Enthusiastic applause.) Private honor is precious; but, as infinitely higher than an individual is the state, so infinitely higher than private honor is the honor of the state. Reproach Virginia who will, reproach her whoever is so inclined, no man can say that her honor has yet been stained. (Vociferous applause.) If I be elected governor of Virginia, then, I tell you bluntly and briefly, if it be necessary to tax you to defend her honor, I shall commend taxation, though it make us groan. (Sensation.) Next to public credit, next to the honor of the state, are her great public works, in the high march of prosperity. You have never yet had—it is unfortunate you never have had—a system of public works. Your works have been begun without regard to their relative importance. You have not completed one before you have begun another and another. Your public works are without termini. Your canals and your railroads are like ditches dug in the middle of a plantation, without outlet at either end. You appropriate for them to-day, neglect them to-morrow, and leave the appropriation of the day after to-morrow to repair decay. It is time that some one or two, or as many as you can, of the public works of the state of Virginia should be completed, in order to ease the taxation of the public. It is time they should be completed, in order to render some profit to the state. All that the state of Virginia has been wanting has been to reach out her arms to the great West—to tap the Ohio river—to join the Big Bend of the Ohio river with your rivers in the East. You have reversed, in times past, the order of true policy. You have said, "Let us have capital—let us have population, and then we will have a city." But you never will have capital—you never will have population, until you have the internal improvements to build up a city. You want commerce. You have bays, quays, roadsteads, which would float the navies of the world; but you have no seat of commerce—no centre of trade has yet pointed its spires to the heavens on the soil of Virginia. That is because you have completed none of your public works. Whatever difference of opinion, then, may have been as to the commencement of your works of state improvement, now that they are begun—now that millions have been spent and wasted upon them—now that you are obliged to be taxed in order to complete them, the sooner you submit to the taxation to complete your primary works the better. And the most expeditious and certainly the most profitable way of completing your works of secondary importance is, to complete those of primary importance. If, then, elected governor of the state of Virginia, I shall use all the influence which I can wield consistently with the public credit, and with the condition of the people, to expedite the completion of all the works of primary importance in the state. Next to your public works and your commerce, your agriculture is the most important. The four great cardinal sources of production—the four great powers of production of national wealth are commerce, agriculture, manufacturing and mining. We have 64,000 square miles as rich in every element of commerce—in every element of agriculture, of manufacturing and mining, as any other 64,000 square miles on the face of the globe; and yet with all four powers in her hand, Virginia has, thus far in her history, relied upon one source alone.

[At this period of the oration the noise and confusion became so great from the press of people in the hall, that Mr. Wise halted in his speech, and invited persons immediately in front of the speaker to take places on the platform, so as to make room for the crowd behind—a movement which procured your reporters seats in a more eligible location. Mr. Wise, resuming said:—]

I was saying when interrupted, that the state of Virginia has every element of commerce, of agriculture, of mining and of manufacturing. On Chesapeake bay, from the mouth of the Rappahannock to the capes of the Chesapeake, you have roadsteads and harbors sufficient to float the navies of the world. From the river of Swans, on whose margin we are, down to the line of North Carolina, you have the Potomac, the Rappahannock, the Penankatank, from Mob jack bay to James river and the Elizabeth river—all meeting in the most beautiful sheet of water of all the seas of the earth. You have the bowels of your Western mountains rich in iron, in copper, in coal, in salt, in gypsum, and the very earth is rich in oil which makes the very rivers inflame. You have the line of the Alleghany, that beautiful blue ridge which stands placed there by the Almighty, not to obstruct the way of the people to market, but placed there in the very bounty of Providence to milk the clouds, to make the sweet springs which are the sources of your rivers. (Great applause.) And at the head of every stream is the waterfall murmuring the very music of your power. (Applause.) And yet commerce has long ago spread her sails and sailed away from you; you have not as yet dug more than coal enough to warm yourselves at your own hearths; you have set no tilt hammer of Vulcan to strike blows worthy of gods in the iron foundries. You have not yet spun more than coarse cotton enough, in the way of manufacture, to clothe your own slaves. You have had no commerce, no mining, no manufactures. You have relied alone on the single power of agriculture: and such agricurture! (Great laughter.) Your ledge-patches outshine the sun. Your inattention to your only source of wealth has scared the very bosom of mother earth. (Laughter.) Instead of having to feed cattle on a thousand hills, you have had to chase the stump tailed steer through the ledge-patches to procure a tough beef-steak. (Laughter.) And yet, while your trust has been in the hands of the old negroes of the plantation; while the master knows as little as his slave about the science, applied science of agriculture, while commerce and manufactures, and mining, have been hardly known, and agriculture has been neglected—notwithstanding all that, and notwithstanding the effect of this has been that you have parted with as much population as you have retained; notwithstanding all this, I say, old Virginia still has a million and a half of population left within her limits. She still has her iron, her coal, her gypsum, her salt, her copper. She still has her harbors and rivers, and her water power, and every source of wealth which thinking men, active men, enterprising men, need apply to.

What boast like that can be made for any other state on the earth? What, then, is our duty as Virginians, as patriots, as men worthy of our fathers—worthy to be the husbands of our wives? What is our duty?

Come to the polls and vote against me and welcome. I am nothing. Record your votes under the influence of any blind prejudice that you please. Record your votes against me. You strike down but an humble man when you strike me down, and though you strike down a man who is too proud to beg you to vote for him, yet he would kneel as a little child and implore you to come to the polls, to do something to put forth your strength to raise up this blessed old commonwealth. (Great cheering.) Her head is in the dust. With all this plentitude of power, she has been dwarfed in the Union; but by her gods! I say that she has the power, now, the energy, the resources—may I say the men? to be put upon the line of progress to the eminence of prosperity, to pass New York yet faster in the Union than ever New York has passed her. (Cheers.) You have been called the "Old Dominion." Let us as Virginians, I implore you, this night resolve that a new era shall dawn, and that henceforth she shall be called the New Dominion. (Cheering.)

Give her commerce, and she will have capital and population; she will have agriculture, mining and manufacturing; and then she will want but one thing more—the enlightenment of her people. (Cheers.) She wants her popular instruction. I do not mean to recommend to you, or to any people within the limits of Virginia, any little day school, night school, common school, a b c, single rule of three, or Peter Parley yankee system of instruction. (Laughter.) I want Mr. Jefferson's policy, that he originally recommended to the state, to be consummated—an enlarged system of science, of literature, of learning, to be given to all classes of our people, to leaven the whole lump. (Applause.) I care not how blue a Federalist that man may be who curses his red waistcoat, but Thomas Jefferson has three things recorded upon his tomb—that he was the writer of the Declaration of the Independence of our country, the founder of the University of Virginia, and the author of the act of religious freedom. (Cheers.) For these three good works alone, every man—Democrat or Federalist—may kneel, patriotically kneel, at his grave. (Cheers.) The great apostle of Democracy never intended that the University of Virginia should be like Michael Angelo's dome in the heavens, without scaffolding or support—never. He intended that it should be a dome over roof and cornice, and walls of colleges and academies, and of common schools; that it should be a dome indeed, but the dome of a grand structure for the whole people. He intended that the University should superintend the colleges, and that there should be a college for every centre; that the colleges should superintend the academies, and that there should be an academy for every centre; that the academies should superintend the common schools, and that there should be a common school for every centre. He knew what equality was. He knew what Democracy was. He knew that the republican institutions of this land were based upon no other, no surer foundation than intelligence and virtue. His Democracy did not drag men down from their elevation into the mire; but his Democracy levelled upwards. He knew that if this man's son had all the means of education, of common school, of academy, of college and of university, and then might travel abroad for his learning, he could not be the equal of the son of the father who had to work for his daily food. He knew that if it was inhuman for the parent to starve the body of a child, it was much more inhuman to starve the mind of a child. (Cheers.) He knew that if you could afford to raise taxes for alms-houses and pauper-houses, to feed the bodies of the poor, it was much more the duty of the state mother to furnish mental food to her children. His Democracy was like the principle of Christian charity—like the great virtue of Christian charity—it elevated men to the highest platform of elevation—high as king's heads; made them sovereigns indeed, to stand equal foot, equal head, uncontradicted, except by the laws of God—with equal opportunities for all. It reached down, to raise men up to the common level of the highest. He knew that property—property which must be taxed for instruction—had no other muniment, no other defence, no other safe reliance for its protection, but intelligence among the people. (Applause.) Is there a rich man, then, in this assembly that loves a dollar better than the intelligence of the people? Is there any old bachelor among you, who has no child of his own, who is too mean to support some poor man's daughter as his wife, or to be rich in having some rich man's daughter to support him? (Laughter.) Is there a man in the state who has already educated his sons, who is now unwilling to be taxed in order that his poor neighbor's children may be educated—educated not only in the common school, but in the academy, the college, the university? If there be, let him remember that before he dies his title to his property may have to be tried by a jury to say whether that property be his own or not, and if God shall let him live till he dies (laughter,) and he can keep what property he has, let him remember that there is such a thing as what lawyers call *devisabit vel non,* that a jury may have to decide whether or not he had sense enough to make his will when he died. An ad valorem tax upon property is the appropriate tax for the education of the children of the people. Property owes its defence to the virtue and intelligence of the people, and property ought, therefore, to be taxed for the education of the people. (Cheers.) We want one school for this state that will revive our agriculture. We want a school like the Mechlin Institute of Prussia—an institute of applied sentence—an institute not to teach political economy and send young gentlemen to the legislature before they have hardly picked in their tuition; but an institute that will teach them domestic ecomomy, the proper relation between floating and fixed capital at home—how much money a man must have to buy—how much land, how much stock, and how many impliments he must have; an institute that will teach the physiology of animals and plants; an institute that will teach natural philosophy and the diseases of animals and plants. Then, gentlemen, the father who has spent his life in acquiring real estate, in spreading out his broad acres, in adding family to family of slaves, may die with a son instructed how to manage the estate. You will then have, or it will be your opportunity to have, the same privilege that the German baron has, of sending your son for his two, or three, or four, or five years' apprenticeship to an institute of that kind that will teach him agricultural chemistry and every other science necessary to enable him to manage an estate of lands and negroes. The present condition of things has existed too long in Virginia. The landlord has skinned the tenant, and the tenant has skinned the land, until all have grown poor together. (Laughter.) I have heard a story—I will not locate it here or there—about the condition of the prosperity of our agriculture. I was told by a gentleman in Washington, not long ago, that he was travelling in a county not a hundred miles from this place, and overtook one of our citizens on horseback, with perhaps a bag of hay for a saddle, without stirrups, and the leading line for a bridle; and he said, "Stranger, whose house is that?" "It is mine," was the reply. They came to another. "Whose house is that?" "Mine, too, stranger." To a third: "And whose house is that?" "That's mine, too, stranger; but don't suppose that I am so darned poor as to own all the land about here." (Laughter.) We may own land, we may own slaves, we may own roadsteads and mines, we may have all the elements of wealth, but unless we apply intelligence, unless we adopt a thorough system of instruction, it is utterly impossible that we can develop as we ought to develop, and as Virginia is prepared now to do, and to take the line of march towards the very eminence of prosperity. She is in the anomalous condition of an old state that has all the capacities of a new one—of a new state that has all the capacities of an old one. Unite with me, then, I implore you; unite with each other; let us as Virginians resolve that there shall be a long pull, a strong pull, and a pull altogether, without distinction of party, without prejudice of party—that there shall be a united brotherhood of Virginians to rear the head of the old mother commonwealth out of the dust. (Cheers.) If I am elected governor of the state of Virginia, it shall be my devotion, my earnest endeavor, in season and out of season to promote her public credit, her internal improvements, her commerce, her agriculture, her mining and manufacturing, and her popular instruction.

Well, now, gentlemen, is not that enough! Are these topics not sufficient for an election for chief magistrate for the state of Virginia? Is there anything else worth considering? With conscientious, with considerate men—with men determined to cast aside minor things, mere prejudices, whether personal or political—is there not enough in these six cardinal points to guide your votes and to govern this election? What more do you want? Why, you are in the habit of discussing federal politics; and permit me to say to you, very honestly and very openly, that next to brandy, next to card-playing, next to horse-racing, the thing that has done Virginia more harm than any other in the course of her past history, has been her insatiable appetite for federal politics. (Cheers and laughter.) She has given all her great men to the Union. Her Washington, her Jefferson, her Madison, her Marshall, her galaxy of great men, she has given to the Union. When and where have her best sons been at work, devoting their best energies to her service at home? Richmond, instead of attending to Richmond's business, has been too much in the habit of attending to the affairs of Washington city, when there are plenty there, God knows, to attend to them themselves. (Laughter.) If you want my opinions upon federal politics, though, I shall not skulk them. The most prominent subject is that of the foreign war. It is said that this administration is a "do nothing administration." To its honor I can claim of every fair-minded man of you—to its honor I can claim that it is at least preserving our neutrality in the foreign war. (Loud and prolonged cheers.) I concur with them in that policy, and here let me say, that, so far as I am concerned, my sentiments are utterly opposed to any fillibustering in any part of the world. (Cheers.)

Then you have the question of the public lands. We are told, now-a-days, that all the old issues are dead. It is not so. If there has been one thing next to the Constitution of the United States more than another among our institutions which has been grand, and great, and good, it has been the operation of the great land ordinance of 1787. It came, like most of the institutions of North America, by inspiration from Heaven. There is no prototype of the land system of the United States in ancient or modern times. There is nothing like it in the feudal system. There is nothing like it in any of the examples of modern Europe. Its very beauty is its simplicity. An eminent domain; a virgin soil, richer than any that God's sun ever shone upon, or heaven's dews ever watered; the simple system of sectioning the public lands by north and south, east and west lines, making them the homes of the brave and of the free, clear of all litigation—selling them at the lowest price, at a minimum that is within the reach of the poorest man, and graduating the price before exposed to sale at the minimum by an infinitesimal graduation—those who have been denouncing the graduation of the public lands ought to remember that there never has been a time when the price of the public lands was not graduated; that they have ever been exposed first to public sale before they have been exposed for sale for the minimum price of a dollar and a quarter. You had an eminent domain, which was a sacred trust, for the common use and benefit of all the states of the Union. You had that eminent domain under your own care, to which the poorest man,

the forlornest man of the east, might go for a home in the west. You had room there for the frontierman, for the actual settler, armed with the simple implement of the logwood axe to hew out unto himself a home for settlement, to strike the light of the log cabin, and to invite the oppressed of every land to our land for an asylum, with a soil rich enough to grow a vine luxuriant enough to shade him and his dwelling all over, where there were none to make him afraid. (Cheers.) If you ask me for my opinion in relation to the public lands, I will tell you that first and foremost, next, at least to preserving the sacred trust as a source of revenue to ease taxation by customs, I would protect, by all the protective policy in my power, the actual settlers upon our public lands. (Cries of "good, good.")

I have been in the west; I have seen the frontiersman; I have broken his bread; I have drank of his cup; I know his enterprise; I know his manhood; I know his privations; I know his courage; I know his endurance; and I know that he is the best of the right arm of the power of his country. (Cheers.) I know that with his logwood axe alone, he has laid the empires of no less than seventeen sovereignties in our confederacy. I would protect him, while at the same time I would conserve the eminent domain of this country, as a source of revenue to be held as legislation of Congress. I would prevent the public lands from being sacred as the revenue by customs. I would protect it from the partial the prey and the plunder of politicians. I would protect them from land-jobbers and politicians. I would prevent them from becoming a source of corruption to Congress, thereby destroying our state rights and our state sovereignty. (Loud cheers.) I would protect them from the electioneering of parties; and any bill that has these ends in view has my concurrence. The President of the United States tells us that 23,000,000 of acres of the public lands have been disposed of during the past year, and that only 7,000,000 have been sold. Thus, without law, while 7,000,000 have been sold, 16,000,000 have been given away; and the price of the public lands, without changing the minimum, has been reduced and graduated with a vengeance.

As to the subject of internal improvements that, too, is alive and kicking. That part of "the American system" is not a dead issue. Congress has been passing harbor and river bills. It is a part of the system of the light-houses of the skies of 1828. It is a part of "the American system," and I thank God that not only has there been a Hickory and a Tyler, but that now there is found a Pierce to thunder his veto against such measures. (Great cheering.)

You are told that the tariff is a dead issue. That, too, is alive. Such are the energies and resources of this country, that we have paid the debt of the war of the Revolution, we have paid the debt of the second war of Independence, and we have paid the debt of the war with Mexico; and now there is a proposition for a reduction of the revenue. A question arises, shall that reduction be made upon the protected or the unprotected class of articles? On that subject, I stand where I have ever stood—a free trade man. (Loud cheers.)

But, gentlemen, I am hurrying over all these topics to get at one which is the subject of the day—the fatal subject of discussion. I mean the inter-state relations of this Union on the subject of slavery. I have had a very severe training in collision with the acutest, the astutest, the archest, enemy of Southern slavery that ever existed. I mean the "Old Man Eloquent," John Quincy Adams. I must have been a dull boy indeed if I had not learned my lessons thoroughly on that subject. And let me tell you that, again and again, I had reason to know and to feel the wisdom and the sagacity of that departed man. Again and again, in the lobby, on the floor, he told me, told me vauntingly, that the pulpit would preach, and the school would

teach, and the press would print, among the people who had no tie and no association with slavery, until, would not only be reached the slave trade between the states, the slave trade in the District of Columbia, slavery in the District, slavery, in the territories, but slavery in the states. Again and again, he said that he would not abolish slavery in the District of Columbia if he could; for he would retain it as a bone of contention, a fulcrum of the lever for agitation, agitation, agitation, until slavery in the states was shaken from its base. And his prophesies have been fulfilled—fulfilled far faster, and more fearfully, certainly, than ever he anticipated before he died. When I left the House of Representatives at that capitol, ten years ago, had I said to Mr. Adams, "Sir, to me it seems that the Congress of the United States can carve out a piece of slavery territory and make it free soil," he would have said, "No, sir; Congress will not dare to attempt such a thing; it would be a *casus belli* if they did." And yet, have you not seen that Congress has carved out, in round numbers, 44,000 square miles from the slave state of Texas? Have you not seen a brigadier general (Riley) of the United States army, with his epaulettes on his shoulders, cocked hat upon his head, and sword at his side, in full panoply of uniform, acting as a brigadier general of the standing army of the United States, go into the territory of California, and there, with the right arm and the left arm of executive power—the army and navy—at his command; have you not seen him, I say, under the pretext that the army and navy could not protect persons and property, proclaim from the camp a territorial Legislature, a territorial judiciary, from *tribunales superiores* down to the *alcade!* Have you not seen him constitute himself chief executive—territorial executive? How dared a brigadier general of the United States standing army thus to assume the power of usurping territorial government? Had he been court martialed he would have produced his order from a Delaware secretary of state (Mr. Clayton) and he would have replied that the *salus populi*—the safety of the people—required this territorial usurpation by a brigadier general of the United States army. Well, if it did require the civil power—as well as the army and navy—why, the plea of necessity was met. There was the Legislature, there was the judiciary, there was the civil executive, as well as the brigadier general, who had at his command the navy and the army that was there. How dared he then, to go further, after the plea of necessity was sufficiently met, and after the safety of the people was secured? How dared he go forth and proclaim the time, place and manner of holding elections? Elections for what? Elections for a Convention. Convention, for what? To form a constitution. A constitution, for what? To create a state—a sovereignty. Yes, by proclamation from the camp of the brigadier general of the standing army of the United States, elective franchise was created. He gave it to Chilean, to Chinese, to Patagonian, to Peruvian, and—last, though not least—to a Georgia representative in Congress (Thomas Butler King.) And after creating suffrage to create a convention—the highest act of the people—convention to create a constitution; constitution to create a state, a sovereign state—the highest act of creation that can be performed by human power—an act next only to those of Deity—no higher act can the people themselves exert—he inducted California a free soil state into the Union. Thus free soilism has been proclaimed from the camp of the standing army. And what has been the result? "Acquiesce" was the word; "acquiesce." They have traded on the pious attachment of the people of the United States to that palladium of liberty, the Union of the states. They have traded upon the feeling of alarm for the Union which was never in danger—never, never. They made "acquiesce" the pass-word for the people. And what did we get in return? We got a free soil law. (Derisive cheers.) We got the grant of the constitution itself—the glorious privilege of catching runaway *niggers*. For that, for that we have submitted to 44,000 square miles of slave state territory being taken and converted into free soil territory. For that we have acquiesced in the proclamation of free soil California from the camp of the standing army of the United States, without authority of Congress. Aye, but they tell me it was all sanctioned by the people. The people! The word people has two significations. It is either a mere aggregate of human beings, or it is an organized aggregate of human beings. Nothing short of an organized aggregate of human beings in California could ever have sanctioned this usurpation; there was no organized aggregate of human beings, either to permit the usurpation or to sanction the usurpation. But we got the fugitive slave act. But how execute it? Can we execute it? A master from the state of Maryland, directly after the act was passed, went to Pennsylvania to recover his property; he was murdered; and judge and jury could not be found to execute the law, to render a verdict or pass judgment upon the crime of murder itself, in that case. At last a Virginia master, from this town, I believe, went to Boston to have the law executed, and to execute it the marshal had to call on the President of the United States—and thank God, there was a Democratic New Hampshire President of the United States, who was ready to obey the call. (Cheers.) The army and navy were ordered to protect the marshal in the performance of his duty. He did perform his duty, at an expense of $13,000 to the city of Boston, and of more than $100,000 to the government and to individuals; and the captive was brought back by reclamation to Virginia. And what has been the consequence? Now we come to the dragon's teeth. Mr. Adams' prediction has been fulfilled. The preachers have begun. The three thousand preachers of Christian politics opened their battery from the press. I have here a specimen of one of their sermons, which I beg leave to read to you. I hold in my hand a discourse called "The Rendition of Antony Burns, its causes and consequences; a discourse on Christian politics, delivered in Williams' Hall, Boston, Whitsunday, June 4, 1854."—I beg you, gentlemen, to remember that date—4th of June, 1854—because some prophecies are made in that sermon which are wonderful prophecies, if this preacher did not know something—(laughter)—"by James Freeman Clarke, minister of the church of the Disciples," published by request—second edition of two thousand—printed at Boston. It commences with introductory services. There is—first the reading the psalms—(laughter)—second, a hymn; third, selections from the prophets; fourth, prayer; fifth, reading of Scripture—selections from the lamentations of Jeremiah—(great laughter)—sixth, a hymn:—

"Men, whose boast it is that ye
Come from fathers brave and free—
If there breathes on earth a slave,
Are ye truly free and brave?

They are slaves who dare not speak
For the fallen and the weak.
They are slaves who will not choose,
Hatred, scoffing and abuse,

Rather than in silence shrink
From the truth they needs must think—
They are slaves who dare not be
In the right with two or three." (Great laughter.)

These are cabilistic terms, gentlemen,—"Two or three." Then comes seventhly, the sermon:—

"Is this the city, which men call the perfection of beauty, the joy of the whole earth? Her gates are sunk into the ground. He hath destroyed and broke her bars. Her kings and princes are among Gentiles. The law is no more. Her prophets also find no vision from the Lord."

That is the text. The preacher says:

"I have invited you here this morning to meditate on the facts of the week—the phenomenon which has occurred in the streets of Boston. The slave power which has triumphed in Congress over the rights of the north, which has violated sacred compacts, and broken contracts, has * * * come north to Boston, taken possession of the court-house, so as to govern our whole police force, our whole military force, and suspend and interrupt the business of our citizens, until its demands can be satisfied. * * * The slave power drove the Indians out of Georgia, brings on a Florida war, and, at last grown bolder, proposes to annex Texas as a slave state, and after a struggle carries the main feature of that transaction. It was done avowedly to prevent the abolition of slavery and to strengthen the slave power. Not only was this purpose declared in Congress by Mr. Henry A. Wise and others, but also by Mr. Calhoun, Secretary of State, in diplomatic correspondence with Mr. Pakenham, the British Minister. * * * A blind adherence to party is another cause of our present position. The mere names of Whig, Democrat, or Free Soiler are now worth nothing."

Do you not hear some talk like that now?

"We must have men to vote for—upright, downright and outspoken. In that is your last hope—your only security."

Again—

"The sibyl, each time we reject her offer, demands a higher price. What she would have done in 1850 she will not do now. What she will do now she will not do five years hence. * * The country is at last awaking. The great west is awaking. Ohio is wheeling into line, and will be perhaps the leader in the coming struggle."

What coming struggle? How did this preacher know that Ohio was wheeling into line as early as the 4th of June, 1854?

Again—

"Northern enthusiasm, when fully aroused, has always been more than a match for southern organization—northern conscience."

Oh! gods! (Great laughter.) Northern conscience! Take a shark skin, and let it dry to shagreen—skin the rhinoceras—go then and get the silver steel and grind it, and when you have ground it, then take the hone and whet it till it would split a hair, and with it prick the shagreen or the shark skin, and then go and try it on northern consciences. (Cheers and laughter.)

"Northern conscience, slow but stubborn, more than a match for southern impetuosity! So may it be still. If right is very apt to be overthrown at first, it is sure of victory in the end—

Careless seems the great avenger,
History's pages but record,
One death struggle in the darkness,
'Twixt old systems and the "word;"
Truth forever or the scaffold,
Wrong forever or the throne,
Yet that scaffold sways a future,
And behind the dim unknown
Standeth God within the shadow,
Keeping watch above his own."

And this is the first time that this preacher of Christian politics has named God in the whole sermon:—

"May to-day, he continues, be a Pentecost to the cause of humanity; to-day may the servants of Christ be every where speaking with one tongue, as the Spirit gives them utterance. May all our devotions and aspirations be—"

This is fusion.

"That all true lovers of liberty—whether they call themselves Whig, Democrat, Free Soiler or Abolitionist—be united in one calm and honest purpose, that once again all may be of one speech and one tongue. We must be united; we must sacrifice everything to unite in one great northern party all the friends of freedom and humanity. Let us forget the past, and gladly receive help from all. Let us reproach none, because those who come in at the eleventh hour—whoever repent and do deeds meet to repentance, even if he has been a servant of kidnappers, a United States Commissioner or Marshal, the editor of a sham Democratic paper, or worse than all, a lower law Doctor of Divinity. Whoever will repent let him be welcome. Let us be calm."

And "calm," there, means not only composed but silent and secret.

"Let us put the calmest, coolest man in front to lead us; let the most cautious advise and tell us what to do; let those of us who for years have been speaking, now listen for words from those whose turn has come to speak. The anti-slavery platform welcomes its new orators from State street and Long wharf. Let us not by any rashness lose the opportunity of uniting all men. As regards the southern threat of dissolving the Union, that has now lost its terror. If we had disregarded it ten years ago we should not have been in such danger of dissolution of the Union as we are to-day. The majority of the north to-day have no objection to a dissolution of the Union. In this community, where one man was opposed to the Union a week ago, a hundred men are opposed to it to-day. The danger of dissolution of the Union now is from the north, not from the south, if some effective measures are not taken to prevent the rendition of another fugitive from the northern states. We can all determine to support no man hereafter for any public office in the federal or state governments who is not openly pledged to five things; first, the abolition of the obnoxious clause of the Nebraska bill; second, the right of trial by jury for fugitives; third, the exclusion of slavery from the territory; fourth, the admission of no more slave states; fifth, the abolition of the Union, if these things cannot be obtained."

That is what they call "Christian politics" in Boston. (Laughter.)

What is the result of such preaching, such teaching, such printing? What has been the result of the pulpit, the school-houses and the press at the north upon this subject? Gentlemen, but a short time back, New England—Massachusetts especially—had but one ism within her limits, and that was Puritanism, the religion of the good old Covenanters and Congregationalists—Puritanism, full of vitality, full of spirituality—Puritanism that made even the barren rock of Plymouth to fructify, that made the New Englanders a strong people, that made them a rich people, that made them a learned people. But since they have waxed fat, since they have begun to build churches by lottery, begun to moralize mankind by legislation, begun to play petty providences for the people, begun to be Protestant Popes over the consciences of men, begun to preach "Christian politics," such as you have heard, Puritanism has disappeared, and we have in place of it Unitarianism, Universalism, Fourierism, Millerism, Mormonism—all the odds and ends of isms—until at last you have a grand fusion of all those odds and ends of isms in the *omnium gatherum* of isms, called Know-Nothingism. (Cheers, laughter, and hisses.) What is it? Now I wish not to offend any man in this assembly, because I would fain believe of our Virginians who are uniting themselves with this association, that their motives and their acts are as innocent as mine. I would fain believe that no man in the state of Virginia means more than simply some political end by uniting himself with this association, and to such men—conscientious, thinking men, who mean no more than to pick up a stick with which to bruise the head of democracy—I will only say, beware! my friends; you may be picking up a serpent that will sting you as deadly as it will democracy. (Cheers and stamping of feet.) I assail no motives here. You may be, according to that passage of Scripture which we sometimes read—that 11th verse of the 15th chapter of 2d Samuel, which tells us that two hundred men went out from Jerusalem with Absalom, when he left his father; that they "went out in their simplicity, and that they knew not anything." (Laughter.) And Bishop Hall most emphatically comments upon that, by saying that the two hundred went out in their simplicity, not knowing anything, and they were merely loyal rebels; but Absalom knew what he was about; he knew something; he knew that when the trumpet blew behind, it should be understood by the people that Absalom reigneth in Hebron; and I tell you that there is an Absalom at work with Know-Nothingism. (Great cheering and some hisses.)

"What is it? Where did it come from? What can it be? Did it fall from the sky? Did it rise from the sea?

I tell you that there is no wonder about it. I tell you that I know it from A to Z. I know where it came from. I know where it was engendered. I know what it has done, and I can exchange with you, my friend, every sign, every grip, every pass. (Laughter.) I know its white triangles and its red triangles, its red arrowtops and its white arrowtops. I know your odd numerals and yonr even numerals. I know your odds from A to M inclusive, and I know your evens from N to Z inclusive. (Laughter.) Now, where did it come from? It is no new thing. It is no strange thing. Although it is a wonder here, it has been operating for years and years in Old England. You that will go to a bookstore and buy Dickins' novel of "Hard Times" will see a portraiture of the thing, and how it has operated in a country with an aristocracy and a queen, with lord proprietors of factories and of lands, which they rent to middle men who grind down the operatives. There, in England, the secret association of the operatives against grinding capital, I grant you, has done much good. There, there is some necessity for it; there, where men's noses are held to the grindstone by oppression; there, where all the luxuries are free, and all the necessaries of life are taxed; there, where the operative is made to bear all the burdens of society; there, where there is a crowned head and an aristocracy —there, dark-lantern, secret association, test oaths have brought forth some reforms. Well, seeing its effect in that country—Exeter Hall—the abolitionists of England sent it over to the preachers of "Christian politics" in Boston and New York, to apply its machinery to the north and the non-slaveholding states. (Cheers and hisses.) They brought it over. They have tried it, and they had it organized as early as June 4th, 1854. They knew its potency. They knew its effect. Therefore it was that Mr. Freeman Clarke could tell you that he knew that Ohio was wheeling into line. This thing was all planned—all organized—and it did sweep Massachusetts, and New York, and Pennsylvania, and New Jersey, and Delaware, and Ohio, and Indiana, and Illinois, and Michigan, and Iowa. It has swept them with the besom of destruction. (Cheers and laughter.)

Go now to Massachusetts, and you find among her hundreds of legislators but one friend of the Constitution left. Sixty-two of these preachers of "Christian politics" have been returned to sit in the seats once filled by such men as John Hancock. There, in the neighborhood of Faneuil Hall, in the land of steady habits—in the land of the Puritans—Theodore Parker, but the other day, received 122 votes to be a chaplain. A man anti-Christ, so much devil incarnate that he can hide neither tail nor hoofs, receives in a Massachusetts legislature 122 votes to be a chaplain. Massachusetts! Massachusetts! the elder sister of Virginia, who in the night of the revolution gave her pass-word for pass-word, sign for sign, cheer for cheer, in the midst of our gloom! Massachusetts has thrown aside her Puritanism, her Christian religion, her constitution, and has given herself up to Know-Nothingism and anti-slavery. (Tremendous cheering.) Let us see the working of Know-Nothingism in Massachusetts. I hold in my hand the official address of his excellency Henry J. Gardner to the two branches of the legislature of Massachusetts. You see here upon one page of it, "not through a glass darkly," but plainly, an intimation of amalgamation itself. "It is a great problem," he says, "in statesmanship wisely to control the mingling of races into one nationality." Can you give that the grip? (Roars of laughter.) Another specimen of Know-Nothingism is a recommendation in this message that the right of suffrage shall be limited to those who can read and write. Do the Know-Nothings of Virginia give that grip too? The only illustrious painting that this country has given to the fine arts has been the picture of the Saviour of mankind healing the sick. This message recommends that the sick foreigner shall be tumbled out of the hospital bed into the Calcutta hole of the emigrant ship, and sent back again to Liverpool! This, then, is a sample of the charitableness and religion of Know-Nothingism. But, gentlemen, here is the governor's doctrine in relation to the Nebraska bill.

Mr. Wise then read a passage from the message in relation to the repeal of the compromise, which the governor characterises as "a violation of the plighted faith of the nation," and declares that "the ultimate effect will be to determine us manfully to demand the restoration of this broken compact, and to jealously guard each and every right that belongs to Massachusetts."

That is in exact correspondence with the preaching of Mr. Freeman Clarke. But the governor goes on:

"While we acknowledge our fealty to the Constitution and laws, the oft-repeated cry of disunion heralds no real danger to our ears."

Of those lights which Massachusetts is jealously to regard, it seems the two cardinal ones are the *habeas corpus* to take the fugitive slave out of the hands of the United States commissioner; and trial by jury, to have the title of the Virginia master subjected to the verdict of twelve abolitionists! "It is submitted," says the governor, "whether additional legislation is required to secure either of these to our fellow-citizens."

Gentlemen, that is not all. This Know-Nothing legislature has just elected one of the most notorious, one of the most inveterate of their abolition leaders, to the senate of the United States, and I beg to read to you a passage from a Boston paper which came to my hand this evening. It is the Boston Daily Chronicle, and I presume no one will say that it misrepresents the position of the Know-Nothings in the state of Massachusetts:

Mr. Wise then read a long report of a lecture on the "evils of and the remedy for slavery," delivered at the Tremont Temple, Boston, by Mr. Anson Burlingame, one of the Know-Nothings elected to Congress, in which he took ground in favor of the repeal of the Nebraska bill, the repeal of the fugitive slave law, the abolition of slavery in the District of Columbia, and the prohibition of slavery in the territories of the United States.

Speaking of the Nebraska bill, this lecturer said:

"One of its fruits was the election of a senator at the state house yesterday, (great applause and calls for Wilson, who was on the platform,) one who would take the place of one who was false to freedom and not true to the slave, (thus denouncing Edward Everett.) He himself, on going to Washington, should so endeavor to conduct himself as to truly represent his native place."

The report continues:—

"After Mr. Burlingame had concluded, Mr. Wilson was called for most heartily, and came forward. He stated that everything Mr. Burlingame had uttered he would endorse. He intended, in accepting his post, to yield nothing of his anti-slavery sentiment to anybody or for anything. He would comprehend in his action the whole country, of every color; but, in saying the whole country, he included Massachusetts and the north." Governor Gardner was called for, and amid loud cheers rose, but modestly declined to speak.

There is a Know-Nothing member elect from Massachusetts to the Congress of the United States. There is a United States senator elect of the Know-Nothings, who confesses the accusation which I make, that the new party of Know-Nothings was formed especially for the sake of abolitionism. (Cheers and hisses.) And there is a Know-Nothing governor—one of the nine who are all ready to take the same ground. (Stamping of feet and some hissing.) Then, gentlemen, I have here an act of the Know-Nothing legislature of Pennsylvania, which proposes to give citizenship to the fugitive slaves of the south. I have here, also, an article which is too long for me to read, exhausted as I am, from the Worcester Evening Journal, an organ of governor Gardner and senator Wilson, which says to you boldly that the American Organ at Washington is a pro-slavery organ, that it is not a true Know-Nothing organ, and that they speak for the north when they claim that they have already one hundred and sixty votes of the non-slaveholding states organized, eleven more than sufficient to elect a president of the United States without a single electoral vote from the slaveholding states.

Now, gentlemen, having swept the northern and the northwestern non-slaveholding states of the Union, the next onset is on the soil of Virginia. This Worcester Journal boasts that Maryland and Virginia are already almost northern states; and pray, how do they propose to operate on the south? Having swept the north—Massachusetts, New York, Pennsylvania, and all those other states—the question was: How can this ism be wedged in the south; and the devil was at the elbow of these preachers of "Christian politics," to tell them precisely how. (Cat-calls, derisive cheers, and other manifestations of the Know-Nothing element of the meeting.) There were three elements in the south, and in Virginia particularly, to which they might apply themselves. There is the religious element—the Protestant bigotry and fanaticism—for Protestants, gentlemen, have their religious zeal without knowledge, as well as the Catholics. (A voice, "True enough, sir.") It is an appeal to the 103,000 Presbyterians, to the 300,000 Baptists, to the 300,000 Methodists of Virginia. Well, how were they to reach them? Why, just by raising a hell of a fuss about the Pope. (Laughter.) The Pope! The Pope, "now so poor that none can do him reverence," so poor that Louis Napoleon, who requires every soldier in his kingdom to be at Sebastopol, has to leave a guard of muskets at Rome! Once on a time, crowned heads could bow down and kiss his big toe; but now, who cares for a Pope in Italy? Gentlemen, the Pope is here. Priestcraft at home is what you have to dread more than all the Popes in the world. I believe, intellectually, and in my heart as well as in my head, in evangelical Christianity. I believe that there is no other certain foundation for this republic but the pure and undefiled religion of Jesus Christ of Nazareth. And the man of God who believes in the Father, in the divinity of the Son, and the Holy Ghost—the preacher in the pulpit, at the baptismal font, by the sick bed, at the grave, pointing

The way to heaven and leading there,

I honor. No man honors him more than I do. But the priest who deserts the spiritual kingdom for the carnal kingdom, he is "of the earth, earthly," whoever he be—Episcopalian, Baptist or Methodist—who leaves the pulpit to join a dark-lantern, secret political society, in order that he may become a Protestant Pope by seizing on political power—he is a hypocrite, whoever he be. (Some applause, and cries of "good.") Jesus Christ of Nazareth settled the question himself. I have his authority on this question. When the Jews expected him to put on a prince's crown and seat himself on the actual throne of David, he asked for a penny to be shown him. A penny was brought to him, a metal coin, assayed, clipped, stamped, with the image of the state, representative of the civil power, stamped with Cæsar's image. "Whose image and superscription is this?" "It is Cæsar's." "Then, render unto Cæsar the things that be Cæsar's, and unto God the things that be God's." (Applause.) "My kingdom is not of this world. My kingdom is a spiritual kingdom." Cæsar's kingdom is political, is a carnal kingdom. And I tell you that if I stood alone in the state of Virginia, and if priestcraft—if the priests of my own mother church dared to lay their hands on the political power of our people, or to use their churches to wield political influence, I would stand, in feeble imitation of, it may be, but I would stand, even if I stood alone, as Patrick Henry stood in the revolution, between the parsons and the people. (Applause and a cry of "I'm with you.") I want no Pope, either Catholic or Protestant. I will pay Peter's pence to no pontiff—Episcopalian, Presbyterian, Baptist, Methodist, or any other. (Applause and cries of "good.") They not only appeal to the religious element, but they raise a cry about the Pope. These men, many of whom are neither Episcopalians, Presbyterians, Baptists, Methodists, Congregationalists, Lutherans, or what not—who are men of no religion, who have no church, who do not say their prayers, who do not read their Bible, who live God-defying lives every day of their existence, are now seen with faces as long as their dark-lanterns, with the whites of their eyes turned up in holy fear lest the Bible should be shut up by the Pope! (Laughter, applause, and derisive cheers.) Men who were never known before, on the face of God's earth, to show any interest in religion, to take any part with Christ or his kingdom, who were the devil's own, belonging to the devil's church, are all of a sudden very deeply interested for the word of God and against the Pope! It would be well for them that they joined a church which does believe in the Father, and in the Son, and in the Holy Ghost. (Good.) Let us see, my friends, what Know-Nothingism believes in. Do you know that, gentlemen? (Holding up a small pamphlet, amid great laughter and excitement. That is your formulary of the Grand Council of the United States of North America, from the press of Damerill & Moore, No. 10 Devonshire street, Boston, 1854.

A voice—"Is it January?"

Mr. Wise—Yes, it is January. It has been used. Here is one of your charters, (holding up a printed document,) and now, if you can see it, you will perceive it has been used by one of your lodges. (Cries of "Read it—drive along, Old Virginny.") Yes I will read from your own book. But I am on the subject of your religion now—you want to put down one of the evangelical churches of the country, which does believe not only in the Father, but in the divinity of Jesus Christ, and in the Holy Ghost—a Trinitarian church. I want to ask the Episcopalians, and the Presbyterians, and the Methodists, whether they are going to put down that Trinitarian church by a secret association? Your sphere consists of the 26 letters of the alphabet. You number your letters from A to M inclusive, with the odd numerals down to 26. Thus, A 1, B 3, C 5, D 7, E 9, F 11, G 13, H 15, I 17, J 19, K 21, L 23, M 25. The last thirteen letters of the alphabet are numbered with even numbers. Thus, N 2, O 4, P 6, Q 8, R 10, S 12, T 14, U 16, V 18, W 20, X 22, Y 24, Z 26. And now let us see how the books read. The first page of the cover of the blue book—and it is not only blue—real Boston blue, but it is a Mazarine blue, (lighter)—contains the following in tabular form. Now listen to Know-Nothing reading. (Manifestations of intense enjoyment among the Know-Nothings, and of interest among the uninitiated, and cries of "go it, old boy.") I will go it, if you will be patient and let me reason with you: 12 16 6 10 9 25 6, that reads "supreme," 4 10 7 9 10 means "order," 4 11, "of," 14 15 6, "the," 12 14 1 10, "star," 12 6 1 2 13 25 9 7, "spangled," 3 1 2 2 9 10, "banner." That is square spelling and square reading. "Supreme Order of the Star Spangled Banner." (Cheers, applause, hisses, and manifestations of all kinds.) The fourth page of the cover, contains the following table—12 6 17 10 17 14, "spirit," 4 11, "of," '76, "spirit of '76." That is the title page and the formulary of the Grand Council of the United States of North America, from the press of Damerell & Moore, No. 16 Devonshire street, Boston. Next come the officers of the Grand Council. President, (that is for the past year, but I believe it still continues,) James W. Barker, of New York. (Cheers.) Vice President, W. W. Williamson, of Alexandria, Va. (Roars of Laughter, cries of "here he is," and "three cheers for Williamson.") Corresponding Secretary, Charles D. Deschler, of New Brunswick, New Jersey. Recording Secretary, James M. Stevens, of Baltimore. Md. Treasurer, Henry Crane, of Cincinnati, Ohio. The Inside Sentinel is John P. Hilton, of Washington, D. C. (Laughter, and cheers from Washingtonians in the crowd.) Outside Sentinel, Henry Metz, of Detroit, Michigan. Chaplain, Samuel P. Crawford, of Indianapolis, Indiana. Now, gentlemen, I want to show you their religion. I read from the blue book—

"The organization shall be known by the name of the Grand Council of the United States of North America. Its jurisdiction and power shall extend to all the states, districts, and territories of the United States of North America. A person, to become a member of any subordinate Council, must be twenty-one years of age. He must believe in the existence of a Supreme Being, as the Creator and Preserver of the universe."

No Christ acknowledged! No Saviour of mankind! No Holy Ghost! No heavenly Dove of Grace! Go, go, you Know-Nothings, to the city of Baltimore, and in a certain street there you will see two churches—one is inscribed, "O Monos Theos"—"to the one God;" on the other is the inscription, "As for us, we preach Christ crucified—to the Jews a stumbling block, and to the Greeks foolishness." The one inscribed "O Monos Theos" is the Unitarian church; the other, inscribed, "We preach Christ crucified," is the Catholic church! (Cries of "good, good," and cheers.) Is it—I ask of Presbyterians, Episcopalians, Methodists, and Baptists—is it, I ask, for any orthodox Trinitarian Christian church to join an association that is inscribed, like the Unitarian church at Baltimore, "O Monos Theos" —to the one God? Is it for them to join or to countenance an association that so lays its religion as to catch men like Theodore Parker and James Freeman Clarke? I put it to all the religious societies—to the Presbyterians, the Episcopalians, the Methodists, and the Baptists—whether they mean to renounce the divinity of Christ and the operation of the Holy Spirit when they give countenance to this secret society, which is inscribed to the one God?

But, gentlemen, these Know-Nothings appeal not only to the religious element, but to the political element—not only to the political element, but to the agrarian element. Not only do they appeal to Protestant bigotry—not only do they ask Protestants to out-Herod Herod, to out Catholic the Catholics, to out Jesuit the Jesuits by adopting their Machiavellian creed, but they appeal to a forlorn party in the state of Virginia—a minority party, broken down at home and disorganized, because their associates have become abolitionized at the North—they appeal to them as affording them a house of refuge. [Cheers and laughter.] There is a paper published in this town by one of the most respectable gentlemen of the state, who some time ago published an article which, I must confess, I did not expect to see in print from his pen. The Alexandria Gazette, one of the most respectable of the Whig papers of the United States, edited by one of the most conservative and respectable gentlemen that I know of among my acquaintance, one who has been advocating the doctrines and practice of conservatism ever since I knew him, is now proposing a fusion between the Know-Nothings and the Whig party, simply for the reason that "the Whigs are tired of standing at the rack without fodder." [Voice in the crowd "Oh, go along," and laughter.] One who used, as I well remember, to denounce corruption and the spoils very sweepingly, is now actually maintaining that the Whigs will not and cannot go upon principle any longer and adhere to conservatism, because they are tired of waiting for office. [Laughter and cheers.] Not only that, but my friend, the editor, has lately published this short article:—

"We are pleased to see that with regard to Mr. Wise, the Democratic candidate for governor, the opposition is generally conducted with entire respect to his character as a citizen and a man, and with a full acknowledgment on all hands of his many excellent personal qualities. The opposition do not think he is the best qualified man for the office of governor, but they admit his talents. In seeking his defeat, they mainly desire to defeat the political organization which he upholds."

Remember that, ye Democrats, who have joined with Mr. Snowden in upholding the Know-Nothing cause—that the very object of the Whigs in joining the Know-Nothing society is to break up the organization to which you belong. [Cheers.] You Democrats have these gentlemen in a minority out of doors, but the moment they get you into a Know-Nothing lodge, they have you in a minority in doors. [Renewed cheers.] But the article goes on:—

"They contend that, as a former violent opponent of the party, at whose head he is now placed, there is too much political inconsistency to entitle him to the position he seeks."

How then, can Mr. Snowden—how can the conservative Whigs of Alexandria, to punish my inconsistency, join hands with Democrats and go over to them in Know-Nothing lodges? [Cheers.] They tell us they cannot give the grip in public to the Whigs of the North, because the Northern Whigs have become abolitionized. Here are two gentlemen who cannot shake hands with one another in our presence—one is a Whig of the North and the other a Whig of Alexandria. They cannot any longer keep up their Whig organization; but let the Whig of the north, abolitionised as he is, become a Know-Nothing, and let the Whig of the South, pro-slavery as he is, become a Know-Nothing, and then behind the curtain, these gentlemen can shake hands and hunny-fuggle with one another. [Much laughter.] This is what is called conservatism. This is what is called consistency. The article continues:

"They are resolved to unite in a strong and determined effort to break up the present political organization, which directs the destinies and controls the action of the state in all its departments. Mr. Wise cannot expect the support of those who desire to see this change effected."

If Mr. Wise cannot expect the support of conservative Whigs, or of any Whig, because the desire of the Whig party in joining the Know-Nothings is to defeat the Democracy, how can they expect Democrats to join them? But there is a last and worst element which they address, for which they can, as conservatives, offer me no excuse, and I come to it boldly. It is the most difficult and the hardest subject to deal with in public in a slave-holding community. Gentlemen, the last constitutional convention of Virginia betrayed the important fact to the north, as well as to ourselves, that out of the 125,000 voters in the state of Virginia, but 25,000 or 30,000, are slave-holding voters. About 1 voter in 5 is a slaveholder. I say it boldly, and no man will dispute it who has been to Norfolk and Portsmouth, that the last and worst element that is appealed to is the agrarian element—appealing to the white laborers of the state against the black laborers of the state. (Cheers.) Go all over the state and tell me where Know-Nothingism is rankest and most violent. [Voice in the crowd, "Down on the wharves," and great laughter.] I tell you that you'll not only find it down on the wharves in Alexandria, as has been said, and well said, in the crowd, but you will find it worse than anywhere else around the wharves of Portsmouth and in Portsmouth navy yard. The very men who, for ten years, have been petitioning the secretary of the navy to forbid the employment of slave labor in Gosport navy yard—the very men who petitioned the last convention to frame a new constitution for Virginia, to make it a part of the organic law of the state that slaveholders should not allow their slaves to be taught the mechanic arts—these are the men who are the very hot-bed of Know-Nothingism.

Voice in the Crowd—Send them to h—ll.

It is impossible to say what effect these three combined elements are to have upon us. I ask the Protestant church, to recur to this religious element, how they expect in future—if they think that Catholicism is not a pure and undefiled religion—to succeed in preaching against the Pope and Catholics? Where a preacher has risen in the pulpit, in times past, to arraign the Pope and the abominations of the church of Rome, he has been regarded as a vital spiritual preacher of Protestantism; he has been regarded as one looking to the spiritual kingdom; but let a preacher now rise and preach against the Pope and against Catholicism, and whether he is sincere or not, his congregation feels that he is preaching for Know-Nothingism. Why, the other day, in Isle of Wight, I saw a man from Canada, or I heard of him there, who was distributing the Bible to the state of Virginia. Well, he may have been the very best colporteur in the world; he may have been a man of as honest intentions as Father Hannell, who is your travelling distributer of the Bible; but he came all the way from Canada down to the Isle of Wight to distribute Bibles? He was asked why he distributed Bibles among us? Did he take us to be heathen? Our churches are distributing the word. Our bishops are distributing the word. The Bible is found in every steamboat saloon, and in every chamber of every hotel in the state. Did he take us to be heathen? Oh, no; he was glad to hear that we had the Bible here, but he thought that perhaps he would be doing us great service to bring the Bible, as the Pope and Bishop Hughes wanted to make it a sealed book. He was called upon to take his departure, as he was known at once to be a Know-Nothing agent. He pretended merely to visit to distribute the Bible, but the fellow was all the time privately carrying his dark lantern and lucifer match in his pocket to apply the test oath. (Laughter.) We gave him warning to go hence, and I hope he has gone. So it is with the preachers—your Protestant preachers. It is utterly impossible that they can make any inroads against the Pope and against Catholics so long as they are suspected of political motives—so long as they are suspected of attempting to become Protestant popes; and to seize political power. What was it, I ask them—what corrupted the Roman church? There was once a time when the Bishop of Rome was the head of a pure, primitive church—when he was armed only with eleemosynary, with spiritual and with ecclesiastical power. But the very moment he laid his hand upon the imperial purple and crown of the Cæsars, that very moment the "whore of Babylon" put on her scarlet and began to play her abominations before the eyes of the people. She played these abominations till the times of Calvin, and Luther, and Melancthon and Roger Williams. These great reformers were men who did not go into secret places, who did not use dark lanterns, who not speak in whispers, but who thundered in the tones of Whitfield himself. The moment the Pope laid hold of political power—the moment he became part and head of the civil state—that very moment the state corrupted the church, and the churchdestroyed the liberties of the state. So it will be here, if, under the pretext of defying the Pope, of proscribing Catholicism, you allow your priests—Protestant or other—to lay their hands upon political power, and put on the imperial purple and the crown of the Cæsars—that very moment the state will corrupt the church, and the church will destroy the liberties of the state. As to the proscription of foreigners, let me ask the Know-Nothings themselves to return to that passage of the Bible to which I have already referred them. If they will take the fifteenth chapter of Second Samuel, and read not only the whole verse, but the whole history of Absalom, the traitor, they will find that while Absalom—not only native born of the land, but native born of the loins of king David—was turning traitor, while the sweet Psalmist of Israel was driven towards the wilderness with his followers, he turned and saw Ittai, the Gittite, and said to him: "Wherefore goest thou also with us? Return to thy place, and abide with thy king, for thou art a stranger and also an exile. Whereas, thou camest but yesterday, should I this day make thee go up and down with us? Seeing I go whither I may, return thou and take back thy brethren: Mercy and truth be with thee." And Ittai, the exile and stranger, who came but yesterday, answered the king and said: "As the Lord liveth, and as my lord the king liveth, surely in what place my lord the king shall be—whether in death or in life—even there also will thy servant be." And remember that the case of Absalom and of Ittai is but the prototype of an Arnold and a Lafayette. (Applause.) Who sent you alliance? You tell the people that Catholics never gave aid to civil liberty; that they never yet struck a blow for the freedom of mankind. Who gave you alliance against the crown of England? Who, but that Catholic king, Louis XVI? He sent you, from the court of Versailles, the boy of Washington's camp, a foreigner who never was naturalized, but who bled at the redoubt of Yorktown. (Applause.) And not only did Lafayette bleed at the redoubt of Yorktown, when an Arnold, a native like Absalom, proved traitor, but when the German, DeKalb, fell at the field of Camden, on southern soil, with fourteen bayonet wounds transfixing his body, and, dying, praised the Maryland militia—Gates, the yankee native, ran seventy-five miles without looking behind. (Applause and laughter.) And not only that: In that intense moment when the declaration of our independence was brought into Carpenter's Hall by Rutledge, and Franklin, and Jefferson, and laid upon the table—that holy paper, which not only pledged life and honor, but fortune, too—realize that moment of intense, of deep, of profound interest, when the independence of this land hung upon the acts of men—when, one by one, men rose from their seats and went to the table to pledge lives and fortunes and sacred honor; at length one spare, pale-faced man rose, and went and dipped the pen into the ink, and signed "Charles Carroll," and when reminded that it might not be known what Charles Carroll it was, that it might not be known that it was a Charles Carroll who was pledging a principality of fortune, he added the words "of Carrollton." (Cheers.) He was a Catholic representative from a Catholic colony. (A voice in the crowd—"But he was a native born American.")

And, sir, before George Washington was born, before Lafayette wielded the sword or Charles Carroll the pen for his country, six hundred and forty years ago, on the 16th of June, 1214, there was another scene enacted on the face of the globe, when the general charter of all charters of freedom was gained, when one man—a man called Stephen Langton—swore the barons of England, for the people, against the orders of the Pope and against the power of the king—swore the barons on the high altar of the Catholic church at St. Edmundsbury, that they would have Magna Charta or die for it. The charter which secures to every one of you to-day trial by jury, freedom of the press, freedom of the pen, the confronting of witnesses with the accused, and the opening of secret dungeons—that charter was obtained by Stephen Langton against the Pope and against the king of England, and if you Know-Nothings don't know who Stephen Langton was, you know nothing sure enough. (Laughter and cheers.) He was a Catholic Archbishop of Canterbury. (Renewed cheers.) I come here not to praise the Catholics, but I come here to acknowledge historical truths, and to ask of Protestants what has heretofore been the pride and boast of Protestants—tolerance of opinion in religious faith. (Applause.) All we ask is tolerance. All we ask is, that if you hate the Catholics because they have proscribed heretics, yout won't out-proscribe proscription. If you hate the Catholics because they have nunneries and monasteries, and Jesuitical secret orders, don't out-Jesuit the Jesuits by going into dark-lantern secret chambers to apply test oaths. If you hate the Catholics because you say they encourage the Machiavellian expediency of telling lies sometimes, don't swear yourselves not to tell the truth. (Cheers.) Here are the oaths—the oaths that bind you, under no circumstances to disclose who you are or what you are, and that bind you not only to political, but to social proscription. Here is your book—your Bible—which requires of you to stick up your notices between midnight and daybreak. (Laughter.) I don't object to secrecy. I am a member of a secret order, and I am proud to be a brother Mason; (loud cheers;) and I am at liberty by my order to say, that as to its ends, its purposes, its designs, Masonry has no secrets. (Renewed cheering.) Its end, its purpose, its aim, is to make a brotherhood of charity amongst men. Its end is the end of the Christian law of religion. I know not how any Mason can be a Know-Nothing. Masonry binds its members to respect and obey the laws of the land in which we live; and when the Constitution of the United States declares that no religious test shall be made a qualification for office, Masonry dare not interpose by conspiring, in a secret association, to attempt to make a religious test a qualification for office. When Virginia has an act of religious freedom—an act that is no longer a mere statute law, but is now a part of the organic law, and which says that no man shall be burdened for religious opinion's sake—Masonry dare not conspire to burden any man for opinion's sake. Masonry has no secrets but the simple tests by which it recognizes its brotherhood. It is bound to respect the law and to tolerate differences of opinion in religion and politics. I do not complain of secrecy, but I complain of secrecy for political objects. What is your object? It is to assail the Constitution of the United States, to conspire to contradict the Constitution and laws of the land; it is to conspire against the Constitution and laws, and swear men by test oaths—the most odious instruments of tyranny that intolerance and proscription have ever devised. It is not only to proscribe Catholics and foreigners, but it is to proscribe Protestants and natives too, who will not unite with you in proscribing Catholics and foreigners. It is further than that: It destroys all individuality in the man. You bring in your noviciate, you swear him to do—what? To give up his conscience, his judgment, his will, to the judgment and the conscience and the will of an association of men who are not willing that others should

8

enslave them, but their test oath enslave themselves. And to what are they sworn? They are sworn to passive obedience—to non-resistance—to take sign and grip. Here is your organization. (Holding up a document.) I will not take time to read it; but I will state the fact that your Grand National Council of the United States is organized by the appointment of thirteen men from each state, a council of thirteen, an oligarchy of thirteen from each state, who assemble outside of the state to form the Grand Council of the United States, with Mr. Barker, of Wall street, New York, as president. Power over original judgment, power over appeal—all power—is concentrated in that National Council. And has it come to this? Has Virginia been so provincialized in the Union that her sons will consent not to be guided by their own individual wills, by their own individual consciences, by their own individual judgments, but consent to qe sworn by a test oath, to take a sign which comes from outside the state, and which may be passed to you from Mr. Barker, of New York.

When that is submitted to by the people of Virginia, no longer call yourselves a free, sovereign, and independent state. You are subdued—you are conquered—you are provincialized—you have lost your individuality. And not only are these appliances brought to bear upon us, but, gentlemen, emmissaries are everywhere at work. The New York Herald has taken up this election, and has proclaimed to the world that it is arranged in New York already, whence the sign will come, I suppose, that Mr. Wise is to be defeated in Virginia. Bennett, the political Fagan, the cross-eyed, whining demon of politics, who has made himself a millionaire by black mail—Bennett, whose paper I never would allow to come into my family—Bennett, who has fed the vultures with the very lambs of society—the man who has regarded no purity, no sanctity, nothing that was holy or sacred—Bennett has dogged me in this canvass, without an open competitor, with his reporter for his paper—sending here that instrument to catch the words of the Virginia stump—our own domestic stump—in order that he might travesty and misrepresent and belie. And, too, at this moment, I have to endure that the Whig presses of the state have forgotten what they owe to the state—not to me—so far as to publish, not only his reports, but his cards, which insult the state as well as me. That is tolerated. I care nothing about that minion of the Herald. I am looking at higher game. I am looking at the Absaloms, at the Arnolds, at the traitors of the north, who, wielding the power of the Herald, have thought to put me down. And I suppose the Know-Nothings are very confident that they will succeed. Let me tell them that I would as lief die a martyr in this cause as in any other cause. Let me say to them, where you have fastened together Whigs and Know-Nothings and Democrats, when you get those who are blindly leaving their party to place themselves in machinery—those who are either seeking office or are disappointed in not getting office—and when you have thus put me down, when you have crushed the slaveholding power in my election, why then follows a total revolution—a social and political revolution, not only in the state of Virginia, but in the whole south. Gentlemen, what is to follow from this? Where is it to end? They have swept the north. They have nine governors. They claim that they have got a majority elected to the next House of Representatives. They are now trying to obtain, by the end of the next three years, a majority in the Senate of the United States; but if I am elected governor of the state of Virginia, what will be the state of things? The next Congress will assemble on the first Monday in December next. If I be elected governor of the state of Virginia, I shall be sworn in on the first of January next. And now I tell you what will be the consequence. When I take the oath to support the constitution of the state of Virginia, I will remember me that I will be invested with the militia power of the state of Virginia, to repel invasion and to suppress insurrection. No man loves and adores the Union of this land more than I do. I have been taught to venerate and to cherish the Union of these states. It is the holiest of all holy things. I would gladly give my life, my blood, as a sacrifice to save it if required. But I know that the main pillars of the Union, the main props and supporters of this palladium, are the pillars of state rights and state sovereignty. (Applause.) If you place me with your sword in hand by that great pillar of Virginia sovereignty, I promise you to bear and forbear to the last extremity. I will suffer much, suffer long, suffer almost anything but dishonor. But it is, in my estimation, with the union of the states as it is with the union of matrimony. You may suffer almost anything except dishonor; but when honor is touched the union must be dissolved. (Loud and prolonged cheering.) I will not say that. I take back the words. I will not allow myself to contemplate a dissolution of the Union. (Renewed cheering.) No, we will still try to save it. But when the worst comes to the worst, if compelled to draw the sword of Virginia, I will draw it; and by the gods of the state and her holy altars, if I am compelled to draw it, I will flesh it or it shall pierce my body. (Enthusiastic cheering.) And I tell you more: we have got abolitionists in this state. (Voice in the crowd—"D—n the Know-Nothings," and great laughter.) If I should have to move, some of the first, I fear, against whom I should have to act, would be some within our own limits. But if forced to fight, I will not confine myself to the state of Virginia. My motto will be—

Woe to the coward that ever he was born,
That did not draw the sword before he blew the horn. (Loud cheers.)

Gentlemen, I was in a very poor plight to speak to you to-night. Perhaps I have spoken already too long, although I have not said half what I would say to you, or produced half the evidence which I have with me. All I have to say to the Democracy is, that all you want is active, earnest organization. (Cheers.) Remember that if these Know-Nothings hold together, they are sworn, compact committees of vigilance. Go to work, then. Organize actively everywhere. Appoint your vigilance committees, but take especial care that no Know-Nothings are, secretly and unknown to you, upon them. (Cheers.) Be prepared. I have gone through most of eastern Virginia, and in spite of their vaunting I defy them to defeat me. (Great cheering.) There are Indians in the bush, but I'll whack on the bayonet, and lunge at every shrub in the state, till I drive them out. (Renewed and enthusiastic cheering.) I tell them distinctly there shall be no compromise, no parley. I will come to no terms. They shall either crush me or I will crush them in this state. (Great applause.) Of the conscientious and considerate and conservative men of the Whig party, I would ask where they can find anything in form, shape, tendency or result, that promises so much destructiveness as Know-Nothingism? I challenge them to compare Know-Nothingism with Democracy, and to tell me what it is in Democracy that they cannot touch in comparison with Know-Nothingism. I will say that I do expect that the Democratic nominations in this election will gain the support of some of the brightest jewels of the Whig party in the state. (Cheers and laughter.) I hail them and extend to them the right hand of fellowship; and I believe that if Know-Nothingism can claim no other good deed, it will at least effect a reorganization of the Democratic party of the state of Virginia upon higher ground, more affiliated, stronger and abler, better to serve itself and the country, than it has been for the last twenty-five years. Let them, then, boast of their 30,000 and 40,000 and 50,000 majorities. We will take our old and usual majority—I will be satisfied with that. (Cheers and laughter.)

And to obtain it, I would not flatter you, the people, "if you were Neptune, for his trident, or Jove for his power to thunder." I will deceive no man; I will hunny-fuggle no voter. (Laughter.) I will condescend to nothing unbecoming a gentleman. I will conduct this canvass throughout in such a manner as will command your respect and preserve my own self-respect. God grant that I may live through the campaign. If I continue to speak as I have been doing, I doubt very much whether I can survive it. But, "sink or swim, live or die," I will do my duty; and "if Rome falls, I am innocent."

Mr. Wise then retired, amidst enthusiastic cheering, and the meeting at once dispersed.

DISTINGUISHED DEMOCRATIC ORATORS OF THE CANVASS.

Among other distinguished gentlemen who took the stump in the eastern part of the State, during the campaign, were the following. Hon. Shelton F. Leake, of Madison; Messrs. James Lyons, and Patrick H. Aylett, of Richmond, (this gentleman especially deserves the thanks of the Democracy for his arduous labours and repeated dissections of Know Nothingism); Maj. James Garland, and Charles Irving, of Lynchburg; Roger A. Pryor, of the Richmond Enquirer; A. D. Banks, of the Southside Democrat; R. K. Meade, of Petersburg; Col. William M. Howerton, of Halifax; Senator James M. Mason, of Frederick; Dr. Clement R. Harris, of Augusta; William M. Treadway, of Pittsylvania; Henry L. Hopkins, of Powhatan, late Speaker of the House of Delegates; William Cabell Flournoy, of Prince Edward; and others.

In the western portion of the State, very great and arduous services were rendered. Conspicuous among the Democratic speakers, was Mr. Elisha W. McComas, who made an active and most successful tour through almost the entire west. Ex-Governor John B. Floyd, of Washington county, did herculean service, and, by his judicious arrangements for the canvass in his district, produced a majority there unprecedented in the political annals of "Little Tennessee." In the northwest, conspicuous among the speakers, were Hon. Sherrard Clemens, of Wheeling, and Mr. Benj. W. Jackson, of Pleasants county. In the Valley, Col. Wm. H. Harman, of Augusta, and James W. Massie, of Rockbridge, were very able and efficient.

The Examiner had the following notice of the canvass in that important district of the State—"Little Tennessee."

GLORIOUS LITTLE TENNESSEE.—We hear daily more and more encouraging tidings from the Democracy of this Heart of Midlothian. In spite of the fallacious asseverations of the Know Nothings to the contrary, Little Tennessee will give the Democratic ticket a majority of two thousand at the very lowest figure. MCMULLIN will beat both his Know Nothing competitors—TRIGG and MARTIN—by a large majority.

The services of Mr. WM. H. COOK, of Carroll county, have been efficient and invaluable in the canvass. He has met TRIGG twice on the stump in a manner that neither his poor victim nor the people who witnessed the onslaught will ever forget. He has had Carroll and Grayson in his especial keeping, and the result in those two counties will attest the effectiveness of his labors in the Democratic cause.

Nor has Col. BEN. RUSH FLOYD, of Wytheville, allowed the imperative calls of his profession to interfere with his duty as a Democrat. His speeches at Wytheville are pronounced the most powerful ever delivered in that county, and has told with crushing effect upon the Know Nothing cause. The election of GRAHAM, in Wythe, is set down as a fixed fact.

THOS. L. PRESTON, Esq., has surprised his warmest admirers by the ability and eloquence of his speeches in denunciation of Know Nothingism. He has gone from precinct to precinct, and man to man, crying aloud and sparing not. The Order boasted that they had secured the county and fettered its voters before the canvass commenced; but Mr. PRESTON has knocked the scales from the eyes of the people, broken up the plans of the enemy, and completely destroyed the work of the Order. His election, in Smyth, we are assured, is a certain event.

But what shall we say of that brave man—that fearless champion of Democracy through evil and through good report—who can neither be driven by treachery nor seduced by flattery from the cause in which he was born and reared, for which he has lived and fought, and which has never yet failed or faltered in his district when *he* was in the field—the ACHILLES of the Southwest—JOHN B. FLOYD?

The secret Order had already stolen a march upon the Democracy in Washington county. They already boasted to have captured and bound and fettered, by oaths and pledges, a majority of the *freemen* of the county. The Democrats were taken by surprise, and had already been surrounded before they knew that the prowling enemy was near them. They turned to FLOYD, and appealed to him, with odds already counted against them, to take the field and attack the enemy in his fortifications. With a noble unselfishness he consented to be a candidate for an office he did not want. He took the stump, spoke in every nook and corner, saw every man, and addressed every dozen men in the county. He burst up lodges, and scattered dismay and consternation among the followers of the dark lantern. He has redeemed the county by a series of speeches surpassing even himself in ability and power, and, as a Whig adversary, distinguished for intelligence, and no friend of Mr. FLOYD, says, never surpassed before in any political contest in this country. He has crushed the puny adversaries that have been pitted against him—as the president of a Know Nothing council and adversary tells it, taking them by couples, and knocking their block heads together, and jarring out every grain of sense they ever contained.

Having secured his own county, he has gone into the unvisited counties of Lee and Scott, crushing out the Order by his ponderous blows, and speaking everywhere with a power never before known there. In Scott, last Monday week, he spoke with peculiar ability, and with such effect that an old Methodist minister exclaimed, as he closed, "God never made the man who ever delivered such a speech as that."

Amongst the distinguished Whigs who took ground against Know Nothingism, and acted with the Democracy, were the following: Thomas J. Michie, of Staunton; Judge Robertson, of Richmond; John Y. Gholson, of Petersburg; and Maj. John T. L. Preston, of the Virginia Military Institute.

We here insert the letter of Mr. Michie, as distinguished for its ability and the influence it exerted over the popular mind.

MR. MICHIE'S LETTER.

STAUNTON, April 9th, 1855.

My Dear Sir:—On my return to-day from Shenandoah, where I had been for the last week, attending a session of the Circuit Court of that county, I received your kind and flattering invitation to address the people of Richmond City.

Permit me to tender to yourself and the committee from whom it emanated, my grateful thanks for the honor you have done me. But I fear that constant and unavoidable professional engagements, will place it out of my power to visit Richmond between this time and the 4th Thursday in May. On the 12th inst., I must be in Rockbridge, and thence to Highland, this place, and Albermarle, in rapid succession. Nothing, I assure you, would give me more pleasure than to address the intelligent people of Richmond, on the interesting questions of the present canvass—to tell them how blighting to the free spirit of our country the secret mystery of Know Nothingism must prove—how demoralizing it will be to our own children, the hitherto high-minded, openhearted, bold youths of Virginia, to be educated in the sneaking arts of secrecy and espionage—to be taught by their fathers to spy out all the political actions of their fellow men. and yet, to keep their own actions and "objects," in reference to matters which necessarily concern all, a profound secret—to publish platforms of *pretended* principles, suited to every latitude and every taste, for the purpose of gaining proselytes, while they feel the degrading consciousness that they are prohibited, by horrible oaths, from ever revealing their real objects and principles outside of their Order—and while a disgusted world is forced to conclude, either that their platforms are filled with false professions, intended to mislead, or that those who publish them are perjured.

Has any party a right to political secrets? In private associations men may conceal matters which concern themselves alone. But politics, relating necessarily to the affairs or conduct of a government, in which every citizen has an equal stake, how can a party be tolerated in withholding, from any portion of our citizens, information on a subject which vitally concerns every one of them? In a small partnership, if a portion of the partners were to conceal from the rest their designs in reference to the social funds, their associates so excluded, would be justified in forming a conclusion of dishonesty, and a court of justice would interfere. In the ordinary intercourse of life, an honest man of ordinary humanity, possessed of a secret which concerns his neighbor's interests, feels bound by a high moral obligation to disclose it to him whom it interests. Yet here is a political party intermeddling in the dark with the affairs of government, which involve your and my life, liberty and property, and those of our children, and of millions of others, and yet they coolly refuse to let us know what their objects are until we shall be informed by such result as they may hereafter produce. By their own showing they are enemies of popular government—for in such a government the whole community participates.

But they show their enmity in various other forms. They practically deny the capacity of the people to govern, and therefore establish aristocratic councils, with a great consolidating and controlling head, located most fitly, somewhere near "the five points" in the city of New York. Power with them, instead of being vested in the people and emanating from them, is vested in these aristocratic councils. The theory of our government requires an appeal from aristocracy to the people. Know Nothingism reverses that theory, by providing in all cases an appeal from the people to aristocracy.

If the people had capacity for self-government, this self-styled American (quære, Aboriginal?) party deny their honesty. Therefore, they are never trusted except under oath. And again, while the spirit of our institutions requires every citizen to exercise his own best judgment in voting for all officers of government—this wonderful invention of Yankeedom requires him to bind himself by solemn oath, not to exercise his own judgment at all, but to give his vote as the majority of a caucus, itself subservient to the mandate of a superior caucus, may order. These are startling novelties to an American ear. Yet, Know Nothingism, bold in this respect alone, in all others skulking, denying its name, denying its association, refusing to make known its objects, hiding in dark caverns with bats and owls, denounces all as anti-American who will not adopt its dogmas! I should like to discuss and dissect the monster, not only under the preceding head, but many others, and especially its Federalism. I should like to show the people of Richmond, and the whole South, the cunning device of the Know Nothing nominee for Governor, instilled into him, no doubt, by the same masters under whom he learned his "Americanism," by which he asks the people of Virginia to deprive themselves of all ground of resistance hereafter, to the Northern plan of intervention in our domestic affairs—by intervening in a crusade against Catholics and foreigners, not because she is suffering any inconvenience from them herself, but in order to rid her sister States of the nuisance.

But I console myself, under my inability to obey your call, by the reflection that if I went, it would only contribute the feeble light of a candle, to that glorious sun which has shone and which continues to shine among you and enlighten you till the day of election. Wise and Douglas, and a host of others, have told you more than I can tell. But as I have been a Whig—only say for me to my old Whig friends, that I have looked carefully under the cloak of Know Nothingism—have lifted with a daring hand the veil that covered the face of the Prophet Sam, and satisfied myself well that it is not Whiggery, as I had always understood it, and as I knew it was understood and professed by thousands of honest and patriotic men, but *monstrum horrendum informi ingens uni lumen redemptum.* Yes, as blind as a bat, and as dark as Erebus. Let them beware of it, as they love their lives and high reputation. History informs us of many secret political parties, but not of one that I remember, which has not been damned by impartial posterity. This party has much besides its secrecy to give it an earlier and deeper condemnation than that which has fallen to the lot of its predecessors. If the Democratic party should follow its lead, what a Hell upon earth their underground fight would make, yet it would plead example, and the responsibility would be Sam's.

With high regard,

THOS. J. MICHIE.

VIRGINIA DEMOCRATIC ORGANIZATION.

The Democratic party, not deeming it wise to despise their secret foe, and wishing to hand down to their children the political escutcheon of their State untarnished, thought it provident and well to organise efficiently, in order to go into a contest with unbroken column and solid phalanx. Accordingly their executive committee for the State met, Feb. 12th, and appointed the following congressional, senatorial and county electors.

CONGRESSIONAL ELECTORS.

First Congressional District—Ro. L. Montague of Middlesex.
Second District—Mordecai Cooke of Norfolk City.
Third District—P. H. Aylett of Richmond City.
Fourth District—R. K. Meade of Petersburg.
Fifth District—A. Hughes Dillard of Henry.
Sixth District—Wm. J. Robertson of Albemarle.
Seventh District—Benj. H. Berry of Alexandria.

Eighth District—Thos. M. Isbell of Jefferson.
Ninth District—Geo. E. Deneale of Rockingham.
Tenth District—Sherrard Clemens of Wheeling.
Eleventh District—Benj. W. Jackson of Wood.
Twelfth District—A. A. Chapman of Marion.
Thirteenth District—Jno. B. Floyd of Washington.

SENATORIAL ELECTORS.

1st	Senatorial District—	L. J. Bell of Accomac.
2d	do.	Hunter Woodis of Norfolk City.
3d	do.	S. Wheeler of Norfolk County.
4th	do.	James F. Crocker of Isle of Wight.
5th	do.	E. W. Massenburg of Southampton.
6th	do.	Thos. Wallace of Petersburg.
7th	do.	Lewis E. Harvie of Amelia.
8th	do.	Alex. Jones of Chesterfield.
9th	do.	Wm. C. Flournoy of Prince Edward.
10th	do.	Wm. B. Baskervill of Mecklenburg.
11th	do.	J. Redd Smith of Pittsylvania.
12th	do.	Wm. M. Howerton of Halifax.
13th	do.	Arch'd Stuart of Patrick.
14th	do.	Austin M. Trible of Bedford.
15th	do.	Thos. K. Kirkpatrick of Lynchburg.
16th	do.	W. R. C. Douglas of New Kent.
17th	do.	John B. Young of Henrico.
18th	do.	Geo. W. Randolph of Richmond City.
19th	do.	John T. Seawell of Gloucester.
20th	do.	R. Claybrook of Northumberland.
21st	do.	Wm. R. Aylett of King William.
22d	do.	Eustace Conway of Spottsylvania.
23d	do.	Eppa Hunton of Prince William.
24th	do.	David Funsten of Alexandria.
25th	do.	Jno. W. Minor of Loudoun.
26th	do.	J. Y. Menifee of Rappahannock.
27th	do.	A. R. Blakey of Madison.
28th	do.	Burrell Snead of Albemarle.
29th	do.	W. D. Leake of Goochland.
30th	do.	B. M. Dewitt of Nelson.
31st	do.	Wm. Lucas of Jefferson.
32nd	do.	G. T. Barbee of Hardy.
33d	do.	Thos. T. Fauntleroy of Frederick.
34th	do.	J. S. Calvert of Shenandoah.
35th	do.	John T. Harris of Rockingham.
36th	do.	Wm. H. Harman of Augusta.
37th	do.	Jas. W. Massie of Rockbridge.
38th	do.	Oliver H. Gray of Botetourt.
39th	do.	Wm. H. Cook of Carroll.
40th	do.	G. W. G. Browne of Tazewell.
41st	do.	Isaac J. Leftwich of Wythe.
42d	do.	Sam'l. V. Fulkerson of Lee.
43d	do.	T. Dunn English of Logan.
44th	do.	R. F. Dennis of Greenbrier.
45th	do.	Jeremiah Wellman of Wayne.
46th	do.	A. J. Smith of Harrison.
47th	do.	James Neeson of Marion.

48th Senatorial District—Benj. Bassell, Jr., of Upshur.
49th do. Wm. G. Brown of Preston.
50th do. Campbell Tarr, Jr., of Brooke.

COUNTY ELECTORS.

Accomac—J. W. H. Parker.
Albemarle—Dr. W. G. Rogers.
Alexandria—George L. Gordon.
Alleghany and Bath—Samuel Carpenter.
Amelia—Wm. Gregory.
Nottoway—Thomas Rowlett.
Amherst—Dr. S. C. Gibson.
Appomattox—S. D. McDearmon.
Augusta—James H. Skinner.
Barbour—A. G. Reger.
Bedford—Samuel G. Davis.
Berkeley—M. S. Grantham.
Botetourt—B. F. Miller.
Craig—Ro. M. Wiley.
Braxton and Nicholas—Jonathan Koiner.
Brooke—Wm. DeCamps.
Hancock—Thos. Bambrick.
Brunswick—Robt. D. Turnbull.
Buckingham—E. W. Hubard.
Cabell—Peter C. Buffington.
Campbell—Wm. T. Yancey.
Caroline—Jno. Washington.
Carroll—Jno. Carroll.
Charles City, James City, and New Kent,—E. Waddill and H. T. Jones.
Charlotte—Wm. H. Dennis.
Chesterfield—Alex. Cogbill.
Clarke—E. W. Massie.
Culpeper—Jno. W. Bell.
Cumberland, and Powhatan,—Creed D. Coleman. Henry L. Hopkins.
Dinwiddie—James Boisseau.
Doddridge and Tyler—Chapman J. Stewart.
Elizabeth City— *Warwick*— *York*— *Williamsburgh*— James B. Hope. Wm. G. Young. J. B. Cosnahan. Talbot Sweeney.
Essex— *King and Queen*— J. M. Matthews. J. M. Jeffries.
Fairfax—Jno. Powell.
Fauquier—Silas B. Hunter.
Fayette and Raleigh—Aaron Stockton.
Floyd—Harvey Deskins.
Fluvanna—Ro. H. Poore.
Franklin—Wm. H. Edwards.
Frederick—F. M. Holladay.
Giles—James Johnson.
Gilmer—Sam'l L. Hays.
Wirt—R. S. Brown.

Gloucester—Wm. B. Taliaferro.
Goochland—W. W. Cosby.
Grayson—Sam'l McCamant.
Green and Orange— } Wyatt S. Beazley. Jno. Welch.
Greensville and Sussex— } O. A. Claiborne. Richmond F. Dillard.
Halifax—Woodson Hughes.
Hampshire—A. W. McDonald, Jr.
Hanover—Edw'd W. Morris.
Hardy—J. F. W. Allen.
Harrison—Robt. Johnston.
Henrico—Dan'l E. Gardner.
Henry—Geo. Hairston.
Highland—Adam Stephenson, Jr.
Isle of Wight—C. B. Haden.
Jackson—H. Fitzhue, Jr.
Jefferson—S. K. Donavin.
Kanawha—Jno. A. Warth.
King George and Stafford—Chas. Mason, Jno. C. Moncure.
King William—Wm. Hill.
Lancaster and Northumberland—Addison Hall.
Lee—S. S. Slemp.
Lewis—Jno. Brannon.
Logan, Boone and Wyoming—St. Clair Ballard, James Shannon.
Louisa—R. B. Waddy.
Loudoun—Geo. Rust.
Lunenbury—Wm. J. Neblitt.
Madison—Thos. J. Humphreys.
Marion—Wm. J. Willey.
Marshall—Bush W. Price.
Mason—John Green Newman.
Matthews and Middlesex—Alex'r K. Sheppard, Geo. L Nicolson.
Mecklenburg—Mark Alexander, Jr.
Mercer—Geo. W. Pearis.
Monongalia—Dr. M. Dent.
Monrce—Nath'l Harrison.
Montgomery—James C. Taylor.
Morgan—Peter Dyche.
Nansemond—H. H. Kelly.
Nelson—Dr. L. N. Ligon.
Norfolk City—Geo. Blow.
Norfolk County—Tapley Portlock.
Northampton—Myers W. Fisher.
Page—Andrew Keysey.
Ohio—John T. Russell.
Patrick—Edward Tatem.
Pendleton—A. S. Norment.
Petersburg—Francis E. Rives.
Pittsylvania—Walter Coles, Jr.
Pleasants and Ritchie—H. C. Creel, L. A. Phelps.
Pocahontas—J. S. Bradford.
Preston—J. A. F. Martin.
Prince Edward, Prince George and Surry—Sam'l C. Anderson, Thomas H. Daniel, Dr. M. Q. Holt.
Princess Anne—E. H. Herbert.

Prince William—Chas E. Sinclair.
Pulaski—R. M. Craig.
Putnam—Dan'l B. Washington.
Randolph—Sam'l Crane.
Rappahannock—Rob't S. Vass.
Richmond City—Wm. F. Watson.
Richmond County and Westmoreland—Henry T. Garnett.
Roanoke—Wm. M. Cook.
Rockbridge—James B. Dorman.
Rockingham—E. A Shands.
Russell—George Cowan.
Scott—H. A. Morrison.
Shenandoah—Sam'l. C. Williams.
Smyth—Hiram A. Greaver.
Southampton—Francis Ridley.
Spotsylvania—Gabriel Johnson.
Taylor—J. T. Curry.
Tazewell—Wm. P. Cecil.
Upshur—Rich'd L. Brown.
Warren—Hanson Dorsey.
Washington—Isaac B. Durun.
Wayne—Jos. J. Mansfield.
Wetzel—Presley Martin.
Wood—John Spencer.
Wythe—Alex. Matthews.

On motion of Mr. Hughes, the following resolution was adopted :

Resolved, That this committee recommends that meetings of the party be called in each of the election districts of the counties, at the earliest practicable day, for the purpose of appointing vigilance committees for the election districts, and that each of such districts appoint two members of a general executive committee for the county, and that the electors for the counties be requested to aid in promoting the object of this resolution.

JOHN RUTHERFOORD, *Chairman.*

WM. F. RITCHIE, *Secr'y.*

At a subsequent meeting they adopted the following address:

To the People of Virginia:

Fellow citizens : The Democratic State Rights Republican party have presented to you their candidates for the Executive offices, which are to be filled by your election, on the fourth Thursday in May next. Those candidates have been selected by our usual organization, as faithful representatives of the principles of our party, and as men eminently qualified to perform all the duties of the high places for which they are proposed. Recognizing the vital importance of the result of the approaching elections to our party and to our country, the "State Democratic Executive Committee" make an earnest appeal for your co-operation in the contest which now engages the attention of the whole Union.

Our party had its origin in the earliest days of the present Confederacy. When the Constitution was first put in operation, two antagonistic parties struggled for ascendancy. One sought to confine the Federal Government within the strict and defined limits of the Constitution,—avoiding the exercise of all doubtful powers, and aiming only at those objects which the framers of the

Constitution had designated in unequivocal terms as legitimate to the Central Government. This party exacted an unhesitating homage to the wisdom of the august authors of that instrument, and sought to administer the government in rigid conformity with the written provisions of the Constitution. The other party sought, by a latitudinarian construction of the Constitution, to obtain in the actual administration of the Federal Government all the power which, in the judgment of those in authority, it might be expedient to exercise. This characteristic division has continued to separate the Democratic party from the old Federal party, and, since its overthrow, from the various parties that have been in opposition to the Democracy.

That the Democratic party is organized upon the true principles of the Constitution, is signally demonstrated by the fact, that it is the only party which has maintained a permanent existence coeval with our present Constitutional system. The history of our party is so fortunately identified with the history of our country, that the prosperity and glory of the one have been coincident with the success of the other. The fact that its leading measures are now in full operation, and have been sanctioned repeatedly by the approval of the country, and that no open organization now opposes them, stamps it as the constitutional party of the Union, and renders it unnecessary to set out her in detail its principles, already so familiar to the people of Virginia.

In the career of its history, the Democratic party has had to encounter the opposition organized in different forms, and bearing different designations. So far, it has overpowered all resistance, and annihilated the national organizations that have opposed it. The Whig party, which for some years past has combined the elements of antagonism to Democracy, has apparently succumbed. The opposition seems once more to be arraying itself in new forms and under new names. Taught by past experience, those who oppose the Democratic party dare not risk themselves any longer upon a fair comparison of principle and policy before an enlightened popular judgment. We have to meet, in the impending canvass, a party which avoids an open encounter, and withdraws from public observation its discussions of political topics and its deliberations upon public affairs. This new party artfully adapts its appeals for votaries to the national and religious prejudices of the country, while it proposes to retain, by the most rigid and imposing party discipline, those who may be enticed into its ranks. If it succeeds in the effort to obtain control over the Federal Government, it must use its powers for purposes not now disclosed—perhaps not contemplated by many of its adherents. It must have its measures upon the great subjects which are so frequently agitated in Congress—the Tariff, the Finances, the Public Lands, Internal Improvements and the Constitutional Rights of the slaveholders. It can have no measures of material importance relating to the avowed objects of its organization—the immigrant and Catholic population. If it goes into power, it goes with purposes unavowed and unknown on those great subjects concerning which its action may be of the last consequence, while it flatters the public prejudices respecting subjects upon which it can really accomplish little or nothing.

The Federal Government, with all its departments combined, can apply no effective remedy for the alleged evils incident to the residence of the immigrant population within our limits. The naturalization laws may be amended or repealed. But irrespective of those laws, the most valuable privileges may still be granted to the alien by the State Governments. The right of residence, the right to acquire and hold lands, and the right of suffrage, may all be bestowed upon the alien by the State authorities, without regard being had to the naturalization laws. The power to refuse residence to the immigrant population appropriately belongs to the State governments. The power of the Federal Government to expel any portion of the alien population, whose residence is permitted by the State Government, was indignantly repelled by the Republican party in 1798. The celebrated alien law provided for the expulsion of a portion of the resident aliens. Both Virginia and Kentucky denounced the law as an unconstitutional usurpation. In the address to the people of Virginia accompanying the resolutions of 1798, it is emphatically declared that "there is nothing in the Constitution distinguishing between the power of a State to permit the residence of natives and aliens. It is, therefore, a right originally possessed and never surrendered by the respective States, and which is rendered dear and valuable to Virginia, because it is assailed through the bosom of the Constitution, and because her peculiar situation renders the easy admission of artizans and laborers an interest of vast importance to her." The fourth Kentucky Resolution of 1798—drawn by Mr. Jefferson—asserts "that alien friends are under the jurisdiction and protection of the laws of the State wherein they are: that no power over them has been delegated to the United States, nor prohibited to the individual States, distinct from their power over citizens." Mr. Madison's Report of 1799 maintains similar positions. It is presumed that this exposition of the Constitutional powers of the State and Federal Governments, over this subject, will not be questioned in Virginia at this day. Each State has the exclusive right to determine for itself, to what extent the residence of alien immigrants in its limits shall be permitted. The Governments of the respective States alone have the right to refuse residence to such of the immigrant population as may be considered objectionable by them. While some of the advocates of a latitudinarian construction of the Federal authority contend that the power of the States over the admission of aliens is limited, in certain respects, by the power of the General Government to regulate commerce, the absolute power of the States to exclude alien paupers and convicts is universally conceded. The power to permit or refuse residence to objectionable aliens belonging thus appropriately to the States, the subject is beyond the control of the Federal Government, and affords no legitimate object for the organization of a national party.

The right to acquire and hold real estate, and the right of suffrage, are equally subject to State authority. The powers of the States over these subjects have been too often exercised and too generally admitted to need any discussion at this time. Probably all the States permit resident aliens to acquire and hold real estate prior to naturalization,—Virginia certainly does. Some of the States confer the right of suffrage upon aliens who have declared their intention to become citizens, while others require them to be fully naturalized before they are allowed to vote. The whole subject of suffrage is exclusively regulated by the State constitutions. It may be confined to native-born citizens, or it may be extended to all resident aliens, at the sole discretion of the State sovereignties. The naturalization laws affect the subject only so far as the State constitutions may direct. It is wholly impracticable for the Federal Government to control the right of suffrage through any laws which it would enact.

Those who seek to curtail the privileges enjoyed by the immigrant population can accomplish no essential object through the agency of the Federal Government. So long as the alien enjoys, under the State government, the right of residence, the right to acquire and hold property, and the right of suffrage, he can experience but little inconvenience from the want of the few additional privileges which full and formal citizenship would confer. The only appropriate theatre for the operations of a party, organized to effect the professed objects of Know-Nothingism, is to be found in the States where the immigrant population abounds, and where the alleged evils of foreignism may exist. Those evils are essentially local, and can be properly remedied only by the local authorities. They afford the appropriate subject for municipal and police regulations. Five-sixths of the foreign- born population of the United States are resident in the non-slaveholding States, and even there nearly one-half of it is accumulated in the cities. The whole of this population in the United States numbers

2,224,648. Of that number, only 43,531 are in the Southern States, with a native white population of 2,342,255, and 105,335 in the Southwestern States, with a native white population of 1,973,531. A considerable proportion of this class of our population in the slaveholding, as in the non-slaveholding States, are congregated in the cities. These facts strongly display how singularly local must be the alleged evils of foreignism. A full investigation, perhaps, might show that the real evils (if such there are) are confined to the cities, which, according to the census returns, contain nearly one half of all the foreign-born residents in the Union. The entire repeal of the naturalization laws would not materially diminish the number of that class of immigrants, who come here seeking employment for their labor, and accumulate in the cities. They come to make a living, not to acquire the right of suffrage—allured by no expectation of easy naturalization, but by the prospect of higher wages and more constant employment than they can find in the country which they leave. Of the foreign-born males over the age of twenty-one, in the city of Boston, the returns for 1845 and 1850, show that five-sixths were unnaturalized. It is fair to presume, that a similar proportion in the other cities have failed to avail themselves of the advantages of our present naturalization laws.

The other ostensible object of the Know Nothing organization is entirely beyond the reach of the Federal Government. It cannot touch Roman Catholicism by any Constitutional action. The folly of attempting to arrest the progress of a religious creed by persecutions and civil disabilities, has been so often demonstrated that it is surprising to see it revived in this age and country. A distinguished advocate of religious liberty declared, nearly a half century ago, that even in Great Britain, nearly all its opponents had been silenced—some had been taught sense, others inspired with shame, until none were left upon the field, except those who could neither learn nor blush. The principles of religious liberty are cherished in Virginia with peculiar affection. Our act for the establishment of religious freedom, asserts in imposing and authoritative language that "the proscribing any citizen as unworthy the public confidence, by laying upon him an incapacity of being called to offices of trust and emolument, unless he profess, or renounce this or that religious opinion, is depriving him injuriously of those privileges and advantages to which in common with his fellow citizens he has a natural right; that it tends only to corrupt the principles of that religion it is meant to encourage, by bribing, with a monopoly of worldly honors and emoluments, those who will externally profess and conform to it, that though, indeed, those are criminal who do not withstand such temptation, yet neither are those innocent who lay the bait in their way." In the struggle which terminated in the complete emancipation of religion in this State, the dissenting Protestant sects, under the energetic lead of the Baptists, bore a conspicuous part. The act for the establishment of Religious Freedom, was eminently a Protestant achievement, and Protestantism in Virginia rudely despoils itself of the fairest ornament with which it is decorated by history, when it violates the letter or the spirit of that celebrated law. The men who now seek to renew the dogmas of religious intolerance, pay an appropriate homage to the virtue and intelligence of this country, when they conceal themselves from public observation. Those who are afraid to meet the Roman Catholic arguments in the field of fair discussion, may well be alarmed at its anticipated progress; but its more intelligent opponents will regard with composure what they consider its errors, so long as reason is left free to combat them. For every Roman Catholic Priest in the United States, there are some 25 Protestant preachers; for every Catholic altar, there are 30 Protestant pulpits. Scarcely one-twentieth part of the population of the Union is attached to the Roman Catholic religion. If Protestantism is not safe with these heavy odds in its favor, its ascendancy will not be maintained by persecutions and civil disabilities imposed upon its opponents. Know Nothingism may do more to advance the Catholic cause than all its Priesthood, and place Catholicism on the right side and Protestantism on the wrong side of the great question of Religious Liberty, by a course so illiberal and unwarrantable. This is attempted to be justified by an absurd exaggeration of the political influence of Catholicism in this country. Mr. Chandler, of Pennsylvania, addressing the House of Representatives a few weeks since, declared that he knew of but one Catholic besides himself, who was a member of that House of Congress. We may, then, at least pronounce the Legislative Department to be free from Catholic control. There seems to be no occasion to organize a new party to protect that branch of the Federal Government, and the Catholic influence is equally feeble in the Executive and Judicial departments.

What then can Know Nothingism accomplish upon the subjects which it undertakes to agitate? It may expel from the Executive department a few naturalized citizens who are incumbents of office,—but as nine-tenths of the Federal offices are said to be already filled by native citizens, that can scarcely be an object worth the attention of a national party. Those who originated and expect to control this organization, must have other and undivulged objects in view. Temporary prejudice and excitement on the subjects of Foreignism and Catholicism may serve to place them in power. How will they use power when so acquired? We may well recall the eloquent warning of a great English statesman, and beware of "so trying a thing as new power in new persons, of whose principles, tempers and dispositions we have little or no experience, and in situations where those who appear most stirring on the scene may not be the real movers." What is this new party expected to do upon those great subjects of practical interest to which we have before referred? The elections in which they have already triumphed afford us sufficient data to infer their policy upon the most important of these subjects—SLAVERY.

Know Nothingism has had its origin and growth in those quarters of the Union where Abolitionism is most powerful. At the very instant that Know Nothingism has swept over the non-slaveholding States, Abolitionism has acquired an ascendency to which it never before aspired. Every election in which Northern Know Nothingism has triumphed, has enured to the benefit of Abolitionism. Every individual whom the Northern Know Nothings have elected to either branch of the Federal Legislature, is committed to the most violent views of the Abolitionists. They have prostrated, wherever they had the power to do so, the same men whom the Abolitionists wished to prostrate. They have sustained every man whom the Abolitionists wished to save. Know Nothingism, in the ascendant throughout the non-slaveholding States, does not elevate into power a single friend to the South. No solitary exception breaks the gloomy uniformity of the scene. Everywhere they are doing the work which Abolitionism has been unsuccessfully attempting for years. And yet we are required to believe that they were not organized to perform this part, but only to do those other things which, as we have endeavoured to show, no such party can effect.

It must be apparent to every intelligent observer that the anti-slavery sentiment now domineers over the public mind in the non-slaveholding States. In all the recent elections in that quarter of the Union, the ordinary political issues have been made subordinate to the slavery subject. Is it not surprising that Southern men should, at such a moment, be expected to waive this issue, and elevate a new party into power, without even inquiring their purposes upon this subject? Just at the time when the Northern States are uniting in an assault upon the vital interests of the South, ought we to abandon the vigilant care of our own affairs, in a gratuitous effort to purge Northern society of a disease which may afflict them, but does not disturb us? We appeal to Southern men, without distinction of party, to ponder the consequences before they co-operate with this organization. The secrecy with which its proceedings are conducted, afford ample ground for caution and suspicion. A party which conceals all its operations and designs from the public, may conceal some of its ultimate purposes from that portion of its own votaries to whom a premature disclosure might be hazardous. The same principle of political ethics, which justifies deception upon those outside the order, might excuse partial concealment from those within. When you enter this order, you assent to the propriety of concealment as an agency in partisan contests. How can you complain when it is practiced upon yourselves by your own confederates? Know Nothingism does not pretend to disclose to its Southern adherents its designs upon any of the questions concerned which Federal Legislation can really affect Southern interests. Will you persist in arming this party with all the powers of the Federal Government, without enquiring and approving its purposes upon those questions, simply because you may happen to agree with its views upon two subjects of no practical importance to you, and concerning neither of which can any material action be had by the Federal Government? The fact, that it discloses to you its views upon those subjects, while it carefully conceals them upon more vital topics, ought, of itself, to awaken your apprehensions. While it attempts to delude you with the fiction that Opposition to Foreignism and Catholicism is an issue which overrides all others, it is actively and rapidly filling the halls of Congress with men pledged to measures of fearful import to your interests.

If the designs of Know Nothingism were even free from censure, it should still be repelled from your midst. In giving countenance to a secret political organization, you are introducing an instrument which may be applied to the most dangerous purposes. Before you bring the wooden horse within our gates, be sure that no armed enemy is concealed in the fatal structure. If any party in our midst ever assails the institution of slavery, its first approaches will be cloaked in a secrecy similar to that which now conceals Know Nothingism. The World's Convention of Abolitionists, at London, recommended the formation of anti-slavery societies in the Southern States. Popular sentiment opposes a formidable and unsuperable barrier to the public execution of this plan. But when the operations of parties have become secret, how soon may we not expect such an organization as the World's Convention has advised? We respectfully and earnestly beg you to consider whether any good which this organization may be expected to effect can compensate for the least of the evils that may follow in its train.

What have we to expect from the action of this party upon those other subjects which the Democratic party has been accustomed to regard as so important in the administration of the Federal Government? After the arduous contests which we have maintained for so many years—just as the Democratic policy is fully established, and the country is gladdening under its influence—shall we blindly elevate into power a party which may revolutionize the whole system? However carefully they may conceal their political views, it cannot be denied that this party is principally composed of the same materials which, combined under a different name, have been heretofore in opposition to the Democratic party. The same indiscriminate hostility to naturalized citizens that now distinguishes Know-Nothingism, characterized the Federal party in the times of John Adams and of the Hartford Convention. The Democracy, under the lead of Jefferson and of Madison, have successfully encountered it heretofore, and are not afraid to meet it again. The annihilation of the Democratic party in the Union is a leading object of the Know Nothing organization. Flushed with its Northern triumphs, it comes here upon Virginia soil to encounter a party that wears the insignia of its victories through half a century, and that has never known defeat. Whenever disaster has overwhelmed the Democracy of the Union, they have always looked to the Party in Virginia to retrieve the fortunes of the day. Once more we are called to perform that duty. If we arrest the progress of this new enemy, and lift the trailing banner of our party, we rally the Democracy of the confederacy for a successful struggle in the Presidential contest of 1856. If we are defeated in Virginia, we disappoint the hopes of the best friends of the Constitution. We are looked to with hope or with fear by the whole confederacy. Let the Democracy of Virginia be equal to the emergency.

JOHN RUTHERFOORD, *Chairman.*

VARIOUS ARGUMENTS AND DOGMAS OF KNOW NOTHINGISM EXAMINED.

We append here sundry articles from the Richmond Examiner touching sundry features of Know Nothingism.

THE KNOW NOTHINGS' OATHS GROSSLY VIOLATE THE CONSTITUTION.—The following schedule contrasts the *nationality* of which the Constitutions of Virginia and of the Union is refulgent in every line and letter, with the explosive, combustible, revolutionary, fanatical and bigoted stuff, with which the Know Nothing ritual is saturated in every section and article.

Know Nothing Constitution.

Art. III. "The object of this organization shall be to resist the insiduous policy of the Church of Rome, and other foreign influences against the institutions of the country, *by placing in all offices in the gift of the people, or by appointment, none but native born* PROTESTANT *citizens.*"

Constitution of the United States.

Art. VI. No religious test shall ever be required as a qualification for *any* office of public trust under this government.

Know Nothing oath.

"You furthermore promise and declare that you will not vote nor give your influence for any man for any office in the gift of the people, unless he be an American born citizen, in favor of Americans ruling America, NOR IF HE BE A ROMAN CATHOLIC."

Amendments to the Constitution of the United States.

Art. I. Congress shall make no law respecting an establishment of *religion*, or the *free exercise thereof;* or abridging the *freedom of speech* or of the press; or the right of the people peaceably to assemble, and to petition the government for a redress of grievances.

Again: "You solemnly and sincerely swear, that if it may be legally, you will, when elected to any office, remove all foreigners and ROMAN CATHOLICS FROM OFFICE; and that YOU WILL IN NO CASE APPOINT SUCH TO OFFICE."

Constitution of Virginia.

Sec. XV. "No man shall be compelled to frequent or support any religious worship, place or ministry whatever; nor shall any man be enforced or restrained, molested or burthened in his body or goods, *or otherwise suffer*, on account of his religious opinion or belief; but all men shall be free to profess, and by argument to maintain, their opinions in matters of religion, AND THE SAME SHALL IN NO WISE AFFECT, DIMINISH OR ENLARGE THEIR CIVIL CAPACITIES."

There could not be a more palpable conflict than that which is here exhibited between the Covenant of nationality and Union, handed down to us by our fathers, and its clandestine assailant. The wonder is, that among an intelligent and patriotic people, so dark and ominous a conspiracy could have acquired the strength it has attained in the land; but what HUDIBRAS said in the bitterness of his cynicism must be acknowledged to be true in the extent to which it applies to the proselytes of this new monstrosity:—

The world is naturally averse,
To all the good it sees and hears;
But swallows nonsense and lies,
With greediness and gluttony.

The Constitution of our country guarantees to every man in the land the right to profess and propagate his creed, provided only that he is a law-abiding citizen. This is as it should be. That great charter of our liberty never contemplated any religious test to constitute a man a suitable person to hold an office under its purview. It is vain to say that you only exercise your rights as freemen to cast your votes for whom you please. In pledging yourselves to exclude all persons from political offices who hold the Romish faith, you do virtually require a religious test. You require at least that your candidate shall be a Protestant. The question is not, if two persons are equally qualified to fill an office, the one a Romanist, the other a Protestant, which of the two you shall choose; but your principles force you to choose a man wholly unfit to fill the place in opposition to a man qualified in every respect to fill it, save that he is a Romanist. You would proscribe a Taney, or a Gaston, for his faith, and in his place elect a man in no respect qualified to discharge the duties of the office. Now if this is not proscribing a man for his religious opinions, the writer is at a loss to know what it is. Leave this whole matter where the Constitution of the country leaves it. Judge each man by himself, and decide upon his own individual merits, but do not proscribe him for his faith. You cannot coerce a man to your opinion. He may adopt your shibboleth for the sake of gain, but you have only made a hypocrite instead of a proselyte.

The purity of religion no less than the welfare of the country would be promoted, by leaving the question of Romanism where our Constitution leaves it. Without the shadow of a doubt, pure religion would be advanced in the same way. An effort to exclude all Romanists from participating in the administration of our government, would only make them combine to accomplish more effectually their object, whereas if left to the silent operation of other influences they would cast their votes as citizens, and not as persecuted religionists. There will always be found men who will bid for their suffrages. In a representative form of government the power of numbers must be felt, and if Romanists cannot elect a man who professes their faith, they will cast their suffrages for one who most nearly reflects their peculiar views, or will do their bidding. In this way a secret Romanist will be elected, instead of an open. Which of the two is preferable? Is it not better to have an open than a secret foe? The truth is, this whole agitation, instead of weakening, will strengthen this sect. It will elevate an unimportant political element, by the power of combination, into one important, if not controlling.

The test of *religious belief* is arbitrary, unjust and oppressive. It is contrary to the Constitution, which expressly forbids that "any *religious test* shall *ever* be required as a qualification to any office of public trust under this government." Every Know Nothing who takes an oath bidding him to try candidates by this *test*, takes an oath against the Constitution of the Union. We do not charge them with intentional culpability in this act, which we know they must commit in thoughtlessness and without due examination, but we warn them against persisting in an oath in direct antagonism to the Constitution of their country.

There are a great many honest men who see the dilemma in which their Know Nothingism places them as good citizens, and yet are deterred from leaving the Order from consciencious scruples in regard to this oath taken in their initiation. An oath to violate one's conscience ought not to be obeyed. The passage from ST. MARK, reciting the occurrence between Herod and the daughter of Herodias, illustrates the fatal consequences of a vicious vow.

"For Herod himself had sent forth and laid hold upon John, and bound him in prison for Herodias' sake, his brother Philip's wife; for he had married her.

For John had said unto Herod: It is not lawful for thee to have thy brother's wife.

Therefore, Herodias had a quarrel against him, and would have killed him, but she could not.

For Herod feared John, knowing that he was a just man and an holy, and observed him; and when he heard him, he did many things, and heard him gladly.

And when a convenient day was come, that Herod on his birth-day, made a supper to his lords, high captains, and chief estates of Galilee;

And when the daughter of the said Herodias came in, and danced, and pleased Herod and them that sat with him, the King said unto the damsel, ask of me whatsoever thou wilt, and I will give it thee.

And he swore unto her, whatever thou shalt ask of me, I will give it thee, even unto half of my kingdom.

And she went forth, and said unto her mother, what shall I ask? and she said the head of John the Baptist.

And she came in straightway with haste unto the King, and asked, saying, I wish that thou give me, by and by, in a charger, the head of John the Baptist.

And the King was exceedingly sorry; yet *for his oath's sake*, and for their sakes which sat with him, he would not reject her."

THE FACTS OF THE CENSUS.—We do not know anything in the course of the history of the country more humiliating than the reflection that in our land, consecrated to equal rights, and boasting its popular intelligence, an unmanly crusade has been gotten up with the avowed purpose of disfranchising a fragment of our people, constituting only twelve and a half per cent. of the whole population, and of persecuting a sect of Christians numbering less than one in one hundred of the Church of Jesus Christ, out of that highest and most sacred of all the liberties for which our fathers fought and shed their blood—the LIBERTY OF CONSCIENCE.

We desire to call the attention of the honest, honorable and magnanimous people of Virginia to the facts of this humiliating subject, as shown by the Census.

1. The foreigners in Virginia number but two and a half in a hundred of her white population; and the foreigners in the United States but twelve and a half in a hundred of the free population of the Union.

2. Except Ireland—which the noble old Whig, HENRY CLAY, once regretted that some great convulsion of nature had not transplated from the side of England to the side of generous Kentucky—and except England, no single State of Europe has given nativity to as many of the residents of Virginia as the Abolition State of Massachusetts.

3. The aggregate number of foreigners in the Southern slave States to the aggregate free population, is less than *two* in a hundred; showing that the Know Nothing movement is of Northern origin, and an ism that the South stands in no need of—saying nothing of the pusillanimity of a popular crusade against a handful of strangers, when the odds are as one hundred against two!

4. The number of Catholic Churches in Virginia is but 17 in an aggregate of 2,386, and these 17 small and thinly attended, being capable of accommodating but 7,930 persons, while the Protestant Churches accommodate 850,156!

5. This is a glaring fact, that there are 87,383 free natives in Virginia unable to read and write; of whom 30,244 (or twice the whole number of male foreigners now in Virginia—15,606) are native white males. If the republican principle of *equal rights* should be violated in order to proscribe 15,606 foreign males, many of them educated and distinguished for learning, talents, and patriotism, it would follow that the principle should be violated also in respect to twice that number of native males unable to read and write.

NATIVITIES.

1. *Virginia* (*whites.*)	*Population.*	*Ratio.*
Born in the State,	813,811	90.95
Born out of the State, but in the United States,	57,582	6.44
Born in foreign countries,	22,953	2.56
Nativities unknown,	454	.05
	894,800	100.
2. *Other States and Territories* (*whites.*)		
Born in the States and Territories,	17,279,829	88.37
Born in foreign countries,	2,240,581	11.46
Nativities unknown,	32,958	.17
	19,553,068	100.

1. *Virginia.*	*Male.*	*Female.*
Born in the State,	404,331	409,480
Born out of the State, but in the United States,	31,084	26,498
Born in foreign countries,	15,606	7,347
Natives unknown,	279	175
2. *Other States and Territories.*		
Born in States and Territories,	8,765,347	8,514,482
Born in foreign countries,	1,239,464	1,001,117
Nativities unknown,	21,591	11,067

The annexed table shows the proportion of native to foreign-born in different sections of the United States, (white and free colored.) The first column represents the native, including unknown; the second, foreign-born; and third, proportion of foreign to native, per cent.:

Eastern,	2,421,867	306,249	12.65
Middle,	5,447,733	1,080,674	19.84
Southern,	2,342,255	43,530	1.86
South Western,	1,973,531	105,335	5.34
N. West and Ter.	5,557,529	708,860	12.75
	17,742,915	2,244,648	12.65

NUMBER OF CHURCHES IN VIRGINIA.

Baptist, 650; Christian, 16; Episcopal, 173; Free, 108; Friends, 15; Germ. Ref., 9; Jewish, 1; Lutheran, 50; Mennonite, 6; Methodist, 1025; Moravian, 8; Presbyterian, 241; *Roman Catholic*, 17; Swedenborgen, 1; Tunker, 8; Universalist, 1; minor sects, 5. Total, 2,386.

The total value of Church Property in Virginia is $2,860,876; of which the Methodists possess $825,000; Baptists, $688,818; Episcopal, $529,450; Presbyterian, $571,165; and Roman Catholics, $126,100.

The total number of Churches in the States and Territories is 38,183, of which 13,338 are Methodist; 9,360 Baptist; 4,863 Presbyterian; 1,461 Episcopalian; and 1,227 Roman Catholic.

The total "Church Accommodations" in Virginia is 858,086; of which 323,708 is Methodist; 257,589 Baptist; Presbyterian, 104,125; Episcopal, 80,684; and Roman Catholic, 7,930.

The number of pupils in the State, attending school, was in 1850, 109,775, of whom 211 were foreign born—ninety-two hundredths of one per cent. of the gross foreign population.

The number of persons—white and free colored—over twenty-one years of age, who were unable to read and write, was as follows: Native, 87,383; Foreign, 1,138; native white males, 30,244; native white females, 46,761. Total, 88,520.

The per cent. of native white and free colored illiterate to total native and free colored population in Virginia is 9.44; the per cent. of foreign do. to foreign do. do. is only half that, or 4.95!

"FOREIGNERS RULE AMERICA."—We find the following table going the rounds of the Whig and Know Nothing papers of Virginia:

Number of foreigners and Americans now holding office under the United States Government at Washington:

Washington, D. C.	*Amer.*	*For.*
State Department,	12	26
Treasury Department,	139	278
Department of the Interior,	338	500
Officers and agents in service of House of Representatives,	10	40
Post Office Department,	11	80
	510	914
Ministers and Consuls,	151	106
Coast Survey,	15	30
United States Mint,	25	12
Light house Board Inspectors and Keepers,	31	392
U. States Revenue and Marine Service,	35	30
	767	1484

The lists of Custom House officers in the different States show—Americans, 215; Foreigners, 1837.

It is printed conspicuously at the head of their leading editorial columns, and must be regarded, therefore, as *the platform of principles* of the Fusionists in the present canvass. It discloses the leading passion that actuates the OUTS, showing that their eyes are intently set upon office, and that their minds are very earnestly exercised with the statistics of office. We doubt not the mass of them believe the truth of the statement, and that some wag of the Order, seeing the vast numbers in their ranks who act upon the principles of the loaves and fishes, has played a trump card in concocting this statement, and in multiplying the real number of foreigners holding office in the land by ten, fifty, or a hundred, in order to whet the appetite of the outs, and prove to their anxious office seeking minds, that there will be vacancies for all and some to spare.

Just for the sake of truth, we shall pick this MUNCHAUSEN bladder of the Fusionists with a bodkin from the Washington *Union*, in the shape of the following *official document.*

POST OFFICE DEPARTMENT.

We begin with the appointment in the Post Office Department:

Clerks,	84
Assistant Postmasters General,	3
Messenger,	1
Assistant Messengers,	2
Watchmen,	3
Laborers,	7
Whole number,	100

Of these, 88 are of American birth, and 12 of foreign birth.

The following are the particulars to be observed:

1. John Marron, Third Assistant Postmaster General, appointed May 17th, 1830; was born in Ireland, came here when eight months old.
2. John Agg, clerk, appointed June 8th, 1851; born in England, resided here for more than forty years.
3. N. Holten, clerk, appointed June 3, 1834; born in Switzerland, resided here 27 years.
4. J. Lawrenson, clerk, appointed April 7, 1834; born in England, came here 3 months old, now fifty years in this country.
5. G. A. Schwarzman, clerk, appointed June, 1848; born in Germany, came to this country 16 years of age, served 10 years in the American army.
6. E. Donelly, clerk, appointed July 1, 1853; born in Ireland, came to this country when 8 years of age, now 32 years in the country.
7. J. R. Condon, clerk, appointed July 1, 1853; born in Ireland, came here about 21 years of age, now 40 years old.
8. J. E. McMahon, clerk, appointed May 2, 1853; born in Ireland, came here an infant, now 22 years of age.
9. James McCorrick, clerk, appointed July 2, 1853; born in Ireland, came here young, now 45 years old.
10. C. McDonnel, messenger, appointed August 10, 1853; born in Ireland, resident in the country 35 years.
11. T. Molchon, watchman, appointed May 22, 1853; born in Ireland, resident in this country many years.
12. James Orr, clerk, appointed August, 1854; born in Ireland, resided here 14 years, served two and a half years in the Mexican war, and was badly wounded.

DEPARTMENT OF THE INTERIOR.

The Interior Department shows the following result:

	American.	Foreign.
Interior Department proper, - -	16	4
Land Office, - - -	112	12

Patent Office, - - -	55	4
Indian Bureau, - - -	17	2
Pension Office, - - -	52	5
Commissioners of Public Buildings, and watchmen, keepers of bridges, &c., under his control, -	21	6
Penitentiary, - - -	13	2
Total,	286	35

THE DEPARTMENT OF STATE.

The following is from the Department of State. It will be observed that the proportion of foreigners holding office under this department is somewhat greater than usual; and the reason obvious: a number of the consulates do not pay a living compensation. American citizens cannot and will not accept of such appointments, and they are given to foreigners simply because no body else will take them:

DEPARTMENT OF STATE, August 28, 1854.

The following is a statement respecting all persons now employed either in or under the supervision of the Department of State:

I.—*Employed Abroad.*

1. Ministers, commissioners, secretaries of legation, and agents connected with them—whole number, 42.

Of these, 4 were born abroad, 3 of whom have been naturalized, and 1, the United States despatch agent in London, has not.

2. Consuls and commercial agents—whole number, 220.

Of these, 49 were born abroad, of whom 21 have been naturalized, and 1 has not; and 1 was born under the flag of the United States; the rest, or 26, may have been naturalized, but of this the department has no evidence.

II.—*Employed in the United States, or their Territories, as Governors, or Secretaries of Territories and dispatch agents—whole number,* 16.

Of whom 13 were born in the United States. The rest, 2 of whom are dispatch agents, were probably so born; but of this the department has no direct evidence.

III.—*Employed in this department—whole number,* 40.

Of these, 6 were born abroad; one of whom came to the United States in his third year, and is of American parents, who at the time of his birth, were temporarily residing abroad; 4 of the others so born have been naturalized, and 1 soon will be:

Clerks.—William Hunter, Rhode Island; A. French, New York; Frs. Markoe, St. Croix, of American parents; A. H. Derrick, Pennsylvania; James S. Mackie, Ohio; J. P. Polk, Delaware; R. S. Chilton, New Jersey; H. D. J. Pratt, Massachusetts; G. J. Abbot, New Hampshire; R. S. Chew, Virginia; Wm. C. Reddal, Virginia; Charles V. Gordon, Virginia; Edmund Flagg, Maine; George Chipman, George Hill, Connecticut; George Bartle, Virginia; L. F. Tesistro, Ireland; Edward Stubbs, Ireland; H. D. Johnson, Massachusetts; R. S. Gillett, New York; C. G. Baylor, Kentucky.

Messenger.—Calvin Ames, Massachusetts.

Packer.—Wm. P. Faherty, Maryland.

Watchmen.—Wm. H. Prentiss, District of Columbia; James Donaldson, District of Columbia; R. Harrison, England; A. Best, Germany.

Laborers.—James S. Martin, Maryland; William Lucus, District of Columbia; E. W. Hansell, Pennsylvania; W. A. Scott, Pennsylvania; Thomas Thomas, Virginia; James Williamson, Virginia; Charles H. Brown, Maryland; John McQuire, Ireland.

Recapitulation.

21 clerks—18 native born; 1 born of American parents, transiently abroad; 2 foreign born. 1 messenger—native born. 1 packer—native born.

2 watchmen—native born; 2 watchmen—foreign born.

7 laborers—native born; 1 laborer—foreign born.

35 in all—30 of whom are native citizens; 5 of whom are foreign.

TREASURY DEPARTMENT.

In the office of the secretary of the Treasury and bureaus, including the offices of the assistant treasurers and mints, there are 430 Americans, 26 foreigners, and 3 not known.

Revenue cutter service—Americans, 65.

Light-house keepers—Americans, 238; foreigners 32; not known, 132.

Customs—Americans, 1,845; foreigners, 227; not known, 20.

Total number of persons employed under the State Treasury, Post Office and Interior Departments, is as follows:

Americans,	3,346
Foreigners,	430
Not known,	330
Whole number of employed,	4,106

In the House of Representatives on the first of October, 1853, there were fifty-four persons employed—all of whom, except one, were Americans.

The statement of the Fusionists is, therefore, shown to be the reverse of truth in every particular item covered by this document from the *Union;* and the inference is, of course, irresistible, that it is so in all its items:—*Falsum in uno falsum in omnibus.* It asserts the foreigners employed in the several departments to be two to one over natives; while the fact is there are seven to one natives over foreigners. It claims that there are nine to one foreigners over natives in the Custom Houses; while the fact is, that there are nine to one natives over foreigners.

For the sake of contrast, we give below the Munchausen statement on the left hand and the official statement on the right. It is amusing.

Look here, upon this picture, and on this:

	Munchausen Statement.		Official statement.	
	Native.	*For.*	*Native.*	*For.*
State Department,	12	26	30	5
Treasury Department,	139	278	430	26
Dep. of Interior,	338	500	286	35
House of Representatives,	10	40	53	1
Post Office Department,	11	80	88	12
Total Munchausen,	510	914	Total true, 887	79
Ministers and Consuls,	151	106	208	54
Light-house keepers,	31	392	238	32
Custom House officers,	216	1837	1845	227

THE ABSURDITY OF FEARING THE CATHOLICS.—It is the characteristic of all one-ideaisms, that they are sure to make fanatics of their advocates; whatever degree of intelligence and elevation of mind and feeling they always before have possessed. We are sure that if there was a broad and substantial foundation of merit and patriotism in the Know Nothing movement, its intelligent members would scorn to appeal to religious bigotry and prejudice for that popular sympathy which the cause would command without such unworthy recourse. Out of about *one million and a half* of human beings in Virginia, there is but the little handful of 7,930—*one half of one per cent. of the whole*—who profess and worship according to the Catholic faith. What must be said of a party which dares not trust its cause to reason and argument in such a State as Virginia; but, to carry its point, is obliged to appeal to the religious feelings, prejudices and jealousy of *fourteen hundred thousand* Protestants against *eight thousand* Catholics, under the cowardly, mean, malignant and false pretence that such a majority is in danger of subjugation from such a handful of proscribed people. If there be real and imminent danger of the sort, where have been the sentinels that are just raising this sudden alarm, for the last ten, or twenty, or fifty years gone by? It has only been within a twelve month that the new party have monopolized to itself all the Protestantism and genuine Americanism of the country, and raised, sudden as a fire-bell at night, the alarm against the wolf—the Pope—the poor Italian Prince PIO NINO. Either the leaders have been long very neglectful of duty and lukewarm in patriotism, or they talk gammon, to gull the ignorant million and alarm the amiable but weak and easily terrified spinsters of the country, when they cry out against the temporal power of the Pope.

Wm. Pitt, while Prime Minister of England, contemplating an act of justice to the Catholics, solemnly proposed a set of interrogatories to several of the most celebrated Catholic Theological Universities in Europe. The following questions were proposed: *First.* Has the Pope, or have the Cardinals, or any body of men, or has any individual of the Church of Rome, *any civil authority*, power, jurisdiction or pre-eminence whatever within the realm of England. *Second.* Can the Pope, or Cardinals, or any body of men, or any individual of the Church of Rome, absolve or dispense his Majesty's subjects from their oath of allegiance, upon any pretence whatever? *Third.* Is there any principle in the tenets of the Catholic faith, by which Catholics are justified in not keeping faith with Heretics, or other persons differing from them in religious opinions, in *any transactions*, either of a public or private nature? To these questions the Universities of Paris, Louvain, Alcala, Salamanca and Valadolid, after expressing their astonishment that it could be thought necessary at the close of the 18th century, and in a country so enlightened as England, to propose such enquiries, severally and unanimonsly answered: 1st. That the Pope, or Cardinals, or any body of men, or any individual of the Church of Rome, has not and have not any civil authority, power, jurisdiction or pre-eminence whatever, within the realm of England. 2dly. That the Pope, or Cardinals, or any body of men, or any individual of the Church of Rome, cannot absolve or dispense his Majesty's subjects from their oath of allegiance upon any pretext whatsoever. And, 3dly. That there is no principle in the tenets of the Catholic Faith, by which Catholics are justified in not keeping faith with Heretics, or other persons differing from them in religious opinions, in transactions either of a public or a private nature. The Pope himself was written to upon the same question, and most solemnly announced that his See asserted no such claim. Surely this is better testimony than the self-contradictory declaration of a Dublin Catholic editor.

We do not rely, however, in a matter of this sort, upon documentary evidence, or newspaper asseveration. We take the ground that the people are themselves sufficient to assert and maintain their independence of Popes of all sorts; and that they are in no danger of being deposed from the sovereignty with which their Maker and their Fathers endowed them in these States. Three thousand and fifty Protestant clergy will in vain hurl their anathemas against them from Yankee pulpits, and one Dublin editor may impotently proclaim the Pope's authority over their temporal concerns, but while they have the right to manage their own affairs, spite of Popes and of secret clubs, they will always be ready and able to maintain and support that sovereignty. It is only an insult to the intelligence, the manliness and the Christian sentiment of the Virginia people to maintain the possibility of a priestcraft domination over them from any quarter or of any sort.

But what are the historical evidences of the truth of this charge, that Catholics are less attached to civil governments entitled to their allegiance, than other denominations? Surely the Catholic subjects of the British crown have had cause of offence against that government in its persecution of Catholic Ireland. Surely the only Catholic province of that government, on this continent, might have been excused, while these persecutions of their Catholic brethren, in Ireland, were going on, for seeking annexation to the United States. Surely the French Catholics of Canada have had incentives of animosity sufficient to shake their allegiance to the British Government in its numberless and bitter wars against Catholic France. Yet what is the present political *status* of Catholic, French, colonial Canada? Hear how Lord Nugent refutes this idea of a *half* allegiance on the part of Catholics:

"Your other colonies revolted; they called on a Catholic power to support them, and they achieved their independence. Catholic Canada, with what Lord Liverpool would call her half-alliance, *alone* stood by you. She fought by your side against the interference of Catholic France. To reward and encourage her loyalty, you endowed in Canada bishops to say mass, and to ordain others to say mass, whom, at that very time, your laws would have hanged for saying mass in England; and Canada is still yours in spite of Catholic France, in spite of her spiritual obedience to the Pope, in spite of Lord Liverpool's arguments, and in spite of the independence of all the States that surround her. This is the only trial you have made. Where you allow to the Roman Catholics their religion undisturbed, it has proved itself to be compatible with the most faithful allegiance. It is only where you have placed allegiance and religion before them as a dilemma, that they have preferred (as who will say that they ought not?) their religion to their allegiance. How, then, stands the imputation? Disproved by history, disproved in all States, where both religions co-exist, and in both hemispheres, and asserted in an exposition by Lord Liverpool, solemnly and repeatedly abjured by all Catholics, of the discipline of their church."—*Lord Nugent's Letter to Rev. Sir George Lee, Bart.*

Men might idly dispute till doomsday over the nice question in political casuistry of the extent of the Papal claim of temporal power outside of Rome. But here are facts which illustrate how devoted Catholics may be and are in the habit of showing themselves in the *practical* matter of allegiance. Yet it is due to candor to admit that there *are* historical instances in which Catholics have refused to obey the calls of the British government. The Irish Catholic Parliament refused to furnish taxes to support the war against the American colonies in their struggle for freedom. Then, too, there is this notable passage in BOTTA, pp. 236-'7:

"General Carleton, finding the Canadians so decided in their opposition, had recourse to the authority of religion. He therefore solicited Brand, the Bishop of Quebec, to publish a mandament, to be read from the pulpit, by the curates, in time of divine service. He desired the prelate should exhort the people to take arms, and second the soldiers of the king, in their enterprises against the colonies. *But the bishop by a memorable example of piety and religious moderation, refused to lend his ministry in this work;* saying that such conduct would be too unworthy the character of the pastor, and *too contrary to the canons of the Roman church.* However, as in all professions, there are individuals who prefer their interest to their duty, and the useful to the honest, a few ecclesiastics employed themselves with great zeal in this affair; but all their efforts were in vain: the Canadians (Catholics) persisted in their principles of neutrality. The nobility, so well treated in the act of Quebec, felt obligated in gratitude to promote in this occurrence the views of the government, and very strenuously exerted themselves with that intention, but without any better success."

It is a well known fact that when Lord HOWE, the first British commander of the forces designated at the breaking out of the American war for the invasion of this country, was ordered by the war department to prepare for embarkation, he wrote that he could not trust the Irish Catholic soldiers of his army, as all their sympathies were with America; and the British government was forced to buy Protestant Hessians at the rate of sixpence a head from the Prince of Hesse Cassel. And the emissaries dispatched to Germany wrote more than once to Lord NORTH complaining bitterly of the German Catholics interfering with the enlistment of soldiers for America.

There are facts, however, still later, and, if possible, still stronger than these.

Catholic Louisiana fought full as bravely and effectually as Know Nothing Massachusetts against Catholic Mexico in the war of 1846-'47. Louisiana furnished seven regiments and 7,041 troops to fight against her brethren of the Catholic faith in that war of races and religions; altho' Know Nothing Massachusetts, in the excess of her zeal against the Pope and his people, furnished but one regiment of 930 men to smite the Mexican priests; and furnished that number only by dint of most strenuous exertions on the part of the patriotic Democrats in her borders. If you ask which three States furnished the largest number of troops in that foreign war against a Catholic nation and a Catholic race, the archives of the country will tell you that they were the Catholic States of Louisiana, Missouri and Texas. These furnished respectively 7,041, 6,441 and 6,955 men, or an aggregate equal to the total number supplied by all the other States in the Union! Besides, it is notorious that the regular army of the United States was made up during that war so exclusively of Irish, (Catholics) that it was difficult to find natives enough for the non-commissioned officers.

Surely the generous people of Virginia will consider the evidence of the muster rolls of the country a better tablet of Catholic patriotism, under all temptations of religious prejudice and bigotry, than the newspaper columns of oath-bound editors. Let those who, for political purposes, are seeking to excite the hatred of the magnanimous Virginia voters against that patriotic people, read these facts of history, and blush for their lack of generosity.

The following articles from the Enquirer discussed other branches of the subject in a most able and conclusive manner.

KNOW-NOTHINGISM AND CATHOLICISM.

Without any very penetrating research or profound philosophy, a person may discover that Know-Nothingism rests upon the vicious principles and practices the very abominations with which the Catholic Church is reproached by its enemies.

It is true both in a logical and historical sense, that Protestantism was a revolt against the moral despotism of the Catholic hierarchy. The church of Rome, at first simple in its ritual, pure in its faith, and spiritual in its aspirations, in time decorated itself with barbaric pomp of ceremonial, and got corrupted by the worldly passion of political ambition. The ignorance, the debasement and the disorders of the Middle Age, favored the pretensions of the Church; as men sought refuge under its wing from the rage of anarchy and the oppression of violence. We speak as a Protestant when we affirm, that the dominion of the Church of Rome in the dark ages, if not in itself legitimate and compatible with the spirit of christianity, was a political contrivance of immense advantage to mankind and to the cause of civilization. We make this assertion on the authority of the accurate and dispassionate Ranke, and we are supported in the position by the facts of history. The spiritual sway of Papacy mitigated the ferocity of feudal tyranny, and put a bridle on the savage passions of uncultivated man. There was no justice but within the precincts of the sanctuary, no religion out of the confessional, no learning beyond the shades of the cloister. The hopes of humanity were preserved from a deluge more destructive than that which swept away the traces of antediluvian existence, and the church was the ark in which the seeds of civilization were saved from the raging elements of universal violence and darkness.

For this great service Humanity must thank the Mediœval Church. But the Church issued from the conflict with pride inflated, ambition stimulated, and with an immense accession of political power. Men recognized their obligation to the Church, and from a feeling of gratitude, as well as superstitious dread of its power, contributed still farther to its aggrandizement. The unclean spirit took possession of the Church, debased its holy nature, and perverted its high purpose. It became corrupt, in proportion as it became rich, and persecuting as it got to be powerful. It arrogated absolute sovereignty over the mind and conscience of men, and established the dread machinery of the inquisition to enforce conformity to its creed and obedience to its will. But the conscience and the reason of men revolted against the despotism of the Church, and Martin Luther raised a cry for the LIBERTY OF PRIVATE JUDGMENT. He asserted the independence of the reason and conscience of the individual man, against the dictation of councils and the authority of the Pope. And he conquered. The living principles of Protestantism, are, perfect freedom of conscience, and the sovereignty of the individual reason. But the Catholic Church too was cleansed of many of its impurities by the spirit of the Reformation, and its pride and its power have melted before the progressive civilization of the age.

In every aspect, Know Nothingism is a preposterous movement. Affecting an apprehension of hierarchical domination, it assails a church which propitiates pity by its very weakness and helplessness. Declaiming against an alliance of Church and State, it drags religion into the arena of politics, and promotes the interests of party by inflammatory appeals to the pious prejudices of Protestants. Denouncing the "insidious policy" and spiritual despotism of the Papacy, it practices expedients of craft and imposture from which a Jesuit would revolt, and enforces a submissive obedience to its will with the cruel intolerance of an Inquisitor.

Protestantism is, in its origin and essential idea, a revolt against any external domination over the reason and conscience of the individual man. Yet, Know Nothingism pretends to serve the interests of Protestantism, by an organization which usurps absolute sway over the mind, and exacts the most rigid conformity to the supreme will of the Order! No stronger contrast can exist, than between the liberal spirit of genuine christianity, which elevates and ennobles the individual with a sense of infinite responsibility and a consciousness of absolute control over his destiny, and the stern despotism of an organization, which strips its votaries of their manhood, denies to them the prerogative of free thought and free speech, and binds them to a passive obedience to the mandates of a superior power.

We do not misconceive the nature of Know Nothingism. Its essential idea is the subjection of the individual to the will of the Order. Before initiation he binds himself by oath, *in all things, political and social, to comply with the will of the Order.* After initiation, he is the abject slave of the Order, and cannot escape from his bondage without the consent of the Order. This is the letter of its constitution: *the Grand Council shall have power to decide upon all matters appertaining to* NATIONAL POLITICS. Thus the individual member barters away his independent judgment, and in *all matters appertaining to national politics* binds himself to submit to the dictation of the Grand Council. If the Grand Council say the Nebraska bill is an iniquity, he can no more dissent from their decision, than a good Catholic can now dispute the immaculate conception of the Virgin. The Catholic takes his religious faith from Popes and Councils; the Know Nothing receives his political creed from a Council too —not a council of men distinguished for piety and learning, but an irresponsible conclave of demagogues, without personal character or public reputation.

Thus is Know Nothingism obnoxious to the very charge of which it accuses Catholicism. Its indictment against the Papacy recites its own crimes against humanity. The Church of Rome was never more intolerant, the Council of the Inquisition never more proscriptive, than this perfidious friend of Protestantism, this treacherous champion of religious liberty.

THE ASSERTED TEMPORAL POWER OF THE POPE.

The Know Nothings of Virginia have placed themselves in the most ridiculous and discreditable position—they have shown themselves to be the most arrant cowards, frightened at the merest shadow. There are only 7,000 Catholics in Virginia, and about 800,000 Protestants—and yet the Know Nothings are alarmed lest the 7,000 should swallow up the 800,000. Truly, as Major James Garland remarked, it would reverse the narrative of the Bible, for it would be nothing less than *Jonah swallowing the whale!* It is difficult to treat this subject in any other light than that of levity and ridicule. But since the *alarming* Catholic influence, and the *overwhelming* temporal power of the Pope of Rome, have been made prominent issues in the present contest, we deem it our duty to refute the absurd and groundless idea by a few *facts* from the records of past and present History. We shall first quote at length a declaration of the English Catholics in 1789, utterly refuting the Know Nothing theory on the subject of the temporal power and influence of the Pope. When we see Catholics, under the monarchical institutions of England, proclaiming that they are entirely free from temporal allegiance to the Pope, is it not absurd to witness the hypocritical alarm *expressed* on this point by Know Nothings in our own country, where religion is free and where Truth is left to combat Error? The following we extract from Rees' Encyclopedia, under the head of "Papists:"

The Declaration and Protestation Signed by the English Catholics in 1789.

We, whose names are hereunto subscribed, Catholics of England, do freely, voluntarily, and of our own accord, make the following solemn Declaration and Protestation.

Whereas sentiments unfavourable to *us*, as citizens and subjects, have been entertained by English Protestants, on account of principles which are asserted to be maintained by *us* and other Catholics, and which principles are dangerous to society, and totally repugnant to political and civil liberty;—it is a duty that *we*, the English Catholics, owe to our country as well as to ourselves, to protest, in a formal and solemn manner, against doctrines that *we* condemn, and that constitute no part whatever of our principles, religion, or belief.

We are the more anxious to free ourselves from such imputations, because divers Protestants, who profess themselves to be real friends to liberty of conscience, have, nevertheless, avowed themselves hostile to *us*, on account of certain opinions which *we* are supposed to hold. And we do not blame those Protestants for their hostility, if it proceeds (as we hope it does) not from an intolerant spirit in matters of religion, but from their being misinformed as to matters of fact.

If it were true, that *we*, the English Catholics, had adopted the maxims that are erroneously imputed to us, we acknowledge that *we* should merit the reproach of being dangerous enemies to the State; but, *we* detest those unchristian-like and execrable maxims: and *we* severally claim, in common with men of all other religions, as a matter of natural justice, that *we*, the English Catholics, ought not to suffer for or on account of any wicked or erroneous doctrines that may be held by any other Catholics, which doctrines *we* publicly disclaim, any more than British Protestants ought to be rendered responsible for any dangerous doctrines that may be held by any other Protestants, which doctrines they, the British Protestants, disavow.

First, We have been accused of holding, as a principle of our religion, that princes, excommunicated by the Pope and council, or by authority of the See of Rome, may be deposed or murdered by their subjects, or other persons.

But, so far is the move mentioned unchristian-like and abominable position, from being a principle that we hold, that *we* reject, abhor, and detest it, and very part thereof, as execrable and impious: and *we* do solemnly declare, that neither the Pope, either with or without a general council, nor any prelate, nor any assembly of prelates or priests, nor any ecclesiastical power whatever, can absolve the subjects of this realm, or any of them, from their allegiance to his majesty King George the Third, who is, by authority of parliament, the lawful king of this realm, and all of the dominions thereunto belonging.

Second, We have also been accused of holding, as a principle of our religion, that implicit obedience is due from us to the orders and decrees of Popes and general councils; and that therefore if the Pope, or any general council, should, for the good of the church, command us to take up arms against government, or by any means to subvert the laws and liberties of this country, or to exterminate persons of a different persuasion from us, *we* (it is asserted by our accusers) hold ourselves bound to obey such orders or decrees, on pain of eternal fire:

Whereas, *we* positively deny that *we* owe any any such obedience to the Pope and general council, or to either of them; and *we* believe that no act that is in itself immoral or dishonest can ever be justified by or under color that it is done either for the good of the church, or in obedience to any ecclesiastical power whatever. *We* acknowledge no infallibility in the Pope; and *we* neither apprehend nor believe that our disobedience to any such orders or decrees [should any such be given or made] could subject us to any punishment whatever. And *we* hold and insist, that the Catholic church has no power that can, directly or indirectly, prejudice the rights of Protestants, inasmuch as it is strictly confined to the refusing to them a participation in her sacraments and other religious privileges of her communion, which no church (as we conceive) can be expected to give to those out of her pale, and which no person out of her pale, will, we suppose, ever require.

And *we* do solemnly declare, that no church, nor any prelate, nor any priest, nor any assembly of prelates or priests, nor any ecclesiastical power whatever, hath, have, or ought to have, any jurisdiction or authority whatsoever within this realm, than can, directly or indirectly, affect or interfere with the independence, sovereignty, laws, constitution, or government thereof; or the rights, liberties, persons, or properties of the people of the said realm, or any of them, save only and except by the authority of parliament; and that any such assumption of power would be an usurpation.

Third, We have likewise been accused of holding, as a principle of our religion, that the Pope, by virtue of his spiritual power, can dispense with the obligations of any compact or oath taken or entered into by a Catholic; that therefore no oath of allegiance, or other oath, can bind *us;* and consequently, that *we* can give no security for our allegiance to any government.

There can be no doubt but that this conclusion would be just, if the original proposition upon which it is founded were true; but *we* positively deny that *we* do hold any such principle. And *we* do solemnly declare, that neither the pope, nor any prelate, nor any priest, nor any assembly of prelates or priests, nor any ecclesiastical power whatever, can absolve us, or any of us, from, or dispense with, the obligations of any compact or oath whatsoever.

Fourth, We have also been accused of holding, as a principle of our religion, that not only the pope, but even a Catholic priest, has the power to pardon the sins of Catholics at his will and pleasure, and, therefore, that no Catholic can possibly give any security for his allegiance to any government, inasmuch as the pope, or a priest, can pardon perjury, rebellion, and high treason.

We acknowledge, also, the justness of this conclusion, if the proposition upon which it is founded were not totally false. But, *we* do solemnly declare, that, on the contrary, *we* believe that no sin whatever can be forgiven at the will of any pope, or of any priest, or of any person whomsoever; but that a sincere sorrow for past sin, a firm resolution to avoid future guilt, and every possible atonement to God and the injured neighbor, are the previous and indispensable requisites to establish a well-founded expectation of forgiveness.

Fifth, And *we* have also been accused of holding, as a principle of our religion, that no faith is to be kept with heretics; so that no government which is not Catholic can have any security from *us* for our allegiance and peaceable behaviour.

This doctrine, that 'faith is not to be kept with heretics,' *we* reject, reprobate and abhor, as being contrary to religion, morality, and common honesty; and *we* do hold and solemnly declare, that no breach of faith with any person whomsoever can ever be justified by reason of or under pretence that such person is an heretic or an infidel.

And *we* further solemnly declare, that *we* do make this Declaration and Protestation, and every part thereof, in the plain and ordinary sense of the words of the same, without any evasion, equivocation, or mental reservation whatsoever.

And we appeal to the justice and candor of our fellow-citizens, whether *we*, the English Catholics, who thus solemnly disclaim, and from our hearts abhor, the above mentioned abominable and unchristian-like principles, ought to be put on a level with any other men who may hold and profess those principles.

The above Declaration and Protestation was signed by one thousand seven hundred and forty persons, including several peers, and two hundred and forty-one clergymen of the Catholic religion.

We come now to a later day, and we produce proof the most undoubted, that the Catholic Church most emphatically repudiates the doctrine that the Pope or the Church could absolve men from any just and binding obligation. The evidence we find in a letter of Michael Doheny, addressed to Henry A. Wise in the New York "Honest Truth." In 1825, the Irish Bishops were summoned before a committee of the British House of Commons. Amongst themselves they selected the most eminent and learned of their body to represent them. Being apprised of the subjects of the enquiry, they had ample time to examine and weigh and duly consider them. Their answers are brifly cited:

Doctor Doyle is asked—

"Can the Pope absolve the king's subjects from their allegiance?" A. "No."

Q. "Is it in his power to deprive the king of his kingdom?" A. "It is not, indeed."

Q. "Can he by any means excuse a Catholic from his allegiance?"

A. "Most undoubtedly not?"

Q. "Is the claim that some Popes have set up to temporal authority opposed to Scripture and tradition?"

A. "In my opinion it is opposed to both."

The Right Rev. Dr. Curtis, Archbishop of Armagl in the same examination, and in answer to the same question, says:

"I do not think it is very conformable to it. I do not say exactly it is opposed to it; but certainly he has received no such power from Christ?"

Doctor Murray, Archbishop of Dublin—

"The Pope's authority is wholly confined to his spiritual authority, according to the words of our Savour, 'My kingdom is not of this world.' His spiritual power does not allow him to dethrone kings or absolve their subjects from the allegiance due to them; and any attempt of that kind I would consider contrary to Scripture and tradition."

Dr. Kelly, Archbishop of Tuam—

"It never was admitted as a doctrine of the Catholic church that the Pope had temporal authority outside his own dominions."

Mr. Doheny also refers to the evidence of the two most eminent men who had theretofore written on the subject in England—Doctor Milner and Father O'Leary—and who had exposed the false pretence that the Pope could dispense with the obligations of an oath. He next comes to our own times and refers to the important case of the College of Maynooth in Ireland. It is (we quote his language) "a Catholic institution, endowed by the ultra Protestant Government of England, and has been now for over half a century the teeming cause of religious acerbity. No wonder that it should, when we consider that by London law a priest was a "felon," to be educated for the priesthood "felony," and to officiate as a priest "high treason." How there came to be a Catholic college is explained in this way:

"Notwithstanding the law, priests were ordained and mass was offered, at first in caves and mountain gorges, and afterwards in out-of-the way places in broad day-light. The priests were educated abroad. France, Spain, Italy, opened asylums of education for the exiled Irish Catholics, and some came home as priests, at the risk of being led to the gallows. Strange things foreshadowed themselves in the literature and feeling of the continent of Europe, and England, beginning to be afraid to hang the priest, and apprehending that his French education was Jacobinical or rather Jacobite, besought her of providing a home education for him, with a view to *denationalize* him. Hence the college of Maynooth—an "invention of the enemy." However, it by no means answered the end. The endowment, up to 1845, was only £30,000 a year. It was then increased to £50,000, but without, as it would seem, becoming any more loyal. Since then, bigotry, biting at the wires of its cage, which grows narrower and narrower daily, has been nibbling at it, and notwithstanding all that has been said and sworn to the contrary, repeating the pretence that the Pope claimed the deposing and absolving power.

"In 1852 a committee was appointed to inquire into the orthodoxy of the College, who have just issued their report. They examined the professors, and asked them the same questions the Bishops answered in 1825.

"I quote first from Doctor O'Hanlon :

"With regard to the first doctrine of Gallican Liberties, is it not a question in dispute among Roman Catholics? It is; tho' we may regard the opinion which attributes either direct or indirect temporal power to the Pope or to the church as being almost obsolete. The only writers who have attempted to revive it in modern times are Dr. Brownson, a recent convert to Catholicity, and an editor of an American review, and the famous Lamennais, who has been condemned by the Holy See, for the extravagance and eccentricity of certain doctrines which he held. I might here observe that in a document addressed from Rome by Cardinal Antoneli, to the Irish Catholic Prelates, so early as 1791, it is expressly affirmed that the Holy See regards that man as a calumniator, who imputes to it the tenet, 'that an oath to kings seperated from the Catholic communion can be violated, or that it is lawful for the Bishop of Rome to invade their rights and dominions.' Pope Gregory XVI., also, not only in his encyclical letter of 1832, but in his reply to the declaration of the Prussian government in 1838, lays down principles which appear to me to be irreconcilable with the opinion which invests the Pope or the church with direct or indirect temporal authority. He adopts the doctrine of Tertullian, and some others of the early fathers, that no cause whatever can justify the deposition or dethronement of a king, and that the people should patiently endure every sort of tyranny and oppression rather than have recourse to so violent and dangerous a remedy. The doctrine is as incompatible with the deposing power of the Pope as it is repugnant to the ideas of political writers of these countries.

"I close with this quotation, hoping that I have satisfied you that in espousing our cause you have not committed yourself to the rant of men like this Brownson, who trade upon credulity and superstition."

This evidence should be sufficient to satisfy all reasonable men, but we mean to clinch the nail and to show what Catholics think and say, here at our own firesides, upon the soil of Virginia, in this metropolis of the Old Dominion. With this object in view, we ask attention to the following correspondence between James Lyons, Esq., and the Catholic Bishop of Richmond. His frank replies to the enquiries addressed to him, should satisfy all but besotted and bigoted Know Nothings, that the charge of the danger to our institutions, from the temporal power of the Pope, are the wildest fancies, the most unsubstantial dreams. No additional word of comment can be necessary to dispel the terrible alarm which has been conjured up by the patriotic and pious managers of the Secret Order, and their zealous co-laborers, the Know-Nothing press and orators :

"RICHMOND, April 18, 1855.

To *Bishop McGill,*

Rev. Sir :—Having heard and read much declamation against the Catholics, because of the alleged temporal power of the Pope, I take the liberty to inquire of you whether the Catholics in Virginia do acknowledge any temporal allegiance to the Pope; and whether, if this country could be and was assailed or invaded by the army of the Pope, (if he had one,) or by any other Catholic power, the Catholic citizens of this country, no matter where born, would not be as much bound to defend the Flag of America, her rights and liberty, as any native-born citizen would be; and whether the performance of that duty would conflict with any oath, or vow, or other obligation of the Catholics?

My purpose is, with your leave, to make this note and your reply to it public.

With high respect, your friend, &c.,

JAMES LYONS."

"RICHMOND, VA., April 19, 1855.

Dear Sir:—The letter, which you have addressed to me, contains three questions, to which you ask an answer, with a view to publication.

First Question.—"Whether the Catholics in Virginia do acknowledge any any temporal allegiance to the Pope?"

To this I answer, that unless there be in Virginia some Italians who owe allegiance to the Pope as a temporal Prince, because they were born in his States, and are not naturalized citizens of this country, there are no Catholics in Virginia who owe or acknowledge any temporal allegiance to the Pope.

Second Question.—"Whether, if this country could be and was assailed and invaded by the army of the Pope, (if he had one,) or by any other Catholic power, the Catholic citizens of this country, no matter where born, would not be as much bound to defend the Flag of America, her rights and liberty, as any native-born citizens would be?"

Answer: To me, the hypothesis of an invasion of our country by the Pope, seems an absurdity; but should he come with armies to establish temporal dominion here, or should any other Catholic power make such an attempt, it is my conviction that all Catholic citizens, no matter where born, who enjoy the benefits and franchises of the Constitution, would be conscienciously bound, like native-born citizens, to defend the flag, rights and liberties of the Republic, and repel such invasion.

Third Question.—"Whether the performance of that duty would conflict with any oath, or vow, or other obligation of the Catholic?"

Answer: Catholics, reared in the Church as such, have not the custom of taking any oaths or vows, except the baptismal vows, "to renounce the Devil, his works and pomps." Persons converted to the faith, or those receiving degrees in Theology, may be required to take the oath contained in the creed of Pius IV. of obedience to the Pope, which, as far as I know, has always been understood and interpreted to signify a spiritual obedience to him as head of the Church, and not obedience to him as a temporal prince. Bishops, on their consecration, also take an oath which, in our country, is different from the old form used in Europe. But none of these vows, oaths, and no other obligation of which I am aware, conflicts with the duty of a citizen of the United States to defend the flag and liberties of his country.

In conclusion, allow me to state that, as we have no article of faith teaching that the Pope, of divine right, enjoys temporal power as head of the Church, whatever some theologians or writers may have said on this point, must, like my answers to your inquiries, be considered as opinions for which the writers themselves only can be held responsible.

Yours, very truly, &c.

J. McGILL, Bishop of Richmond.

To JAMES LYONS, ESQ."

THE WINCHESTER CONVENTION.

About five months after the Democratic state ticket was put forth, on the 14th March, the Know-Nothing party, trying to imitate as much as possible the Hartford Convention, of Federal blue-light notoriety, assembled in secret at the town of Winchester, for the purpose of nominating a state ticket. Never before in the history of Virginia did any party, for the purpose named, assemble in privacy and secrecy to make a state nomination. We suppose that the famous Gun Powder plot could not have been concocted under more binding oaths and cautious secrecy. Guy Fawkes himself would have owned its organization as his handiwork. We have never seen the names of but *three* delegates that were present, and these were appended to the schedule of Basis Principles which was soon promulgated in the name of the convention and to the correspondence informing the candidates of their nomination. Who were there, and what was said and done, in all human probability will never be known to the generation now in existence. There could be nothing discovered by examining the registers of the hotels, for the delegates used fictitious names in recording themselves. What shall we think of a state convention which meets and registers under aliases? Are we to believe that this party loves darkness rather than light because their deeds are evil?

The Examiner contained the following amusing notice of the body and its actions:

THE WINCHESTER CONVENTION.—After long and painful labors, commenced in the long coffin-like garret of Stebbins' china-shop, in this city, some weeks since, and adjourned over, for reasons unknown, to Winchester, a salubrious village of this state, the Know-Nothings have made their anxiously expected nominations.

A Winchester paper describes this gathering of midnight accouchers as a slim, dreary and melancholy squad of battered Whigs, the aggregate record of whose disappointments and defeats would fill a volume considerably exceeding the dimensions of the doom's-day book. There were about as many Know-Nothings in attendance, that paper says, as there were delegates to the celebrated Hartford Convention; and, of that number, it is said that there was *a solitary Democrat*, whose local habitation and name we have not heard. The rest were, of course, hungry and famished Whigs—ex-congressmen, ex-state senators, ex-members of the House of Delegates, ex-sheriffs, ex-constables, ex-magistrates, ex-coroners and ex-militia officers of every rank. It was a grand carnival of political cripples, the maimed, mutilated remains of defeats and disappointments without number. Dante, in his excursion through the infernal regions, might have stumbled upon such a conclave of the political damned, drinking hot brimstone punches, and toasting, at their leisure, on gridirons and pitchforks; but never before in this state was there such a lifeless convention. The congressional, senatorial and muster precincts gave up their dead, and we question whether there was as much vitality in the whole convention as there is in one healthy Democrat.

We have said that this melancholy assemblage of Chelsea invalids was Whig. Its presence perfumed the little town of Winchester with the odor of church-yard Whiggery. The maimed survivors of many a sad and luckless fight, with the gallant Virginia Democracy, were seeking prominent places in the council chamber of the Know-Nothings, as the afflicted of scriptural times struggled to be in the front rank around the healing waters of Bethesda. No man, we venture to say, from what we have heard of the Winchester Convention, could have been present, and beheld that collection of Whig partisans and leaders, without denouncing Know-Nothingism as the very latest and most vicious invention of the old Federal enemy, that turns up with a new name, but the same old principles and vices, every few years.

There was nothing Democratic about it. The shameful spectacle was presented to an intelligent people, of delegates appointed by secret lodges, bound by frightful oaths, pledged upon the Holy Word of God to the work of proscription and persecution, meeting with closed doors, and seeking to take from the people all free agency in the selection of their representatives. It presented the contrast of Cataline's gathering of disaffected and disappointed colleagues to that of the people of Rome flocking in the open air to listen to the fearless eloquence of Cicero. There are times beyond question—times when nations, like individuals, become the victims of temporary insanity—when Reason, tired of sitting on her throne, vacates it for a while, when Folly "takes the chair," and misrule becomes the order of the day. Good and true men are, at such moments, disregarded; and the temporary sovereign appoints befitting courtiers. Such dynasties compress much evil in the few months of their existence, and then are overthrown and become, a by-word and reproach.

Secret conclaves to select candidates for the people, in a country where the purity of the elective franchise depends upon its freedom from mystery and concealment, illustrate the inauguration of such an unfortunate era as we have just referred to. It is a new phase of that spirit of political folly and error which made the unreflecting and unprincipled fall down and worship log-cabins, coon-skins, hard cider, and other barbarous symbols, in 1840. It is a revival of that incarnation of insincerity, fraud and duplicity—"the no party movement"—by which the Whig party skulked into power in 1848, and then laughed at the silly Democratic gulls who were seduced from their party but to rue their treason in sackcloth and ashes.

The Winchester Convention, in spirit, intent and arrangement, was a new device—a fresh snare of Federalism set for that class of Democrats who have again and again been caught and plucked by a political adversary, who, like the modern Greek, substitutes cunning for boldness and courage. The solitary Democrat who is said to have formed the popular element in this Convention of, it is said, sixty-eight delegates, properly represents the exact proportion of Democracy in the Know-Nothing party in Virginia. It is made up in the ratio of sixty-eight parts of rank, bitter and most uncompromising Federalism to one of bogus, pinchbeck Democracy. The Federal pill is coated, not with fine white sugar, but with a compound of treacle and coffee brown. This new organization the late ludicrous Convention at Winchester has convinced every body, possesses no actual strength in Virginia. The proud, inflexible, consistent Henry Clay Whigs will never give up the banner of "the old Clay Guard," torn and ragged as it is, to march under the black flag of a secret society. The unambitious, intelligent gentlemen of the Whig party, men depending upon their plantations, not upon office for support, would sooner die than exchange pass-words, oaths and grips with slippery professional politicians in the garrets of china shops. They hold too sacred the memory of their great leaders to deny the name given them by the noble Kentuckian, and become Know-Nothings. In spite of the example of the solitary Democrat in the Winchester Convention, nine hundred and ninety-nine of our party would consider it a profanation to abandon the faith of their fathers, and become disciples of Judson, the convict, Bennet, the outlaw, and Ullman, the Hindoo, and regard such a solicitation as affording ample justification for knocking the verdant author of the proposition down. Know-Nothingism may fester in the towns and villages, among Whig shopkeepers, but there is a power in the country, among the Democratic farmers, that will crush it out.

Sam's Unsuccessful and Successful Courtships.—It is a perfectly notorious fact, that long before the Winchester Convention, the chief conspirators of the new order of Jesuits, in this state, like the "Father of Evil," went about covertly throwing temptations in the way of nearly every available and distinguished Democrat. Acting upon the Walpole theory, that "every public man had his price," they essayed to secure for their purpose a strong, healthy Democrat—thus confessing that there was no member of the order who possessed the confidence of the people—not one who was sufficiently strong to bear the odium and opprobrium of avowed Know-Nothingism.

At the very time when they were everywhere boasting of their strength, they were seeking for what they did not have in their organization—viz: a prominent Democrats. We could name a dozen Democrats who indignantly spurned their proposals, and kicked their bribes out of doors. They crawled about like poor, rejected suitors, humbly entreating prominent Democrats to accept their nominations. But of the members of our party, with a single grain of vitality, not one would touch their offer. It was only when they went down among the dead men that a few hungry ghosts snapped at their proposals.

Letcher, Holladay, Brockenbrough, Leake, and other leading Democrats, are known to have declined the "honor of the alliance." Never was an ugly and uncouth suitor so unfortunate as was Sam. He ran the gauntlet of "kicks," and became the by-word and the laughing-stock of all well-to-do Democrats. His efforts to "get a live Democrat" were as fruitless as were the attempts of men of little capital and less credit to raise their bank kites during the monetary pressure of December. Sam's addresses were all rejected, and his notes of entreaty protested by all of our first and second class Democrats. In the early days of his courtship, Sam, like other unsuccessful gentlemen of our acquaintance, looked too high. He fancied for his first loves Democrats in the bloom of youth, with good prospects, and a very broad margin between themselves and a state of collapsed and toothless old fogyism. He professed to turn up his priggish little Federal nose, (mushroom and *parvenu* as he is,) at the elderly and neglected maiden and widow-ladies of our party, who, for the last quarter of a century, have vainly pined for a suitor, however uncouth and valueless the much courted article. Soured by a thousand disappointments, left behind, outstripped by younger and more vigorous rivals, these forgotten old Democratic spinsters and mouldering widows, would have taken the devil for a partner, rather than not have at least one grab at the fleshpots. When a hard and melancholy experience had taught Sam that no Democrat who had anything to lose by accepting his "honorable proposals" would listen to them, he, for the first time, discovered that there was a small but excessively *recherche* assortment of *verde antiques*, coyly ogling him from the back benches, and recalling his youthful recollections of the song about—

Four-and-twenty old maids
  All in a row,
Dressed in yellow, pink and red,—
  Poor old maids.

With whatever indignation blushing young misses like Holladay, Letcher, Brockenbrough, &c., &c., had repelled his advances, it was obvious that these ladies were of much easier dispositions, and they had what Sam wanted [but in an eminently diluted state]—to wit: "Democratic blood."

Like the venerable females of a certain Italian city, who, when it was sacked by the French, after boldly waiting at the street corners all day, in the midst of the invaders, without experiencing any violence at their hands, went home grumbling that "they had heard the French were wicked fellows, but that they had not found them so," these antiquated Democrats had not seen much of Sam's reputed gallantry. Still they hoped on, and when Sam had failed to get the young ladies, in a fit of desperation he put the whole battalion of "venerable and unrecognized merit" in a flutter by seeking a consort from their midst. "Really," said Miss Madison Monroe Flexible, to her aged friend, Miss Jefferson Giles Castaway, "this fellow Sam is a very nice young man," and she flirted with the aforesaid Sam after a very spavined and octagenarian fashion. And let us not be understood as blaming any of these venerable spinsters and matrons for their choice. Let no Democrat, in the flush and vigor of early youth, sit too harshly in judgment upon those who, after pining, neglected and disregarded, for half a century, waiting for an eligible Democratic offer, in despair accepts even Sam. Pity the sorrows of our venerable friends, recollect their long, dismal years of dreary waiting, youth sobering into middle age, middle age turning into the sear and yellow leaf of old age—and Sam the first offer. Ye young, admired and vigorous Holladays, Letchers, Leakes, &c., rejoicing in a plenitude of eager beaux, think kindly and sorrowingly of the forlorn and bereaved widow Beale, whose cheerless and neglected fireside in the far west Sam has gladdened by his refreshing presence. Recollect the long and involuntary solitariness of that estimable person, and drop a tear rather than a curse upon the sin of disappointed old age.

For when time and disappointments have sapped the best of us—when we have waited long and waited vainly for the expected bridegroom, and he overstays his time, we may at a weak moment pounce upon the first substitute that turneth providentially up. For there cannot be much love between Sam and his new brides. He took, we incline to the opinion, the venerable Beale and the flexible Patton, because the fresh, the young, the vigorous of our party refused him, and they, heaven forgive their old souls, took Sam because it was obvious that no Democratic suitor would ever claim their hands. It will be a barren union, and we predict a speedy divorce *a vinculo matrimonii*. They may not live long enough to repent of their marriage with a fellow of low degree, but Sam will find that his Democratic consorts will bring him nothing but the recollections of their early loves and disappointments, and that he will stand forth in the list of Beale's lovers, and alas for his prospect for domestic happiness! Mr. Patton treasures tender souvenirs of more political loves than did the scandalous Don Giovanni of affairs of the heart.

Nor, if the character of Sam's Democratic conquests are understood by the public, will they allow him much peace upon their slender jointures of respectively fifteen hundred and seven hundred dollars per annum, whilst the Whig wife of his bosom, the lucky and fascinating Flournoy, will get five thousand dollars a year, and a house besides. Whether successful or unsuccessful, he is destined to have no peace in his polygamous household. If Brigham Sam comes home ladened with the *opima spolia* of Democracy, the disinterested Beale will flare up when she looks up from behind her official wash-tub and contrasts her homely attire and seven hundred dollars per annum, with the costly outfit and plentiful pocket money of Mrs. "Sam" Flournoy. Nor will the generous and impulsive Patton regard the trifle of one thousand five hundred dollars per annum a sufficient recompense for his having given his talents and respectability to a plebean like Sam. Indeed, much to the discredit of Sam, it is rumored that the haughty Patton, whilst requiring the most ardent manifestations of affection from Sam, gives him nothing but the Platonic power of a *name*, and treats his warm-hearted advances with marked coolness.

It is idle for any rational man to suppose that antiquated but aristocratic political dowagers, like Sam's legal consorts, when they bestow the odds and ends of worn out political affections upon such a mushroom, ever bring with them a large dowry of love. The idea of such a thing is laughable. Those who, in the enthusiastic and disinterested desertion of early blushing love, gave their hearts to the gallant Jackson, then transferred their more experienced and matured affections upon the irresistible Clay, and then distributed the small residuum of middle aged esteem among such men as Polk, Cass and Pierce, have nothing that is worth bestowing upon Sam. We regret to disturb his polygamous bliss by croaking predictions of unhappiness—but the truth must be told.

THE WINCHESTER TICKET.

The result of this notable gathering was the nomination of the following gubernatorial ticket, viz:

For Governor—THOMAS S. FLOURNOY, of Halifax.

For Lt. Governor—JAMES M. H. BEALE, of Mason.

For Attorney General—JOHN M. PATTON, of Richmond.

The country had been led to expect that none but new men, uncontaminated by party and undistinguished as partizans, would have been presented by an organization which eschewed all partisan prejudices and disavowed all partisan affiliations and objects. We shall discover, in the comments of the Democratic press upon these nominations, whether these anticipations were realized. The Examiner received the announcement of the nominations in the following strain of ridicule and narrative:

THE WINCHESTER TICKET.—The elements of the Know-Nothing ticket present a laughable illustration of Sam's utter disregard of his solemn pledges. The chief object we have heard for months past of this new organization was the killing off of old and decayed politicians, and the promotion of fresh, talented and accomplished men, able and ambitious, yet bearing about them the marks of no disappointments and defeats. We expected that the Know-Nothings would not be mere political resurrectionists, and that they would at least refrain from giving the people of Virginia the dry bones of the forgotten dead.

We had been led to believe that their nominees would possess all the freshness, youth and virgin purity of the early spring flowers that so sweetly and modestly peep out of the bosom of mother earth about the Ides of March. Indeed, like a gallant young fellow, we all expected Sam's Winchester nominees to be a charming bouquet of early spring flowers—not a *hortus siccus* of badly preserved specimens. Is there any of the violet's freshness about Flournoy, or of the lily's virginity about Beale, or of the daisy's simplicity about Mr. Patton? We have a ticket made up of the survivors of past honors and offices—from the head to the tail of the ticket we have "ex-honorables," all of whom had to be exhumed for their new missions. They were dug up, for there was no germinating or sprouting elements in them. As far as Messrs. Patton and Beale were concerned—we speak knowingly when we say that, as far as their political prospects in the Democratic party were concerned—they were as dead as any ancient Theban that Gliddon ever unrolled. A close examination of the ticket will convince our readers of the truth of what we say.

THE NECROLOGY AND RESURRECTION OF THOMAS STANHOPE FLOURNOY. It must have struck every one very forcibly when the Winchester ticket was announced, that it was constructed precisely like that famous animal, the Kangaroo, with all of its strength in its hind legs and tail, for, by some singular freak, Mr. Patton, a man of distinction and decided talents, but of flexible back-bone, was put at the tail, and Mr. Flournoy at the head of the ticket. The Kangaroo illustration will, however, help us to an explanation, for, as in the case of that animal, whilst the hind legs and tail perform all the hard work, the weak and idle fore paws, being nearest the mouth, secure all the food.

This interesting fact explains the construction of the ticket.

The majority of Whig Know-Nothings who effected the Winchester nominations were too keen for the spoils to give the executive chief office to the political friends of the minority of Democratic Know-Nothings.

The spoils department of the hybrid triumvirate is, as a matter of course, in the hands of a bitter, uncompromising Whig. Flournoy takes the oyster, and the two shells are divided with the most refreshing generosity between Patton and Beale, or rather Beale and Patton, for they appear to have put poor Mr. Patton to the foot of the table—even Beale taking precedence. To give the remnants of the Federal party in this state a chance at the flesh-pots of the state offices, the Federal Know-Nothings put one of their own men at the head of the distributing department. They had an eye, every one of them, doubtless, to the fish, flour, guano, tobacco, and lumber interests of the Old Dominion. Hence they have put Lepidus in the chair, and Anthony and Augustus at very humble side tables.

If the ticket triumphs, Lepidus gets five thousand dollars, a handsomely furnished house, and control over the much coveted flour, guano, lumber, tar, and tobacco, whilst Anthony gets what will be equivalent to an overseer's wages every other year, and Augustus receives the salary of a tide waiter in the custom-house. Standing in front of his palace with a plate of broken victuals, Lepidus will whistle, and a huge flock of starving Whig cormorants will flutter around him, each of whom will receive more than either of the other members of the triumvirate.

We shall make no excuse for briefly attempting to explain to our readers who Mr. Flournoy is! He is, in the first place, a gentleman by birth and education, and like Mr. Patton, (and for aught we know to the contrary, Mr. Beale,) a man upon whose private character there is not a spot or blemish. In chivalry and integrity he is every way the equal of Mr. Wise, or of any other Democrat or Whig in Virginia. But he is the very embodiment of Whiggery, a man, we believe, in whose veins there flows as much Federal blood as in those of any man in the commonwealth. He hates and loathes Democracy as he does a mean action, or even the Pope or an Irishman. His Federalism has been of the most consistent character, and his comparative obscurity alone prevents every Democrat from associating his name with bank, tariff, distribution, and the rest of the Federal abominations now dead and buried.

In that section of Virginia in which Mr. Flournoy once figured as a politician, his memory is cherished through the broad expanse of several muster precincts, by the shattered remains of his party. For Mr. Flournoy's political life was of insect duration, and it was as brief as the constitution allowed. A valorous Democratic lion and chivalrous unicorn of the same political family were seven years ago fighting for a seat in Congress from the strong Democratic Halifax district; Mr. Flournoy slipped in and transferred, for the brief period of two years, his obscurity from the county courts of Halifax and Charlotte to the halls of Congress. Our memory retains no vivid or distinct recollection of what he did during his two years of public life.

Like most lucky men who have crept into office through a split or cleft in the Democratic party, Mr. Flournoy tried to repeat the experiment a second time, but "the party" closed upon him with the grip and snap of a first rate steel trap, and after a few convulsive jerks and wiggles, Flournoy died. Politically he was declared, by competent judges, "a beautiful corpse," which, no doubt, he was.

His intended victim, but actual conqueror, that old and honored Democrat, Averett, thinking that the rash young man was dead as Julius Cæsar, extricated him from the trap which had closed with such fatal force upon him, buried him with pious and affectionate care, heaped up the dirt, and patted the mound as smoothly as possible, and wiping a tear from his eccentric-looking spectacles, went his way to Washington. It may be well to make a note of the fact, that the ever true and faithful Powell acted the sexton to Goggin that same year, but had to keep his purturbed ghost still with a cedar stake. Although as decently interred as man could have been, and killed, to boot, by a regular old school physician, Flournoy would not lie still and let the worms have their due, and the time which Averett spent, much to the benefit of his constituents as a true southern representative, in Washington, the restless Flournoy spent in scratching out of his narrow red-land tenement. And when the estimable doctor once more started upon a grand tour through his district, the ghost of Flournoy, "thin and shadowy, traveled by his side." "Averett, does murder sleep?" shrieked the ghost of Flournoy; and the dead man followed the living one, going through all the motions of a candidate for Congress, in a most shocking and heart-rending manner.

But the people were so much shocked at the apparition of their beloved and lamented Flournoy, flitting about from court-house to court-house, and shrieking its sepulchral notes from stump and hustings, that they determined, from feelings of humanity, to dispel the delusion under which the apparition labored, by electing Averett a second time. They did so, and the troubled ghost, exorcised of the ugly demon of ambition, sunk with a sigh into its grave, and Averett again heaped up the clay, and left the now quiet dead for a second visit to Washington. There was something so amiable, refined and respectable in the appearance of Flournoy's ghost, that Averett treated it with a mildness which, in the parallel case of Goggin, Powell could not consistently with his own welfare employ.

Thus terminated the brief and troubled career of the politician Flournoy. He came upon the stage when his favorite federal measures were tottering to their fall, and he went down with them, involved in the common ruin of his party. Several times since his death there have been ugly splits in the Democratic party in Flournoy's old district, but there was no Flournoy to slip into Congress. Nothing short of the trumpet of the Know-Nothing "Gabriel" could have aroused him from his long sleep. For years ambition came not near the grave of Flournoy. All of him that was political, his friends said, was dead, very dead, and in the counties of the Halifax district the legal Thomas Stanhope Flournoy practiced his profession, we have heard, in a quiet, but most orderly and respectable manner. All political dress having been cast out of him, his explorations in the technical jungles of the Code, and his struggles in the quagmires of Mayo's Guide, are said to have been most creditable.

Honest and industrious in the plain and unornamented details of his profession, he is said to have secured the confidence of Whigs and Democrats.

The fates, as we have seen, had decreed, however, that at the dead hour of midnight, the Know-Nothings should dig up the political remains of Flournoy, and thus end his career of usefulness as an attorney, without imparting over two months and a half of galvanic political vitality to the bones of the deceased.

From the thousand rumors which have found their way to the public, from the secret eouncils of the Know-Nothing Convention, we entertain no doubt of its having resolved itself into a committee of resurrectionists, surgeons and practical anatomists, to overhaul, compare and examine the remains of every Whig politician in Virginia of the least note or notoriety. It is suspected that, knowing the character of the subject with which they had to deal, the delegates were well provided with all the implements for body-snatching, and with dark lanterns, chloride of lime, galvanic batteries and volatile salts. Each delegation, it is supposed, brought its local dead, and a sweet set they must have been. Phew! Winchester will smell of them as long as Hartford will be fragrant with the odor of the old blue light Federalists. And what a set of mummies must have been then and there unrolled! What a charnel-house; what a rich rare and varied assortment of "Whig ex-honorables" in every stage of decay. The catacombs of Paris, the pyramids of Egyptian Cheops, must hereafter hide their diminished heads. The anatomical museums have been all eclipsed. To catalogue and systematically arrange this strange collection of relics of mortality, would be a task beyond our capacities. A second Tamerlane could scarcely make a decent pyramid of those battered skulls.

The purpose and design of the collection was to ascertain whether there could be found, within the limits of the commonwealth, the remains of a single Whig sufficiently well preserved to respond, by a few muscular jerks, to the strongest charge af a Know-Nothing battery. Long and vain is said to have been their labors. Down among the dead men they worked long and sadly. There was hardly a semblance of life in the whole collection. They were as dead as if the ball of a Minie rifle had passed through the skull of each of them. They were of the earth, earthy.

The Valley delegation, it is said, brought, wrapped up in one of poor Fillmore's castaway suits, the gigantic bones of the once lively and ever astute Stuart, but the electric shock called into play no tough muscle still clinging to its appropriate bone. The canvass for the Reform Convention had left nothing in those remains for a battery to get a muscular jerk out of.

The Red Land district, it is surmised, respectfully submitted a petition in *forma pauperis* for an examination of Goggin's coffin, but a few broken bones and a little dust alone remained of that gallant Whig.

The faithful delegation from ever loyal Screamerville pressed proudly forward with the sarcophagus of the terrible Botts, exclaiming, "Here's a man buried, but not dead—he'll kick and jump for you without touching him up with your infernal machine—he's alive, we tell you, don't you hear how he kicks and bellows to get out." But the whole college of surgeons, holding up their hands and screwing down the corners of their hypocritical mouths, said: "Oh, you are mistaken; Botts has been dead these many years—that's an evil spirit you hear kicking up that muss in his coffin, and, to keep it from getting out, drive in a few more nails!" And, as the indignant and sorrowing Screamervillians tottered off with the vivacious Botts, the chief doctor, placing his finger to the side of his proboscis, said *sotto voce*, with a wink, "Botts aint dead, but he's dangerous," and the sixty-eight Whigs and the solitary Democrat said, "Amen!" And, if street rumors are to be credited, the neglected Botts, although his sarcophagus was not opened, or the galvanic battery of the resurrectionists applied, is keeping up an awful shindy on his own hook, and frightening the secret order more than he did when he smashed their crockery over the china shop of Stebbins of Shockoe Hill.

And thus the convention proceeded in its melancholy work, passing on from Pendleton to Strother, from Strother to Rives, and with no success. The mystery of Flournoy's nomination has not leaked out, but it is supposed that some desperate individual threatened that if they did not make a selection, he would uncork that powerful narcotic, "the extract of Sheffey," and the whole college, with a shriek of horror, declared that the remains of the next of the Whig defuncts should be honored with their choice, and Flournoy's coffin was the next in order.

The Apotheosis of Beale.—The nomination of J. M. H. Beale, of Mason, was the most natural thing in the world. They could not do without a man from the portion of the State in which he lives, and Beale caught their eye, having fallen from grace in the Democratic party and kicked up a little filibustering campaign in his Congressional district, which had at the last accounts resulted in the partial defection of Mr. J. M. H. Beale. A gentleman perfectly familiar with that section of Virginia from which Mr. Beale hails, tells us, that after a long and arduous canvass, Mr. Beale may emerge the triumphant leader of from five to twenty followers. Although a very well disposed person, and we hear, of good moral character, he is not a man whose most intimate friends have ever suspected of the smallest *scintilla* of talent. And when, in addition to this, we tell our readers what everybody in his Congressional district knows, that he is a worn out, broken down politician, turned out to graze by his party, they can form some idea of his strength in the West. It is the strength of a cob-web to hold an eagle, or of a child to check a locomotive.

The only recommendation of Mr. Beale was, we imagine, that he was out on his own hook—solitary and alone—for Congress. Or it may have been a delicate compliment to the lone Democrat of the Winchester Convention, that led that body to nominate Beale. That poor delegate having seen half a hundred Whig coffins opened, his associates may have, in compliment to his fortitude, exhumed Beale. But if they thought to weaken the Democratic party in the West by nominating Mr. J. M. H. Beale, that particular mistake may be put down as the richest in the whole Winchester comedy of errors. We can almost, in imagination, hear the peals of inextinguishable merriment with which the unflinching Democracy of the Trans-Alleghany country will greet Sam's expedient of seducing them by the blandishments of the complimentary Beale.

We heard, some years ago, of a young gentleman's essaying to turn over the Natural Bridge with a crowbar, but that young man's verdancy was not equal to that of the Winchester Convention in using Mr. Beale for turning over to Know-Nothingism the ever faithful West. We can see the hardy Democracy of that section of the state pulling down the lower eyelid, and revolving the four digitals, with the thumb resting on the proboscis for an axis, and asking the unlucky Beale "if he sees anything green." Whatever may be his idea of colors, the unseduced Democracy of Western Virginia will make him feel very blue before they are done with him. But enough of Mr. Beale. We should, perhaps, for the sake of our readers, have, before saying a word about him, recollected that "*de minimis lex non curat.*" Perhaps, however, the space devoted to him will be pardoned by those who, unlike the people of his own section of country, do not know what a harmless old gentleman he is.

Hon. John M. Patton, the Nnow-Nothing Candidate for Attorney General.—The offence of Beale, in accepting the nomination of a secret Whig organization, is a very small matter. It is one of those trivial, harmless misdemeanors over which the mayor exercises jurisdiction, a case for the local reporters of the daily papers, deserving a record in "Howison's Calendar of Crimes," and nothing more.

But acceptance of a nomination from such a party by a Democratic gentleman of Mr. Patton's ability, position, education, and antecedents, is an offence calling for harsh comment and the strongest language of reprobation. From what we have heard of Mr. Beale, we suppose that he does not understand the bearing of his defection if his example should be followed. But a man of Mr. Patton's sagacity must have long since discovered that Know-Nothingism, North, South, East and West, is a dangerous conspiracy, having for its object the overthrow of the National Democratic party. Thus far that secret organization to which he has lent the influence of an honored name, has been the deadliest and most cruel foe to slavery and the Union. At midnight, and stealthily as a serpent, it has sought to undermine that great temple, dedicated to religious liberty, which Jefferson and Madison reared with such anxious and patriotic care. He has seen it, like some frightful reptile, creeping South, everywhere crushing in its folds the National Democracy. He has seen that it has everywhere availed itself, in the free States, of the temporary unpopularity of the Democratic party—an unpopularity growing wholly out of that party's devotion to the South. One by one he has seen the firm friends of the South defeated by the most reckless and unprincipled of fanatical Abolition agitators. He has seen the secret and stealthy foe drag down the flag of our party in New Hampshire, upon whose granite hills it had floated for more than half a century. He has seen that no political services, however eminent, have saved the friends of the South from the deadly hate of Know-Nothingism.

He has heard its proud and insolent boasts, that in Virginia, yes, that the enemy of religious liberty will wrest the land of Jefferson from his followers and his disciples. The infidels are to climb over the walls of the sacred city, and desecrate the memory and destroy the principles for which the illustrious dead of our own state struggled through evil and good report. He knows that if the Democratic garrison stands firm, we can "laugh a siege to scorn"—but that if that noble party gives way in Virginia, all is lost—yes, all is lost; and that the National Democratic party falls beneath the feet of a secret political inquisition. At such a moment, when the election in Virginia is to decide the fate of Democracy and the Union, Mr. Patton has lent the influence of his name to the secret foe.

Is it strange that this monstrous and unprovoked defection should excite the surprise, the grief, the pity, the indignation of those brave and loyal Democrats who, at this crisis in the history of our party, expected, as in times gone by, to have heard Mr. Patton fighting for the principles, the altars, the household gods of Democracy.

When in the midst of a battle, with a powerful and dangerous foe, we have expected prodigies of valor from a favorite General, and the startling news of his desertion is reported, is it strange that we should pity a man so dead to the good opinions of the world as to desert at such a time.

We envy not the notoriety of that unfortunate human being who shall, by binding himself to this Know-Nothing movement, defeat the Democratic party in Virginia. Men have, by the magnitude of their offences, been occasionally hanged in chains by history, for the edification and amazement of posterity—but the Democrat who lets the enemy into this old citadel, will hang higher than any historical character of our acquaintance, either of ancient or modern times.

It is useless for the apologists of Mr. Patton to say that he is "not a Know-Nothing, and that the office of Attorney General is not a political office." He is on the same ticket with Flournoy and Beale; his and their fortunes are idissolubly connected, and if the opposition ticket to the regular Democratic ticket triumphs, Mr. Patton triumphs. And if he is not a Know-Nothing, we cannot commend that caution which induces him to accept the aid of the party without incurring the odium of membership. We intend to indulge in no abuse of Mr. Patton, for respectability and talent entitle him to some esteem, even in the unhappy position which he now occupies.

If over the ruins of the proud old Democratic party of Virginia, he is willing to walk into the office of Attorney General, and become the recipient of the magnificent salary of fifteen hundred dollars a year, let him, let him do so.

But the future of a man, in his position, cannot be enviable, whether successful or not. On the contrary, the rankness of his offence will be the same. For the secret organization, under whose black wing he rests, must run its career, from the cradle to the grave, in a few short years. Antagonistic parties and associations, to the National Democratic party of this country, have sprouted up and rotted down again and again. These short cuts to preferment, end invariably in quagmires, as the examples of Wilmot, Foote, &c. &c., sufficiently demonstrate. It is, perhaps, fortunate that the tastes of men differ; but, for one, we would not, for the Presidency and fifty thousand dollars per annum for life, be pointed at whilst living, and remembered when dead, as the Democrat who broke down the Democratic party in Virginia, and held office during the reign of the Know-Nothings. Of such living, as well as posthumous honors and fame, we are (thank God) not covetous.

THE COUNCIL OF TEN.

The following able discussion of the dangers of the Know-Nothing plan of organization was republished with great effect in Virginia, from a New Hampshire journal:

[From the New Hampshire Patriot.]

About five hundred years ago a fearful and mysterious tribunal, bearing this name, was established in the republic of Venice. It gradually acquired despotic control over the government and the people. Its deliberations and its actions were alike enveloped in the profoundest secrecy. Its meetings were held in secret; it received denunciations against the most virtuous and patriotic citizens in secret, and in secret it conducted its victims, in silence and in gloom, to a sudden and mysterious death. It inquired, sentenced, and punished according to what is called "reasons of state." The public eye never penetrated its mysteries; the accused was rarely heard; he was never confronted with witnesses; the condemnation was secret as the inquiry, and the punishment undivulged like both. This tribunal gradually acquired control of every branch of the government, and exercised despotic power over every question. It annulled at pleasure all decrees, degraded members from their offices, and even deposed and put to death the chief magistrate. It was an object alike of terror and detestation to those whom it oppressed under the pretext of protecting their rights. And yet its diabolical cunning prolonged its existence until the genius of Napoleon prostrated it in the dust, with so many other relics of cruelty and intolerance.

People of New Hampshire! there exists at this moment among you a *Council of Ten*, as fearful and as pregnant with danger to your liberties as was that of Venice to her oppressed citizens. You have been accustomed, in the bounty of your hearts, to look upon this republic as beyond danger. In company with your fellow-citizens of other states, you have successfully resisted foreign intervention, and repelled with triumph the conquering legions of the most arrogant nation on the earth. You have advanced your triumphant banners to that proud city which Cortez gloried in adding to the Spanish empire. You have scattered the seeds of civilization throughout realms before untrodden by any human footsteps but those of the Indian. You have seen your population advancing, your wealth increasing, and your country teeming with the fruits of physical and intellectual labor. And you fondly think that you are safe; that each of you and your children are, for long years, to have a share in a government the very breath of whose nostrils is freedom of opinion—one of whose cardinal doctrines is an open and fearless avowal of principles; and you are proud that you live under a constitution which permits you to reward intelligence and uprightness by selecting for your public trusts those among you who are marked by such qualities.

But be not deceived! The sceptre is even now passing from your grasp, and will be irrevocably lost unless you trample in the dust the traitors who are clutching at it with all the despair of disappointed ambition. An unholy cabal of fifth rate pettifogging lawyers, mouldy political hacks, and Mammon-seeking parsons, is seeking to wind the coils of the serpent around you, and to strangle you in its embrace. The grand council of Know-Nothings have sworn by the only God they worship—that is, themselves—undying hatred to political freedom and popular supremacy. These decayed aristocrats, these shameless bigots, these ravening political banditti, these utterly desperate traitors to the country that gave them birth, are organizing a scheme whose details would strike terror into your hearts if fully disclosed. They have combined to destroy every institution that stands in their way, and to prostrate every man who will not do their bidding. Every town has its branch of the conspiracy. Secret signs and pass-words and mummeries are used to impress the imagination, and unlawful oaths are administered binding the unhappy members to subject themselves like slaves and vassals to the dictation of this terrible oligarchy. Meanwhile the Council of Ten, the controling power of this infamous conspiracy, squats in its noisome retreat like a toad sweltering in its own venom, or a bloated spider spinning its web over the state. It sends forth its decrees to its bond slaves. "Prostrate," it says, "this man, for he has too much education! Destroy that one; he is too intelligent! Ruin your best friend, for he has too much independence!" And with the spectacle before it of triumphant tyranny and bigotry in Massachusetts, it confidently expects a like victory over the freemen of New Hampshire! But you had better write your names in characters of blood upon your thresholds, and escape with your wife and children to some far country by the light of your burning houses, than crouch to this insolent oligarchy! Why would you live here when life has lost all that is worth living for? when you may be stabbed by an assassin in the back, or slain by an unseen arrow from him you supposed your dearest friend? Are you content to crawl out at twilight like birds of evil omen, to creep into blind alleys, to hover around the back "slums" of your cities and villages, to start at every passing tread lest some honest man should see you, to move with muffled face and stealthy step, and double upon your tracks as if you were a thief with the officers of justice in pursuit of you, and with this sickening consciousness of shame to group your way to the den where such animals herd, and with trembling hand give the mystic signal which admits you into this community of sin? And when you are admitted, and the door of the pandemonium is closed, are you content to leave all hope behind you, and renew before God the oath you have taken to do the bidding of your disreputable tyrants? It is incredible that any one worthy of the name and rights of a freeman can do this. You will not cast this disgrace upon the mothers who bore you, and whose veins are filled with the blood of '76. You will not thus bastardize your descent from the men of the revolution! No, leave that to the abolitionists, who, with philanthropy upon their tongues, have treason and murder in their hearts! Leave it to the traitors who prayed that the Mexicans would welcome your fellow-citizens "with bloody hands to hospitable graves."

Is it supposed that this language is too strong, and that these are unwarrantable charges? Depend upon it, the half is not yet told. No faction in the history of our country has ever struggled through its vicious life that has been one-half so dangerous as this secret organization. Its only avowed bond of union is a shame and disgrace. It is a standing libel upon all that has made America the refuge of the oppressed. By it every man is proscribed who is either a Catholic himself or whose wife is a Catholic. This includes the patriotic Gaston of North Carolina, the venerable Charles Carroll of Carrollton, and other signers of the immortal Declaration of Independence, as well as the present admirable and learned chief justice of the United States, and many others as pure and patriotic men as can be found in the country. And every man is to be proscribed, no matter how honest and intelligent, who came to this country at the age of twenty, until he is forty-one years old! What shall we say, then, of the devoted Lafayette, the gallant Sterling, the chivalrous Montgomery—of Pulaski, the brave and generous—of the statesman Gallatin?—of the thousands of noble souls who shed their blood for us, and counselled with our fathers in the stormy days of the republic? But no! "America for the Americans," and the "Americans for the Know-Nothings!" This is the secret spur—this is the "exceeding great reward," that they shall lay the rod on the backs of the people, and the people shall kiss it, and smile and beg them, if it is not too much trouble, to lay it on a little harder! This they anticipate, and this they are determined to accomplish, though all the rights of humanity, the constitution, the laws, every public right, every private right, should stand in their way. The paltriest pettifogger—the shabbiest political hack—is of more value than every man among us who ever breathed the air of Europe, in the eyes of this ruthless and intolerant Council of Ten.

Hereafter, when this wretched faction fills a dishonorable grave, and its carcass reeks with political corruption, how can any man stand up before the world without hiding his face, when it is cast up to him that he has labored to introduce that worse than Egyptian slavery, when a free citizen dare not vote as he desires, but obeys the insolent orders of this tyrannical Council of Ten? What will become of American honor, at home and abroad, when a mob of despotic adventurers shall make the laws? The follies and absurdities of Jacobinism in France were so extreme that it was said of it that "it would have been a farce if it had not been for murder." And so with this faction; its silly pass-words, its ridiculous ceremonies, its contemptible balderdash, would make it only a laughing stock, if all this nonsense did not conceal a deep-laid conspiracy against freedom. Compared with their intolerant proscription, Austrian tyranny is endurable, and police spies become respectable. But, thank God, there is life and vitality in American freedom yet. Altered, indeed, radically changed, must we be from the principles of our glorious ancestors, if our political liberties are to be delivered, bound and unresisting, into the custody of such a set of political jailors. There are despotisms maintained by such genius and adorned by such brilliancy that the imagination is led astray and the mind bows to a superior intellect. But what honor can there be, what redeeming considerations can there be, in subjection to a political mob which shamelessly disavows all political principles, whose only rallying cry is proscription, whose candidates for office are selected not because they are men of education, or talent, or sagacity, or integrity, but because they are destitute of all these? Among the rabble of the Boston delegation to the Massachusetts legislature we look in vain for one man of character, one man of intelligence, one man of experience, one man possessing anything like the proper fitness for a representative of a great city. Did the city of Boston, did the commonwealth of Massachusetts, ever, of their own free will, elect such a legislature as that about to assemble there, or can we conceive of their doing so, except at the irresponsible dictation of this modern Council of Ten?

People of New Hampshire! To each and all of you we say, "touch not this accursed thing!" It will one day, should you do so, cause you to cover your heads with shame. Like a bubble of deleterious gas, it will explode, leaving behind it nothing but a pestilential odor. The finger of Providence has pointed out this country as the place where Catholicism may be purged of its abuses, and absorbed without harm into the system. Millions of poor and humble men in Europe are looking hitherward as the place where they and their children may enjoy those privileges of freedom denied them at home. But if you are content to kiss the rod that smites you, to place your republican freedom at the feet of a tyrannical oligarchy, if you can forget that there is scarcely a hill or a valley in New England but tells of some struggle of your fathers against religious and political intolerance, then is this such a country, then are you such a people, as will entirely suit the purposes of this obscure, shameless, and persecuting Council of Ten.

To the same purport was the following article which appeared in the Richmond Examiner:

Secret Societies and Republican Institutions—The Thirty Tyrants of Athens—The Council of Ten of Venice—The Supreme Know-Nothing Council of Thirteen of the United States.—The introduction of Secret Societies into the bosom of free communities, for the attainment of political ends, is the first symptom of the decay of free institutions, and the chief instrument in their corruption and overthrow. We are not left to conjecture: we are not condemned to perform the whole experiment of Know-Nothingism in order to ascertain its effects. We are not sentenced to submit to the manipulations of that hidden band of political jugglers in order to learn the results of their skill. The testimony of history, the experience of other nations, furnish all necessary instructions on this point. It might almost be asserted that in almost every republic which the world has yet seen, the first sign and chief agency of the decay of freedom was the prevalence of secret associations for the attainment of political purposes—chiefly for the acquisition of political offices. In Athens, in Rome, perhaps in Carthage, in Milan, Florence, and Venice, Secret Societies first introduced disorder, dissension, disorganization, and civil war into the republic, and then inaugurated despotism, either by their own acts, or by the consequences of their acts.

It must necessarily be so. As long as Republican institutions flourish, as long as they are acceptable to the people, the regular and constitutional modes of procedure, in the election to offices as well as in all other respects, are followed with reverence and acquiescence. It is only when those constitutional methods cease to be respected by a portion of the people that they are rejected, and the invention of secret machinery for election is applied. This is at once an innovation at variance with free government, destructive of it, and adopted in a spirit of conscious or unconscious hostility to it. It is the substitution of new and unconstitutional modes of election, (or nomination, which is in spirit, if not always in effect, the same thing,) and of legislation for the republican practices previously in force. It is an attempt to arrest the legitimate development of free institutions by secret and underhand practices—and the moment that fidelity to a secret league or bond is regarded as paramount to the fidelity due to the Constitution and State, patriotism is at an end and the bonds of political organization is snapped like rotten flax. The Constitution ceases to be to each man the supreme authority, and the object of supreme attachment. His allegiance has been transferred to a secret league—the secrecy of whose deliberations, measures, and action, places them equally beyond responsibility and the reach of public sentiment. If the secret association is able to control the elections, the secresy of their action disfranchises to all intents and purposes all who are not affiliated with them, and prescribes all political action and legislation without other restraint than the ineffectual opposition which may be offered in secret conclave. To maintain secrecy, and secure efficiency of procedure, the numbers who have the direct control in determining nominations, and in regulating the policy to be pursued, must be limited. The tendency of either success or defeat will be to restrict more and more the members of the directing council.

Thus the ultimate effect is to substitute a hidden oligarchy, like the Council of Ten at Venice, for the regular executive authorities and the republican organization. If the secret association is not able to control the elections, it introduces factious oppositions, jealousies, unexplained and therefore irremediable dissensions, into the bosom of the community. And, after the first step of secret operation has been taken, the other steps of illegal practices, fraudulent misrepresentations, and criminal resistance, follow naturally and unsuspiciously, and are taken before the members of the secret society are aware themselves of the tendency of their course. Thus secret political societies, commencing in the distrust and repudiation of constitutional authority and constitutional procedure, first disorganize the society in which they occur, undermine its free institutions, cashier its open, candid publicity of action, and finally eventuate in an oligarchy, which sometimes continues dominant, but more frequently transfers its power into the hands of a despot.

This was the course of affairs at Athens, and in many other States of Greece, from the time of Pericles to the ascendancy of the Thirty Tyrants, directly put in power and sustained by the Hetæriæ or secret political associations of Athens. This was the progress of events at Rome from Cincinnatus to Julius Cæsar. And similar was the history of Venice before the Inquisition, of Milan before the Visconti, and of Florence before the ascendancy of the second house of the Medici. In every instance secret societies—originating among professed conservatives, or mainly sustained by them—provoking the establishment of other secret societies—opposing the regular constitutional action of the ancient republican institutions—sapping these institutions—allying themselves with foreign enemies for the attainment of party ends and the conquest of the offices—abhorring the freedom and the Constitution of their country—sheltering or instigating crime—corrupting juries and coercing false verdicts—were the instruments in introducing at last the despotism of a few, after having ruined both the morals of the citizens and the prosperity of the state by intestine broils and commotions.

This is the clear and distinct testimony of the past. It is only necessary to read the detailed histories of Greece, Rome, and the Italian Republics, in order to see the course and tendency of Know-Nothingism—if not crushed like a young crocodile in the egg. The option presented to the American people—and now more particularly to the people of Virginia—is simply a choice between discord and anarchy under Know-Nothing impulses resulting in the abrogation of the Constitution and the establishment of an oligarchy (more terrible in the exercise of its unlimited powers, because the Secret Council may be unknown) and the maintenance of the Republican government, the free constitution, and the liberal principles conquered by the blood of patriots and martyrs.

This is the only choice. If Know-Nothingism is sustained, farewell to the liberties of America. The two things are absolutely and essentially incompatible. They can no more co-exist than fire and water. The Know-Nothings among many other things which they do not know, do not know this. The heat, fanaticism, and mingled credulity of partisans may prevent many from recognizing it, who would otherwise apprehend it at once. But history, experience, philosophy, reason, assert that there is no other alternative. If Know-Nothingism is perpetuated, Republicanism is at an end. If Republicanism is to be preserved, Know-Nothingism must be promptly and effectually crushed. The evidences which it has furnished in its brief career, are sufficient to illustrate and confirm these allegations, though they might not have been sufficient to suggest them without the testimony of history. What constitutional provision—what Republican principle—what political or social interest—what obligation between man and man has been respected, when it interfered with the purposes of the secret rulers of this secret organization?

These remarks are made not in the spirit of party—not as a mere Democratic utterance, but as the plain, indubitable warnings derived from the lessons of other free states, which have declined from the influence of such a society as the Know-Nothings in their midst.

In a second notice, the Examiner dwelt more upon the details of the antecedents of the Winchester ticket. We append also two notices of the ticket from the Enquirer and Lynchburg Republican:

SOME OF THE ANTECEDENTS OF THE KANGAROO TICKET.

The people were promised a ticket of fresh names by the Know Nothings. They were to be allowed to vote for men who had never been contaminated in the slightest degree by party politics, or implicated by the remotest participation in the struggles of the old organizations for place, plunder and patronage. But these brave promises have been forfeited in a manner as unblushing as amusing. Instead of a ticket as fresh and pure as butter just from the churn, we have the most rancid platter of long packed away and accidentally raked up stuff that was ever offered in the political market.

Mr. FLOURNOY is discovered to be one of the oldest and lamest Whig stagers in the State. In 1837 he sought to represent Halifax county in the House of Delegates; and failed of election by the small poll of 206 in more than 800 votes cast. The next year he ran the same race again, and the result was still worse, the vote being: For EDMUNDS, (Dem.,) 553; for TAYLOR, (Dem.,) 533; for SIMMS, (Whig,) 310; for FLOURNOY, (Whig,) 295; the spavined FLOURNOY being the very hindmost nag. Set back by a hint of this emphatic description from the people and his immediate neighbors, he remained quiet for several years, until a split in the Democratic ranks of the Halifax Congressional district tempted him once more into the field, when he was accidentally elected by a beggarly majority of two or three votes—which made the first and last of his successes in his own bailiwick. This irresistible and invincible tried it a second time for Congress in 1949, and Dr. AVERETT beat him 9 votes. He tried it again in 1851, and the Doctor smashed him to the tune of 300 majority. From this statement it will be perceived that FLOURNOY'S mission on this naughty earth, is to be beaten to a jelly by the great Democratic party, and he has not yet fulfilled his mission. Yet his present, is drolly advertised as his "first appearance on the stage." His want of strength at home has kept him in a state of pickled and rancid obscurity so long that the public has forgotten his existence altogether; and the burning zeal which the braggarts and trumpeters who do the boasting for the new party, represent that his nomination has elicited throughout the world and among the rest of mankind, when tested by these domestic facts, turns out to be a fox-fire commodity.

Mr. PATTON is an old stager still more unlucky in his destitution of the quality of freshness, than the Napoleon of minorites in Halifax. Of which of the "old and broken down parties," which are the so great abhorrence of Know Nothings, has he not been part and parcel in his tortuous partisan career? He has tried all parties, and carried off, as he successively left them, some of the mud and contamination of all. The colored chart of his political history is as variegated as JOSEPH'S coat of many colors; or as the chameleon phases of Know Nothingism in the several States of the Union—by virtue of which facile adaptation to the prevailing local prejudice and passion, it sweeps the thorough Abolition State of Massachusetts with as overwhelming a majority as it boasts its ability to carry the staunch slave State of Virginia. The idea of Mr. PATTON'S being unsoiled by the dust, and unsophisticated in the wiles of party strife, is droll enough. Why, it was only since the abolition of the executive Council, and the old Constitution, that he ceased to hold office; and, as late as 1850, in the great movement for reform, which even dashed its refreshing waves over starched and conservative Richmond, he ran and was beaten on the fogy ticket—under the flag that he still flaunts and swears by—of UNEQUAL RIGHTS and PARTIAL SUFFRAGE among the grown up white men of Virginia.

But BEALE is the very Koh-i-noor in this cabinet of fossil remains. Where will you find—what is a broken-down, worn-out politician, if BEALE is not a genuine specimen? While in the Valley, he rode the Democratic party as the Old Man of the Sea rode SINBAD. He stuck to it like sponge to the ocean rock, and sucked it like the daughter of the horse leech. They choked him off finally in the Valley, and he sought new victims farther west. He forced himself on the party, in the Kanawha district, without a call or a Convention, at the instant ROBERT A. THOMPSON started for the West, and gained his election at last by a promise to give way to men acceptable to the Democracy for the future. He went before the Democratic Sectional Convention, in 1852, for the Board of Public Works in Col. ARMSTRONG'S district, but was thrust out of it with as little ceremony as FALLSTAFF was turned hissing-hot into the Thames. Since that occurrence, he has been as discontented and restless as a bear with a sore head; and, despairing of further favor among the Democracy, has been bountiful of blandishments, smirks and smiles for the Know Nothings. They have caught at the bait, and put BEALE, the worn-out, cast-off, and broken-down, number two on their ticket of *fresh* men. They are welcome to BEALE.

Such is the ticket that was to be free from all party taint, from fleshpot odor, and from loaf-and-fish contamination? If such a ticket should sweep Virginia, under Know Nothing auspices, then it may indeed be time to return to Mr. PATTON'S old doctrine of UNEQUAL RIGHTS und LIMITED SUFFRAGE, and to make a man's poverty and want of education, as well as his alienage, a disqualification for suffrage and for office.

Those who are curious in regard to the metamorphoses of fossil politicians are likely to have their curiosity abundantly gratified with the relics of Mr. PATTON'S early opinions of politics and politicians, that will be recovered from antiquity during this canvass. Here is a specimen of his satire in 1848 against the prospective Know Nothing party, its "Delphic oracles," and "Sybilline leaves." Here is his funeral oration over the great Whig party "quietly inurned in the tomb of all the Capulets," and his requiem over their "defunct and buried principles." Here are the words in which he expressed his witty abhorrence of the trick of the Whig party, in 1848, in practicing the deception of the cat in the fable, and "hiding itself in the meal tub" of no partyism. Here is his prophetic denunciation, in advance, of Know Nothingism, in boasting itself to be a great and prodigious "conservative" party, but "*without political principles*," and therein so unlike the "*little* conservative party *with principles*," of which himself was so bright and shining a light. Here is his biting sarcasm upon the "*blind man's buff*" party, then rejoicing in the character of *no partyism* and now relapsed into the darker mystery of Know Nothingism. Here is Mr. PATTON's pungent jeer of the Whig party for accepting in General TAYLOR a candidate who "took especial pains to declare that he could not be the exponent of their doctrines,"—a fact in politics that never had its counterpart until Mr. PATTON, disclaiming Know Nothingism and all affiliation with it, coolly consents to be their passive nominee, and to be elected if they have votes enough to make him Attorney General. And more than all, here is Mr. PATTON's eloquent, but, as it turns out, empty exhortation to the Democracy *not to abandon their principles*, seeing that "*one defeat, while standing by their principles and never surrendering their principlss, is worth more than a thousand victories achieved by the abandonment of them all.*"

Mr. PATTON said, in 1848, in addressing a Democratic meeting in Richmond:

"We come to proclaim our unchanged and *unchangeable adherence* to those great principles of Republican government, of practical expediency, and of constitutional construction, of which he (President Polk) has been for the last three years the exponent—principles which we deem *essential to the perpetuity of Republican government, and to the union of the States.* (Cheers.) We have no disputes to settle—no conflicting claims of rival candidates for the Presidency to decide—*no Delphic oracles to expound*—(laughter) and *no Sybilline leaves to interpret.* (Laughter.) I presume we shall have no *thunder* (laughter) to shake our nerves, (laughter) and no flashes of lightning to bewilder our senses. (Laughter.) There are no dark and portentous clouds lowering over us which require a thunder-storm to dispel. (Cheers.) The only clouds we have are light and floating vapors, far above our *heads*, which may make it doubtful with those that are not weatherwise whether the day is to be clear or cloudy, but which the first rays of a *Democratic Sun* will dissipate, and show that the skies are *bright and brightening.* (Cheers.)"

The Whig Convention had "quietly laid the great embodiment of Whig principles on the shelf," and had "solemnly announced as their favorite candidate a gentleman who, with the frank and honest plainness of a gallant soldier, takes especial pains to declare that he will not be their candidate [laughter]—that he will not be the exponent of their doctrines, [laughter] and that his life has been hitherto so much spent in the field that he has not had time to 'consider or investigate great plitical questions,' nor has he attempted to do so. Notwithstanding this, they proclaim Gen. Taylor as their first choice. To this complexion the principles of the great Whig party have come at last! [Laughter.] Thus ends the great chapter of Whig principles, [laughter] quietly 'inurned in the tomb of all the Capulets' by its own friends, and their embodiment quietly laid on the shelf! [Laughter.] I think we may say of these defunct and buried principles—

'Great Cæsar dead and turned *from* clay,
May stop a hole to keep the wind away.'

"But, gentlemen, *it becomes us more steadily to maintain our own principles.* Since Æsop's Fables, having been quoted by Gen. Taylor, are likely to become a political text-book, I think we may draw a lesson of instruction from that renowned writer on civil government. [Laughter.] We are told in a notorious fable of Æsop, of an animal more dangerous *while hid in a meal tub* than when running about with a bell around its neck. [Laughter.] *Timeo Danaos et dona ferentes.* I am afraid our political opponents, dead, though their present principles be, may rise up again under their present, or *in some other form.* They may possibly assume the name of *the great conservative party*, as suggested by their President. [Laughter.] I was, myself, once a member of a *little* conservative party, [laughter] and I have no objection to a little conservative party with principles, but *object decidedly* to a great big one *without political principles.* [Laughter.] But, inasmuch as they may be indisposed to take either of these names, they may adopt the suggestion of another distinguished champion of the late 'indomitable Whigs,' and take the cognomen of the "*blind man's buff.*" Therefore, gentlemen, it is not the less necessary that we should maintain, *proclaim* and *stand* by our principles—that we should adopt the means necessary to concentrate public opinion upon a man available to *sustain our principles,* and to take care *not to abandon our principles* in order to get an available man. We should not have a man who has formed no opinions, but one who has formed opinions, *is ready to avow them,* and has proclaimed them in his past actions, in the public councils. [Cheers.] To such a man let us give our support, fearless of defeat, but prepared for either fortune. If we are destined to triumph, it will then be our proud boast, that it is a triumph of principle—and, if destined to defeat, we shall still have the proud boast, and the consolation, too, that one defeat, WHILE STANDING BY OUR FLAG, AND NEVER SURRENDERING OUR PRINCIPLES, IS WORTH MORE THAN A THOUSAND VICTORIES ACHIEVED BY THE ABANDONMENT OF THEM ALL.—[Long continued cheering.]"

THE HYBRID TICKET.

The Know Nothing nominations have provoked from the Democratic press just such a display of defiant opposition as we anticipated. The device of an amalgamation ticket, while it has offended the pride and repelled the sympathies of intelligent and independent Whigs, has not conciliated the least favor with the Democratic party. The association of Beale and Patton with a malignant Whig was not only a crime in morals but an egregious blunder in policy. It is not only a violation of principle and a mockery of every idea of political honesty, but it is a refinement of artifice, which, instead of damaging the party against whom it is directed, will wound and embarrass the cause it is designed to promote. What must be the feeling of every honest Whig to whom this hybrid ticket is presented? Will he not reject it with an indignant protest against so shameless a barter of *principles* for *spoils?* He is not so smitten with a lust for plunder as to sacrifice the convictions of his judgment and the pure affections of his heart, to any expedient which hungry politicians may think essential to the acquisition of power. There are Whigs in Virginia who have caught something of the chivalrous character of Clay. There are Whigs in Virginia who will never betray a cause in a crisis of peril, nor confederate with an obnoxious party on a promise of a division of the spoils. These gentlemen see much disgrace but discover no advantage in the coalition with Know Nothingism. "But stay," whispers a Whig politician; "it is true we claim no principle and avow no party purpose, but we play a game of profound policy. Observe a staunch Whig at the head of the ticket, and a couple of fishy Democrats at the tail. Flournoy will engross all the power and patronage of the State, while Beale and Patton, like the prodigal son who deserted his father's house, are feeding on husks and herding with the harlots of our party, without the dignity of respectable association or the luxury of a liberal reward. As we deny them any political power, so have we effectually robbed them of the influence of personal character, by bribing them to perform this venal service. They are the helpless instruments of our pleasure, and if they choose, have not the ability to oppose any resistance to the execution of our grand scheme OF EXPELLING THE GOTHS AND VANDALS, AND RESTORING THE ASCENDANCY OF WHIG MEASURES AND WHIG POLICY." To this development the honest Whig will reply: "That he scorns to perpetrate a fraud upon the people; that if his principles have not enough of wisdom to command the public confidence, he will not seek to impose them upon the State by the secret agency of a corrupt conspiracy; that he will not disgrace himself and his cause, by the false pretences of a perfidious policy;

that he is resolved, at least, to save his honor if his party must sustain defeat." This is the feeling and this the resolution of the independent and incorruptible Whigs of Virginia. They will not degrade themselves by the support of the Know Nothing nominees.

On the other hand, the Democracy feel the indignity of the proffered bride, and instead of being propitiated by the Democratic tail of the Know Nothing ticket, they are excited to greater energy and enthusiasm in support of their own candidates and cause. In every quarter of the State curses loud and deep are muttered against Beale and Patton, and vows of vengeance on their despicable treachery. The Democratic papers of the State manifest a zeal and ability in their assaults on the mongrel ticket, which betoken the pervading discontent of the popular mind. We have distinguished many of their stirring articles for publication in this paper, but are compelled to suspend our purpose in consequence of the pressure on our columns. We can assure our friends that the Opposition will reap no advantage from the expedient of a hybrid ticket.—*Richmond Enquirer.*

THE MERMAID TICKET.

Since the publication of the Know Nothing ticket, we have been vexing our curiosity to find some prototype to it in the physical, animal, or mineral kingdom. We have found one after much agony of brain. It is the mermaid. This animal has a doubtful existence. So has the Know Nothing ticket—its paternity being a matter of speculation. The mermaid is a sea animal, represented to have the head and body of a woman with the tail of a fish. This Know Nothing ticket has the head of a Whig, while its tail is certainly composed of *fishy* Democrats. Nor does the analogy cease here. The mermaid is associated with that public imposter and general circulator of impositions, Phineas T. Barnum. This mermaid ticket is presented to the world under the auspices of a set of politicians whose experiments upon popular curiosity and credulity have been as numerous as those of Barnum. It is like the mermaid in another light. One of the amusements of this half woman and half fish is to attract persons to its embrace by singings of the sweetest melody, and when its fated admirers come within reach of its scaly tail, to coil it round them, and dive with them to the depths of the sea, and there feed upon the bodies of the deluded victims. So it is with this political mermaid ticket. It too sings songs of American melody, but woe to the deluded wretch who listens to their treacherous music. Once within their slimy embrace, it will sink with them into the slime of Ocean's bed, and their gorge at leisure upon their unfortunate victims. We might run out this and other analogies, but the present is sufficient for to-day.—*Lynchburg Republican.*

The Enquirer, in a subsequent article, discussed Mr. Flournoy's antecedents, as follows :

HISTORICAL RESEARCHES OF THE HON. THOMAS S. FLOURNOY.

Silence is at length broken. Know Nothingism speaks through its avowed organ. Its recognized candidate "endorses, fully, the basis of principles of the American party," and adopts them as his own. Nay, more, he expounds and enforces them, and invokes in their behalf the "teachings of all history." We design for the present merely to explore the depths of his historical researches. Hereafter we may work still further the rich mine revealed in his letter of acceptance.

After advocating an exercise of Federal power for the purpose of checking foreign immigration, and thus conceding that the Federal Government may use its power to increase or diminish at pleasure the population of a State, he continues in this fashion :

"Intimately connected with this question of foreign immigration, is the growth of the Roman Catholic Church in our country. Despotic, proscriptive and intolerant, its ascendancy, as all history teaches, has ever been destructive of freedom of opinion ; while I would uncompromisingly oppose any interference with the rights of its members as citizens by any legislative enactment, yet by a full and independent exercise of the right of suffrage and the appointing power they should be excluded from the offices of the Government in all its departments."

Analyze this paragraph and we get the following result. All history teaches that the Roman Catholic religion has ever been destructive of freedom of opinion, and therefore, " that its members should be excluded from the offices of the Government in all its departments." In other words, a due regard for public safety requires the total exclusion of Roman Catholics from all participation in the Government of the country.

Before proceeding to notice this most extraordinary dogma, we protest against a misconstruction of our design. We are not, and never can be, the apologists of the Roman Catholic religion. We are essentially Protestant, reared under Protestant influences and bound by the strongest ties of affection and reason to Protestantism. But we detest the rank injustice to Roman Catholics, daily and hourly perpetrated by the Know Nothing party, and now officially promulgated by its representative.

History does not teach that free institutions are incompatible with the predominance of Roman Catholicism, as the Hon. Thomas Stanhope Flournoy maintains.

Indeed, the contrary is so notorious as to excite suspicion that history was not one " of the quiet pursuits of private life" from which he " was unwilling to have his attention withdrawn." We fear that his attention was directed more to the new Code and Mayo's Guide, than to the teachings of Hume and Hallam. We shall, therefore, take leave to give him an elementary lesson in history.

Nothing is more distinctly taught by history than the inability of the Romish Church to cope with free principles, supposing them, for argument sake, to be hostile. And that Roman Catholics themselves have waged the war in behalf of freedom against the head of their Church.

To prove this, we shall select the history of a period beginning three hundred years before the advent of Protestantism, when the Romish Church was in the plenitude of its power, spiritual and temporal ; and we shall take the country whose history is best known to us.

We maintain, in opposition to the historical theory of the ex-honorable candidate, that nearly all, if not quite all, of the essential principles of our Republican institutions originated among Catholics, and were developed by them. We take it that freedom of person, and security of property, stand foremost in the catalogue of these principles if they do not constitute their sum total. According to Hallam, a Protestant and the most impartial of historians, these two principles were recognized and secured by Magna Charta, three centuries before the reformation. He says, that "the essential clauses of Magna Charta, are those which protect the personal liberty and property of all freemen by giving security from arbitrary imprisonment and arbitrary spoliation." (Hallam's Middle Ages, page 342.) He then quotes from the Charter of Henry III. substantially the same with Magna Charter, this passage : " No freeman shall be taken or imprisoned, or be disseized of his freehold, or liberties, or free customs, or be outlawed, or exiled, or any otherwise destroyed; nor will we pass upon him, nor send upon him, but by the lawful judgment of his peers, or by the law of the land." "It is obvious, (says Hallam,) that these words, interpreted by any honest court of law, convey an ample security for the two main rights of civil society. From the era, therefore, of King John's Charter, it must have been a clear principle of our constitution, that no man can be detained in prison without a trial. Whether Courts of Justice framed the writ of habeas corpus in conformity to the spirit of this clause or found it already in their register, it became from that era the right of the subject to demand it." "That writ is the principal bulwark of English liberty." Thus it seems, according to this Protestant historian, that the principal bulwark of English liberty was erected by the hands of Roman Catholics. Other clauses of the Charter protected the subject from absolute spoliation and excessive fines, and "fourscore years afterwards (says Hallam) *the great principle of parliamentary taxation was explicitly and absolutely recognized.*"

The principle which caused the American Revolution, and is justly regarded as the corner stone of our present institutions, was explicitly declared and absolutely recognized by Roman Catholics two centuries before Protestantism was born.

Nor was this passion for liberty, a passing flame, but a deep, unwavering, permanent attachment. Recurring again to Hallam, page 343, we find it stated that "the Great Charter was always considered as a fundamental law. But yet, it was supposed to acquire additional security by frequent confirmation." And what part did the Catholic Clergy act, with regard to it. The historian says "from the great difficulty of compelling the King (Henry III.) to observe the boundaries of law, the English Clergy, (Catholic of course,) to whom we are *much indebted for their zeal in behalf of liberty during this reign*, devised means of binding his conscience, and terrifying his imagination by religious sanctions. The solemn excommunication, accompanied with the most awful threats pronounced against the violators of Magna Charta, is well known from our common histories."

Not so. Mr. Flournoy never heard of it or dreamt of it, else he would not have maintained from the "teachings of history," that no Roman Catholic should be permitted to hold office.

A cursory glance over the succeeding pages of the same historian, shows the progressive developement of free principles. The admission of the Commons to Parliament, the incorporation of Towns with exemptions from arbitrary control; the division of Parliament into two houses—the illegality of raising money without consent of Parliament—the necessity that the two houses should concur for any alterations in the law, and the right of the Commons to enquire into public abuses, and to impeach public counsellors; all of these principles were established upon a firm footing by the close of Edward III.'s reign, or about 150 years before the reformation.

Hallam closes the history of the Plantagenets with this remarkable declaration, written as if to rebuke prophetically, the false and fanatical charges against the Catholics now in vogue:

"It were a strange misrepresentation of history to assert that the constitution had attained anything like a perfect state in the 15th century; but I know not whether there are any essential privileges of our countrymen, any fundamental securities against arbitrary power, so far as they depend upon positive institutions, which may not be traced to the time when the house of Plantagenet filled the English throne." (page 450.)

When it is remembered that the last of the Plantagenets fell on the field of battle, on the 22d day of August, 1485, more than forty years before the reformation in England, it will be seen that Hallam's statement is equivalent to a declaration that all the essential privileges of Englishmen, and all their fundamental securities against arbitrary power were established by Roman Catholics and secured by constitutional guarantees.

The answer which will probably be made, strengthens our argument. It will be said that these institutions were founded in spite of the Pope and that Innocent formerly annulled Manna Charta. Granted, but this only proves the utter inability of the Pope to suppress free principles among his undisputed subjects; and when, in the utmost plenitude of his power, spiritual and temporal, he was powerless against Catholics, would he be stronger against a mixed population like our own? But why recur to history for a demonstration of the impotency of the Romish Church against free principles? Have we not seen it dethroned in the very seat of its power, and is it not now upheld by French bayonets? Could it suppress free institutions in the Kingdom of Sardinia, or Switzerland, or prevent the present revolution in Spain? How absurd to suppose that the people of the United States are in danger from a power too feeble in its strongholds to effect the purposes ascribed to it. How absurd to fear injuries from a decayed institution which it could not inflict in the height of its power. How wicked to pretend such fear for the purpose of producing sectional hate and riding into power on a predominant faction?

History teaches that England when wholly Catholic, gave birth to and reared free government in spite of the Pope. Therefore, Virginia, containing 49 Protestants to 1 Catholic, is in danger from the Papal power! This is the premise and this the argument of Know-Nothingism.

MR. FLOURNOY'S ACCEPTANCE.

Mr. Flournoy signified his acceptance of the Winchester nomination in the following letter. This document derives greater significance from the fact, that it was the only expression of opinion in any form which Mr. F. vouchsafed in the paper during the whole canvass:

[CORRESPONDENCE.]

WINCHESTER, March 14th, 1855.

To the Hon. Thos. S. Flournoy:

DEAR SIR:—The undersigned, a committee appointed for the purpose, take pleasure in informing you of your unanimous nomination, by the Convention of the American Party of Virginia, which met on yesterday at this place, as "the American candidate for the office of Governor of this State;" and request your acceptance of the nomination.

Very respectfully, &c.

ANDREW E. KENNEDY,
GEORGE D. GRAY,
JOSIAH DABBS, } Committee.

HALIFAX C. H., March 22d, 1855.

Messrs. Andrew E. Kennedy, George D. Gray and Josiah Dabbs:

GENTLEMEN—I have just received your letter of the 14th, informing me of my nomination by the Convention at Winchester, for the office of Governor of this State, and requesting my acceptance.

It was well known to all who communicated with me upon the subject, that for reasons entirely personal to myself, I had no desire to occupy such a position. As far as it is above any merit which I possess, and as worthy as it is of the ambition of any man, I was unwilling to have my attention withdrawn from the quiet pursuits of private life, and earnestly hoped that the Convention would have selected some one more suitable in every respect than myself to represent the American party. But my entire confidence in and earnest desire for the success of the principles of that party, upon which, in my humble judgment, depend the protection of the rights of the States, and the preservation of the Union, induce me to accept the nomination.

In doing so, it is proper that I shall express my opinions upon the subjects which most interest the people of the State.

I am in favor of a general system of popular education.

I am in favor of completing the leading lines of internal improvement, now under prosecution, with as much dispatch as the financial condition of the State will justify, keeping always in view the preservation of her faith and credit.

I endorse fully the Basis of Principles of the American party, believing them to be the most conservative presented to the consideration of the country since the establishment of our independence.

The rapid increase of Foreign immigration is well calculated to excite alarm, and the power of the Government, both State and Federal, should be exerted to check it. It seems almost impossible to doubt that the influx of between four and five hundred thousand Foreigners into our country annually, will ultimately be subversive of our Republican institutions. Washington, Jefferson, Madison and Jackson gave early warning to the country of the danger to be apprehended from foreign influence. The naturalization laws should either be repealed or so modified, and such restrictions imposed as to avert the evil.

The South is especially and deeply interested in this question. This immense annual addition to our population settle in the non-slaveholding States and the extensive territories of the West and North-west, out of which Free States will, in consequence, be more speedily formed, increasing with fearful rapidity the balance of power against us.

Intimately connected with this question of foreign immigration, is the growth of the Roman Catholic Church in our country. Despotic, proscriptive and intolerant, its ascendancy, as all history teaches, has ever been destructive of freedom of opinion, and while I would uncompromisingly oppose any interference with the rights of its members as citizens, by any legislative enactment, yet by a full and independent exercise of the right of suffrage and the appointing power, they should be excluded from the offices of the Government in all its departments.

It may be said that there are comparatively but few Foreigners and Roman Catholics in Virginia. She is not acting for herself alone. She is a leading member of this great sisterhood of States, and her action will be felt for weal or woe, by them all. Her destiny is identified with theirs, and she cannot look with indifference to the fact, that the great valley of the Mississippi, watered by twenty thousand miles of navigable rivers, and the immense and fertile Territories, stretching beyond to the Pacific, capable of sustaining a population of one hundred millions, are rapidly filling up with this class of people.

I will advert particularly to one other principle of the American party—the "non-intervention of the Federal and State government with the municipal affairs of each other." The strict observance of this principle will make the union of the States perpetual.

I shall not have it in my power to meet the people of the State and discuss these questions with them face to face. It is now but about sixty days to the election, and if I were to devote every day to the canvass, I should not be able to visit much more than a third of the counties. An additional, and with me an important reason, is, that I shall be fully occupied in preparation for, and attendance upon the Courts in which I practice, until the election shall have passed.

If with these opinions, and this position, the people of Virginia shall elect me to the distinguished office of Governor of the Commonwealth, I will discharge its duties with fidelity, and what ability I possess. I will endeavor to advance the prosperity, guard the honor, and protect the interests and institutions of Virginia, by all the power vested in me, and I shall do all that I can consistently with her interest and honor for the preservation of the Union.

Very respectfully, your ob't serv't,

THOS. S. FLOURNOY.

The editor of the Examiner criticised, in the following searching and scathing manner, Mr. Flournoy's letter on its publication:

THE STATESMANSHIP OF MR. FLOURNOY.

We have expressed our respect for the personal character of Mr. Flournoy. That he is a man of integrity, intelligence, talents, a genial temperament and an honorable reputation, we desire at all times to be understood as cheerfully conceding; and we trust that nothing we are about to say, or shall utter during the present canvass, (which promises to be the most acrimonious ever known in Virginia) shall be construed as, in the least degree, retracting or qualifying this concession.

Entertaining these sentiments of personal esteem for Mr. Flournoy, we cannot but express our surprise at the production, printed in another column, purporting to be from his pen, and addressed to three persons understood to be corresponding secretaries of the Know Nothing Convention of Winchester.

It is a palpably just and a very lenient criticism of Mr. Flournoy's letter accepting the nomination of the Winchester Convention, to say that it is weak in tenor and shallow in statesmanship. Indeed, it would be beneath especial notice but for the position of its author. That single circumstance alone, entitles it to the searching examination which we shall give it. It gives us pain to use this bluntness in regard to a letter emanating from one who aspires to be the Governor of Virginia. We had hoped, for the credit of the State, that at a time when the eyes of the whole Union are riveted anxiously upon Virginia, when the entire American people are eagerly scanning the men aspiring to fill the distinguished office in this Commonwealth which has been illustrated by Henry, Jefferson and Giles, and in a canvass that is national, not only in the intense and far-pervading interest it has excited, but in the great principles of representative government it involves, we should have had some other response, from a leader of one of the contending organizations, than a letter abounding in the shallowest partisan politics, and announcing sentiments which, if gravely propounded twelve months ago in Virginia, before fanaticism had taken partial possession of the public mind, would have branded him as an idiot, a maniac, or a monster.

He Adopts the Low Dogmas of the Know Nothings.

Mr. Flournoy declines to discuss the momentous questions at issue in this canvass, "face to face" with the people, on the miserable, hackneyed plea, that a load of *nisi prius* practice presses upon his shoulders. What is this practice—what are the few fees he may earn by pursuing it, to the stern obligation he is under as a republican citizen, an honest man, and a professing Christian, to justify to the people of Virginia the felonious blows and stealthy assaults by which his secret clubs and midnight accomplices are attacking the vital principles of religious freedom and representative government? Heralded as a Presbyterian, as a member of a denomination illustrious for its services in the cause of religious toleration, he owes it to his own church—nay, he owes it to all Protestantdom to explain why he repudiates a principle which they claim as their own peculiar gift to freedom, and why he accepts, to the shame of his religion, from church burning ANGEL GABRIELS, NED BUNTLINES and BILL POOLES, of the North, the barbarous doctrines of proscription and intolerance which he shamelessly avows in his letter. He owes this justification to the people of Virginia: for when has a candidate for her most distinguished honor ever insulted them before by invoking the low passions of intolerance and bigotry to aid his partisan pretensions? When did WASHINGTON, or JEFFERSON, or RANDOLPH, or any honorable name that graces the annals of our State, ever descend to denounce in a campaign circular, *even the Catholics*, for the sake of securing public office, and winning the suffrages of the generous Virginia people? We know that midnight clubs are in the habit of lashing themselves into fury, and that partisan demagogues of the cross-roads and the campaign journals delight to bellow and rant themselves into notoriety, over this newly vamped Catholic question; but that a man of elevated character and liberal scholarship, esteemed fit to fill an exalted office of Virginia, should stoop to lay his tongue and draggle his reputation in such filthy mire, is a shame that we trusted would be spared to our State.

He Assails the Freedom of Religion.

He maintains that Roman Catholics "should be excluded from the office of the government in all its departments," and promises fidelity and vigilance in this brave work. That any sect of Christians should be proscribed for their religious faith, is a sentiment which we thought had been scouted out of our country as long ago as the establishment of our free institutions, which even England is become ashamed of and restive under, and of which the only remaining stronghold, home and sanctuary at the present day is God-forsaken Spain and her sister despotisms of Europe. The present is the first occasion, in Virginia, for a century, in which a person holding an honorable position in society, above the level of the JACK CADES and Z. JUDSONS of the mob, has stooped to appropriate it as a political hobby, and to claim it as a partisan shibboleth.

He Declares for the Perpetual Agitation of a Bigoted Sentiment.

Mr. FLOURNOY'S mode of effecting this shameful proscription is as unstatesmanlike as it is unmanly. He would accomplish his object by incessant demagogue *agitation*; but would "uncompromisingly oppose" effectuating it by the direct and honorable means of "legal enactment." What is worthy of being done at all, is worthy of being done well; and it is sufficient to damn any scheme of public policy, that it is too vicious, unjust, and unrighteous to be carried into a law. And how pitiable and unmanly is the statesmanship which propounds a measure of reform, but skulks from the only bold, honorable and efficient means of carrying it into effect! That he shrinks from carrying his scheme of politics out into practical legislation, proves that it is agitated for anything else but the public good, that it is agitated exclusively for the ends of demagogues. In the benignancy of his *statesmanship* he would sow the elements of discord and strife broadcast over the community, and make it the leading effort of his diplomacy to keep the flames thus enkindled ever burning and exploding. He would not execute the victims of his proscription by a single blow of the axe or the guillotine, but roast them leisurely upon the slow fires of the rack, that he might continue to gloat over their tortures! Consummate is that *statesmanship* which studies to supply a perpetual incentive to strife, hatred and mob-violence between class and class, sect and sect, race and race, in the bosom of the same community! We know of no better definition of demagogueism than it is *agitation for the mere purpose of fermenting ill-blood and strife between class and sects, as the means of elevating the agitators to office.* It is a sort of politics that might be tolerated in irresponsible clubs convened in secret, and in vapid partizans of low degree; but that a man of education, aspiring to the control of public affairs, should have proposed it in a public letter over his own name, is an event that shocks the moral sentiment and patriotic composure of all conservative citizens. We are sorry that a man has been thought worthy of grave public responsibilities in Virginia whose moral obliquity is such that he plumes himself upon advocating the very plan of politics which he vaunts it as a virtue that he "uncompromisingly opposes making the subject of legal enactment,"—because, of course, it is too intolerant, despotic, proscriptive and bigoted to deserve place upon the statute book!

He Propounds an Abolition Scheme of Politics.

Mr. FLOURNOY's positions on the subject of immigration are ridiculously weak, absurd, and untenable. Borrowing the idea of Governor *Smith*, he says:

"The South is especially and deeply interested in this question; this immense and annual addition to our population settle in the non-slaveholding States and the extensive territories of the West and North-West, out of which Free States will, in consequence, be more speedily formed, increasing with fearful rapidity the balance of power against us."

In a previous paragraph he "endorses fully" the "Basis of Principles of the American party," one of which runs thus:

"No obstacle should be interposed to the immigration of all foreigners of honest and industrious habits;"

which language is coupled with a clause excepting "paupers and criminals" from the privilege.

Excepting paupers and criminals, which men of all classes and parties in the Union would join him in excluding from our shores, Mr. FLOURNOY would let foreigners into the country *ad libitum.* What then is his position? Conceding that immigration goes almost altogether to the North, and that little of it comes to the South, his masterly statesmanship proposes to agitate in Virginia a subject peculiarly northern and domestic, and strictly within the scope of State and police regulation—a doctrine of abolition invention and utterly abhorrent to all Southern ideas of State sovereignty. He would prosecute this mad policy under the pretext, and in the dog-in-the-manger spirit, of checking a more "rapid increase of political power in the North" than in the South. It is humiliatingly in conflict with the *chivalrous* temper of the South to resist a movement, right, and worthy of "full endorsement" in itself, from the mean motive of jealousy; but such is Mr. FLOURNOY's statesmanship and Virginian manliness!

But is Mr. FLOURNOY ignorant of the fact that so long as honest and industrious foreigners are let into the North *ad libitum*, which he approves, the mere denial to them of the right of suffrage and official position cannot prevent that augmentation of Northern representation in Congress, of which he complains? Is this Governor of Virginia, expectant, ignorant of the notorious constitutional fact that it is *population* and not *suffrage* which determines the ratio of representation in Congress? Has he not yet learned in the horn-book of constitutional law, that five *slaves* even, count as many as three whites in determining Southern representation in Congress; and that immigrants once landed at the North, without naturalization, count as much in augmenting Northern representation in Congress as if each could vote for every office in the country? We all know that the Know Nothing party belie by their action every principle avowed in their BASIS, and that plausible schedule, chiefly of truisms that nobody will dispute, is put out as a decoy for the shallow and unthinking; but we really did not think that Mr. FLOURNOY would commit himself in black and white to a pretext so transparent and disreputable, as that a denial of office and suffrage to immigrants could swell the rapid increase of the Northern balance of power. The Basis principle which he "fully endorses" admits all honest and industrious immigrants, and itself permits to be accomplished the very evil of which he complains, whether the immigrant ever afterwards secures a vote and office or not.

He Borrows a Bad Argument from Governor Smith.

But imitators and quacks are prone to get swamped in quagmires. Mr. FLOURNOY borrowed Governor SMITH's idea without having the sagacity to perceive the necessity of borrowing also the limitation which that gentleman coupled with the stolen article. Governor SMITH did not, like his imitator, "endorse fully" the Basis Principles of the new party, but only approved some of them. *He* goes a bow-shot beyond the decoy doctrine, and, so far from protesting that "no obstacle should be interposed to foreign immigration," &c., "deprecates immigration as a great calamity," declaring it to be "our highest duty to *arrest the importation of foreigners.*" Poor Mr. FLOURNOY appropriates Governor SMITH's argument of unduly augmented Northern representation in Congress, but stumbles and fractures his skin over the "*no obstacle*" clause in his own Baais Principles.

He and Gov. Smith both Tumble into an Abolition Heresy.

It is an easy but unpleasant task, to show that Gov. SMITH, in taking this position on the immigrant question, bids farewell to State Rights politics. It is monstrous for a Southern man to propound a doctrine requiring the Virginia people to interfere with a strictly domestic question of the North, upon the whining plea—of envy and jealousy, that the North is outstripping us in the march to empire. It is calling upon the South to violate a principle of politics which she has considered of vital importance to her safety, and *that,* from the meanest and most pusilanimous of all motives. With what indignation would we ourselves resist the like doctrine, if brought to bear by the North against our own physical development? What if Virginia, as is not unlikely, should herself take steps to import miners, artificers, manufacturers and laborers from overstocked Europe, for the development of her own latent wealth;—and if the Abolitionists of the North, borrowing the policy of George III., should demand of Congress to exclude this foreign immigration, on the Smith-Flournoy-Know Nothing Ground, that it would unduly augment Southern representation in Congress? Would Virginia tamely submit to the insolent demand and gratuitous insult? How has she not resented the conduct of the Abolitionists, bottomed on the similar plea of checking the extension of *slave* power, in imposing the Missouri Compromise upon us, in urging the Wilmot Proviso almost to the disruption of the Union, in resisting the purchase of Florida and Louisiana, the annexation of Texas, and the conquest of Mexico, and in now attempting to thwart in advance the honorable purchase and acquisition of Cuba?

He Borrows a Mean Sentiment from the Abolitionists.

The strength of the Sourthern cause has heretofore consisted much in the meanness of the motive with which our progress has been resisted by the Abolitionists. Let us not permit DELILAH to shear us of our strength. Let us not borrow the meanness, the politics and the policy of Abolitionism, by shamelessly avowing our jealousy of Northern progress and prosperity, and by interfering with their domestic concerns, professedly but to cripple them, and not to benefit ourselves. Foreign immigration is a subject strictly of State economy, and no Northern State will or Southern State should consent to surrender the supreme control of it. When Massachusetts, through Congress, shall dictate to Virginia to what classes of people her ports shall be opened, what races of men shall vote and shall hold office, what shade of opinions shall disqualify for enjoying the rights, privileges, and franchises of citizenship, Virginia will have surrendered to the last demand of abolitionism, and been despoiled of the last attribute of State sovereignty.

He Invites the North to Stop Prospering, in Order to Appease the Jealousy of Virginia.

But, instead of such a rotten doctrine, does our model State Rights Governor, expectant, mean to maintain that agitating this question here in Virginia is calculated to bring about the exclusion of immigrants from the North by voluntary legislation on the part of Northern States? If so, in what a contemptible attitude does the proposition stand? He raises a huge clamor in Virginia about the rapid increase of political power in the North from immigration, for the purpose of inducing those people *themselves* to destroy the main agent of their own growth and progress! He agitates here to induce them to cease to grow and prosper, in order to gratify Mr. FLOURNOY'S puerile statesmanship, and to sooth Virginia's dog-in-the-manger spirit. Of all the absurd and stupid propositions we ever heard, it is this of Mr. FLUORNOY, borrowed from Governor SMITH, that by agitating and raising a hello—hello *here in Virginia* about the great augmentation of northern power from immigration, we shall induce them to lay a suicidal axe at the roots of their own amazing prosperity!

And yet he turns up at last a State Rights Man!

After announcing these rank and fanatical doctrines of Federal interference and inter-State interference, it is a mockery of State-Rights politics, and an insult to popular intelligence—only equaled by the late similar profession of WILSON of Massachusetts—for Mr. FLOURNOY to declare:

"I will advert particularly to one other principle of the American party—the 'non-intervention of the Federal and State government with the municipal affairs of each other.' The strict observance of this principle will make the union of the States perpetual."

The force of impertinence could no further go!

He Desires Virginia to Scour the Great West on a Tour of Proscription.

Mr. FLOURNOY takes still further pains to proclaim this rotten Abolition doctrine of interference in the domestic affairs of other States. The following ambitious, sophomeric sentences have a prominent place in his remarkable letter:

"It may be said that there are comparatively but few foreigners and Roman Catholics in Virginia. *She is not acting for herself alone.* She is a leading member of this great sisterhood of States, and her action will be felt for weal or woe, by them all. Her destiny is identified with theirs, and she cannot look with indifference to the fact, that the great valley of the Mississippi, watered by twenty thousand miles of navigable rivers, and the immense and fertile Territories, stretching beyond to the Pacific, capable of sustaining a population of one hundred millions, are rapidly filling up with this class of people."

So, then, our chivalrous Commonwealth, under the guidance of his resplendent statesmanship, is to assume the honorable office of common scold and intermeddler, and to go forth into the West and North-west, berating Catholics and shoo-shooing foreigners—like depredating poultry—out of their gardens and potato patches! A fit Governor for such a Commonwealth, would be amiable Mr. FLOURNOY—the statesman.

Virginia is to go out into the West and North-west, a jealous, scolding Juno, attended by her Know Nothing Argus of an hundred eyes, threading their twenty thousand miles of navigable rivers, expelling "foreigners" from a land they may have held since De Soto and La Salle, and "excluding Catholics from the offices of government in all its departments." We pity the spirit of narrow jealousy and intolerance which dictates such a policy as much as the ignorance it betrays. Mr Flournoy will be surprised to learn that there is scarcely a square inch of the countries here mentioned in which the Catholic citizen is not protected and guaranteed in all the rights, immunities and privileges, political and religious, of the most favored citizens of the United States, by express compacts, sacred, inviolable, irrepealable and perpetual.

He is taught a Lesson of Some Importance to a Statesman from the Archives of the Country.

We shall first apprise our Governor expectant of the existence of a clause in the celebrated ordinance of 1787, "for the government of the territory of the United States north-west of the Ohio river" in the nature of a perpetual compact, framed by some of the best men and purest patriots with whom God ever blessed the earth. The first—*first* article of that venerable statute runs thus:

"Art. I. No person, demeaning himself in a peaceable and orderly manner, shall EVER be molested on account of his mode of worship or religious sentiments, in the said territory."

We trust that no demagogue will interpose here, the shallow quibble, that to insult a citizen, with the declaration that his religious sentiments render him an unsafe depositary of official reponsibility, is not *molesting* him on account of his religion.

Again, that vast territory, acquired by the Louisiana purchase, stretching from the Pacific to the Mississippi, embracing Oregon, Texas Missouri and all the intermediate domain, which was ceded by France, and was first settled, as was the northwest country just mentioned, by Catholics, is subject to the following solemn stipulation, being the third article in the Louisiana Treaty of the 30th April 1803:

"Art. 3. The inhabitants of ceded territory shall be incorporated in the Union of the United States, and admitted as soon as possible, according to the principles of the Federal Constitution, to the enjoyment of ALL the rights, advantages and immunities of citizens of the United States; and, in the meantime, they shall be *maintained* and *protected* in the free enjoyment of their liberty, property, and the *religion which they profess.*"

Instead of maintaining and protecting them, according to the spirit of this solemn compact, in this religion, Mr. FLOURNOY proposes, on *account of it,* to proscribe them from office and degrade them from the rank of sovereign citizens.

Proceeding farther in this interesting historical enquiry, we find another portion of the Union, watered in part by the Mississippi, consecrated perpetually to religious toleration. The Treaty of Feb. 22, 1819, with Spain, under which we acquire Florida and a large adjacent territory, contains these two articles:

"Art. 5. The inhabitants of the ceded territories shall be secured in the *free exercise* of their religion, *without* ANY *restriction;* and all those who may desire to remove to the Spanish dominions shall be permitted to sell or export their effects at any time whatever, without being subject, in either case, to duties."

"Art. 6. The inhabitants of the territories which His Catholic Majesty cedes to the United States, by this Treaty, shall be incorporated in the Union of the United States, as soon as may be consistent with the principles of the Federal Constitution, and admitted to the enjoyment of ALL *the priviliges, rights, and immunities* of the CITIZENS of the United States."

And coming still further down, even to our own time, we find that our vast acquisition from Mexico, an empire, itself, in the magnitude of its area, its population and wealth, to be indelibly stamped with an holy canon of religious toleration. In the Treaty of May 30, 1848, with the Mexican Republic, under which, auriferous California became a part of our Union, occurs the following golden provision:

"Art. 9. Mexicans who, in the territories aforesaid, shall not preserve the character of citizens of the Mexican Republic [but shall elect under the preceding clause to be citizens of the United States,] * * * shall be incorporated into the Union of the United States, and be admitted at the proper time (to be judged of by the Congress of the United States) to the enjoyment of all the rights of citizens of the United States; according to the principles of the Constitution; and, in the meantime, shall be maintained and protected in the free enjoyment of their liberty and property, and SECURED IN THE FREE EXERCISE *of their religion without restriction.*"

As reference is repeatedly made in these documents to the *rights, privileges* and *immunities*, of the citizens of the United States, as guaranteed by the Constitution thereof, it is a fitting conclusion to such solemn stipulations to support them by the provisions on this subject of that palladium of liberty and compact of fraternal Union between the States. The sixth article of that instrument declares—

"Art. VI. No *religious test* shall *ever* be required as a qualification to *any* office of public trust under this government."

And the very first article among the amendments which were added to the instrument, out of the abundant caution and jealousy of our fathers, which had special reference to such intolerant movements as that of the latter day Know Nothings, places religious freedom first in its enumeration of the inviolable franchises of a free people:

"Art. I. Congress shall make no law respecting an establishment of religion, or the FREE EXERCISE THEREOF; or abridging the *freedom of speech*, or of *the press;* or the right of the people peaceably to assemble, and to petition the government for a redress of grievances."

Thus it seems that every foot of territory in this broad and glorious confederacy is consecrated by the most solemn and holy compacts to the LIBERTY OF CONSCIENCE. Thus it is apparent that Mr. FLOURNOY'S mushroom part of *religious intolerance*, though boasting its NATIONALITY, has not a spot of the consecrated soil of the American Union on which to plant its flag-staff.

Mr. FLOURNOY will now perceive, that it would have been the more prudent part for him to have pursued the policy of Mr. PATTON, and, if accepting the disreputable nomination at all, to have held his silence in regard to the principles of proscription and tyranny that are coupled with it, upon which the fathers of his country so solemnly pronounced their anathema maranatha. Even if Mr. FLOURNOY should have deceived himself into a declaration that he did not desire this nomination for the office for which he is named, can any one else believe that so intelligent a person as himself *could* be sincere in such a profession, while consenting, for the sake of securing the position, to endorse the infamous and damnable doctrines to which he has now set his name, and which will stigmatize that honorable name long after his body shall have returned to the dust from which it came?

He Goes to Sea on a Frail Raft of Rotten Logs.

Mr. Flournoy borrows his principles of State policy from Mr. Wise, making up no issue on State questions, and standing exclusively, in this canvass, on the Know Nothing principles of

Religious Intolerance,
Unequal Rights,
Secret Politics.

MR. PATTON'S SPEECH AT RICHMOND, ACCEPTING THE NOMINATION.

This oration is remarkable as the only one delivered by any of the Winchester candidates during the progress of the canvass, if we except one or two other speeches of Mr. PATTON, delivered on the very eve of the election. It therefore merits a conspicuous place in this compilation, and we lay it before our readers *in extenso*, following it up by a very searching review of it from the Richmond Examiner.

Fellow-citizens—fellow-citizens of the American party and of all parties: I regret that, upon this first occasion of the assembling of the American party, and of the great body who are sympathizing with the American party, that it is my lot to be the only one of the nominees of the Winchester Convention present to receive your greetings on this occasion. I should have been much better pleased, and especially gratified, if the distinguished leader, who has been chosen as your political standard-bearer in the present canvass, had been present to address you; a gentleman so much more able to address you than I am, so as to do justice to your views, and so much better qualified to gratify the expectations of this large and crowded assembly, by an address worthy of the meeting, and worthy of the great subject.

I came here, gentlemen, rather for the purpose of vindicating myself for assuming the position which I have assumed, and of vindicating you for having placed me in that position. My nomination by the Winchester Convention, as a candidate for the suffrages of the people of Virginia, was as unexpected as it was unsought by me, withdrawn as I had been for several years —for two or three years at least—from any active participation in the political controversies of the country. Absorbed in the laborious, overwhelming and almnst crushing duties of an arduous profession, I had paid very little attention to the progress of political events. I knew scarcely anything of the issues which were about to arise, and which were likely to guide the people in the coming election. In that position I sought no office, and expected none from any party, or a nomination from any party. I held out no inducements to those who, in behalf of this new American party, called upon me for the purpose of ascertaining whether I would accept this office of attorney-general. I sincerely and most frankly discouraged the idea, and told them very frankly that I had not even read the Basis Principles which they had put forth as containing the objects for which this organization was formed, and which they were endeavoring to accomplish. I was told that this great organization desired, or at least a portion of the members of the Convention at Winchester, and probably the whole body, would desire to confer this nomination on me, if I was willing to accept the office, without any regard to my political opinion or my political course; that it was an office wholly disconnected with political controversy, in reference to the discharge of the peculiar duties which devolved upon it; that it was an office which had no patronage connected with it, and that, estimating very highly (much more highly than I had vanity to aspire to) my qualifications and fitness for the office, they desired to confer it upon me, in reference to their estimate of my qualifications and fitness for it, without reference at all to any political object. I told them that if, under these circumstances, as it was an office in the line of my profession—an office which, although I had no particular desire to obtain, it would yet not be unacceptable to me—if the Convention chose to confer upon me the nomination, I would accept it, assuring them at the same time that it would be incompatible with my business to engage in the political canvass in the way of discussion, and that, in my estimate, it was not desirable or proper that a candidate for an office of that sort should be mixed up in the angry political strife of parties. I most sincerely desired to occupy that position absolutely and entirely. It has not seemed good to the leaders and mouth-pieces of the party on the other side that I shall be permitted to occupy that position. I have been assailed with a fierceness of denunciation, and with a virulence of invective, and coarseness and illiberality of abuse, that has never been surpassed, if indeed it has ever been equaled. My motives traduced—eagerness for office imputed to me—ambitious aspirations—suffering humiliation in consenting to take an inferior office with a tide-waiter's salary, to serve under another leader with the high and important and splendid office of governor of Virginia, with a vast munificent pecuniary compensation.

You have seen what *eagerness* I displayed to get the nomination of attorney-general. And now let me bring to the notice of this vast assembly, and to those who have been disposed to impute to me ambitious motives and eagerness for high office, one or two papers, which is all the answer I mean to give to those charges.

I received, on the evening of the 13th March, from Winchester, the following telegraphic dispatch from a friend of mine, who was a member of the body:

"Will you accept the nomination for governor? Reply immediately to this."

I immediately sent the following by telegraph:

"I would not accept the office of governor if every man in Virginia were to vote for me."

By an ingenious perversity of accusation, it might still be said that I was like Cæsar, rejecting the crown because I knew I could not get it.

On the same evening, not very long after I had received the telegraphic dispatch which I have just read, I received this note from a gentleman in Richmond:

"I have just received a dispatch by telegraph that you were nominated for governor, and requested to communicate it directly."

As soon as I received this note, instantly, for the purpose of preventing any inconvenience to the Winchester Convention, such as would result from their making a nomination which would not be accepted, probably causing them to assemble again there or somewhere else to make another nomination, I sent the following reply:

"I regret the information your note contains. Several times during the last fifteen years I have declined being a candidate for governor when my friends thought I could be elected. I will not accept the office of governor under any circumstances, and though every man in the state were to vote for me. Excuse the apparent peremptoriness of this note."

These are my aspirations for the office of governor, and you can now well form a notion how great was my *mortification* at being passed over for this high office and offered the humble office of attorney-general. It is proper to state that the information that I was nominated for governor was a mistake, which of course I did not know until the following day. There was, as I understand, no such nomination, and the distinguished gentleman who has been nominated, and is so worthy to receive the suffrages of the American party, was the decided choice of the Convention at all times. I do not know that there was a single man who was favorable to my nomination, except the particular gentleman who sent me the dispatch.

Besides all that, it is now said that I am animated by aspirations for the Senate. I say here and now, as I have said repeatedly in the course of the last fifteen years, when my friends desired to put me in nomination for that office, as I said about the office of governor, I would not have the office of senator if every man in the Legislature of Virginia voted for me.

I was then nominated for this office under the circumstances to which I have referred, by a large, respectable, intelligent and patriotic body of men, as much so to the extent that I have information in regard to them, as any body of men in any quarter, any state, or anywhere else in the world—a body of men representing, as I understand now, (for I Know-Nothing about the supposed elective strength of the American party,) fifty or sixty thousand of the free citizens of this commonwealth. I have repeatedly said, in talking of this organization, without knowing anything at all of its objects or purposes, but having heard merely the rapid way in which it advances in the hearts and affections of the people elsewhere, that its objects must be patriotic. Were they otherwise, I could not believe that it could have enlisted so effectually the aid and support of the people of Virginia. It has surpassed the most extravagant idea that I could form of its progress in this state, my opinion having been that the sparseness of the population and the difficulty of communication between our people, would form almost an insurmountable barrier to its extension. I had not the least idea of hope (if I may use that word) that when my nomination was made upon this ticket, there was a reasonable probability that the ticket would prevail. Now, I understand that the body of men who nominated me represented 50,000 persons at least in the commonwealth of Virginia, who have become united to the order, and among them some fifteen or twenty thousand Democrats. I received the nomination, then, of this body of gentlemen representing this vast portion of the people of Virginia, composed of all parties, and I could not feel myself altogether at liberty to refuse to permit such a body of gentlemen of all parties, irrespective of the political basis they might have in this movement, to present my name to the people of Virginia as a candidate for an office wholly disconnected with political parties or strife, and utterly void of all political patronage. And yet that act, the act of permitting my name to be presented to the people of Virginia, has been denounced as an act of treachery to party and a violation of party obligations. I never entered into any party obligations which would prevent me from allowing a majority of the people of Virginia to elect me to any office which I was willing to take, no matter who may have made the nomination, or when or where they may be denounced. I have read the Constitution of Virginia several times, and I find there that the office of attorney-general is to be filled by the votes of the people of Virginia, and not by the Democratic Convention. He little knows my antecedents who does not know that I have never permitted myself to be governed or controlled by the dictates of a party, in regard to party nominations or party measures, anywhere or on any occasion.

It is said I have received rewards of party, and have rendered very little service for them. What party reward did I ever receive? I am charged with ingratitude to the Democratic party. I was never elected to but one office, and that office, like this of attorney-general, not political—I mean the office of councillor of state—and I was elected to that office by a fraction of the Democratic party, with the united vote of the Whig party, beating the caucus nominee of the party. [Mr. P. did not refer to his service in Congress. To prevent misapprehension, it is proper to say that he was never elected to Congress by a party vote. He was elected by the people four terms—three terms without opposition—once against the opposition of a most popular, distinguished and thorough-going party man of the Democratic party; and was, at all times, supported in the independent course he pursued in Congress, (independent of party, he means,) by the great body of both parties.] And I was elected and re-elected to that office five times, every time, except one, by almost the unanimous vote of both parties, without a nomination even against me. On one occasion there was a nomination of a Democratic gentleman against me: a very ardent, consistent and thorough supporter of Democratic principles, who got "twenty-nine votes," and I all the balance. At these elections the Whig party were in the majority twice. I do not mean at all to say anything whatsoever to detract from the liberality, from the friendly feeling, from the liberal support that I received, from the liberal members of the Democratic party, as well as the Whig party, during those elections. But I never was elected by a party vote—never in my life. I never was the favorite of the ultra men of any party assembly, because I did not recognize the despotism of party obligations, and because I always spurned their denunciations, whenever they were directed against me, for a preference of what my judgment approved as demanded by the true interest of the country.

I *have* changed my party position, therefore. During the eight years of my service in Congress—during a portion of the time when Gen. Andrew Jackson was in the zenith of his power, and when to oppose him was like bearding the lion in his den—it can be seen, by reference to the journals of that time, that I voted indifferently, as I thought, with the one party as the other: and it was because of this that the great, aud illustrious, and patriotic man, Henry Clay, who was always my warm friend, (and deeply did I regret very frequently that I could not consistently, with the opinions and principles which I entertained, support him for the presidency,) in the most friendly spirit and the facetiousness of his genial nature, said to me one day, "How are you *to-day*, Mr. Patton?" and that joke, which I told so much to the amusement of my friends in private ten years ago, was told with very amusing effect by John Hampden Pleasants in the Whig, on the day after I made the *great somerset* from the Whig party into the Democratic ranks, when I made a speech at the Exchange in 1844. And this joke, which was so good-humoredly published ten years ago, our Democratic friends seem to have taken hold of for the first time. They seem to have brought it up with a gusto, as if they never had heard of it. They must be very much in want of something to amuse them, when they had to revive my old, stale and thread-bare jokes for the purpose of creating a little merriment.

Gentlemen, this habit of resistance to party dictation exposed me during all my political life to the severe criticism of the press; and they have also brought along with them something which, perhaps, I ought to take as a full equivalent—the good natured, extravagant and equally unmerited praise of the party press.

I have thus received alternately the applause of Mr. Thomas Ritchie and that again of John Hampden Pleasants; and have received alternately their denunciation, too—denunciations from whom were calculated to carry some terror with them. I have heard the thunder of Democratic denunciations rolling over my head, threatening to exterminate me, when Jupiter Tonans, the Olympian Jove of Democracy, Thomas Ritchie, wielded the thunderbolt. I have had the lightning of Whig denunciation to flash in my eyes when it was struck forth by the electric genius of John Hampden Pleasants. I was assailed violently by both, but it gave me great pleasure to see that after the storm of prejudice and passion and political strife had passed away, it was my good fortune to enjoy, in a very high degree, the respect and confidence and friendship of both these gentlemen, which was cordially reciprocated by myself. And now, when I have survived "heaven's artillery," do you think I am going to be killed, or frightened, or hurt, by firing crackers or sky-rockets, and least of all by pop-guns loaded with sliced potatoes, and very soft and small potatoes at that.

It has been said that curses loud and deep from the Democratic party are poured forth against me—I suppose melo-dramatic curses put forth for stage effect. But if there be any gentleman of the Democratic party, whose respect is worth anything, that has lost his own self-respect so far as to deal in curses against me, let me say to him that he had better remember the Eastern apothegm, that "curses, like chickens, go home to roost." As for myself, I regard the curses of an angry partizan just as much as I do the raving of a maniac, or the howling of a hungry hyena. "They pass by me as the idle wind, which I respect not." And there is a consolation accompanying all this denunciation. If I am to be considered, (and I don't care a pinch of snuff whether I am to be so considered or not,) as driven out of the Democratic party, (it certainly required no very strenuous exertion to accomplish that end,) I have the comfort of knowing that I enjoy in this calamity the company of 20,000 (as I am told) of that old and respectable party, as steadfast, true and conscientious as any other equal number who still adhere to it.

And now, gentlemen, I ought, perhaps, after saying this much about political intolerance, say what is perfectly just perhaps to all parties, and certainly to the Democratic party, that whatever other sins they might have been guilty of, they do not bear *malice*. Let any politician, no matter how reprobate he may have been in his opinion—no matter what his political offences may have been—come to the High Priest of the Democratic party, and say, "Purge me with hyssop and I shall be clean, wash me and I will be whiter than snow," he will be sure to receive the merciful response, "Though thy sins be as scarlet, they shall be white as snow; though they be red like crimson, they shall be as wool." For verily, (at this time particularly,) there is more joy in the kingdom of Democracy, or rather, perhaps, I should say in the popedom of Democracy, for they seem to launch their fulminations in the same spirit and tone as if they conceived themselves, like his holiness, the Pope and vicegerent of God, whose decrees and bulls of excommunication proclaimed eternal damnation—for verily "there is more joy over one sinner that repenteth, than over ninety and nine just men that need no repentance." And if there shall be here and there occasionally an acquisition of some seceding Know-Nothing, or obdurate Whig that comes to be purged with hyssop, they are thrown in absolute ecstacy and paroxysms of joy.

Well, gentlemen, there is perhaps something too much of this. I have given this matter connected with myself more consideration than it deserved. I desired, gentlemen, to be saved the necessity of having to say anything in respect to this nomination for attorney-general, or in respect to any matter connected with this canvass. I certainly have no design to say at any time, here or anywhere else, anything in disparagement of the claims of the distinguished gentleman who has been nominated by the Staunton Convention for the office of attorney-general, or anything, in the slightest degree, to derogate from the fidelity with which he will discharge his duties, if a majority of the people of Virginia prefer his filling that office; and still more, emphatically, I have nothing to say and mean to say nothing intended or calculated to induce any man to vote for me, or to prevent any man from voting against me, for that office, if he prefers my competitor to fill it.

I said to you, gentlemen, that when I was nominated for this office I had seen none of the discussions which had grown up in Virginia, or anywhere else, in regard to this American party. I have been so much absorbed with my own business, that I do not think I have read a governor's message for several years, nor a presidents message; and the time when I read a speech in Congress, is a period which runs back to a time that my memory "runneth not to the contrary." I have, however, read somewhat carefully, at various times since my nomination, the principles and basis of the Know-Nothing or American party, and I have no hesitation in saying that with one or two exceptions in regard to the mode of action of the party, and the extent to which they are proposing to go, as a rule for themselves in their organization, the principles and basis of that party meet my entire approbation. I see nothing inconsistent with those unchanged and unchangeable principles of state rights Virginia republicanism which I have always cherished and still cling to.

I have looked a little into the grounds upon which this organization and its principles have been assailed in the canvass, and have been amazed at the strange misconception and the singular perverseness of argument by which it is sought to be maintained, that the principles of this organization are violative of the Constitution and of the Bill of Rights, and that they lead to the destruction of civil and religious liberty.

The last time I was in this building—certainly in connection with any political organization—the cry was then "Young America," and I was hardly permitted to be considered as a fit associate for the genius of true Democracy, because I did not join in a cry which I had not the most distant understanding of the meaning of, except that I had some vague idea that it was gotten up for the purpose of making Stephen A. Douglas president of the United States; and as that was a purpose which I had never conceived, and most probably never would, I was regarded as an "*old fogy*."

Since then there seems to have been some change in the relation of parties and in the issues. We hear no more of these unchanged and unchangeable principles of Virginia state rights republicanism as questions of party controversy, or as the watchword of the Democratic party. And now, since old America and young America have come together, and that young America with a little more prudence and discretion than she manifested before, did come to take counsel of old America; and when they have both joined hands together to form a great American party, those who then made this cry about young America say no more about it, but seemed disposed to embrace in their comprehensive patriotism *old* Europe, *all* Europe, Asia, part of Africa, all creation, and the rest of mankind.

I said, gentlemen, that in regard to some of the details of this basis of principles of Know-Nothingism, I was not prepared to adopt them in all their breadth and length. I do not bind myself by any pledge, either written, spoken, or sworn—that I never will, under any circumstances, vote for foreigners for any office. That is a matter that I will leave altogether at my discretion. Were I to act otherwise, I should be abandoning the ground which I have maintained all my life, and upon which I can now stand up and defy those Democratic denunciations that are hurled against me. I have never been in a party caucus in my life, in Congress or out of it.

While *these* are *my* views of party obligations and the means of carrying out objects of party organization, I have no right to be a censor upon those who, as party men, pursue a different course and entertain other opinions. The American party chooses to hold their meetings in secret, as the Whig and Democratic party have been and are in the habit of holding secret caucuses, by night or day. This party enter, it is said, into mutual obligations as to their party action. No matter what is their form, they can't be held more binding than the Democrats claim to hold the implied obligations of their party. A violation of them, by disobeying the behest of the party, quitting it, is followed by the most vehement denunciation—while this party, as I understand, allows every man to go out of the party when he pleases, and his obligations are at once at an end, without denunciation. With the Democratic party it does not seem to be so, for although there is no oath taken, no pledge registered, no man that acts with them can dare to defy their behests and dissent from their decrees. If he does—"Off with his head. So much for Buckingham."

The freedom of thought and opinion which they allow at this day is happily illustrated in an anecdote which is told of one of Napoleon's marshals, when Napoleon was a candidate for the First Consulship for life. It was to be determined by universal suffrage. Marshal Augekaw addressed his division in the following words: "Soldiers, there is an election to-day to determine whether Napoleon shall be Consul for life. It is to be a matter of the free choice of the people. You will march to the polls and vote just as you think proper; but if you vote against Napoleon, I will shoot you as soon as you come back." While I do not, and cannot according to my notions about party engagements, come under its obligations, I agree that, as a general rule, yours is a proper principle of action, and shall probably act upon it practically myself. There may be occasion under some very peculiar circumstances which should induce a departure from that course, in respect to the exclusion of a foreigner from all political offices. But I maintain against the world in arms, that free citizens of this country, native or foreign, have the right to enter into such an agreement without violating the rights of any other citizens, and without infringing upon any principle of the constitution or the bill of rights, or any other guarantee.

It is to my mind one of the strangest and most extraordinary perversions of principle that ever has been seriously insisted upon, that the rights of foreigners are affected because a portion of the people of Virginia, who regard it as a question of high and important public policy, say, and unite themselves together for the purpose of maintaining the principle, that foreigners should not be allowed to have the political offices of the country.

For what are the rights of foreigners? The rights of foreigners under our laws are to come here and acquire a residence and carry on their business under the ægis and protection of our laws,—to sit down under their own vine and fig tree, and after spending the term of probation fixed by law to entitle them to the right of suffrage, to exercise that right, and, so far as the Constitution permits, to be capable of election to any office *if the people choose to confer it upon them*—and because a portion of the people, in the exercise of their fundamental, indisputable and essential rights, say we won't vote for you for political offices, they are represented as acting in direct conflict with the Constitution and the principles of civil liberty. Foreigners have exactly the same right, when they become citizens, to say we won't vote for you, and I suppose nobody would pretend to say that was a violation and invasion of your rights.

Why, gentlemen, do you know—and I suppose you don't, for you *Know Nothing*—do you know that this principle, so destructive of the rights of foreigners, which you have advocated and which you state is one of the rules of action of your organization is not your thunder at all. You are the copyists merely. You have borrowed the *thunder*, and of whom do you suppose? We have a Constitution here which, as I told you sometime ago, I had read once or twice, and we find in that Constitution that no person shall be eligible to the office of governor unless he have attained the age of thirty years, is a *native citizen of the United States*, and has been a citizen of Virginia so many years. The lieutenant governor shall be elected at the same time, and for the same term, and his qualifications and manner of election shall be the same; so that here is the Know Nothing principle—so fatal and destructive to the right of foreigners, so consistent with equal rights of all citizens—incorporated into the fundamental law of the land; so that if you wanted to vote for foreigners, every one of you, the Constitution forbids your doing so for the office of governor or lieutenant governor of the commonwealth.

Well, now, you have only carried it a little further than the Constitution. The Constitution does not prohibit you from doing as you propose in regard to voting. It is a matter left to the exercise of your will. It is perfectly competent for the citizen, in the exercise of his fundamental and essential right to select for himself any particular individual to vote for. The principles which govern his action in this regard cannot of course be affected by any constitutional enactment, nor can they, by any means, be said to conflict with any provision in our Constitution. But lest you might, peradventure, put a foreigner into the office of governor, or lieutenant governor, our legislators have put an insuperable barrier in the Constitution—you cannot do it.

And now, gentleman, who do you suppose inflicted this violation of the rights of foreigners, and incorporated it into the Constitution? In the convention which formed the Constitution, it was moved by Mr. Hunter, to amend the report by striking therefrom the word "native," so as not to permit foreigners to be elected to the office of governor.

Mr. Letcher moved to amend the amendment by striking out in the 2d and 3d lines the words, "shall be a native citizen of the United States."

The question upon the adoption of the amendment being put to the Convention, was decided in the negative.

The question then recurring upon the motion of Mr. Hunter, was decided in the negative: ayes 49, noes 52.

Those who voted in the negative were Messrs. John Y. Mason, (President,) Banks, Beale, Bocock, Botts, Bowls, Braxton, Burgess, Richard C. Boyd, Chambers, Chambliss, Chilton, Cocke, Deneale, Douglas, Edmunds, Edwards, Faulkner, Finney, Floyd, Fultz, Fuqua, M. R. H. Garnett, Muscoe Garnet, Goode, Hall, Hill, Kenny, Leake, Lucus, McCandlish, Wm. Martin, Moore, Newman, Price, Reeves, Saunders, Scoggin, Frances, W. Scott, Shell, Berry H. Smith, James Smith, Archibald Stuart, Taylor, Tunish, Turnbull, J. Watts, Whittle, Whilley, Wingfield, Wise, Woolfolk, Wysor.

We find among those whose names are recorded in the negative the *elite* of the Democracy. The exclusion of foreigners, this dangerous violation of the rights of foreigners kept in the Constitution by the reform Convention of Virginia, which boasted its pre-eminent defence of equal rights! Can it be possible? Tell it not in Gath. Proclaim it not in the streets of Askalon. You Know-Nothings *do know nothing*. It is not your invention at all. Listen to it, you foreigners who have been deluded and bamboozled by this clamor, that the American party were your peculiar enemies, because they were depriving you of your equal rights. Those very people who have aroused your prejudices and excited your passions, not content with saying that they would not vote for you for the office of governor as private citizen, have actually put it into the Constitution that you shall not be voted for by anybody. Let the Hon. S. A. Douglas hear it, and learn that if his gallant and brave and patriotic fellow-citizen, General Shields, were here in Virginia, although he were ready to shed, as I have no doubt he is ready to shed, a hogshead of blood, if he had it, in defence of the country—if he were here a citizen of Virginia, he would be incapable by law—by the Constitution—of receiving the office of governor, or the comparatively insignificant office of lieutenant governor, although every American in the State were anxious to make an exception in his favor to this generalrule, in consideration of his great gallantry and patriotism. This has been done, not by the *accursed Know-Nothings*, but by a majority of the Convention of Virginia, who have engrafted it into the Constitution to stand for all time.

But, gentlemen, nor was the reform convention entitled to this discovery of wisdom and prudence of putting some safe guarantees against permitting the high political offices of the country to be filled by foreigners. You have a similar provision in the Constitution of the United States and the Constitution of Virginia of 1831, and you have a piece of legislative history in the law of Virginia even still more striking and remarkable. In the year 1786 the Legislature of Virginia passed this law, and I desire you to consider the views which seemed to have governed the legislators of that day. I will read the statute to which I refer:

"The Speaker read from 'Henning's Statues at Large,' as follows:

"1st. Whereas it is the policy of all infant States to encourage population among other means by an easy mode for the admission of foreigners to the rights of citizenship; yet wisdom and safety suggest the propriety of guarding against the introduction of secret enemies, and of keeping the offices of Government in the hands of citizens intimately acquainted with the spirit of the Constitution and the genius of the people, as well as pernanently attached to the common interest.

"2. Be it therefore enacted by the General Assembly, that all free persons born within the territory of this commonwealth, all persons not being natives, who have obtained a right to citizenship under the act entitled, An act declaring who shall be deemed citizens of the commonwealth, and also all children wheresoever born, whose fathers or mothers are or were citizens at the time of the birth of such children, shall be deemed citizens of this commonwealth, until they relinquish that character in manner hereinafter mentioned; and that all persons other than alien enemies who shall migrate into this state, and shall before some court of record give satisfactory proof by oath, (or being Quakers or Mononists, by affirmation,) that they intend to reside therein, and also to take the legal oath of affirmation for giving assurence of fidelity to the commonwealth, (which oaths or affirmations the clerk of the court shall enter on record, and give a certificate thereof to the person taking the same, and shall, on or before the first day of October annually, transmit to the Executive a list of the persons who shall have taken the said oath or affirmations, reciting their nation and occupation (if any) to be by them entered in a book to be kept for that purpose, for which he shall receive the fee of one dollar;) shall be entitled to all the rights, privileges and advantages of citizens, except that they shall not be capable of election or appointment to any office, legislative, executive, or judiciary, until an actual residence in the state of FIVE YEARS from the time of taking such oaths or affirmations aforesaid; nor until they shall have evinced a permanent attachment to the state by having intermarried with a citizen of this commonwealth, or a citizen of any other of the United States, or purchased lands to the value of one hundred pounds therein."

Mr. Patton proceeded:—That was the idea of the patriots and sages of the revolution, at that early period, when the policy of this infant state was especially to encourage immigration. That law continued in force in Virginia certainly until 1852, when Congress passed its naturalization laws. And it seems to have been supposed by very eloquent lawyers and able men, that this law was still in force, notwithstanding the passage of the naturalization laws by Congress; it was re-enacted in '92, which was before the naturalization law, and continued in the Code of 1819, prepared by Watkins Leigh, one of the ablest jurists of the country. It remained in the statute book until 1850, when the revisors of that time, finding it there, and believing it was supperseded by the naturalization law of Congress left it out of the Code. But there it stands as a monument of the opinions of the then illustrious sages of the revolution. This law was made about the very time—whether it was one of the laws reported by the committee, I don't know—that Jefferson, Pendleton and Wythe were appointed to revise the laws of Virginia. Here is the Know-Nothing principle with a vengeance!

Gentlemen, this cry about the rights of foreigners is all gammon. Nobody proposes; no man that I have ever seen; no paper that I ever read, advocating or sustaining this Know-Nothing or American party movement, has said or written anything indicating a purpose to violate any rights of foreigners. A foreigner has no right in this country except what the laws give. It is wholly a matter of domestic policy, and for the consideration of the people of the United States, under what circumstances they will admit foreigners into the country, or whether they will admit them at all—whether, when they come here, they will allow them to become citizens—upon what terms of probation, and under what forms and conditions. My opinion is, that viewing the vast increase in immigration—the change in our condition; the vast numbers and rapid increase of our own population—that the time has arrived materially to change our naturalization laws—to increase very considerably the length of probation, before admission to the rights of citizenship, and provide other and more efficient securities, that those who are to receive these rights are fit depositaries of them by their moral character—knowledge of the principles of our institutions, and imbued with devotion to our constitution.

These are matters, however, of detail to be disposed of by Congress. It would be premature for me to undertake to consider or define any specific views as to the proper provisions. They must be left to the wisdom of Congress exercised with a full view of the exigencies of the country at the time.

I believe that there are some over-zealous advocates of the American party, who go to extreme lengths, such as preventing the immigration of foreigners out and out, and repealing the naturalization laws. Now I am in favor of neither. I do not understand the Virginia American party to be in favor of either. I say, let the foreigners come, and if I could remember here, I would speak over again that speech which seemed to have been admired so much by my Democratic friends. I would say, let them come, and forbid them not—the industrious and pains-taking German from his fader land, the gay Frenchman from the fertile plains and vine-clad hills of his beautiful France, the whole-souled and gallant Irishman—let them come. But let them come with a means of living; let them come to better their fortune by their industry, adding to the industrial products of the country itself, by becoming permanently located amongst us, by raising families amongst us; and when they have stayed here a sufficient length of time—all the time prescribed by our laws, and have given proper assurances, such as the details of the law of Congress may prescribe, that they really understand the principles of our government, and properly estimate the value of our system, let them be received as citizens amongst us. But take care. I would appeal to every industrious, intelligent and sober-minded foreigner himself, if this is not a principle which is necessary for his and the rights of his children—take care that our shores be not flooded by the paupers and criminals cast off by the old, declining governments of Europe—sent here to be supported by us, and to fill our poor-houses, and our penitentiaries. And if there be any foreigner who is not satisfied about that, I pray and beseech him to read Valentine Heckler's letter. In my poor estimate, it is worth all the speeches that have been made or will be made from now until Christmas upon that subject.

Talk about violating rights, &c., gentlemen, I have no hostility to foreigners. Why should I? My father was a Scotchman, and my grandfather was a Scotchman, and the first, I believe, the only general officer who died in battle in defence of the country in the revolutionary struggle. These propositions, as I understand them, are just as essential for the true interests, and for the protection of the true rights of foreigners who come here and become established amongst us, as they are for natives, and nothing but a misconception and misunderstanding of the true purposes and objects of this association, could have possibly created such a storm among a considerable portion of foreigners, or any other persons.

As to the religious question, gentleman, I am afraid that I cannot consider myself entirely fit to consider such a subject as that; I am afraid, God help me, I have not much religion of any sort, though I see that somebody has made the wonderful discovery that the Winchester ticket is made up of a Methodist, a Baptist, a Presbyterian and Episcopalian. I believe I am myself nearer the Episcopalian than any other; I don't live more than a square and a half from the church. Now, I understand that nobody belonging to this much and terribly abused party—for I think it is and has been the worst abused that ever has risen in the country, not excepting the Abolitionists, who deserve it most richly—I do not understand that any man belonging to this organization desires to interfere with any civil or religious rights of Catholics, any more than with the civil and religious rights of Protestants. Nobody disputes the right, or designs to interfere with the liberty, of the members of that Church in worshiping God according to their own consciences. Nobody designs to interfere with their right to believe that what is proclaimed by the Pope as religious faith, is an infallible truth. No person desires to interfere with their belief that they must take their conviction of religious duty from the Pope and not from the Bible. Nobody denies their right to believe in transubstantiation or consubstantiation, or in the Immaculate Conception of the Virgin Mary, which has been recently declared by his holiness the Pope, or any other article of faith.

So far as any person undertakes to say that he will not vote for a Catholic, he exercises his undeniable right. It is equally competent for persons outside the order to take that position, nor do I believe that they would be guilty, if they choose to take such a position, of any violation of the rights of Catholics, either civil or religious. How far the charges of temporal allegiance on the part of Catholics to the Pope are justified, I am not aware. It is strange that while some Catholics deny the temporal authority of the Pope over them, others of their own church, some of them high in position, do maintain that they are thus bound.

Well, I know not who is right and who is wrong about that; but this I do know, that if it is established that we have a body of men here who are under the temporal authority of a foreign potentate, or any other religious head, domestic or foreign, in the exercise of their civil rights, it would be a justifiable ground upon which we should abstain from conferring any office of political power or influence upon any such man—I care not whether he be Catholic, Presbyterian, Episcopalian, Methodist, Baptist, or of any other religion. Just convince me that, as a religious congregation or body, they are controlled by a Pope abroad or a Bishop here, and I would give none of them my vote for any office of political power or trust, because that is to us a dangerous exercise of the right of citizenship, dangerous to them, dangerous to civil liberty, dangerous because it is a practical union of church and state, under which, wherever it exists, the tree of liberty withers and dies. With such convictions, I cannot hesitate to adopt that portion of the Know-Nothing platform which refers to religious toleration. It is this:

"That the American doctrine of religious toleration, and entire absence of all proscription for opinion's sake, should be cherished as one of the very fundamental principles of our civil freedom, and that any sect or party which believes and maintains that any foreign power, religious or political, has the right to control the conscience or direct the conduct of a freeman, occupies a position which is totally at war with the principles of freedom of opinion, and which is mischievous in its tendency, and which principle, if carried into practice, would prove wholly destructive of religious and civil liberty."

Well, then, gentlemen, another great and formidable ground of assault upon this American party—upon those 40, or 50, or 60,000 of the people of Virginia, is, that they are laboring in the cause of Abolitionism. Fifty thousand Virginia gentlemen of intelligence, of property, of character, combined to promote the cause of abolitionism! Terrible conspiracy, most dangerous and mischievous politicians! Why, gentlemen, the very fact of the composition of this order is a standing refutation of this most singular imputation. But if you wanted any other evidence of it just take the testimony of Mr. Greely, or Weed, the peculiar organ of W. H. Seward, or Wade of Ohio, or Giddings, all of whom denounce this American party as the deadly enemy of the abolition party.

I received a newspaper this morning, I believe, containing the last fulminations (for they seem to have some Popes among the abolitionists) of Mr. Giddings upon the subject. I will read them for you, together with some remarks from the Chicago Journal, an abolition paper. Speaking of the Know-Nothings, he says:

"There are few foreigners whom I would be less willing to trust in office, than those who are so active in their efforts to arouse the popular feeling against our emigrant population, while themselves remain perfectly quiet, and see our native born Americans, (that is, runaway negroes,) from Ohio, and other free states, seized and sold into interminable slavery; aye, they not only remain quiet under such insults, but insist that the people shall not discuss the impropriety of such a crime."

"I would a thousand times rather vote for an honest lover of liberty, though a Catholic, than for many Protestant Doctors of Divinity, who have so long denied our obligation of God's 'higher law,' and endeavor to reconcile us to the infamous fugitive slave enactment. The time has arrived when men should be judged by their *action* by their political conduct, rather than by prejudices attached to a name or sect."

The Chicago Journal—an Abolition print—quotes a passage from Gov. Smith's speech in defence of Know-Nothingism, and says:

"There it is in a nut shell. Foreigners who come to this country, settle in free states, with instincts against slavery,

"For these instincts the South is to hunt them down, while freemen at the North shout forth the 'tally ho!' to the chase. Aside from the oath-bound, proscriptive intolerance of the order, there seems enough in its slavery instincts to cause all friends of freedom to view its progess with alarm."

That, continued Mr. Patton, is the testimony upon the one side, and then we have our Virginia papers denouncing this party and the leaders of the party without measure, and denouncing it as an abolition party. There really seems to be something very amusing and curious in the idea of seeing this great American omnibus moving along upon the railroad, which people believe is going to lead to the terminus of triumph and success, and the leaders of the Virginia Democracy trying to pull it off the track because it is loaded with runaway slaves, carrying them to the North, while on the other side we have Greely, Giddings, and all that party pulling at it with all their might, because it is catching runaway slaves to bring them back. Well, if they will keep on pulling in that way, one pulling on one side and the other on the other, as action and re-action is equal, "with a long pull, a strong pull, and a pull altogether," the car will be kept steady in its course, and will arrive at its destiny without any sort of difficulty.

But, this oath-bound organization, as Mr. Giddings calls it. Well, gentlemen, as I said before, I do not belong to this secret organization. I never belonged to a secret society in my life, although most of my family were Masons. I have some sort of scruples and fastidiousness which prevented me at all times from going into any place to assume any secret engagement. But, surely we are not going at this time of day to denounce secret associations as dangerous and mischievous, and ruinous to the country merely because they are secret. I hope we are not to have the Anti-Masonic party revived. The question whether the secret character is objectionable or not depends upon the objects of the organization. The reason which they had to make it secret, assume any secret engagement, is manifest to all who can estimate the extraneous influences of party, and the consequences of an open repudiation of former party fealty.

But we are justified in taking it for granted that there is nothing dangerous in it, as good fruits come out of it; and I would no sooner believe that my venerable friend (pointing to Dr. Merritt on his left,) if he be a Know-Nothing, which I do not know, but suppose, I would just as soon suspect my venerable friend would be a member of a secret association, red with conspiracy against the liberty of the country, as I would believe that you, or you, or you, (pointing to several prominent Masons,) or any other gentleman not belong to this organization, would unite in such a conspiracy. Gentlemen, this is all stuff.

We know what this secrecy is, and what it was for. They have proclaimed their principles and basis. They proclaim that it is a peculiar organization for building up a party to sustain certain principles. If these principles are good, of what importance is it, that they choose to go together and consult about them, and discuss the ways and means to procure their ends in secret. Is not every political association practically secret in its operations and its communications with other associations affiliated with it, and in all the machinery calculated to give effect and success to their political objects? We know that it is. We know that the great mass of the party have nothing to do with all this preliminary management, and in truth know nothing about it.

No, gentlemen, we know what the object of this secrecy is, or at least I think we do, and I think it is stated in a very able letter, issued recently from some council in New York. It gives very fully the objects of this organization, and the reasons of its secrecy. I will read you some extracts copied into the Lynchburg Virginian, from a Pennsylvania paper, which is opposed to this Know-Nothing organization. It is perfectly well known that it was designed to protect those who were desirous of joining this party from the terrors and denunciations of the old parties to which they might belong. Possibly there are many men, honest, industrious and sober men, men whose bread depends on not quarrelling with their party, who, though desirous of joining this new organization, could not do so unless they could be protected from the consequences of an open avowal of the fact that they had joined the new party. [The remarks of the Pennsylvania paper were read.] I will now read from the Lynchburg Virginian some commentary on the extract which I have referred to:

"We need only look over the columns of any Democratic press in the state, to perceive how necessary it was that the members of the new party should protect themselves behind the shield of secrecy. Whenever a Democrat is discovered in connection with the movement, regardless of his rights as a citizen, and his feelings as a man, he is stigmatized as a miscreant and traitor, and held up to the scorn and contempt of the world. The rigor of its party discipline is such that few men are bold enough to incur the vindictive and relentless penalties of absolving their allegiance to the Democratic organization. The law of Russian despotism which makes it a capital offence for a subject to quit the realm, without permission of his imperial master, is not more stringent or more rigorously enforced than the obligation of the Democratic fealty, which demands a perfect and perpetual adhesion. The regulations of military service have been adopted into their code—and deserters are either shot without mercy, or drummed out of camp with the ignominious notes of the rogue's march. It would have been impossible for the American organization to have obtained recruits from that party, had they not been protected by an obligation of secrecy, in withdrawing from one body and uniting with the other. And if the object and principles of the party are in themselves patriotic and proper, this condition of membership will be excused as a necessary and sole means of promoting their strength—and the only proper subject of enquiry and comment remaining is as to the purposes, not the character, of the organization."

Besides all that, we now have it pretty well understood that the purposes and objects of this secrecy having been attained, and the party being strong enough to sustain itself, the veil of secrecy will soon be removed. And then everybody will probably wonder what a great fuss was made about this secrecy, which at last may turn out to have been no secret at all, except in regard to some particular modes and details of proceeding.

Now, gentlemen, I believe I have said pretty much all that I designed to say, though I may have forgotten something. One of the papers of the city, a very respectable paper, and edited by a very able, amiable, facetious gentleman, published some time ago, a speech of mine, made here at this place, in good humored raillery of the Taylor Convention, a speech which I suppose must have been considered by my Democratic friends as exceedingly funny, considering the vast amount of *printed laughter* which it seems to have occasioned. Well, now, in perfect good humor towards Mr. Hughes, for whom I entertain feelings of kindness and respect, I beg leave to say that it is a little strange to me, that while he was making himself so merry over it, it never occurred to him that there was another convention to which that speech about the cat in the meal tub might possibly have some application, as well as the Taylor Convention. There was a certain Convention which assembled not very long ago at Staunton, where there was also a cat in the meal tub, and there was a certain Archibald-Bell-the-cat, who threatened to hang the bell around puss' neck, at the Convention, so that there should be no mouse running about there nibbling at the cheese without danger of being caught. But some considerations overruled this bold intent. Harmony was thought more expedient than the assertion of principle, or like Bob Acres, his courage oozed at his fingers' ends. Nobody knows to this day what are the principles of the Virginia Democracy upon Hunter's land bill.

There is another matter suggested by this reference to the land bill which presents considerations of great importance in reference to the question of foreign immigration. One of the most mischievous habits of legislation has grown up in Congress in reference to new territories in the west and north-west—and a course of legislation inconsistent, as it seems to me, with the spirit of the Constitution.

I allude to the organizing territories so that every foreigner—although he may have only been in the country a short time (six or twelve months) I believe, becomes a voter in these territories. It is in those states, built up by that population to a great extent—a population who cannot speak our language, or read or write any language—a great many of them—it is in, I say, those states, built up by a population of this cast, that a great and important political power is growing up which, before many years at the present rate of immigration, would have the power to control the destinies of the country. And besides all that, in connection with this course of legislation in regard to the territories, we have projects of practical agrarianism appropriating the public lands to all who will go and settle upon them without price or at merely nominal prices, furnishing bounties to immigration and thus filling up those states to a large extent with such foreign population, and stimulating into a natural and artificially rapid growth those states, thus increasing the preponderance of political power against the southern states.

Such are the views presented by ex-governor Smith, expressed in a spirit of manly firmness and independence. I honor him for it, and hope and believe that he will be able to breast the storm and carry his election triumphantly. What better illustration can you have of the arbitrary power assumed by party, than that such a man as ex-governor Smith has had abuse and invective poured out upon him, notwithstanding his unflinching, enduring, undeviating devotion to the Democratic party, because he will not vote for a gentleman for govornor who has been nominated by them? No man has rendered more party service than he has. And now for this single act of disobedience towards a decree of party, he is to be hunted down with indignation and fury.

Gentlemen, I understand that some laudable and disinterested anxiety was expressed to know what my views were upon the Kansas and Nebraska bill.

Well, really, I did not expect that such an inquiry would be made of me, being merely a candidate for the attorney-generalship. But disposed to gratify all rational curiosity, I will give my experience on that subject. I never read either the Kansas or Nebraska bill, if there are two of them. All I know about it is, that a particular object was to repeal the Missouri Compromise, and I confess I did not see any great importance in that eompromise law, as I always considered that the Missouri was unconstitutional. In truth, I know very little about the Kansas and Nebraska bill; but finding that the great body of the southern delegation were in favor of it, I also was anxious for the passage of the bill. I don't see what importance it is to those who make the inquiry to ascertain my views in this matter, since I do not think they would vote for me if I was for or against it. It cannot be of any importance to them either way, for Gen. Millson, who voted against, and my friend, John Caskie, who voted for it, receive their support alike.

I am sorry that I have consumed so much of your time. There are other gentlemen whom you will be glad to hear, and it is proper, therefore, that I should give way. I desire simply to say, that all this time I have been discussing questions unconnected with the office of attorney-general. I certainly do not desire any gentleman to give me his vote upon mere party grounds. I feel very little concern about the office. If the people of Virginia choose to elect me to it, I shall endeavor to discharge its duties the best I can. I certainly think I will be able, as I should strive, to deal out equal and exact justice to all men of all parties, Democrats and Whigs, natives and foreigners, Wise men and Know-Nothings.

From the Examiner, April 10, 1855.

MR. PATTON AND HIS CLIENTS.

We have discussed the "statesmanship" of Mr. FLOURNOY. Friends and neighbors of that gentleman have complained of the severity of our strictures. The complaint is unjust and unwarranted. We have said nothing impeaching Mr. FLOURNOY'S private character. His public character is public property. We have said naught of his public character that was not strictly legitimate—nothing that was not allowable of a candidate for high public trust and popular suffrage—nothing that was not entirely just in respect to an educated Virginia gentleman, who had adopted the truculent politics of a Northern party or mob that burns churches, desecrates the ballot box, peers into the private sanctities of the woman's chamber under pretence of religious zeal, and prefers for office the Deist, the Atheist, the Infidel and the Abolitionist rather than Christians of the faith of ROGER B. TANEY, WILLIAM GASTON, Sir THOMAS MORE, and CHRISTOPHER COLUMBUS.

We have now to discuss the sentiments of Mr. PATTON as proclaimed at length in the African Church, in this city. His speech in that building on Tuesday night last is fully reported in last Friday's Richmond *Whig*, to which we refer the reader of the following paragraphs. Reciprocating fully and cordially the sentiments of kindness and respect expressed for ourselves by Mr. Patton on that occasion, we shall endeavor to characterize his remarks with a frankness and fairness befitting those sentiments. We declare in the outset, however, that in order to do so we shall have to treat the whole speech as an elaborate joke.

We heard that speech with infinite satisfaction. We saw with pleasure that Mr. Patton could not bring himself to endorse the politics of the Know Nothing party. From beginning to end, it was the speech of an advocate for a prisoner in the box; and it committed Mr. Patton to the tenets of Know Nothingism no more than his pleadings for the worst criminals at the bar of justice have committed him to the crimes which his professional duty required him to extenuate and whitewash. We expected his clients to growl and rebel at this treatment. We confidently expected that the speech would be suppressed. We felt it in our bones that his words had fallen upon the exuberant feelings of the meeting like a shower bath. We saw it become quieter, tamer, cooler, at every sentence that fell from his lips; for he denied any membership in the Order; he entered a *caveat* against secret politics and religious bigotry; he pointedly rebuked the over-zealous advocates of a repeal of the naturalization laws (Mr. Flournoy inclusive); and, so far from *arresting* immigration, he was especially sweet upon the "industrious, pains taking German," "the gay Frenchman from the vine clad hills of beautiful France," "the whole souled and gallant Irishman," of whom he cried "let them come and forbid them not."

We did not expect his clients to stand this. We thought they would certainly resent such a damning with faint praise as Mr. Patton gave them. We thought they had some self-respect, and would send their lawyer howling home, and suppress his white-washing, patronising oration, teeming with ill-disguised reproach and repudiation. We thought Mr. Patton had mistaken the temper and spirit of his client. But *we* were wrong and Mr. Patton was right. An accomplished and experienced lawyer, he managed the case exactly to the liking of his client. He took SAM out of the jail, dungeon, or culvert damp and dark in which he had been confined so long, had him cleansed, shaved, shirted, slicked up, and brought him into court clothed and looking the counterfeit of a gentleman. He dressed up SAM's dilapidated reputation in the most artistic and ingenious manner of the legal profession, taking occasion and pains as he proceeded to smooth down and pare off the angularities and monstrosities of the poor fellow's character. The effect upon SAM was electric. The rascal really thinks he has been made an honest man of, and shouts the praises of his lawyer in the most boisterous and immoderate manner at the corners of all the streets. The fellow will soon get to thinking that he is on visiting and wine-drinking terms with his lawyer; but it will only be, we fear, to get himself summarily "sot back" by one of those charming "hints" common in the land of "the whole-souled and gallant Irishman."

But we must examine the speech in the order in which it was delivered. SAM was not the only client of Mr. Patton on the occasion. Mr. Patton felt the necessity of defending Mr. Patton, spite of the old Spanish proverb, "the lawyer that argues his own cause has a fool for his client." There are criminal cases so monstrous and ugly that the legal profession often shrink from their defence. And where the lawyer's own conscience is not troubled with qualms of the sort, an indignant and outraged public frowns often upon his acceptance of a retainer. It is in such cases, and in such cases only, that the attorney feels obliged to preface his argument for the criminal with a labored exculpation of himself. Accordingly, Mr. Patton's defence of SAM is prefixed by a painful apology for his own participation in the ugly case.

It is true that Mr. Patton sets out with the grand airs of a Cæsar or a Cromwell, refusing crowns and rejecting diadems in a lofty, wholesale, and amusing strain; but he soon relapses into the attorney, and plays that character out to the end, with a truthfulness and consistency worthy of his great reputation at the bar. Our Cæsar proves conclusively that the crown *was* offered to him, thus:

"Let me bring to the notice of this vast assembly, and to those who have been disposed to impute to me ambitious motives and eagerness for high office, one or two simple papers, which is all the answer I mean to give to those charges.

"I received, on the evening of the 13th March, from Winchester, the following telegraphic despatch from a friend of mine who was a member of that body:

'Will you accept the nomination for Governor? Reply immediately to this.'

"I immediately sent the following by telegraph:

'I would not accept the office of Governor if every man in Virginia were to vote for me.'"

He did that part majestically, and with the genuine stage strut, for he had evidently been studying the Cæsarean *role* of disinterested virtue; for it was uppermost in his mind. He continues:

"By an ingenuous perversity of accusation, it might still be said that I was like Cæsar, rejecting the crown because I knew I could not get it.

"On the same evening, not very long after I had received the telegraph despatch which I have just read, I received this note from a gentleman in Richmond:

'I have just received a despatch by telegraph that you were nominated for Governor, and requested to communicate it directly.'

"As soon as I received this note, instantly, for the purpose of preventing any inconvenience to the Winchester Convention, such as would result from their making a nomination which would not be accepted, probably causing them to assemble again there or somewhere else to make another nomination, I sent the following reply:

'I regret the information your note contains. Several times during the last fifteen years, I have declined being a candidate for Governor when my friends thought I could be elected. I will not accept the office of Governor under any circumstances, and though every man in the State were to vote for me. Excuse the apparent peremptoriousness of this note.'"

Protestations of this sort are so frequent in our day, that we believe it has become a conventional understanding in society not to credit them from whomsoever they proceed. Mr. Patton's refusal of the *chance* for office in a doubtful contest, is not the first instance of a similar discretion by many ten thousands; and unluckily, his antecedents in the particular of office-holding are against him. For nearly a quarter of a century the fascinations of office overcame this platonic disdain of Mr. Patton; and the world is too uncharitable to suppose that a man who could consent to be a member of the House of Representatives at Washington for eight years, and to endure the petty vexations of a Virginia Executive Councillor for fifteen years of his life, could repent him of that mode of living, in old age, even in respect to so illustrious and lucrative a position as the Governorship of Virginia.

Indeed, the whole effect of this mock pageant—of this billing and cooing on the part of delegates in Winchester, and this virtuous coyness on his own side, is destroyed by a subsequent revelation in his speech. For, after proving, by a very plausible set of facts, that he did refuse the crown, he destroys the whole effect of the scene by letting out the fact that the crown, though refused, was never offered him:

"It is proper to state, that the information that I was nominated for Governor was a mistake, which of course I did not know until the following day. There was, as I understand, no such nomination, and the distinguished gentleman who has been nominated, and is so worthy to receive the suffrages of this American party, was the decided choice of the Convention at all times. I do not know that there was a single man who was favorable to my nomination, except the particular gentleman who sent me the despatch."

Thus it is plain that Mr. Patton but enacted the part of a mock duke in his lofty rejection of the crown. The Whigs of the Winchester conclave knew what they were about in playing off these mysterious telegraphic missiles. Their Democratic confreres were doubtless supposed to make a muss against Flournoy's being entrusted with the spoils department of the ticket. Under these circumstances, the dispatches to Patton and his prompt waiver of the place designed for Flournoy, must have worked like a charm.

The *role* had been rehearsed thoroughly beforehand, and Mr. Patton might have done a deal of mischief by disturbing the arrangement. He had been called upon in person before the 13th of March; let himself reveal the protocol:

"I held out no inducements to those who, in behalf of this new American party, called upon me for the purpose of ascertaining whether I would accept the nomination for Attorney General, &c., &c. I was told that this great organization desired, or at least a portion of the members of the Convention at Winchester, and probably the whole body, would desire to confer this nomination upon me if I was willing to accept the office, without any regard to my political opinion or my political course, &c., &c. I told them that if the Convention should choose to confer upon me the nomination, I would accept it, assuring them at the same time that it would be incompatible with my business to engage in the political canvass in the way of discussion, &c., &c."

Such was the understanding before the 13th of March, and Mr. Patton was too acute to disturb or change it on the spur of a telegraphic dispatch received late in the night of that eventful day. Mr. Patton rejected the crown. He protests he did not want it and would not have it. Many will believe him and many will not. The fable of the fox and the grapes stands in the way, and the uncharitable perversity and cynical common sense of plain people who do see something illustrious, honorable and enviable in eminent position, *will* gloss the highest acts of disinterested virtue with the rouge of selfishness.

This chronicle of his disdainful refusals of the highest office Virginia can confer—an office which was not too contemptible for Thomas Jefferson, Patrick Henry, John Tyler the elder, James Monroe or Wm. B. Giles—was not felt by Mr. Patton to be sufficient to sustain the argument he was submitting on this subject. He went on to tax still more the already strained credulity of his hearers. It seems that Mr. Patton, not content to reject with disdain the chair which a Jefferson and a Giles have been proud to occupy, has repeatedly declined to be the Colleague of Clay, of Webster, of Calhoun, of Dickinson, of Dallas, of Badger, of Berrein, of Crittenden, and of other secondary persons of that calibre, in the annoying duties and obscure character of Senator of the United States. He lets the world into a secret it never would have dreamt of, thus:

"And besides all that, it is now said I am animated by aspirations for the Senate. I say here, and now, as I have said repeatedly in the course of the last fifteen years, when my friends had desired to put me in nomination for that office, as I said about the office of Governor, I would not have the office of Senator if every man in the Legislature of Virginia voted for me."

The Senate of the United States will doubtless be profoundly mortified to learn this determination of Mr. Patton.

"Upon what meat doth this our Cæsar feed,
That he is grown so great."

It is evident that it was as little a part of the scheme of the Know Nothings to confer the vexatious troubles of a Federal Senator upon Mr. Patton as it was to confer upon him the spoils-distributing duties of Governor. The telegraphic missiles of the 13th of March, and the sham suggestion of his name for the head of the ticket in the Winchester cabal, were plainly but intended to deceive and quiet the forlorne but grumbling Democrat or Democrats who were entrapped in that conclave and bound by big oaths to submit to its Whig preferences and arrangements.

Mr. Patton, not content with breaking loose from the Democracy and from the Richmond Junto, of which he was a member in 1852, seems determined to vex and harrass his old associates even as members of his own Order. He magnanimously yields the Federal Senatorship in advance to George Washington Summers, and leaves his Democratic Know Nothing associates completely in the lurch as to that office, which will be clearly theirs by right if they succeed in carrying the next General Assembly. For, in that event, when the Councils shall convene here from all parts of the State next winter, to dictate to Virginia legislators the votes they shall cast in the Senatorial election, this public, solemn pledge and disdainful declension beforehand of the position, on the part of Mr. Patton, will throw the gates wide open for the triumphant election of the very man whom they and the Commonwealth three years ago indignantly repudiated at the polls. For, if the Democratic Know Nothings shall remonstrate at the election of Summers to the Senate, the ready and silencing answer of their Whig managers will be—"Patton does not want the office. Patton turns up his nose at the Senate of the United States. He as good as tells you, you must vote for Summers. He wants to be rid of the annoying solicitations every body besets him with about that plaguy seat in the Washington Capitol. Do give the man a little peace and rest. Patton had as lief go to the Penitentiary as to the Senate of the United States."

Well, then, Mr. Patton declined the Governorship that was not offered to him in favor of Mr. Flournoy who got it—notwithstanding the electric despatches, and in strict pursuance of the protocol held previously to the 13th March. He declines the Senate of the United States also, in advance, in favor of the peremptory precept dictating votes to Virginia legislators—of the next winter's Know Nothing secret councils that shall flock to Richmond, in case they carry the General Assembly—declines the Federal Senate in favor of a Know Nothing Western nominee, say of George W. Summers. But Mr. Patton did accept the Attorney Generalship, and that with a thank ye, too. He is evidently flattered by that nomination. In the exuberance of his gratitude he condescends to vouchsafe his imprimatur of respectability to a "body of men" who were ashamed to show their faces by daylight in a small village, and to write their true names upon the tavern registers of the town. He is very marked in his manner of giving a good character to the suspicious gentry who found it convenient to travel with an *alias*. They are his clients of whom he says:

"I was nominated for this office under the circumstances to which I have referred, by a large, respectable, intelligent and patriotic body of men, as much so, to the extent that I have information in regard to them, as any body of men in any quarter, any State, or anywhere else in the world—a body of men representing, as I understand now, (for I Know Nothing about the supposed elective strength of this American party) 50 or 60,000 of the free citizens of this Commonwealth."

After so emphatic an endorsement from a rejector of crowns and avoider of Senates, who will say that the Know Nothings are not respectable people? They nominate Mr. Patton to get a dash of respectability, and of course are in ecstacies over the fullness and completeness of his certification of character.

But Sam is not at all discriminating in these demonstrations of gratitude. Mr. Patton is very explicit in confining his encomiums to the immediate "body of men" assembled at Winchester. He accepts their nomination without the principles of their *party* "annexed." Attorney-like, he had not condescended to read Sam's "papers" until after his retainer, and he takes the most cruel pains, in consenting to appear in Sam's case, to give the cold shoulder to the fellow's gutter politics. Previously to the Winchester Convention, he talked out flat on this subject:

"I sincerely and most earnestly discouraged the idea, and told them very frankly that *I had not even read the basis principles* which they had put forth to the public as containing the great objects for which this organization was formed, and which they were endeavoring to accomplish."

They replied, importunately:

"That this office was an office *wholly disconnected with political controversy*, in reference to the discharge of the peculiar duties which devolved upon it; that it was an office which had no patronage connected with it, and that, estimating very highly, much more highly than I had vanity to aspire to, my qualifications and fitness for the office, they desired to confer the office upon me in reference to the r estimate of my qualifications and fitness for it, *without reference at all to any political objects*. I told them that if, under these circumstances, as it was an office *in the line of my profession*, an office which, although I had no particular desire to obtain it, would yet not be unacceptable to me, &c., &c."

After the nomination was announced to him, he wrote a letter, most cruelly and pointedly ignoring Sam's principles; and, in his speech, thus describes his feelings in accepting Sam's case, keeping still a cold shoulder upon the fellow's politics:

"I could not feel myself altogether at liberty to refuse to permit such a body of gentlemen of all parties, *irrespective of the political basis they might have in this movement*, to present my name to the people of Virginia, as a candidate for an office *wholly disconnected with political parties or strife*, and utterly rid of all political patronage."

Thus Mr. Patton gave his clients distinctly to understand in the protocol previous to the Winchester Convention, in his letter of acceptance, and in his speech at the African Church, that he joined in with them only as counsel, and would not consent to adopt their politics. Before the protocol, poor devils, he had never heard of them, or thought enough of their affair to read over their basis principles. He had no time to bestow on such trifles as the Know Nothing movement, and his valuable thoughts were too much absorbed with the cases of other clients to think of the case of Sam—the promising progeny of a New York Penitentiary jail-bird.

But we are not done with Mr. Patton's defence of himself. He entertains the same imperial repugnance to party ties as to the glittering honors which such men as Jefferson and Monroe, Webster and Calhoun have not despised. His morals on this subject are very elevated and yet very convenient:

"And yet that act, the act of permitting my name to be presented to the people of Virginia, has been denounced as an act of treachery to party, and a violation of party obligations. I never entered into any party obligations which would prevent me from *allowing a majority of the people of Virginia to elect me to any office which I was willing to take*, no matter who may have made the nomination, or when or where it may be announced."

That is capital. It is so characteristic. His allegiance to party ceases at the moment his party sinks into a minority. He never "enters into a party obligation" save with the understanding that he is to play quits whenever he sees the majority on t'other side. Soldiers who have done thus have been classed by history in the catalogue of Arnolds, Georgeys and Dalghetties; and we are very glad that Mr. Patton has taken pains to establish the understanding that he goes over to the Know Nothings simply as an attorney.

Of course all who have acted upon the rule of Mr. Patton, just laid down, can safely proclaim as he does:

"He little knows my antecedents who does not know that I have never permitted myself to be governed or controlled by the dictates of a party, in regard to party nominations or party measures, anywhere or on any occasion."

Such words would sound handsomely in the mouth of any but a Know Nothing nominee. Whatever Mr. Patton's antecedents may do in vindication of his abandoning the Democratic party, his "present cedents" present a beautiful illustration of his disgust of party. He who quits either of the old political organizations of this country, founded each by great and good men, with avowed measures, avowed principles, avowed membership, with open and public tactics as to all their meetings and arrangements, great and small, with newspapers to make public all that is said in town, in country, at night and by day—in order to join a secret, oath bound cabal, originated by a New York penitentiary convict, loving darkness rather than light for the initiation of accomplices, the concoction of schemes and the devising of tactics, that conceals its every step and act in secrecy, whose novitiates are sworn to deny their complicity, and would be perjured if responding frankly and truly to a legitimate enquiry—he who abandons either of the old political organizations to join this underground midnight movement, whatever other motives may be attributed to him, cannot be said to do so from disgust *at party*. And though Mr. Patton may deceive himself by such a delusion, he must expect, as he certainly must endure, the uncharitable reflections of the world.

Can Mr. Patton believe he is manifesting a disgust of "*party*" by accepting overtures and nominations from Know Nothing clubs—the most intense, intolerant, proscriptive, exercising, inexorable system of party drill ever invented?—Is there no such thing as party in Know Nothingism? Out of his own mouth shall he be judged; for in the following rather grandiloquent sentences he himself recognizes a new party servitude:

"I have been so much absorbed with my own business that I do not think I have read a Governor's Message for several years, nor a President's Message, and the time when I read a speech in Congress, is a period which runs back to a time that my memory 'runneth not to the contrary.' I have, however, read somewhat carefully at various times, *since* my nomination, the principles and basis of this *Know Nothing* or American PARTY, and I have no hesitation in saying, that with one or two exceptions in regard to the mode of action of THE PARTY, and the extent to which they are proposing to go, as a rule for themselves in their ORGANIZATION, the principles and basis of that PARTY meet my entire approbation."

There it is—*Party, party, organization, party.* Already is Mr. Patton immersed quadruply in the toils of party. He has leaped out of the Democratic frying-pan only to land in the live coals of Know Nothing strife, passion, religious hate, and social prejudice.

If Mr. Patton loathes and disgusts at party, he is much to be commiserated in his present allegiance. What a bitter rebuke is all his fine talk about party tyranny, upon the intolerant, fierce proscriptive partisanship of his new confederates! Did he know that he had accepted the support of an Order which prescribe the following qualifications for membership, carrying *party* not only into public affairs, but into the domestic household and leveling its brutal proscription at wives and mothers? According to the ritual:

"A person to become a member of any Subordinate Council must be twenty-one years of age; he must believe in the existence of a Supreme Being as the creator and preserver of the Universe; he must be a native born citizen; a Protestant *born of Protestant parents;* reared under Protestant influence, and *not united in marriage with a Roman Catholic: Provided, nevertheless,* that in this last respect, the State, District, or Territorial Council shall be authorized to so construct their respective constitutions as shall best promote the interest of the American cause in their several jurisdictions: *And provided, moreover,* that *no member who may have a Roman Catholic wife shall be eligible to any office in this Order.*"

And again, his new friends are required to swear thus:

"*Obligation.*—You, and each of you, of your own free will and accord, in the presence of Almighty God and these witnesses, your left hand resting on your right breast, and your right hand extended to the flag of your country, do solemnly and sincerely swear that you will not, under any circumstances, disclose in any manner, nor suffer it to be done by others, if in your power to prevent it, the name, signs, pass words, or the secrets of this degree; that you will, *in all things, conform to all the rules and regulations of this order,* and to the Constitution and By-Laws of this or any other Council to which you may be attached, so long as they do not conflict with the Constitution of the United States, nor that of the State in which you reside; that you will, under all circumstances, if in your power so to do, *attend all regular signs and summonses that may be thrown or sent out by a Brother of this or any other degree of this Order; that you will support, in all political matters, for all political offices, 2d degree members of this Order*, providing it be necessary for the American interest; that if it may be done legally, you will, when elected to any office, *remove all foreigners, aliens or Roman Catholics from office; and that you will, in no case, appoint such to office.* All this you promise and declare on your honor as Americans to sustain and abide by, *without any hesitation or mental reservation whatever.* So help you God, and keep you steadfast."

Is not this party proscription with a vengeance? But Mr. Patton complains bitterly of the crimination and denunciation that have been visited upon himself for leaving party. Let him read the terrible curses he will receive if, in his partialities for a majority, he should soon abandon his new allegiance:

"To all the foregoing you bind yourselves, under the no less penalty than that of being *expelled from this Order, and of having your name posted and circulated throughout all the different Councils of the United States, as a PERJURER, and as a TRAITOR to GOD and YOUR COUNTRY, as a being unfit to be EMPLOYED in any BUSINESS TRANSACTION, as a person unworthy the confidence of all good men, and as one at whom the finger of scorn* should ever be pointed. So help you God!"

Such is the machinery which is to help Mr. Patton into the Attorney Generalship!!

We cannot pursue this black and horrid aspect of the subject farther without transcending the rule of kindness and respect towards Mr. Patton with which we set out.

We are glad to see Mr. Patton dodging the real politics of the Know Nothing party, and confining his encomiums to the Basis Principles which they put out as a decoy to beguile simpler men than he. That basis is not necessarily offensive or objectionable, and we are ready to join Mr. Patton in endorsing every word and line it contains except the first article, and a few clauses in the preamble, provided they are construed in the spirit of enlarged statesmanship and of sincere patriotism. We have not room to-day to point out the glaring discrepancies between their secret ritual and this tempting sign-board which they post before the doorway that leads down into their secret caverns of shame.

We have only space left for a few of the cutting and pointed rebukes he gave his clients in the course of his argument of their ugly cause.

He will not even accept their Basis Principles unconditionally:

"I said, gentlemen, that in regard to some of the details of this basis of principles of Know Nothingism, I was not prepared to adopt them in all their breadth and length; or to bind myself by any pledge, either written, spoken or sworn,—that I never will, under any circumstances, vote for foreigners for any office. That is a matter that I will leave altogether at my discretion. Were I to act otherwise, I should be abandoning the ground I have maintained all my life, and upon which I can now stand up and defy those Democratic denunciations that are hurled against me."

Sam of course did not applaud that passage. We thought we detected a suppressed groan, but may have been mistaken.

Mr. Patton does not know why he cannot himself join secret societies, or how to describe his scruples and fastidiousness about that matter; but certain it is he does not like Dr. Fell:

"Well gentlemen, as I said before, *I don't belong to this secret organization.* I never belonged to a secret society in my life, although most of my family were Masons. I have *some sort* of scruples and fastidiousness which prevented me at all times from going into any place to assume any secret engagement."

Did ever lawyer, who *somehow* could never have behaved so himself, more ingeniously console a trembling criminal with the hope of having a felonious act attributed, by a lenient jury, to a lofty motive? Yet Mr. Patton was evidently a little blind to this policy of his client, having a personal appreciation of the reason alleged for secrecy:

"It is perfectly well known that it was designed to protect those who were disirous of joining this party from the terrors and denunciations of the old parties to which they might belong. Possibly there are many men, honest, industrious, and sober men, men whose bread depends on not quarreling with their party, who, though desirous of joining this new organization, could not do so unless they could be protected from the consequences of an open avowal of the fact that they had joined the new party."

Mr. Patton takes care to hint in the most delicate manner, and yet most emphatically, to Sam, that secrecy *will not do;* and that, as soon as his promising outlaw shall wash his face and comb his soap-locks, he had better come boldly out of his hiding places like an honest man:

"Besides all that, we now have it pretty well understood that the purposes and objects of this secrecy having been attained, and the party being strong enough to sustain itself, the veil of secresy will be removed."

How terribly does he rap Sam over the knuckles in the following handsome sentences, redolent with true American feeling, and glowing with sound Democratic sentiment:

"I believe that there some over over-zealous advocates of this American party [Mr. Flournoy is among them] who go to extreme lengths, such as preventing the immigration of foreigners out and out, and repealing the naturalization laws. Now, I am in favor of neither. I do not understand this Virginia American party to be in favor of either. I say, let the foreigners come, and if I could remember here, I would speak over again that speech which seemed to have been admired so much by some of my Democratic friends. I would say, let them come, and forbid them not—the industrious and pains-taking German from his fader land, the gay Frenchman from the fertile plains and vine clad hills of his beautiful France, the whole-souled and gallant Irishman—let them come."

It is true, that Mr. Patton after thumping Sam soundly with these notable paragraphs, went on to palliate the fellow's conduct and to delicately instruct him how to behave himself in the future conduct of the canvass. We hope Sam will profit by the advice, and take his instructor's lecture in the spirit of a true penitent.

Let him take Mr. Patton's advice. Let him throw away his barbarous ritual picked up in the purlieus of New York city—come out from his secret hiding places—cease his slang about the unfitness of good Christians of the Catholic or any Church for office, and agree to recognize merit in the pains-taking German, they gay Frenchman, and the whole-souled Son of Erin. Sam will then be a gentleman. His will then be a strong, respectable and potential party, able to effect good ends by reputable means. He will then have reason to chant everlasting hosannas to Mr. Patton, and that gentleman will not only consent to be his counsel, but his friend, admirer and probably his boon companion.

THE NATIONALITY OF THE DEMOCRATIC PARTY IN 1855.

The nationality of the democratic party in 1855 presented a remarkable and admirable contrast to the anti-slavery fanaticism of the Know Nothing party in the Northern States. In every free state of the Union the Democratic party passed resolutions fearlessly endorsing the Nebraska and Kansas bills. That there may be hereafter no mistake upon this subject, we publish resolutions of the democracy of nearly all the free states upon the vexed questions of slavery and the repeal of the Missouri Compromise. They were collected from the principal leading newspapers of the Union during the Canvass in Virginia.

OHIO.

Resolved, That the right of the people to govern themselves, and frame their own laws—a principle re-established by the passage of the act to organize the Territories of Kansas and Nebraska—meets our cordial approbation, and we declare our determination to adhere to such principle, no matter what miserable subterfuge our enemies may invent to cloak their opposition to it.

Resolved, That we witness with painful feeling the formation of a secret political organization in this Union under the name of "know nothings," or "sons of the sires of '76," whose principles, so far as we can judge, being antagonistic to the liberal principles of the democratic party, and if carried out, subversive of the constitution of the country, merit and receive our unqualified condemnation.

ILLINOIS.

The democrats of Illinois, lately in convention assembled, resolved as follows:

Resolved, That, abiding by the free spirit of our constitution, which recognises no religious test as a qualification for office, and proscribes no citizen on account of the place of his birth, we shall ever oppose every attempt, whether open or secret, to deprive our adopted citizens of the full right and privilege of native-born citizens, and hold in abhorrence the recent organization of the "know nothing" society, believing their design to be fraught with evils to the country.

Resolved, That our liberty and independence are based upon the right of the people to form for themselves such government as they may choose; and that the great privilege, the birthright of freedom, the gift of heaven, secured to us by the blood of our ancestors, ought to be extended to future generations, and no limitation ought to be applied to this power in the organization of any Territory of the United States, of either a territorial government or State constitution, provided the government so established shall be republican, and in conformity with the constitution of the United States.

PENNSYLVANIA.

Resolved, That we adhere as firmly as ever to the Compromise of 1850 and the platform laid down by the National Convention of 1852; and that, in the passage of the much abused Nebraska bill of 1854, we fail to discover, as is alleged by the whig press, any departure from the principles or policy there so strongly and patriotically inculcated by the wisest and best men of the nation of both the great political parties.

Resolved, That a candidate before the people who may be openly or secretly allied to the proscriptive, intolerant faction commonly called 'know nothing,' is unworthy the support of any democrat, and should be opposed by every true friend of his country, of every party and faith.

VERMONT.

Resolved, That the passage of the Kansas-Nebraska bill by Congress is in strict accordance with the constitution of the United States and the principles of self-government and non-intervention by Congress in the domestic concerns of the States, devised by the framers of our government.

DELAWARE.

Resolved, That President Pierce, by enforcing economy in the conduct of the various departments of the public service, by bringing to justice persons who had plundered the treasury under the preceding administration, by vigorously enforcing the laws, by fearlessly using the power vested in the Executive by the constitution for the arrest of improper legislation, and by lending his influence and wielding his power for the perpetuation of the principle of the Compromise of 1850 embodied in the Nebraska bill, has proven himself an honest man, a faithful public officer, a sound republican, and a sagacious statesman.

MICHIGAN.

Resolved, That, believing the interests of the country required the speedy settlement of the broad expanse of territory lying between the western States and the Rocky mountains, we cordially approve of the establishment of territorial governments in that region; and that Congress, in according to the people of the Territories of Nebraska and Kansas the right to fix and regulate their own domestic institutions, gave us the strongest proof of its determination to maintain the great republican principle of the Compromise of 1850.

MASSACHUSETTS.

Resolved, That the constitution recognizes the principle of self-government and the power of the people, in whatever bond united with each other, whether in State, county, town, district or territory, to control their own institutions; that on this principle alone the colonies entered upon the struggle for independence, the confederation was established, and the federal constitution adopted; that only by a rigid regard for this principle can we hope to preserve our liberties against usurpation, rivalries, and anarchy; and that confidence in this principle, old as our country, enforced by Jefferson, sustained by Jackson, leads us to look with pride and satisfaction on every measure of the administration calculated to give it a bold and unflinching support, removing every vestige of federal folly from our legislation, and extending the same rights and privileges to new States and Territories which were claimed by, and secured to, the people of Massachusetts and all her sister States when they were united in this confederation.

NEW JERSEY.

Resolved, That our senators and representatives in Congress, who have in the legislation of 1854 stood by the compromise measures of 1850, and so manfully maintained the right of the people of the Territories to make the laws relating to their domestic concerns, and by which alone they are to be governed, deserve the approbation and high commendation of the lovers of the Union as faithful servants of the people whom they represent.

Resolved, That the national course of the federal administration, its measures and policy, based as they are on the constitution, and recognising as they do the rights of the States and the principles of strict construction, ever sacred to democracy, as well as the rights of American citizens everywhere, deserve the high commendation and cordial support of the nation.

Resolved, That we will oppose by all proper means any candidate for office who favors the repeal or modification or change of the fugitive-slave law passed in 1850, and also any candidate who shall favor or advocate the repeal, change, or modification of the right of the people of the Territories of Nebraska and Kansas, or any other Territory, to legislate for themselves upon all subjects not prohibited by the constitution of the United States.

Indiana.

3. *Resolved,* That the removal of the "Missouri restriction"—a measure that has stultified American pretences, innovated the constitution of our country, that was conceive at the shrine of an unholy ambition for the "balance of political power," brought forth at an evil hour, when might rudely cast principle in the dust—is a theme deserving the gratulations of all mankind, and those who brought forth and successfully carried out its obliteration merit a meed of praise never ending and without bounds.

4. *Resolved, further,* That the "Nebraska-Kansas" bill as passed, is a return to first principle, that was unwisely violated, and places the soil where the constitution found it, and where the God of Nations designed and ordered it—to be "inherited" and governed by those who live on and draw their subsistence from it.

5. *Resolved,* That in this new northern party, styled "republican," alias "fusion," we think we see that which threatens the Union! A northern party once formed and successful, a correlative southern party must of necessity follow; when the name of Union would be a mockery, and it would remain only in the memories of those who survive it. Called by whatever name such a party may be, disunion is its tendency, and it therefore merits, and should receive, the unqualified reprobation of every American and lover of American institutions.

6. *Resolved,* That, in selecting a candidate for Congress in this district, it is the sense of this meeting that such a one be chosen as will fully reflect the veiws herein set forth, taking high, bold ground in support of the Kansas-Nebraska bill as passed; and that our delegates to the congressional convention be, and are hereby, instructed to act accordingly.

Iowa.

Resolved, That, as, in the acquisition of territory, all sections of the Union contributed their proportion, whether the purchase was made in blood or treasure, so, in our opinion, ought citizens of all sections of the Union have the right to equal participation in the benefits of such acquisition, controlled in the exercise of their rights by the constitution of the United States, as exemplified by the principles of the Compromise of 1850, and as carried into effect by the Nebraska bill.

Wisconsin.

Resolved, That we shall, as a measure of justice to the North and the South, oppose all attempts to repeal the fugitive-slave law—believing that the repeal of that law would have the two-fold effect of unjustly depriving the South of her property, and of adding largely to a population whose increase in the North must be deprecated by all who do not desire the spread of licentiousness, pauperism, and crime.

Resolved, That we recognise in the Nebraska bill, the fugitive-slave law, and the existing laws for the naturalization of foreigners, the leading issues in the approaching congressional contest; and that we here take our stand firmly in favor of their maintenance, and require our candidate to defend them before the people.

Maine.

The Aroostook district democrats passed the following resolutions at their convention at Houlton, Maine, on the 24th :

Resolved, That the doctrine of the sovereignty of the people is the very basis of republicanism, and the integrity and security of State rights the only safeguards against the federal tenets of consolidation.

Resolved, That the administration of President Pierce merits the undiminished confidence of the democracy, and his strict-construction principles entitle him to exalted rank among the truest defenders of the constitution.

New York.

Resolved, That the democrats of New York repeat here the expression of their unchanged devotion to the principles of the national democracy, as laid down at the Baltimore Convention of 1852, and as approved by the united democracy of this State in its conventions since; that we recognise in that platform the only sure foundation of a national party, and the only bulwark against the uniting and dangerous agitation of sectionalism on one side, and the insidious encroachments of the federal powers upon the rights of the States on the other, and as the best guarantee that a political organization can give of its fidelity to the Union and the constitution.

Resolved, That we consider the introduction of the clause in the Nebraska and Kansas bill repealing the Missouri Compromise as inexpedient and unnecessary; but we are opposed to any agitation having in view the restoration of that line, or tending to promote any sectional controversy in relation thereto: and we congratulate the country that the results to grow out of that measure are likely to prove beneficial to the people of the Territories; and that while we maintain our position, that opinions in regard to the power of Congress in this matter are not tests in regard to democracy, we regard the act of renunciation by Congress of the power it has heretofore exercised over the subjects as the practical surrender of a formidable function on the part of the federal government, and the accession of a right on the part of the incipient sovereignties that are to constitute the States of the Union, the exercise of which can, in all probability, result only auspiciously to the people of the Territories and the peace of the Union.

During the canvass there were many exceedingly able communications published in the *Examiner* and *Enquirer*, from which we extract the following, which excited much attention, and was widely copied by the press of this State.

REASONS WHY I AM A DEMOCRAT AND NOT A KNOW NOTHING.

I presume there is no doubt of the death of the Whig party, as a national party, unless it is silently lurking in the secret bed of Know Nothingism.

This idea a number of bold and conscientious Whigs, in the country, utterly repudiate; and they would despise the day that disclosed the fact of a great national party being concealed in the womb of Know Nothingism. However, this cannot be doubted, that every voter who goes to the polls, in May next, will vote, not directly as Whig or Democrat, but as Know Nothing or anti-Know Nothing. He who wishes a secret political party to rule this free, proud and independent nation, votes for, and he who opposes secret, oath-bound political societies, against Know Nothingism. The one votes for freedom, the other for tyranny. Every voter, then, should stop and consider well before he casts his influence at the ballot box in favor of such organizations; for, when schism, persecution, anarchy and bloodshed result, it will be a poor excuse to say, "I misunderstood the object of my vote." Let them remember that eternal vigilance is the price of liberty, and that freemen should always be on their guard for fear of being carried away by appearances, and thereby bring ruin and destruction upon this happy land. For the old Whig party every one entertained the highest opinion. It was a noble foe—open, bold, generous and national—a party consecrated to history by the immortal minds of Hamilton, (a foreigner,) Clay, Webster, and others no less distinguished in war or in peace. This party is no longer in existence—the *Know Nothings have deliberately murdered it* in cold blood, and desecrated the tombs of Clay and other great leaders of the popular mind. Know Nothingism has swallowed it up in its all-capacious and devouring maw. What say the Whigs of 1840? What say the Clay, the Webster, the Fillmore Whigs? Where are those Whigs who have repeatedly declared they "would be Whigs as long as they lived?" Oh, consistency is a jewel; and, to preserve your consistency, you cannot forsake your old party. But you join the Know Nothings. Then, you have forsaken your old party, or recognize in this new secret society the former Whig party. Which? There is a number of Whigs, who, if they knew that their old party had become metamorphosed into this new party, would despise the very name of Know Nothingism as long as they lived.

The great contest, then, hereafter, in the country, will be between the Democratic party and the Know Nothing organization. The old Whig party will divide between the two—some going one way, and some another. I propose to give a short expose of the principles and condition of the two leading parties, and, at the same time, showing wherein they differ, and wherein they agree.

KNOW NOTHINGISM VERSUS THE DEMOCRATIC PARTY.

The true origin of this Know Nothing party is, of course, unknown; but, I presume, there is no doubt of its having been born among the abolition and corruption of the North, aided by disappointed office-seekers, who wished a promotion to some office in the country. However, the place of its birth is of no importance. It is enough to know its principles, its objects, its workings and its fruits, and, from these, we can judge of its character and destiny. Of the Democratic party, the whole country understands its principles, and knows perfectly well what it has done; and its proud achievements are marked on the map, and its glory bounded by the glory of the country. What a difference between the two! Look at the contrast! The last is open, bold and fearless in all it does and thinks; the first, secret, timid and fearful. The one discusses the important matters of State before the world, the other plots where none can see or hear. The one unbosoms itself to its foe, and challenges refutation and argument before the sovereign voters of the land; the other, like a snake in the grass, is sly, sneaking and cunning, watching a favorable opportunity to leap upon its adversary, and do it a fatal injury by inflicting its poisonous fang. The acts and views of the one are open for attack from any quarter; the other, conscious of its weakness, binds its members under sacrilegious oaths not to disclose its proceedings to the public. The one is an open, bold, independent foe; the other crouches, sneaks and deceives. Which do you prefer?

But I object to the Know Nothing party—

First. Because I believe it contrary to the spirit of the Constitution. What says the Constitution? What says the Know Nothing Constitution? Let us compare them:

Constitution of the United States.

Art. VI. No religious test shall ever be required as a qualification for *any* office of public trust under this government.

Constitution of Virginia.

Sec. XV. "No man shall be compelled to frequent or support any religious worship, place or ministry whatever; nor shall any man be enforced or restrained, molested or burthened in his body or goods, *or otherwise suffer*, on account of his religious opinion or belief; but all men shall be free to profess, and by argument to maintain, their opinions in matters of religion, AND THE SAME SHALL IN NO WISE AFFECT, DIMINISH OR ENLARGE THEIR CIVIL CAPACITIES."

Know Nothing Constitution.

Art. III. "The object of this organization shall be to resist the insidious policy of the Church of Rome, and other foreign influences against the institutions of the country, *by placing in all offices in the gift of the people, or by appointment, none but native born* PROTESTANT *citizens.*"

Know Nothing oath.

"You furthermore promise and declare that you will not vote nor give your influence for any man for any office in the gift of the people, unless he be an American born citizen, in favor of Americans ruling America, NOR IF HE BE A ROMAN CATHOLIC."

Again: "You solemnly and sincerely swear, that if it may be done legally, you will, when elected to any office, remove all foreigners and ROMAN CATHOLICS FROM OFFICE; and that YOU WILL IN NO CASE APPOINT SUCH TO OFFICE."

The direct and irreconcilable antagonism between the Federal and State Constitutions and the Constitution and Ritual of Know Nothingism is palpable to the plainest understanding. The objects and declarations of this Order conflict not only with the abstract principles, but with the actual provisions of the government. Know Nothingism *does* prescribe a religious test as a qualification to office. Know Nothingism *does* molest and burthen men, and *does* diminish their civil capacities on account of their religion.

For this reason, then, I object to the Know Nothing party.

Second. I object to the Know Nothing party because of its Oaths. I had always thought it clearly established that extra judicial oaths were anti republican, anti scriptural, unchristian and opposed alike to sound policy and law, human and divine. The great Author of the Christian religion has said, "swear not at all, neither by heaven, nor by the earth, nor by thy own head, for thou canst not make one hair white or black; but let your communication be yea, yea; nay, nay: *for whateoever is more than this cometh of evil.*" Learned divines and commentators of every persuasion concur in interpreting this passage as a complete prohibition of all voluntary oaths, and in placing those who deliberately take an oath, except under the authority of the State or Church, upon the same footing with profane swearers and blasphemers. Why have oaths? Is it because you believe every person prone to tell a falsehood, and you wish to prevent it. It is a solemn thing to take an oath. And it has long been discussed whether, in a court of justice even, oaths were not contrary to the divine law. If there is a doubt here, surely every individual should be exceedingly careful how he swore in unimportant matters, or in matters where there is no necessity for oaths. Is not marriage a solemn, important and binding institution? Why are not oaths administered here?—for the simple reason, they are *unscriptural.* Is not the right of baptism, joining the church, and ordination of ministers, serious and important acts? Why are not oaths required here?—for the simple reason, they are *unscriptural.* Is the reader aware that courts of justice in our land have already decided that a Know Nothing is an incompetent juror to try the life of a Catholic foreigner, and this because of the oath that the Know Nothing organization imposes upon its members. Is it possible that this is true—that the oath of a Know Nothing prevents him from doing justice to a fellow being? And is this the organization that ministers of the gospel defend? Is this the party that is to rule our country? Gov. Wright, of Indiana, left the Methodist church because the man sent to minister to him in *holy* things was a Know Nothing. Do you blame him? When the clergy begin to turn Know Nothings, they will find many more of their flock who will turn their backs, not upon the House of God, *but upon the prostitution of the pulpit.*

Thirdly. I object to the Know Nothing party because of its secrecy. Why secret? Would you be ashamed for the acts and proceedings of your meetings to be exhibited before the scrutinizing gaze of the world? If so, you acknowledge error and shame for your conduct. Do you wish, and is it the object of the organization to break down the Democratic party? If so, you should acknowledge it, and not declare otherwise to the candid world, for this is gross deception. Is your object spoils or self-promotion? If so, you are corrupt. Is it your object to purify and purge the politics of the day, and to defeat rascality and demagogueism? If so, your object is good, but you will find it a hard task. The Democratic party has tried to do this, and has only partially succeeded. The Whig party could not do it. And how do you expect to accomplish such a work? If you claim the power to alter the human heart and passions, and can succeed in doing so, you will do more than the Christian religion itself can do after many centuries hard labor. You can *try* to prevent it; so does the Democratic party *try* to prevent them both. Man is *still man* wherever you find him, and wherever you find him *there* you will find both "demagogueism and rascality." I presume the Know Nothings are *men;* if so, you will find as many demagogues, office seekers and rascals among them as in any other party, and probably *more,* for they have left the Democratic party and joined the new party, believing it *will* soon have the "loaves and fishes" to distribute. It is true, the Know Nothings may *try* to prevent these evils; but if they say they can, they are superior to the Christian religion, and they can perform works of supererogation. Wherever man is, there is corruption, vice, intrigue and rascality. What all-seeing Jupiter have these Know Nothings found who can tell at first view whether a man is a demagogue or not? What crucible, what purifying process have they, through which a man passes and then comes forth pure, incorruptible and undefiled? It is sheer nonsense to claim such a power. But why did you join them? Are you an office seeker? Then always "acknowledge the corn." Did you join from curiosity? Your motive then was wrong, and, being satisfied, you should immediately amend your act. Did you join without duly considering its aim and tendency upon our Constitution, our rights, or interests?—or without fairly considering its effects, its acts or its fruits? If so, you are still wrong, and have allowed some one blessed (or rather cursed) with a little gift of gab to take advantage of your ignorance and weakness. How do you know that this has not been done in your case merely for the purpose of electing some demagogue to office. Have you joined them to secure your election to Congress, the Legislature, magistracy, clerkship, constableship, or to be elected as a director, steward, collector, treasurer, or to any office of any kind? Then always proclaim it openly and boldly, and never say again you intend to put down demagogues or *office seekers*. This is corruption *per se*. There is not one in the Know Nothing organization who will say or acknowledge that he is an office seeker; yet we confidently believe there are more office seekers, and more corruption inside the pale of this party than out of it, including all classes, of all ages.

But why so *secret?* Is it because you fear that great disgrace and ignominy will hereafter cluster around the very name of Know Nothing? Ah! this is the true secret of all the secrecy of this secret organization. Well, I am inclined to think with you, and by all means enjoin secrecy, profound secrecy, to save the good name in after years. There is a difference between the secrecy of Know Nothings and those meetings usually called "caucuses." About the proceedings of the first you can find out nothing; in the case of caucuses, any member will tell what was done, and, indeed, the entire proceedings are usually published. In the first case, the secrecy *continues*, in the last, it is *temporary*, and its acts in a short time are known to the world. There is also a marked distinction between Know Nothingism on the one hand, and Masonry or Odd Fellowship on the other. The first is political, the last are not. What is done inside the first very materially affects the "outsider," by throwing him out of office. What is plotted, planned, and done inside the Know Nothings affects materially the wishes and rights of him who does not belong to the organization. Do you not thrust him out of office, and this, too, when he may be dependent upon the very proceeds and profits of this office for daily sustenance for himself and family? Is not this hard? When he meets you in the street and shakes you warmly by the hand, he places his confidence in your friendship, while all the time you may be connected with a secret organization aiding to deprive him of his office, and consequently of his daily supplies of food and clothing. Does not this tend to engender ill feelings in society, in the same family, and to lessen the confidence of man in his fellow man? In Odd Fellowship you do not do this, but exactly the reverse, for you aim in this organization to benefit and help your friend. How can you then

> "Carry smiles and sunshine on your face
> When discontent sits heavy at your heart?"

Fourth. I object to the Know Nothings because of their opposition to the Catholics. It is something remarkable that the "basis principles of the American party," as published and scattered throughout this State, does not even mention the Catholic Church. Thus the *only Know Nothing principle* in the whole platform is left entirely out of the question, unless it was intended to be inferred from the fourth article. And is it possible that this mighty bugbear to the country—this very subject of Catholicism, about which they are continually gabbing—this only fundamental principle of the party—is left *only to be inferred from the platform?* Why was not the opposition to the Catholics expressly laid down in broad terms? This anti-Catholic resolution (as I infer from the *last* part,) is the *only* plank, the *only* principle, that the Know Nothings can claim as exclusive property. Who ever heard of a party with *one* principle before this organization was hatched from Abolition spawn? But to the point. This opposition to a religious sect is inconsistent with the spirit of Christianity, the genius of our government, and the spirit of our institutions. It is assuming the Bible cannot work out its own destiny. It is setting up an earthly tribunal to pass sentence upon an individual's religious opinions. It is the same spirit of intolerance that lit the fires of Smithfield, and that brought many to a speedy death under the executioner's axe in the reign of *Protestant* Elizabeth and the French Revolution of '89. Opposition to a religious sect but tends to increase its strength, and calls from it a more determined resistence. The sympathies of all are, more or less, on the side of the persecuted. It should be remembered too, that this same Pope, concerning whom so much is said, has to keep a foreign army around him to prevent his own Catholic subjects from dethroning him; and yet the cry is, "the power of the Pope." England, of all other countries, should fear the Pope, if he does assume the right to alter governments or dethrone kings; and yet, England has tried to disfranchise the Catholics in the realm. She has done so, but after several years' experience she came to the conclusion that the Catholics were as good citizens as the Protestants; and upon bringing the Emancipation Bill before Parliament, the ablest Protestants in both houses advocated its passage, and by a large majority the Catholic subjects were relieved of their civil disabilities. On this occasion the Catholic religion underwent the severest scrutiny. The committee on the part of Parliament summoned a large number of Catholic priests, professors in colleges, and intelligent lay members, before them, by whom the temporal or civil power of the Pope was absolutely denied. Alexander Pope, the poet, and a Catholic by profession, also denied it. The Pope himself was written to, and he denied it as being a part of the Catholic creed. A few days since Mr. Chandler, in Congress, whom the *National Intelligencer* last year considered a man of the highest character, also denied it upon the floor of Congress, and read extracts from many Catholic works, conclusively showing that they do not recognize it as a part of their creed to interfere with matters of government.

But suppose the Catholics do advocate the union of Church and State, and that they are trying to get possession of this country. The idea is still whimsical and absurd. This country was discovered in 1492, and at that time there was neither a Catholic nor Protestant in the country. At present (1855) the population of the country is 24,000,000. Drop 4,000,000 for slaves, and we still have 20,000,000 of whites. There are 1,570,000 Catholics in the country, which, taken from the 20,000,000, leaves over 18,000,000 of anti-Catholics, or those opposed to the Catholics. Since the discovery of the country to the present time, 365 years have passed. Then, in 365 years, the Protestants or anti-Catholics have increased to 18,000,000, and the Catholics to only 1,500,000. If then, they continue to increase in the same ratio, 365 *years hence* there will be 36,000,000 of people opposed to the Catholic Church, and only 3,500,000 of Catholics. Do the Know Nothings fear the Catholics when, in *three hundred and sixty-five years hence*, the Catholics will number only 3,500,000, and the anti-Catholics, or *those opposed to the Catholic Church*, will amount to the enormous sum of *thirty-six millions?* These facts might be enlarged on, but we deem them sufficient.

Fifth.—I am opposed to the Know Nothings because they have *a party with only one principle, and that an objectionable principle.* As before remarked, this Catholic question is the only principle of this new party, and this, I endeavoured to show in the last paragraph, was utterly untenable and whimsical, as well as unchristian and anti-republican. In regard to the other resolutions laid down in their platform, they are either assumed or borrowed from other parties, and the Know Nothings have no right to claim them as exclusive property. For instance, take the sixth, which reads thus:

"That the Bible in the hands of every free citizen is the only permanent basis of true liberty and genuine equality."

Have the Know Nothings a right to claim this, and say that every other party denies the happy influence of the Bible on "liberty and genuine equality." It cannot be a principle solely their's until some other party denies it; for, if both parties adopt it and claim its utility, it is a principle of both parties—common to both—and neither has the exclusive right of property. Now, I would ask, when did the Democratic party ever object to or deny this principle? Why it has never been denied by the Democratic party at all; but this party looking upon it as a common principle, has never thought proper to incorporate it in its platform, no more than a resolution that "every master should rule his slave, and that the slave should not rule the master;" or that "a man can look upon the sky or his wife if he chooses." These, too, would be good principles, but they are the principles common to every freeman. But, again, I should like to know how it is that the members of the Know Nothing order care more about the Bible than other persons, outside of the organization, who have always been members of the Church. Irreligious skeptics inside the organization, and some of whom are regardless of the Bible, and yet they care more about it than an outsider of some Christian persuasion. No; the truth is this: it is as much one party's principle as the other's—as much Whig or Democratic as Know Nothing, and as much mine as their's.

So it is with other principles in the platform. They do not belong to the Know Nothing any more than to the Democratic party. Some of them, indeed, are taken from the Democratic creed. As, for instance, "religious freedom," and "State Rights." Who wrote the celebrated act of religious freedom in Virginia? The father of the Democratic party. Which party has for years been struggling for the true doctrine of State Rights? The Democratic party. Each article in the platform may be discussed in the same way. As to "availability, Red Republicanism, demagogueism, and corruption,"—the Democratic party has been trying to prevent these evils, and as the people become more enlightened and virtuous, we may expect a reform, and not until then. These evils are already festering like an ulcer upon the face of Know Nothingism. As regards the "*non*-union of Church and State, the doctrine of State Rights, and the education of the people,"—they form a part of the Democratic creed and practice, and always have. Indeed, on some of these points the platform is objectionable, because it does not go *far enough*, and is not sufficiently explicit *for good and genuine Democracy*. Why, then, join a secret organization under sacreligious oaths? Why dodge around the corners at night or run across the streets through the mud, to avoid being seen on council nights? This is noble, high-born and chivalrous. Is it not? This, no doubt, is *one of the beauties of Know Nothingism.* What you do, do openly and above board like a man.

In regard to foreigners and the voting laws, two-thirds of the Know Nothings disagree with their platform;—some want 21 years previous residence, and some 14, and some wish to keep foreigners out of the country altogether. Upon this subject members of the Democratic party also differ—some for 21 years, some for 14, some for 10, and some prefer that the foreigner should be allowed to vote, but not hold office; still the party is willing to discuss the subject before the people on the hustings and in our legislative halls, and as the majority of the people think best, they are willing to sanction. Here I must be more explicit. Naturalization merely confers the right of transmitting property, serving on jury, sue and be sued, and the pledge on the part of the government for protection." I presume no one will say that the honest and good foreigner should not be *naturalized* for 21 years. This would be cruel and unhumane. Five years previous residence should entitle him to the rights of naturalization. This right of passing "a uniform rule of naturalization" belongs to Congress, though the States sometimes confer upon a foreigner some of the privileges of naturalization even before he has been naturalized by Congress. But, in regard to the voting power, this is granted only by the terms of the constitution in our State, and, to alter the law, a convention must be held and the constitution altered. I claim to be a Democrat in the strict sense of the word, and yet I would favor a law of this kind! "Five years previous residence should be required before the rights of naturalization should be conferred on a foreigner. He should not be allowed to vote at all unless he came to this country before he was 21 years of age; and those who came before that age should be required 14 years previous residence." I take 14 as a compromise between 7 and 21, and think that a sufficient length of time. On this point some Democrats may agree with me and some disagree, and they, like myself, are willing to leave the whole subject open for discussion before the people, and for their action. This question of naturalization and voting is a question of expediency, and is similar to the one agitated in the late Reform Convention, by both Whigs and Democrats. I mean "white and mixed basis." It was a question for the people, and not a party issue, for the simple reason that different individuals entertained different views on the subject in the same party.

Sixth.—I object to Know Nothingism because it practices a general system of deception in the community. I have long since determined never to ask a man, "are you a Know Nothing?" unless I am quite certain he does not belong to the council. And for this reason, that if he does belong to them, he will reply, "I don't know anything about them," or some other similar equivocal expression, which I regard as contrary to the principles of honor and the Bible; and the individual who does thus equivocate commits a *known positive sin*. When asked the question, the Know Nothing well knows my meaning, and by equivocating he emphatically deceives me; and what is deception? Answer it in your consciences. I dare assert it, as my opinion, that few persons who do not belong to this new party ever believe one word another says in regard to the Know Nothings, even if the Know Nothing belongs to the Church. This is hard, but it is true, as the reader well knows. I regret it.

This position might be fortified by scriptural quotations, and by extracts from learned writers on the subject, but it would take up too much space. One sentence, however, from Dr. Wayland, who says:

"The obligation to veracity does not depend upon the right of the inquirer to know the truth. Did our obligation depend upon this, it would vary with every person with whom we conversed; and in every case, before speaking, we should be at liberty to measure the extent of our neighbor's right, and to tell him the truth or falsehood accordingly. You cannot do that which God has forbidden."

Members of the church especially should guard themselves. I do not believe that the Know Nothings intend wrong, but in the excitement of party spirit and useless enthusiasm, they have overlooked this point. A word to the wise is sufficient.

Seventh.—I object to Know Nothingism because it prevents a free exercise of voting. The elective franchise is the birthright of freemen. Its free and unrestrained use is the palladium and only security to our liberties and institutions. Control the ballot box by oaths, and you promote chicane, abolition, and demagogueism by oaths. It has been acknowledged by members of the Know Nothing organization, that if a nominee is made by the party they are compelled to vote for him or not vote at all—any how, I presume, they are bound by oaths, if they do vote, to vote for a Know Nothing. They cannot vote for an outsider, even if he sustains the platform. Does this not restrict the free exercise of the voting power? The only way a Know Nothing can be independent in his vote is to leave the organization. When the great security of our liberties is thus restrained, who does not fear the ultimate result? The sea may be quiet and calm now, the breezes fair, the prospect bright and beautiful, yet take care, that in the last effort to strike the harbor, already in view, the gallant vessel does not go down the fearful abyss, dragging with it death and destruction.

Eighth.—I object to Know Nothingism because of its "fruits." By their fruits ye shall know them. What are the fruits? Abolition and Proscription. The Know Nothings triumphed in Massachusetts. What was the consequence? The Governor swears eternal enmity to the South, and regards "papacy and slavery" the two evils which this new party is bent to exterminate. The Legislature of this State elected Henry Wilson to the U. S. Senate, who says he looks forward with a hope, that soon the "sun will rise on the last master and set on the last slave." In Michigan, Wisconsin, Delaware, Pennsylvania and Illinois, where this new party was successful, what has been the result? Abolition, Freesoil, anti-Nebraska men have been elected, and the Governors recommending to the Legislatures in their messages eternal hatred and opposition to the South. We know of no man who has been elected at the North by this new party, unless he first proclaimed himself determined to oppose the extension of slavery and the rights of the South. They are turning out of office the conservative men, and placing in their stead the rankest Freesoilers. But what is very objectionable in this new party, is the fact that they are bound by oaths either to support the nominee for the Presidency or withdraw from the party. Take care that this feature of being bound by oaths is not an Abolition trap to abolitionize the South, or sever in pieces the Union of the States. I believe the Know Nothings of the South will go with the South, but are they not giving their influence to an organization which, at the North, is pledged against the South, by strong and binding oaths? How do you not know that this system of oaths was not devised for the express purpose of binding together the Abolition vote of the North? If so, farewell, a long farewell, to the Union—to the glory of this great nation.

Ninth.—I object to the Know Nothing party because of *its corruption and demagogueism.* It is a well known fact, that all the disappointed office-seekers, demagogues, and corrupt politicians of the Democratic party, have joined this new organization, for the purpose of spoils or self-promotion. Of course the Know Nothings did not know it at the time, for they would not tell their object, and it was impossible for the "incorruptible" party to see a man's motives or secret intents. The transfer of disaffected Democrats to the secret invincibles is of daily occurrence, and when they do get a Democrat in their council they rejoice over him as over a "lost sheep." But what does the Democratic party think of such men? Read the following from the Lynchburg *Republican:*

"J. M. H. Beale.—We see extracts from a letter of this individual going the rounds of the press. Mr. Beale was once a Democratic member of Congress. His career in that body was so obscure that we never heard or saw anything about it, except that he went off from the South on the Compromise, and was suspected of being in the same category with Foote, Cobb, and other spavined patriots. We suppose that the true explanation of his Know Nothing proclivities, as with every other politician, is, that finding himself unable to get office in the regular way, he is willing to identify himself with any organization which promises to gratify his weak ambition and inordinate vanity. All of these "one idea" excitements are beneficial to the Democratic party, in producing the self-destruction of such weak and selfish members as Mr. Beale, and ridding the party of their annoyances. For one, we are glad to see such characters as Mr. Beale saving the Democratic party the necessity of killing them, by killing themselves. We have always thought that persons whose execution was necessary, should be allowed the privilege of suicide."

I have thus hastily given *some* reasons why I object to the Know Nothing organization—an organization with no fixed principles, and destined to do more harm than all the corruption and trickery of demagogues. I do fear it. Not as an individual, but as a citizen. I do not fear the individual members, but I fear the result of the secret oath-bound political society that unites them. I have no doubt of the patriotism, of the honor, of the integrity of most of its members; but they are deceived, and are using means to effect ends which may result in a universal vortex of destruction to the country, and to the peace and security of our firesides and homes. But in this dark political storm through which our country is now passing, our trust is in the integrity, purity, conservatism and nationality of the *Democratic party. In hoc signo vinces.*

Having given *nine* good reasons why I am not a Know Nothing, I propose now to give *twelve* good reasons for the "Faith that is in us."

THE DEMOCRATIC PARTY.

This is an old, settled, national, conservative party, that has boldly stood by the Constitution for a series of years, and repeatedly saved the country, when threatened with destruction by opposing principles. Its policy, its aims, its objects, its acts, stand out in grand relief to the gaze of an admiring world. Its principles are fixed, and have been well tested by the people of the country. It is open, bold and independent, and crouches before no foe, nor acknowledges any superior opponent. But why favor this party? In stating my reasons under this head, I shall say but little by way of explanation, as this party is well known and all its principles have been thoroughly discussed before the people, through the press and in the halls of State.

I favor the Democratic party—

First.—Because it is not secret.

Second.—Because it does not bind its members by sacrilegious oaths.

Third.—Because it is in favor of "Religious toleration," and does not proscribe the Catholic or any other Church. Thomas Jefferson wrote the celebrated act of religious toleration upon the statute book of the State.

Fourth.—Because it supports the Constitutions of the land, and is not contrary to their spirit.

Fifth.—Because it has many great national principles, and is not a "*one* principle party."

Sixth.—Because it does not practice a general system of deception in the country.

Seventh.—Because it does not prevent a free and unrestrained use of the elective franchise.

Eighth.—Because of its glorious "fruits." The Democratic party has enlarged this country from thirteen original colonies to thirty-one independent States; and increased its population from four millions to twenty-four millions. Under the guidance of its principles, commerce, the arts, manufactures, education and christianity have flourished.

Ninth.—Because it is now the purest party, and has in its pale less corruption and demagogueism. The Know Nothing excitement is but a political tornado to purify and purge this good old national party.

Tenth.—Because it opposes the union of Church and State; and not only the Catholic, but any other Church whatever may be its creed. This fact no Democrat will deny.

Eleventh.—Because it believes in and has established the doctrine of State Rights, although for a long time bitterly opposed by another party. The Democratic party struggled for years to confirm this cherished principle upon the minds of the people.

Twelfth.—Because it believes "that the Bible in the hands of every free citizen is the only true basis of liberty and genuine equality." And by this is meant, not to *force* the Bible on any one, but that the party believes in the happy influences of the Bible on liberty and its grand Republican tendency.

Thirteenth.—Because it favors and fosters education—the education of the masses "as necessary to the right use and continuance of our liberties."

Fourteenth.—Because its members are not ashamed to own that they belong to the party, but are proud of the cognomen of "*Democrats.*"

Fifteenth.—Because it is a party proud of its origin, proud of its achievements, proud of its men, proud of its glory, proud of its history, and proud to know that it is able and will crush to earth the Know Nothing Hydra, and forever remain the invincible defender of the Constitution, the rights of the States and the rights of the people.

In laying down these principles I have omitted the great, fundamental and long-contested doctrines of the party, such as Free Trade, anti-Bank, &c., for the reader is no doubt well conversant with these leading principles. This, then, is a party intimately interwoven with our country's history, and can present a long list of great, national principles.

MADISON.

The following communication, which appeared in the Richmond Enquirer of the 19th of March, was subsequently published in pamphlet form, and justly regarded as one of the most able and useful documents of the campaign:

"All states that are liberal of naturalization towards foreigners are fit for empire. The Roman plant was removed into the soil of other nations. It was not the Romans that spread upon the world, but it was the world that spread upon the Romans—and *that* was the sure way of greatness."—[1 *Lord Byron's Works*, 37.

Messrs. Editors:—The present canvass in Virginia involves considerations of the uttermost moment. In the course of my researches into one of the most prominent issues presented, I have fallen upon some facts which I have not seen presented anywhere, and which may be of utility to the people. I have not the time now to elaborate the suggestions which may be made. My object is to present a manual of authorities for the campaign—authorities which may not be accessible in many parts of the commonwealth. I shall be content, therefore, with the mere presentations of many points, with the proof on which they are based, leaving out any obvious reflections of my own.

My first position is, that the whole scope, end and aim of the new organization of Protestant Jesuits in this country, for the abolishment of the laws in regard to naturalization, and the exclusion of all foreigners and Roman Catholics from office, is, instead of an *American*, essentially a *British* idea. All its principles are borrowed from Britain. There is not an original plank of *native* growth in the whole platform.

What are their principles, as published in the Know-Nothing and American Crusader, at Boston?

1. "Repeal of all naturalization laws."
2. "None but *native* Americans and Protestants for office."
3. "War to the hilt on Romanism."
4. "The amplest protection to Protestant interests."
5. "Citizenship granted to foreigners only by SPECIAL act of Congress."
6. "The doctrines of the revered Washington and his compatriots."

These, for the present, will suffice. Now, whence are these doctrines derived?

In England, naturalization cannot be performed but by act of Parliament. The applicant must reside 14 years in the country, and present proof of his good character. The whole doctrine of perpetual allegiance is an English doctrine. Expatriation is an American doctrine. It was this impulse which first peopled this continent. Our ancestors claimed the right to enter the social compact wherever their own feelings should dictate, and their own views of personal aggrandizement or enjoyment would be best promoted. In this way they established a premium for good government exceedingly beneficial to the whole human race. The intelligent and enterprising in every department of life found less difficulty in offering their allegiance to that state which would afford them the best protection in the enjoyment of the fruits of their talents and industry. The admission of such a principle into the general policy of nations did not militate against the real welfare of any, because the great mass of mankind were still held by those bonds to their native soil, which exist among every people, and strengthen from day to day in the various relations of kindred: friends, countrymen and community of interests. At the same time it afforded a facility to those who felt that their exertions might be successfully prosecuted, and would be better appreciated and rewarded in distant climes, to withdraw from the country in which their energies have no free scope and adequate encouragement. It was thus the general amelioration of mankind was most effectually promoted. [Blackstone, 276.] The proposition now is to abandon this whole doctrine—to destroy this great American example, and go back to English policy—to the jealousies and exclusions which always exist among barbarous nations, to the narrow and illiberal systems of China and Japan.

But, as if this was not enough, the proposition goes still further, and all the prejudices, all the enmity, all the machinery of the *Orangeman* in Great Britain must be palmed off upon our people as *American?* I wish I had time to go into a full investigation of this matter. It presents a most inviting field, but I can only give it to you in glimpses.

In England there is a union of church and state. After the establishment of the church of England under Henry the Eighth, the whole object of Parliament was to enforce uniformity to the faith of the kingdom. Penal statutes were directed, not only against Roman Catholics, but against all dissenters from the Church of England. These are all given at large in Hallam's Constitutional History, but I will refer now only to those in regard to Catholics. They were deprived of all means of educating their children, at home or abroad. They could not be guardians to their own or other persons' children. They were all disarmed. The priests were all banished. The holiest feelings of nature were outraged; the son was turned against his father. Any son of a Catholic who would turn Protestant succeeded to the family estate. From that moment it could not be sold, or charged with debt or legacy. A child who turned Protestant was taken from the father and the mother, no matter how young, and given to a Protestant relation. No Protestant could marry a Catholic. No Catholic could purchase or lease land for more than thirty-one years. If the profits of the land amounted to a rate above that fixed by law, the farm belonged to the first Protestant who made the discovery. No Catholic could hold any office of trust, honor, profit or emolument. He could not vote. A Catholic's wife who turned Protestant had an increase of jointure. No Catholic could keep a school. Catholic priests who turned Protestants received $150 a year from the kingdom for life. A reward of $ 250 was provided for the discovery of a Catholic bishop, and $100 for a Catholic priest! Any justice of the peace could compel a Catholic above 18 years of age to reveal the hiding-place of any priest, where mass was celebrated, where schools were kept. On refusal to answer, he was imprisoned for a year. Nobody could act as a trustee for a Catholic. No Catholic could be a juror. No Catholic could take more than two apprentices, except in Ireland, in the linen trade. Popish horses could be taken for the militia and used without pay. No descendant of a Papist could vote without taking the oath of allegiance, taking the sacrament of the Lord's supper according to the Church of England, and renouncing the doctrine of transubstantiation. No Catholic could be a lawyer. No lawyer could marry a Catholic without being considered one, and subject to all penalties as such. No Catholic could marry a Protestant—any priest who celebrated such a marriage was *hanged!* Instances are innumerable where the defendant has pleaded in a criminal trial that the deceased was an Irishman and a Catholic, and, therefore, he had a right to kill him. [Hallam, Sydney Smith, Howell's State Trials.] He was compelled to pay a tithe of all his products to support the Church of England. Every tenth potato belonged to a sect which first made him a slave and then a beggar. The sayers and hearers of mass, whether in public or private, were for the first offence to suffer confiscation of all their goods, together with corporeal punishment, at the discretion of the magistrate. For the second offence they were to be banished. For the third they were to be hanged. John Knox, the great reformer of Scotland, inculcated as a most sacred duty, in 1564, incumbent on the civil government in the first instance, and if the civil government is remiss, incumbent on the people, to extirpate completely the opinions and worship of the Catholics, and even to massacre them, man, woman and child! [Edinburgh Review, September 1826, page 167; Cook's Church of Scotland.]

Of these monstrous provisions, Blackstone says, [2 Black. 58,] "If a time should ever arrive, when all fears of a pretender shall have vanished, and the power and influence of the Pope shall become feeble, ridiculous and despicable, not only in England, but in every country of Europe; it probably *then* would not be amiss to review and soften these rigorous edicts—for it ought not to be left in the breast of every merciless bigot to drag down the vengeance of these laws upon inoffensive though mistaken subjects, to the destruction of every principle of toleration and religious liberty."

For four hundred years these disgraceful acts remained unrepealed. *Now*, England herself sees the folly, and her writers acknowledge the impolicy of them. In 1839, the last dyke which surrounded this infamous system was broken down by Catholic emancipation; and now the Catholic, the Methodist, the Presbyterian, all dissenting sects, even the Jews, have the honors of Parliament open to them.

For six hundred years, united as she was in church and state, England tried the policy of exclusion. Many of the highest offices in the kingdom could be occupied alone by members of the established church. By the test act, all officers of state had to take the oath of allegiance, partake of the sacrament of the Lord's supper, and renounce the doctrine of transubstantiation. It excluded, not merely Catholics, but all dissenting sects.

Under the assaults of the best and most gifted of her sons, these too fell. The language of the great Fox, on this subject, is so appropriate, that I must give it. He says, [Speech on the Test Act,] "No human government has jurisdiction over opinions as such, and more particularly over religious opinions. It had no right to presume that it knew them, and much less to act on that presumption. When opinions were productive of acts injurious to society, the law knew when and where to apply the remedy. If the reverse of this doctrine were adopted, if the actions of men were to be prejudged from their opinions, it would sow the seeds of everlasting jealousy and mistrust; it would give the most unlimited scope to the malignant passions; it would incite each man to divine the opinions of his neighbor, to deduce mischievous consequences from them, and *then* to prove that he ought to incur disabilities, to be harrassed with penalties, and to be fettered with restrictions. From this intolerant principle had flowed every species of sectarian zeal; every system of political persecution; every extravagance of religious hate. Let not Great Britain be the last to avail herself of the general improvement of the human understanding. Indulgence to other sects—a candid respect for their opinions—a desire to promote charity and good will—were the best proofs that any religion could give of its divine origin."

The test act was not repealed until 1828, notwithstanding all the efforts made against it, and the beneficent influence of our example. The Orange lodges were composed of Protestants entirely. They were directed against the Catholics, and embodied in the organization all the prejudice and injustice comprehended in the test act itself, and in the penal laws against Catholics. They are the origin of the Know-Nothings, sons of the Supreme Order of the Star Spangled Banner, sons of the sires of 1776, or by whatever other name they may be designated. They were bound together by similar oaths to those which now bind their brethren in this country; and while they are denouncing the Irish, and Ireland, they are guilty of stealing the very machinery by which they are held together, from another soil,—from Irish ingenuity and Irish bigotry. While they profess to be an American party—they are, in fact a foreign party, borrowing the very principles of their creed from those they do bitterly denounce. They are, in truth, *American Orangemen*, with the profession on their lips that none but Americans ought to rule America, when they themselves are ruled, governed, and sustained by a system of policy which was considered so dangerous, even to the liberties of the British subject, that these very Orange lodges were put down and suppressed by prohibitory and penal statutes in 1825, by the votes of a Protestant parliament.

I have not the time now to go into details in regard to the Orangemen. The curious in such matters may obtain full information form the history of the Rebellion in Ireland. I must, however, give one of their toasts, from which the character of the association, and the spirit which pervaded it, may be inferred. It was drank with great solemnity and joy, at civic feasts on the 1st day of July, the anniversary of the battle of the Boyne, every man kneeling as he repeated the words. They were put together in 1689. It ran thus: "The glorious, pious and immortal memory of the great and good King William, who saved us from Pope and Popery, brass money, and wooden shoes. He that won't drink his toast, may the north wind blow him to the south, and a west wind blow him to the east; may he have a dark night, a lee shore, a rank storm, and a leaky vessel to carry him over the ferry to hell; may the devil jump down his throat with a red hot harrow, that every pin may tear out his inside; may he be jammed, rammed and damned into the great gun of Athlene, and fired off into the kitchen of hell, where the Pope is roasting on a spit, and the devil is pelting him with Cardinals."

It was in an age and among a people where such laws were tolerated, and where such sentiments were indulged, not only towards Catholics, but towards all other non-conforming or dissenting sects, that our fathers first sought this land. The Puritans or Presbyterians found themselves hedged round with penalties quite as unjust as those which girt the Catholic like a belt of fire. Until the settlement and the revolution in this country, no nation seems to have had the least conception, or made the slightest advances, towards religious toleration. Even Bacon, far in advance of his age, as he was upon most subjects, contended that unless there was uniformity in the churches of the colonies with the creed of England, religion itself would be nugatory. He makes the relaxation of some laws a matter of expediency, to recover the hearts of the Irish, but loses sight of the great principle.—[2 Bacon, 189.]

Until the year 1836, to deny the doctrine of the Trinity was, by the English law, a crime punishable with fine and imprisonment. Speculative writers had indeed announced the idea of toleration, and among them as the first, Sir Thomas Moore, in his Utopia; but the suggestion had no response from the government. The prevailing idea, among all churchmen, was, that "liberty of conscience and toleration are things only to be talked of, and pretended by those that are under; but none like or think it reasonable that are in authority. 'Tis an instrument of mischief and dissettlement, to be courted by those who would have change, but no way desirable by such as would be *quiet*, and have the government undisturbed."—[Quoted 3, Hallam's Cons. His. 232.]

The period then before the settlement on this continent was one of intense religious persecution throughout the whole of Great Britain. From the restoration to the year 1685, fifteen thousand families had been ruined by a refusal to conform to the established church, and for the same period, five thousand persons had died victims from imprisonment from the same cause.—[1 Neil's His. Puritans.]

A state of things so utterly overwhelming naturally led to an investigation of intellectual and spiritual rights; of the sanctity of conscience; of all the responsibilities which are intrinsic and unborn—and from these flowed the external, but more ramified prerogatives and privileges which attach to and belong to the man. In 1604, three hundred Puritan ministers had been either silenced, imprisoned or exiled. That Virginia and some of the northern colonies did depart from the very principle which cut them off from the fatherland, is true; it was to have been expected; and perhaps to that very cause we may attribute, in some measure, the early assertion and maintenance of that freedom of religion and of conscience which has made this land the favored spot of all the world. It was reserved for the Catholics to set the first example. Lord Baltimore, in November, 1632, founded his province on the broad basis of freedom of religion, and introduced into his fundamental policy the doctrine of general toleration and equality among *Christian* sects. He does not appear to have gone further; and we have thus given, says Judge Story, "The earliest example of a legislator inviting his subjects to the free indulgence of religious opinion. This was anterior to the settlement of Rhode Island, and therefore merits the enviable rank of being the first recognition among the colonists of the glorious and indefeasible rights of conscience. Rhode Island (in 1644) seems without any apparent consciousness of co-operation to have gone further, and to have protected an universal freedom of religious opinion in Jew and Gentile, in Christian and Pagan, without any distinction to be found in its legislation."—[1 Com. on Cons. 95.]

It is needless, however, to multiply these details. It is sufficient now to say that American policy and principle created a broad division between all that was established in England. It was not toleration of sects which we encouraged, but it was perfect freedom of religion, perfect freedom of conscience. The man who was held responsible to God, and not to government—to eternal truths, not to evanescent laws. This, this is the true American principle. It constitutes our great characteristic as a people. Shall we abandon the American platform, and go back in the history of the human race four hundred years, to that very system of intolerance which England, herself, after a trial of centuries, has abandoned with every badge of infamy?

But let us pass on. The Declaration of Independence was declared, and among the grievances therein recited, we find it charged against the King of England, that "he has endeavored to prevent the population of these states; for that purpose obstructing the laws for the naturalization of foreigners; refusing to pass, others encouraging their migration hitherto, and raising the conditions of new appropriation of lands."

Mr. Madison, too, in enumerating the defects of the confederation, says: "Among the defects severely felt was want of an uniformity in cases requiring it, as laws of naturalization and bankruptcy."—[2 Madison Papers, 712.]

We have now come to the formation of the Federal Constitution. We can now consider what were "the doctrines of the revered Washington and his compatriots." Washington was the President of that Convention. His assent was given to the Constitution as it passed.

By it the President and Vice President are required to be native-born citizens of the United States. There seems to have been no debate upon this proposition.

A foreigner, however, is eligible to the House of Representatives, after being seven years a citizen; and he is also eligible to the Senate after being one nine years.

In the debates which took place on the various propositions which were submitted before the clause was passed in its present shape, we shall see that all those who were afterwards distinguished as Federalists announced themselves in favor of a policy as narrow and exclusive as that of Great Britain, in this as in all other respects; while those who advocated a generous system—an American system—were afterwards quite as much distinguished in the adherence to Republican or Democratic principles. It is true parties were not then formed, but we shall discern the seminal principle of those which divide this country at this very hour, by whatever names called.

Mr. Governeur Morris, (Fed.)—moved to insert fourteen years, instead of four years' citizenship, as a qualification for senators, urging the dangers of admitting strangers into our public councils.—[3 Mad. Papers, 1273, et seq.]

Mr. Pinkney, (Federalist)—seconded him. As the senate is to have the power of making treaties and managing our foreign affairs, there is peculiar danger and impropriety in opening its door to those who have foreign attachments.

Mr. Madison, (Republican)—was not averse to some restrictions on this subject, but could never agree to the proposed amendment. Should the constitution have the intended effect of giving stability and reputation to our government, great numbers of respectable Europeans, men who loved liberty and wished to partake its blessings, will be ready to transfer their fortunes hither. All such would feel the mortification of being marked with suspicious incapacities, though they should not covet the public honors. He was not apprehensive that any dangerous number of strangers would be appointed by the state legislatures, if they were left at liberty to do so; nor that foreign powers would make use of strangers as instruments for their purposes.

Mr. Butler, (Federalist)—Was decidedly opposed to the admission of foreigners without a long residence in the country. They bring with them not only attachments to other countries, but ideas of government so distinct from ours, that in every point of view they are dangerous. He mentioned the great strictness observed in Great Britain on this subject!

Dr. Franklin, (Republican)—-Was not against a reasonable time, but should be very sorry to see anything like illiberality inserted in the Constitution. The people in Europe are friendly to this country. We found, in the course of the revolution, that many strangers served us faithfully, and that many natives took part against their country. When foreigners, after looking about for some other country in which they can obtain more happiness, give preference to ours, it is a proof of attachment which ought to excite our confidence and affection.

Mr. Randolph, (Republican)—Never could agree to the motion for disabling foreigners for fourteen years from participating in the public honors. He reminded the Convention of the language held by our patriots during the revolution, and the principles laid down in all the American Constitutions. He would go as far as seven years, but no farther.

Mr. Wilson, (Republican)—Said he rose with feelings which were perhaps peculiar, mentioning the circumstance of his not being a native, and the possibility, if the ideas of some gentlemen should be pursued, of his being incapacitated from holding a place under the very Constitution which he had shared the trust of making. He remarked the illiberal complexion which the motion would give the whole system, and the effect which a good system would have in inviting meritorious foreigners among us, and the discouragement and mortification they must feel from the degrading discrimination now proposed.

Governeur Morris, (Federalist)—The lesson we are taught is, that we should be governed as much by one's reason and as little by one's feelings as possible. He ran over the privileges which emigrants would enjoy among us, though they should be deprived of that of being eligible to the great offices of government, (as in England,) observing that they exceeded the privileges allowed to foreigners in any part of the world. The men who can shake off their attachment to their own country can never love any other.

On the motion of Mr. Morris, the vote stood: New Hampshire, New Jersey, South Carolina, Georgia—Ayes 4. Massachusetts, Connecticut, Pennsylvania, Delaware, Maryland, Virginia, North Carolina—Noes 7.

Mr. Rutledge.—Seven years' citizenship having been required for the House of Representatives, surely a longer time is requisite for the Senate, which will have more power.

On the question for nine years: New Hampshire, New Jersey, Delaware, Virginia, South Carolina, Georgia—Ayes 6. Massachusetts, Connecticut, Pennsylvania, Maryland—Noes 4. North Carolina divided.

On the 13th August, 1787, the question again came up on motion to strike out 7 and insert 4 years, as the required term for citizenship of a member of the House of Representatives.

Mr. Madison (Republican)—Wished to maintain the character of liberality which had been professed in all the constitutions and publications of America. He wished to invite foreigners of merit and republican principles among us. America was indebted to emigration for her settlement and prosperity.

Mr. Wilson (Republican)—Remarked that almost all the general officers of the Pennsylvania line of the late army were foreigners, and no complaint had ever been made against their fidelity or merit. Three of her deputies to the Convention—Morris, Fitzsimmons and himself—were also not natives.

On the motion to make the term 4 years instead of 7, the vote stood: Connecticut, Maryland, Virginia—Ayes 3. New Hampshire, Massachusetts, New Jersey, Pennsylvania, Delaware, North Carolina, South Carolina and Georgia—Noes 8.

Such, then, were the sentiments of the "revered Washington and his compatriots," on this great issue. But we are not left there as to the position of Washington. It were a bootless task to give from his writings what his opinions were. Garbled extracts have been paraded before the people, without relation to the context, to give some color of authority to the designs of this resuscitated American, Orange, Protestant, Jesuit organization; but they can impose only on those who perversely shut their eyes against all knowledge. One example in point may suffice for the end which we have now in view. In December 1789, while Washington was president, he addressed a letter to the Catholics of the United States, in which he said: "As mankind become more liberal, they will be more apt to allow that all those who conduct themselves as worthy members of the community, are equally *entitled to the civil government.* I hope to see America among the foremost nations in examples of justice and liberality. And I presume that your fellow-citizens will not forget the patriotic part you took in the accomplishment of their revolution, and the establishment of their government, or the important assistance they received from a nation in which the Roman Catholic religion is professed." [12 Writings of Washington, 178.]

We come now to that provision of the Constitution in regard to a religious test.

Mr. Pinkney moved that no religious test shall ever be required as a qualification to any office or public trust under the United States.

Mr. Sherman thought it unnecessary, the *prevailing liberality* being a sufficient security against all such tests. It is remarkable that the motion was agreed to *nem. con.* without another word on the subject. Little did the framers of that instrument suppose that, in less than a century, an organization should arise, the object of which is to do indirectly the very thing which it was supposed could not possibly be done directly, even without the constitutional guarantee which now exists.

It is equally remarkable, too, that in all the debates upon the adoption of the Constitution, there is nothing said upon the power conferred on Congress to pass uniform laws in relation to naturalization. The clause in regard to the test, however, did undergo a very rigid examination, and it may be well to show the spirit which prevailed at the time in regard to it. We will commence with Massachusetts. [2 Elliot's Debate, 156.]

Rev. Mr. Backus.—I beg leave to offer a few thoughts upon the Constitution proposed to us; and I shall begin with the exclusion of any religious test. Many appear to be much concerned about it; but nothing is more evident, both in reason and the holy scriptures, than that religion is ever a matter between God and individuals; and that, therefore, no man or set of men can impose any religious test without invading the essential prerogatives of our Lord Jesus Christ. Ministers first assumed this power under the Christian name, and then Constantine approved of the practice when he adopted the profession of Christianity as an engine of state policy. And let the history of all nations be searched, from that day to this, and it will appear that the imposing of religious tests hath been the greatest engine of tyranny in the world.

Next Connecticut—[2 Elliot, 203.]

Oliver Wolcott.—For myself I should be content either with or without the clause in the Constitution which excludes test laws. Knowledge and liberty are so prevalent in this country, that I do not believe that the United States would ever be disposed to establish one religious sect and lay all others under legal disabilities. But as we know not what may take place hereafter, and any such test would be destructive of the rights of free citizens, I cannot think it superfluous to have added a clause which secures us from the possibility of such oppression.

Next Virginia—[3 Elliot, 113. Do. 313.]

Mr. Madison.—I confess to you, sir, that were uniformity of religion to be introduced by this system, it would, in my opinion, be ineligible; but I have no reason to conclude that uniformity of government will produce that of religion. This subject is, for the honor of America, left perfectly free and unshackled. The government has no jurisdiction over it—the least reflection will convince us there is no danger on this ground. Happily for the states, they enjoy the utmost freedom of religion. This freedom arises from that multiplicity of sects which pervades America, and which is the best and only security for religious liberty in any society. For, where there is such a variety of sects, there cannot be a majority of any one sect to oppress and persecute tne rest.

Next North Carolina—[4 Elliot, 196.]

Mr. Iredell used this comprehensive and elegant language: "Every person in the least conversant in the history of mankind, knows what dreadful mischiefs have been committed by religious persecution. Under the color of religious tests, the utmost cruelties have been exercised. Those in power have generally considered all wisdom centred in themselves, that they alone had the right to dictate to the rest of mankind, and that all opposition to their tenets was profane and impious. The consequence of this intolerant spirit has been that each church has in turn set itself up against every other, and persecutions and wars of the most implacable and bloody nature have taken place in every part of the world. America has set an example to mankind to think more rationally—that a man may be of religious sentiments differing from our own, without being a bad member of society. The principles of toleration, to the honor of this age, are doing away those errors and prejudices which have so long prevailed even in the most intolerant countries. In Roman Catholic lands principles of moderation are adopted which would have been spurned a century or two ago. It will be fatal, indeed, to find the time, when examples of toleration are set even by arbitrary governments, that this country, so impressed with the highest sense of liberty, should adopt principles on this subject that were narrow, despotic and illiberal."

These, then, were the sentiments of the compatriots of Washington. I commend them to the state of his birth—in this fatal hour of the republic—when the poisonous drops of a horrid fanaticism, and a not less horrid bigotry, are distilled into the ears of the people—when an "airy devil hovers in *her* sky and rains down mischief!" Shall *we* go forward to that crag which beetles over an unfathomable abyss, or shall we stand now and forever as a commonwealth upon our glorious act of religious freedom?

"Shall we, on this fair mountain, have leave to feed."

My next point is, that the principles of the Orange Americans, that "America shall be ruled by Americans;" that "foreigners ought not to be eligible to office," and "that all public positions ought to be filled by natives of the soil," are nothing more than revivals of the doctrines of Federalism, *British* Federalism in its worst type: of that party in this country which has had so little of Americanism about it, that in every war that we have ever had, it has been against that very flag which is now used as a symbol, a desecrated symbol, in their Jesuitical orgies, and demagoguical mysteries. What are the proofs?

On the 3d day of May, 1798, Harrison Gray Otis, of Massachusetts, a Federalist, and afterwards a member of the infamous Hartford Convention, introduced into Congress this resolution:—[Annals 5th Congress, page 1570.]

"Resolved, That no alien born, who is not at present a citizen of the United States, shall hereafter be capable of holding any office of honor, trust or profit under the United States."

The Democratic party then, as now, took ground against this most illiberal exclusion. We shall show this by the debates.

Mr. Venable, of Virginia, (Democrat,) did not think the House were authorized to enact such a principle into a law. If taken up at all it ought to be considered as a proposition for amending the Constitution. If it was thought necessary by gentlemen to amend the Constitution in this way, why not make the proposition? After foreigners were admitted as citizens, Congress had not the power of declaring what should be their rights; the Constitution has done this. Foreigners must therefore be refused the privilege of becoming citizens altogether or admitted to all the rights of citizens.

Mr. Otis, of Massachusetts, (Federalist,) had no idea this proposition could be considered as a proposition to amend the Constitution. If the House had the power to amend the naturalization law, and extend the time of residence necessary to entitle an alien to citizenship, they could certainly extend it to the life of a man. The idea of citizenship did not always include the power of holding offices. In Great Britain no alien was ever permitted to hold an office; he wished they might not be allowed to do it here!

Mr. Venable, in reply. He did not believe Congress had the power of saying men who were entitled to hold offices by the Constitution shall not hold them.

Mr. Macon, of North Carolina, (Democrat.)—If a man is a citizen he is eligible to office agreeably to the constitutional rule, and that could not be altered by law. If the people choose to elect a foreigner as a member of the Legislature, if he had been a citizen seven years, Congress could not say he should not be eligible.

Mr. Otis, in continuation.—"What advantage was derived to this country from giving foreigners eligibility to office? The people of this country were certainly equal to the legislation and administration of their own government. He had no doubt many aliens would become very valuable acquisitions to this country; but he had no idea of admitting them into the government. Great Britain was very careful of the avenues which led to her freedom. Aliens were there excluded from holding all places of honor, profit or trust. It had not only been thought good policy in times past to encourage foreigners to come to this country, but also to admit them into the Legislature and important offices. But now America is growing into a nation of importance, and it would be an object with foreign nations to gain an influence in our councils; and before such an attempt was made it was proper to make provision against it!"

How many speeches have we lately heard which are like this one of Mr. Otis!

It seems, too, that another plea, very commonly put forward was then in vogue too.

Mr. McDowell, of N. C., (Democrat.)—"It has been said our population was now sufficient, and that the privileges heretofore allowed to foreigners might now be withdrawn. In some parts of the country this might, in some degree, be the case; but he knew there were other parts which wanted population."

Robert Goodloe Harper, South Carolina, (Federalist,)—"Believed it was high time we should recover from the mistake which this country fell into when it first began to form its Constitution, of admitting foreigners to citizenship. He believed the time had now come when it was proper to declare that nothing but birth should entitle a man to citizenship in this country. This was the English doctrine. He was for giving foreigners every facility for acquiring property, of holding this property, of raising their families, and of transferring their property to their families. He was willing they should *form* citizens for us; but, as to the rights of citizenship, he was not willing they should be enjoyed except by persons born on the soil. If the native citizens are indeed adequate to the performance of the duties of the government, he could not see for what reasons strangers are admitted. None but persons born in the country should be permitted to take part in the government. He moved to amend by adding the following words: 'or of voting at the election of any member of the Legislature of the United States, or of any state.'"

The alien law was then under consideration, upon which, and the sedition law, Virginia passed her renowned resolutions in 1798. We need not now allude specifically to its provisions. It gave the president power to order all aliens he may judge dangerous to the United States, or that he may suspect to be so, to depart out of the country in such time as he himself may specify. And if ordered to depart, and he remained without a license from the president, he was to be imprisoned for a term of three years, and forever debarred of all the privileges of a citizen.

The debates show that the Democratic party opposed this act, and it became one of the grand lines of demarcation in 1800. The liberal policy established by our fathers was not sufficient for the Federalists, who desired to make America conform to Britain in regard to aliens, in regard to a bank, in regard to the whole governmental policy. Here, again, the Democratic party, in peace as in war, were the American party, as they are now, and as we trust ever shall be. But to the proofs:

Mr. Allen, of Connecticut, Federalist, [Annals of 5th Congress, 1798,] "alluded to the vast number of naturalizations which lately took place in this city (Philadelphia) to support the party opposed to the president (John Adams) in a particular election."

Have we not heard similar language used in our day by the men in favor of the same course of policy?

Mr. Sewell, (Democrat.)—"What is to be feared from the residence of aliens among us? Anything to ruin the country? He acknowledged many inconveniences arose from this circumstance, but more from their own unnatural children, who in the bosom of their parent conspired her destruction."

Then, it was the cry of the French, now it is the power of the Pope, which is made the pretext for this new agitation. Listen!

Mr. Allen, of Connecticut, (Federalist.)—A person in this city, who has too respectable a standing, and who is doing too much business in it, has declared that he wished to see a French army land in this country, and that he would do all in his power to further their landing. He had heard nearly the same thing from another quarter. Not that he was himself afraid of being assassinated or having the city burnt.

Mr. Gallatin, (Dem.) of Pennsylvania.—This bill was not only contrary to every principle of justice and reason, but to the plain provisions of the Constitution. The Constitution says "that no person shall be deprived of life, limb or property, without due process of law." But here persons may be deprived of their liberty without any process of law, or being guilty of any crime.

Mr. Livingston, (Dem.) of N. Y.—He esteemed it as one of the most fortunate occurrences of his life, that after an inevitable absence from a seat in that house, he had arrived in time to express his dissent to this monstrous bill. It would have been a source of eternal regret and the keenest remorse if any private affairs had deprived him of the opportunity of recording his vote against an act he believed in direct violation of the Constitution, and marked with every characteristic of the most odious despotism. By this act the president alone is authorized to make the law—to fix in his own mind what acts, what words, what thoughts or looks shall constitute the crime contemplated by the bill, that is, the crime of "being suspected to be dangerous to the peace and safety of the United States." This comes completely within the definition of despotism—an union of legislative, executive and judicial powers.

Mr. Tazewell, (Dem.) of Virginia—Knew of but one power given to Congress by the Constitution which could exclusively apply to aliens, and that was the power of naturalization. Whether this was a power which excluded the states from its exercise, or gave to Congress only a concurrent authority over the subject, he would not now pretend to say. But it neither authorized Congress to prohibit the migration of foreigners to any state, nor to banish them when admitted. It was a power which could only authorize Congress to give or withhold citizenship. The states, notwithstanding this power of naturalization, could impart to aliens the right of suffrage, and the right to purchase and hold lands. There was in this respect no restraint upon the states.

At the same session the sedition law passed—a law aimed at the natives, as the other was aimed at the foreigners. It provided that any one who should write, print, utter or publish, or cause or procure the same to be done, any malicious writing against the government of the United States, or either house of Congress, or the president, should be punished by a fine not exceeding two thousand dollars, and by imprisonment not exceeding two years. It is not necessary now to dip into the debates on this branch of the subject. It would extend this paper longer than we desire. It is sufficient to say that the same principles were involved—the same division of parties took place—the same liberality was advocated by the American Democratic party—and the same narrowness and exclusion found advocates among those who, instead of mapping out a system of Americans and America, looked to England for the great principles of their public action. The feeling of the time may be deduced from a letter of Timothy Pickering to Alexander Hamilton, both noted Federalists.—[6 Hamilton's Works, 303.]

"The alien bills introduced into the houses of Congress have undergone such alterations I do not know their present form. Of one thing, however, you may rest assured, that they will not err on the side of severity, much less of cruelty."

Here, perhaps, it may be well for a moment to pause, and dwell upon a most remarkable prediction made by Duncan of Ohio, in a speech delivered in the House of Representatives on the 19th of February, 1845.—[Appendix 28 Congress, vol. 14, page 413.]

"Indulge me while I expose a few of the corrupt and iniquitous measures which have ever marked the course of the Federal party, not only to secure their elections, but to secure their favorite measures. It is a fundamental principle of Federalism, that the want of intelligence of the common people makes them unfit for self-government; and they being of the uncommon class, should of right be the governors. Hence it is, that all their means to secure their elections and their favorite measures, are directed to the supposed ignorance and stupidity of the people—that they *know nothing!* I will trace up some of those means from an early period of our government, by which the Federal party may be known under whatever name they may have assumed, or may hereafter assume for political deception; for so long as they shall be known by their true name, and their principles are known to correspond with their name, the Democracy must and will triumph.

"I begin with the unprincipled practice they have of changing their name. They have changed their name with the periodical return of every presidential election: and this for the purpose of concealing their principles and deceiving the people. Their last name was Whig, and that name they kept as long as it would answer any purpose; but they will never fight another battle under the banner inscribed Whig again. Having exhausted the political vocabulary, they will return to the abuse and persecution of the Irish and Germans which characterized the party in the administration of the elder Adams. Nothing is longer to be feared from a change of name. The people contemplate them as they do a stranger, who gives himself a new or different name in every town or village through which he passes. They look upon him as a scape-gallows or horse-thief who merits the rope or the penitentiary."

The best commentary upon this passage, is the following editorial from the New York Express, a Whig paper, of the date of the 14th of February last:

"It gives us no pleasure to refer to the past glory of the Whig party, or to write the obituary of that which we have joyed in and joyed over; but we conduct a newspaper, not a Book of Lamentations, and we cannot shut our eyes to continually occurring facts. The Whig platform, 'previously spit upon,' to quote the coarse phrase of a city contemporary, has now been so shattered by the withdrawal of its main protective tariff plank, that there is not enough left of the corpse, we fear, for any species of political anatomization. Internal improvement is a vague idea; a protective tariff is abandoned even in New England, where the manufacturers say it is not only not needed, but has become an embarrassment, just as in England when the Peelite manufacturers turned their somerset and flung out the banner of free trade. Massachusetts now stands with Alabama on the tariff. The currency issues have been superseded by the railroads and magnetic telegraphs, which do away with all necessity for any great regulator of the domestic exchequer. Indeed, there is not a Whig principle that Clay and Webster fought for, that is not dead and buried! Nevertheless, Whig hosts will hover for months over the tombs of Clay and Webster, and the principles buried with them; for mourners of parties, like other mourners, are the last to believe in the dissolution of death."

Such being the condition of the Whig party, what course remained but to do what Duncan said they would do: go back to the old principles which we have shown to be British, and not American, and abuse and persecute the Irish and Dutch, with an addition of British, not American, disqualifications against Catholics? They hoped in this way to seduce off a sufficient number of unsuspecting Protestant Democrats to give them the balance of power. It was the last resort of Federalism; and, to crown all, they steal their very war-cries of hostility against the Pope, of his power to exempt his subjects from the oath of allegiance, from the bigotry and intolerance of England. This device was used there for centuries, and after being reduced so low that no respectable man in that kingdom will use it, it is vamped up and paraded here as something new, patriotic and American! I wish I had the time to go into this branch of the subject, but I must postpone it to a future paper.

On the slavery question—on the extension of territory—on foreigners—the old Federal party occupied precisely the same grounds now occupied by the Protestant Jesuits of the north. I design hereafter, if I can find the leisure, to show this in detail; but I must for the present confine myself to the latter branch of the subject alone.

Let us pursue still further the history of parties on the alien question. Virginia declared her sentiments in the resolutions of Madison in 1798, to which, in spite of Federal jeers and jibes, we are forced back more and more every year for an exposition of the true powers and functions of this confederacy.

In the language of one of these resolutions, "the General Assembly protests against the palpable and alarming infractions of the Constitution, in the late case of the alien and sedition acts, passed at the last session of Congress, which exercise powers nowhere delegated to the federal government, and by uniting legislative and judicial powers to those of executive, subverts the general principles of a free government."

Alexander Hamilton, true to the instincts of Federalism, could not let these sentiments pass. He refers to Jefferson's opinions on emigration, expressed in his notes on Virginia, which are quoted now in all the American Orange councils as indicating his approval of their work, and then makes these animadversions on the passage of the message we have quoted, in which we shall see the very language now used by them and their adherents upon this subject. He says:—[7 Hamilton's Works, 771.]

"It is certain that had the late election been decided entirely by native citizens and native votes; had foreign auxiliaries been rejected on both sides, the man who ostentatiously vaunts that the doors of public honor and confidence have been burst open to him, would not now have been at the head of the American nation. The pathetic and plaintive exclamations, by which the sentiment is enforced, might be liable to much criticism, if we are to consider it in any other light than as a flourish of rhetoric. It might be asked, in return, does the right to asylum or hospitality carry with it the right to suffrage and sovereignty? And what, indeed, was the courteous reception which was given to our forefathers by the savages of the wilderness? When did these humane and philanthropic savages exercise the policy of incorporating strangers among themselves on the first arrival in the country? When did they admit them into their huts to make part of their families? And when did they distinguish them by making them their sachems and chiefs?"

We have now traced the division of parties on this subject to the time of Jefferson, by an appeal to the record, and by undoubted authorities. We may hereafter carry the parallel down to our own days. It can be done most conclusively, but we must reserve other views for another occasion. To show how consistent Federalism was on this subject, it is only necessary to refer to the proceedings of the Hartford Convention. We shall select two resolutions, as in point.

The first was, that "the most inviolable secrecy shall be observed by each member of this convention, including the secretary, as to all propositions, debates and proceedings thereof, until this injunction shall be removed, suspended or altered."

The next is, "That no person who shall hereafter be a naturalized citizen of the United States shall be eligible as a member of the Senate, or the House of Representatives of the United States, nor be capable of holding any civil office under the authority of the United States."

At this point we must close, leaving other views for the future. We have written mainly for the benefit of the young men of the state, over whom this American Orange organization is most zealously striving to obtain control. By subtle appeals to their patriotism—to their native pride—to their holy zeal for the land of their birth, they seek to draw them into a crusade against the purest principles of our constitutional faith—against the very heart of the nation. Let the young men of the state go back to the precepts and doctrines of our ancestors, as herein delineated, and then decide for themselves the question whether they will follow those who have proven themselves to be the lights of the universe—immortal not less in their consciousness than in their maintenance of the right in religion as well as in the state; or whether they will forswear the ancient colors of the republic, and go back in the history of the human race four hundred years, to the exclusions, the penalties and disabilities, both political and religious, which, instead of being indigenous to our soil, are but poisonous exotics transplanted from Great Britain! Believe me, this is not an age to deprive humanity of any of its dear-bought privileges. Human ingenuity may go very far, but no mode can be devised to justify persecution—to sanctify bigotry, or deify the crimes which we may commit on our fellow men. Passion and prejudice may go far, very far too; they may establish parties, they may give them temporary success, but they will realize the reflections of Sandoval to Henry:

"Always strivest thou to be great
By thine own act,—yet art thou never great,
But by the inspiration of great passion;
The whirl blast comes, the desert sands rise up
And shape themselves; from earth to heaven they stand
As though they were the pillars of a temple
Built by Omnipotence in its own honor!
But the blast pauses, and their shaping spirit
Is fled: the mighty columns were but sand,
And lazy snakes trail over the level ruins!"

In reply to the arguments, empty declarations, and bold assertions of the Know Nothings respecting the temporal power of the Pope, the Examiner published the following editorial:

COMFORT FOR THE FRIGHTENED—CHEER FOR THE FAINT-HEARTED.

There is a convenient provision in the *secret* constitution of the Know Nothing Order, (not promulged, however, in their published Basis Principles,) allowing their grand National Council to grant dispensations to the Councils in the States, exempting them from such provisions of that instrument as may not be locally popular. Accordingly, the Councils of Louisiana, a State settled chiefly by French Catholics, have a dispensation from all those articles of their constitution which are proscriptive of *Catholics*, and would exclude that sect from office and from suffrage. So that in the very State in which—if there were real danger from the temporal authority of the Pope, that danger would be imminent and appalling,—this valiant order of Protestant lions are roaring as gently as sucking doves against the Romish hierarchy.

While the Order in Louisiana are courting Catholic votes with commendable assiduity, their brethren in the State of Virginia are in a terrible state of alarm on the subject of a Popish invasion, and are quoting newspaper authority from Dublin, to show that the Pope does claim the power to depose sovereigns from their thrones—a power that might be exerted with dreadful effect upon the sovereigns of Screamersville, Butchertown, and the Hanover Slashes.

When we hear intelligent Virginia gentlemen, entitled to be respected for candor on every other subject, inveighing against Popes and Catholics, as inimical to the State Government of Virginia, and threatening to the official safety of Governor Joseph Johnson, we are tempted to inquire in derision and compassion, why this valorous assault on eight thousand Catholics in Virginia? while their order have not the honesty, the candor, the patriotism, or the courage to lift a finger against that denomination in Louisiana, where they are really numerous and strong, and where, if their ascendancy were really dangerous to free institutions, it would deserve their attention.

But proving the hypocrisy of Know Nothingism, by pointing to the changing hues of its chameleon charlatanry in different quarters of the Union, may not suffice, as it should do, to remove the apprehensions of weak minded, but well meaning Virginians about Popish and Catholic machinations against their government and liberties. If these were indeed in danger from such a source, it is very plain from the conduct of the Know Nothings in the State of Louisiana that safety is not to be sought in that weather-cock Order, but that it rests where the safety of all liberty and liberal governments rests—in the strong arms and brave hearts of a free people. This Know Nothing clamor about the Pope and his authority, is a pusillanimous outcry, appealing to the fears of the people against a sort of danger from which their own bravery and intelligence are ever the sole and the all sufficient safeguard.

The Know Nothings, for the want of better authority, are parading an editorial article from a foreign newspaper, entitled the Dublin *Tablet*, asserting the power of the Pope in temporal affairs, and especially his power to depose rulers. The assertion and the explanation of the power claimed are both embodied in the following sentence from the Dublin article:

"The deposing power does actually exist at present; it is publicly taught in every state that considers itself free. It is the doctrine of Americans, for they deposed George III. It is the doctrine of Englishmen, who deposed James II.; and of Frenchmen, for they have deposed the dynasty of the Bourbons. The Spaniards admit it, for Queen Isabella's throne is in danger. The difference between the modern and mediæval world consists in this. We vest this in the people; our ancestors, more wisely, in the Pope. In England, the deposing doctrine is made a law of the kingdom, to be put in force whenever the reigning sovereign prefers his soul to the sceptre. Kings, of course, have done their utmost to discredit the doctrine, and they have gained for themselves, instead of it, the scaffold and the sword. The divine right of certain families to govern nations according to their will is refuted, not by argument, but by exile or a violent death. If kings prefer this solution of the difficulty to that which mediæval principles offered, that is their affair. This, however, is certain, the Pope was more patient and considerate than the people are, and a deposition is less injurious to society than a bloody revolution. A deposition does not necessarily involve a change of dynasty, but in general, revolution does; and perhaps kings might, on reflection, prefer to lose the crown to themselves only, to losing it for the family as well."

It is very plain that this witness, whom the Know Nothing journals, for the want of a better, have lugged in to their support, and are vouching with so much gusto, means to assert only some such power for the Catholic Christians, under dispensations from the Pope, as all free people claim in regard to the civil authority—"the same power as does actually exist among all people claiming to be free"—a power like that which the South claims, of secession from the Union, and which the people of every free country claim, *of political revolution* in the failure of all other means of redress.

This accidentally discovered and solitary witness of the Know Nothings, therefore, proves no practical claim of temporal power on the part of the Pope, and only raises a nice question of political casuistry, the discussion of which now would be as useless as a discussion of the abstract doctrines of State secession and of popular revolution. A great noise was made in England, more than fifty years ago, about this very idea of the Pope's temporal authority, and evidence was taken which is certainly entitled to more weight than the loose and irresponsible editorial of a Dublin editor.

Mr. Pitt, as Prime Minister of England, contemplating an act of justice to the Catholics, solemnly proposed a set of interrogatories to several of the most celebrated Catholic Theological Universities in Europe. The following questions were proposed: *First*, Has the Pope, or have the Cardinals, or any body of men, or has any individual of the Church of Rome, *any civil authority*, power, jurisdiction or pre-eminence whatever, within the realm of England? *Second*, Can the Pope, or Cardinals, or any body of men, or any individual of the Church of Rome, absolve or dispense his Majesty's subjects from their oath of allegiance, upon any pretence whatever? *Third*, Is there any principle in the tenets of the Catholic faith, by which Catholics are justified in not keeping faith with Heretics, or other persons differing from them in Religious opinions, in *any transactions* either of a public or private nature? To these questions the Universities of Paris, Louvain, Alcala, Salamanca and Valadolid, after expressing their astonishment that it could be thought necessary at the close of the 18th century, and in a country so enlightened as England, to propose such enquiries, severally and unanimously answered: 1st, That the Pope, or Cardinals, or any body of men, or any individual of the Church of Rome, has not and have not any civil authority, power, jurisdiction or pre-eminence whatever, within the realm of England. 2dly, That the Pope, or Cardinals, or any body of men, or any individual of the Church of Rome, cannot absolve or dispense his Majesty's subjects from their oath of allegiance upon any pretext whatsoever; and 3dly, That there is no principle in the tenets of the Catholic Faith, by which Catholics are justified in not keeping faith with Heretics, or other persons differing from them in religious opinions, in transactions either of a public or a private nature. The Pope himself was written to upon the same questions, and most solemnly announced that his See asserted no such claim. Surely this is better testimony than the self contradictory declaration of a Dublin Catholic editor.

We do not rely, however, in a matter of this sort, upon documentary evidence, or newspaper asseveration. We take the ground, that the people are themselves sufficient to assert and maintain their independence of Popes of all sorts; and that they are in no danger of being deposed from the sovereignty with which their Maker and their Fathers endowed them in these States. Three thousand and fifty Protestant clergy will in vain hurl their anathemas against them from Yankee pulpits, and one Dublin editor may impotently proclaim the Pope's authority over their temporal concerns, but while they have the right to manage their own affairs, spite of Popes and of secret clubs, they will always be ready and able to maintain and support that sovereignty. It is only an insult to the intelligence, the manliness and the Christian sentiment of the Virginia people to maintain the possibility of a priestcraft domination over them from any quarter or of any sort.

But what are the historical evidences of the truth of this charge, that Catholics are less attached to civil governments entitled to their allegiance, than other denominations? Surely the Catholic subjects of the British crown have had cause of offence against that government in its persecutions of Catholic Ireland. Surely the only Catholic province of that government, on this continent, might have been excused, while these persecutions of their Catholic brethren, in Ireland, were going on, for seeking annexation to the United States. Surely the French Catholics of Canada have had incentives of animosity sufficient to shake their allegiance to the British government in its numberless and bitter wars against Catholic France. Yet what is the present political *status* of Catholic, French, colonial Canada? Hear how Lord Nugent refutes this idea of a *half* allegiance on the part of Catholics:

"Your other colonies revolted; they called on a Catholic power to support them, and they achieved their independence. Catholic Canada, with what Lord Liverpool would call her half-allegiance, *alone* stood by you. She fought by your side against the interference of Catholic France. To reward and encourage her loyalty, you endowed in Canada bishops to say mass, and to ordain others to say mass, whom, at that very time, your laws would have hanged for saying mass in England; and Canada is still yours in spite of Catholic France, in spite of her spiritual obedience to the Pope, in spite of Lord Liverpool's argument, and in spite of the independence of all the States that surround her. This is the only trial you have made. Where you allow to the Roman Catholics their religion undisturbed, it has proved itself to be compatible with the most faithful allegiance. It is only where you have placed allegiance and religion before them as a dilemma, that they have preferred (as who will say that they ought not?) their religion to their allegiance. How then stands the imputation? Disproved by history, disproved in all States where both religions co-exist, and in both hemispheres, and asserted in an exposition by Lord Liverpool, solemnly and repeatedly abjured by all Catholics, of the discipline of their Church."—*Lord Nugent's Letter to Rev. Sir George Lee, Bart.*

Men might idly dispute till doomsday over the nice question in political casuistry of the extent of the Papal claim of temporal power outside of Rome. But here are facts which illustrate how devoted Catholics may be and are in the habit of showing themselves in the *practical* matter of allegiance. Yet it is due to candor to admit that there *are* historical instances in which Catholics have refused to obey the calls of the British Government. The Irish Catholic Parliament refused to furnish taxes to support the war against the American Colonies in their struggle for freedom. Then, too, there is this notable passage in BOTTA, p. 236-7.

"General Carleton, finding the Canadians so decided in their opposition, had recourse to the authority of religion. He therefore solicited Brand, the Bishop of Quebec, to publish a mandament, to be read from the pulpit, by the curates, in time of divine service. He desired the prelates should exhort the people to take arms, and second the soldiers of the king, in their enterprises against the colonies. *But the bishop, by a memorable example of piety and religious moderation, refused to lend his ministry in this work;* saying that such conduct would be too unworthy the character of the pastor, and *too contrary to the canons of the Roman Church.* However, as in all professions there are individuals who prefer their interest to their duty, and the useful to the honest, a few ecclesiastics employed themselves with great zeal in this affair; but all their efforts were vain; the Canadians (Catholics) persisted in their principles of neutrality. The nobility, so well treated in the act of Quebec, felt obligated in gratitude to promote in this occurrence the views of the government, and very strenuously exerted themselves with that intent on, but without any better success. The exhortations of Congress did not contribute alone to confirm the inhabitants in these sentiments, &c. &c.

"General Carleton, perceiving that he could make no calculation upon being able to form Canadian regiments, and knowing, withal, that there existed in the province certain loyalists, who would have no repugnance to taking arms, and other individuals whom interest might easily induce to enlist as volunteers, resolved to employ a new expedient. He caused the drums to beat up, in Quebec, in order to excite the people to enroll themselves in a corps to which he gave the name of the *Royal Highland Emigrants.* He offered the most favorable conditions. The term of service was limited to the continuance of the disturbances; each soldier was to receive two hundred acres of land, in any province of North America he might choose; the king paid himself the customary duties upon the acquisition of lands; for twenty years, the new proprietors were to be exempted from all contribution for the benefit of the crown; every married soldier obtained other fifty acres, in consideration of his wife, and fifty more for account of each of his children, with the same privileges and exemptions, besides the bounty of a guinea at the time of enlistment. In this manner, Carleton succeeded in gleaning up *some few soldiers;* but he was reduced to attach much more importance to the movements of the Indians"—

—who proved themselved genuine "Native Americans."

It is a well known fact that when Lord Howe, the first British commander of the forces designated at the breaking out of the American war for the invasion of this country, was ordered by the war department to prepare for embarkation, he wrote that he could not trust the Irish Catholic soldiers of his army, as all their sympathies were with America; and the British Government was forced to buy Protestant Hessians at the rate of sixpence a head from the Prince of Hesse Cassel. And the emissaries despatched to Germany wrote more than once to Lord North complaining bitterly of the German Catholics interfering with the enlistment of soldiers for America.

There are facts, however, still later, and, if possible, still stronger than these.

Catholic Louisiana fought full as bravely and effectually as Know Nothing Massachusetts against Catholic Mexico in the war of 1846-'47. Louisiana furnished seven regiments and 7,041 troops to fight against her brethren of the Catholic faith in that war of races and religions; altho' Know Nothing Massachusetts, in the excess of her zeal against the Pope and his people, furnished but one regiment of 930 men to smite the Mexican priests; and furnished that number only by dint of most strenuous exertions on the part of the patriotic Democrats in her borders. If you ask which three States furnished the largest number of troops in that foreign war against a Catholic nation and a Catholic race, the archives of the country will tell you that they were the Catholic States of Louisiana, Missouri and Texas. These furnished respectfully 7,041, 6,441 and 6,955 men, or an aggregate equal to the total number supplied by all the other States in the Union! Besides, it is notorious that the regular army of the United States was made up during that war so exclusively of Irish, (Catholics) that it was difficult to find natives enough for the non-commissioned officers.

Surely the generous people of Virginia will consider the evidence of the muster rolls of the country a better tablet of Catholic patriotism, under all temptations of religious prejudice and bigotry, than the newspaper columns of a raw Irishman in Dublin. Let those who, for political purposes, are seeking to excite the hatred of the magnanimous Virginia voters against that patriotic people, read these facts of history, and blush for their lack of generosity.

The arguments employed in Virginia to shew that the Know Nothing party in the free States sympathised and co-operated with the Abolition or anti-Nebraska party, were supported by the most overwhelming and conclusive proof. The evidence of this unholy alliance, we herewith spread before our readers without comment.

CHANG AND ENG—SAM AND THE WOOLLY-HEADS—A CHAPTER OF DEATH WARRANTS.

What a sad story are the accounts from every quarter of the North, telling of Sam's affiliations! And how cruelly inopportune are these accounts for his followers in Virginia! Behold in the following schedule the record of the strolling Yankee Abolitionist's delinquencies at the North. We begin with New York.

THE VOICE OF THE NEW YORK LEGISLATURE.

The following resolutions were passed by the Legislature of New York before their recent adjournment. The negative vote in the Senate was five to nine out of some thirty in the affirmative, and in the House it ranged from about eleven nays to sixty yeas. The very few Democrats in the Legislature voted generally against the resolutions, and the Seward Whigs and the Know Nothings seem to have gone in a body for them:

Whereas the passage of the bill organizing the Territories of Kansas and Nebraska, and repealing that portion of the Missouri Compromise which prohibited the existence of slavery within their limits, for the purpose of permitting its establishment upon their soil, was a gross violation of good faith, and inflicted grievous wrong upon free labor and free principles throughout the Union;

[Passed—yeas 61, nays 9.]

And whereas this act and the spirit in which it was consummated demonstrate the determination of the slaveholding interest to use the power of the Federal Government to promote the indefinite extension and permanent establishment of slavery;

[Passed—56 to 15.]

And whereas Congress, having no power or right to interfere with slavery as it may exist in any State, is expressly commanded by the Federal Constitution to make all needful rules and regulations concerning the Territories of the United States: Therefore;

[Passed—69 to 1.]

Resolved, (if the assembly concur,) That the people of the State of New York, represented in senate and assembly, demand of Congress the enactment of a law declaring that slavery shall not exist except where it is established by the local law of the State—thus restoring, by positive statute, the prohibition of slavery from the Territories of Kansas and Nebraska.

[Passed—65 to 11.]

Resolved, (if the assembly concur,) That the people of the State of New York, represented in senate and assembly, will not consent to the admission into the Union of any State that may be formed out of the Territories of Kansas and Nebraska, unless its constitution shall prohibit the existence of slavery within its limits.

[Passed—58 to 11.]

Whereas the repeal of the Missouri Compromise and the repudiation of a solemn legislative compact by the slaveholding interest, for the extension of slavery, has released the free States from all obligations that may be expressed or implied in any compromises on the subject of slavery outside of the federal constitution: Therefore, be it

[Passed—55 to 12.]

Resolved, (if the assembly concur,) That while the people of the State of New York, represented in senate and assembly, recognize, and have always respected, the obligation of that prohibitory clause of the Constitution of the United States which declares that "no person held to service or labor in one State, under the laws thereof, escaping therein, be discharged from such service or labor, but shall be delivered up on claim of the party to whom such service or labor may be due," they regard the law of 1850, which provides for employing the whole power of the federal government in the recapture of fugitive slaves, as a violation of the Constitution, an encroachment on the rights of the several States, an outrage upon the principles of justice, and disgraceful to the spirit and civilization of the age in which we live; and that, in their opinion, the welfare of the Union and the principles of republican liberty demand its repeal.

[Passed—53 to 15.]

Two other resolutions were adopted as a sort of blind to indicate that the Seward party are not favorable to the Know Nothings, and these resolutions will doubtless be quoted as such in the slave States. They object simply to secret societies, but do not denounce the war upon religious belief, upon emigration, or upon adopted citizens.

We next go to Massachusetts.

MEETING AND ACTION OF THE KNOW NOTHING STATE COUNCIL OF MASSACHUSETTS.

The Boston *Chronicle* makes the following statement of the transactions of this body:

"Senator Wilson made a speech in opposition to debarring all persons from office who are not native born. The General said that his nativism, when it carried him to an endeavor to make a twenty-one year naturalization law, carried him far enough, and as far as the party of the South and West would agree to. Mr. Ely, of Boston, urged the propriety of excluding all aliens from office, but the views of Mr. Wilson seem to have the more adherents in the meeting.

"We understand, also, that the delegation from this State was instructed to urge upon the National Convention the opening of the doors of the lodges for the future, and to do away with much if not all of the present secrecy. *Resolutions were passed in favor of the abolition of slavery in the District of Columbia, and in all the United States Territories; declaring that no more slave States can be admitted into the Union, but that slavery may be unmolested where it now exists. Furthermore, that these resolutions* MUST BE INSISTED ON *at any cost, even to the dissolution of the Convention.*"

The *Evening Telegraph* says of the election:

"It is rumored to-day that there were about three hundred votes thrown for the officers. The tone of the council was decidedly anti-slavery. Henry J. Gardner, of Boston, Henry Wilson, of Natick, Edward Buffington, of Fall River, John W. Foster, of Brimfield, Henry H. Rugg, of Dennis, Andrew A. Richmond, of Adams, and Augustus C. Carey, of Ipswich, were chosen the delegates to the national council in June next at Philadelphia. A. B. Ely, Esq., made an anti-slavery Know Nothing speech. Strong anti-slavery resolves were passed in the evening without a dissenting vote. Some who were hunkerish hitherto admitted it was no use—the order must take anti-slavery ground.

"It is evident from the action of the council, if it is correctly reported, that the anti-slavery men in the Order have the power, and will use it, to put down whoever shall set himself against the anti-slavery sentiment of the State."

The *Courier*, that staunch Whig organ of the true Daniel Webster type, then adds, and we commend its testimony to the Southern Whigs:

"As from the beginning, we have never looked upon the Know Nothing organization in this State in any other light than as an organization which was controlled entirely by abolitionism, we are not at all surprised at the result of the election, which is fairly set forth in the latter paragraph from the *Telegraph*. Jonathan Pierce, who voted against the adoption of the Loring resolves, is superseded in the office of president by an Abolitionist, and Messrs. Warren, of the Senate, and Mullin, of the House, who voted the same way, have been most unceremoniously discarded. No person who voted in the negative upon that matter has been rechosen, and the leaders of the party are determined to make the Order in Massachusetts thoroughly anti-slavery. How they are to fellowship with the anti-Seward 'Hindoos' of New York, and with such men as Mr. Sollers, of Maryland, and Mr. Ligon, of Virginia, will be known when they meet in national council."

THE KNOW NOTHINGS OF NEW HAMPSHIRE TAKE SIDES WITH FRED. DOUGLASS AND THOS. JAMES, FREE NEGROES AND FREE SOILERS.

The American party of this State have, in State Council, adopted resolutions protesting against the repeal of the Missouri Compromise, and against the Nebraska bill and Fugitive Slave Law, and pledging the party to resist the further extension of slavery.

The following are the resolutions passed by the State Council, at a meeting held at Concord, on the first and second days of May. They are published by a vote of the Council:

Whereas, there appear to exist in the minds of a portion of the community some doubts as to the position of the American party in regard to slavery and its extension over new territories, therefore,

Resolved, That the American organization, as constituted and existing in New Hampshire, is not based on one idea alone, but comprehends every principle that will promote the political welfare of a free people.

Resolved, That the declaration of Independence, the tones and deeds of the founders of the Republic, all indicate that our forefathers intended that slavery should be sectional, not national—temporary, not permanent.

Resolved, That as a political party, pledged to regard and watch over the best interests of the whole Union, and to labor for its integrity and perpetuity, we solemnly protest against the repeal of the Missouri Compromise, the Kansas-Nebraska bill, and the Fugitive Slave law, as violations of the spirit of the Constitution, and tending to disunion and the destruction of the free institutions of the country.

Resolved, That we never will, under any circumstances, consent to the admission of slavery into any portion of the territory embraced in the compact of 1820, and from which it was then excluded by the mutual agreement of both the Northern and Southern States.

Resolved, That any attempt to commit the American party of New Hampshire to the advancement of the interest of slavery, to ignore it as a political question, or to enjoin silence upon us in regard to its evils and encroachments, deserves and shall receive our earnest and unqualified disapprobation.

ELECTION OF A KNOW NOTHING GOVERNOR IN CONNECTICUT—HIS OPPOSITION TO THE KANSAS-NEBRASKA ACT.

The Legislature of Connecticut last Thursday elected Wm. T. Minor, American, for Governor for the ensuing year. The vote was as follows: Minor, 117; Ingraham, (dem.,) 70.

The telegraph says that the message of the Governor recommends that the proposed amendment to the constitution extending the right of suffrage to colored persons, and requiring persons to be able to read and write before being admitted as electors, be allowed to go to the people. He considers that, in the recent election, the people reiterated their emphatic condemnation of the act organizing the Territories of Nebraska and Kansas. He enters largely into the consideration of the pernicious influence arising from the extent and character of the foreign immigration.

SENATOR WILSON, OF MASSACHUSETTS, STILL AS THOROUGH A KNOW NOTHING AS VILE AN ABOLITIONIST, AND THE ALLEGATION THAT HE HAS ABANDONED THE ORGANIZATION PRONOUNCED A FALSEHOOD AND A FORGERY.

When the notorious Henry Wilson was first elected Senator of the United Statesby Hiss and his brethren of the "*American*" party in the Massachusetts Legislature, the Southern Know Nothing press vociferated with one united voice his soundness on the Slavery question.

The new Senator soon dashed these fine asseverations by attending a lecture of Burlingame, the Abolitionist, in Boston, and volunteering to endorse with savage emphasis, as cruel as it was defiant and insulting to his Southern adulators, every word that lecturer had said in a rabid, red hot abolition diatribe.

This was not enough to satisfy the more incredulous and infatuated of his Southern admirers, and when Senator Henry Wilson, the Abolitionist and leader of the "*American*" party, reached Washington, one of the high priests of the Councils of the Order there, sought him out, conversed with him cheek by jowl in a long sitting, discovered to his great delight that the Boston Senator was a great stickler for State Rights, and at once addressed him a letter enquiring his views on the whole subject of inter State and federal and State interference.

The reply was written, and was very full and explicit in proclaiming doctrines of State Rights, coupled and combined with ill-disguised Abolitionism of the most rabid sort. Forthwith, a few of the Southern Know Nothing press began to claim Wilson as safe and trustworthy on State Rights principles, notwithstanding his endorsement of Burlingame; but the knowing ones, more astute than the common herd, discovered a cat in the meal. The State Rights doctrines of Wilson sounded grateful enough; but the legs and claws and head and teeth of Abolitionism were too apparent, and they advised against meddling with Wilson.

It turns out since, by the by, that the advocacy of State Rights principles as laid down in the Know Nothing basis platform, has suddenly become a universal thing among the Abolitionists. They are driven to assert those doctrines, as they construe them, as the only means of *nullifying* the Fugitive Slave Law in the free States. There is a notable difference, however, between *their* doctrine of State Rights and the Virginia doctrine. They assert the right of the States to the exclusive regulation of all their affairs *notwithstanding the Federal Constitution:* whereas the true Virginia doctrine asserts the right of the States to regulate their internal affairs under the Constitution strictly construed.

The vapid and meaningless generalities of the State Rights clause in the Know Nothing basis of principles render that article acceptable to the most violent Abolitionists of the North, while they tend to beguile into a false security and confidence the honest members of the Order at the South. Giddings himself is a State Rights man in the radical, Abolition sense of the word, as well as Wilson. Every vile Aolitionist of the North endorses the Know Nothing article of faith upon this subject.

Well, *revenons a moutons,* Wilson's State Rights letter of February last, written in Washington, to Vespasian Ellis, afforded a crumb of comfort to his Southern confreres, the less scrupulous of whom pronounced him safe though an Abolitionist; and so the matter stood until sometime after the adjournment of Congress, and Wilson's return home, when this State Rights Know Nothing and Abolition Senator broke out afresh somewhere in Massachusetts with the most fierce and vindictive declarations of Abolitionism and hatred to the South.

Of course nothing was left to his Southern Know Nothing "*brethren*" but to repudiate him outright. And that was done in a summary and convenient manner; for, in the great secret laboratory of lies which Sam operates somewhere underground, a paragraph was concocted, which is found below, for general circulation through the Southern Know Nothing papers, alleging that Wilson had denounced and renounced the "*American* party" as "perilous to the anti-slavery sentiment." The forged paragraph was attributed to the Boston *Telegraph,* and quoted by all of Sam's journals in Virginia as from that newspaper. Many of them were *hoaxed*—badly hoaxed—we are sure; but some of them must have been *particeps criminis* in the falsehood and forgery. It is incumbent upon them all to make their peace with an honest public by explaining the fact of their palming the forgery upon their readers.

Now read the following extract from the Boston *Telegraph* itself, in its issue of Friday, May 4, 1855. The italics are its own:

"The latest manœuvre of the Know Nothings in Virginia, consists in a representation that Senator Wilson of this State has abandoned the organization. We find the following in the Petersburg (Va.) *Intelligencer:*

'**But our object in writing this article was not to discuss the comparative unworthiness of Wilson and Sumner, but to congratulate the American party upon the welcome intelligence that has reached us of the abandonment of their ranks by this man Wilson. The Boston Telegraph is first rate authority on this point, for it is the Abolition organ in Massachusetts, and a special admirer of Wilson. What will the anti-Americans of the Wise school say to the following refreshing and cheering announcement? We give it to them as a sweet morsel to roll under their tongues:**

SENATOR WILSON DENOUNCES THE AMERICAN PARTY.

[From the Boston Telegraph.]

'Gen. Wilson gave the closing lecture of the anti-slavery course, last evening, at the Temple. He explained for himself the position with regard to slavery that he had occupied for twenty years, and called upon all to oppose any party that should try to smother the anti-slavery sentiment. He assumed that this course had been the death of the two great, parties, *and must be of the other party now forming*. He said *this party was perilous to the anti-slavery sentiment*, and called upon the anti-slavery party to *kill off* the *American* dough faces, as they had the others.

'Let it be remembered by the people of Virginia that Senator Wilson has within the last ten days publicly proclaimed in Boston that *the American party was perilous to the anti-slavery sentiment!* Put this in you pipes and smoke it at your leisure, ye devotees of Henry A. Wise !'

Gen. Wilson has never made any such declaration as is above attributed to him, and the extract which is credited to the Boston Telegraph never appeared in this paper until now. We are unable to say whether it is a forgery, or whether it did appear in one of the other Boston papers.—*Boston Telegraph.*

Such is the indignant repudiation, by the Boston *Telegraph* itself, of this unblushing fabrication; and the appointment, by the Know Nothing State Council of Massachusetts, last week, at Boston, of this same Henry Wilson as one of their delegates to the Philadelphia National Convention, finishes the whole story. We have already published the following announcement:

BOSTON, May 2.—The Know Nothing State Convention met this evening, and was largely attended, and its action was decidedly anti-slavery. Governor Gardner and Senator Henry Wilson are among the delegates appointed to attend the Know Nothing Convention to be held in Philadelphia in June. A. B. Ely made an anti-slavery Know Nothing speech. Strong anti-slavery resolutions were passed, and it is generally admitted that the Order must take position upon the anti-slavery platform.

Wilson, the Abolitionist, is not only still in full communion with the Order, but one of its chosen and most exalted exponents. He will meet the delegates from Virginia at the approaching National Convention, and will there maintain the necessity of Abolitionizing the Order, and "taking position upon the anti-slavery platform." We shall see whether he succeeds; and we have this to say, that if delegates from the Virginia Councils shall consent to sit in deliberation with Wilson and his Abolition colleagues from the North, it will be an insult to Judas Iscariot to call them traitors.

JUDGE IT BY ITS FRUITS.

If—according to it the only boon it asked in the outset—we judge it by its fruits, it can only be pronounced a rabid Abolition and Freesoil party everywhere North of the Potomac—which is everywhere that it has borne fruit at all. The triumph in which it won the greatest *eclat* was the election of Pollock, in Pennsylvania, over Gov. Bigler, the Democrat and leading champion in that State of the Nebraska-Kansas act. In the first Message of this first *eleve* of the Order, and as the first fruit of the tree, he denounced the Nebraska Bill as "an attempt to extend the institution of slavery," and "a violation of the plighted faith and honor of the country;" expressed his "opposition to the extension of slavery into territory now free;" demanded for the fugitive slave "the trial by jury and the writ of *habeas corpus;*" and summed up his farrago of abolition with the declaration that all these abominable incendiarisms were sanctioned by his election. To fill up the cup of disgust and execration as to Pennsylvania, a Know Nothing member of the Legislature at Harrisburg, hating the South more than the foreigner, and by way of demonstrating his conviction that the black race whom the South enslaves, are more capable of citizenship than men of his own color and blood, introduced a bill for giving "all male colored persons, of African or mixed blood, all political, civil and religious rights as fully and amply as they are held and enjoyed by any person or persons" in that Commonwealth.

As to the State of New York, the news is gone abroad that many of the Freesoil members of the Order have determined to secure the re-election of Seward to the Senate, by casting the requisite number of Know Nothing votes in his favor; and the bitter deprecations of the New York *Herald* of so damning a result, confirm the well-grounded apprehension.

In Ohio, the complicity of the Order with the worst enemies of the South in the recent elections is notorious. The *State Journal*, organ of the Freesoil, fusion party in the State, declares and avows in plain terms:

"So far, in this State, and in the free States generally, *the "Know Nothings" have co-operated and worked faithfully with the anti-Nebraska and anti-slavery feeling of the people.* They have shown themselves true republicans by *casting their weight uniformly in favor of freedom.*"

In Massachusetts, which seems to be as emphatically the cradle of treason in this its day of infamy, as it was the cradle of liberty in the day of its honor, the Order has elected a low-bred, presumptuous, unlettered JACK CADE to the Executive office; and elected to the Legislature, some sixty out of those three thousand and fifty clergymen of New England, who last year protested against the Nebraska Bill, and threatened Congress with the vengeance of Almighty God for meditating a simple act of justice to the South. This Governor Gardner—the seedy fruit of this tree of evil—makes haste in his first message to urge the restoration of the Missouri Compromise, and to claim for the fugitive negro the writ of *habeas corpus* and the trial by jury—in the same breath that he urges the disbanding of that very Irish soldiery who defied the rescuers of Burns, anathamatizes foreigners in bad English, and urges the *dispulsion* of every foreign language from popular use as tending to preserve—horrible to relate!—"unassimilating elements of character."

"*Jack Cade.* Fellow Kings, that Lord Say has gelded the Commonwealth, and made it an eunuch; and, more than that, he can speak French, and therefore is a traitor.

"*Stafford.* O, gross and miserable ignorance.

"*Cade.* Nay, answer, if you can; the Frenchmen are our enemies: go to, then, I ask but this: can he that speaks with the tongue of an enemy be a good counsellor, or no?

"*Dick, Smith and all.* No, no; and therefore we'll have his head."

This Legislature of Massachusetts, composed of *three hundred and seventy-six* Know Nothings to *one* Democrat, have elected Henry Wilson, one of the most rabid Freesoil demagogues in all New England, to the Federal Senate, as the successor of Edward Everett. In the Know Nothing caucus which decreed the election of Wilson to the Senate, the chief officer of the Order in Massachusetts avowed that they were, "*all Freesoilers;*" and other members asseverated that the overwhelming success of the Order in the elections of that State had been due "*to the passage of the iniquitous Nebraska bill.*"

The evidence of the complicity of this Secret Order with the enemies of the South in the Northern States is overwhelming and irresistible. The Southern man who refuses to believe a fact attested by such palpable results—who refuses to accept the Order's own challenge, and to judge it by potent and notorious facts—is willingly blind to the truth, and like the five living brethren of Dives in hell, would not be persuaded though one rose from the dead.

The Hon. L. M. Keitt, of South Carolina, in a speech delivered in the House of Representatives on the 3rd of January 1855, thus strongly arrays the evidence of the identity of the Abolition and the Know Nothing parties of New England.

What, too, have been the practical results of this new party? In Massachusetts alone it has been victorious through its own strength; and what see we there? Is not the abolition and free-soil flag the only one flying? How stand its members elect? I read an extract from the correspondent of the National Era (an abolition paper) of November 23, 1853. The writer is stated to be John G. Whittier, co-editor, I believe, of the Era, and a distinguished abolitionist of Massachusetts, who, as much as any man, is booked up in reference to its politics, particularly freesoil:

"C. L. Knapp, of the eight district, is an old liberty-man, true as steel. DeWitt in the Worcester district, Trafton in the eleventh, Comins in the fourth, Damrell in the third, and Burlingame in the fifth district, are also free-soilers. N. P. Banks, Jr., is triumphantly re-elected from the seventh district against the combined opposition of the Pierce democracy and the whigs. He goes back to Washington an anti-administration fusionist. Buffington, of the second district, and Morris, of the tenth, are reliable anti-slavery whigs. Of Davis, of the sixth, and Hall, of the first, we have no very definite knowledge.

"Gardner, the governor elect, stands openly pledged against the Nebraska fraud and the fugitive-slave law. His past history has been evidently that of a pro-slavery whig; but we speak now only of his present position. Brown, lieutenant governor, is a free-soil democrat and fusionist. Of the senators and representatives elected, enough is known to be tolerably certain that a reliable man will be chosen to the United States Senate, and effectual provision made for protecting the inhabitants of the State against the fugitive-slave hunt."

Thus have *acted* the Know Nothings of Massachusetts. How spoke they. I will read the resolutions of a Know Nothing convention in Norfolk, Massachusetts:

"*Resolved*, That we hail with hope and joy the recent brilliant successes of the republican party in the States of Maine, Iowa, Indiana, Pennsylvania, and Ohio, and we trust those victories are a foreshadow of others soon to come, by which the free States shall present one solid phalanx of opposition to the aggression of slavery.

"*Resolved*, That in the present chaotic condition of parties in Massachusetts, the only star above the horizon is the love of human liberty and the abhorrence of slavery, and that it is the duty of anti-slavery men to rally around the republican party as an organization which invites the united action of the people on the one transcending question of slave dominion which now divides the Union."

"Whereas Roman Catholicism and *slavery* being alike founded and supported on the basis of ignorance and tyranny, and being, therefore, natural allies in every warfare against liberty and enlightenment: therefore, be it

"*Resolved*, That there can exist no real hostility to Roman Catholicism which does not embrace slavery, its natural co-worker in opposition to freedom and republican institutions."

How spoke Gardner, their governor elect, in reply to the charge that he had aided in the rendition of Burns? He says, in a letter to Mr. Wilson, a free-soil leader?

"Were the same charge made against yourself, it could not be more groundless than it is against me. The power of language does not permit me to express the utter loathing I have for the conduct attributed to me. Far sooner would I be the poor quivering wretch on the road again to the agony of bondage than a volunteer guard to aid in his return. He who invented the charge grossly slandered me; they who repeat it, or believe it, do not know me.

"It is not true that I am, or have ever been, in favor of the fugitive-slave bill. I never voted for a man who favored it, knowing such to be his views, and I must very much change before I ever do. I never, by word, act, or vote, favored its passage, and I am an advocate of its essential modification, or, in lieu thereof, its unconditional repeal. Returning from Canada last June, I read in the cars that there was a petition for its repeal at the Exchange News Room, and on my arrival, before even going to my place of business, I hastened to the Exchange, and signed the petition."

Among the most prominent leaders of the Know Nothing party in Massachusetts, in 1855, was the Hon. Amos Burlingame, now a member of Congress from that State.

The Boston *Telegraph*, of the 3rd of February 1855, gave the following sketch of the anti-slavery lecture delivered by that gentleman at the Tremont Temple, on the evening of the 2d of February :

Before introducing Mr. Burlingame, Dr. Howe stated that a letter had been received from Hon. N. P. Banks, in which he announced his inability to deliver any lecture in the anti-slavery course, on account of the necessity for his presence at Washington during the coming week. In his place Frederick Douglass has been engaged for next week.

Mr. Burlingame was received with hearty applause. He commenced by saying, that in speaking for freedom he should not be choice in the selection of terms by which to characterize slavery. Slavery had betrayed us, and the time had come for an outraged people to express their sentiments in language not to be misunderstood. Mr. B. ascribed the origin of slavery to Pope Martin V., who issued a bull sanctioning African slavery. It was also sanctioned by several of his successors. It was brought to this country under the cross, and in the garb of humanity, but it never was sanctioned here by positive law. He then asked what is slavery? In the language of Wesley he would answer, "The sum of all villanies." The fitness of this description was then shown by a reference to facts. Our fathers hated it, and hoped it would soon die away. But Colten gave it a pecuniary power, and the slave representation a political power, which has controlled the whole country, and prevented its advancement. But for its influence, this nation of twenty-five millions would have been forty millions. The prosperity of the North was contrasted with the poverty of the South. The idea of force being used by the South to extend slavery was ridiculed. The power of the South is a political one, and with that she has smitten our commerce, our manufactures, and every interest of freedom. The very nullification buttons worn by the South Carolinians in 1832 were made in Connecticut, and their cannon came from Woonsocket, and were cast off guns at that. He alluded to the mobbing of Judge Hoar in Charleston, and the neglect of the government to protect him and the cause he represented, while to enforce an odious law in this city, a cannon manned by aliens was planted in Court square, while our own brothers were called out by illegal orders to be a body guard to them. Some, he said, censured the soldiers on that occasion, but the censures should rather fall on those who issued the illegal orders. On the chief magistrate they had already fallen like a thunderbolt. In this connection Dr. Adams was spoken of as being disloyal to every Northern sentiment. The means by which slavery has secured the control of the general government were then spoken of. The men of the South are men of one idea. They make politics their study, while at North the reverse is true. As a remedy for all this, we must study politics. He could not agree with Wendell Phillips in his plan of dissolving the Union, nor with Ralph Waldo Emerson in his proposition to purchase the slaves, as a remedy for slavery. If asked to state specifically what he would do, he would answer—1st, repeal the Nebraska bill; 2d, repeal the fugitive slave law; 3d, abolish slavery in the district of Columbia; 4th, abolish the inter-State slave trade; next he would declare that slavery should not spread to one inch of the territory of the Union; he would then put the government actually and perpetually on the side of freedom—by which he meant that a bright-eyed boy in Massachusetts should have as good a chance for promotion in the navy as a boy of one of the first families in Virginia. He would have our foreign consuls take side with the noble Kossuth and against the papal butcher Bedini. He would have judges who believe in a higher law, and in anti-slavery constitution, an anti-slavery Bible and an anti-slavery God! Having thus denationalized slavery, he would not menace it in the States where it exists, but would say to the States, it is your local institution; hug it to your bosoms until it destroys you. But he would say you must let our freedom alone. (Applause.) If you do but touch the hem of the garment of freedom we will trample you to the earth. (Loud applause.) This is the only position of repose, and it must come to this. He was encouraged by the recent elections in the North, and he defended the "new movement," which he said was born of Puritan blood, and was against despotism of all kinds. This new party should be judged, like others, by its fruits. It had elected a champion of freedom to the United States Senate for four years, to fill the place of a man who was false to freedom and not true to slavery. For himself he could say that so long as life dwelt in his bosom, so long would he fight for liberty and against slavery. In conclusion, he expressed the hope that soon the time might come when the sun should not rise on a master nor set on a slave.

It will be recollected that Henry Wilson was elected to the United States Senate by the Know Nothing members of the Legislature of Massachusetts.

Upon the occasion of Mr. Burlingame's lecture, in response to a call from the audience, he responded as follows:

Mr. Chairman and Ladies and Gentlemen:—This is not the time nor the place for me to utter a word. You have listened to the eloquence of my young friend, and here to night I endorse every sentiment he has uttered. In public or in private life, in majorities or in minorities, at home or abroad, I intend to live and to die with unrelenting hostility to slavery on my lips. I make no compromises anywhere, at home or abroad. I shall yield nothing of my anti-slavery sentiments to advance my own personal interests, to advance party interests, or to meet the demands of any State or section of our country. I hope to be able to maintain on all occasions these principles, to comprehend in my affections the whole country and the people of the whole country, and when I say the whole country, I want everybody to understand that I include in that term Massachusetts and the North. This is not the time for me to detain you. You have called on me most unexpectedly to say a word, and having done so, I will retire, thanking you for the honor of this occasion.

The "*American Organ*," the central organ of the Know Nothing party of the United States, published at Washington, thus endorsed the senator from Massachusetts:

We know too little of the antecedent of Mr. Wilson, to say that he has or has not been hitherto regarded as a freesoiler in his political proclivities, but we do know enough to say that within the last year a mighty revolution has been in progress, and that thousands upon thousands have abandoned their former political platform, and now stand upon the national platform of the "American party!" We know, also, that our friends, as well in Massachusetts as here, believe that whatever may have been the former opinions of Mr. Wilson, he will now sustain the National platform of our party.

But again: The "American Reformation," now in progress, is sustained by men of all the various political complexions that have existed in our country. All meet and harmonize upon the great platform of the American party, without enquiry into the antecedents of any member of this party. Whoever binds himself to sustain the principles of our party, becomes an "American," and is admitted into full communion with "Americans." We have formed this party on the basis of a total abandonment of all former party ties, and the adoption of a common standard of faith and action.

Who, then, shall deny the right of Mr. Wilson, or of any other man, to leave other affiliations, and to associate with men who are pledged to sustain "American" doctrines, and to repudiate former affiliations?

* * * * * * * *

We freely welcome all patriotic Americans into our ranks, and we only ask that they adopt and carry into practice our "American principles," and stand firmly upon our American platform. That Mr. Wilson, as an "American" senator, will faithfully and firmly adhere to our principles, we entertain no manner of doubt.

We copy from the Washington correspondent of the *Philadelphia North American*, the points which Hon. Henry Wilson elaborated in a speech delivered in the Senate of the United States, soon after his entrance into that body:

"He wishes the fugitive act repealed.

"He wishes slavery in the District of Columbia abolished.

"He wishes the Wilmot proviso established.

"He wishes all new slave States excluded.

"He wishes all connection between the general government and slavery abolished.

"He wishes agitation of slavery continued until these objects are accomplished.

"He understands these views to correspond with those of the Know Nothings as a party, so far as they have taken any position on the question."

The *Richmond Enquirer*, speaking of the Abolitionism of Senator Wilson, and of the Massachusetts Know Nothings, presented the evidence upon which it based its charges in the following forcible manner.

Now, let us examine what mighty reasons the South has to "rejoice" over the election of such a man. The Boston Courier, one of the most respectable Whig papers in the country, says of Wilson, the Senator elect:

"*He does not renounce one iota of the ultra Abolition principles which he has been inculcating throughout his political career, and by which he has approached his present eminence*, but he adopts certain vague ideas, which may be holden by men of any party, and sends them forth as the sum and substance of his conversion to Americanism."

The Boston Advertiser, another influential Whig paper, questions Wilson's claims to be regarded as an exponent of the principles of the new "American" organization; for in one of his speeches he asserted distinctly, "I care nothing about the place where a man was born," and he was enthusiastic in the reception of Kossuth, an "imported political demagogue," a class of people who, the Know Nothing Governor Gardner says, should be discouraged. Again, in the summer of 1852, the Freesoil National Convention at Pittsburg, of which Gen. Wilson *was President*, unanimously adopted the following resolution:

"Resolved, That 'emigrants and exiles from the Old World should find a *cordial welcome* to homes of comfort and fields of enterprise in the new; and *every attempt to abridge their privilege of becoming citizens and owners of the soil among us, ought to be resisted with inflexible determination.*'"

It seems, therefore, that it was Wilson's unadulterated *abolitionism* that cleansed him of his anti-"American" principles, and secured his election. This is farther made manifest by the developments in the Know Nothing caucus to nominate an United States Senator. We have once before published these startling facts, but we do so again, to refute the jesuitical efforts of Southern Know Nothing organs to blind the South to the damning anti-slavery movements of their New England "American" allies:

"Mr. Prince of Essex took the floor. He spoke strongly in favor of Gen. Wilson's election, and deprecated any yielding to the South upon this question.

"Senator Pillsbury of Hampden, humorously alluded in medical terms to the pumping process which had been made by the Senator from Suffolk (Warren) on Wilson. It would seem that he was not satisfied with what he pumped out; but, to his mind, the candidate came out of that contest as bright as light from a taper, and he might say, "Get thee behind me, tempter." Relative to the argument of the Senator from Middlesex, (Baker) he wished to say that he, nor no man from his section, could have come here, if he had been only an American. *It was because the party was anti-Slavery, as well as American, that it had got the majority.*

"Jonathan Pierce, Esq., the head of the Order in Massachusetts, next spoke. It had been said if he opposed Wilson, he himself would be ruined. He thanked God, no party of men had power to do that to him. He only wished Gen. Wilson was as good a Native American as himself. *It had been said this Free Soil movement would cut us up;* I doubt it, *for we are all Free Soilers ourselves.* He had been advised to close the doors and keep certain men out of the Order. He had said no—let them all come in. A man is not a Senator for a single State, he is a Senator of the whole Union.

"J. Q. Griffin, Esq., of Charlestown, said: Now, relative to Wilson's antecedents, he submitted there was no statute of limitations bearing upon the position or sentiments of members of this party. There was as much need of this party before last year as during that year. And he would say, and all would bear him out, that if it had not been for the passage of the infamous Nebraska bill, and the utter meanness of Pierce's National Administration, the revolution would not have so speedily taken place, though it might have come in time. He wanted a man right on this question—the one now prominent, worthy to stand by the side of CHARLES SUMNER!"

Here is one of the *sweet* "fruits of the mighty revolution," over which the Washington Organ "rejoices," and which has sent to the U. S. Senate an abolitionist, "*worthy to stand by the side of* Charles Sumner!" Will not Virginians turn away, with alarm and disgust, from an association whose Northern brethren perpetrate such monstrous acts and are whitewashed therefor, by Southern Know Nothing organs?

Among the first triumphs of the Know Nothings, were the election of their gubernatorial candidates in the States of Pennsylvania and Delaware; and in the inaugural addresses of Governor Pollock of Pennsylvania, and of Governor Causey of Delaware, we have the first official enunciation of the doctrines of the anti-slavery Know Nothings of the free states. We therefore publish extracts from their inaugural addresses:

INAUGURAL ADDRESS OF GOVERNOR POLLOCK, OF PENNSYLVANIA, TUESDAY, JAN. 16, 1855.

* * * * * *

Republican institutions are the pride, and justly the glory of our country. To enjoy them is our privilege, to maintain them our duty. Civil and religious liberty—freedom of speech and of the press, the rights of conscience and freedom of worship—are the birthright and the boast of the American citizen. No royal edict, no pontifical decree, can restrain or destroy them. In the enjoyment of these blessings, the rich and the poor, the high and the low, meet together—the constitution, in its full scope and ample development, shields and protects them all. When these rights are assailed, these privileges endangered, either by mad ambition, or by influences foreign to the true interests of the nation, and at war with love of country—that noble impulse of the American heart, which prompts it to revere home and native land as sacred objects of its affections—it is then the ballot box in its omnipotence, speaking in thunder tones the will of the people, rebukes the wrong, and vindicates the freedom of the man—the independence of the citizen. To the American people have these blessings been committed as a sacred trust; they are, and must ever be, their guardians and defenders. The American citizen, independent and free, uninfluenced by partizan attachments, unawed by ecclesiastical authority or ghostly intolerance—in the strength of fearless manhood, and in the bold assertion of his rights—should exhibit to the world a living illustration of the superior benefits of American republicanism; proclaiming a true and single allegiance to his country, and to no other power but "the God that makes and preserves us as a nation."

Virtue, intelligence and truth are the foundation of our republic. By these our institutions and privileges can and will be preserved. Ignorance is not the mother of patriotism, or of republics. It is the enemy and destroyer of both. Education, in its enlightening, elevating and reforming influences, in the full power of its beneficent results, should be encouraged by the State. Not that mere intellectual culture that leaves the mind a moral waste, unfit to understand the duties of the man or citizen, but that hither education, founded upon, directed, and controlled by sound and elevated moral principle—that recognizes the Bible as the foundation of true knowledge, as the text-book alike of the child and the American statesman, and as the great charter and bulwark of civil and religious freedom. The knowledge thus acquired is the proper conservative of States and nations; more potent in its energy to uphold the institutions of freedom and the rights of man, than armies and navies in their proudest strength.

The framers of our constitution understood this, and wisely provided for the establishment of schools and "the promotion of the arts and sciences, in one or more seminaries of learning," that the advantages of education might be enjoyed by all.

To improve the efficiency of this system, not only by perfecting our common schools, but by encouraging and aiding "one or more" higher literary institutions, in which teachers can be trained and qualified; and to increase the fund appropriated to educational purposes, are objects which will at all times receive my willing approval. Money liberally, yet wisely, expended in the pursuit and promotion of knowledge, is true economy. The integrity of this system and its fund must be preserved. No division of this fund for political or sectarian purposes should ever be made or attempted. To divide is to destroy. Party and sectarian jealousies would be engendered; the unity and harmony of the system destroyed, and its noble objects frustrated and defeated. Bigotry might rejoice, patriotism would weep over such a result.

* * * * * * * *

Pennsylvania, occupying as she does an important and proud position in the sisterhood of States, cannot be indifferent to the policy and acts of the national government. Her voice, potential for good in other days, ought not to be disregarded now. Devoted to the Constitution and the Union—as she was the first to sanction, she will be the last to endanger the one or violate the other. Regarding with jealous care the rights of her sister States, she will be ever ready to defend her own. The blood of her sons, poured out on the many battle fields of the revolution, attests her devotion to the great principles of American freedom—the centre-truth of American republicanism. To the constitution in all its integrity; to the Union in its strength and harmony; to the maintenance in its purity, of the faith and honor of our country. Pennsylvania now is, and always has been, pledged—a pledge never violated, and not to be violated, until patriotism ceases to be a virtue, and liberty to be known only as a name.

Entertaining these sentiments, and actuated by an exclusive desire to promote the peace, harmony and welfare of our beloved country, the recent action of the National Congress and Executive, in repealing a solemn compromise, only less sacred in public estimation than the constitution itself—thus attempting to extend the institution of domestic slavery in the territorial domain of the nation, violating the plighted faith and honor of the country, arousing sectional jealousies, and renewing the agitation of vexed and distracting questions—has received from the people of our own and other States of the Union, their stern and merited rebuke.

With no desire to restrain the full and entire constitutional rights of the States, nor to interfere directly or indirectly with their domestic institutions, the people of Pennsylvania, in view of the repeal of the Missouri compromise, the principle involved in it, and the consequences resulting from it, as marked already by fraud, violence and strife, have re-affirmed their opposition to the extension of slavery into territory now free, and renewed their pledge "to the doctrines of the act of 1780, which relieved us by constitutional means from a grievous social evil; to the great ordinance of 1787, in its full scope and all its beneficient principles; to the protection of the personal rights of every human being under the constitution of Pennsylvania, and the constitution of the United States, by maintaining inviolate the trial by jury, and the writ of habeas corpus; to the assertion of the due rights of the North as well as of the South, and to the integrity of the Union."

The declaration of these doctrines is but the recognition of the fundamental principles of freedom and human rights. They are neither new nor startling. They were taught by patriotic fathers at the watchfires of our country's defenders, and learned amid the bloody snows of Valley Forge and the mighty throes of war and revolution. They were stamped with indelible impress upon the great charter of our rights, and embodied in the legislation of the best and purest days of the republic; have filled the hearts, and fell burning from the lips of orators and statesmen, whose memories are immortal as the principles they cherished. They have been the watchword and the hope of millions who have gone before us—are the watchword and hope of millions now, and will be of millions yet unborn.

In many questions of national and truly American policy, the due protection of American labor and industry against the depressing influence of foreign labor and capital—the improvement of our rivers and harbors—the national defences—the equitable distribution of the proceeds of the public lands among the States, in aid of education and to relieve from debt and taxation—a judicious Homestead bill—reform in the naturalization laws, and the protection of our country against the immigration and importation of foreign paupers and convicts in all these, we, as a State and people, are deeply interested; and to their adoption and promotion every encouragement should be given.

INAUGURAL ADDRESS OF GOV. PETER F. CAUSEY, OF DELAWARE, AT DOVER, JANUARY 16, 1855.

* * * * * * * * *

As the servant of a gallant and patriotic people—as the Chief Magistrate of a State, whose spirit and genius, and not her metes and bounds, have determined her position in the national estimate—it would not become me to comment upon the conflicts of faction. Not such was the recent election in this State. But the history of the popular mind of a commonwealth is the history of its life, its honor and its fortunes, and a great organic movement of that mind, such as we now witness—one that uplifts, sweeps, and bears onward with it the community and its interests—may not, upon such an occasion, be ignored. We have seen a re-assertion of the declaration, and a re-enactment of the struggle for independence. It would be injustice to the people of Delaware to be silent on the progress and triumph of that sentiment which, kindled at the altar-fires of the revolution, has spread with miraculous speed from heart to heart; has united our American people in the holy brotherhood of patriotism, and has secured the triumph—not mine—not any man's—not the victory of art or eloquence, of parties or politicians—but of a free people, in whose hearts the American spirit, too long smothered under the ashes of exhausted factions, has burst forth, and asserted its own purity and power. This affords just grounds for an exultation, in which every American is privileged and may be proud to share, for in it no old party has been exalted; it brings to no true American citizen occasion for regret or mortification, no memory of wrong, and no fear of injustice. As a broad and bright assertion of the principles of American liberty—the only true liberty which the world knows, or has known—springing freshly from the people, and faithful to all the noble and time-abiding sentiments that render the voice of native masses, when spontaneous and unperverted, the voice of eternal right—it must be recognized as a triumph in which every real American has an equal interest, and an equal claim.

When, under the influence of a sentiment so lofty, the people of a State confide their highest office to the hands of one of themselves, in trust that it shall be administered in the same pure and exalted spirit, his solicitude must bear some relation to the exultation of his patriotic pride, and the fervor of his gratitude. Such is the anxiety with which I approach the duties that must, for a time, be mine. He whose task it is to guard the untarnished honor of Delaware, has a high and holy trust. The stranger who consults the chart of our Continental Republic, hardly discovers our State amid her leviathan sisters; but he who studies the history of American valor, American devotion, and American statesmanship, sees her pictured a giant on every page. Those who won the laurels of our liberty in our revolutionary struggle, who saw the declaration carried by her vote, and knew no field from Long Island to Camden and Eutaw where Delaware did not leave her martyrs, and always nearest the foe—no crisis in her councils where Delaware did not maintain the cause of the country—no exigency where Delaware was not among the foremost of the confederacy in defence of the Union—have done her ample justice; and their children, of whatever section of our common country, will rejoice that, in the present crisis, when the cause of American independence against foreign domination has again invoked the patriot spirits of the land, Delaware has been the foremost State to record her vote openly and boldly on the side of her country. Sister commonwealths have followed and will follow with a noble ardor, and, in after times, when the children of our little State shall exult over the many triumphs of her patriotism, it will not be forgotten that, in the gathering of the nation's millions for the public and fearless re-assertion of unshackled independence, Delaware, as a State, led the van; Delaware struck the first blow—Delaware won the first victory.

The issue which has been so harshly forced from abroad, upon our people, has no feature in common with our past political controversies—the mere domestic contests which have recognized a generous and fraternal difference of opinion among those who agree in a united devotion to our native land. The present is a resistance to invaders who unite foreign minds and hearts in allegiance to a foreign prince and pontiff, and standing between the American parties have dictated their own terms, and asserted their own superiority. Under these influences the ballot box has been corrupted by their frauds, or subjected to their violence; American politics have been stained with vices foreign to the American character; and a large portion of our most virtuous citizens have revolted in disgust from the exercise of privileges so shared, and so degraded; and the highest places of the republic have been abandoned to foreigners or their flatterers, some of whom have dared to assert the alleged prerogative of a foreign pontiff to free American citizens from their allegiance to the government of their country. In our foreign policy, the settled principles of American statesmanship are well nigh lost sight of; foreigners have been selected to represent the country at the principal courts of Europe; and in the gratification of feelings unshared by our people, they have made the American name a reproach throughout a large part of the civilized world. American principles and policy, feelings and interests, have been merged in their alien opposites, and in the press and on the platform, foreign influences have overswayed the control and directed the action of parties and the selection of candidates. The result of this conspiracy against the original and native American liberty has been to establish, in this country, a foreign-political party, substantially, though not nominally, devoted to foreign interests, and preferring persons of foreign birth. If its recognized advocates have as yet failed to proclaim allegiance to a foreign monarch, they have made, in most of the States, efforts to overthrow the American system of public instruction; have sought to exclude the Bible from the American schools; and have freely denounced the most cherished principles of American religious liberty; and all this, it should be remembered, has sprung from those to whom all that our fathers have won, and that is dear to us, was freely offered; all this was foreign in its origin, authors and acts—all this was unprovoked, wanton, long and patiently endured —endured till foreign demagogues claimed our country as their own, and made our right and our safety the counters with which they played the game of foreign politics.

At length the reaction and the rescue came. Its history is an exalted evidence of the fitness of the American people, for the most trying exigencies of self government. No son of the soil can regard it, and its proof of American intelligence, patriotism and virtue without pride and exultation. It borrowed no aid, it knew no leader, it sought no counsel. The movement burst, like a bolt, from the overcharged cloud of American wrongs—sudden, spontaneous and universal; it knew no parent but the old and ever true American heart. It had, and it needed, no organ, no orator, no oracle, no leader, no aid. The American people, North and South, East and West, finding the cup of foreign arrogance and usurpation overrunning, quietly stepped forth by myriads from their homes, and recorded the decree. It can never be revoked. It can never be regretted. Hereafter it will be pointed to as the noblest evidence of American intelligence, patriotism and independence; and when so remembered, Delaware will not be forgotten as the foremost to impress upon the cause the broad seal of a commonwealth's sanction.

That triumph, should it prove to be national, will impose many and majestic duties. The first will be to surround, as with a wall of fire, which no pollution can invade, that Holy of Holies—the ballot box, and closely succeeding will rise the duty of regulating immigration; of closing the avenues which have communicated with the prisons and lazar-houses of Europe; of defeating the ungenerous policy by which foreign princes force us to receive the moral abominations which their overcloyed country vomits forth, constraining us to support their paupers, and to expose the property and lives of our peeple to the ruffian skill and desperation of their transported felons. As a tax and a peril the heaviest and worst, as a wanton wrong and outrage, it should be redressed in the first hours of realized national American victory.

But the more pervading and vital triumphs of the second American revolution will be those which will establish, as the settled policy, foreign and domestic, of the nation, the saving principle of American Independence, as applied, not only to the right of suffrage, but to the privileges, sacred and inestimable, of our honest hardhanded home labor. The policy by which our country has been, in its trade, its currency, its varied industrial pursuits, agricultural, mechanical, and otherwise, and in its social habits of expenditure, and luxury, thrust into and made a part of Europe, is a treason against American honor and American interests. It is a repudiation of all the peculiar advantages bestowed by Providence, in requital of the virtues of our fathers upon our young and then unburthened country. We have, to gratify the schemes of politicians, and to glut the greediness of money changers, invited aud drawn upon our country a common and almost an equal share of the evils which attend, as their parasite and clinging curses, the wasting crimes and vices of Europe. Our true independence, real happiness and secure policy are to be realized only by fostering our own American homes—their industry, mutual relations, and mutual self-reliance. In regard to every political virtue and hope, to all of pride and confidence associated with that American liberty which—as the earthquake shakes and the tempest overshadows all else of the civilized world—grows brighter and dearer to us, it is apparent that the time has arrived when our country must separate her policy from the intrigues and machinations of Europe—from the strategy and corruption by which European councils and interests boastfully betrayed the independence of American industry, and made our land a tributary, as it now unhappily is, to England and France; forced upon us, with their luxuries, their vices; and added to the usurpation, the heavy imposition of a monstrous and perpetual debt—a debt shared by every American; a debt which drains our country of its specie, and which subjects it, throughout every fibre of its giant frame, to the agony of such a financial convulsion as that which now afflicts us. Vain will be the patriotic throbbing of the great American heart, and vain the vigor of the American arm to re-achieve American Independence, until our land shall have been made independent in that form which all power has its source—her industry.

Then, and only then, will she cease to be a European colony; then will she be the America of our fathers—truly independent—rich in her own resources—secure in her own strength, and happy in her own freedom. The crimes and oppressions, the wrongs and wars of Europe may terrify and torture their own world; but not a ripple of the storm will break upon our shores. Till that consummation shall have been effected, our duty will be unfulfilled, and our triumph—however glorious—incomplete; the oracles of our American patriarchs and prophets will remain empty, and the real mission, holy, calm and beneficent, of our American destiny unachieved.

In the federal Union, the general and State governments, revolving in their appropriate orbs, neither unite nor clash—their mutual influence induces a mutual interest, and the individual States watch with anxiety the disk, darkened or lustrous as her councils determine, of the central orb. The history of Delaware, in her relations with the general government, has always been interesting and conspicuous; and in every crisis it has been her fortune to prove—as the most illustrious republics of the past, not excelling Delaware in extent of territory have also shown—that real greatness consists in the exaltation of virtue and spirit, and not in vastness of proportion. In the present aspect of our general government, there is more for hope—that hope which always abides with a confidence in the people—than for present felicitation. Abroad and at home, the government has been so administered, as to leave to the people ample scope for the exercise, through their representatives, of their wisdom and love of country. In the trials which the feebleness and faults of an unhappy administration have imposed upon the country, Delaware will again, we may confidently trust, be found as in all the past, at her post—true to the exalted obligations of the constitution. But it may be remarked, as an illustration of the extraordinary power and success of our system, and of the entire reliance due to American prudence and patriotism—that never has our country been so secure as when her danger seemed greatest. The perils which were imagined in regard to the Union, only demonstrated manifestly that it was immovable as the hills; every indication of weakness or folly in the government has given to the people an opportunity, never expected, of proving the all sufficiency of their wisdom and devotion.

The *New York Herald* was regarded in 1855, as the most powerful, dangerous, and influential Organ of the Know Nothing party in the United States. We therefore publish an editorial from that paper, regretting the alliance which existed between the Know Nothing and Abolition parties in the free States.

THE KNOW NOTHINGS OF THE NORTH—MOVEMENTS ON THE SLAVERY QUESTION.

We published, some days ago, the inaugural message of Mr. Gardner, the Know Nothing Governor of Massachusetts. Our readers will remember that upon the Nebraska question he betrays the wrath of a Freesoiler, and boldly declares himself in favor of the restoration of the Missouri Compromise. We give to-day an extract on the Slavery question, from the inaugural of Mr. Pollock, the Know Nothing Governor of Pennsylvania, in which we are informed that Pennsylvania, in her late election, has repudiated the Nebraska bill, reaffirmed the Missouri interdict, and decreed a radical modification of the Fugitive Slave law, notwithstanding which the Governor has no recommendation to make upon the subject.

These declarations, "by authority," from the elect of the Know Nothings of the North, go very far to show that this new American party are still embarrassed, to a considerable extent, with the widely diffused anti-slavery sentiment of the Northern States, and especially with the remains of the anti-Nebraska epidemic, which entered so largely into the late elections from Massachusetts to Kansas. The same Freesoil concessions have been exhibited in the late nomination, by a caucus of the Massachusetts Know Nothing Legislature, of General Henry Wilson, heretofore a leading anti-slavery man, as their candidate for the United States Senate. There has been a rebellion, however, and a split upon this nomination, and the final result will probably be the election of a Senator less decidedly tinctured with anti-slavery antecedents and principles than Wilson. At all events, the trouble concerning this gentleman, shows that the Know Nothings of Massachusetts are aware of the importance of maintaining, as far as possible, in this Senatorial election, the attitude of non-intervention upon the slavery question.

In these Know Nothing messages of Messrs. Gardner and Pollock, and in this nomination of Wilson, there is a manifest disposition to conciliate the free-soil and anti-slavery sentiment of the North. Nor is it surprising that this should be the case, considering the fact that the Know Nothings entered into the late elections side by side with the anti-slavery forces rallied throughout the North upon the anti-Nebraska furor. In the outset, all great revolutions are crude and encumbered, more or less, with incongruities and inconsistencies. So this new party, from the throes of parturition, comes into the world somewhat lacking the elements of perfect symmetry and harmony, although the bantling possesses a vigorous vital system, and all the requisites of superior manly strength. Now, the anti-Nebraska agitation is dying out—the popular mind soon wearies of impracticable abstractions. Public opinion in these United States is eminently practical and utilitarian, national, patriotic and conservative. A little resolution and unity of action on the part of the Northern Know Nothings are all that is now wanted to cleanse their skirts of the last remaining vestiges of anti-slavery doctrines and affiliations.

Since our November election there has been some trouble among the Know Nothings of this State, traceable to the slavery controversy. Hence those outside Know Nothing Lodges, the object of which is a diversion from this new party in favor of the re-election of Wm. H. Seward. And so, in Iowa, an anti-slavery Whig has been elected to the United States Senate, from the support of the Know Nothings, in the place of Dodge, Nebraska administration Democrat. Such combinations of anti-slavery men and Know Nothings have had in view the great object of "crushing out" the greatest imbecile spoils coalition at Washington, and in this light they may be considered as the necessary preliminary steps in clearing the track for the projected national revolution of 1856.

The *Examiner* summed up the acts of the Know Nothings of the free States during the years 1854 and 1855 in the following admirable manner.

WHAT HAVE THEY DONE?

The Know Nothings have within the last twelve months made sufficient progress, in many of the State and city elections, to develope their plans and inaugurate their men; and from Maine to California we challenge the friends of the Order to point to a single instance of their having performed the first creditable act of reform. In Massachusetts their triumph was complete, and, with a half dozen exceptions, the Legislature is there composed of members of the new Order. In that State they have removed Judge Loring for enforcing the Fugitive Slave law—they have taken the first step toward practical amalgamation by placing negro and white children in their common schools upon terms of equality—they have elected to the Senate a man who endorses the horrid blasphemy of a wretch who wants an anti-slavery God, and an anti-slavery Bible—they have violated the sanctity of the dwelling of a few unprotected females and offered rudeness to the persons of sick children and helpless women—they have legislated with closed doors, disbanded the Irish companies who protected the person of Col. Suttle, and placed his fugitive slave, Anthony Burns, safely on board a vessel bound for Alexandria—and elected to the Legislature sixty or seventy of the Clergymen who signed the famous anti-Nebraska protest.

In New Hampshire, led on by a fugitive slave and the notorious John P. Hale, they have crushed the National Democratic party, and the re-election of Hale to the U. S. Senate, is regarded as a fixed fact.

In New York they have elected William H. Seward, and, by uniting with the fanatical Maine Liquor Law men, destroyed a legitimate branch of business employing 40,000,000 of dollars per annum, and thrown out of employment 150,000 laborers.

In Maine they have passed the following resolutions, breathing the fiercest spirit of hostility to the South :

Resolved,

"1. That slavery *has no legal tenure* either under State or Federal jurisdiction, and therefore exists only by sufferance.

"2. That our Senators in Congress be instructed and our Representatives requested to use all practicable means to secure the passage of the following enactments:

"First. An act repealing all laws of the United States authorizing slavery in the District of Columbia.

"Second. An act repealing the act of 1850 known as the Fugitive Slave Law.

"Third. An act forever prohibiting slavery or involuntary servitude, except for crime, within the territories of the United States."

In Michigan they have passed resolutions precisely similar to those of Maine. In Illinois and Iowa they have elected to office the boldest and most odious of the Abolition party. They have Abolitionized Pennsylvania. In Ohio they mobbed that true friend of the South, the chivalrous Mitchell, and in Rhode Island they attempted to destroy the house of the Sisters of Charity, and were checked by the military companies of the city of Providence.

They have already destroyed the peace and harmony of the American people, arraying neighbor against neighbor, and son against father. They have, by persecution and intolerance, alienated the affections of loyal and patriotic foreigners from our institutions, and declared the Constitution and the act of religious toleration null and void. In the brief history of this new Order there is nothing good. Its career has been one of fanaticism and folly, its progress that of a deadly enemy of our institutions, over the ruins of all which we hold sacred in history and tradition.

THE FOUR ISMS UNITED.

In the free States the Democratic party in 1855 had to contend against an alliance of Maine-lawism, Know Nothingism, Abolitionism and the remnants of the old Whig party.

The *Nashua Gazette* drew the following admirable picture of the allied forces of 1855:

Temperance, Know-Nothingism, Niggerism, and Whiggery.

In this vicinity, Temperance, Know-Nothingism, Niggerism and Whiggery are all united and acting cordially together for the overthrow of the Democracy; and doubtless the same is true of other sections of the State. The chief manager of the Temperance organization, the man of all work, imported from the West to direct our political affairs under the pretence of promoting the temperance cause, (Rev. E. W. Jackson,) is devoting his whole time and efforts in perfecting this combination to break down the Democratic party. It is stated, upon good authority, that he offered his services and the influence of the Temperance organization to the Whigs, some weeks ago, before they concluded to go into the "Order." He is a Know-Nothing, and attended the late Convention of that Order at Great Falls; a "leaky" Temperance Know-Nothing says he was a delegate to the Know-Nothing State Convention, which met on Tuesday last at Manchester, for the nomination of candidates for State officers, members of Congress, &c. He is a professed Abolitionist, and a political priest and Pharisee of the most Jesuitical type. He declares in the Temperance organ that he and his friends will support no candidate who is not an open and reliable friend of a stringent prohibitory liquor law. Yet when he became a member of the Know-Nothing organization he took the following oath:

"*Obligation.*—You, and each of you, of your own free will and accord, in the presence of Almighty God and these witnesses, your right hand resting on this Holy Bible and Cross, and your left hand raised towards Heaven, or *if it be preferred*, your left hand resting on your breast, and your right hand raised toward Heaven, in token of your sincerity, do solemnly promise and swear, *that you will not make known to any person or persons any of the signs, secrets, mysteries, or objects of this organization*, unless it be to those whom, after due examination, or lawful information, you shall find to be members of this organization in good standing; that you will not cut, carve, print, paint, stamp, stain, or in any way, directly or indirectly, expose any of the secrets or *objects* of this Order, nor suffer it to be done by others if in your power to prevent it, unless it be for official instruction; that so long as you are connected with this organization, if not regularly dismissed from it, you will, in all things, POLITICAL or SOCIAL, so far as this Order is concerned, *comply with the will of the majority*, when expressed in lawful manner, *though it may conflict with your personal preference*, so long as it does not conflict with the Grand State or Subordinate Constitutions, the Constitution of the United States of America, or that of the State in which you reside; that you will not, under any circumstances whatever, knowingly recommend an unworthy person for initiation, nor suffer it to be done if in your power to prevent it. You furthermore promise and declare that you will not vote nor give your influence for any man for any office in the gift of the people, unless he be an American-born citizen, in favor of American-born ruling America; nor if he be a Roman Catholic; and that you will not, *under any circumstances, expose the name of any member of this Order, nor reveal the existence of such an organization.* To all the foregoing you bind yourselves, under the no less penalty than that of being expelled from this Order, and of having your name posted and circulated throughout the different Councils of the United States *as a perjurer, and as a traitor to God and your country; as being unfit to be employed and trusted, countenanced or supported, in any business transaction; as a person totally unworthy the confidence of all good men, and as one at whom the finger of scorn should ever be pointed.* So help me God."

By this oath this reverend politician and all other members of the Order have sworn, "in the presence of Almighty God," to vote for such candidates as may be selected by the Know-Nothing Convention. If they nominate the greatest rumsellers ever defended by Jack Hale, this leader of the Temperance cause has *sworn to support them!* If they select open and notorious rum-drinkers and opponents of a prohibitory law, *he is bound by a most solemn oath* to support them! He is a ranting Abolitionist and anti-Nebraska man; yet if they nominate avowed Nebraska men, he has *sworn before God* to give them his cordial support! And such is the position of every other Temperance man and Abolitionist who belongs to this Order—a position which this reverend gentleman has knowingly induced very many of them to place themselves in.

Now, who can doubt, when an intelligent man pursues such a course, that he *designs* just what must inevitably follow? Rev. Mr. Jackson has not been the dupe of others in this matter, but, on the contrary, has designedly used the influence of his position to thus virtually *force* Temperance men into the support of the factions now banded against the Democratic party.

But has he used nothing *but* his influence? It is known that efforts have been made to raise "a million fund," upon which a certain per cent. may be assessed to be expended in promoting the success of the Temperance party. Quite a large sum has been subscribed towards that fund, and Rev. Mr. Jackson is said to be the sole manager, depositary, and disbursing agent of the money paid in. And for what purpose, and in what manner, is that money now being used? Is it true that it is being expended for political purposes—to pay his salary and expenses and "incidentals," while engaged mainly in promoting the schemes of the political organizations opposed to the Democracy? This is openly stated to be the fact; and the course of Mr. Jackson but tends to corroborate the statement. Let true, honest, and single-minded Temperance men enquire into these matters before they lend themselves further to the promotion of the political and mercenary schemes of the demagogues for whose use the Temperance organization is now being perverted.

We learn that among the delegates from Concord to the Know-Nothing Convention at Manchester, besides Rev. Mr. Jackson, was Ephraim Hutchins, late Whig postmaster there, a leading member of the Whig State committee, and an active member of the Convention which nominated James Bell for Governor! Among them were, also, some of the leading Freesoilers. Thus the heads, "the central cliques," of Whiggery, Niggerism, and Temperance are united and active in this dark conspiracy against the rights of the people and the Republican institutions of the country. Let honest men of all parties, and especially Democrats, look and reflect upon this fact, and let it nerve their arms and confirm their resolution to fight manfully against this corrupt and wicked combination of unprincipled men for the promotion of mercenary objects.

THEIR PLATFORM IN VIRGINIA.

Having now shown the attitude of the Know Nothing Party in the Northern States, we close this review by publishing their officially promulgated Basis of Principles in Virginia. It was an emanation from the Winchester Convention.

THE CONVENTION OF THE AMERICAN PARTY OF VIRGINIA,

Which met at Winchester, on Tuesday, the 13th of March, appointed the undersigned a committee, to make publication, over their names, of the following:

Basis Principles of the American Party of Virginia.

Determined to preserve our political institutions in their original purity and vigor, and to keep them unadulterated and unimpaired by foreign influence, either civil or religious, as well as by home faction and home demagogueism; and believing that an American policy, religious, political and commercial, necessary for the attainment of these ends, we shall observe and carry out in practice, the following principles:—

1. That the suffrages of the American people for political offices, should not be given to any others than those born on our soil, and reared and matured under the influence of our institutions.

2. That no foreigner ought to be allowed to exercise the elective franchise, till he shall have resided within the United States a sufficient length of time to have become acquainted with the principles and imbued with the spirit of our

institutions, and until he shall have become thoroughly identified with the great interests of our country.

3. That whilst no obstacle should be interposed to the immigration of all foreigners of honest and industrious habits, and all privileges and immunities enjoyed by any native born citizen of our country should be extended to all such immigrants, except that of participating in any of our political administrations; yet all legal means should be adopted to obstruct and prevent the immigration of the vicious and worthless, the criminal and pauper.

4. That the American doctrine of religious toleration, and entire absence of all proscriptions for opinion's sake, should be cherished as one of the very fundamental principles of our civil freedom, and that any sect or party which believes and maintains that any foreign power, religious or political, has the right to control the conscience or direct the conduct of a freeman, occupies a position which is totally at war with the principle of freedom of opinion, and which is mischievous in its tendency, and which principle if carried into practice would prove wholly destructive of our religious and civil liberty.

5. That the Bible in the hands of every free citizen, is the only permanent basis of all true liberty and genuine equality.

6. That the intelligence of the people is necessary to the right use and the continuance of our liberties, civil and religious, hence the propriety and importance of the promotion and fostering of all means of moral culture, by some adequate and permanent provision for general education.

7. That the doctrine of availability now so prevalent and controlling, in the nomination of candidates for office, in total disregard of all principles of right of truth, and of justice, is essentially wrong, and should be by all good men condemned.

8. That as a general rule, the same restrictions should be proscribed to the exercise of the power of removal from office, as are made necessary to be observed in the power of appointment thereto; and that executive influence and patronage, should be scrupulously conferred and jealously guarded.

9. That the sovereignty of the States should be supreme in the exercise of all powers not expressly delegated to the Federal Government, and which may not be necessary and proper to carry out the powers so delegated, and that this principle should be observed and held sacred in all organizations of the American party.

10. That all sectarian intermeddling with politics and political institutions, coming from whatever source it may, should be promptly resisted by all such means as seem to be necessary and proper for this end.

11. That whilst the perpetuity of the present form of the Federal Government of the United States, is actually necessary for the proper development of all the resources of this country, yet the principle of non-intervention, both on the part of the Federal Government and of the several States of the Union, in the municipal affairs of each other, is essential to the peace and prosperity of our country, and to the well being and permanence of our institutions, and at the same time the only reliable bond of brotherhood and union.

12. That Red Republicanism and licentious indulgence in the enjoyment of civil privileges, are as much to be feared and deprecated, by all friends to well regulated government and true liberty as any of the forms of monarchy and despotism.

13. That the true interest and welfare of this country, the honor of this nation, the individual and private rights of its citizens, conspire to demand that all other questions arising from party organizations, or from any other source, should be held subordinate to and in practice made to yield to the great principles herein promulgated.

ANDREW E. KENNEDY, of Jefferson,
GEORGE D. GRAY, of Culpeper,
JOSIAH DABBS, of Halifax.

THE METROPOLITAN DISTRICT.

Various circumstances combined to render the canvass in the Richmond or Metropolitan Congressional District, one of profound interest to the whole State. The great circulation of the Democratic press published in Richmond, and the fact that the Know Nothing party boasted of its perfect invincibility in that district, attracted all eyes to its candidates and aspirants for Congress.

As an entertaining and amusing chapter, illustrative of the party feeling in the district, we give two of the *Examiner's* articles upon the factions and rivalries which disturbed the tranquility of the Know Nothing councils of Richmond:

The Know Nothings, we have every reason to believe, have to brave a sea of trouble. Rampant and perfectly ungovernable aspirants for the nomination for Congress, render the councils as tempestuous as the cave of Æolus. If what we hear is true, the friends of Messrs. Botts, Crane and Scott, are in a precious stew. Messrs. Crane and Scott have not left their destinies to be controlled by the stars and their friends. Both have sought, by deeds of mighty valor, to build up reputations in the provinces. They have held forth long and frequently to admiring audiences, and the people have been left in great uncertainty as to their respective merits. Scott makes, we learn, usually a speech of one hour and a quarter, well digested, full of facts and scraps from newspapers and almanacs. All of this *materiel* he has carefully and systematically arranged, and he runs out with the regularity of an hour glass. When the exigencies of the debate require a reply, he reverses his hour glass and the sands of his discourse pour back again. He is courteous and gentlemanly, but deficient in vivacity and fluency. Mr. Adoniram J. Crane, on the contrary, is affluent of words, and really has gotten together a large collection of clap trap, broken beads, bits of tinsel, fragments of red wax, pieces of differently colored glass, and other odds and ends, which, when he pours them forth, do look very pretty and dazzling to the eye of the unthinking. There is neither logic nor connection in his ideas, but he has a great deal more declamation than Scott, and possesses a creditable share of intellectual cultivation. He does not measure his discourses by the hour, but runs like an endless chain pump—the same buckets and the same links coming up every few minutes. Hence, when we attend public meetings in Richmond, and the disciples of Sam want a regular blow out, we hear the name of "Crane!" "Crane!" "Crane!" frequently repeated—but we never hear the first feeble cry for Scott. Scott is strong in the provinces where the people like the strong pork and beans of "facts and arguments;" but Crane's fancy touches tickle the descendents of Botts' old guard. They shout for Judson Crane, just as their fathers used to scream for Botts—when his envious lieutenants used to sit neglected on the back benches, without a call. Besides, Scott is regarded as a sort of interloper, having recently made a descent upon Richmond from the hills of Powhatan. His sign still glistens, on Governor street, with the fresh paint of yesterday, whilst A. Judson Crane's shingle looks as old and veteran as his services to Botts. Scott has not figured in our city courts, whereas the professional services of Crane are frequently called into requisition by the unwashed of the extremities of the city. Scott's affection for Botts is said to be of a doubtful character, whereas Crane has illustrated his devotion in a thousand ways. He has sat at the feet of Gamaliel long and faithfully. In times gone by, he is said to have perpetrated a biography of his majesty, and being a man of classical education, which Botts is not, he is supposed to have often taken the Immortal's thunderbolts in a rough state, and polished them for general circulation. We have long thought that Botts' ragged mantle would sit becomingly on Crane. Scott's services to the party are acknowledged in the counties, but the sages who deliberate at the African church know him not. He has again and again ravaged the counties of the district, devouring Democratic electors and candidates for Congress, like a new Dragon of Wantly—but the people of Richmond have never seen him do it.

He was reported, during the Congress of 1852, to have swallowed our Congressional elector, Mr. Robert G. Scott, eleven times, and to have skinned him alive eight times—albeit a mild tempered man. During the present canvass he has devoured Judge Caskie in a great many instances, but yet the city people are skeptical, and do not put much faith in the correspondents of newspapers. If Scott would make arrangements to swallow Judge Caskie some evening at the African church, it would put his stock up amazingly. Adoniram's prospects would also be improved, if he was to demolish Mr. Aylett in that sacred edifice. Both had better try it at an early day. We believe the victims are prepared to meet their fate with becoming resignation.

But Crane has not been at all behind Scott in the Dragon of Wantly line. He went to Petersburg one afternoon to sup upon the remains of Senator Mason, and it was with great difficulty that he was kept from his atrocious and cannibal designs upon that estimable gentleman's body. The kindness of the Democracy of Petersburg having rescued Senator Mason, and deprived our friend of his anticipated supper, he hastened, hungry as a boa constrictor, to Caroline, and in the sight of a great crowd, crushed and skinned our Congressional elector, Mr. Aylett, and ravenously swallowed his mangled remains. Scarcely had we recovered from the shock of this bereavement, when we heard of his frightening to death two or three Democratic orators in New Kent, and the very next evening he was in Petersburg, unmercifully devouring Senator Mason's speech, and speaking so eloquently that a letter writer mentions an unfortunate man who, having had his jaw fractured by the accidental discharge of a pistol, quite forgot the pain in his ecstatic admiration of Mr. Crane's harangue.

It will thus be seen, from this hasty parallel after the manner of Plutarch, that both Scott and Crane have great claims at this time, and that both of them have performed eminent services. Crane and Scott are the Achilles and Hector of the aspirants. There are others who are said also to hone after the fleshpots in a very meek and quiet manner, but who are, we fear, mouldering in the shade of Scott's greatness and Crane's eloquence. An occasional groan from an old Botts man evinceth the wrath of a few of the faithful at Crane's having, tired of long waiting, now set up shop for himself with a fair prospect of supplanting his old patron in business.

Mr. Harmer Gilmer having won many laurels by his manly and patriotic correspondence with "*A Southern Matron*," and achieved all that a diplomatist could, in his famous negotiations for Mt. Vernon, would not, it is supposed, indignantly reject a nomination for Congress, provided that accomplished unknown, "*The Southern Matron*," does not desire it. But Mr. Gilmer has only made one speech of half an hour's length, whereas Messrs. Crane and Scott have expended many thousand cubic feet of gas for their country. There is a fitness of things in Crane's succeeding to the fading glories of Botts, which the Know Nothings will certainly recognize. Mark the prediction. We stand ready to welcome the young phœnix when he springs from the ashes of the old.

"HURRAH FOR BOTTS!"*

Gordon Cummings, the celebrated lion killer, who spent seven years in Africa slaying all sorts of wild animals, somewhere describes the consternation produced among all inferior wild beasts by the appearance and roar of a full grown, tawny lion. One evening when he was anxiously awaiting near a pool of water for his game, he was amused by the performances of sundry jackalls, wolves, hyenas, and other subordinate beasts of prey. The jackalls lorded it in quite a magnificient manner over a pack of timid wild dogs; the hyenas treated the rascally looking wolves with aristocratic contempt, and the wolves revenged themselves by their contemptuous treatment of a few stray foxes. Suddenly, in the midst of this entertaining comedy, a terrific roar is heard, and a huge lion bounds into the throng, with flaming eyes, and erect, vibrating tail. In a moment the whole scene changes—the hyenas skulk off, the jackalls take to their heels, the wolves disappear, and the wild dogs, protected by their insignificance, retire to a neighboring hill and bay alternately at the rising moon and the hungry lion.

Since our last issue a somewhat similar scene has been enacted in this Congressional district. Presuming that the immortal Botts was looking so intently upon the glittering fringe of a prospective nomination for the Presidency, that he had forgotten this Congressional district, a choice assortment of subordinate aspirants had appeared upon the stage, and were furnishing a capital gratuitous entertainment for the people of the surrounding counties. In the absence of razor strap orators, and greased rope itinerants, these gentlemen afforded huge amusement to our unsophisticated country friends. And the rivalry of these gentlemen was so transparent that it was seriously apprehended that after they had devoured all of the Democratic electors and candidates, they would swallow each other and produce "an aching void," such as that which the Kilkenny feline combatants are said to have created at the termination of their little controversy. Botts out of the way, this Congressional district seemed a "pent up Utica," too small to contain two such Cæsars as A. Judson Crane and Wm. C. Scott. Two suns or two moons, would not have surprised people more than the appearance of two men of such transcendant ability at the same time. Their reputation was the growth of a day. It took their most intimate friends by surprise. The moment the rumor spread that Botts was out of the way, these gentlemen outgrew their small clothes, and their greatness spread over the land with marvellous rapidity. Their inflation was as rapid as that of a balloon, and Jack's wonderful bean stalk was rather a slow affair when compared with the rise of these gentlemen. Until yesterday, never were the chances of success more nicely balanced, than between Crane and Scott. One reigned supreme in the city, whilst the other lauded it in the provinces. One wore the scalp of a United States Senator, of a candidate for the mayoralty, and of a Congressional elector at his girdle; the other scoured the counties with the skin of another Congressional elector, for a waistcoat, and the legs of a distinguished candidate for Congress dangling out of his mouth. Both were working with an energy that prompted success, but we fear that both have been suddenly cut down in the flower of their youth. On Tuesday morning, Botts gave one of his old fashioned roars, and, by nine o'clock the same day, Crane and Scott needed the services of Coroner Wicker. Thus we have seen, on a bright spring morning, two belligerent turkey cocks writhing and twisting each other's necks in deadly conflict, struck down by the fowling piece of a cruel sportsman. Botts again in the field, Crane falls prostrate before his omnipotent I am, and poor Mr. Scott retreats to Powhatan to digest his bloody repasts in private. Vanity of vanity,

* Old Screamersville war cry.

all is vanity! Who knoweth what a day may bring forth? Yesterday, Crane and Scott were Sam's greatest pets; to day, and none so poor as to do them reverence. Oh, cruel Botts! oh, unhappy Crane! oh, miserable Scott!

We had just announced the speedy appearance of the young phœnix when the old bird, with a few lusty blows from his still vigorous wings, extinguishes the funeral pile, and with slightly singed plumage, drives his dreadful beak and terrible claws plump through the tender body of the aspiring lieutenant.

For no one can read the wrathful *manifesto* of Botts and not recognize the willingness of that gentleman to accept the nomination; and as he stands head and shoulders above such men as Crane and Scott, and as there is more capacity in the parings of his nails than in all the rest of the Whig party together, his nomination may be regarded as most probable. For, although at this time, when the people are given to doing funny things, and when the political cauldron is boiling, we may expect strange things to happen and queer nominations to come to the surface, there is nevertheless a weight of Whig consistency and genuineness in the ring of Botts' metal that the subordinates cannot resist. They may scour the district, and illustrate their "gift of the gab" at every cross-road, but when the old lion (dilapidated as he is) of Whiggery sends forth one of his terrible roars and treads the accustomed war path with as firm a tread as ever, in an instant Adomiram and the gentleman "*late of Powhatan*" are forgotten, and the old guard, the veterans of Screamersville, the heroes of ever faithful Butchertown, the patriots of Rocketts, and the partisans of the Slashes, instinctively send up the old shout of "*hurrah for Botts.*" There is an affection, a faithfulness about these old chaps which the juveniles who yell for Crane, and the old country people to whom Scott administers almanacs and newspaper scraps, never dreamt of. The hearts of the old respectable, consistent Clay Whigs, still belong to Botts. He is the embodiment of the most respectable elements of Whiggery, and in this district he is still invincible. He possesses stores of strength that the fire flies who have recently sought to illumine the dark subject of Know Nothingism never dreamt of.

Look at the weight and respectability attached to the card in which Botts has just crushed out the prospects of the Cranes and Scotts of this district. They indicate that the nomination will be given to John Minor Botts beyond a question of doubt. The old spirit flames out in his *pronunciamento*. Know Nothingism has not purified him of a drop of his deep rooted prejudice, and we find the usual slap at the enemies who have always beset his path.

The unconquerable Whiggery of the venerable and invincible gleams forth in striking contrast with the cowardly silence of the Know Nothings upon great principles and measures. He grapples with the sub-treasury and the tariff in the real old fashioned way; as Whigs were wont to do in the days of Clay and Webster. He pitches into Democracy boldly and courageously, and feeling that he is a foeman worthy of our blade, we are inclined to yell out, as his old guard used to do, "*Hurrah for Botts.*"

If Botts receives the nomination, as no doubt he will, we shall have to use longer artillery than we had designed employing in this district. Small fowling pieces, with dimunitive loads of ordinary powder and mustard seed shot, we had deemed sufficient for the game which was anticipated. But we must get a Minnie rifle and Dupont's best, now, for Botts is very different game from that which we had expected to hunt after.

The appearance of Botts renders it necessary that we should take an affectionate farewell of those disconsolate young gentlemen, Crane and Scott, to whom we recommend an attentive perusal of "Love's Labor Lost." They will now have, we fear, nothing to remind them of their labors but indigestions and nightmares, those inevitable consequences of cannibal feasts and indiscriminate gluttony. When Scott had no one to oppose him but Crane, the offence of his *squatting upon Adoniram's property* was denounced as a most grievous intrusion. But when the ferocious old guard of Botts open upon him there will be no mercy shown. With brief recollections of the manner in which they used to crucify Botts' ambitious and refractory lieutenants, we compassionate poor Mr. Scott—we do indeed. We almost imagine that we already hear the ever faithful and eloquent Perrin, the friend of Clay, and the *fidus Achates* of Botts, in classic alternations from Latin to English, pouring his lard like streams of burning invective upon Mr. Scott, for moving into the Immortal's district to get to Congress. Gods! what a theme for the Old Guard—what an offence in the estimation of the faithful—what a scarlet crime in the eyes of indignant Screamersville—*a stranger seeking to reign in the kingdom of his Serene Highness*, Botts I.!

And Adoniram, young friend by adoption, "well beloved of Mahomet," Luther's ever faithful Malanothon, biographer, thunderbolt polisher to his Majesty, will you swallow you disappointment, and, with a face expressive of castor oil, salts and senna, love and disappointment, affection and desperation, conceal your griefs, and cry with the rest, "*Hurrah for Botts!*" How will you bear this cruel treatment of him to whom you have devoted so many years of useful friendship?

We know that this trial of temper and test of devotion is a terrible one, but take the advice of a well-wisher. Stick to Botts—never hoist the flag of rebellion—show, as you have always done, the loyalty of your friendship—wait but a little longer, and you will bask in the sunshine of the Immortal's eternal gratitude—sacrifice your very excellent prospects—go in heart and soul for Botts—and the Old Guard will agree with their sons, that you deserve to succeed to all of Botts' popularity and honor. The présent is a critical period in your fortunes, and no man ever lost by a graceful and timely act of magnanimous self-sacrifice for a friend. You could have swallowed Scott and Gilmer, but no one ever expected that you could resist the will of the political Gamaliel, seated at whose feet you have drank in so much wisdom and statesmanship. We entreat you, *don't be rash*.

The Political Entomology of "Our District."—We must solicit the indulgence of our readers for furnishing them in each issue of our paper with a fresh chapter upon the ever changing phases of the Congressional nomination battle of the bats and owls of this district. We must, however, beg them to remember that, in devoting so much time to such trivial matters, we humbly imitate the examples of many most illustrious authors and eminent men. Have we not the elaborate epic of the "Battle of the Frogs and Mice;" Gulliver's account of the wars of the Blufuscans and the Lilliputians, about the best method of breaking an egg; a classic author's history of the feuds of the cranes and pigmies; Dickens's sketch of the rival candidates for the office of Beadle; Shakspeare's "Mid-Summer's Night Dreams," and "Much Ado about Nothing?" Have we not in every issue of Bell's Life in London carefully prepared reports of fights between rats and terriers? and are there not well authenticated accounts of men having lost and won thousands of pounds upon a fight between crickets, or a race between two maggots extracted from a rotten hazlenut? Let these precedents be our excuse. We take the same pleasure in the political entomology of this district, that naturalists do in studying the habits of beetles and bed bugs.

We are happy in the refreshing conviction, that the Know-Nothing councils of this district are about as harmonious as were the famous cats of Kilkenny. An army of candidates for the nomination have scattered dismay and discord through the ranks of the enemy. Sampson's foxes with fire brands fastened to their tails, never produced such wide-spread alarm and consternation as these vociferous candidates have done. We have already recorded the mighty deeds of the famous squatter from Powhatan, Scott, and the not less valorous and voracious pet of the hungry Adoniram, who has achieved greatness in a day. We have now to announce that Mr. Harmar Gilmer has recently greatly distinguished himself by his cannibal performances on the South-Side—having somewhere near Farmville swallowed the Hon. Kidder Meade, one day, and lunched upon the attenuated remains of the Hon. Wm. O. Goode the next; thus depriving of his legitimate food the facetious and jocose Tazewell, who is announced by the Know-Nothing papers as "running with his tail curled," a compliment which he doubtless deserves and appreciates.

Abandoning, for a time, the patriotic and man-milliner duties of his high diplomatic connection with the treaty for the cession of Mount Vernon, he is said to have snapped up our unfortunate friends, Meade and Goode, like a hungry pike. We, therefore, hail him as an honorable member of that order of cannibals, of which Messrs. Scott and Crane are the founders. He has proved himself their equal, and we take the liberty of entering him for the nomination. It is distinctly understood that no man can become a candidate for the nomination unless he can furnish to the Convention satisfactory evidence of having swallowed or skinned a Democratic orator within the six weeks preceding the 5th of May. Have Messrs. Coleman, Perrin, Rhodes and Griffin, either skinned or swallowed any one yet. If they have not, the sooner they begin the better.

We have been assured by a friend, that the Whig did not slay Botts on last Tuesday morning, but that its rifle ball merely stunned him. It is suspected that he was restored to consciousness by the felonious attempts of two distinguished cannibals to skin and swallow him, whilst he lay upon the Potter's field where the Whig had cast his apparently lifeless remains. We regret to say, that Messrs. Crane and Scott are strongly suspected of this horrible crime. They are supposed on Tuesday morning to have been wandering about seeking for fresh victims, when at the same instant they espied the prostrate body of the "Immortal," and both, with a cannibal yell of joy, pounced upon him, Adoniram making an incision between the ears to skin him scientifically, whilst Mr. Scott, in his eagerness to swallow him, and not wishing to disturb Mr. Crane, commenced with the supposed defunct's feet. These violations of his sacred person, restored the Immortal to consciousness. They were like the application of volatile salts to a fainting woman's nose. One blow and a kick sent the luckless swallower and the ungrateful skinner fifty feet in opposite directions, and the Immortal sprang to his feet, irritated beyond measure by the treatment which he had sustained.

We, therefore, take pleasure in announcing that our illustrious friend, is not yet dead, and that he again treads the old war path, in a most wrathful and dangerous mood. These attempts to rule him off, and diabolical efforts to skin and swallow him, have merely irritated him, as gad flies excite the rage of mighty bulls. We delight to believe that Botts knows his rights as a freeman and a Know-Nothing, and that he does not intend to be ruled off. The bullet of the Whig merely flattened against his intellectual skull, as do those of a western hunter against the frontal bones of the hardy buffalo. We believe that he will now wage a war of extermination "on the faction which has always sought (his) my destruction and overthrow," and that he will be backed by the very strongest and most efficient men of the order. He will make the district too hot for the squatter from Powhatan, and hang the rebellious Adoniram in chains, or quarter him, as the old king's of England used to do their enemies. Long may Botts live, for there are many uses to which he can be turned.

The indications of a Know-Nothing now of no ordinary magnitude, cannot be mistaken. If Botts does not receive the much coveted nomination, he will leave the order so shattered and torn by dissensions, that there will be no chance for any one else. The members of the Old Guard whom we occasionally meet on the street, wear a grim, firm, defiant, air—a rule or ruin look, that leaves no question as to what they will do if the Immortal is cast overboard. We have a right, as Botts' most consistent and faithful organ, having always hailed his nominations with pleasure, and felt inexpressibly gratified when he was soundly beaten by Judge Caskie, to insist that he shall not be killed off. When the post of danger requires a man of nerve and pluck, an interesting protege is always placed in the front rank. Upon such occasions the Scotts stay quietly enough in Powhatan, and the Cranes are models of humble devotion to the Immortal. But now that there is some remote prospect of success, Botts is to be inhumanly sacrificed, and all Screamersville thrown into convulsions of grief at the massacre of her noble son. As the only organ of the neglected Botts, we call upon the Old Guard to rally, and if the rebels with Adoniram, Gilmer and Scott at their head, continue to resist, we command them to "head them or die." Let this language of your illustrious leader be inscribed upon your banners, and the dangers now menacing your chieftain will disappear like morning clouds. Let the Slashes be aroused, let Hell town wax hot, let Rocketts take the field, let Screamersville move forth like an army with banners, let Butchertown, led on by the faithful Heckler, emulate Darby town in deeds of mighty valor, and Botts will win the nomination.

As it is not in mortals, however, always to command success, should the indignant order prove too strong for our protege, and eject him from their culvert hissing like a red hot shot from a cannon's mouth, we again affectionately proffer to him the sanctuary of Democracy. If the high honor of taking Botts, the most incorrigible of sinners, to the altar of Democracy is vouchsafed to us, it will constitute the proudest duty of our life. We shall lead forward the sobbing and penitent old gentleman, blubbering over the recollection of his unnumbered political transgressions with the delight of a pious parson who has at last beaten down the last barrier erected by Satan around the soul of a hardened reprobate.

We now confess—what we have long concealed within our own breast—that the great object of our life has been the conversion of Botts. We have always had a mysterious presentiment that he would die a good Democrat, and as the carniverous Adoniram says that "the Whig party has died of corruption," we feel assured that if the Know-Nothings kick Botts out, he will petition to lay his battered head on the great bosom of Democracy.

It is all nonsense to say that Botts is too old to turn Democrat, and that gentlemen at sixty are not equal to feats of ground and lofty tumbling. There have been instances of men commencing the study of the law at that age, and becoming eminent jurists. Would it not be a cheering spectacle to behold Botts a regular attendant at Democratic gatherings and love-feasts, working on vigilant committees, attending nominating conventions, and applauding the speeches of our young orators, from a modest back bench in the African church. Promotion, we admit, would be slow in the Immortal's case, but if he was to join us now, and live to the good old age of ninety, we would make him chairman of a ward committee, or use our influence to have him rewarded by some post-office appointment in the provinces.

P. S.—Since writing the above we have seen the Lynchburg Virginian's awful account of the manner in which Adoniram, on Thursday night, in the presence of the goodly people of Lynchburg, swallowed our friend, Mr. Shelton F. Leake. The account should have been headed "How Jonah swallowed the Whale;" and be interpreted by contraries as Irish dreams are interpreted. The astonishing rapidity with which this modern scourge of Democracy thins our ranks is frightful. Boa-constrictors, after they have crushed and swallowed their prey, remain torpid for weeks, whilst the slow work of digestion is going on; but Crane snaps up the most plethoric orator, swallows him whole, as if he were a minnow, digests him in five minutes, and at once proceeds to transfix the next victim, as if he had eaten nothing for a month. Like Tamerlane, he has reared a pyramid of scalpless skulls, which far surpasses in height those of even Scott or Gilmer. Look at the following pyramidical statement, and see how Adoniram leads the column. To Judson's list we ought to add the prospective victims, Hunter, Judge Douglas, and six other U. S. Senators:

Tamerlane Adoniram's	*Scott's.*	*Gilmer's.*
S. F. Leake,		
J. M. Mason,		
P. Henry Aylett,	0	0
John D. Munford,	00	00
Douglass of New Kent,	000	Goode,
Douglass of King William,	Caskie,	R. K. Meade.

The Scrub Race for the Nomination.—The scrub race for the Know-Nothing nomination for Congress in this district is becoming every day more and more ludicrous and amusing. A new pony, or an ambitious Shetland, is entered almost every morning, and the excitement promises to become terrific before the 5th of May, when the judges propose making the award. There have been many entries recently from the provinces. Forgetting that he was merely put forward to be well beaten in the last election, the friends of Clayton G. Coleman have entered that highly respectable but rather slow horse. Chesterfield, we learn, proposes to put forward Holden Rhodes, and we imagine that the ever faithful, eloquent and full blooded Whig, Samuel Perrin, of Hanover, and the not less faithful Fendal Griffin, will be duly put upon the turf.

Our last article upon this subject left the indomitable Botts with erect mane, vibrating tail, and unearthly roar like a lion in the path, frightening into the jungles such small fry as the exotic Scott and the vociferous Crane. But, sad to relate, whilst this dilapidated, although still formidable lion was frightening all the inferior rivals out of their wits, the Gordon Cummings of the Whig was taking a deadly and unerring aim at him, and at the report of that sportsman's editorial rifle, on last Tuesday morning, Botts keeled over dead as a mackerel, and his conquerer at once dragged his carcase to the nearest Potter's field, where, we fear, by this time, under the hot suns of the last three days, it is becoming animated with insect life. In the name of all that remains of Botts, in the name of the old guard, in the name of the few floating fragments of the old Whig party, we ask why did our friend of the Whig kill Botts by an editorial filled with damning hints of his want of availability, and suspicions of his being chest foundered and spavined. We fear that there is a conspiracy in this district to deprive Botts of his rights, to declare him dead, to publish his obituary notice as Dean Swift did that of Partridge, the almanac maker, whilst the man was alive and hearty. We begin to fear that Know-Nothingism in this district is a diabolical conspiracy against Democracy and Botts, that the Whig party has been disbanded to get rid of that brave and glorious old Whig, and that he is to be cast adrift for the sake of the shoal of minnows now nibbling at Judge Caskie. How can the old Clay Whigs give in their adhesion to a new party which thus turns the cold shoulder upon the acknowledged leader of the old Whig party of this state? If the new order actually proposes to confer the offices of the country upon their ablest men, how supremely funny is it to thrust Botts aside, refuse to allow him to be entered for the race, and to wrangle about the men whom the boiling cauldron of Know-Nothingism have brought to the surface in this district within the last few weeks.

Let all who have been prominent in the Whig party read their fate in that of the "Immortal," whose immortality has been snuffed out. Botts' "extreme opinions" we take to have been a bold, manly vindication of Whig measures, when men of less moral courage had fled into the dark caves of the new order. The new order has treated Botts most inhumanly, and, to all intents and purposes, has ostracised him, as if he was a "foreigner or a Roman Catholic." For we expect that in the oath of the third degree, recently instituted, there is a provision that Botts is never to be elected to office. All of our poor friend's advances having been rejected, his want of qualifications having been officially announced, we cannot see how he can—even if they will allow him—remain in such an order.

They have disbanded the party of his long and never changing affections—they have buried Whiggery—even the ungrateful Adoniram declaring that "it has died of corruption"—and why should Botts be chained, like a blind Samson, in this new temple of the enemy, to be made the sport and laughing-stock of boys and renegade Democrats? Why does he not grasp the pillar to which he is chained, imitate the slayer of the Phillistines, topple over the temple, and crush the bats and owls that infest it. Has Botts turned a priest or a woman, that he will permit these slights and insults to go unpunished?

Would it not be best for him, if he is in this humble and Christian mood, to put on the apparel and take the staff of a pilgrim, and with feeble steps and supplicating voice, petition for admission into the sheepfold of Democracy? Often times has he devoured our flock and laid waste to our lambs, but it was always as a bold, hungry wolf—never as an assassin in sheep's clothing. We can offer him no office, but the sanctuary of Democracy is always open to the penitent and destitute. He has no organ in this city—the Know-Nothing papers repel his advances—but has the Examiner ever deserted him? Have we not for seven years cheered him on in his wars against the rebellious lieutenants, and against that faction which, we are informed in all of his epistles to the public, "is seeking his (my) destruction at the expense of the party." Is there an instance of the Examiner having deserted Botts? For a time we had but one rival in consistent affection for Botts—and that was Adoniram. But we feel proud of the fact, that our advocacy of Botts has survived even the love of Adoniram, for we fear that he will not follow our advice by clinging to the shipwrecked fortunes of his old commander. Of all of Botts' friends, the Examiner alone remains consistently faithful. We have seen Screamersville and Rocketts desert—Darby Town deny its lord—Hell Town grow cold in its affections—and even Adoniram hoist the flag of rebellion, but the Examiner stands firm. "Hurrah for Botts!"

Overthrow of the Legitimists—Downfall of Botts—Triumph of Tylerism—Squatter Sovereignty above par.—On Saturday night the Know-Nothings met in council to immolate Botts, to inaugurate squatter sovereignty and Tylerism, and to exterminate the last vestige of Whiggery from this district. The result tells how complete was the overthrow of the old *regime*. That Corsican usurper, the squatter from Powhatan, has seized upon the throne of the Bourbons, and Botts, Perrin, Griffin and Crane, have been exiled from the land of their fathers. The provinces proved too strong for Botts' strongholds in this city, and Butchertown, Screamersville and Rocketts were routed by the regiments from the rural districts. The Old Guard, demoralized, dispirited and disheartened by the defection of lieutenant Adoniram, fought not with their accustomed valor, and unused to the bush-ranging tactics of the new order, were no match for Scott's squirrel-hunting militia from Louisa and Goochland.

It is rumored that the contest waged most fiercely between the friends of Scott, Botts and Adoniram, but we have not heard it hinted that Messrs. Gilmer, Perrin, Rhodes and Coleman were suggested to the Convention in the very mildest manner. Nor, from what we have heard, do we imagine that the merits and services of Adoniram were properly appreciated by that august body, which played the part of Paris, and awarded the prize, to the disgruntlement of the rest of the neglected goddesses, to the fair claimant from Powhatan. We fear, had Mr. Crane sedulously harangued at our country court-houses respecting the cleansing virtues of grease-extracting soap, or beaten a tin pan for the delectation of his provincial auditors, that either of those enlivening and intellectual recreations would have furthered his prospects fully as much as his carniverous performances appear to have done. The people appear to have fancied Scott's facts, figures, scraps, almanacs and paragraphs far more than they did the damp oratorical pyrotechnics of the neglected Crane.

We tender to our disconsolate friend Adoniram our affectionate condolences, and the solemn assurances of our most distinguished commiseration. It is only with the aid of a slop bucket to receive the briny freshet of one eye, and of a sponge and large red bandanna to absorb the lachrymose deluge of the other, that we are able to pen this doleful narrative of his death and sufferings. It is painful—it is heart-rending—it is grief absolutely insupportable—to reflect that all of his labors were thrown away upon a perverse and ungrateful generation of vipers. Our blood boils with indignation at the thoughts of the infamous treatment which he has received from those for whom he abandoned the civilized duties of his profession and turned cannibal. For naturally our friend is not addicted to swallowing human beings like a boa constrictor, scalping them like a lawless Mohawk, or to devouring steaks fresh from the thighs of fat Democratic orators, as if they were from the rump of a prize ox.

This dietetic system we know must have been repugnant to all the civilized instincts of his refined nature. And what has been his reward for thus cannibalizing and gorging himself with the bodies of men, whose disconsolate wives and fatherless children will hand down the name of Adoniram, black with curses and wet with the tears of the afflicted, to posterity. Tamerlane, like Adoniram, erected a pyramid of human skulls; but the bloody Tartar won empires and wealth, whereas Adoniram has won nothing but indigestion, night-mares and a sore throat. Without knowing what was to be his melancholy fate, he was setting the districts to rights and devouring the enemies of the man who has squatted on his domain, and robbed him of his anticipated congressional laurels. It turns out that poor Adoniram was merely a hard-working, energetic laborer for a gentleman who, although not twelve months a resident of the district, has managed to triumph over the leaders of the old Whig party.

What melancholy evidence does this nomination afford of the decay of Whig greatness in the metropolitan district. Here, where for twenty-five years the city orators and lawyers have looked down and sneered contemptuously at their provincial brethren, we have an ordinary country gentleman, with none of the graces of metropolitan oratory, plain and prosy as the heaviest of county court lawyers, respectable, honorable, and decent, but nothing more, squatting in the midst of all the Whig lights of the bench, the bar and the hustings, and bearing off the palm, when there was not one of the late prominent Whigs of the district who would not have given his eyes for the nomination.

Mr. Scott, from what we have seen and heard of his history and antecedents, is a gentlemanly, educated, middle-aged man, of some forty-five or fifty years of age, who served a term or two in the Legislature very many years ago, and again represented Powhatan in the House of Delegates within the recollection of ourselves. His private virtues have secured him many devoted personal friends, and to these unobtrusive virtues he is doubtless indebted for his nomination. Through life we learn that he has been the victim of a very entertaining delusion, to the effect that nature designed him for a public speaker, when she intended nothing of the sort. His life has been a prolonged struggle and dispute with nature upon this subject, but like Mrs. Partington in her celebrated contest for supremacy with the Atlantic ocean, nature has thus far held her own, and Mr. Scott, although well informed and thoroughly posted, speaks in a very spavined and deplorably dull manner. Adoniram is equal to a dozen of him on the stump, and Botts to fifty thousand of him anywhere but in the caucus of the culvert.

A forgotten circumstance in the history of Mr. Scott, as related to us by a friend, furnishes a clue by which his nomination can be explained and cleared up. It was to crush poor Botts to the very earth, to add insult to injury, to add that last straw under which the back-bone even of the camel snaps, that Mr. Scott was nominated, if the following statement be correct—if it is not, we shall correct it in our next issue. It has been stated to us by a gentleman of this city: "That Mr. Wm. C. Scott was, in 1844, a red hot ultra Tylerite, and was a member of that funny little convention which nominated John Tyler for re-election in opposition to Henry Clay and James K. Polk." Was or was he not a member of that convention? Did he or did he not occupy, in 1844, for a time, a position of antagonism to Botts and all the leaders of the Whig party of this district in his devotion to the fortunes of John Tyler?

The information which we have received comes in such a form and from such a source that we feel constrained to propound these questions: If, when Botts and the old guard, in the prime and vigor of the Immortal's best days, were thus bearded by the squatter from Powhatan, and the latter was then a Tylerite, and committed the deadly and unpardonable sin for which Mr. Wise has been so often and unmercifully denounced, what will the Botts men do? How will they brook this most humiliating of all the insults yet thrown in the face of Botts? To forget the transcendent talent of Botts, to fail to reward the gluttony of Crane, to pass by the splendid claims of Perrin, Gilmer, Griffin, Coleman, Rhodes, were detestable crimes,—but for the Know-Nothings to import a Tylerite from Powhatan, and make an idol of the man, was a more hideous iniquity than infanticide or parricide.

Gentlemen of the old guard, indomitable survivors of the grand Clay army, behold your leader—a stranger and a Tylerite! Oh, Botts! venerable and remarkable old man, has it come to this, that one of the humblest of the followers of your old foe should be placed over your head? How have the mighty fallen! Who expected to live long enough to see Botts doing homage to "*a Tylerite*," and Adoniram Crane in a state of insurrection and rebellion? Where can Botts fly?—what is to become of him? Know-Nothingism throws a Tylerite at his head—Adoniram swears that the Whig party has died of corruption, and the old guard fly before the undisciplined militia of the counties. Oh Richard, oh my prince, they are all deserting thee! Believe not their false promises of election to the Senate of the United States, for the same promises, flattering, but false, have been made to every grumbling old Whig in the state.

At the command of Gen. Tyler Scott, late of Powhatan, you must fall into the ranks, or have your sturdy head chopped off. You are now the lieutenant of a Tylerite—a sepoy of the household of the usurper, who sits upon your old throne and cracks the whip over your venerable head, and will touch you on the raw if you do not pull steady in the traces. If, venerable, neglected, and badly treated friend, you need just at this time a safety valve for the escape of any superfluous wrath which may have collected since last Saturday night, we conjure you to *wallop Adoniram*. Spring upon him with the yell and erect, vibrating tail of a wounded and enraged lion, insert your teeth in the nape of his neck, and shake him either into subjection or to a jelly. The experiment would be a safe one, for Adoniram, like yourself, oh Botts! seems to have no friends. At him, old Bengal! Give it to him, antique Lybian!

The attempt of the Know-Nothing party to array the prejudices of the Protestant clergyman of this state against the Democratic party, were incessant, but in most instances unavailing. The press of the new organization in vain attempted to arouse the prejudices of the various Protestant churches against the doctrines of religious toleration and religious liberty.

Some of the strongest arguments against the peculiar opinions of the Know-Nothings, were embodied in the communications which appeared in the Examiner and the Enquirer, from the pen of eminent clergymen. We select the following from a number which were published during the canvass:

Patriotic Sentiments of an Eminent Clergyman in Virginia.—As a clergyman of an inveterately Protestant denomination of Christians, I have been politely requested by a distant friend, who belongs to the same church, to give him, through the columns of your paper, my views of the new half religious and half political chain of secret clubs, called Know-Nothings. I should have very little objection to complying with this request, reasonably made, at any time; but feel the less disposed to decline, when requested by one of those whose official teacher I am by the constitution of a church which we have both voluntarily joined.

The church with which we are both connected is as thoroughly Protestant as any on earth. It has as little of persecution upon its historical escutcheon as any other church which is so old. I fear, however, that it has some spots of this kind. I blush more when those spots of persecution come before my mind than for anything else of the past. If one fervent prayer ascends from my heart to the Father of Mercies, concerning the social shape of religion in our country, it is that it may never dip its hand in blood, that it may never become a suppliant to the populace in the political club, and that it may never permit itself to be upheld by those arguments of tyrants or imbeciles: civil disabilities for opinion's sake. Such a resort is indeed capable of no other construction than as a confession of weakness. When recently the Spanish Cortes had up the subject of religious liberty in Spain, and after the discussion, deliberately resolved not to grant it, what Protestant puts any other construction upon it than that they declined to grant religious liberty, for fear the people would become Protestant? If they thought truth would uphold Roman Catholicism, they would not wish to uphold it by civil pains and penalties. So it is with the Know-Nothing movement in the United States. It has unquestionably grown out of a want of confidence in the moral power of truth to uphold Protestantism. It has sprung up in the northern cities, where the principles of revealed religion have notoriously not much more positive power than they have in Papal countries. It has grown up among those who say they will trample the Bible under their feet, if it does not support the Maine Liquor law—or if it does not support Abolition—or whatever else may be the peculiar phase of their personal fanaticism. When truth retreated to a distance from their mental visions, and they lost confidence in its power to withstand Popery, then they invented the scheme of withstanding the Catholics by a civil disability, a secret club, and a midnight oath. The writer is too much of a Protestant to be a Know-Nothing. He has a confidence too entire and unshaken in the power of the truth alone. He does not believe that this night club, this awful oath, or this infliction of civil disabilities on Catholics, is necessary to retain the power of Protestantism in this country. He protests against the inference that Protestantism needs any such assistance. He protests against the imputation of the persecuting spirit of Know-Nothings to religion. It has grown out of the wane of religion. It springs from nominal Protestants, who care, and think, and know nothing about the moral, and spiritual, and rational power of religion, except that it is a strong principle. Their object is probably not the advancement of true religion; for if it was they would very easily see that persecution will do more than any thing else to build up the Roman Catholic church.

And, if such was their object, they would see that the prevalence of Protestantism in this country, through the means of civil disabilities, would be just as hollow, and just as worthless, and just as empty a thing, as is the prevalence of Catholicism in Spain by civil disabilities. You must forever keep up the prop of civil disability when it is once set under, or else the whole frame will fall. The history of the world shows, beyond a doubt, that there is always a reaction in the reasons of men, against that religion which the strong arm of power proposes to them. Cicero says the state religion of old Rome was totally hollow, and the augurs knew it. There is a majority of dissenters from the state religion to-day, in England, and in Scotland, and an overwhelming majority in Ireland: there is said to be the same in Spain and Italy, if the hearts of men could speak out; and there would have been in France, but for the existence there of something like religious freedom.

The writer sends up fervent prayers to the Disposer of events, that this country may not be left to the judicial blindness of Know-Nothingism, to persecute the Catholics into prosperity; to confess the weakness of naked truth; to depart from the great American principle of perfect religious freedom; to come down from our high and pure and noble position, and dabble in secret conclaves, in silly fears, in weak and nervous alarms. Know-Nothingism has not, then, grown out of religion. It did not start in the Protestant church. All it had to do with religion, was to observe that the religious prejudice of the country was a strong lever with which to work another purpose. It made use of that lever as a tool, just as the political parties had made use of military renown as their lever before.

Their purpose, probably, is to play with the raw head and bloody bone fears of the Pope, which infests the dreams of nervous people, in order to cajole the country, and get on their side the religious prejudice, and, in the mean time, to do their real work in secret.

The liberties of this country may be in danger from Popery. No man can well think too hardly of that inveterate system. But does it make a great deal of difference to us, whether our liberties are taken away by secret Jesuit clubs, or by secret Know-Nothing clubs? But this quarrel with foreigners is a northern affair altogether. We never had much temptation to it, here in the South, where the social spirit is as much more benign as the climate is. After all, it is not the religion of the foreigners which is objected to. And if it was, I believe that John Mitchel's religion is just as good, to all practical intents and purposes, as Ward Beecher's religion; and his politics ten thousand times more patriotic than Ward Beecher's. John Paul Jones was a better American, to my heart, though born in Scotland, than "Hull, the traitor," though born in Massachusetts. I think that the Marquis La Fayette was a far better American, though born in France, than Benedict Arnold, though born in Connecticut. I give the preference to Count Pulaski, Baron Steuben, and "lighthorse" Lee, though they were foreigners, over Aaron Burr, Gen. Winder, and Gen. Wilkerson, though native Americans.

The people here used to know that religion and patriotism were not to be ascertained by these external circumstances. The traitors whom this counrry has to fear, are not foreigners. They are men who were born and live where Hull and Arnold were born and resided. Their treason is deep, deliberate and meditated for a long time.

The clamor against foreign traitors, from whom no man can show us a single case where we have suffered anything recently, or much ever, or been ever in any great danger, is all a make-weight. That clamor is but a mere availability. It is but a new form of appeal to military glory. It is the dust with which the eyes of the southern people are to be blinded, while in secret club we shall be abolitionized, as they boast that we shall be. It is a peice of cold, cautious, yankee cunning, by which the northern people, at one stroke, get us to help them against their rivals in labor, the immigrant foreigners, and by which they will soon ask us for another tariff of protection to American industry; by which they yoke us to their car to make us fight their social battles; by which they gull and blind us to their real designs against our domestic peace and prosperity; and by which they sport with us as their tools, and avail themselves of our deep and positive religious convictions, in which they have no sympathy, and which they admire only for their strength as political engines. May a Higher Power deliver us from that deep blush with which we shall be suffused, if our church—boldly, deeply, thoroughly Protestant as she is—falls into the trap in the slightest degree, and becomes the catspaw of northern treasonable designs. And may that kind Power open speedily the eyes of the people, to see in the light of every public development yet made by Know-Nothingism, what the real object of the movement is! And may the sacred subject of the man's religious faith be once more withdrawn from the secret club-room, from the political caucus, and from the popular hustings, into that retirement to which it has a right, under the really, though not under the so-called, American principle! I do not know whether I have fully responded to my friend. If not, I hope to hear from him again. ROCKINGHAM.

AN APPEAL TO THE CLERGY.

Gentlemen: It is rumored that many of your body have become associated with that political organization commonly called the Know-Nothings. If this is true, or if you sympathise with them, the writer of this deeply regrets your position. No one entertains a higher opinion of your integrity than he. No one felt more indignant than he, when a Senator of Virginia assailed you in the councils of the nation, styling you "a proud and self-opinioned body." This assault was unstatesmanlike, as it was undiscriminating and unjust. What if some of the Northern clergy signed an anti-Nebraska memorial, shall the whole class be proscribed for the sins of these fanatics? It is not true that the clergy, as a body, are too proud and self-opinioned to listen to the truth. They yield a ready assent to the voice of reason, but they will not abide dictation. They may be drawn by a straw; they cannot be driven with a weaver's beam. And especially they will not listen with very great meekness to a rebuke from those who, as the representatives of the nation, unblushingly trample the laws of God and man under their feet by legislating on the Sabbath. They know their rights, and knowing will defend them.

But while this is true of you, gentlemen, may there not be occasions when you might adopt an opinion too hastily with reference to the great political movements of the day. Such was, doubtless, the case with some who signed that odious anti-Nebraska memorial. They signed it without considering its import, and afterwards regretted their course. So may it be with you. You may have adopted an opinion with reference to the principles of the self-styled American party, which is erroneous. The writer of this address, therefore, respectfully asks you to listen to what he has to say in opposition to the principles of this new party. The leading points of difference between this organization and those parties which have hitherto controlled the interests of the country, are—*First*, opposition to Roman Catholics, so far as to prevent any professing that faith from holding any political office in the gift of the people. *Secondly*, excluding every man from participating in the administration of the government of the country, who was not born on American soil.

With reference to the first, that of excluding Romanists from participating in the administration of our government, the writer would here avow, that there breathes not that man on earth more invincible than he, in his hostility both to Romish doctrines and Romish practices. He believes that Romanists are plunged into the deepest and most ruinous errors; but he does not believe that men are to be won from error by political proscription. Satan argued on more philosophical principles, when he told God that if he would put forth his hand and afflict his servant, that Job would curse him to his face. The mistake of Satan lay in the application of the principle to the peculiar case of the man of Uz, and not the statement of the principle itself. The man of Uz saw the loving hand of a father in his sorrows, but unfortunately the rod which is laid on the Romanist, is not wielded by paternal hands.

This subject has its political as well as its religious aspect. So far as its political aspect is concerned, this may be said: that the Constitution of our country guarantees to every man in the land the right to profess and propagate his creed, provided only that he is a law-abiding citizen. This is as it should be. That the great charter of our liberty never contemplated any religious test to constitute a man a suitable person to hold an office under its purview. It is vain to say that you only exercise your rights as freemen to cast your votes for whom you please. In pledging yourselves to exclude all persons from political offices who hold the Romish faith, you do virtually require a religious test. You require at least that your candidate shall be a Protestant. The question is not, if two persons are equally qualified to fill an office, the one a Romanist, the other a Protestant, which of the two you shall choose: but your principles force you to choose a man wholly unfit to fill the place in opposition to a man qualified in every respect to fill it, save that he is a Romanist. You would proscribe a Taney, or a Gaston, for his faith, and in his place elect a man in no respect qualified to discharge the duties of the office. Now if this is not proscribing a man for his religious opinions, the writer is at a loss to know what it is. Leave this whole matter where the Constitution of the country leaves it. Judge each man by himself, and decide upon his own individual merits, but do not proscribe him for his faith. You cannot coerce a man to your opinion. He may adopt your shibboleth for the sake of gain, but you have only made a hypocrite, instead of a proselyte. If a man's religious opinions warp his judgment or blind his reason, so that in the face of truth, and at the expense of justice, he would favor his co-religionist, then hurl him with indignation from his seat as a perjured wretch, who has desecrated the ermine. But if he be faithful to his trust, and decide by law and equity, between man and man, then do not put him under the political ban because he differs with you in his religious views. Truth will be promoted by this course.

Again, look at this subject in its religious aspect. What is the language of your great commission?—"Go ye into all the world, and preach the gospel to every creature." You believe the Romanist in error, and so he is. But how will you reclaim him? How can you get his ear to pour into it the life-giving truths of the gospel, while you proscribe him politically? Do you not understand human nature well enough to know that a man shuts up, and locks, and bars, and bolts his heart against the truth, the moment you assume towards him a hostile attitude? Treat him with kindness, and you will have won his ear by first winning his heart. No compromise of truth is demanded. But bear in mind that the gospel is a message of love, and its ministers should be "wise as serpents and harmless as doves." Besides, what more do you want? Are you not free as the air you breathe? Have you not the best arena in the world on which to meet and grapple with error? How is error to be put down? Is it not by presenting truth, its great and omnipotent antagonist, in such a way as to commend itself to the conscience of man? Are you afraid that truth will not reach the Romanist? Then surely you adopt a singular method by which to reach him. Did Paul act so at Athens? Did the Son of God act so in Judea? "Away with coward wiles!" The truth is great, and will prevail. Enlighten the people. Meet error in the public assembly, meet it in the pulpit, meet it in the public conveyance, meet it by the fireside, and leave the results to God. If any people on earth have high vantage ground on which to stand and battle for the truth, we are that people. We have an unshackled press; we have a people who throng the hustings; we have a people ready to listen to any who can instruct them. It does not agree with the genius of our government to meet open error by secret political conclaves. What is the chief glory of our nation? It is that every subject is openly and freely canvassed. When error mounts the car to traverse the length and breadth of the land, you can send truth with lightning speed along the telegraphic wires to anticipate it, or prove its effectual antidote.

Besides, your course has not only an unhappy effect on the Romanist himself by steeling his heart against you, but you are awaking a sympathy in his behalf in the bosom of myriads who are outside of the Romanish communion. The writer of this has had occasion to notice the effect of your principles on others. You not only, as the great and magnanimous Chalmers says, "transform a nation of heretics into a nation of heroes," but you engender sympathy for them among neutrals—you make men read with avidity such speeches as Chandler's and swallow as truth everything which is said in defence of Romanism. Such is human nature. You are thus playing directly into the hands of your foes. The Romanists want to be persecuted. They will fatten on it. They will appeal to it as a proof of apostolicity. They will draw round them thousands by the bonds of sympathy whom they will yoke to their car, and by whose aid they will spread their sentiments through the length and breadth of our land.

Still more, the moment you league the cause of religion with any political party, you diminish the power of the truth. When religion became connected with the state, in the days of Constantine, it became corrupt. It was not the church which made advances to the state, it was the state to the church. The monarch of christendom thought that he could have a powerful engine to carry out his designs in the religious prejudices of his subjects. He accordingly courted the alliance. The consequence was, that an ecclesiastico-political government was formed, and true religion was obliged to flee for safety to dens and caves of the earth. It has been so in all ages. Whenever the church of God has abandoned her own divinely appointed agencies and formed unholy alliances with Belial, she has lost the prestige of her glorious name, and the shekinah of the divine presence departed from her. Gentlemen, beware how you allow a conglomerate of all creeds and isms, socialists, infidels, and political demagogues to lure you into their toils. Pure are you in your motives, but wofully are you in error if you think this the best means to serve your country, or spread the religion of Jesus Christ. Adhere closely to the instructions of the Divine Author of your faith. Preach the gospel. "The weapons of your warfare are not carnal," nor political. "What concord hath Christ with Belial, or what part hath he that believeth with an infidel?"

Finally, consider the vast assimilative powers of your country. It is emphatically Protestant in its complexion, though tolerating every creed under its banner. Thousands of foreigners seek our shores. In a few years these become completely assimilated to our government and prevailing religious views. In a few years, multitudes who were reared under Romish influences abroad, become Protestants. Five hundred Roman Catholic children in one of our western cities, lately marched in the Free School procession, each with a Bible under his arm; thus under the silent operation of educational, social, and religious influences, ten Romanists annually become Protestants to one Protestant who becomes a Romanist. Let these influences alone. Why interpose, by drawing unnecessary and invidious distinctions, which, instead of attaching the Romanists to you, will only irritate him, and repel him from you. You know that his superstition is "to be destroyed by the spirit of Christ's mouth, and consumed by the brightness of his coming." Labor to hasten this great event by the spread of the gospel, but do not compromise the dignity of the truth by entangling alliances with men, who with a new-born zeal for Protestantism, are yet adopting principles and practices essentially Jesuitical.

But the writer must reserve for another number his views on the Know-Nothing policy touching foreigners. In the meanwhile, gentlemen, he hopes you will review your position on this whole subject, and no longer allow men to mix religious issues with political questions. Be assured they do not have at heart the welfare of religion. They are only using it as an element to promote their own ends, and when it ceases to advance these, they will leave it to its fate. Respectfully,

VERITAS.

DR. R. J. BRECKENRIDGE—POLITICIAN.

Mr. Editor:—A letter purporting to be written by the great and justly distinguished Dr. Ro. J. Breckenridge, has been copied from the Kentucky press into the papers of Virginia, just on the eve of the election, and for the purpose of affecting it. This policy is certainly a shrewd one. No name in America carries such weight with it in large sections of the southern community as the name of this unquestionably great and brilliant man. For years the ablest and fiercest champion of Protestant Christianity in this country, distinguished for controversial talent, high in social position, reputation, and purity of character, and speaking from the leading chair in a large Protestant school of theology, his endorsation of the political movement designated by the name Know-Nothingism, is calculated to do infinite mischief to the cause of truth, by throwing an air of respectability even upon those peculiarities which some of its own advocates deprecate as foreign to the spirit of our government, and especially by creating the impression that this movement against the Catholic church is endorsed by the Protestant ministry at large. It is to do what in us lies, to counteract these impressions, and as a Protestant minister, who by no means stands alone in opposition to a political movement for the suppression or restraint of Popery, to protest, in the name of the great doctrines of religious liberty, against all such constructions of the views of the Protestant clergy. No doubt there are thousands of those who do sympathize with this movement; but it is equally true that there are fully as many, perhaps more, who dread to lose an end proper in itself pursued by improper means, and who dare not desire the ostracism of the Papacy itself at the expense of those great principles of religious liberty which lie at the foundation of all the prosperity enjoyed by every ecclesiastical organization in the land. We do not mean to follow Dr. Breckenridge through his remarks in the way of reply. Indeed his letter is nothing but a series of terse and animated statements, giving the views which he has taken of the present crisis in political affairs, and not the reasons upon which they are founded. But we except to the whole spirit of this article, as well as to the movement it endorses; but particularly to the apology which he makes for that feature in the organization for which no apology can ever be made, for which no atonement can ever be rendered but a peremptory and final abandonment of the whole of it.

We cannot endorse Dr. Breckenridge's sanction of a political movement to stay the progress and power of the Catholic church. It contains a confession of weakness in the moral machinery of the Protestant churches, an inability to meet all the influences of the great apostacy or the institutions of this nation, which we feel intensely to be a misrepresentation of the facts. There is a power in the Protestant church alone, unaided by a political move, which needs only to be fully and wisely expended, to demonstrate the entire want of any necessity to supplement her weakness by a political crusade. The simple and sufficient condition of the preservation of the republic from the arts of Romanism, is the extension of the Protestant church, the full support of the great Domestic Mission enterprises of the various Protestant denominations. If Protestantism cannot maintain itself in a fair field against Popery, it ought to perish. But there is no need for any such catastrophe: it does possess that capacity; and it is a practical acknowledgment of Protestant weakness, which is as unjust to the Protestant church as it is proscriptive to the Catholic, to represent the destruction of the political franchises of the Catholic citizen as essential to the prosperity of the Protestant religion, or to the conservation of any of the great social or political interests which are dependent upon it. Such a dependence we do believe to exist between the Protestant religion and the institutions of this country: they were established together on this continent, and they will stand or fall together. But so long as the Protestant religion is a living and vital element in forming the character and controling the action of the masses of American citizens as it is at present, so long will the institutions of this nation, the nationality, the Federal Union and the Protestant civilization, of which Dr. Breckenridge speaks, be safe under the moral and spiritual power of the Protestant churches, unaided by any political disabilities inflicted upon the individual Catholic citizen.

We do not mean to say that no political action is never to be taken against the Catholic church or against any Protestant church. But we do mean to say that such political action against any ecclesiastical organization ought to be local and temporary, and above all things discriminated by the practical action of the organization, and not by its principles when held in theory. We do not hesitate to say, if the Catholic church is coming into the political field as such, its members voting on a principle discriminated by their ecclesiastical relations, then it ought to be met on political grounds and resisted with political weapons. We would say this for the same reasons and with equal emphasis of any Protestant church. We would say it of a Masonic order which should engraft a political character on its Masonic capacity. Nay, more, it is unquestionably true that the Catholic church does lay claim to temporal power, holds the state as auxiliary to the church, and under pretence of deciding his duty, announces the right to control the whole action of man, which is susceptible of a moral character. There is this much of the truth in the theory of Know-Nothingism, but it does not answer the purpose of that party. With the fatality which seems to attend all its reasonings from its premises, the modern reform fails to see the true logical result of its premise. The principle which we have enunciated as controling political opposition to all ecclesiastical bodies, Catholic or Protestant, makes all such opposition local, temporary, defined by the previous action of the church itself, not by its theoretical principles, controlled absolutely by that action, stopping when it stops, progressing when it progresses, and ceasing forever when it ceases. To ostracise a Catholic for theory not embodied in practice, no matter how objectionable that theory may be both on political and religious grounds, is to punish crime in embryo; it is to assume the office of deity and judge criminalities of the soul before they are embodied in action or subject to the cognizance of human tribunals. All interference with principles of such magnitude as the liberty of conscience and religious worship, ought to be rigidly adjusted to the strictest limits of the practical exigency that demands it. If the Catholic church has been tampering with politics in any other state, let it be met there; but it would be wrong to suffer the demand for such opposition to extend beyond the exigency which demands it, and to call for the ostracism of the church in Virginia, unless it can also be shown to have been tampering with politics here. Until this is proved, a political disfranchisement of her members to any extent is a violation of the law of religious liberty, and a high misdemeanor. There is no demand whatever for a great national movement against the Catholic church. There may have been cause for local and temporary displays of political opposition to it, but certainly none for an opposition co-extensive with the republic. It is in the main a corrupt movement of unprincipled politicians to excite the Protestant feeling of the country and ride into power upon the tide.

The remark thus made, that the inference of Know-Nothingism in relation to the political opposition to the Catholic church, was a logical blunder from its own premises, which only warranted a local and limited opposition, not a permanent and universal ostracism of individual Catholics, is equally true in relation to the other great issue it has raised as to the foreign population. On all its positions it is logically required to go a great deal farther than it dares attempt. In one case the *premise* is, the Catholic church is incompatible with the existence of the republic; the *inference* is that *no* Catholic shall be eligible to office. The true and legitimate inference is, the Catholic church ought not to be tolerated at all!

The premise assumed in this case is, that the foreign element in our population is dangerous to the government: the inference drawn is the reduction of a part of the rights of citizenship in foreigners already here, and an extension of the term of naturalization. The true inference is the prohibition of all emigration for the future, and the avoidance of everything that would exasperate the foreign element already in the midst of us, the careful observance of everything which would tend to strengthen their attachment to the institutions of the country. How well the modern reform in the political world is accomplishing these ends, it is easy to determine. Leaving in the hands of the Catholic and foreign citizens all the rights of citizenship except one, giving them the power to vote, allowing them, in other words, all their power to do mischief, and exasperating them to use it by the ostracism of their religion and birth, condensing the Catholic and foreign element into a political body, distinct from the mass of the nation, and animated with all the hostility which is natural to men under an attempt to diminish the equality of their rights with other citizens; producing all these ruinous results, Know-Nothingism is par excellence the perfection of political wisdom, the certain salvation of the country! If the abandonment of one of the greatest of the great principles of our political system, if political proscription for religious opinion is to be substituted for the great doctrine of unequivocal liberty of religious belief, irrespective of all political or civil responsibility, then the existence of this government is brought into infinitely more peril than that from which the new party would deliver it. Dr. Breckenridge intimates that if the question had arisen as to the eligibility of a Chinese or a Mahommedan, less difficulty would have been found in settling it. We reply, that the general principles involved would have been settled by the settlement of a previous question; and that is, whether we should admit a Chinese or a Mahommedan, Pagans and Idolators, to the rights of citizenship at all in a Christian supporting country. This determined in the affirmative, it is absurd to question the propriety of allowing by vote what is allowed by law. If there is any reason why they should be excluded from any of the common rights of citizenship, it is a reason why they should be excluded from all of them. If it is right to allow them to vote, it is right to allow them to be voted for: the one right is almost the correlative of the other. Any argument which would prove a man disqualified for office, would equally prove him disqualified to vote. If, then, this opposition to Catholics and foreigners is to be maintained, let it go far enough to accomplish the ends which are alleged to be sought. It is unwise in the extreme to leave all their power for mischief in their hands, resulting in part from their simple existence in the country as a part of the population, and in part from the privileges which are still to be left them; it is unwise to leave them their power for mischief and exasperate them to use it by a crusade against their full political equality with citizens of other religious opinions.

But we must not protract these remarks. We cannot close them, however, without protesting, in opposition to the endorsement of Dr. Breckenridge, against the propriety of a secret organization as a mode of political action, and especially against the particular oath of that modern party binding its members to concealment of the objects of the order, the order itself, and their personal connection with it. What are the objects of this order which have not been proclaimed? If those which are blazoned on their banners are not all of their objects, what are the rest? If they are, why have these been proclaimed in the teeth of that oath? Is it a secret police, as we have heard it intimated? Does not the possibility that this order may have ultimate ends in view which they have not yet discovered, demonstrate the impropriety of that mode of organization which would allow of such concealment and require it to be maintained by an oath? If ever any principle was at direct and practical war with the very foundation of the American republic, it is this principle of an oath-bound secret organization. It will place the legislation of Congress in the hands of an irresponsible association of its members—into a body unknown to the Constitution of the United States, and whose avowed object is to annihilate all distinction between a minority and a majority, by an oath requiring the unlimited surrender of the minority! The Congressional Council will be under orders of the General Council; and the result will be that the Congress of the United States will become, under the full success of Know-Nothing principles, a mere registry of decrees to a body in the heart of the country—unknown to the Constitution—existing no one can tell where—aiming at no one can tell what. It strikes a deadly blow at that great fundamental maxim of the government—the necessity of the intelligence of the people as an essential of republican liberty. What matter how much intelligence the people may have, if political men will conceal from them the facts upon which to employ their intelligence in the formation of a judgment and the adoption of a policy? The two duties are essentially correlative. If it is the duty of the people to require knowledge of any party claiming their suffrages before they endorse them, it is the duty of that party to give it. No party has the right to retire into the dark, bind itself to secrecy under oath, unfold what they please, and conceal what they please from the people; nor have the people one shadow of a moral right to give their sanction to that of the propriety of which they are not fully informed. Moreover, if their principle of secrecy is legitimate for one party, it is legitimate for all; every party may adopt it; the Sag. Nicht clubs of the foreigners of the West are wholly justified; and the whole political destinies of the country may be controled by secret oath-bound organizations, a hybrid mixture of Masonry, and a political caucus with all of good in either spoiled by the conjunction! Can any man in this nation contemplate such a prospect—the legitimate results of the principle of organization adopted by the Know-Nothing party—without emotions of alarm amounting to terror? Yet Dr. Brickenridge would place such a principle on the footing of the vote by ballot! This is the most remarkable instance of the power of prejudice to extinguish the power of perception, in an intellect of the highest order, we have ever encountered. Dr. Johnson's belief in the Cock-Lane ghost is hardly comparable to it.

In conclusion, we must say that the issues pledged upon the fidelity of the Democratic party of Virginia, cannot be fully estimated in their intrinsic value. We trust they will show at the polls that Dr. Breckenridge has been premature in his claim of conquest for Know-Nothingism over the Democracy of the Old Dominion. Be the fate of the party victory or defeat in the ensuing election, the war upon the heresies of the new party will have just begun. The great principles of religious liberty and open organization in political parties, in a republican government, will never be abandoned until they are embodied in practice as well as commended in theory—two things which the Know-Nothing party have taught us to consider carefully apart from all connection with each other. Let the whole power of the party be strained to the uttermost; let all the objections to the candidate, which might have been enough to have justified inaction in his support in ordinary times, now give way in a crisis which involves the very existence, not merely of Democratic measures, but of the fundamental principles of all republican institutions. It is a great battle. God help the right.

A Protestant Minister.

The pretensions of the Know Nothings to peculiar reverence, for the teachings of the Bible, were vindicated in the *Examiner* in the following editorial :

A SERMON FROM LEVITICUS FOR "SAM."

When the *sans culottes* of the secret order of Jacobins were, with foul and bloodstained hands, dragging the noble, beautiful and gifted Madame Roland to the guillotine, and in the name of liberty moistening the streets of Paris with the blood of the Girondists, that illustrious woman, gazing at the bright deadly steel that was soon to sever her fair head, exclaimed, "Oh ! Liberty, how many crimes have been committed in thy name !" When we find a secret order in our midst, in the name of the Bible and of patriotism, practising proscription, intolerance, and worse than savage inhospitality, the fearful truth of Madame Roland's dying words must come home to every calm and dispassionate friend of religion and liberty.

The Know Nothings, in the name of the holy Christian religion, and in the name of patriotism, propose disregarding the plainest teachings of the priest and the true meaning of the host. Particularly do they proclaim that their midnight mission is the purification of the Church, and the preservation of our civil liberties. Like Henry VIII., who, according to Hume, exhibited his impartiality by hanging Catholics and burning Protestants, they claim the title of "defenders of the faith."

Professing to regard the pure teachings of the Bible as of paramount importance to everything earthly, seeking to purge the land of Jesuits and heretics, their principles are utterly at variance with the teachings of that human law maker, who, upon Mount Sinai, received from a Supreme Being the living word. This "*Lion of the North and Bulwark of the Christian faith*" plants its standard, or rather organizes its conspiracy, upon the disregarded teachings of God through his chosen instrument. The Know Nothing who, amid the imposing mysteries and solemn ceremonies of midnight initiation, swears with uplifted hand to defend the true teachings of the Bible, in the same *formula* swears to violate one of the most simple, plain and intelligible lessons of that sacred volume. Whoever, therefore, takes the oaths required by this order, pledges himself to violate the Constitution, and to maintain doctrines irreconcilable with every species of Christian faith, whether Protestant or Catholic—for neither Catholics nor Protestants openly deny the very strongest and plainest doctrines of the Holy Bible. "Sam," however, as he is familiarly termed, has taken the field not only against the Catholic religion, the Constitution and Democracy, but also against *Moses and the Prophets.*

One of the pretexts of "Sam" for his hostility to the Catholics, is that they exclude the Bible from their schools—a grave and heavy fault—one to be looken into and punished. But if the Catholics are to be proscribed for this crime, what punishment should not Sam receive for rearing the structure of his order, digging its very foundations out of the disregarded, despised teachings of the great and inspired law-maker?

The civil polity of Moses, that which followed as a natural sequence to the Ten Commandments, the code framed in accordance with the organic law of Mount Sinai, certainly deserves the respect of Protestants. We, therefore, respectfully ask the disciples of Sam. to reconcile their teachings with the following precept of Moses. Let them take their revered, but too often desecrated Bible, upon which they swear their deluded victims, and turn to the Book of Leviticus, 19th chapter, 33d and 34th verses, and explain to us what Moses meant in the verses aforesaid:

"IF A STRANGER SOJOURN WITH THEE IN YOUR LAND, YE SHALL NOT VEX HIM; BUT THE STRANGER THAT DWELLETH WITH YOU SHALL BE UNTO YOU AS ONE BORN AMONG YOU, AND THOU SHALT LOVE HIM AS THYSELF, FOR YE WERE STRANGERS IN THE LAND OF EGYPT. I AM THE LORD THY GOD."

This language, we humbly suggest, is peculiarly simple, and it scatters the teachings of Sam like a bombshell. Sam is a true Protestant; he boasts that his grandfather was a Protestant, his grandmother was a Protestant, and that his mother, father, uncles, aunts, cousins, nephews, wife, children and grandchildren, are of the same persuasion. Sam and his brethren are the old guard of the Bible, defending the pure, unadulterated faith, flashing the bright sword of a pure and undefiled religion in the eyes of all who question anything which the sacred volume contains from Genesis to Revelations. It is therefore to be presumed, that having wandered often over this holy dominion, having consecrated himself to the sacred work of defending the Bible, Sam is prepared to reconcile this text from Leviticus with his elegant sermons against foreigners and "strangers that are sojourning in the land." All of this he, doubtless, is prepared to do; although, for reasons to us inexplicable, Sam has vouchsafed no revelations respecting this passage from Leviticus. Recollect, Sam, thou "guard of the Bible and defender of the faith"—Leviticus, 19th chapter, 33d and 34th verses. We know that it is hard, Samuel, either in courts of law or in social converse, to get intelligible answers from you. But the Bible, Sam—the Protestant Bible—you certainly will not say that you "Know Nothing" about that. In the name of Moses, we, therefore, pious, religious, consistent Sam, venture to ask you a few simple questions concerning the 33d and 34th verses of the 19th chapter of Leviticus, which, Sam, it may be well to state, incidentally, may be in what is called among good Protestants and sincere haters of the Pope, the Old Testament.

Do you or do you not "*vex strangers who sojourn with thee in your land?*" You swear to turn them out of office. You swear to proscribe them, do you not? Do you regard such treatment as a vexation or a pleasantry where the ejected "stranger" happens to starve in consequence of your "little pleasantry" in turning him out of office.

Moses, you will observe, (perhaps you "Know Nothing," biblical Sam, of Moses,) says, under special instructions from God, that "*the stranger that dwelleth with you* SHALL BE UNTO YOU AS ONE BORN AMONG YOU." Do you not not proclaim "*that strangers who dwelleth among you* SHALL NOT BE UNTO YOU as those who were born among you?" Do you not in every thing which relates to your creed, fly in the face of divine law, denying the wisdom of God and man?

Have you not organized your midnight Order for the express purpose of casting the stranger out—of showing him by hateful and unconstitutional acts that you do not intend to treat him as if he was *born among you?* Is it not most remarkable that, as a self-elected defender of the faith, you propose to set aside the law of Moses to amend the word of God, and declare with the superior sagacity of a Know Nothing that you are more knowing in your generation than Moses was in his? (What is your opinion as to Moses being a fogy?) Do you entertain as low an opinion of the book of Leviticus as you do of the Constitution? Do you regard Judson, Bennett, Clayton, Wilson and Vespasian Ellis as much better law makers than Moses? Is the blue book of your Order higher and better authority than the Old Testament? But most scriptural Sammy—thou modern evangelist of the dark lanterns and frightful oaths—Moses also says, in his old-fashioned way, thou shalt "*love the stranger sojourning in thy land as thyself.*" Dost thou obey the Bible in this regard? Do you love Irish, Dutch, Spanish, Italian, French, Swiss, Danish, Norwegian, Scotch, Patagonian, Chinese, Mexican "strangers" *as you do yourself?* Have you a great love for the ALIEN, an overflowing affection for the foreign born, or have you not *sworn*, yes, sworn, in your midnight deliberations, to persecute the strangers "within your gates?" Of these matters, however, of course, you "Know Nothing." If you love the strangers, how have you shown your affection? By burning their churches, denying them bread, driving them from the ballot box, denying them the rights of citizenship, and mobbing them in the streets of your great cities. In thus treating them, how have you interpreted the Bible?—certainly not as Protestants—but rather, (we regret to say it, Sam,) as hard-hearted, cruel disregarders of the spirit of Christianity.

The 33d and 34th verses of the 19th chapter of Leviticus apply so forcibly and appropriately to Sam's position in this country, that we almost feel inclined to believe that Moses, rending the veil which hides the future from ordinary mortal eyes, must have foreseen the rise and progress of Sam, and thousands of years ago provided for his annihilation. For after thus advising the Israelites, he concludes the 34th verse thus: "*For ye were strangers in the land of Egypt.*" How significant the warning, how impressive the reminiscence. The chosen people of God were once aliens and foreign born in the land of Egypt. Pharaoh and his people were *native Egyptians*, proud of their nationality, insolent and tyrannical, lauding it with a high hand over the poor Israelites, denying them social and political rights, making them hewers of wood and drawers of water, grinding the strangers into the dust, practising modern Know Nothingism without its secrecy, in a bold, open, cruel oppression of the "strangers sojourning among them." The wrath of God fell upon the Know Nothings of the order of Pharaoh; plague followed plague, and pestilence, famine and war desolated the land of the oppressors. Death visited the household of every *native Egyptian*; a leader chosen by God led the oppressed through a sea whose waves, at His command, opened a way for their retreat, and closed over the hosts of the pursuing enemy. This may seem fanciful and far fetched, but it should teach the oppressor and the Know Nothing that "*we were strangers in the land of Egypt.*" This fair land was not God's heritage to us. The *native* Americans have passed away, and we European interlopers have built up our palaces upon the sites of their wigwams,—cities stand where the villages of the natives once stood, and the ploughshare is driven over the burying grounds of those to whom God gave the land.

We are strangers of yesterday in this land;—war, pestilence and famine, introduced by ourselves, have swept those from the land to which God gave them title-deeds. The relics, the monuments, the antiquities of America are not ours. "SAM," a miserable European exile of yesterday, flying from worse than Egyptian bondage at home, to this land of the oppressed of every clime, denies the same precious privileges to the exile of to-day. In doing this, he forgets his origin, the character of our institutions, and the history of the land which he inhabits. He disregards the Constitution, and he forgets the divine teachings of God and of Moses. Hence this sermon.

To the charge every where preferred by the Know Nothings, that the *Examiner* and the *Enquirer* were Catholic organs, the *Examiner* published the following reply:

CIVIL INCAPACITATIONS TEND ONLY TO BEGET HABITS OF HYPOCRISY AND MEANNESS. OPINIONS OF RELIGION SHALL IN NO MANNER DIMINISH OR AFFECT THE CIVIL CAPACITIES OF THE CITIZEN.—*Virginia Act of Religious Toleration.*

Nothing dies so hard and rallies so often as Intolerance.—*Sydney Smith.*

"Catholic organ!" is the favorite ejaculation of the advocates of intolerance against their opponents in the present canvass. The epithet supplies the place and substitutes the purpose of argument in the mouths of men weak enough in mind to fear that these free and powerful States are in danger of temporal subjection from the poorest and weakest of the European Princes. Historical lore they indeed have at command to foment this morbid apprehension: but it is lore borrowed from the dark ages and from persecuting, intolerant Europe—it is lore that has lost its terrors even on the intolerant side of the Atlantic, when Catholic Emperors have repeatedly taken the Pope—that most formidable temporal prince, prisoner in his sacred city, and led him into ignominious captivity; and where, even within the recollection of very small children, that same Potentate, whose authority is pretended to overshadow all the goverments of the earth, was driven out of Rome by a handful of domestic revolutionists.

Native born Americans who terrify at the thought of a Papal subjugation, must be excused for rummaging up the exploded and forgotten lore of benighted and intolerant ages, and for denouncing as "Catholic organs," those who laugh at their folly and deride their farrago of nonsense about Popish invasion and subjugation.

The Rev. Sydney Smith, a staunch supporter of the English Church Establishment, has supplied us with language suitable to the cases of these cowardly terrorists, in the following happy description of a modern Know Nothing:

"Philagatharches is an instance (not uncommon, we are sorry to say, even among the most rational of the Protestant dissenters) of a love of toleration combined with a love of persecution. He is a dissenter, and earnestly demands religious liberty for that body of men; but, as for the Catholics, he would not only continue their present disabilities, but load them with every new one that could be conceived. He expressly says that an Atheist or a Deist may be allowed to propagate their doctrines, but not a Catholic; and then proceeds with all the customary trash against that sect which nine school boys out of ten now know how to refute. So it is with Philagatharches;—so it is with weak men in every sect. It has ever been our object, and (in spite of misrepresentation and abuse) ever shall be our object, to put down this spirit—to protect the true interests and to diffuse the true spirit of toleration."

So here is a "Catholic organ," after the Know Nothing sense of the word, in the person of a staunch clergyman of the Episcopal Church of England.

In the same sense, Thomas Jefferson, who drew the Virginia act of religious toleration, the pith and gist of which stands at the head of this article cf ours, and who is generally understood to have been a Free Thinker on the subject of religion and church government, was also a "Catholic organ." Indeed, if this Know Nothing idea be true, that all defenders of religious freedom are "Catholic organs," we fear it will turn out, at last, that the proscribed denomination are very formidable in this matter of *organship.* George Washington and the whole convention of conscript fathers who formed the *American* Constitution containing provisions in favor of the *free exercise of religion* and denouncing religious tests, against which the Higher Law Know Nothings of our day swear so great an oath, were in that sense "Catholic organs." Madison and Jackson, as will appear in another place in this sheet, were likewise in the same category of "Catholic organs."

Not only were all good men of our earlier history amenable to this charge, but many bad men also; for the famous Thomas Paine wrote himself down a "Catholic organ" repeatedly and unmistakably, in defending the liberty of conscience; as, for instance, thus:

"Toleration is not the opposite of intolerance, but is the counterfeit of it. Both are despotisms. The one assumes to itself the right of withholding liberty of conscience, and the other of granting it. The one is the Pope armed with fire and faggot, and the other is the Pope selling or granting indulgences. The former is Church and State, and the latter is Church and traffic.

But toleration may be viewed in a much stronger light. Man worships not himself, but his Maker; and the liberty of conscience, which he claims, is not for the service of himself, but of his God. In this case, therefore, we must necessarily have the associated idea of two beings: the mortal who renders the worship, and the immortal being who is worshipped. Toleration, therefore, places itself, not between man and man, nor between church and church, nor between one denomination of religion and another, but between God and man: between the being who worships, and the being who is worshipped: and by the same act of assumed authority, by which it tolerates man to pay his worship, presumptuously and blasphemously sets itself up to tolerate the Almighty to receive it.

Were a bill brought into any parliament, entitled, 'An act to tolerate or grant liberty to the Almighty to receive the worship of a Jew or Turk;' or, 'to prohibit the Almighty from receiving it;' all men would startle and call it blasphemy. The world would be in uproar. The presumption of toleration in religious matters would then present itself unmasked: but the presumption is not the less because the name of 'man' only appears to these laws, for the associated idea of the worshipper and worshipped cannot be separated. Who, then, art thou, vain dust and ashes! by whatever name thou art called, whether a king, a bishop, a church or a state, a parliament or any thing else, that obtrudest thine insignificance between the soul of man and its Maker? Mine own concerns. If he believes not as thou believest, it is a proof that thou believest not as he believeth, and there is no earthly power can determine between you.

With respect to what are called denominations of religion, if every one is left to judge of its own opinion, there is no such thing as a religion that is wrong: but if they are to judge of each other's religion, there is no such thing as a religion that is right; and, therefore, all the world is right, or all the world is wrong. But with respect to religion itself, without regard to names, and as directing itself from the universal family of mankind to the divine object of all adoration, it is man bringing to his Maker the fruits of his heart; and though those fruits may differ from each other like fruits of the earth, the grateful tribute of every one is accepted.

A bishop of Durham or a bishop of Winchester, or the archbishop who leads the dukes, will not refuse a tythe—sheaf of wheat, because it is not a cock of hay, nor a cock of hay, because it is not a sheaf of wheat, nor a pig, because it is neither one nor the other; but these same persons, under the figure of an established church, will not permit their Maker to receive the varied tythes of man's devotion.

One of the continual choruses of Mr. Burke's book is "Church and State:" he does not mean some one particular Church, or some one particular State, but anti-Church and State: and he uses the term as a general figure, to hold forth the political doctrine of always uniting the Church with the State in every country, and he censures the National Assembly for not having done this in France. Let us bestow a few thoughts on this subject.

All religions are, in their nature, kind and benign, and united with principles of morality. They could not have made proselytes at first by professing anything that was vicious, cruel, persecuting or immoral. Like everything else they had their beginning: and thus proceeded by persuasion, exhortation and example. How is it then that they loose their native mildness, and become morose and intolerant?

It proceeds from the connection which Mr. Burke recommends. By engendering the Church with the State, a sort of mule animal, capable only of destroying, and not of breeding up, called the church established by law. It is a stranger, even from its birth, to any parent mother on which it is begotten, and whom in time it kicks out and destroys.

The Inquisition of Spain does not proceed from the religion originally professed, but from the mule animal engendered between the Church and State. The burnings in Smithfield proceeded from the same heterogeneous production: and it was the regeneration of this animal in England afterwards, that renewed the rancour and irreligion among the inhabitants, and that drove the people called Quakers and Dissenters to America. Persecution is not an original feature in any religion, but it is always the strongly marked feature in all law religions, or religions established by law. Take away the law establishment, and every religion re-assumed its original benignity.

In America, a Catholic priest is a good citizen, a good character, and a good neighbor; an Episcopalian minister is of the same description; and this proceeds independently of the men, from there being no law establishment in America.

If we also view this matter in a temporal sense, we shall see the ill effects it has had on the prosperity of nations. The union of Church and State has impoverished Spain. The revoking the edict of Nants drove the silk manufacture from France into England: and Church and State are now driving the cotton manufacture from England to America and France. It is by observing the ill effects of it, in England, that America has been warned against it, and it is by experiencing them in France, that the National Assembly have abolished it: and, like America, have established universal right of conscience, and *universal right of citizenship.*"—*Paine's Rights of Man, part* 1*st.*

But better men and better moralists than Paine proved themselves "Catholic organs" in full as decided and able and instructive a manner. One of the most lucid and popular authors upon subjects of casuistry and religion, Dymond, writes thus:

"A few, and only a few, sentences, will be allowed to the writer upon the great, the very great question of extending religious liberty to the Catholics of these kingdoms. I call it a very great question, not because of the difficulty of deciding it, if sound principles are applied, but because of the interests that are involved, and of the consequences which may follow if those principles are not applied.

It is the writer's conviction, that full Religious Liberty ought to be extended to the Catholics, because it ought to be extended to all men.

If a Catholic *acts* in opposition to the public welfare, diminish or take away his freedom; if he thinks amiss, let him enjoy his freedom undiminished.

To this I know of but one objection that is worth noting here—that they are harmless, only because they have not the power of doing mischief, and that they wait only for the power to do it. But they say this is not the case; we have no such intentions! Now, in all reason, you must believe them, or show that they are unworthy of belief. If you believe them, Religious Liberty follows of course. Can you then show that they are unworthy of belief. Where is your evidence?

You say their allegiance is divided between the king and a foreign power. They reply '*It is not.*' We hold ourselves bound, in conscience, to obey the civil government in all things of a temporal and civil nature, notwithstanding any dispensation to the contrary, from the Pope or Church of Rome.

You say their declarations and oaths do not bind them, because they hold that they can be dispensed from the obligation of an oath by the Pope. They reply '*We do not.*' We hold that the obligation of an oath is most sacred; that no power whatever can dispense with any oath by which a Catholic has confirmed his duty of allegiance to his sovereign, or any obligation of duty to a third person.

You say they hold that faith is not to be kept with heretics. They reply, '*We do not.*' British Catholics say they have solemnly sworn that they reject and detest that unchristian and impious principle, that faith is not to be kept with heretics or infidels. These declarations are taken from a 'Declaration of the Catholic Bishops, the Vicars, Apostles, their co-adjutors, in Great Britain, 1825.' They are signed by the Catholic Bishops of Great Britain, and are approved in an 'address' signed by eight Catholic Peers, and a large number of other persons of rank and character.

Now, I ask of those who contend for the Catholic disabilities, what proof do you bring that these men are trying to deceive you? I can anticipate no answer, because I have heard none. Will you, then, content yourselves by saying, we will not believe them? This would be at least the candid course, and the world might then perceive that our conduct was regulated not by reason, but by prejudice or the consciousness of power. It is unwarrantable to infer, *a priori*, and contrary to the professions and declarations of the persons holding such opinions, that their opinions could induce acts injurious to the common weal. But, if nothing can be said to show that the Catholic declarations do not bind them, something can be said to show that they do. If declarations be indeed so little binding upon their consciences, how comes it to pass that they do not make those declarations which would remove their disabilities, get a dispensation from the Pope, and so enjoy both the privileges and an easy conscience. Why, if their oaths and declarations did not bind them, they would get rid of their disabilities to-morrow! Nothing is wanting but a few hypocritical declarations, and Catholic Emancipation is effected. Why do they not make the declarations? *Because their words bind them.* And yet, (so gross is the absurdity,) although it is their conscientiousness which keeps them out of office, we say they are to be kept out because they are not conscientious! I forbear further inquiry, but I could not with satisfaction, avoid applying what I conceive to be the sound principles of political rectitude to this great question; and let no man allow his prejudices or his fears to prevent him from applying them to this, as to every other political subject. Justice and Truth are not to be sacrificed to our weakness and apprehensions; and I believe that, if the people and legislature of this country (Great Britain) will adhere to justice and truth with regard to our Catholic brethren, they will find, ere long, that they have only been delaying the welfare of the Empire"—*Dymond's Essays on Morality.*

Religious Toleration before the American Revolution.—More than a hundred years before the declaration of independence, the American colonies asserted, and the British monarchs granted, the great doctrines of religious tolerance. In 1662, the sovereign of England declared "the principles and foundation of the charter of Massachusetts to be the freedom of liberty of conscience!" But from the moment that the idea of making an English settlement in Maryland occurred to the just and high-souled Calvert, Lord Baltimore, which was early in 1600, the idea of religious toleration became as precious to American adventurers and settlers as the air which they breathed or the lives they had dedicated to the New World. In 1636, every other country in the world had persecuting laws but Maryland; and at that early day the oath of a governor of Maryland was: "I will not, by myself, or any other, directly or indirectly, molest any one professing to believe in Jesus Christ, for or in respect of religion. At a moment when the overthrow of the monarchy in the mother country was about to place in the hands of Cromwell, the embittered enemy of the Romism church, unlimited power, the Catholics of Maryland (April 21, 1649) placed the following law upon their statute-book: "And whereas the enforcing of the conscience in matters of religion hath frequently fallen out to be of dangerous consequence in those Commonwealths where it has been practised, and for the more quite and peacable government of this province, and the better to preserve mutual love and amity among the inhabitants, no person within this province, professing to believe in Jesus Christ, shall be any ways troubled, molested or discountenanced, for his or her religion, or in the free exercise thereof." The "friends of prelacy" who were disfranchised in Massachusetts, and the Puritans who were "vexed" in Virginia, were welcomed to equal political and civil liberty in Catholic Maryland. The manner in which Lord Baltimore was persecutcd and denounced—thrown out his rights by usurpers—and in turn proscribed by the very persuasion he had tolerated and protected—and yet his noble and constant adherence to the doctrine of religious freedom and political equality, whether in public or in private life—are embalmed in the history and in the remembrance of the world.

High upon the roll of fame will shine the name of Lord Baltimore, made glorious in the person of Sir George Calvert, and sustained in that of his son, Cecil Calvert. At a time when the nation was overrun with the foes of the holy right of the freedom of conscience, Lord Baltimore set an example that to this day bears perennial blessings upon all. Ever green be his immortal memory! The ingrates who assail the reputation of the illustrious dead—their rude ribaldry over his honored grave—their ignorant denial of services that are printed in the pages of impartial history—will not deprive him of his claims upon the gratitude of all generations of civilized and Christian people.

The progress of religious toleration in New England was marked by gigantic and almost incredible perils. The heart sickens over the recital. And in proportion as we feel proud and glad at the exhibition of the Catholic Calvert's liberal and generous policy in Maryland, we are oppressed and grieved by the details of Catholic persecutions in England during the reign of Mary. But the religious toleration which flourished under a Catholic proprietor in the New World grew up defiantly in the face of Catholic illiberality in the Old World. It was precious in both cases; but more perilous to maintain and to defend in the latter than in the former. Nor were the Puritans mnch safer under the Protestant rule of Elizabeth. Proscriptive decrees were passed against them commanding conformity, and some of their most beloved leaders were executed. But still their increase in numbers could not be arrested. Under James they suffered fearfully; and, finally, in order to worship God without the fear of man, and to be able to assert the divine right of conscience, in 1607 a number of reformers fled to Holland, where they arrived after terrible privations. They remained in Holland about eleven years. In 1620 they left for the New World, and soon after their arrival established themselves at Plymouth. Their sufferings for long years, from the climate, from starvation, from the ravages of the Indians, and from their distant foes, as we read in their sad but eloquent story, make the heart bleed. Throughout all, they asserted and maintained that principle of religious toleration to preserve which they fled from their fatherland. Population advanced slowly for long years; few followed their despairing fortunes: but through all "they worshiped God under their own vine and under their own fig tree, with none to molest or to make them afraid." It would compensate for the trouble if some eloquent writer would go back to those days of the past, and contrast the perils and the persecutions endured by these early Christians—the loss of fortune and of life—to sustain a principle now madly assailed by those who boast at the same time of being the offspring of such ancestors, and trample their holiest prerogative under foot as if toleration were the teaching of sin itself!

In 1631, however, there reached the shores of Nastaket one of those men whose character impresses itself upon coming generations, and whose virtues outweigh all the honors of merely military chieftains. He was the champion of religious toleration, and almost its martyr. He contended for it against all local fanaticisms, offended his own friends by his heroic fortitude, and was finally expelled from the Massachusetts colony for his adherence to this immortal doctrine. We allude to Roger Williams. Let those who now scoff at the right of conscience, and who dare to lay their hands upon that sacred element of freedom—let them contemplate the character and the example of this heroic spirit; and if they do not feel overwhelmed with the consciousness of their own insignificance and ingratitude, we shall be deceived. Behold the picture of this brave and noble leader as drawn by the glowing pencil of Bancroft: "In 1631 he was but little more than thirty years of age; but his mind had already matured a doctrine which secures him an immortality of fame, as its application has given religious peace to the American world. He was a Puritan, and a fugitive from English persecution; but his wrongs had not clouded his accurate understanding; in the capacious recesses of his mind he had revolved the nature of intolerance, and he, and he alone, had arrived at the great principle which is its sole effectnal remedy. He announced his discovery under the simple proposition of the sanctity of conscience. The civil magistrate should restrain crime, but never control opinion; should punish guilt, but should never violate the freedom of the soul. The doctrine contained within itself an entire reformation of theological jurisprudence; it would blot from the statute-book the felony of non-conformity; would quench the fires that persecution had kept so long burning; would repeal every law compelling attendance on public worship; would abolish tithes and all forced contributions to the maintenance of religion; would give an equal protection to every form of religious faith; and never suffer the authority of the civil government to be enlisted against the mosque of the Mussulman or the altar of the fire worshiper, against the Jewish synagogue or Roman cathedral. * * *

"But the principles of Roger Williams led him into perpetual collision with the clergy and government of Massachusetts. It had ever been their custom to respect the church of England, and in the mother country they frequented its service without scruple; yet its principles and its administration were harshly exclusive. Williams would hold no communion with intolerance; for, said he, 'the doctrine of persecution for cause of conscience is most evidently and lamentably contrary to the doctrine of Christ Jesus.' * * * * * * * * * * * *

"But the controversy finally turned on the question of the rights and duty of magistrates to guard the minds of the people against corruption, and to punish what would seem to them error and heresy. Magistrates, Williams protested, are but the agents of the people, or its trustees, on whom no spiritual power in matters of worship can ever be conferred; since conscience belongs to the individual, and is not the property of the body politic; and with admirable dialectics clothing the great truth in its boldest and most general forms, he asserted that the civil magistrate may not intermeddle even to stop a church from apostacy and heresy; 'that this power extends only to the bodies and goods and outward estates of men.' With corresponding distinctness, he foresaw the influence of his principles on society. 'The removal of the yoke of soul-oppression,' to use the words in which, at a later day, he confirmed his early view, 'as it will prove an act of mercy and righteousness to the enslaved nations, so it is of binding force to engage the whole and every interest and conscience to preserve the common liberty and peace.' * * * * * * * * * * *

"When summoned to appear before the general court, he avowed his convictions in the presence of the representatives of the state, 'maintained the rocky strength of his grounds,' and declared himself 'ready to be bound and banished, and even to die in New England,' rather than renounce the opinions which had dawned upon his mind in the clearness of light. At a time when Germany was the battle-field for all Europe in the implacable wars of religion; when even Holland was bleeding with the anger of vengeful factions; when France was still to go through the fearful struggle with bigotry; when England was gasping under the despotism of intolerance, almost half a century before William Penn became an American proprietary, and two years before Descartes founded modern philosophy on the method of free reflection, Roger Williams asserted the doctrine of intellectual liberty. It became his glory to found a state on that principle, and to stamp himself upon its rising institutions in characters so deep that the impress has remained to the present day, and can never be erased without the total destruction of the work. The principles which he first sustained amidst the bickerings of a colonial parish, next asserted in the general court of Massachusetts, and then introduced into the wilds on Narragansett bay, he soon found occasion to publish to the world, and to defend as the basis of the religious freedom of mankind; so that, borrowing the rhetoric employed by his antagonist in derision, we may compare him to the lark, the pleasant bird of the peaceful summer, that, 'affecting to soar aloft, springs upward from the ground, takes his rise from pale to tree,' and at last, surmounting the highest hills, utters his clear carols through the skies of morning. He was the first person in modern, christendom to assert in its plenitude the doctrine of the liberty of conscience, the equality of opinions before law, and in its defence he was the harbinger of Milton, the precursor and the superior of Jeremy Taylor." * * * * * *

[After being expelled from Massachusetts, Roger Williams went out to seek a home for himself:]

"It was in June that the law-giver of Rhode Island, with five companions, embarked on the stream; a frail Indian canoe contained the founder of an independent state and its earliest citizens. Tradition has marked the spring near which they landed; it is the parent spot, the first inhabited nook of Rhode Island. To express his unbroken confidence in the mercies of God, Williams called the place PROVIDENCE. 'I desired,' said he, 'it might be for a shelter for persons distressed for conscience.'"

These are taken from examples of American history long before the revolutionary war, and before the declaration of independence. We shall reserve to another occasion the reproduction of the model character of William Penn—a portrait entitled to a high place in the galaxy of which Calvert and Williams were unfading stars. But what a retrospect is opened to the inquiring mind by these reminiscenses! We see a simple Bible truth—a plain principle in politics—prevailing over bigotted and cruel kings. We see the wisest statesmen of a brilliant reign yielding to this principle; men perishing for it at the burning stake in order that posterity might feel its value; others stealing off to strange lands with their feeble wives and little children; others hunted like wild beasts, and finally Christians flying for a refuge from intolerance to a far-distant world—a new asylum—and meeting there the rigors of a harsh climate, of prostrating diseases, of savage foes—all that the seed of religious freedom and liberty of conscience might not perish, but might be the beginning of a great nation in the future under the canopy of whose institutions all nations might find a home, safe from king and Kaiser, screened from fanaticism and hatred, and equal alike before God and man!

One of the first bad deeds of the Know Noth ng Governor of Massachusetts, after his election in 1855, was the disbanding of several military companies, composed of foreign born citizens.

John Mitchell, the Irish patriot and refugee, published the following admirable and scathing article upon the subject in his paper, *The Citizen*.

DISARMING OF CITIZENS—THE FIRST STEP TOWARDS DESPOTISM.

He must be a grossly ignorant Celt, indeed, who does not know the principles of Republican freedom better than Mr. Gardner, Governor of Massachusetts. Mr. Gardner holds "that the foreigner shall enjoy all the blessings of this country; but that the *natives* shall continue to administer the laws, according to their own judgment and the example of their fathers." Therefore Governor Gardner has not the least idea what the blessings of this country are (or rather *were*) when he excludes from the number of those blessings the equal capacity of all citizens to "administer the laws" and to do every other civic duty and exercise every other civic right. When he presumes to cite the example of his fathers for this, if he means the Pilgrim Fathers, he is right enough;—for they had little notion of republican freedom or any other freedom—but if he means the Fathers of the American Revolution, then he blasphemes his fathers and stultifies his fathers' son. His fathers did not call a naturalized citizen "the foreigner;" his fathers did not claim for natives the sole administration of the law. His fathers knew what were the blessings of the Revolution they achieved and of the country they created; and they made laws *inviting* all mankind to come and participate in those blessings upon equal terms. His fathers little thought they would be so unlucky as to beget a Know Nothing.

However, he has begun the work; knowing nothing, and we suppose caring nothing, how it may end. "To cultivate a living and energetic nationality—to develop a high and vital patriotism," he has commenced his term of office by issuing an order to disband all militia companies of the State, whose members were *born* in other lands—or as he clearly expresses it, "Companies composed of foreign birth." Whether he has by law the power to carry his ukase into effect is another question, which we are glad to see will be tried with him; but in the mean time, so far as in him lies, he revokes the invitation of his fathers *after* it has been accepted by millions of men—after they have abandoned the crowded and crushed lands of Europe, their home, their kindred, and what citizenship they had there,—and declares his resolution to *cheat* them, by penal disabilities and disqualifications, which would make them citizens but in name, helots in fact.

This is what Governor Gardner calls Americanizing America. But he has other plans, this learned Governor—"To retain the Bible (that is the Protestant Bible) in our Common Schools, and to keep entire the separation of the Church and the State." Obviously he is in a state of the most innocent unconsciousness that these two suggestions destroy one another. To expend the taxes of the whole people in maintaining institutions (call them schools or conventicles, or what you will) that only a part of the people can use by reason of some one sort of religion being taught there—this is not separation, but connexion, of Church and State. We do not mean to make an elaborate criticism on the Massachusetts inaugural. It is all like what we have quoted—ignorance, bad sense, bad feeling, and bad English. But what we do mean to do is to address a few words of advice to naturalized citizens in the premises.

It may be assumed that Governor Gardner's principles and measures will in the present temper of the public mind, be popular, and be imitated in other States. In fact Know Nothing Governors may even attempt to improve upon them, and invent some original and more ingenious oppression. It would not be easy, just now to go too far in that direction. It is full time that the people against whom all these blows and insults are aimed should take counsel together, should ascertain whether they are indeed citizens in the true and full meaning of the term, if not, then what position they are to consider themselves as holding in America henceforth,—and in the mean time what measures can be taken to avert the evils which the present proscription may bring upon themselves and their adopted country.

In the first place we must remark the fact which no doubt Governor Gardner knows well enough—that the separate military organizations, whether of Irish or of German citizens, although certainly an evil, are fully as much owing to the separate organizations of native Americans as to any disposition on the part of either Irish or Germans to isolate themselves. There are companies in New York which do not admit a foreign-born soldier, and doubtless in Boston too. These native Americans will not take the word of command from a foreign-born officer; so that if a naturalized citizen, no matter how educated and intelligent, were even admitted into those corps he must be a full private. The plain consequence is that naturalized citizens desirous of bearing arms under the flag of their adopted country, if they will not submit to humiliation, *must* form corps of their own. We say this is an evil; but it is directly produced by the intolerance of the natives; yet the natives think themselves entitled to cry out in condemnation of it.

Since the CITIZEN was established, seeing that the existence of separate Irish, German and Native American companies could not be helped, we have earnestly endeavored to impress upon the Irish soldier, what indeed we believe every Irish soldier feels without being tutored—that he bears arms solely for his adopted country, whose laws he is bound to obey, and whose flag and constitution he is to defend with his life. We have loudly condemned the anomaly and absurdity of what is called "the Irish vote," (another mischief invented and used by American politicians) and exhorted our countrymen *not* to vote in masses or in batches, as Irishmen, nor suffer electioneering intriguers to "make capital" of them by a few blarneying phrases. We have preached to them that here they are never to forget they are Americans, and exhorted them to be obedient to the laws, and to rely on the justice of their fellow citizens and on the majesty of the constitution.

We repeat that advice still more earnestly *now*. Let no irritation at an insolent aggression tempt us to be false to the obligations we have taken upon us. In the difficulties that are approaching, let the Know Nothings be still, as they are now, wholly in the wrong.

But what is of more importance still—submit to no brand of inferiority, no shadow of disparagement, at the hand of these natives. You are their equals by law; you are their equals every way. Disbandment of a military company is a direct imputation of *misconduct:* and we are happy to find that Col. Butler of Lowell refuses to brook the outrage. He declines to transmit the order for disbandment to his captains, invites a Court Martial, and appeals to the law—for there is still an appeal to the law. And the Shields' Artillery of Boston have taken like action in the case. If, however, the final decision be against them and against Col. Butler, and if the military companies of foreign birth are actually disarmed and disbanded, then for every musket given into the State Armory, let three be purchased forthwith; let independent companies be formed, thrice as numerous as the disbanded corps—there are no Arms Acts here yet—and let every "foreigner" be drilled and trained, and have his arms always ready. For you may be very sure, (having some experience in that matter) that those who begin by disarming you, mean to do you a mischief.

Be careful not to truckle in the smallest particular to American prejudices. Yield not a single jot of your own; for you have as good a right to your prejudices as they. Do not, by any means, suffer Gardner's Bible to be thrust down your throats. Do not abandon your post, or renounce your functions, as citizens or as soldiers, but after resort to the last and highest tribunal of law open to you; keep the peace; attempt no "demonstrations;" discourage drunkenness, and stand to your arms.

It is hardly to be conceived that the madness of faction and the insolence of race will proceed to such a length as to disarm independent companies, or private men. If they *do,* then the Constitution is at an end—the allegiance you have sworn to this Republic is annulled.

Would to God that thoughtful and just Americans would bethink themselves in time. They are strong: they far outnumber the foreign born: they are proud and flushed with national glory and prosperity: doubtless they *can* if they will, do great and grievous wrong to a race that has never wronged them:—but seriously, earnestly we assure them, the naturalized citizens will not submit. This senseless feud must be reconciled: there must be peace: peace or else a war of extermination. We are here on American ground, either as citizens or as enemies.

HAS EMIGRATION INJURED OUR COUNTRY?

It is stated—we know not how truly—that the Legislature of Wisconsin has unanimously passed resolutions against any alteration of the naturalization laws. This item of news has suggested some reflections on the subject of emigration, which may not be inapplicable to present politics.

In 1840 the entire population of Wisconsin was 30,945.

In 1850 the entire population of Wisconsin was 305,391—being an increase in ten years of 886.88 per cent.!

Of this 305,391 souls, 110,477 were born in foreign countries, and but 54,479 within the State of Wisconsin.

There are many other evidences of the value of emigration which deserve notice.

Chicago, that wonder of the lakes, which twelve years ago was no larger than an ordinary village, and which is now one of the great depots of the far West, had a population of 30,000 two years ago. Of this number about one half is composed of citizens born in other countries.

Take next the city of Milwaukie, Wisconsin, which has only risen into notice within a few years, and we find there a population of 20,000 three years ago, of which 12,782 are adopted citizens from Germany and Ireland.

Cincinnati, the queen city of the West, has a population of 115,435, of which 54,500 are adopted citizens from Germany and Ireland.

St. Louis is another wonder. In 1852 it had a population of about 78,000, of which 38,397 were born in foreign countries—chiefly from England, Wales, Ireland and Germany.

New Orleans has a population of 50,470 native-born to 48,601 foreign-born—mainly from Ireland, France and Germany.

Detroit numbers 11,055 native to 9,927 foreign-born.

Boston has 88,948 native to 46,667 foreign-born.

Philadelphia has 286,346 native to 121,699 foreign-born.

It appears, says the Compendium of the Census, compiled by Mr. DeBow, that there were, in 1850, in the United States, 961,719 persons born in Ireland; 278,675 born in England; 70,550 in Scotland; 29,868 in Wales—making a total for Great Britain and Ireland of 1,340,812, which is considerably more than one half of the total foreign-born residents in the United States. If British America be added, (147,711,) there will be a total of 1,488,523, which makes two thirds of the total foreign-born. From France there are 54,069; from Prussia, 10,549; from the rest of Germany, 573,225; and some 80,000 from other countries, including Mexico.

Closely and inseparably connected with this view of the subject, are the enormous and increasing resources opened by this emigration to our commerce, manufactures, agriculture, and hence to the revenues of the general government. The amount of shipping employed is itself an item worthy of reflection. New York, which is the point at which most of the emigration from the Old World arrives, thence to take its departure over the States of the Union, had in 1821 a tonnage equal to 21,726,634, and in thirty years after (1851) its tonnage was equal to 106,568,635! This ratio holds good as to other cities. We have no data by which to estimate the large amount of coin that follows and accompanies emigration to the United States; and this is an element of first-rate importance. Arrest emigration and the first interest to feel the blow will be that of commerce.

What emigration has done for agriculture, the statistics of the Western States will show to the curious inquirer. Every foot of uncultivated soil that is rescued for the purposes of civilization by the teeming thousands that pour into the wilderness of the far West is made to add to the enormous products that have made this the granary of the world, *and to every other interest in every State of the Union*, because where these masses of citizens do not produce they consume, giving to manufacturers a market on the one hand, and aiding to feed starving millions upon the other.

There is probably no element that enters so largely, and at the same time so convincingly, into the discussion of the question of the value of emigration to the United States, as that which relates to the public lands. Here is a subject worthy of the noblest efforts of the intellect. Regarded from every point of view, it inspires the most profound ideas, and fills the mind of the citizen with sublime anticipations of his country's greatness. Indissolubly connected with the question of revenue, it suggests to us a bulwark against a world in arms. In peace it promises to support a government without taxation, and so enforces the great idea of free trade with the nations of the earth. In war it furnishes us with the means to protect ourselves against the invader. Every year fills up new expanses of the public domain; and yet, as State after State is recovered from the gloom and the desolation of centuries of ignorance and of neglect, other regions are opened to the energies of our race, startling all the peoples of the globe with stories of illimitable natural resources. The policy of the government has not fallen below the majestic dignity of this subject, in all its relations, social and political. Chiefly, however, has it been considered as belonging to that class of interests which look beyond the present, and connect themselves with the future. The following brief and striking paragraph in the President's last annual message contains a volume of food for patriotic thought:

"During the last fiscal year, eleven million seventy thousand nine hundred and thirty-five acres of the public lands have been surveyed, and eight million one hundred and ninety thousand and seventeen acres brought into market. The number of acres sold is seven million thirty-five thousand seven hundred and thirty-five, and the amount received therefor nine million two hundred and eighty-five thousand five hundred and thirty-three dollars. The aggregate amount of lands sold, located under military scrip and land warrants, selected as swamp lands by states, and by locating under grants for roads, is upwards of twenty-three millions of acres. The increase of lands sold over the previous year is about six millions of acres; and the sales during the two first quarters of the current year present the extraordinary result of five and a half millions sold, exceeding by nearly four millions of acres the sales of the corresponding quarters of the last year."

It is not necessary that we should retrace the history of emigration for the last twenty years, and especially for the last ten. years, to show how and by whom these lands are purchased. While the government liberalizes its laws, cheapens its public lands, and peacefully treats with the aborigines, the doctrines of our forefathers are equally respected and applied, and the oppressed and down-trodden of the Old World come hitherwards *to help the cause of enlightened liberty on these shores, and to find homes for themselves, with none to molest or to make them afraid.* We thus fulfil ennobling duties to ourselves and hold out ennobling inducements to all our fellow-beings. We reduce our public debt, lighten the burdens of taxation to our citizens, open the pathway to religion and civilization, where for thousands of years untutored nature reigned supreme, and reward those who have fought our battles against the common foe. Who does not see how such a picture held up before the hunted and the starving masses of ancient kingdoms is like a voice from God himself calling them hitherwards? It is He who speaks in these wonderful and manifold evidences of His goodness and His glory. And when the emigrants come, answering to us, as the agents of the Supreme Ruler, do they take from us without giving in return? Do they not aid to make the wilderness blossom as the rose—to dig the canal—to heave the ponderous granite from its time-worn caves—to stretch the long line of railroad—to pay taxes—and to contend against our enemies at home and abroad? But more than this: Leaving the material advantages thus given on the one hand, and returned a thousand-fold upon the other, to those who delight in such calculations, who will estimate the general advantage to those rational principles of freedom, and of civilization and of law, secured to us by these additions to our population? Exceptions, indeed, there are to this rule—deplorable exceptions. And so were there exceptions after the revolutionary war among a native-born people, who rebelled in the face of sacred obligations, and resisted the delegated authority with the strong arm. But the problem has been too fully and too clearly solved in regard to emigrants to this country. Here all nations mingle and make up a race such as the sun has never shone upon, and the feature that towers most prominently in all the States—that arrests and converts, if it does not denounce and overwhelm, every element of foreign tumult transported here—is the feature that when men would be truly free they must be obedient to the laws they themselves have made, or sworn to respect. And this is the rock upon which for fifty years a popular government has stood, and upon which it now stands stronger than ever. This, too, is the rock upon which absurd prophesies and craven fears have been shivered to atoms.

The narrow bigot, or the selfish demagogue, may choose to extract apprehensions from these observations, but we advise him to adjourn his criticisms. We advise him to leave as a legacy to the future his present persecutions and plots; and there can be little danger of the issue; for if he *will* try his theories now, he must rest on a more enduring basis than mere proscription and envy. He must erect his standard higher than the secret cells of midnight schemers. He must raise his voice in a purer atmosphere than that which exhales from oath-bound orgies. He may riot for a day in the excitement resulting from intoxicating prejudices and glittering promises. But he must oppose arguments to facts, truth to history, great thoughts and practical benefits to the solid and inspiring record that we hold up before his eyes. Who cannot realize such a prospect in the not too distant future, when the Pacific slope will swarm with human beings; when the untrodden empires that now belong to our country will be peopled with freemen; when we have rescued the suffering nations of this hemisphere, by the force of a peaceful example, from the sword and the bayonet; when our lakes, on all their borders, will fulfil the destiny that awaits them, and renew there the glories of the ancient republics; when in all the world there is no tyrant; and when there need be no emigrants to this land, because toleration, equality, and peace will be the common blessings of the whole family of man?

HOSTILITY TO EMIGRATION.

The following powerful articles appeared in the *Washington Union* during the canvass in Virginia, and as they have been ascribed to two of the most distinguished statesmen of the Democratic party, we republish them. In learning and research, they equal any writings of the canvass.

Hostility to Emigration—To the Extension of the American Union—To the Rights of the States and the Rights of the Citizen—And, Finally, to the Constitution of the United States—Now, as heretofore, Integral Portions of Federal Creed.

Now that a party has arisen in our midst, boldly avowing the worst doctrines of the old alien law, and striking down its victims by an illegal secret process, it will serve a good purpose to trace its relationship to the federal sources from which it springs. We cannot better illustrate and establish the parentage of this party than by again taking up the subject upon which we yesterday addressed some observations to the readers of the *Washington Union*. This party is federal in its origin, in its instincts, and its designs; but in nothing can this be more clearly shown than in its relations to the future disposition of the public lands, in its hostility to emigration, in its abolition proclivities, and in its opposition to the erection of new States. General Hayne, of South Carolina, in his great speech in reply to Mr. Webster in 1830, eloquently pointed where the federal party and where the Democratic party respectively stand on the question of the public lands. What was true of both in 1830, is faithfully correct in regard to them in 1855. We copy from that speech as follows:

"When the gentleman refers to the conditions of the grants under which the United States have acquired these lands, and insists that, as they are declared to be 'for the common benefit of all the States,' they can only be treated as so much treasure, I think he has applied a rule of construction too narrow for the case. If, in the deeds of cession, it has been declared that the grants were intended 'for the common benefit of all the States,' it is clear from other provisions that they were not intended as so much property; for it is expressly declared that the object of the grants is to erect new States; and the United States in accepting the trust, bind themselves to facilitate the formation of those States, to be admitted into the Union with all the rights and privileges of the original States. This, sir, was the great end to which all parties looked, and it is by the fulfilment of this high trust that the common benefit of all the States is to be best promoted. Sir, let me tell the gentleman that in the part of the country in which I live we do not measure political benefits by the money standard. We consider, as more valuable than gold, liberty, principle and justice."

This is the Democratic idea. Observe, next, how clearly the old federal idea, often tried, and fatally failing on each successive trial, is given by the same masterly hand:

"The lands are, it seems, to be treated as so much treasure, and must be applied to the common benefit of all the States. Now, if this be so, where does he derive the right to appropriate them for local and partial objects? How can the gentleman consent to vote away immense bodies of the public lands for canals in Indiana and Illinois; to the Louisville and Portland canal; to Kenyon College in Ohio; to schools for deaf and dumb, and other objects of a similar description? * * * * Sir, the true difference between us I take to be this: the gentleman wishes to treat the public lands as a great treasure—just as so much money in the treasury—to be applied to all objects, constitutional and unconstitutional, to which the public money is now constantly applied. I consider it as a sacred trust, which we ought to fulfil on the principles for which I have contended."

What followed all these efforts to convert the proceeds of the sales of the public lands into a common fund for the purpose of bribing local interests and propitiating the electoral votes of certain States for presidential favorites? We had a long procession of expedients to tax the products of labor; a high and exorbitant tariff; a system of internal improvements; and a settled effort, on the part of the federal leaders, to build up a gigantic "national bank," to oppress labor, and to aid the few at the expense of the many. In the meanwhile, the Democratic party, led in that day by such men as Benton, Forsyth, Grundy, and Wright, labored with herculean energy to preserve this fund from the public lands for two great objects: 1st, that by the encouragement of actual settlers new States might be added to our Union; and, 2dly, that our public debt might be extinguished. What American citizen does not, at this day, regard our public lands, and the manner in which, under Democratic auspices, they have been disposed of, with pride? The able Commissioner of the General Land Office, John Wilson, in his last annual report, speaks of the blessings which the present system has conferred upon our country as follows:

"The true policy of the land system is, first, to encourage the actual settlement and improvement of the public domain. This may be done by such amendments to the preemption laws as experience may prove necessary for the purpose, and by which every actual settler may secure his improvements in a reasonable time, without risk of competition from speculators.

"And, second, to aid in providing the necessary facilities for intercommunications, and for the transportation of the products of the lands to market. Although the railroad excitement, in many cases, has been carried to excess, experience has proved that grants for such purposes, when carried out in good faith, are alike beneficial to the people, the States, and the general government.

"To prevent mere speculation, and to secure an equivalent to the government for the lands granted for those purposes, some modifications in the acts making them seem proper—as, for instance, that no grant should be made except on the application of the legislature of a State; that the lands should be taken in alternate sections within a certain distance on each side of the improvement, the minimum price of the remaining sections to be doubled throughout the whole extent of the grant; and the lands to be certified to the States as the work progresses, with a provision of forfeiture in case of failure.

"It is impossible to portray the vast benefits already derived by the West from this system. Immense regions have been disposed of that were thought to be wholly unsalable because of the difficulty of access; and so numerous are the applications for these lands, that in some cases, for want of time, they cannot be acted on for months after they are made."

At this point we come to the efforts now making by the new secret party to arrest emigration from the Old World, by which the wilderness is redeemed to civilization, industry encouraged, the public revenues increased, and the way gradually but surely prepared for the abolition of all indirect taxes in the shape of tariffs upon our people. Defeated before, and with results that we can never too highly appreciate, the federal leaders are now trying to arrest emigration, so that this noble policy may be destroyed. Mr. Benton charged these leaders, twenty-five years ago, with being guilty of the same monstrous offence denounced against the King of England, by the signers of the Declaration of Independence, in the following words:

"He has endeavored to prevent the population of these States, for that purpose obstructing the laws for the naturalization of foreigners; refusing to pass others to encourage their migration hither, and raising the conditions of new appropriations of lands."

His Majesty, the King of England, professed, like the federal leaders of old, and the present secret party under the control of federal and abolition leaders, to be affectionately devoted to this country. He, too, wanted "Americans to rule America," (meaning himself and his mercenaries.) The federalists desired to limit the boundaries of the Union, and the new party toils to effect the same object, even while the whole world acknowledges the wisdom of our policy in regard to the oppressed of other nations, in stopping all emigration to the United States.

Strange, too, that from the very Massachusetts which now sends the rankest enemies of the Union to the Congress of the United States, and the most relentless foes of the adopted citizen, the first voices were raised against the expansion of our beloved Union. John Quincy Adams admitted this in October of 1813, while American minister at the Russian court. Speaking of the growth of western States, and admiring at that distance the sublime spectacle, he exclaims: [How true is this voice of the past in its application to the Massachusetts of 1855!]

"If New England" (says Mr. Adams) "loses her influence in the councils of the Union, it will not be owing to any diminution of her population, owing to these emigrations to the West. It will be from the partial, sectarian, or, as Hamilton called it, clannish spirit, *which makes so many of her political leaders jealous and envious of the South.* This spirit is in its nature narrow and contracted, and it always works by means like itself. Its natural tendency is to excite and provoke a counteracting spirit of the same character; and it has actually produced that effect in our country. It has combined the southern and western portions of the United States, not in a league, but in a concert of political views adverse to those of New England. The fame of all the great legislators of antiquity is founded upon their contrivances to strengthen and multiply the principles of attraction in civil society. Our legislators seem to delight in multiplying and fomenting the principles of repulsion."

The doctrines of Massachusetts abolitionism have, we regret to say, since made rapid progress in those free western States whose progress they so long and so violently resisted. Their avowed hostility to emigration, however, after a long silence on that favorite federal dogma, must show to the West that the "snake is only scotched, not killed;" and that opposition to the rights of the South is now, as ever, closely identified with animosity to the growth of the West.

The same leaders were anxious in 1786, 1787, and 1788 to surrender the navigation of the Mississippi to Spain.

The same federal leaders, in the first ordinance for the sale of the public lands, refused to sell a less quantity than six hundred acres, and also refused to reduce the price for actual settlers.

The course of such men as Josiah Quincy, of Boston, and those who believed in his doctrines, and followed his example in opposing the acquisition of Louisiana, is an event familiar to the youngest readers of political history. The element that controlled them then was hostility to the admission of a flourishing people and a noble region into the Union; and they contended with memorable bitterness against that memorable acquisition. In the midst of the excitement on this question, however, Thomas Jefferson was chosen President. To obtain Louisiana was a matter of the greatest importance, commercially and politically. "The West," says Mr. Benton, "was filling up with people, and covered over with wealth and population. It was no more the feeble settlement which the Congress of the Confederation had seen, and whose rights, few as they were to the free navigation of the Mississippi, had given birth to the most arduous struggle ever seen in Congress. States had superseded these infant settlements. Ohio, Kentucky, and Tennessee had been admitted into the Union; the Territories of Indiana, Illinois, and Mississippi were making their way to the same station. The western settlements of Pennsylvania and Virginia lined the left bank of the Ohio for half the length of its course. All was animated with life, gay with hope, independent in the cultivation of a grateful soil, and rich in the prospect of sending their accumulated products to all the markets of the world, through the great channel that conducted the King of Rivers to the bosom of the ocean. The treaty with Spain had guaranteed this right of passage."

In 1802 this right was violated and New Orleans was suddenly closed against the States and Territories alluded to above, thus producing dismay, disaster, and bankruptcy. Mr. Jefferson took bold and rapid measures to acquire Louisiana. He sent Livingston and Monroe to France to negotiate the purchase; and in the Senate of the United States, on the confirmation of these two distinguished gentlemen, every federal vote from the free States, including nearly all from New England, was cast against them! The result is known, and Louisiana was acquired; but not without a fierce and relentless opposition from the federal leaders in Congress. Massachusetts was the first State to raise its voice against the admission of Louisiana as a State of this Union. We copy the following resolutions, reported to the Massachusetts legislature by Josiah Quincy, Ashmun, and Fuller, on the part of the Senate, and Messrs. Thatcher, Hall, and Bates, on the part of the House, recorded in the Boston Sentinel, June 26, 1813:

"Resolved, (as the sense of this legislature,) That the admission into the Union of States created in countries not comprehended within the original limits of the United States is not authorized by the letter or the spirit of the federal constitution.

"Resolved, That it is the interest and the duty of the people of Massachusetts to oppose the admission of such States into the Union as a measure tending to the dissolution of the Union.

"Resolved, That the act passed the 8th day of April, 1812, entitled 'An act for the admission of Louisiana into the Union, and to extend the laws of the United States to the said State,' is a violation of the constitution of the United States; and that the senators of this State in Congress be instructed, and the representatives be requested, to use the utmost of their endeavors to obtain a repeal of the same."

Without going out of the way to show the advantages to the whole North, of the measures which gave us control of the Mississippi, and of the treaty that gave us Louisiana, and without pointing to the cultivated and liberal States that now occupy the domain thus recovered from a monarchy, the reader of the present day cannot fail to see the analogy between this act of the Boston federalists and their present crusade upon Kansas and Nebraska.

But, as if to show how this ancient hostility to emigration, to the acquisition of territory, to the erection of new States, and to the spread of liberal principles over the continent, sympathizes with the present organized secret warfare upon the adopted citizens, and the hostility to new States, let us present another evidence.

The same Massachusetts, by a vote of 260 to 90, in the house of representatives, sent delegates to the Hartford Convention on the 15th of December, 1814; and the next day, while Jackson was preparing for the battle of New Orleans, with the adopted citizen and the native American by his side, that convention

"Resolved, That the most inviolable secrecy shall be observed by each member of this convention, including the secretary, as to all propositions, debates, and proceedings thereof, until this injunction shall be suspended or altered."

A few days afterwards, on the 24th of December, it was resolved:

"That it is expedient to make provision for restraining Congress in the exercise of an unlimited power to make new States and admit them into the Union."

And on the 29th of December, of the same year, the same convention proposed:

"That the capacity of naturalized citizens to hold offices of trust, honor, or profit, ought to be restrained."

Other movements, and more sectional and treasonable, were advocated, and adopted. But we rest here.

It needs only to complete this convincing record that we should show that the same federalists have continued their war upon emigration, upon the expansion of our country, upon the adopted citizens, and upon the Union of these States, down to this moment of time. They opposed the annexation of Texas and the acquisition of California, and are as ready to denounce the peaceful purchase of Cuba as they were to resist the great triumph that gave us Louisiana. They are organized all over the North to set the laws of Congress at defiance, and rejoice at the success of their fusion with the Know Nothings because it enables them to throw their abolition and disunion disciples into Congress. They are, therefore, united in a persistent war upon the established rights of the South, and in opposing the admission of any more slave States into the Union, even at the risk of a dissolution of the confederacy. Identified with the hostility to the Irish in New York, when the latter would not join in the crusade against Jackson for his war upon the bank; refusing to make good the destruction of a Catholic convent destroyed by a Boston mob; the aiders and the abettors of the nativist movements of 1841 and 1844-45; they are once more in the lead of a secret society, which, like their own Hartford Convention, plots treason against the constitution and the rights of the citizen in the dark, and publicly elevates bold and reckless factionists and demagogues to commanding positions in the national legislature, whence they may scatter fire and death over the South, and hurl anathemas against the rights of conscience.

We have deemed this glance at the history of the past, as contrasted with existing parties and schemes, eminently due to the cause of truth. We commend it to the consideration of the Democratic party of the whole Union. We ask those who have been misled, by the cry of a "new party," into the Know Nothing lodges, to observe how completely they have fallen into the hands of the advocates of those very doctrines against which Jefferson protested, and over which the Democratic party has been gloriously and ultimately victorious ever since the constitution of the United States was accepted as the fundamental law of the American republic.

ONE OF THE VICTORIES OF THE NEW PARTY.

While the Mexican war was at its height, a gentleman at the head of one of the departments under President Polk resigned his commission in the civil service of the country, and was appointed a brigadier general in the American army. He was an Irishman born. He had made a most favorable impression while discharging his official duties in Washington. He was among the very few of our adopted citizens who held prominent position in this country. The State which had presented him to the President as eminently worthy of his confidence, had herself shown her appreciation of his high ability and unexceptionable deportment; and the result proved that her estimate of the man was just. After having served with Generals Taylor and Wool on the other line, he landed with the American army at Vera Cruz under command of Gen. Scott, and was warmly eulogized for his gallantry at the capture of that city and the castle of San Juan de Ulloa, in March of 1847. When Gen. Scott issued his brilliant order (No. 111) of the 17th of April, in which, with almost prophetic inspiration, he sketched the very details of the great victory that awaited him at Cerro Gordo, he selected this brave Irishman as one of the leaders in that eventful struggle. He said:

"The second (Twigg's) division of regulars is already advanced within easy turning distance towards the enemy's left. That division has instructions to move forward before daylight to-morrow, and take up position across the national road in the enemy's rear, so as to cut off a retreat towards Jalapa. It may be reinforced to-day, if unexpectly attacked in force, by regiments—one or two—taken from Shields' brigade of volunteers. If not, the two volunteer regiments will march for that purpose at daylight to-morrow morning, under Brigadier General Shields, who will report to Brigadier General Twiggs, on getting up with him, or to the general-in-chief if he be in advance."

This order was executed to the letter. The party under Twiggs and Shields were the advance party; but while leading his troops to the conflict, under the heavy fire of the enemy, General Shields fell, as it was supposed, mortally wounded.

"Brigadier General Shields, (says General Scott, in his report of the day's operations,) a commander of activity, zeal, and talent, is, I fear, mortally wounded.

And again, the commander says, in another report:

"The brigade so gallantly led by General Shields, and, after his fall, by Colonel Baker, deserves high commendation for its fine behavior and success."

General Twiggs said: "Of the conduct of the volunteer force under the brave General Shields, I cannot speak in two high terms."

General Patterson united in these strong commendations of the courageous general. And the whole country soon responded to the sympathy and solicitude which his dreadful wounds and his noble bearing had secured for him in the American army.

The Illinois general slowly recovered, however. His escape from death was miraculous, and we shall never forget how the intelligence of his restoration to health thrilled the American people.

The next great battles were those of Contreras and Churubusco. Here we find the gallant Shields once more ready for action, though still weak and suffering from his wounds. It is remarkable that, after having been carried in an ambulance from Jalapa to Puebla, bleeding and suffering from his wounds, he insisted upon going into the fight, and did so, when so weak and wasted that his physicians declared it impossible for him to survive? Again General Scott paid him the highest compliments for his skill and daring in fulfilling his orders. This was on the 19th of August, 1847.

On the 28th of the same month, General Scott once more reports to the Secretary of War—and this time he writes "from the gates of Mexico." What does he say of Shields? We copy from his despatch:

"Shields, the senior officer of the hamlet, after Smith had arranged with Cadwalader and Riley the plan of attack for the morning, delicately waived interference; but reserved to himself the double task of holding the hamlet with his two regiments, (South Carolina and New York,) against ten times his numbers on the side of the city, including the slopes to his left, and, in case the camp in his rear should be carried, to face about and cut off the flying enemy."

And again, speaking of the grand finale of that day, Gen. Scott says:

"Shields, too, by the wise disposition of his brigade, and his gallant activity, contributed much to the general results. He held masses of cavalry and infantry, supported by artillery, in check below him, and captured hundreds, with one general, (Mendoza,) of those who fled from above."

Referring to the fifth victory of that glorious day, Gen. Scott says:

"It has been stated that some two hours and a half before Pierce's brigade, followed closely after the volunteer brigade, both under the command of Brigadier General Shields, had been detached to our left to turn the enemy's works, to prevent the escape of the garrisons, and to oppose the extension of the enemy's numerous corps from the rear, upon and around our left.

"In a winding march around to the right this temporary division found itself on the edge of an open, wet meadow, and in the presence of some 4,000 of the enemy's infantry, a little in the rear of Churubusco, on that road. Establishing the right at a strong building, Shields extended his left parallel to the road to outflank the enemy towards the capital. But the enemy extending his right, supported by three thousand cavalry, more rapidly (being favored by better ground) in the same direction, Shields concentrated the division about a hamlet, and determined to attack in front. The battle was long, hot, and varied, but ultimately success crowned the zeal and gallantry of our troops, led by their distinguished commander, Brigadier General Shields. Shields took 300 prisoners, including officers."

General Worth spoke highly of the gallant bearing of Pillow, Shields, Cadwalader, and Pierce in this fierce engagement. His praises were re-echoed by Generals Twiggs and Smith. General Shields, in his own report, which is a model of its kind, presents a graphic and beautiful sketch of the battle.

But we find General Shields in the last, as in the first, conflict. In the terrible attack upon the city of Mexico he was in the advance with the veteran Quitman and the accomplished Persifer F. Smith. General Scott refers to him warmly, and says, in one part of his report of the battle, "General Quitman, being in hot pursuit—gallant himself, and ably supported by Generals Shields and Smith—Shields badly wounded before Chepultepec and refusing to retire," &c.

General Quitman writes: "In directing the advance, Brigadier General Shields was badly wounded in the arm. No persuasions, however, could induce that officer to leave his command and quit the field." And again: "Until carried from the field on the night of the 13th, in consequence of the severe wound received in the morning, he was conspicuous for his gallantry, energy, and skill."

SPEECH OF MR. RUFFIN.

The speech of Mr. Thomas Ruffin of North Carolina was used with great effect in the Virginia canvass, and doubtless in every Southern State, in the conflicts of the Democracy with Know Nothingism. Its distinguished ability eminently entitles it to a place in this compilation:

Speech of Hon. Thos. Ruffin, of North Carolina, Delivered in the House of Representatives, February 27, 1855.

[The House being in Committee of the Whole on the state of the Union.]

Mr. Ruffin. Mr. Chairman, I rise in my place for the first time since I have had a seat upon this floor, with the view of submitting a few remarks. I do not propose to discuss the question immediately before the Committee, and shall avail myself of the privilege now accorded me, to consider another question. Since I have been a member of this House, it has acted upon many important questions. Being loth to trespass upon the time of the House, I have contented myself by giving a silent vote upon all of them. These were questions which had heretofore entered, more or less, into the political discussions of our country, and upon them my opinions were not unknown to my constituents. Since the commencement of the present session of Congress we have heard discussions in this Hall upon questions which were thought to have been settled long ago. I allude more particularly to those great questions of religious toleration and naturalization.

I had thought that the question of religious toleration was settled by the Constitution of the country, and that American citizens had always proudly boasted that here, every man had the right to worship Almighty God according to the dictates of his own conscience, and that this right was not only guaranteed by the fundamental law of the land, but was regarded as inherent and inalienable.

And, Mr. Chairman, I had thought that the naturalization laws, passed under the administration of Jefferson, amended and perfected by subsequent legislation, had given general satisfaction to the country, with the exception of a small faction. Throughout the country, discussion on these questions has been revived of late.

To keep pace with the spirit of the times, early in the present session honorable gentlemen were struggling to get the floor to bring them before the House for its consideration.

The honorable gentleman from Tennessee (Mr. Taylor), more fortunate than his competitors, succeded in his efforts, and, having obtained the floor, introduced a bill proposing an alteration of the naturalization laws.

Sir, that gentleman is responsible for the introduction of the subject here, or if he prefers it, he is entitled to the distinguished honor of having been the first to introduce this measure into the House at the present session of Congress.

And again, Sir, not long since a series of resolutions embodying certain principles in relation to these questions was offered by the honorable gentleman from Pennsylvania, (Mr. Witte). I was called upon to vote for the suspension of the rules to enable the House to consider those resolutions, and it is not out of place here that I should give the reasons which influenced me in giving the vote which I gave on that occasion. These are generally known as the anti-Know Nothing resolutions.

I can conceive of no evil, either real or imaginary, existing or supposed to exist in this country, which will justify American freemen in the formation of secret oath-bound political societies. They may do for the despotism of Russia; they may do for Austria; but there can certainly be no necessity for such in our land.

No, sir, in our country where every man has the right to speak, print, and publish whatever he may see fit, only being liable for the abuse of that privilege, and where, to use the language of an old revolutionary writer, "The press glows with freedom's sacred zeal,"—here, sir, there can be no necessity for resorting to institutions of this kind with a view of controlling the legislation of the country. Those who framed our government wisely provided the means of altering such laws as needed amendment. They are open to repeal, or alteration; but, sir, this can be done through the ballot-box in the sunlight of broad day. Our institutions depend for their success on the virtue, intelligence, and patriotism of the people; and when the time comes in which they will desert the usual mode, do away with the open action of day and resort to these secret cabals to influence the legislation of the country, then, in my opinion, the days of the republic are numbered. He has read history with but little profit, who has not observed that in every country where the people have lost their liberties they have brought such misfortune upon themselves. When they have become demoralized and ready for a change, then the turmoil of the times has given birth to some adventurer who boldly usurps their liberties, assumes the management of their affairs, and concentrates all political power in himself. Learning lessons of wisdom from the records of the past, let us strive to escape the calamities that have befallen other republican governments.

What master spirit devised this organization? I do not know that this is a question of any great importance. I do not think that the author is entitled to any great credit for originality, I do not undertake to say whether it is taken from the forms and ceremonies adopted by Catiline and his co-conspiritors at Rome, or whether it is like unto the societies formed in certain districts of England to protect labor against capital, or whether, as seems most probable, it has for its prototype the order of religious Jesuits, as depicted in the "Wandering Jew," and that the federal treasury is the Renepont inheritance, which it is using its appliances and secret machinery to get possession of.

I was forcibly struck with the similarity between the two orders, the religious Jesuits and the Know Nothings, in the speech of the honorable gentleman from Alabama (Mr. Smith), and I am sorry that he is not present this evening. From his graphic description in his defence of the Know Nothing order, we see that it makes use of the same appliances to accomplish its objects as the religious Jesuits which order he set out to denounce. In one portion of his speech, he says, that the Know Nothings are formed for the purpose of making war against the religious Jesuits. Both seemed to be the same in organization. Each is after power and spoils. Each is enshrouded in the garb of mystery.

One hides its iniquities under the cloak of religion; the other under a most exalted devotion to country. Each teaches the practice of falsehood, craft, and deceit. Each binds its members by a mighty oath, the violation of which they assume to punish. The one claims devout piety, the other intense patriotism.

The gentleman from Alabama says, that "when you fight the devil you have the right to fight him with fire." That seems to be in fact an acknowledgment on his part that the new order was taken from the other one. But will this principle hold good? Fight the devil with fire—perpetrate an evil to obviate the consequences of another one—commit one fraud to nullify another? The gentleman is a distinguished lawyer and I would ask him whether he would consider it right to meet a forged bond with a forged release? The principle is the same. That was said to have been a practice at one time quite common among the British lawyers in the East Indies. It has never been introduced into this country and I trust that it never will be. It is unsound in morals. It is a sentiment unfit to be proclaimed in the presence of the representatives of the people here in this Hall.

He also says in the course of his speech that these religious Jesuits were organized by thwarted military aspirants after the reformation. I would ask whether this order of political Jesuits, of which the gentleman is champion upon this floor, was not organized after the great political revolution which swept federalism out of power in 1852. Until this power was ground down, until Democracy was in the ascendancy, we never heard of any such order as this.

But to go on with the simile. The Gentleman says, that these religious Jesuits were taught to ingratiate themselves into the confidence of men of power and influence, or, to use his own language, "to cultivate their friendship, probe their designs, and communicate their secrets." How stands the order that he defends? Is it not well known to Gentlemen on this floor who were candidates in the late elections for Congress, that these Know Nothings formed this plan; pretended to be their friends, went into convention pretending to be Democrats, assisted in making the nominations, drew their secrets and all their plans from them, obtained all the information they could from them, and after night-fall skulked into the Know Nothing lodges and communicated those secrets! This is a notorious fact and cannot be denied. I say, that it is beneath the dignity of American gentlemen and honorable men to resort to such means in midnight lodges for any purpose. Do we not know that they make it a boast in Pennsylvania that in the Gubernatorial election there, they took the distinguished Democratic candidate, Governor Bigler, from one county to another, and his pretended friends of one lodge handed him over (if I may use the expression) to the tender care of his professed friends of another lodge who would take him in special charge, and in the language of the Gentleman from Alabama, "cultivate his friendship, probe his designs, and communicate his secrets." Sir, this indicated a degree of proficiency in Jesuitism that would have gladdened the heart and raised a ghastly smile even on the countenance of old Rodin himself. [Laughter.]

The Gentleman from Alabama justifies the oath of this order, and says, that it finds its justification in the practices of its adversaries. Is not that sound doctrine to hold forth in an American Congress? Finds its justification in the practices of its adversaries! The religious Jesuits are the adversaries he speaks of.

The Gentleman says also, that "an oath solemnly taken is an element of purity." Well, Sir, if a solemn oath was what they sought for, this order should not have stopped at the oath of the Jesuits, but gone a few centuries further back and adopted the oath which Cataline administered to his co-conspirators when they met in the back-room of the house of one Sempronia, a Roman bawd—in a place, as the historian says, every way suited for the purpose, and well adapted to their occult and dark practices, for there, after administering a mighty oath, just as the Know Nothings administer it, they sealed that oath by drinking from bowls, draughts of wine mingled with human blood! Was that an element of purity? Did that oath make them pure? Why, Sir, if the history of those times are correct, they were men of desperate fortunes and abandoned characters—men dangling loose upon society, who were ready for any change of affairs that promised to benefit themselves.

Then, Sir, the Gentleman says that secrecy is the great element of success, and that the "Order should preserve in their halls the most inviolable secrecy," all the time acting upon the old doctrine that the end will justify the means. Now, Sir, if this is not Jesuitism, I do not understand what is the meaning of the term. But the Gentleman says that it finds its great justification of secrecy in the fact that it is warring against Jesuits. Warring against Jesuits! If the religious Jesuits are what the Gentleman represents them to be, and if these political Jesuits of Know Nothingism are what I believe them to be, I Sir, should look upon a contest between them with perfect indifference. I would look upon it as American citizens now generally look upon the war going on between Russia and England, or as a Western hunter would look upon a fight between a bear and an alligator, or a mink and a polecat. [Much Laughter.] Every objection that the Gentleman has urged against the Jesuits seems to apply with equal force to the Know Nothings. They are neither of them suited to our country and they cannot flourish here. One is the counterpart of the other, and Sir, as my friend from the Red River district of Louisiana, (Mr. Roland Jones) says, that the men of my State are fond of making quotations from Hudibras, let me say to the Gentleman from Alabama, of the Know Nothings and Jesuits, that:

"They are so near akin,
And like in all as well as sin,
That put them in a bag and shake 'em,
Himself on the sudden would mistake 'em,
And not know which was which, unless
He measured by their wickedness." [Laughter.]

Who set on foot the organization in the United States? We first find it springing up in the North, in the old hot-bed of federalism. It had been conquered under every name by the Democratic party. It was the old Federal party and was conquered under that name. It assumed the name of National Republican, then Whig, and then degenerated into isms. The Whig party had become almost extinct at the North. There was in fact but one party there and that was the Democratic party. All the others were but isms.

Mr. Washburne, of Illinois. Will the Gentleman tell me in which State at the North the Democratic party now exist?

Mr. Ruffin. I think it does in Illinois, judging from the late election there. [Laughter.]

Mr. Washburne. I suppose the Gentleman refers to the election of an anti-Nebraska Senator. [Renewed laughter.]

Mr. Ruffin. No, Sir, I do not, but I will come to his election by and by.

Mr. Florence. I will say to the Gentleman, that it exists in Pennsylvania, thank God!—"its banner torn but flying." [Great Laughter.]

Mr. Washburne. In what part of Pennsylvania?

Mr. Florence. In the First Congressional District. [Renewed laughter.] That will do. Now let the Gentleman from N. C. go on.

Mr. Ruffin. The Democratic party being triumphant at the North, there was a fusion of all the isms to oppose it. This organization sprang up. It offered great inducements. There were a host of old political hacks out of office, men who had lived all their lives out of the public crib. They had then nothing to resort to. The Democratic party was in power in the general government and at that time, in most of the States, and these old political hacks, who were wandering about like stray spirits on the Stygian banks, thought it a fine chance to join in a new venture, and they joined this organization. I say, Sir, that it is taken from the old Federal party. That party has never been eradicated at the North. It is true, the old tree of federalism is dead, its leaves have long since withered and been wafted away upon the winds of Heaven, its boughs have crumbled and fallen, and its aged trunk lying prostrate has mouldered into dust, but from its prolific roots has sprung up this bastard slip of Know Nothingism. It has incorporated into its platform, planks from that old party.

Mr. Campbell. Amen! [Laughter.]

Mr. Ruffin. Anti-naturalization! Where is that taken from? It is a plank of the black cockade federalism of the days of the elder Adams, and the order finds a bright example of secrecy in the blue-light federalists who met in the Hartford Convention to plot treason against the Government.

It has flourished in that section of country fruitful in isms, in abolitionism, freesoilism, atheism, women's-rightism and every other ism imaginable. These, Sir, have given it its strength there, in that section of our country where men meet together in convention and declare "there is no God;" where agrarian mobs, the very scum of the earth, parade the streets by thousands, recognizing no distiction between *meum* and *tuum*, and crying aloud for a division of property. In that section of country where weak-minded men, crazy fanatics, meet in convention with strong-minded women clothed in boots and breeches, to discuss the important question of women's rights. [Laughter.]

Inaugurated under these auspices, how can it be conservative? Sir, the idea is preposterous. It professes now to be the only true National Conservative Union party—whereas it is a sectional radical destructive party. It is an abolition, disunion scheme, and in every step, its progress gives unerring indication of a settled purpose to sever asunder the ties which bind these States together.

It has given strength to the abolitionists of the North, and now it has the unblushing effrontery and daring impudence to offer itself to the South as something which is conservative, something which is designed to place in their hands and the hands of their friends, the power of the General and State Governments. Sir, I for one, never had any confidence in it from the beginning, for it came from the wrong quarter.

"Timao Danaos et dona ferentes."

I was satisfied that within the cavity of that wooden horse were concealed the elements of abolitionism. It was absurd to believe that the abolitionists of the North, when they had for years and years in their weakness, waged an offensive war against the South, would now in the pride of their strength—after their shattered ranks had been recruited by untold thousands, after the embattled hosts of Know Nothingism had flocked to their standards, not in straggling parties like deserters, but in solid column with flags flying and drums beating—be so magnanimous as to raise the long siege, and celebrate it with a peace offering. I for one, Sir, as a Southern man, cannot trust it. Was I not right, Sir, in my opinion at that time? I say that I was. Recent developments have proved this beyond all doubt. The Know Nothing party of the North has never aided in the election of a single friend of the Nebraska bill to either House of the Congress of the United States. I again assert that it has not. I challenge successful contradiction from any quarter and pause for a reply. They have elected no man who is willing to give the South the rights guaranteed to it by the Constitution of the United States. Maine, Pennsylvania, New York, Ohio, Indiana, Iowa and Wisconsin have returned to this House men who are pledged to vote for the repeal of the Fugitive Slave Law which we regard as the very bond which binds the Union together. In the above named States it has aided abolition in striking down the true friends of the Constitution, and filling their places with a dangerous class of politicians.

Let us see what a Northern Editor says about its doings in the North :

"But if we lacked positive proof of the feelings of the masses of the party in regard to slavery, the late elections in this and other States of the Union show the liberal tendencies of the whole party. In New York the American party polled 122,000 votes, but they aided the anti-Nebraska party in that State in returning to the next Congress twenty-nine men opposed to the admission of slavery into Kansas. In Pennsylvania we saw a like result; while in Illinois, by the aid of this movement, the Douglasites were completely routed ; and so in Michigan, where the whole State was carried for freedom by the council fires of the American party."

But Sir, we are sometimes pointed by Southern Know Nothings to the Massachusetts election, and gravely told that the Know Nothings in that State have sent a new delegation to Congress with but two exceptions. I am not aware of any alteration in this respect so far as liberality and nationality are concerned. No Sir, these Yankees of Massachusetts are cunning men and they followed the example of the skilful huntsman who, when his hounds are flagging in the chase blows them off, lets slip the leashes and hies on a fresh pack, the more speedily to hunt down his prey. The people of Massachusetts no doubt thought that their representatives here, being removed from the fanaticism which surrounds them at home, had become less zealous and were rather flagging in the chase, and therefore considered it better to send on a new set. [Laughter.]

But, Sir, if any body has doubted this abolition sentiment of Know Nothingism, let us look at the recent elections carried by these Know Nothings. Look at the men elected by them,—Harlan, the fusionist in Iowa. Trumbull, the man of "isms," in Illinois, over the gallant Shields, whose body is scarred with wounds received in defence of the flag of his adopted country. Durkee, the Abolition agrarian in Wisconsin. Wilson, the embodiment of rampant freesoilism in Massachusetts, the latter elected by a Legislature in which there was but one Democrat, and—it is said—but some five or six old line Whigs. Are the Know Nothings not responsible for the election of these men ? Are they not responsible for the election of this Mr. Wilson to the Senate of the United States ? Yet another election ! that of Seward, the "Jupiter Tonans" of abolition, the "higher law" Senator, who, in the intensity of his hatred of the South, stands a head and shoulders above them all. The Know Nothings had made a boast that they would defeat him,—that they would show their nationality in that election,—that they were going to take the arch-agitator from the Senate of the United States, and put a conservative in his place. That election was looked to with probably more interest than any Senatorial election ever held in any of the States of this Union. We all recollect Tuesday, the 6th of February,—I believe that was the day. It was at all events a dark and gloomy day. It was known that the election for United States Senator from New York was to be held that day in Albany. The hour had arrived. The telegraphic office in this capital was, on that occasion, an interesting place. Numbers of politicians might be seen wending their way there—your Southern Know Nothings and your Northern Know Nothings. They were there about the time when they expected the announcement to come. They were watching with straining eyes, and palpitating hearts, and half-suppressed respiration. The mystic wire is watched with the fixed gaze of intense anxiety. A message comes rushing upon the wings of the lightning. The suspense is but short. "The sybil speaks, the dream is o'er." The dispatch is read. It was a sweet morsel to your freesoil Know Nothings. They hearkened to it as the prodigal son to his father's testament. They gulped it down with all imaginable avidity. It was as sweet to them as the manna from Heaven to the hungry Israelites in the wilderness. But how was it to the Southern Know Nothings? Ah! it was a bitter pill for them. They had to swallow it down, but oh! what rueful grimaces and contortions of countenance, it was like gall and wormwood to a sick and fainting girl.

Now, Sir, let us see what is thought of him as a national man in the North. I read an extract from one of the New York Journals. I do not know whether it is Know Nothing or not, but I suppose it is, at all events it was, allied with them in the grand contest.

Speaking of the Senator from New York, it says:

"He has pressed with equal ardor the claims of Commerce, Agriculture and Manufactures—he has vindicated with equal zeal, the just rights and interests of the West and South, and those of the East and of the North. There is not at this day, in the Senate or in public life, a statesman of more ability—more laborious and conscientious in his discharge of public duties, or more thoroughly and truly national in all his views, than Governor Seward."

And again, what a Know Nothing Journal means by conservatism:

"The slavery question cannot affect the American party, for its whole power and all its hopes are north of Mason and Dixon's line. Its aspirations are for freedom, and when the party is accused of being pro-slavery, let its defenders point the men who utter the base lie to every election that has occurred since the party sprung into existence."

Also, what is meant by "ignoring slavery."

"The party never has, and we hope never will, fulminate anti-slavery resolves for the purpose of humbugging the masses, but it will do right, move right, and act right, and in every free State in the Union it will give new protection to every citizen within its borders. Its first great national aim is to procure an alteration of the naturalization laws, and upon that point they will know no sectional division; but upon the great question of freedom and slavery, every northern American freeman will raise his voice for liberty, and Banks, DeWitt, and Trafton will utter upon the floor of Congress the sentiments of this new party. That foreign element that has given the pro-slavery Democratic party the control of this country will soon lose the means of augmenting its numbers; and when that is effected, freedom in this republic is secure. The prize we are battling for is 'liberty to all;' and when Americans rule America we shall obtain it, and not till then."

Thus we learn what is meant by their "ad captandum" expressions—conservative indeed! "lucus a non lucendo" called conservative for the same reason that a certain mythological character was called Midas, from a Greek word meaning to eat, because he could not eat. What can Southern men promise themselves by affiliating with this "Order?" If the people of the South act with their usual foresight, they will fly from it as from a raging pestilence, and shun a "Know Nothing" lodge room as they would the charnel-house of a small-pox hospital.

I have thought from the beginning of this new movement that it was an emanation from the filth and corruption of rotten and festering isms, and that it was a mere *ignis fatuus*, fetid miasma springing up from moral and political decay, corruscating and shining in the darkest hour of night, but disappearing before the light of morn. It is not to be expected that the people of the South are to be blinded and led by this jack with a lantern into the bogs and marshes of Abolitionism; nor will they follow Sam with his dark lantern into the midnight conclave of the Know Nothings. But they tell us that these men are native Americans, and that we are not to suspect them. Is it not true that much the larger portion of the Abolitionists of this country are native-born Americans. Some of the leading spirits who figure in this Know Nothing party are foreigners, although the party itself profess such a holy horror for all foreigners. The Crusader, a Know Nothing paper at New York, is edited by one Caselli, and has for its chief contributor Father Gavazzi. It would require but little credulity for one to infer from the columns of the New York Herald, that a leading spirit in the councils of the order might be found in its editor. Bennett, an unnaturalized foreigner, and a political Ishmaelite, whose hand has been against every man, and every man's hand against him, has probably done more towards furthering the progress of this order than any man in the United States. History will record two remarkable things of this order, one is that professing to be composed entirely of native Americans, its chief pillars of support are foreigners; and the other is, that it is a society of political Jesuits, professedly formed for the purpose of waging war against religious Jesuits.

The friends of the "order" say that it is necessary to establish their secret societies to protect ourselves against foreign influence. In the section of the country in which I live, we have none of this foreign influence, and we are not troubled with anything of the kind. What foreigners we have among us are generally intelligent and educated people, men of character, and I suppose one reason of it is owing to the fact of the existence of the "peculiar institution" among us which I regard as one of the greatest moral, social and political blessings that was ever vouchsafed to man, and another reason is owing to the fact that we have not encouraged these men to come as they have in some of the Northern States where they are now complaining of them so much. Why do we not know that two or three years ago the people of some of the Northern cities regarded foreign fiddlers and show girls as beings worthy of adoration, almost of worship; then coming from the other side of the Atlantic was of itself a certain passport to the highest honors.

We all recollect with what exultation it was heralded through the land when the "Swedish Nightingale" touched the American shores. No one has forgotten the grand demonstration that was made in the great commercial emporium of New York, when the literati, the elite, aristocracy and upper tendom of of that city flocked in her train in greater numbers than ever the Pagans followed after the car of Juggernaut. It was but a few years ago that they introduced at the North, a member of the British Parliament, to lecture upon the subject of abolitionism. The people of the North are alone responsible for the introduction into the country of that class of turbulent and vicious foreigners, of whom they now complain so loudly.

Here I will say, that I am as much opposed as any man can be to the introduction into this country of the vagabonds, felons, paupers, and convicts of the Old World. I say, let the government pass such laws as it has authority and power to do under the constitution, let the States and your municipal corporations, pass such laws as they please, to suppress the introduction of this class of foreigners; but do not persecute the well-disposed foreigners on this account. You will find it no easy matter to stop the importation of convicts and paupers, and when you try it you will ascertain that it will be something like the slave trade. Mercenary men will fit out vessels in the port of New York to bring convicts and paupers of Europe to this country, as they now fit out slavers to sail to the coast of Africa to get slaves for the markets of Brazil and Cuba. I do not care what kind of laws you pass against the importation of felons and convicts, you will find Yankee captains visiting the ports of Europe, and having their agents in its cities to contract secretly with the public authorities to rid them of their convicts and vagabonds by bringing them to our seaports—the more risk the higher will be the price of passage, and a brisk trade will soon be "opened up" by these enterprising men. You may have laws upon your statute books, for punishing in the severest manner those who engage in the importation of foreign criminals. You may for what I care, if you can find warrant for it in the constitution, put this importation of felons on the same footing with piracy—you may take the vessels of the navy and scour the high seas in search of the violators of the law—you may, whenever you find a "live cargo" of criminals on board a ship, string up your Yankee skipper to the yard-arm, and pitch his body to the fishes of the sea. Even then, sir, I fear it will be difficult to stop the importation. Sir, there are now men at the North who have grown rich by the importation of this class of foreigners. Punish those who engage in it. Do not adopt the plan recently proposed by the philosopher, Horace Greely. That amounts in substance to reducing the poorer class of foreigners to slavery, and if it is carried out, New York will become a great slave market—white men will be sold at the block.

I am opposed to making slaves out of any class of white men on earth. I know of no good reason for prohibiting the immigration of well-disposed foreigners to this country, to assist in developing its resources. A large portion of the foreigners in the West are German farmers, and they are known to be good citizens. I for one, can see no reason why an orderly and well-disposed class of our population should be persecuted because mercenary men in the commercial cities will violate the rules of decency and propriety by bringing a different class of foreigners here. Enforce your naturalization laws. We hear a great deal said about its having been always customary to naturalize any man who desired to be naturalized. In that part of the Union in which I reside, I rejoice to say that the naturalization laws of the Federal Government are enforced to the very letter—just as strictly as any law we have upon the statute book of our State. If you will impeach your judges when they violate their duty, and make them enforce the law, we can then have none but a good class of naturalized citizens, and no man unless he proves a good character, and is well disposed to our institutions, &c. can get his naturalization papers. I do not understand this sudden change of opinion in regard to foreigners. Twelve months ago the case of Martin Kostza was before this House, and gentlemen then seemed to be exceedingly anxious to curry favor with foreigners. Why this sudden change? Is it because military companies composed of naturalized citizens stood in serried ranks in Boston, to maintain the laws, and protect the officers of the Government in the discharge of their duties, when a Southern man was there seeking to claim his property under the Constitution? Is it because these naturalized Irishmen prevented a blood-thirsty mob of native-born traitors from rescuing a fugitive slave? Is it because Bachelder who was assassinated by that mob was a native of Ireland?

Yes, Sir, because these men kept off abolition traitors, we hear this cry against them, the fact is notorious that one of the first act of the Know-Nothing Governor of Massachusetts was to disband their military companies. I suppose another reason for the outcry against foreigners is because they generally vote the Democratic ticket. In the last presidential canvass the Whig candidate proclaimed a new principle on this subject. He was for admitting to the rights of citizenship all who had served in the army for a certain length of time, and but a short time at that. The Whigs then said he was right—they then said that service for a few months in camp—(the last place to learn the operation of our institutions)—should entitle a foreigner to citizenship. Such of them as have joined this "new movement" now say let no one who is born abroad ever be naturalized.

Yes, Sir, it is because they cannot get the sturdy Germans and generous Irish to sing the peans of federalism that they are prejudiced against them. The ways of federalism are the ways of inconsistency; before an important election it has a high appreciation of adopted citizens—it is then greatly fascinated with the "rich Irish brogue, and the sweet German accent," but the election over, and how is it then? Why, Paddy becomes a "splay-footed Irish bog-trotter," and Hans a "damned lop-eared Dutchman." [Laughter.] Why are efforts now made to raise a party opposed to religious toleration.

And here again I must be permitted to say that I have no relation or connection, so far as I know, either among the living or the dead, who ever was a member of any Catholic church, and while I yield to no man in the ardent and sincere hope that the day will come when the Protestant religion shall have its churches and altars in every part of the Globe; yet, Sir, I do not believe that either the fostering hand of the government or a persecution of other churches would expedite its onward progress. I never will join in persecuting any man for his religious opinions. That is a matter between him and his God. In the part of the country in which I live, and I dare say, in the whole State which I have the honor in part to represent, there is not a master who would dictate to his slave the manner in which he shall worship God, or the church to which he shall belong. This new fangled doctrine of the Know-Nothings to hunt down men on account of their religious opinions is a monstrous proposition. It is at utter variance with the whole spirit of our government.

And where did this proscription against the Catholic religion originate? It originated in the same section of the country, at the North, where those three thousand and fifty abolition clergymen got up a traitorous petition to the Congress of the United States. No Catholics joined them. No Catholic signed that petition. But, Sir, this seems to be an effort either to make them join the abolition party, and engage in an abolition crusade against the South, or that they will drive them from the country by persecution. Opposition to this religion is held out to us of the South as the reason why we should join this "Know-Nothing" order. As the Catholics do not wage a war against us, I, for one, am opposed to waging war against them. As long as they obey the Constitution and the laws, their rights should be respected by every man. It is a deep laid scheme, all these ghost tales, cock-and-bull stories, and old wives' fables about the Jesuits and Catholics of the United States. All designed to operate on the prejudices of the people. They expect them to operate as a charm upon the South, and in that way to throw us off our guard. We have much stronger reasons for apprehending danger from the machinations of the 3050 wooly-headed abolition clergymen who with the wierd sanctity of bigotry and fanaticism are disseminating treason from their pulpits, than from the tiara that encircles the brow of the feeble and harmless old man at Rome, thousands and thousands of leagues by land and sea, far, far away from our shores.

But, Sir, in this connexion let us see what is going on in New England—a newspaper has this advertisement:

"SLAVERY AND POPERY.—Rev. Thomas James, a fugitive slave, will address the citizens of various towns upon Slavery and Popery, and show their bearing on the nation."

And then follows a list of appointments. If a Southern minister should desire to preach from one of their pulpits the privilege would be denied him, yet this negro can use them.

I have seen it stated frequently in the papers, that in the great State of New York, free negroes had actually formed "Know-Nothing" lodges. This is the conservative party which the people of the South are invited to join, so as to wage war against the Pope. Sir, we have enemies a plenty at our own doors without looking across the waters to find others. How is it proposed to sustain the Know Nothing party? By boasting and threats. The gentleman from Maryland (Mr. Sollers) would have us believe that this party is one of gigantic power, and that he who has any hopes of a political future should not be so rash as to combat it. He says "it has gone sweeping like a whirlwind" and "annihilating all its opponents." He appeals to the fears of gentlemen, and talks to them of political graves—let him take heed lest when looking around for burial places for others, he shall himself be consigned to a political grave as deep as the "gloom where dreary chaos reigns" and where he may be even beyond the reach of that politico geological explorer of whom he spoke, who at some future day is to search for the opponents of Know Nothingism among the fossil remains of an extinct race. I, Sir, tender my thanks to the eloquent gentlemen from Mississippi and South Carolina (Mr. Barry and Mr. Keit) for their exposition of the objects and aims of the Know Nothings, and for their moral courage in being first on this floor to assail the principles of this new order—with keen blades and stalwart blows they shivered into fragments the crazy mail that but feebly protected this staggering carcass of galvanized federalism, and exhibited it in its nakedness and hideous deformity to the gaze of the world. The order had not then so fully developed its anti-slavery sentiment. The gentleman clamed for it "*intense nationalty.*" We were to hear no more of the invasion of Southern rights, if they dared make the attempt he himself would meet his Northern friends at Mason & Dixon's line, not as brothers but with "banner, brand and bow." Let him adhere to this determination when the rights of the South are invaded—let him be prepared to defend them—when the Scotts cross the border line, let him as a true knight, wind the cornage horn.

Know Nothingism professes to be eminently patriotic, struggling for the common weal, not for office. Well, Mr. Chairman, why is it, that wherever they have reached power they have proscribed all, from the highest officials even down to the hog constables of the little towns. Anticipating a majority in the next House of Representatives, there are already hosts of applicants for the places within its gift. Yes sir, if all the men who aspire to these offices were formed into regiments and drilled for a few weeks, General Scott could take them to the Crimea and carry Sebastopol by storm.

They are looking after all the places, from the Speaker's chair down to the humble office held by the sable high priest who ministers at the altars of the temple of Cloasina in the basement of this Capitol. (Laughter.)

Look at their election in this city? It was an extraordinary affair. They seemed to be after the Exchequer, the first thing, like Sir John Falstaff. They desired to get the control of the funds of the Washington National Monument. They banded together in this capital and proscribed such men as General Winfield Scott, Mr. Seaton, Gen. Jones, Elisha Whittlesay and others, to make room for such renowned and august individuals as Vespasian Ellis, French S. Evans, "et id omne genus."

Yes sir, General Scott was proscribed—the eagle was stricken from his eyre to put the mousing owl there. This plot is said to have been concocted at the National Council of Know Nothings held at Cincinnati. What right had these intolerant proscriptionists to take in charge the Monument to Washington? Let his own words rebuke them. I read from a letter written by the Father of his country to a committee of the Baptist church of Va., after paying a high and just compliment to the Baptist for their patriotism and liberality, he says:

"If I could have entertained the slightest apprehension that the Constitution framed in the convention where I had the honor to preside might possibly endanger the religious rights of any ecclesiastical society, certainly I would never have placed my signature to it; and if I could now conceive that the General Government might ever be so administered as to render the liberty of conscience insecure, I beg you will be persuaded that no one would be more zealous than myself to establish effectual barriers against the horrors of spiritual tyranny and every species of religious persecution; for you doubtless remember I have often expressed my sentiments that every man, conducting himself as a good citizen, and being accountable to God alone for his religious opinions, ought to be protected in worshipping the Deity according to the dictates of his own conscience."

Mr. Chairman. I have heard many strange sentiments expressed in this hall, but there was one uttered by the gentleman from Mass. (Mr. Banks) which for boldness and originality, surpasses all others. After speaking of the power, the secret plans, the covered cavernous ways of the order, he says—

"Sir, it is the people who are passing through these avenues, those who make judges and district attorneys, and they will take care of them all. They will take care of the juries and sheriff's as well as judges."

The startling announcement has been made by a representative on the floor of the American Congress, that this secret order is to take charge of the judges and juries of the country. Yes sir, it is to lay its ruthless hand upon the judicial ermine. When that is done, our laws will not be worth the paper on which they are written. If the judges of the courts are to be overawed by the combinations and machinations of midnight conspirators, what becomes of our individual safety? Is such an association fit for American citizens? Can it be commended to the South? The judiciary is the great shield of our protection. Destroy it, and the Constitution would be no more than a rope of sand.

They took care of Judge Loring. This is an illustration of the state of feeling existing in what is called the Athens of America. There a judge is proscribed for doing what he conscientiously believed to be his duty. He did his duty and I presume that no man will here deny it. He delivered up to his owner, after a patient hearing of all the facts, the fugitive slave, Anthony Burns; and, for this, he is proscribed and hunted down as a wild beast. That is what is meant by the taking care of judges. Is not a Know Nothing association illegal? It has been so held by one of the ablest jurists of the country. Judge Porter, of Pa., once a member of the Cabinet, in a late charge to a grand jury in reference to it, used this language:

"If any number of men combine to form themselves into an association by agreements, vows, or oaths to control the opinions and votes of any portion of our citizens in the exercise of their suffrages, so that they shall vote not according to their own choice or the dictates of their own consciences, but as a majority of such association shall determine, it is a conspiracy, and punishable as such by indictment.

And you will remember that it is the agreement to do the act that constitutes the criminality, even if the act itself be not done. It may be well here to observe that if any person or persons shall have unthinkingly, unadvisedly, or without being aware of the criminal character of such an act, joined such association, or taken upon himself any such vows, obligations, or oaths, they are not binding upon him in law, and ought not to be in morals. He will enact the part of a good citizen by eschewing all such fellowship or association, and abandoning the illegal enterprise."

This Know Nothingism is a step in advance of Jesuitism, it combines higher law "ism"—it claims supremacy over all laws. Is such an institution to be tolerated:

Is law to be perverted from its course?
Is abject fraud to league with brutal force?
Is freedom to be crushed, and every son
Who dares maintain her cause to be undone?
Is base corruption creeping through the land
To plan and work her ruin underhand?

Mr. Chairman. In the sincerity of my heart, I hope the people of the South will take warning, and not affiliate with such an organization. I have reason to believe that many good and patriotic men in the South, of both political parties, have joined this new movement. It is to be hoped they will take warning in time. I beseech them to study more closely the aims of this order, before deciding in its favor. I beseech them to test "Sam" by his principles, and they will find that, like the evil spirit when touched with the spear of Ithuriel, he will squat, toadlike, to the earth. They will find that "Sam," the good genius of the order, has flirted and caressed with every "ism" of the day. Sir, I proclaim it with pride, that the State which I have the honor, in part, to represent has, at all times and under all circumstances, been true to the Constitution and the Union—she is eminently conservative, and no "ism" ever got foothold there, and for this she has been charged with being always asleep. Better, far better, that she should sleep on, than to arouse from her slumbers to find herself locked in the meretricious embraces of that graceless libertine, dubbed by its godfathers with the euphonious and classical sobriquet of "Sam." I have too high a regard for my native State, to suspect, for even a moment, that her people will be controlled by such influences. North Carolina will do nothing to endanger the liberties of her people and the union of these States—nothing to tarnish the bright escutcheon of her ancient renown. In the olden time, she was the first to rise up against the oppressions of the British King—within her borders the first declaration of independence was made—the hills of Mecklenberg first re-echoed the hosannas of a people who had declared themselves free and independent, and along Carolina's mountain passes, first reverberated the sacret hymn of freedom, "nature's melodious anthem" as her patriotic sons hailed with soul stirring shouts the newborn Goddess of American liberty. The men of that day met openly and boldly, and God forbid that their descendents should discard the noble example.

If there are laws requiring repeal or amendment, why not go about the work openly as heretofore? The time is not auspicious for the Southern people to inaugurate new practices. It is said, that in the Know Nothing councils the majority govern absolutely, and that the National Council governs the State councils. Who can tell what mandatory edicts this National Council may issue? Northern Know Nothings control it—Northern Know Nothings are in favor of excluding all persons who cannot read and write from voting. Will their Southern brethren stand with them on that platform. The North has kept the South poor by high protective tariffs and navigation laws—has drawn from it that wealth which would have enabled it to educate all its people, and now, because we have a large number of persons who have not received the benefits of an education, the Northern Know Nothings arrogantly propose to add insult to injury, by declaring to us who are to be admitted to the right of suffrage. They had as well let us alone; we can manage our own affairs. The Whigs of the South have, heretofore, advocated principles. Why quit them now? Why should any Southern Democrat quit his party now? It has proved itself equal to every emergency. Under its principles the country has prospered. It is the party of progress, of State rights—of the Constitution—pledged to maintain all its guarantees. General Pierce has proved true to the principles upon which he was elected—true to the Constitution, and consequently to the South. If he has lost ground, he lost it by maintaining the rights of the South. He has proved himself a friend to the South. Ingratitude is not a trait in Southern character, and every true Democrat in the Southern States will sustain his administration, so long as he stands on that great platform, the "Constitution of our country," and administers the Government upon the principles of that instrument.

LETTER OF HON. A. H. STEPHENS, OF GEORGIA.

Equally effective was the following able letter, in the canvass in Virginia and other Southern States.

CRAWFORDVILLE, GA., May 9th, 1855.

Dear Sir :—Your letter of the 5th inst. was received some days ago, and should have been answered much earlier, but for my absence from home. The rumor you mention in relation to my candidacy for re-election to Congress, is true. I have stated, and repeated on various occasions, that I was not, and did not expect to be, a candidate—the same I now say to you. The reason of this declaration on my part, was the fact, that large numbers of our old political friends seemed to be entering into new combinations with new objects, purposes and principles of which I was not informed, and never could be, according to the rules of their action and the opinions I entertain. Hence my conclusion, that they had no further use for me as their representative; for I presumed they knew enough of me to be assured if they had any secret aims or objects to accomplish that they never could get my consent, even if they desired it, to become a dumb instrument to execute such a purpose. I certainly never did, and never shall, go before the people as a candidate for their suffrages with my principles in my pocket. It has been the pride of my life, heretofore, not only to make known fully and freely my sentiments upon all questions of public policy, but in vindication of those sentiments thus avowed, to meet any antagonist arrayed against them, in open and manly strife—"face to face and toe to toe." From this rule of action, by which I have up to this time been governed, I shall never depart. But you ask me what are my opinions and views of this new party, called Know Nothings, with a request that you be permitted to publish them. My opinions and views thus solicited, shall be given most cheerfully, as fully and clearly as my time, under the pressure of business, will allow. You can do with them as you please—publish them, or not, as you like. They are the views of a private citizen. I am at present, to all intents and purposes whatsoever, literally one of the people. I hold no office nor seek any, and as one of the people I shall speak to you and them on this, and on all occasions, with that frankness and independence which it becomes a freeman to bear towards his fellows. And in giving my views of "Know Nothingism," I ought, perhaps, to premise by saying, and saying most truly, that I really "know nothing" about the principles, aims or objects of the party I am about to speak of—they are all kept secret—being communicated and made known only to the initiated, and not to these until after being first duly pledged and sworn. This, to me, is a very great objection to the whole organization. All political principles, which are sought to be carried in legislation by any body or set of men in a republic, in my opinion, ought to be openly avowed and publicly proclaimed. Truth never shuns the light nor shrinks from investigation—or at least it ought never to do it. Hiding places, or secret coverts, are natural resorts for error. It is, therefore, a circumstance quite sufficient to excite suspicion against the truth to see it pursuing such a course. And in republics where free discussion and full investigation by a virtuous and intelligent people is allowed, there can never be any just grounds to fear any danger even from the greatest errors in religion or politics. All questions, therefore, relating to the government of a free people, ought to be made known, clearly understood, fully discussed, and understandingly acted upon. Indeed, I do not believe that a republican government can last long, where this is not the case. In my opinion, no man is fit to represent a free people who has any private or secret objects, or aims, that he does not openly avow, or who is not ready and willing, at all times, when required or asked, candidly and truthfully, to proclaim to the assembled multitude not only his principles, but his views and sentiments upon all questions that may come before him in his representative capacity. It was on this basis that representative government was founded, and on this alone can it be maintained in purity and safety. And if any secret party shall ever be so far successful in this country as to bring the government in all its departments and functions under the baneful influence of its control and power, political ruin will inevitably ensue. No truth in politics can be more easily and firmly established, either by reason or from history, upon principle or authority than this. These are my opinions, candidly expressed.

I know that many good and true men in Georgia differ with me in this particular—thousands of them, I doubt not, have joined this secret order with good intentions. Some of them have told me so, and I do not question their motives. And thousands more will, perhaps, do it with the same intentions and motives. Should it be a short lived affair, no harm will or may come of it. But let it succeed—let it carry all the elections, State and Federal—let the natural and inevitable laws of its own organism be once fully developed—and the country will go by the board. It will go as France did. The first Jacobin Club was organized in Paris on the 6th of November 1789, under the alluring name of "the Friends of the Constitution," quite as specious as that we now hear of "Americans shall rule America." Many of the best men and truest patriots joined it—and thousands of the same sort of men joined the affiliate clubs afterwards—little dreaming of the deadly fangs of that viper they were nurturing in their bosoms. Many of these very men afterwards went to the guillotine, by orders passed secretly in these very clubs. All legislation was settled in the clubs—members of the National Assembly and Convention, all of them, or most of them, were members of the clubs, for they could not be otherwise elected. And after the question was settled in the clubs, the members went next day to the nominal Halls of Legislation nothing but trembling automatons, to register the edicts of the "Order," though it were to behead a monarch, or to cause the blood of the best of their own number to flow beneath the stroke of the axe. Is history of no use? Or do our people vainly imagine that Americans would not do as the French did under like circumstances? "Is thy servant a dog that he should do this thing?" said the haughty, self-confidant Hazeel. Yet, he did all that he had been told that he would do. "Let him that thinketh he standeth take heed lest he fall." Human nature is the same compound of weak frailties and erring passions everywhere. Of these clubs in France, an elegant writer has said:

"From all other scourges which had afflicted mankind, in every age and in every nation, there had been some temporary refuge, some shelter until the storm might pass. During the heathenism of antiquity, and the barbarism of the middle ages, the temple of a god or the shrine of a saint, afforded a refuge from despotic fury or popular rage. But French Jacobins, whether native or adopted, treated with equal scorn the sentiments of religion and the feelings of humanity; and all that man had gathered from his experience upon earth, and the revelations he hoped had been made him from the sky, to bless and adorn his mortal existence, and elevate his soul with immortal aspirations, were spurned as imposture by these fell destroyers. They would have depraved man from his humanity, as they attempted to decree God out of his universe. Not contented with France as a subject of their ruthless experiments—Europe itself being too narrow for their exploits, they send they propagandists to the new world, with designs about as charitable as those with which Satan entered Eden."

This is but a faint picture of some of the scenes enacted by that self same party, which was at first formed by those who styled themselves "the friends of the Constitution." And where did these "secret Councils" we now hear of come from? Not from France, it is true—but from that land of *isms*, where the people would have gone into anarchy long ago, if it had not been for the conservative influence of the more stable minded men of the South? And what scenes have we lately witnessed in the Massachusetts Legislature, where the new political organism has more fully developed itself than any where else. What are its fruits there? Under the name of "The American Party," they have armed themselves against the Constitution of our common country which they were sworn to support—with every member of the Legislature, I believe, save eight belonging to "the order," they have by an overwhelming majority vote deposed Judge Loring, for the discharge of his official duty, in issuing a warrant as United States Commissioner, to cause the arrest of the fugitive-slave Burns. In reviewing this most unheard of outrage upon the Constitution, the "National Intelligencer," at Washington, says it "shudders for the Judiciary." And if they go on as they have begun, well may the country "shudder," not only for the Judiciary, but for everything else we hold most sacred. "If these things be done in the green tree, what may you expect in the dry."

But I have been anticipating somewhat. I was on the preliminary question; that is, the secrecy which lies at the foundation of the party—that atmosphere of darkness in which "it lives, and moves, and has its being," and without which probably it could not exist. I do not, however, intend to stop with that. I will go further, and give, now, my opinions upon those questions, which are said to be within the range of its secret objects and aims. The principles as published (or those principles which are attributed to the Order, though no body as an organized party avow them,) have, as I understand them, two leading ideas, and two only. These are a proscription by an exclusion from office of all Catholics, as a class, and a proscription of all persons of foreign birth, as a class; the latter to be accomplished not only by an exclusion from office of all foreigners who are now citizens by naturalization, but to be more effectually carried out by an abrogation of the naturalization law for the future, or such an amendment as would be virtually tantamount to it. These, as we are told, are the great ostensible objects for all this machinery—these oaths—pledges—secret signs—equivocations—denials, and what not. And what I have to say of them, is, that if these indeed and in truth be the principles thus attempted to be carried out, then I am opposed to both of them, openly and unqualifiedly.

I am opposed to them "in a double aspect," both as a basis of party organization and upon their merits as questions of public policy. As the basis of party organization, they are founded upon the very erroneous principle of looking, not to how the country shall be governed, but who shall hold the offices—not to whether we shall have wise and holdsome laws, but who shall "rule us," though they may bring ruin with their rule. Upon this principle, Trumbull, who defeated Gen. Shields for the Senate in Illinois, can be as good a "Know Nothing," as any man in the late "Macon Council," though he may vote as he doubtless will, to repeal the Fugitive Slave law, and against the admission of any slave State in the Union; while Shields, who has ever stood by the Constitution, must be rejected by Southern men because he was not born in the country? Upon this principle a Boston Atheist, who denies the inspiration of the Bible, because it sanctions slavery, is to be sustained by Georgia "Know Nothings" in preference to me, barely because I will not "bow the knee to Baal," this false political god they have set up. The only basis of party organization is an agreement amongst those who enter into it upon the paramount question of the day. And no party can last long without bringing disaster and ruin in its train, founded upon any other principle. The old National Whig party tried the experiment when there was radical differences of opinion on such questions, and went to pieces. The National Democratic party are now trying a similar experiment, and are experiencing a similar fate. This is what is the matter with it. Its vital functions are deranged—hence that disease which now afflicts it worse than dry rot. And what we of the South now should do is, not to go into any "Know Nothing" mummery or mischief, as it may be, but to stand firmly by those men at the North who are true to the Constitution and the Union, without regard either to their birth place or religion. The question we should consider is not simply who "shall rule America," but who will vote for such measures as will best promote the interests of America, and with that the interests of mankind.

But to pass to the other view of these principles—that is, the consideration of them as questions of public policy. With me, they both stand in no better light in this aspect than they do in the other. The first assumes temporal jurisdiction in "*forum conecientiæ*"—to which I am quite as much opposed as I am to the spiritual powers controlling the temporal. One is as bad as the other—both are bad. I am utterly opposed to mingling religion with politics in any way whatever, and especially am I opposed to making it a test in qualifications for civil office. Religion is a matter between a man and his Creator, with which governments should have nothing to do. In this country the Constitution guarantees to every citizen the right to entertain whatever creed he pleases or no creed at all if he is so inclined, and no other man has a right to pry into his conscience to enquire what he believes, or what he does not believe. As a citizen and as a member of society, he is to be judged by his acts and not by his creed. A Catholic, therefore, in our country, and in all all countries ought, as all other citizens, to be permitted to stand or fall in public favor and estimation upon his own individual merits. "Every tub should stand upon its own bottom."

But I think of all the christian denominations in the United States, the Catholics are the last that Southern people should join in attempting to put under the ban of civil proscription. For as a church they have never warred against us or our peculiar institutions. No man can say as much of New England Baptists, Presbyterians or Methodists; the long roll of abolition petitions, with which Congress has been so much excited and agitated for years past, come not from the Catholics; their pulpits at the North are not desecrated every Sabbath with anathemas against slavery. And of the three thousand New England clergymen who sent the anti-Nebraska memorial to the Senate last year, not one was a Catholic as I have been informed and believe. Why then should we Southern men join the Puritans of the North to proscribe from office the Catholics on account of their religion? Let them and their religion be, as bad as can be, or as their accusers say they are, they cannot be worse than these same Puritanical accusers, who started this persecution against them say that we are. They say we are going to perdition for the enormous sin of holding slaves. The Pope with all his followers cannot I suppose, even in their judgment, be going to a worse place for holding what they consider the monstrous absurdity of "immaculate conception." And for my part I would about as soon risk my own chance for Heaven with him, and his crowd too, as with these self-righteous hypocrites who deal out fire and brimstone so liberally upon our heads. At any rate I have no hesitancy in declaring that I should much sooner risk my civil rights with the American Catholics, whom they are attempting to drive from office, than with them. But sir, I am opposed to this proscription upon principle. If it is once begun there is no telling where it will end. When faction once tastes the blood of a victim it seldom ceases its ravages amongst the fold so long as a single remaining one, be the number at first ever so great, is left surviving. It was to guard against any such consequences as would certainly ensue in this country if this effort at proscription of this sect of religionists should be successful, that that wise provision to which I have alluded was put in the fundamental law of the Union. And to maintain it intact in letter and spirit with steadfastness at this time, I hold to be a most solemn public duty.

And now, as to the other idea—the proscription of foreigners—and more particularly that view of it which looks to the denial of citizenship to all those who may hereafter seek a home in this country and choose to cast their lots and destinies with us. This is a favorite idea with many who have not thought of its effects, or reflected much upon its consequences. The abrogation of the naturalization laws would not stop immigration, nor would the extension of the term of probation, to the period of twenty-one years do it. This current of migration from East to West, this Exodus of the excess of population from the Old to the New World, which commenced with the settlement of this continent by Europeans would still go on. And what would be the effect, even under the most modified form of the proposed measure—that is of an extension of the period from five to twenty-one years, before citizenship should be granted? At the end of the first twenty-one years from the commencement of the law, we should have several millions of people in our midst—men of our own race—occupying the unenviable position of being a degraded caste in society, a species of serfs without the just franchise of a *freeman* or the needful protection due to a *slave*. This would be at war with all my ideas of American Republicanism as I have been taught them and gloried in them from my youth up. If there be danger now to our institutions, (as some seem to imagine, but which I am far from feeling or believing,) from foreigners as a class, would not the danger be greatly enhanced by the proposed remedy? Now it is true they are made to bear their share of the burthens of Government, but are permitted, after a residence of five years, and taking an oath to support the Constitution, to enjoy their just participation in the privileges, honors and immunities which it secures. Would they be less likely to be attached to the Government and its principles under the operation of the present system, than they would be under the proposed one which would treat them as not much better than outcasts and outlaws? All writers of note, from the earliest to the latest, who have treated upon the elements and component parts, or members of communities and States, have pointed this out as a source of real danger—having a large number of the same race, not only aliens by birth but aliens in heart and feeling, in the heart of society.

Such was, to a great extent, the condition of the Helots in Greece—men of the same race placed in an inferior position, and forming within themselves a degraded class. I wish to see no such state of things in this country. With us at the South, it is true, we have a "degraded caste," but it is of a race fitted by nature for their subordinate position. The negro, with us, fills that place in society and under our system of civilization for which he was designed by nature. No training can fit him for either social or political equality with his superiors; at least history furnishes us with no instance of the kind; nor does the negro with us feel any degradation in his position, because it is his natural place. But such would not be the case with men of the same race, and coming from the same State with ourselves. And what appears not a little strange and singular to me in considering this late movement is, that if it did not originate with, yet it is now so generally and zealously favored by so many of those men at the North who have expended so much of their misguided philanthropy in behalf of our slaves. They have been endeavoring for years to elevate the African to an equality socially and politically with the white man. And now, they are moving heaven and earth to degrade the white man to a condition lower than that held by the negro in the South. The Massachusetts "Know Nothing" Legislature passed a bill lately to amend their Constitution, so as to exclude from the polls in that State, hereafter, all naturalized citizens, from whatever nation they may come; and yet they will allow a runaway negro slave from the South the same right to vote that they give to their own native born sons! They thus exhibit the strange paradox of warring against their own race—their own blood—even their own "kith and kin," it may be, while they are vainly and fanatically endeavoring to reverse the order of nature, by making the black man equal to the white. Shall we second them in any such movement? Shall we even countenance them so far as to bear the same name —to say nothing of the same pledges, passwords, signs and symbols? Shall we affiliate and unite ourselves under the same banner, with men whose acts show them to be governed by such principles, and to be bent upon such a purpose? This is a question for Southern men to consider. Others may do it if they choose; but I tell you, I never shall; that you may set down as a "fixed fact," —one of the fixedest of the fixed. I am not at all astonished at the rapid spread of this new sentiment at the North, or rather new way of giving embodiment and life to an old sentiment, long cherished by a large class of the Northern people, notwithstanding the paradox. It is true, "Know Nothingism" did not originate, as I understand its origin, with the class I allude to. It commenced with the laborers and men dependant upon capital for work and employment. It sprang from the antagonism of their interests to foreigners seeking like employments, who were underbidding them in the amount of wages. But many capitalists of that section, the men who hold the land and property in their own hands, wishing to dispense with laborers and employees, whose votes at the polls are equal to their own, seized upon this new way of effecting their old, long-cherished desire. And the more eagerly as they saw that many of the very men whom they have ever dreaded as the insuperable obstacle between them and their purpose, had become the willing, though unconscious instrument of carrying that purpose out, which, from the beginning, was a desire to have a votingless population to do their work, and perform all the labor, both in city, town and country, which capital may require. And as certainly as such a law shall be passed, so far from its checking immigration, there will be whole cargoes of people from other coutries brought over, and literally bought up in foreign ports—to be brought over in American ships to supply the market for labor throughout all the free States of the Union. The African Slave Trade, if re-opened, would not exhibit a worse spectacle in trafficking in human flesh, than those most deluded men of the North who started this thing, and who are now aiding to accomplish the end, may find they have but kindled a flame to consume themselves. The whole sub stratum of Northern society will soon be filled up with a class who can work, and who, though white, cannot vote. This is what the would-be lords of that section have been wanting for a long time. It is a scheme with many of them to get white slaves instead of black ones. No American laborer, or man seeking employment there, who has a vote, need to expect to be retained long when his place can be more cheaply filled by a foreigner who has none. This will be the practical working of the proposed reformation. This is the philosophy of the thing. It is a blow at the ballot box. It is an insidious attack upon general suffrage. In a line with this policy, the "Know Nothing" Governor of Connecticut has already recommended the passage of a law denying the right of voting to all who cannot read and write. And hence, the great efforts which are now being made throughout the North, to influence the elections, not only these, but in spending their money in the publication of books and tracts written by "nobody knows who," and scattered broad-cast throughout the Southern States, to influence elections here by appealing to the worst of passions and strongest prejudices of our nature, not omitting those even which bad and wicked men can invoke under the sacred but prostituted name of religion.

Unfortunately for the country, many evils which all good men regret and deplore, exist at this time, which have a direct tendency, wonderfully to aid and move forward this ill-omened crusade. These relate to the appointment of so many foreigners—wholly unfit, not only to minister offices at home, but to represent our country, as Ministers, abroad. And to the great frauds and gross abuses which at present attend the administration of our naturalization laws—these are the evils felt by the whole country, and they ought to be corrected. Not by a proscription of all foreigners without regard to individual merits. But in the first place by so amending the naturalization laws, as effectually to check and prevent these frauds and abuses. And in the second place, by holding to strict accountability at the polls in our elections, all those public functionaries, who either with partisan views, or from whatever motive, thus improperly confer office, whether high or low, upon undeserving foreigners, to the exclusion of native born citizens, better qualified to fill them. Another evil now felt, and which ought to be remedied, is the flooding, it is said, of some of the cities with paupers and criminals from other countries. These ought all to be unconditionally excluded and prohibited from coming amongst us—there is no reason why we should be the feeders of other nations' paupers, or either the keepers or executioners of their felons—these evils can and ought to be remedied without resorting to an indiscriminate onslaught upon all who by industry, enterprise and merit may choose to better their condition in abandoning the respective dynasties of the Old World in which they may have chanced to have been born, and by uniting their energies with ours, may feel a pride in advancing the prosperity, development and progress of a common country not much less dear to them than to us. Against those who thus worthily come, who quit the misruled Empires of their "father land," whose hearts have been fired with the love of our ideas and our institutions even in distant climes, I would not close the door of admission. But to all such as our fathers did at first, so I would continue most freely and generously to extend a welcome hand. We have from such a class nothing to fear. When in battle or in the walks of civil life did any such ever prove traitor or recreant to the flag or cause of his country? On what occasion have any such ever proven untrue or disloyal to the Constitution?

I will not say that no foreigner has ever been untrue to the Constitution; but as a class they certainly have not proven themselves so to be. Indeed, I know of but one class of people in the United States at this time that I look upon as dangerous to the country. That class are neither foreigners or Catholics—They are those native born traitors at the North who are disloyal to the Constitution of that country which gave them birth, and under whose beneficent institutions they have been reared and nurtured. Many of them are "Know Nothings." This class of men at the North, of which the Massachusetts, New Hampshire and Connecticut "Know Nothing" Legislatures are but samples, I consider as our worst enemies. And to put them down, I will join, as political allies now and forever, all true patriots at the North and South, whether native or adopted, Jews or Gentiles.

What our Georgia friends, whether Whigs or Democrats, who have gone into this "New Order," are really after, or what they intended to do, I cannot imagine. Those of them whom I know have assured me that their object is reform, both in our State and Federal Administrations—to put better and truer men in the places of those who now wield authority—that they have no sympathies as party men or otherwise with that class I speak of at the North—that they are for sustaining the Union platform of our State of 1850, and that the mask of secrecy will soon be removed when all will be made public. If these be their objects, and also to check the frauds and correct the abuses in the existing naturalization laws, which I have mentioned, without the indiscriminate proscription of any class of citizens on account of their birth place or religion, then they will have my co-operation, as I have told them, in every proper and legitimate way, to effect such a reformation. Not as a secretly initiated co-worker in the dark for any purpose, but as an open and bold advocate of truth in the light of day. But will they do as they say? Will they throw off the mask? That is the question. Is it possible that they will continue in political party fellowship with their "worthy brethren" of Massachusetts, Connecticut, New Hampshire, and the entire North? Every one of whom elected to the next Congress is our deadly foe! Do they intend to continue their alliance with these open enemies of our institutions and the Constitution of the country under the totally misnamed association of the "American Party"—the very principle upon which it is based being anti-American throughout?

True Americanism, as I have learned it, is like true Christianity—disciples in neither are confined to any nation, clime, or soil whatsoever. Americanism is not the product of the soil, it springs not from the land or the ground; it is not of the earth, or earthly; it emanates from the head and the heart; it looks upward, and onward, and outward; its life and soul are those grand ideas of government which characterize our institutions and distinguish us from all other people; and there is no two features in our system which so signally distinguish us from all other nations, as free toleration of religion and the doctrine of expatriation—the right of a man to throw off his allegiance to any and every other State, Prince or Potentate whatsoever, and by naturalization to be incorporated as citizens into our body politic.

Both these principles are specially provided for and firmly established in our Constitution. But these American ideas which were proclaimed in 1789 by our "sires of '76," are by their "sons" at this day derided and scoffed at. We are now told that "naturalization" is a "humbug," and that it is an "impossibility." So did not our fathers think.

This "humbug" and "impossibility" they planted in the Constitution; and a vindication of the same principle was one of the causes of our second war of independence. England held that "naturalization" was an impossible thing. She claimed the allegiance of subjects born within her realm, notwithstanding they had become citizens of this Republic by our Constitution and laws. She not only claimed their allegiance, but she claimed the right to search our ships upon the high seas, and take from them all such who might be found in them. It was in pursuit of this doctrine of hers—of the right of search for our "naturalization" citizens—that the Chesapeake was fired into, which was the immediate cause of the war of 1812. Let no man then, barely because he was born in America, presume to be imbued with real and true "Americanism" who either ignores the direct and positive obligations of the Constitution, or ignores this, one of its most striking characteristics. As well might any unbelieving sinner claim to be one of the faithful—one of the elect even—barely because he was born somewhere within the limits of Christendom. And just as well might the Jacobins, who "decreed God out of his Universe," have dubbed their club a "Christian association," because they were born on Christian soil. The genuine disciples of "True Americanism," like the genuine followers of the Cross, are those whose hearts are warmed and fired—purified, elevated and ennobled—by those principles, doctrines and precepts which characterize their respective systems. It is for this reason that a Kamschatkan, a Britton, a Jew, or a Hindoo, can be as good a Christian as any one born on "Calvary's brow," or where the "Sermon on the Mount" was preached! And for the same reason an Irishman, a Frenchman, a German or Russian, can be as thoroughly "American" as if he had been born within the walls of the old Independence Hall itself. Which was the "true American," Arnold or Hamilton? The one was a native and the other was an adopted son. But to return. What do our Georgia friends intend to do? Is it not time that they had shown their hand? Do they intend to abandon the Georgia Platform, and go over "horse, foot and dragoons" into a political alliance with Trumbull, Durkee, Wilson & Co? Is this the course marked out for themselves by any of the gallant old Whigs of the 7th and 8th Congressional Districts? I trust not, I hope not.

But if they do not intend thus to commit themselves, is it not time to take a reckoning and see whither they are drifting? When "the blind lead the blind" where is the hope of safety? I have been cited to the resolution which, it is said, the late Know Nothing Convention passed in Macon. This, it seems, is the only thing that the 600 delegates could bring forth after a two days "labor"—and of it we may well say, "*Montes parturient et ridiculus mus nascitur*"—"The mountains have been in labor and a ridiculous mouse is born." It simply affirms, most meekly and submissively, what no man South of Mason and Dixon's line for the last thirty-five years would have ventured to deny, without justly subjecting himself to the charge of incivism—that is, that "Congress has no constitutional power to intervene by excluding a new State applying for admission into the Union, upon the ground that the constitution of such State recognizes slavery." This is the whole life and soul of it, unless we except the secret blade of Joab which it bears towards Kansas and Nebraska, concealed under a garb.

It is well known to all who are informed, that in the organic law of these territories the right of voting, while they remain territories, was given to all who had filed a declaration of intention to become citizens. This was in strict compliance with the usual practice of the Government in organizing Territories; and under this provision that class of persons are now entitled to vote. Kansas, in two elections under this law has shown that an overwhelming majority of her people are in favor of slavery, notwithstanding the Executive influence of the Freesoil Governor (Reed) whom Mr. Pierce sent out there to prevent it; but whom the people have lately driven, as they ought to have done from the country. Now, then, when Kansas applies for admission as a Slave State, as she doubtless will, a Southern "Know Nothing," under this Resolution, can unite with his worthy brethren at the North, in voting against it upon the ground that some have voted for a Constitution recognizing slavery, who had not been "naturalized," but had only declared their intention. For this Resolution in its very heart and core, declares that the right to establish Slave institutions "in the organization of the State Governments, belongs to the native and naturalized citizens," excluding those who have only declared their intentions. A more insidious attack, was never made upon the principles of the Kansas and Nebraska Bill. And is this to be the plank on which Northern and Southern "Know Nothings" are to stand in the rejection of Kansas. But to the other and main objection, why did it stop with a simple denial of the power of Congress to reject a State on account of slavery? Particularly when it had opened the door for the rejection of Kansas on other grounds by way of pretext? Why did it not plant itself upon the principles of the Georgia Resolutions of 1850, and say what ought to be done in case of the rejection of a State by Congress because of slavery? So far from this it does not even affirm that such rejection by their "worthy brethren" of the North would be sufficient cause for severing their party affiliation with them for it?

Again I would say, not only to the old Whigs of the 7th and 8th Congressional Districts, but to all true Georgians, whether Whigs or Democrats, Union men or Fire-Eaters, whither you are drifting? Will you not pause and reflect? Are we about to witness in this insane cry against Foreigners and Catholics a fulfilment of the ancient Latin Proverb. "*Quem Deus vult perdire prius dementat!*" "When the gods intend to destroy they first make mad?" The times are indeed portentous of evil. The political horizon is shrouded in darkness. No man knows whom he meets, whether he be friend or foe, except those who have the dim glare of the covered light which their secret signs impart. And how long this will be a protection even to them, is by no means certain. They have already made truth and veracity almost a by-word and a reproach. When truth loses caste with any people—is no longer considered as a virtue—and its daily and hourly violation are looked upon with no concern but a jeer or laugh, it requires very little forecast to see what will very soon be the character of that people. But, sir, come what may, I shall pursue a course which sense of duty demands of me. While I hope for the best, I shall be prepared for the worst; and if the worst comes, with my fellow citizens, bear with patience my part of the common ills. They will affect me quite as little as any other citizen, for I have but little at stake; and so far as my public position and character are concerned, I shall enjoy that consolation which is to be derived from a precept taught me in early life, and which I shall ever cherish and treasure, whatever fortune betide me.

> "But if, on life's uncertain main,
> Mishap shall mar thy sail,
> If, faithful, firm and true in vain,
> Woe, want, and exile thou sustain,
> Spend not a sigh on fortune changed."

Yours, most respectfully,

A. H. STEPHENS.

Col. T. W. THOMAS, Elberton, Ga.

From the Richmond Examiner, May 1, 1855.

KNOW NOTHING HUMBUGS EXAMINED AND EXPLODED.

The present canvass has been prodigiously fruitful in all sorts of Roorbacks, humbugs, misrepresentations and even downright falsehoods. The whole land teems with garbled extracts, apochryphal pamphlets, Munchausen paragraphs, and statements of the most transparent and egregious absurdity. To crush this prolific brood, would require the labors of a dozen regiments of men, like the hero of the Augean stables. We propose examining, at this time, three of the most current and common place, which we read every day in our exchanges.

When a Democratic editor or newspaper points to the identity of the Know Nothing and the old Federal parties, as far as their common hostility to foreign immigration is concerned, he is invariably told that, although the objections to immigration fifty years ago were absurd, yet that the causes which made immigration desirable have ceased, the land has inhabitants enough, and that we should keep the domain for our children. Without stopping to point out, for the fiftieth time, that the repeal of the naturalizations laws will, in no manner diminish or affect immigration, let us see whether our landed estate is already filling up too rapidly.

The census of 1850 furnishes us with the following facts, which effectually demonstrate the absurdity of this argument of the Know Nothings:

Area of the United States, 3,306,865 of square miles or 2,116,383,600 acres.

Number of acres in farms,	293,560,614
Number of acres improved,	113,032,614
" " unimproved,	180,528,000
Total in farms, as above,	293,560,614

It has therefore required, from this official statement, 320 years to bring 113,032,614 acres under cultivation, and we have yet left the small number of *two billions three millions* of unimproved lands. We are therefore certainly not in imminent peril of our dense population covering our limited possessions two or three layers deep, and the excess slipping off into the Atlantic and the Pacific oceans. The absurdity of this humbug of Know Nothingism might be rendered still more glaring by a calculation, demonstrating how greatly the two billions of unimproved acres, might be made to add to our national wealth, by cultivation and population; but the good sense of our readers will render such an argument unnecessary.

II.

The second humbug maintains that immigration has increased the pauperism of this country, and that New York and the New England States are taxed to support the paupers of Europe. The simple fact that immigration profitably employs a large portion of the marine of the free States, renders their railroads and canals valuable, and enriches thousands who, in the shape of boarding house keepers, agents, runners, and store keepers, prey upon the immigrants after their long sea voyages, would be a sufficient refutation of this assertion. But there is still more conclusive evidence. The German emigrants alone bring into this country annually, it has been estimated, 11,000,000 of dollars in gold and silver. The commissioners of emigration for the State of New York so state. But the enemies of immigration, pinned to the wall by this fact, say the Irish paupers, not the Dutch, are the rascals who are devouring the substance of New York and New England.

Here, again, stubborn and unquestionable facts nail the falsehood to the counter. The following letter, from the President of the Irish Emigration Society of New York, effectually spikes that gun:

OFFICE IRISH EMIGRATION SOCIETY,
New York City, Jan. 4, 1855.

Dear Sir:—In reply to yours of the 1st instant, addressed to the lamented president of the Irish Emigrant Society, lately deceased, relative to the receipt and disbursement of the funds received and disbursed on account of emigrants arriving at this port, I beg leave to state—

That in May, 1847, the State Legislature organized the commissioners of emigration, and passed laws requiring that for each alien passenger landed at this port the owners and consignees of the vessel bringing them should pay to the commissioners of emigration—first, $1 per head, with 50 cents each for hospital tax, to support the Quarantine Hospital, which latter was decided to be illegal and was abolished; then it was increased to $1 50, and at the last session it was further increased to $2, (which tax is included by the owners and masters of vessels in the passage money,) and giving the commissioners authority to disburse all such moneys received by them, for care and support of all emigrants chargeable to them, and to every city, town, or county in the State, for a period of five years from the date of their arrival at this port.

The amounts received by the commissioners of emigration and disbursed by them for the support of emigrants, since their creation in May, 1847 are as follows:

In 1847,	193,293 00
1848,	311,002 38
1849,	315,876 16
1850,	358,010 36
1851,	469,538 27
1852,	555,911 96
1853,	571,651 92
1854,	688,802 98
	$3,464,187 03

Which have been all disbursed, less the amount of $64,000 now on hand, for the care, maintenance, and support of emigrants arriving at this port, and chargeable in the various counties of this State, and in forwarding them to their friends and to places where they may get employment.

In reply to your second question, I beg leave to inform you, that since the creation of the commissioners of emigration, the city authorities have paid no money on account of alien passengers arriving at this port, nor has the city incurred any expense for their support; on the other hand, the commissioners have paid since May, 1847, to the various public institutions in this city, for the care of such emigrants, chargeable to them, as they could not take care of in their own institutions, such as lunatics blind, deaf and dumb persons, $93,-490.

* * * * * * * *

With great respect, yours truly,
AND. CARRIGAN,
President Irish Emigrant Society.

Really, the President of the Emigration Society is too cruel. He proves that a tax laid upon the immigrants more than pays all their expenses, that there is now on hand a surplus of 64,000 dollars, and that there has been paid to the charitable institutions of the State of New York, for their disinterested care and support of the "pauper Irishmen," the sum of 93,500 dollars.

This then is a truthful picture of Irish pauperism, and New York philanthropy. How stands the matter in the slave States? Are we taxed for the support of the German and Irish pauper immigrants? Baltimore is the port, at which we suppose nine-tenths of the European paupers are landed. The following is a letter from the President of the Maryland Emigration Society:

BALTIMORE, Jan. 3, 1855.

Dear Sir:—I received yesterday your favor of the 29th ult., asking information about the amount of head-money paid by emigrant passengers and its application. In reply, I can only give you the amounts collected, which have been as follows:

In 1850, - - - -	10,015 11
1851, - - - -	12,505 20
1852, - - - -	20,128 71
1853, - - - -	17,185 77

being at the rate of $1 50 for each passenger. A portion of these sums—say two-fifths, or sixty cents per head—has been annually paid over to the several beneficial societies, and the German Society has been the recipient of some five or six thousand dollars per annum.

I am not aware that our city authorities have been put to any expense on account of emigrants. There is no special provision made for them, and it is left to the German, Hibernian, St. Andrews, and other charitable societies, to assist the sick and indigent.

The balance of the head-money, with the exception of trifling donations in some instances made to Dutch passengers, is applied towards the support of the Baltimore city and county almshouse.

I have not yet ascertained the exact number of passengers which arrived at this port during last year; it has been somewhat greater than during the preceding year, and the collections will probably reach $20,000.

It will afford me pleasure to give you any further information on the the subject of emigration at my command; and I remain, with sincere regards,

Your obedient servant,
A. SCHUMACHER.

Far from being a tax upon the people of the slaveholding State of Maryland, we find that a large part of this "head money," or tax upon the immigrants, is actually applied "towards the support of the Baltimore city and county almshouse," the "foreign paupers" furnishing their mite towards the support of the indigent native Americans.

III.

The third Roorback and humbug of the Know Nothings, is "that the influx of foreigners depreciates the price of labor." This is the rankest and most transparent nonsense which we have yet heard, even from the Order which has inaugurated misrepresentation as one of their cardinal virtues. The price of labor is, like everything else that can be bought or hired, regulated by the demand for it. If immigration did not open new resources by bringing immense tracts of land under cultivation, by opening roads for the exchange of commodities between the various portions of the country, and by an increased home consumption, it would necessarily come to pass, that a constant influx of foreign mechanics and laborers would soon glut the market and depreciate the price of labor.

But the fact is, that the wages of labor have increased more rapidly, during the last seven years, than they have ever done, and yet, during the last seven years, immigration has also more rapidly increased than at any subsequent period of our history as a nation. We shall not insult the intelligence of our readers by elaborating the argument which this fact will prove to every sensible man.

From the Richmond Examiner, May 15, 1855.

EQUAL RIGHTS AND EQUAL LAWS.

Equal Rights and Equal Laws—these things have ever been the dearest to the heart of the race whose descendants we are. In all eras, under all climates, in every alteration of society, that key-note recurs in the grand symphony of its utterance and action. Equal Rights and Equal Laws! These words sum up the political system of the American States and the American people. To them they represent all things that are good in government. They have fought for them, and toiled for them, and paid for them in money and in blood; till they thought the principles those words express were so won to their possession, so wrought into their flesh, so mingled with the life stream that they were sending down to after ages, that all the waters of the multitudinous seas would never wash them out, nor all the drowsy syrups of the East erase them from the memory of any posterity of theirs. But that heroic hope was only a glorious, noble dream. Their children have already forgotten the Declaration of Rights which do pertain unto the people of Virginia, and unto their posterity.

As the white cloud by day and the pillar of fire by night were insufficient to assure the wanderers in the desert of the presence in their midst of the God of Abraham, Isaac and Jacob, and they must needs make a golden calf to worship in his stead, and choose other leaders than the Lord's anointed; so are we discarding the maxims of our fathers which have brought the Republic to its present power, as worn out trumpery unsuited to its now exalted estate, and adopting a new class of dogmas, at war with the example of our ancestors, substituting narrow counsels for noble and exalting sentiments, strife for harmony, intolerance for charity, privilege for equality, birth for merit, hypocrisy for faith, and making the name *American* instead of a symbol of all that is generous, brave, hospitable, self-reliant, enterprising, excellent, elevated, and free in conscience, in effort, in enterprise, in aspiration, in ambition, in the person and in the soul—a confined idea, limited between narrow latitudes and longitudes, synonymous with Ishmaelite and cur, and expressive only of jealousy, selfishness, ill-nature, inhospitality, meanness of instinct and narrowness of soul.

And that which makes the blood of the patriot boil with the fiercer indignation in contemplating the conduct of the advocates of this total change in the genius and spirit of our institutions, is to see them hypocritically attempting to impose the belief upon the ignorant and simple, that their new-fangled dogmas have the sanction of the founders of the Republic.

Equal Rights and Equal Laws for all free citizens, was the cardinal maxim and fundamental principle ruling the whole conduct of the framers of our institutions. They prescribed no test of religious faith as a qualification for office or citizenship. They expressly forbade that so proscriptive, so unjust, so insulting a test should ever be applied to the freemen of our country. Although the Republic was then weak and the Pope was strong, and although taunted by the Arnolds of *those* days to measures of intolerance, they refused to require an oath purging even the Catholic conscience of its imputed transcendental allegiance to its spiritual Ruler. They left these measures of proscription to be taken by new light statesmen of the present hour—when ours has become the strongest power on earth, and the Pope the weakest potentate—when Protestantism has come to number in proselytes and creeds as the sands of the sea, and, growing up like the spreading oak, is stretching out its limbs to the four winds of heaven, and like the banyan tree of India, is reaching forth its arms, and striking down its roots into all regions of the earth. They left the people the option to choose from among the members of all the different religious persuasions, whomsoever themselves and not unequal laws should adjudge "most honest, most capable and most faithful to the Constitution." They left it to modern bigots, by demagogue oaths and unequal laws, to cut the people off from one entire religious persuasion in their elections of public servants; and to prescribe a rule and enforce an oath, which, if Brigham Young and Judge Taney were rival candidates for office, would command them—THE PEOPLE—to vote for the polygamist, the outlaw, the impostor, the whoremonger, the adulterer, the brute and the infidel, rather than for the man—*clarum venerabile nomen gentibus, et multum nostræ quod proderat urbi.*

The same great principle of equal rights and equal laws for free citizens was carried by our fathers into their welcome to the emigrant. They required a probationary residence of the foreigner as requisite to the attainment of citizenship, it is true; but, once a citizen, they made the emigrant a peer of the proudest native in respect of all the privileges and franchises of the citizen. True it was, that our fathers, in consideration of the tender years of the Republic, its infancy and weakness, the power of hostile governments whose tyranny it had escaped by miracle, the jealousy with which the monarchies abroad regarded our free institutions, and the danger of insidious efforts from that quarter to undermine our liberties unawares to our people while few and feeble, ordained that the Federal executive and some of the State executives should be native male citizens. But there they stopped, and that was the single exception which they engrafted upon that wonderful system of legislation, which they planted upon the foundation stone of Equal Laws and Equal Rights. With that single exception, they left the unrestricted choice of their public servants to the people—to the judgment, the discernment, the discrimination, the patriotism, the justice, the WILL of the people. Proceeding upon the great American maxim, of the capacity of the people for self-government, they did not essay to prescribe to them from what class of citizens they should select their servants, or by what accidents of birth or privilege they should restrict their choice. They left it to the innovating demagogues of the present day to deny the capacity of the people for self-government, and to hamper the POPU-

LAR WILL and paralyze the elective franchise by unequal laws and extra-judicial oaths, under which, if the felon *Native American*, E. Z. C. Judson, and that great and generous foreigner, the Marquis LaFayette, were rival candidates for office, the people would be compelled, in the exercise of the highest function of the American freeman, to exalt the convict and proscribe the hero—under which base laws and oaths restricting the people in the exercise of the elective franchise, if all the foreigners wafted by ship loads to our shores were Gallatins and DeKalbs, and all our natives were Garrisons, Phillipses and Burns rescuers and rioters, they—the people—would be compelled to hurl the Gallatins from power and substitute an infamous litter of Wilsons, Hisses and Folsoms in their places. Yes, our fathers left it to the innovators of the present evil hour, to deny to the people the liberty of choosing their public servants according to their judgment, patriotism and WILL, and, distrusting the great, primary American doctrine—the capacity of the people for self-government—to fetter the people's judgments, their wishes and their choice with unequal laws and extra-judicial oaths.

In their desperation, these innovators are now vouching, at this late hour of the Virginia canvass, and as a last recourse to support a failing cause, certain resolutions of the Virginia General Assembly of 1799, proposing to exclude foreign-born persons, thereafter to come into the country, from the two houses of Congress and the Executive and Judicial offices of the federal government, running in these words:

"The general assembly, nevertheless, concurring in opinion with the legislature of Massachusets, that every constitutional barrier should be opposed to the introduction of foreign influence into our national councils:

Resolved, That the constitution ought to be so amended, that no foreigner who shall not have acquired rights under the constitution and laws at the time of making this amendment, shall thereafter be eligible to the office of senator or representative in the Congress of the United States, nor to any office in the judiciary or executive departments.

Agreed to by the Senate, January 16, 1799."

The resolution was adopted by that immortal body, just after their memorable contest over the Alien and Sedition laws, and was doubtless offered by the illustrious Virginians of that day, in the generosity of victors to the vanquished, as a testimonial of a spirit of compromise and concession on their part towards a fallen adversary after his ignominious defeat. The resolution proposed to extend the exception already mentioned in respect to the presidency of the Union and Governorship of some of the States—an exception to the great American doctrine of equal laws and equal rights—to the subordinate offices of the federal Executive, and to the federal Judiciary and the federal Legislature. It was a concession on the part of those illustrious men to the advocates of the Alien and Sedition laws, which their own after conduct proves that they themselves considered unwise and unnecessary. They themselves condemned it as a temporary indiscretion, and left it to sink into sudden and incontinent oblivion. The resolution has slept the sleep of death upon the statute book ever since. It is as obsolete as its cotemporary measures of National Bank and Protective Tariff; and was buried still-born by the very statesmen who are now appealed to as its authors.

But mark the disingenuousness of this effort of the latter day Know Nothings to array this resolution against the doctrine of equal rights and equal laws, and to set the illustrious statesmen of '98 and '99 at war with themselves. The resolutions of the Massachusetts Know Nothing Legislature of '99, to which this Virginia resolution responded, had invited those statesmen to do a mean thing, an unjust thing, an infamous thing—had invited them to exclude foreign born citizens, already naturalized, and already entitled under the Constitution as it was, and the laws as they stood upon the statute book, from an equal participation in the offices, privileges and franchises of the country. In short, the Massachusetts Legislature of that day recommended the proscriptive principle which is incorporated in the following article of the Know Nothing creed:

"You, of your own free will and accord, in the presence of Almighty God and these witnessess, your right hand resting on this Holy Bible and Cross, and your left hand raised toward Heaven, in token of sincerity, do solemnly promise and swear that you will not vote, nor give your influence, for any man for any office in the gift of the people unless he be an American born citizen, in favor of Americans ruling America."

—an oath which cuts at the very roots of those solemn guarantees of the Constitution which have already given to the alien born citizen heretofore naturalized, the free, unrestricted benefit of the same equal laws and equal rights which is enjoyed by the native citizen—an oath retrospective in its operation, *ex post facto* in its disfranchisements, violative of vested rights, and repudiatory of the long standing compact between our country on the one hand, and the domiciliated emigrant on the other, who has sought its shores under the allurement of those guarantees of equality and hospitality which shone forth from the Constitution in letters of gold, so refulgent as to have tempted him to forsake home and kindred, to have forsworn sovereign and allegiance, and to have sought a country then offering citizenship and equality, but now proposing to degrade him into an exile and a Helot.

That was the proposition of the Massachusetts Legislature to the illustrious Virginians of '99; and now mark the noble language in which they replied, and ponder the resolution which it has suited the Know Nothings to suppress, and which precedes the one printed above, on which they rely to sustain their measures of proscription and intolerance:

"The general assembly of Virginia, considering that the privation of personal rights solemnly sanctioned by the Constitution of the United States, is arbitrary and unjust; that the right of election to office, is one of the most important secured thereby to the citizen; and that it ought not to be destroyed or impaired, especially by regulations having a retrospective operation:

Therefore, Resolved, That the proposition from the legislature of the State of Massachusetts, having for its object the exclusion of certain citizens from their eligibility to offices, which [eligibility] they now actually possess, and the exclusion of other persons who may become possessed thereof upon the performance of certain conditions held out to them by existing laws; [meaning the naturalization laws]—thus, by a retrospective regulation, improper in itself, and inconsistent with the spirit of all our civil institutions, infringing the rights of persons solemnly guaranteed by the constitution and laws—is arbitrary and unjust; and, that it ought not to receive the approbation of the general assembly."

Then follow the resolutions already quoted. Let the Know Nothings read these passages and hang their heads for shame, that they ever appealed to the authority of the Virginta statesmen of 1799 to sustain their schemes of proscription.

From the Washington Union.

VIOLENCE THE NATURAL CONSEQUENCE OF THE KNOW NOTHING ORGANIZATION AND DOCTRINES.

The public press has recently been filled with the gross and sickening details of riot and crime in our cities and towns, growing out of the new Know Nothing organization and the spirit its movements have provoked. It has been found that even in this country, which proudly boasts that the law of the land is supreme and acquiesced in by all, the constituted authorities are found incompetent or unwilling to repress disorder and protect from violence the lives and property of the citizens. We question much whether, during the last year, under the autrocrat of Russia, or him of France, more frequent or more flagrant outrages upon the rights of personal liberty and property have taken place than those who have brought the blush of shame to the cheek of every true American citizen. Private houses are given to the flames, churches are destroyed, murder stalks boldly forth, unrepressed and unpunished; whilst the authors of these outrages, not satisfied with such achievements, find ample time for attacking the peaceful assemblages of their opponents, and for even blackening the character of those native Americans who will not join with them in the cry, that every Catholic woman who goes to confession is lewd, every priest a sworn foe to our liberties, and every Roman Catholic an incipient traitor to the constitution.

There is at least one fortunate feature in all this spectacle of calumny and crime. It is leading men everywhere to reflect upon the causes and progress of these moral heresies, and to bestir themselves to the task of their removal. The calm and reflecting of all parties are beginning to appreciate the fact that our free institutions, won by the blood of our fathers, are only to be preserved by our own constancy, zeal, and vigilance. It is not enough to chant pæans to the names of Washington, Patrick Henry, and Jefferson, but we must bring home their teachings to the popular heart, and by the example of their tolerant and liberal doctrines shame those to silence who have either forgotten or repudiated the principles ingrafted upon our constitution by those illustrious patriots.

The connexion between the doctrines of the Know Nothing or native American party, and the recent developments of crime and outrage, is too obvious to be overlooked. What is "Know Nothingism" but the turning of the bad passions of our fallen nature into a particular direction? The evil feelings of malice and hate, and intolerance to our opponents, to which humanity is but too prone, have been industriously stimulated and concentrated upon the adherents of a particular faith, and upon the helpless and unfortunate emigrant, who, fleeing from tyranny and thanking God that his feet have at last touched the soil of freedom, finds to his dismay that the spirit of persecution is before as well as behind him, and meets with a scourge where he hoped for an asylum. And this is republican hospitality! A constitution and laws which offer heart and hand to the emigrant and the Roman Catholic, but a secret organization aspiring to override both constitution and laws, which substitutes for the olive branch of peace the sword and dagger of relentless bigotry! When men, instead of being taught to feel their own sins, to amend their own lives and purify their own conduct, are, on the contrary, daily and hourly admonished by their leaders that there is a class of their neighbors whose faith is so full of pernicious error, and yet so rapidly increasing, and that it must be put down, not by argument, by the light of holy example, or by the generous rivalry of deeds of charity and mercy, but by denying to the adherents of these presumed heresies all posts of trust and honorable preferment—thus making them the only pariahs, or outcasts, in a land of equality—is it strange that the growth of malice and hate should be rapid, and quickly bring forth its appropriate fruit of riot, sedition, calumny, and murder? This lesson, which all history teaches us, was familiar to our forefathers, who wisely ingrafted its consequence of religious toleration upon the constitution; but we have among us, it seems, a class for whom history affords no warnings for toleration, but only precedent for revenge and persecution, and who use daily for their purposes the names of our revolutionary patriots whilst they studiously disregard their precepts.

There is another reason why these consequences should ensue. The Know Nothing organization is a secret one. It repudiates any appeal to argument or public discussion, but aims to obtain its proselytes by private appeals and cajolery, and to compass its objects by secret and irresponsible machinery. Is it wonderful, therefore, that these men, when met with the calm voice of reason, should fly to passionate invective to drown the voice of conscience, that they should interrupt by violence those public meetings and discussions, whose effects they so justly fear as entirely to discard them from their plan of operations, or that they should finally, when all other means have failed, resort to the pistol and the knife?

It will be obvious, too, that the weapons of violence are much more readily and conveniently handled by them than those of logic and argument. It may take a man a month or more to familiarize himself with the writings of our fathers and the principles of the constitution, and his studies may even then add but little to his Know Nothing zeal; but the sorriest and simplest of the "order" can readily handle a pistol or a bludgeon. A Know Nothing may argue with an Irish Catholic by the hour, and fail to convince him that he is an idolater or a traitor, and therefore a fit subject for proscription; but a resort to the knife settles the question speedily for all practical purposes, and your dead Irishman will hardly disturb by his replies the convictions of his antagonist, so pointedly and eloquently expressed. Five hundred pistols may be fired, and as many Irishmen made to bite the dust in less time than it will take to produce a good argument in favor of religious proscription. The midnight lamp wasted in the vain and fruitless attempt to find in the writings of Washington and Jefferson a sanction for the establishment of a "religious test" for office, may be conveniently and fitly employed in firing the Irishman's house, where his wife and children find a miserable shelter from the elements, or in burning the edifice in which he offers that sacrifice of prayer and penitence which the Know Nothing bigot, kindly assuming the province of Deity, unhesitatingly rejects as hypocritical or idolatrous. It may cost them some pains to read the constitution or the Gospel of Peace? and is it singular that they shirk the disagreeable task for the easier one by far, to them, of reading the heart of man and pronouncing upon his motives and his integrity?

Men, too, are beginning to ask, where is all this violence and crime to end? If the Catholic is to be attacked, who, indeed, will be safe? Murder does not always draw nice dictinctions, and the demon of hate and religious bigotry, when one object is exhausted, readily conjures up another. The man or villain who, by setting fire to the houses of Irishmen, acquires a fondness for such glowing spectacles, will not always be content with such narrow limits for his taste, but will apply his principles and his torch to those who are guiltless of one drop of Milesian blood. It is, we doubt not, susceptible of demonstration that the house of an Episcopalian or a Methodist will burn as readily as that of an Irish Romanist, and we suspect that his blood will in the end be fully as acceptable and sweet to many of those who are prominent in this work of hâte. We will not inquire whether it is better to be a drunkard, or rowdy, or Know Nothing assassin, than an Irishman, or whether the man who rejects the Saviour and spurns the sacrifice of Jesus Christ (but who, despite his deism or atheism, finds a ready welcome in their "order") is more worthy of trust and confidence than the Roman Catholic; but surely we may be excused for turning to the Presbyterian, the Methodist, the Baptist, the Unitarian, and indeed every sectarian who may encourage this movement, and asking them this question: Is it so short a time since your faith has felt the iron heel of persecution that you are ready and eager to apply to others those practices of persecution and proscription of which your fathers in England and elsewhere so justly complained? and if so, in what sense can you call yourselves followers of Him who said to you and to all men, "*Do unto others as you would that they should do unto you—this the second and great commandment?*"

A NATIVE PROTESTANT.

From the Richmond Examiner, April 24, 1855.

DUPLICITY BETTER THAN NATIONALITY.

Honesty is not the better policy in these days, if we take the successes of Know Nothingism as testing the rule. Ingenious Sam has adopted the tactics of the horse gangs, and as these wonderful travellers (on other men's animals) have a different name for every county they traverse, so Sam has a different schedule of policy for every State in the Union. Already are seven programmes of his Basis Principles extant; and as not half of Sam's tactics and principles are yet dragged out to light, it is fair to presume that the number of his Bases of Principles is at least thirty, the number of the States, and probably as many more as there are unorganized territories in the Union.

In respect to Catholics, the policy of the "Traveller" is peculiarly characteristic. Beginning in Massachusetts, where Puritan bigotry is not relaxed in tension since the expulsion of Roger Williams, and the hanging of defenceless and toothless old maidens for "witchcraft," he carries on his persecutions for opinion's sake, openly and avowedly, by sending special committees, attended by courtezans and prostitutes, to spy out the secrets of private female schools, conducted by Catholic ladies. There is no nice distinction there between Catholic religion and Catholic politics. It is the genuine spirit of persecution of the old, cruel, shameless, barbaric type, of the Praise God Barebones era. It is not merely Catholic voters, Catholic officers, and Catholic politicians, that are the objects of Know Nothing hostility in Massachusetts, but Catholic women and children, old men and old ladies, old maids and young virgins.

The whole American public have heard what Know Nothing legislators have done in the way of persecution in Massachusetts. Fancy the feelings of our countrymen abroad when the accounts from Boston shall reach them in Europe. But here is what a Boston Know Nothing editor says, and such is the language of the whole New England Know Nothing press:

"The Nunnery, the Convent, and other monastic systems have had full swing in Sardinia. And this for generations—for ages. What has been the result? These things: corrupt morals; debased public sentiment; violation of the most sacred laws; destruction of virtue; pollution of female virtue; general decay of noble and refined sentiments; sensuality; profligacy; vitiation of the social fabric. Much else. But these in chief. The people of Sardinia see this. They look back on centuries and see it. It is met with everywhere. The church is corrupt. Society is corrupt. Religion, morality, virtue, the true, the hallowed, the beautiful is corrupt. Hence the passage of a law of reform; a law of suppression. It has come to this: Either these places must be abolished or corruption stalk unfettered over the land. The better cause has prevailed. Hitherto we have seen little to admire in Sardinia. It has little in history but to blush and weep over. But an act has now risen which looms up like a Bunker Hill Monument."

Catholic schools "must be abolished." The convent-burning scenes of Charlestown must be re-enacted, and women and children must become again the victims of outrage from heroic, brutal, profane Sam, Apostle of Protestantism and Pharisee of 1855. Not Catholic schools only, but Catholic churches too must come down in New England; for the few that were sacked and destroyed by Sam in 1854, under the instigation of Gavazzi, the foreigner, and the "Angel Gabriel," the other foreigner, will not appease the ferocity of the unwashed felon against Catholic martyrs of obstinate consciences.

Yes, the latter half of the nineteenth century is witnessing a renewal of the persecutions of the dark ages; and this "free" land of ours, consecrated so solemnly to liberty, is witnessing already the public violation by political parties and loud-mouthed partizans, of the sacred liberty of conscience.

As the demon of intolerance progesses Southward, however, thanks to the good genius of Southern institutions, he is compelled to disguise, by every possible artifice of duplicity, the loathsomeness of his purposes. In Virginia, he professes not to touch the conscience of the Catholic, but only his franchises. He does not play Paul Pry in Catholic schools, or burn to the ground Catholic churches; but he simply utters the exclamation, "Lord I thank thee that I am not as wicked as these bigoted Catholics;" and appropriates the spoils of office to himself. The Massachusetts basis principle is to burn Catholic churches and corporeally examine Catholic female teachers and pupils. The Virginia Basis Principle is to denounce Catholics as great political knaves, rifle them, in a sort of pick-pocket patriotism, of all the offices they hold, and sing psalms of hallelujah to the Act of Toleration and the names of Washington and Jefferson. Occasionally, but very rarely, and that only in remote districts, where wholesale lying is not apt to be found out in time to be exposed, they put forth such monstrous falsehood as the following, which we take from a Know Nothing document sent us from the county of Patrick. Munchausen the Second addresses his "fellow citizens of the county of Patrick, and all lovers of their country," in the following amusingly mendacious strain. We italicise the gems in this Cabinet of

SAM'S SPECIMEN LIES, DESIGNED TO SHOW HIS VENERATION FOR THE VIRGINIA ACT OF RELIGIOUS TOLERATION.

"It is often the case, fellow citizens, that these ruffianly Priests go to common free schools, taught by the charity of some good Protestant ladies for the purpose of educating the poor, and break it up *by cowhiding all its pupils.* The daughter of an old magistrate, near a town called Ballinrobo, collected a school in which she taught the children of the poor. In the goodness of her heart, she took pity upon the poor ignorant children of the neighborhood, and desired to learn them to read, that they might peruse the word of God. The Priest, of the Parish entered the school house one day, and asked if the children were taught to read with the view of reading the Bible. On being informed that they were, he whipped every child out of the house. He denounced from the altar a school house under the care of the wife of the sheriff of Galway, and whipped a respectable old man for permitting his children to go it. Now, fellow citizens, is all this sober truth, or is it enormous fiction? It is possible that such outrages can be suffered to exist in a civilized community? Yes, fellow citizens, they do exist in their startling and hideous reality, and were it not for fear of *spinning* this address out to a too great length, I could tell you of wrongs that these Bible-hating Priests do, of crimes they commit, and of misery they entail upon every people over whom they have control, that would make your hair rise on your head. And the alarming fact stares us in the face, that the despots and tyrants of Europe are in league with the Roman Catholics annually to send over to this country hundreds and thousands of their paupers, criminals and persons of abandoned characters, that our country may be overrun by foreigners and Roman Catholics, that the government may be overthrown, and that the Roman Catholic religion may become the established religion of the United States. When these things shall come to pass, (and may God in his mercy forever forbid it,) then all Baptists, Presbyterians, Methodists, and all other Protestant denominations will be persecuted and hunted down like the beasts of the forest, for every Roman Catholic Priest and Bishop regards them as heretics, and *they take an oath to persecute by fire and sword all heretics and enemies of their church.*"

Beautiful language is this for the latitude of Virginia, and for the latter half of the XIXth century!

Such is the spirit of Know Nothingism towards Catholics where those people are few and weak; and it would naturally be inferred, from the intemperate hostility to Catholics of these suddenly enlisted champions of Protestantism, that where their party did come in contact with the hated church, in States where it was really formidable by its numbers and political influence, and where, if all they charge in Massachusetts and Virginia be true, they could carry on their system of persecution and intolerance to some good purpose, the order would be especially savage and bloody minded with the Catholics. For, if the country does really need to be cleared of the Catholic faith, and if the safety of the country really requires that its offices should be taken out of the hands of Catholics, the work of reformation should go on hottest where Catholics are most formidable, and where they participate most largely in the administration of public affairs. Yet, in Louisiana, where the Catholics do muster in force, and where there is important work for the Know Nothings, that valiant Order turn up advocates in fact of religious toleration, and are even more tolerant of the proscribed religion than the Democratic party itself. In the Basis Principles of the Order for the southern and much the larger portion of that State, there is no article denouncing the Catholic Church, and the councils are actually talking of nominating a Roman Catholic gentleman for the office of Governor.

Under that convenient article in their secret ritual, authorizing them to so construct their constitutions as to exempt Catholic men, WIVES and MOTHERS from their brutal system of proscription, where the INTEREST of the Order demands such exemption, they have consulted discretion rather than valor, and resolved to embrace Catholics as brethren in the bonds of patriotism and equals in the qualifications for office. Here is the constitutional provision of the Order on this subject of which they have availed themselves in Louisiana:

"He (a member) must be a native born citizen; a Protestant born of Protestant parents; reared under Protestant influence, and not united in marriage with a Roman Catholic: Provided, nevertheless, that, in this last respect, the State, District or Territorial Council shall be authorized to so construct their respective constitutions as shall best promote the American cause in their several jurisdictions; and provided, moreover, that no member who may have a Roman Catholic wife shall be eligible to any office in the Order."

We have received the following letter from the editor of one of the most influential, able and respectable journals of the Southern country, which shows how the double faced party has profited, in the State of Louisiana, by this convenient article in their constitution:

THE KNOW NOTHINGS HOIST THE WHITE FLAG WHERE THE CATHOLICS MUSTER IN FORCE.

NEW ORLEANS, April 16th, 1854.

Dear Sir :—

Your letter of the 7th instant, addressed to Mr. ————, was handed by him to me, with a request that I would endeavor to procure such reliable information as would enable me to answer it for him.

There is not the slightest doubt that, in the lower portion of the State of Louisiana, including this city and the Parishes which are mostly peopled by the so-called Creoles, there is no clause in the obligations of the members of the Know Nothing Order proscribing the Catholic religion or its followers on account of their religious belief. I knew this for months past, having received positive assurances from acquaintances who avowed their connection with the Order.

But, in order to "make assurance double sure," I resolved that I would appeal to some of the recognized leaders of the Order among us, and obtain from them such confirmatory information as they might be willing to afford me.

One gentleman, who is widely known throughout the State for his former zeal in Native Americanism and his present activity in the Know Nothing cause, and whose name has been brought forward prominently as the candidate for Governor of the State, on their ticket, told me, in answer to my question as to the religious test, that here the members did not take any such obligation; that, in order to obtain the support of the Whig Creoles, who were generally Catholics, it had been from the first excluded, except in so far that a "confessing Catholic" was not admitted to the Order; but that, for some months past, even that question had not been put to the applicant; all that was required being that he should be in favor of the policy of the Order as to foreigners and the Naturalization laws. When I stated to him that some of the presses in the northern portion of the State which advocated the Order, had permitted attacks on the Catholic religion and the rights of its professors, he replied that some of the country lodges had gone to work and organized themselves without having first properly informed themselves of the true objects of the movement in regard to religion; but that at present, means were being taken to procure uniformity and harmony in the work and aims of the lodges throughout the State, and that it would be required of the country lodges to give up all pretensions to introduce any religious test into the obligations of their members.

Another gentleman, who I had reason to know was one of the first to introduce the Order into this State, and who informed me that the lodge over which he presided contained over fifteen hundred members, confirmed fully what the other had said as to the absence of any religious test, especially against the Catholics, and said that on one occasion he had compelled a judge, in this city, who, in addressing his lodge, had attacked the Catholic religion, to resume his seat, as he would not permit any such violation of the real objects of their association as an attack on any man's religion.

Both the gentlemen to whom I have referred, emphatically stated that if the Order in the North and West did not yield to the demand of the Louisiana members, to give up the obligation proscribing the followers of the Catholic or any other religion, the latter would be compelled to break off from them, and act independently. And both stated that this demand would be made at the first National Council of the Order.

I have not thought it necessary to extend my inquires farther, as the highly respectable character of the gentleman who told me what I have above related, and the feeling of absolute certainty which I felt as to the entire truth of what they stated, disposed me to think that I could gain no additional information, on the points you mentioned, from others.

I am, sir, respectfully, your obedient servant,

JNO. H. CLAIBORNE.

R. W. HUGHES, ESQ., Editor of the Examiner, Richmond, Va.

From the Richmond Examiner, April 17, 1855.

FOREIGNERS AND THE SOUTH.

We should fear the Greeks though bearing gifts. We should beware of the North, though approaching us in the name of nationality and friendship. We should distrust the wooden horse of Know Nothingism, with insidious Northern fanatics in its belly, though offered as a holocaust to restored peace and harmony. We should eschew this Yankee scheme of politics, though proffering safety and protection to the South. We should neither touch nor handle the viper, though counterfeiting venomous hostility to its mother—though pretending to bite and snap at Abolitionism.

Why should the South join her bitter revilers in a hue and cry against foreigners? Fifty of the very New England clergymen who denounced her institutions to Heaven and threatened Congress with the vengeance of Almighty God for meditating a constitutional law of justice to the South, are leaders of the infamous Massachusetts Legislature in visiting persecution and outrage upon foreigners. Is it from such Know Nothings as these that slaveholders expect an effective warfare upon Abolitionism? Are these a new spawn of "Northern men with Southern principles?"

Not long ago all Boston was up in arms against the federal authorities in an attempt to rescue a slave from his master. An Irish regiment of volunteer soldiers and Catholics were chiefly instrumental in vindicating the majesty of the law and restoring the slave to his Southern owner. A "whole souled and gallant" Irish lad bared his breast to the native American mob and poured out his life's blood in defence of the rights of the South. The Know Nothing Legislature of Abolition Massachusetts, with a malignity of vengeance which history cannot parallel, has disbanded that Irish regiment and denied the privilege of citizenship to all foreigners, for the part they acted in the rescue of Burns. Is the South to lick the hand that smites her? Is she to ally herself in a league of persecution and extermination with her enemies and revilers, against the little handful of persecuted strangers who dared to take her part at the expense of life and disfranchisement? Shame! eternal shame upon the craven men of the South who shall do so mean a thing! Let us not take our politics from Massachusetts and the Know Nothing anathematizing clergy of her Legislature. Let us rather take it from the Bible, and treat the foreigner kindly and hospitably, obeying the command of that Book—"Be not forgetful to entertain strangers, (foreigners,) for thereby some have entertained angels unawares."

Why are Northern Abolitionists and Know Nothings persecuting and proscribing foreigners and Catholics? It is because they have always refused to join with them in their outcry against slavery and the South. Of all the mobs that have hounded and howled at the heels of Southern men that have gone to the North for their property, who has ever heard of a mob of foreigners? How many instances have there been, like the memorable one of Burns, at Boston, where Irishmen have vindicated the Constitution and law against the fiendish clamor of raging and gnashing hell-hound mobs of native Abolitionists. Call the Northern Know Nothing the American party? It is American in but one sense of the word, and that the meanest, shabbiest and most sneaking. It is the *Yankee* party. To persecute and proscribe foreigners is not an American policy, because it is not a Southern policy; and nothing can be truly American which is not heartily Southern. To persecute and proscribe foreigners is only a Yankee policy. Yankees at the South join in it. Yankees at the North join in it. The Know Nothing is a Yankee policy. The Know Nothing is "THE YANKEE PARTY."

The foreigners and Catholics at the North have never joined in the Abolition crusade against us. Three thousand and fifty Yankee pulpits, filled—we will not say by Protestants, but filled by Infidels—are constantly belching forth fire and brimstone, hell and damnation against the South. Theodore Parkers, Antoinette Browns and Horace Greeleys, too pious to take the sacrament of the Lord's Supper, from disgust at the intoxicating wine in use at the Holy Table, fulminate anathemas upon the South and slavery, day and night, in season and out of season, from the pulpit, from the hustings, and from the press, until our Southern people can no longer travel at the North without encountering insult at every step and hour. But who has ever known the Catholic pulpit to court popular favor by such incendiary means; and who has ever known Irishmen to join in this crusade of insult and aggression upon the South? These two persecuted classes have made themselves obnoxious to the Northern populace, and hateful as Mordecai the Jew in the sight of Haman, to their incendiary preachers and politicians, by sternly and nobly standing aloof from the fanaticism, and interfering, when they interfere at all, only to defend the integrity of the Constitution .and to assert the might of the violated law. Who ever heard of an itinerant Irish lecturer against slavery? Who ever heard of a political sermon against this constitutional institution from a Catholic pulpit? How consonant with the whole tenor of Irish conduct on this question was the prompt, the gallant, the unselfish and the pecuniarily suicidal denunciations of John Mitchell, against the revilers of the slaveholders! Well might Lord Carlisle in his leave-taking lecture at Boston, after a thorough tour of this country, declare that "the worst enemy of the Abolitionist was the Irishman, and the most staunch defender of slavery was the Irishman." The party which denounces, disfranchises, persecutes and proscribes the Irish Catholic, whatever else it may be, is not a Southern party. If it take root at the South, the fact will only confirm the slander that republics of self-governing people are ungrateful; it will be a Southern party with Northern principles; it will be a YANKEE PARTY *on Southern soil.*

Look to those States of the North where the foreign population holds a larger ratio than elsewhere, and where they exercise the greatest degree of political influence—look to the vigorous young States of Illinois, Indiana, Wisconsin, Iowa, and Michigan, as contrasted with Ohio, New York, and the States of New England; and, until this new crusade arose to temporarily unite the popular masses with Abolition natives, in a common crusade against the Democratic party and the foreign voters usually acting with them, those States which had the largest infusion of the foreign element in their populations, are found to have been the staunchest defenders of constitutional politics and Southern rights. We speak, of course, of the ratio of foreign population actually and permanently settled down in homes of their own, as distinguished from foreigners living from hand to mouth by working on railroads and laboring in other migratory employments.

What though the increase of this element be indeed rapid, as asserted by Ex-Governor Smith, and, second-hand, by Mr. Flournoy; will the Virginia politician object to a gradual and healthful augmentation of our natural friends in the Northwest? The fact is notorious, that foreigners at the North stand aloof from the Abolition movement, and that the staunchest Democratic anti-Abolition States of that section of the Union are chiefly those in which foreigners, who have found permanent homes, constitute a larger proportion than elsewhere of the whole population.

We are agitating in the South against foreignism as an evil, although foreigners are our staunchest friends at the North, where they number 2,201,118 in the census of 1850, and although the evil at the South is so small and trifling as to constitute less than two per cent. of our popnlation, and numbers a grand total in all the South of but 43,530 souls! We have never known a more monstrous piece of folly and blindness than this enlistment of Southern men in a Yankee crusade against foreigners. We can only imagine a single ground on which it can be plausibly excused; and that is, that the evil of foreignism is so entirely Northern and so microscopically Southern, as to induce the notion that immigrants seek the North from a natural repugnance to our people and institutions. But who can believe such a charge? An Irishman prejudiced against a Virginian or a Kentuckian! The thought is as monstrous as the notion itself is false and unnatural. Immigrants go to the North because emigrant ships land them at Boston, New York and Philadelphia; and because, the North being engaged most largely in manufactures, mines, internal improvements, and the mechanic arts, all requiring cheap white labor, they find employment in that quarter of the Union more promptly and surely than in the agricultural South. When they can find work at the South, they never hesitate to migrate hither; and no Southern man has ever yet heard of a foreigner leaving the South from preference for the North. No man has ever yet heard of foreigners, like Yankees, coming in sheep's clothing to sympathize with our slaves, and clandestinely shipping them off from their owners by underground railroads.

DYING WAILS FROM THE CULVERT.

Some unknown friend—probably a repentant Know Nothing about to bolt the Order and come over to the Democracy—has contrived into our possession a curious budget of documents, yet damp from the press, intended, no doubt, to be poured out in deluges over the State of Virginia, upon the eve of the election. To be forewarned is to be forearmed—and on that principle we lay the precious batch before our readers, in order that the Democracy may have a knowledge of the weapons with which they are to be assailed in the dark, before yet the blows are dealt.

The documents breathe a savage and truculent spirit enough; but we are very sure that though venomous as serpents they are harmless as doves. We have rarely seen a paper so overflowing of gall and bitterness and wormwood, and yet so imbecile and impotent to subserve any effective purpose, as SAM'S *First Epistle to the Hindoos.*

It is as unlike *Paul to Timothy* as could be conceived, through it breathes out fire and slaughter as fiercely as SAUL of Tarsus on his way to Damascus. How awfully savage is it on that mythical body, "the Anti-American Junto" of Richmond. We have heard a great deal of the JUNTO. It is said that *we* have had something to do with the killing of the old iniquity. That fact was announced in the New York *Herald* five month ago, and seeing that the *Herald* is chief organ of the Know Nothings in North America, the fact of the Junto's demise is undeniable. The Junto is a myth—a ghost, beyond doubt or cavil; and yet it is amusing to see how it still haunts the imagination of SAM. He can't divest himself of the idea that the monster is still alive, and protests to his people that it is "daily and nightly manufacturing and sending into all parts of the State secret ROORBACKS—outrageous villifications—shameless misrepresentations—unmitigated falsehoods—miserable resorts—shameless tricks—total fabrications—men of straw"—and legions of similar hobgoblins. To say that SAM is frightened and in despair, would be telling but half the story. SAM is frantic. See how he raves. The *italics*, SMALL CAPS, and CAPITALS are all his own :

SAM'S FIRST EPISTLE TO THE HINDOOS.

Richmond, May 12, 1855.

DEAR SIR : We have just learned from authority of the most undoubted character, that the Anti-American Junto of this city are *daily* and NIGHTLY manufacturing and sending into all parts of the State SECRET ROORBACKS, containing the most outrageous villifications of our Order, the most shameless misrepresentations of its objects and aims, and the most UNMITIGATED falsehoods in relation to its present standing and position. The object of this letter is to warn you, and through you, every member of your Council, and every friend of the American cause, to beware of the legion of Roorbacks which they will start, in the desperation of what they fear, and we believe, to be *their* LAST *expiring effort!*

One of their miserable resorts has been exposed to us this morning. They have already issued a large number of secret circulars, setting forth that there have been *several thousand* withdrawals from the American Councils, and that a few days before the election, *a list of these withdrawals will be furnished to the under strappers of the Junto.* The object of this cannot be doubted. It is to spread dismay through the ranks of Americans, and discourage and unnerve the efforts of our leading men. Now, without any hesitation, we pronounce the whole thing *as miserable and shameless a trick as ever issued even from the corrupt source from which it emanates.* We *know* what we say, and speak from the record when we declare, that they cannot parade the names of a thousand members in the whole State of Virginia, (out of 75,000,) who have withdrawn from the Order. We know it to be a total fabrication, a *shameless Roorback*, and ARRANT FALSEHOOD! They may parade the names of thousands, but we declare most *positively* and EMPHATICALLY, that if so, four-fifths will prove MEN OF STRAW—men who were never men of our Order—who have not withdrawn, or who never had existence anywhere except in the very fertile imaginations of our most *reckless* and UNSCRUPULOUS adversaries!

But here we will ask, even if they could parade the names of 5,000 who had withdrawn from the Order, *what* would that amount to? Would not even that number leave us 70,000 *good and true men in the Order*, which, with 30,000 outsiders, whom we know will go with us, will make a total of 100,000, *or enough to bury this miserable Junto, with its myriad corruptions, too deep to be even smelt again?*

But, sir, we tell you again, that they cannot parade one thousand actual withdrawals, if their earthly existence depended on it.

We beg to call your attention to a circumstance which alone should establish the villainy of this transaction. If this report—this list of names—is *honest*, CORRECT, TRUE—*why*, WHY have they not published them in their papers in time to have their genuineness examined, and TRUTH OF FALSITY TESTED. Both the Daily Post and Whig of this city, have repeatedly called on the Junto papers to *publish the names and localities* of the "WIIHDRAWALS" which by scores and fifties they were heralding through their papers, but without giving either *names* or LOCALITIES. These, they were not only CALLED UPON, but DARED to give. They were finally goaded into making positive declarations in the following instances, which were the only positive ones now recollected :

(Here follow the alleged charges, followed by most ferocious refutations.)

Here, then, sir, we have at much length taken pains to dissect the *four* Roorbacks which the enemy have dared to locate—read them attentively, and judge for yourself. *Falsus in uno, falsus in omnibus.* [Bad Latin, SAM.] False in one, false in all.

Finding it would never do to present the names and localities of their sham defection, followed as they were by such immediate and complete exposures, they have, it seems, concluded to issue an advance circular, CLAIMING *several thousand withdrawals, and promising to give the names in a* SECRET CIRCULAR *just before the election, when it would* BE TOO LATE TO EXPOSE THEIR FALSITY.

Then again, sir, we repeat, sound the news in advance through your Councils. Watch for Roorbacks of every possible description, and BELIEVE NONE YOURSELF, nor allow any others to be imposed upon by such base means. Recollect that with our opponents it is a death struggle, and as drowning men catch at straws, they will endeavor to seize hold of every imaginable pretext and falsehood which promises to give them *even a single vote.*

Gird on your armour then—return blow for blow, like brave soldiers, confident of Victory. Remember that while you are fighting, your brothers here and elsewhere are battling manfully in a common cause—a cause which involves the fate of our Union, our Bible, and our Faith. Let this, then, animate your hearts, and nerve your arms, in what we sincerely believe to be a contest involving mightier interests than any before tested since "the days that tried men's souls." Remember! that

To fight
In a just cause, and for our country's glory,
Is the *best* office for THE BEST OF MEN;
And to decline when these motives urge,
Is infamy beneath a coward's baseness.

Respectfully and fraternally,

C. A. ROSE,
P. POINDEXTER,
RO. D. WARD.

SAM's second epistle is not so savage as the first, but far more pithy, effective, and to the point. It is evidently the composition of higher grade of Jesuits than the boquet above. We have not the pleasure of a personal acquaintance with Mr. 17–:–3.21.12.2.7; or with Mr. J–!–6.12.13.2.7.1.8; or even with Mr. &c.–17–26.12. Tt. They are in a terrible state of alarm at the fancied thorough organization of the Democracy, and have taken measures suited to such an emergency. We publish the document entire, and as it is always lawful to fight the Devil with his own weapons, we trust the suggestions of the "*undersigned,*" Messrs. 17–:–3.21.12.2.7, J–!–6.12.13.2.7.1.8, and &c.–17–26.12.Tt, will not be lost on the Democracy:

SAM'S SECOND EPISTLE TO THE HINDOOS.

RICHMOND, May 9th, 1855.

Dear Sir:—The undersigned, claiming no other excuse than the general good of the American party, have taken the liberty to request you and————— of your county, to act as a special county committee, for the purpose of effecting an immediate and, if possible, a thorough organization in your county, unless you have already done so. We respectfully ask your earnest attention to the following:

We have as glorious a cause as ever moved the American people since the days of '76—a cause which must commend itself to the American people, and which must, as a matter of palpable necessity, become the dominant party in the land. The present struggle is one which more completely involves the fate of our Union, our Bible, and our Faith, and all else that we hold near and dear, than any other that has occurred since the United States became a nation: for it is a struggle which is to foreshadow the end—of which this is but the beginning.

But, strong as is our position, high and holy as our mission is, and as much as it commends itself to the people, we beg our friends not to rely too confidently to its inherent strength alone. We have an enemy ever watchful, ever vigilant, ever untiring, and ever, as now, utterly unscrupulous. They are old tacticians, who having long succeeded by "management," will now, in their hour of peril, resort to every means that unscrupulous knavery can suggest, or the most untiring energy carry out.

The enemy, too, are completely organized, and that in the most thorough and efficient manner. Their "modus operandi" is secret and effective—is confided to a few and proper hands. They first have a State Central Committee, who appoint sub-committees in every county, who in turn appoint sub-committees in every precinct. These precinct committees' first business is, to ascertain the number of Whigs outside the order, and the number of Democrats in. Each man on this list is put under the special care of one, two or three men best calculated to exert an influence upon him, who are instructed to use the argument best calculated to influence him against the American party. These committee-men, on some plausible excuse visit the persons under their particular charge. To the Whigs outside, they will urge the folly, the madness and impolicy of sacrificing their cherished principles—the principles of that "noble old party," "the brave party of principle," &c., to a new party, whose aims are mysterious, and whose designs they know not of. To the Democrats inside, the American party will be denounced as a Whig trick, the same miserable old blue light, Hartford Convention, Federal and Bank Whig party. They will denounce it as unchristian, unpatriotic and unconstitutional. They will declare it abolitionism in disguise, and importation from the North, from England, &c., &c. They will misrepresent its principles, its aims and its acts. They will swear it has driven every national man from the United States Senate—that it elected Seward and Wilson, and probably Sumner, and Trumbull, and Durkee, and Chase, and Hale, and Wade, and Fessenden, and a host of other abolitionists, who, so far from being Know Nothings, are among their most intensely bitter opponents. They will beseech them to come out from among a set of "*lousy, Christless, Godless plotters,*" conspirators, traitors, midnight assassins and prostitutes of the pot-houses.

In this manner, and in this style, they will visit, and are now daily visiting, every inside Democrat, and outside Whig in the State. Every device will be resorted to, to "wean those weak in the faith." They will not only visit our members, but will stay with them, eat with them, drink with them, and sleep with them. Sometimes they will double or triple teams, and bring double and triple batteries to bear on the more obstinate and difficult—will seek to frighten the timid, seduce the fishy, and "fatigue" and worry the true and honest ones out of the party.

Thus will the most powerful political machinery that political tacticians ever did invent, or ever can invent—that of direct personal appeal, entreaty and compulsion—be brought to bear, with concentrated force, upon the members of our organization in every section of the State. It is idle to say that such means, so constantly and so perseveringly applied, will be without effect, unless they are promptly and effectively met by the vigilance of our friends in every county of the State.

The only way to check this influence is to meet it promptly, and in that view we most earnestly and respectfully request your attention to the following

SUGGESTIONS.

That on the reception of this you will hold an immediate conference with ——————— of your county; and that you together shall appoint a committee of ——— active, intelligent and efficient men in each precinct of the county, who will act as a precinct committee, and who will fully and efficiently carry out the following suggestions by all honorable means:

1st. To make a perfect list of every man who will vote the American ticket.

2nd. A similar list of every man who will vote the Anti-American ticket.

3rd. A doubtful list, embracing every man, whether now with or against us, who can be swerved or induced in any manner; to place each man on this list under the care of some one, two, or more men, who will make it their special business to see, talk and even labor with every man or men placed under their charge, with a view to the following results:

1st. If an American, to protect him from the arts of the enemy, and to keep the wavering firm in the faith.

2nd. To influence as many of the Anti-Americans to vote with us as possible.

3rd. To induce as many as will not vote with us not to vote against us—if they will do us no good, at least to do us no harm.

4th. And finally, to see that every American vote is brought out and polled on the day of election.

☞ Please instruct the committee of each precinct, immediately after election, to send full returns of their precincts, addressed to the Editors Daily Whig, Richmond, and all will thus know by extras issued from that office the result in a few days after election.

17–:–3.21.12.2.7
J–!–6.12.13.2.7.1.8 } *Committee.*
&c.–17–26.12.Tt. &c.

What a pity to take away these young men's Bibles! To steal their purses is to steal trash; but to take away their Bibles—what a cruelty!

Epistle third is an eloquent dissertation from Sam on the importance of a single vote. He has been boasting of his fifty and eighty thousands for months past, and professing a generous willingness in his bets with the Democracy to give odds of fives and tens of thousands against himself; but since the late terrible reaction commenced, and his men have forsaken him by entire lodges and councils, Sam is firmly convinced that he cannot spare a single vote; and vouchsafes a special epistle to the faithful, on the necessity of getting out every vote he can call his own. Democrats of Virginia, learn a lesson for yourselves while reading

SAM'S THIRD EPISTLE TO THE HINDOOS.

RICHMOND, May 14th, 1855.

Dear Sir:—The object of this communication is to call your especial attention to the possible importance of every single vote in your, and every other precinct in the State, accompanied by such illustrations as occur to us at the moment:

In 1797, the President was elected by a majority of three in the electoral college—in 1801, by seven. Virginia was carried in 1840 by 500 votes. In 1844, 5,000 votes in New York, out of 550,000, or one in 55, made Mr. Polk President; hence, had this vote been cast for Clay, he would have been elected by five votes.

Some ten years ago, Marcus Morton was elected Governor of Massachusetts by a majority of one. In many other instances, ten votes have decided the fate of the gubernatorial election.

Mr. Benton was made Senator by one vote. Many other Senators have been elected by majorities of from one to ten.

In 1846, the candidates for Congress tied each other in two instances in a single State, and two were elected by one majority, and three more were elected by majorities of from three to twenty. In the same State, in 1848, there was one tie, three were elected by one majority, and several others by majorities of from five to fifty. On one occasion, a distinguished Virginian was elected to Congress by five majority, and at the next term defeated by seven. A hundred instances could be given of members of Congress elected by majorities of from one to five votes, and a thousand where majorities of one to five have carried State Senators, and members of the different Legislatures.

In the coming election, we expect to see several of our candidates for Congress, Senate and House, elected by very small majorities, perhaps by a single vote. Remember then, sir, that the failure to vote in a single instance, in your precinct, may lose us a Delegate, Senator, Congressman, and even U. S. Senator. The election of Flournoy, however, if our strength is polled, is as certain as the rising of to-morrow's sun.

Probably, in Virginia, an average of five of our voters in each precinct will resolve to stay at home, each thinking his own vote can make no great difference; but remember that there are 1,000 precincts in the State, and that a loss of five votes in each precinct would be 5,000 in the State, or more votes than made Mr. Polk President in 1844.

Then, sir, we call on you and your friends, and the friends of the cause, to *work*, WORK, WORK! See that every vote, in every precinct in your county, is brought out. Your brothers call on you to work for us as we work for you!

The Junto is setting day and NIGHT. The lights in their culvert are never suffered to go out. They set us an example. Let us improve it.

Confident of Victory, we are yours, &c.,

C. A. ROSE,
P. POINDEXTER, } Committee.
RO. D. WARD,

☞ Call the Council together the night before election.

LETTER FROM THE HON. DANIEL S. DICKINSON ON KNOW NOTHINGISM.

The following letter, first published in the Tallahasse Floridian and Journal of August 4th, was written in June 1855.—*Ed. N. Y. Daily News.*

My Dear Sir: On my return to my residence a few days since, from a professional engagement abroad, I found your favor of a late date inquiring for my views touching the principles of the "American" or "Know Nothing" organization. Before I found time to answer, I was hurried to this place to attend the Court of Appeals now in session, where the business in which I am engaged affords little time or opportunity for correspondence. I will, however, as I have no concealments upon public questions, borrow a moment from my pressing duties to say quite hastily, that I have no knowledge concerning the Order to which you allude, except such as is acquired from publications purporting to give information upon the subject, and must therefore confine myself to such points as are embraced within this range. It is generally understood and conceded to be a secret society or organization, designed to act politically in the contests of the day. Of this secret feature I entirely disapprove, and am unable to understand by what necessity, real or supposed, it was dictated, or upon what principle it can be justified. Free public discussion and open action upon all public affairs, are essential to the health—nay, to the very existence—of popular liberty; and the day which finds the public mind reconciled to the secret movements of political parties, will find us far on our way to the slavery of despotism. If good men may meet in secret for good purposes, we can have no assurance that bad men, under the same plausible exterior, will not secretly sap the foundations of public virtue.

Whether I am in favor of their platform upon the question of domestic slavery, must depend upon what it is; or rather, whether they are in favor of mine. If their platform is to be regarded as including, upholding or justifying such political monstrosities as the "personal liberty bill," recently passed into a law by the Massachusetts Legislature over the veto of Governor Gardner, then I pronounce it treason of the deepest dye—treason, rank, unblushing and brazen—deserving of public reprehension and condign punishment. If upon this subject their platform conforms to resolutions recently published, purporting to be the voice of a majority of the Convention assembled at Philadelphia, it is in substance the same upon which I have stood for years—upon which I did not enter without counting the consequences, and which I intend to relinquish only with life. I have not now these resolutions before me, but as I recollect them, I approve them in substance as sound national doctrine. I ignore no part of the Federal Constitution, either in theory or in practice, to court the popular caprices of the moment, to gain public station, or to minister to the necessities or infirmities of those in power. Nor can I distrust the soundness of principles approved upon full consideration under a high sense of duty, because others may choose to adopt and embrace them.

I cannot believe that any good can be accomplished by making the birthplace a test of fidelity or merit. It does not accord with, but is at war with the genius of our institutions. That abuses have been practiced by the appointment of foreigners to places of trust, before sufficiently familiar with our Constitution, laws, and social system, or to which, from circumstances, they were unsuited, is probable. This, however, is, in some respects, common to native as well as naturalized citizens, and arises not from a defective system, but from its erroneous administration. It is in both respects the natural result of placing in the hands of the incompetent the distribution of public patronage.

Upon the subject of naturalized citizens, I have been governed by considerations of justice and duty, and have designed to observe the spirit of my country's Constitution. When members of Congress engage in a steeple chase, to see who should propose earliest, give most, and vote loudest, to feed suffering Ireland from the federal treasury a few years since, not finding any warrant for such proceedings I voted against it, and let public clamor exhaust itself upon my head in denunciations. When I learned that the foreigner who had in good faith declared his intentions of citizenship, by setting his foot upon a foreign shore in case of shipwreck, without any intention of remaining abroad, lost the benefit of his proceedings, I introduced and procured the passage of a bill to redress the grievance. These principles have governed my public conduct, and now guide my opinions. The Constitution, administered in its true spirit, is, in my judgment, sufficient for the protection of all, whether native or naturalized, and for the redress of all political evils which can be reached by human government.

I have the honor to be,

Your friend and servant,

D. S. DICKINSON.

A MONSTROUS FRAUD.

The following article from the Cincinnati *Enquirer* will throw a new light upon the Know Nothing villainy practiced in the circulation of the Cincinnati *Times*, through Virginia, designed to operate on the election of next Thursday. The *Times* is an abolition paper, and, in its issues "circulated at home, and through the free States, asserts that the Secret Order is *anti-slavery*." The Cincinnati *Enquirer*, in a previous article, said that "the greatest care is taken at the office of the *Times*, not to allow a copy of the issue, intended for the Virginia market, to be seen in Cincinnati, where its sentiments would be injurious to the Know Nothing cause and prejudicial to the interests of the paper." This *Times* Roorback, sent to Virginia, is one of the most infamous frauds ever resorted to by a party, and the following exposure should arouse every honest Virginian to an indignant reprobation of an organization, based upon trickery and deception :—*Richmond Enquirer.*

Virginia Election—The Spurious Edition of the Times sent to that State.—Infamous Fraud.

We have received a letter from Wheeling in relation to the *Weekly Times* of this city, with which the Know Nothings are flooding the State of Virginia. This issue of the *Times* is filled with articles endeavoring to prove that the Know Nothings of the North are pro-slavery. The *Times*, however, which is circulated, at home and throughout the *free* States, asserts that the order is *anti-slavery*. A gross fraud is, therefore, being practised upon the Virginians, which, if they are true to themselves, they will resent. Like "orator Puff" the Times has two tones to its voice, and puts on two faces—one for the North, the other for the South. The Times which is sent to Indiana *contradicts* the Times which is sent to Virginia. It would be a terrible thing for that journal if, by some mistake of its mailing clerks, the editions should get transposed—the slavery Times finds its way to Indiana and the anti-slavery times to Virginia.

We shall endeavor to procure a copy of the Virginia edition, and make some extracts from it for the benefit of its Northern Freesoil readers, who will start in amazement at finding such sentiments advocated in that sheet. The Virginians, by the time of the election, will be pretty well informed of this dirty Abolition trick to wheedle them out of their votes, and we are confident it will react upon its perpetrators. Our friends in Virginia are making a most gallant struggle to preserve that State from the enemy and we have every assurance of their success. Our Wheeling correspondent says that "the prospects for carrying the State in favor of Wise are very flattering. I think his election is certain, beyond doubt. The only question is, how large will his majority be?" The Richmond Enquirer, the central democratic organ, whose conductors are always excellently informed in Virginia politics, estimates Mr. Wise's majority at fifteen thousand over his Know Nothing competitor. Mr. Wise himself, after travelling most of the State, is sanguine of twenty thousand. The recent municipal election at Harper's Ferry, which resulted in favor of the Democrats, is a significant indication, and shows that the popular current is running in the right direction.—[*Cincinnati Enquirer.*

CONGRESSIONAL CANVASS.

The Congressional Districts of Virginia, in 1855, were the theatre of great political excitement, and in nearly all of them the Know Nothings brought forward candidates of their own party, and boldly predicted the defeat of at least eight of the Democratic candidates for Congress.

I. Judge THOMAS H. BAYLY, of the county of Accomac, the representive of that district in Congress for the last ten years, was a candidate for re-election in the first district without regular opposition, although Messrs. GARNETT and MONTAGUE received handsome complimentary votes in portions of the district where Judge BAYLY'S views upon the principles of the Know Nothing party were not popular with the Democratic party. It was a source of deep regret, with many of Judge BAYLY'S political friends, that he avoided making a direct issue with the Know Nothing party, and actually expressed himself favorably to some of their doctrines. The result of his course during the canvass, was eminently favorable to his individual interests, and he was elected to Congress without, as we have said, any regular opposition.

The congressional elector in this district was ROBERT L. MONTAGUE, one of the most fearless, able and energetic Democrats in the State. He was, some years ago, a distinguished member of the Legislature from the counties of Middlesex and Matthews; and is a lawyer of extensive practice and great popularity. During the last canvass, his services as a speaker were of great advantage to the Democratic party of the first district.

II. In the second district, Gen. MILLSON, of the City of Norfolk, was the nominee of the Democratic party for Congress. In this district the Know Nothings were confident of success, and nominated Mr. WATTS, of Norfolk, as their candidate, a gentleman of considerable talent, who was a prominent member of the Reform Convention of 1850. It was supposed that Gen. MILLSON'S vote as a member of Congress, against the Kansas Nebraska bill, would materially diminish his prospects of success, as it had excited a strong prejudice against him with many leading members of his party. But the Democratic party of his district, feeling assured that Gen. MILLSON'S course upon that question was the result of his ultra and impracticable pro-slavery views, rather than of sympathy with the Freesoil party, re-elected him to Congress by a large majority. The result in this district was as unexpected as it was gratifying to the Democratic party.

MORDECAI COOKE, of Norfolk city, a lawyer of distinction, and an efficient elector during the presidential canvass of 1852, was the elector in this district; but was prevented by ill health from taking any part in the canvass.

III. In the third district, Hon. JOHN S. CASKIE, so widely known as an eloquent, chivalrous and able champion of Democracy, was a candidate for re-election, his course as a member of Congress having given universal satisfaction to the Democratic party of the Metropolitan District. The Know Nothings were, in this district, confident of defeating Judge CASKIE, and this anticipation of a long and certain victory, afflicted the Know Nothing councils with a number of aspirants, whose claims were urged with great zeal by their respective friends.

The most prominent of these gentlemen were A. J. CRANE, Hon. J. M. BOTTS, and WM. C. SCOTT, of the City of Richmond. The latter gentleman had been, for a short time, a citizen of Richmond, and formerly represented the county of Powhatan for many years in the Legislature with considerable ability. He was also the Know Nothing elector for the district, and was actively engaged in the canvass for several weeks before he received the nomination of his party for Congress. Mr. SCOTT is a gentleman of good education, unblemished private character, and remarkable for the accuracy of his political information. He was the most available of all the prominent Know Nothing politicians of the district, and received the full vote of his party. The discussions of Messrs. CASKIE and SCOTT were conducted with great courtesy and good feeling, and in no previous canvass were the speeches of Judge CASKIE more eloquent and effective than in that of 1855. He was re-elected to Congress by a handsome majority.

The elector in this district was Mr. P. H. AYLETT. His labors were arduous and incessant during the entire campaign, and were as effective as his brilliant talents, united with such untiring service, was calculated to be. Nor did Mr. AYLETT confine his exertions to his own field of labor, but accepted many invitations from different quarters of the State, everywhere vindicating his high reputation for talents and powers of oratory.

IV. In the fourth district, Hon. WILLIAM O. GOODE, a gentleman of great political experience, ripe years, and of State reputation, was the Democratic candidate for Congress. Mr. GOODE was a member of the Convention of 1829 '30, and of 1850, and was for many years a distinguished member of the Legislature, and had served in Congress two sessions with distinction. He was opposed by Mr. TAZEWELL of Mecklenburg, a young gentlemen of great facetiousness, whose anecdotes during the canvass, were exceedingly entertaining, and pleasing to his auditors. The district was regularly canvassed by the candidates, and Mr. TAZEWELL was beaten by about two thousand majority. "Alas poor Yorick."

The elector in this district was Hon. RICHARD KIDDER MEADE of Petersburg, formerly a prominent member of Congress, and distinguished leader of the States Right party. He canvassed the district with great activity, and contributed largely to the extraordinary triumph of the Democratic party on the Southside.

The *Southside Democrat*, published in Petersburg, was edited with signal ability during the canvass, and was regarded as one of the best campaign papers in the State. It was edited by Messrs. BANKS and KEILY.

V. Hon. THOS. S. BOCOCK, for six years the able and efficient representative of a large portion of the fifth district, was a candidate for re-election. The candidate of the Know Nothing party, was Mr. N. C. CLAIBORNE, of Franklin, once a prominent and popular member of the Democratic party, and for many years a member of the Legislature; he was also a member of the Reform Convention of 1850. At a weak and unlucky moment, Mr. CLAIBORNE yielded to the blandishments of the Know Nothing party, and fell from the respectable position which he once occupied in our party. He received the nomination of the Know Nothing party, beating, it is said, a talented young Whig lawyer of Pittsylvania, Mr. CARRINGTON. Mr. CLAIBORNE occupied an awkward position during the canvass, in consequence of his having attended the Democratic Convention at Staunton; although, it was said, at that very time a member of the secret order. He took a prominent part in that convention for Mr. LEAKE. After the nomination of Mr. WISE, it is said that Mr. CLAIBORNE publicly declared his willingness to support that gentleman, and declared himself ready to "scour" the mountains of Franklin for the nominee of the Staunton Convention. The unfortunate position of Mr. CLAIBORNE rendered it necessary for Mr. BOCOCK and the Democratic press of the State to handle that gentleman with gloves off. The following editorial from the *Lynchburg Republican*, will afford our readers some idea of the scathing and merciless manner in which Mr. CLAIBORNE was dealt with.

POLITICAL PURIFICATION—N. C. CLAIBORNE.

The particular attention of our readers is invited to the following graphic sketch of the political career of Mr. Claiborne, the Know Nothing candidate for Congress in this district.

"The scripture moveth us in sundry places" to deal gently with the frailties of our fellow men. We confess and claim much of this milk of human kindness, and extend a scriptural toleration to their short comings. But there are some things which we are not at liberty to leave unexposed.

The Know Nothings set up to purify the politics of the country, and to consummate this purification have nominated as their candidate for Congress in this district, N. C. Claiborne, Esq. An examination of the record of Mr. Claiborne presents some rare developments, and shows that he is perhaps about the only man now running for office in Virginia whose past conduct and present position exhibit an entire unconsciousness that there is such a thing as political principle. The honesty of most politicians situated as he is would be seriously impeached. But the application of such a standard to Mr. Claiborne would not in our judgment be just. We do not believe that Mr. Claiborne has good political principles. We do not believe that Mr. Claiborne has bad political principles. In fact from an intimate knowledge of his character we are satisfied that he has none at all, and never did have any. He was once elected to the Legislature pledged to oppose the Virginia and Tennessee Railroad. He went to the Legislature—voted for the road—and ran again for the Legislature as its peculiar champion, never once exhibiting a consciousness of his change. He came out a candidate for the late reform Convention upon the White Basis at one court and a speech against the White Basis at the next court—he advocated Mr. Wise in 1851 and opposed him in 1854—connected himself with the Know Nothing organization before the Staunton Convention—avows the fact in his public speeches—avows at the same time that he announced in that body his intention to support its nominees—and seemed utterly unconscious of the conflict of obligations thus voluntarity assumed. He sent Mr. Bocock word that he approved cordially his representative conduct from Staunton, and at that same time and place, Mr. Bocock charges him with having declared that he intended opposing him and he does not seem conscious that here is a question worth explanation. He seems to look upon political honor in the same light in which Falstaff regarded personal honor. "Can Honor set a leg? No. Or an arm? No. Or take away the grief of a wound? No. Honor hath no skill in surgery then? No. What is Honor? A word. What is that Honor? Air. A trim reckoning. Who hath it? He that died on Wednesday. Doth he feel it? No. Doth he hear it? No. Is it insensible then? Yea to the dead. But will it not live with the living? No. Why? Detraction will not suffer it—therefore I'LL NONE OF IT. Honor is a mere escutcheon, and so ends my catechism."

Thus soliloquized Falstaff, and thus we should judge thinks N. C. Claiborne of the honor of politics. And this man is put up for Congress to purify politics.—*Lynchburg Republican.*

Mr. BOCOCK was re-elected by an overwhelming majority, and since the election, Mr. Claiborne has disappeared from public view. Mr. Bocock's majority was upwards of 1800 over Mr. Claiborne.

Mr. HUGHES DILLARD, of Henry County, a lawyer of distinction and a Democratic elector in 1852, was the elector in this district, and delivered several addresses of marked ability. He is at this time a distinguished member of the Legislature of Virginia.

VI. In the sixth district, Hon. PAULUS POWELL, than whom there is not a more faithful and fearless representative in Congress, was a candidate for re-election, having redeemed that district again and again by his energy and popularity. POWELL like BOCOCK was opposed by a gentleman who was for many years a highly respectable member of the Democratic party. Dr. L. N. LIGON, of Nelson County, was the candidate of the Know Nothing party. Like Mr. CLAIBORNE, Dr. LIGON was a member of the Staunton Convention, and was friendly to Mr. WISE in the early part of the canvass.

He was nominated by the Know Nothings, and at once accepted the nomination and entered upon the canvass. He was defeated by Mr. Powell, who was re-elected to Congress by a large majority.

The following articles appeared during the canvass in the *Lynchburg Republican* and *Charlottesville Jeffersonian* relative to Dr. Ligon.

MR. LIGON.—Mr. Ligon wanted to be one of the Board of Public Works. There seemed no prospect for him in the Democratic ranks. There was just as little prospect for him in the Know Nothing order. But the Know Nothings did have a "forlorn hope," which they were willing to give him, and Mr. Ligon, like the old maid of fifty praying for a husband, being willing to take "Any body, Good Lord," agreed to it. That place was a candidacy for Congress. Let us look at Mr. Ligon's claims upon the Know Nothings:

1st. Mr. Ligon was a member of the Staunton Convention. A motion was made in that body to make the nomination of Mr. Wise unanimous. Mr. Ligon did not oppose it. Unless he intended to sustain it, he was bound as an honorable man to have made known his opposition.

2d. He was appointed Elector for the county of Nelson by the Democratic Executive Committee. Unless he declined it, the failure to decline was equivalent to an acceptance. He did not decline, so far as we can learn, unless it has been very lately.

3d. He met Mr. Wise at Lovingston—toadied him no little—applauded his speech—and bore himself as one of his best friends.

4th. Until within the last six weeks he has been notoriously supporting Mr. Wise, and equally notoriously denouncing the Know Nothings.

5th. We have heard that so venomous was his opposition to Know Nothingism, that he declared he would as soon see a son of his a horse-thief as a Know Nothing.

6th. He received for circulation documents against the Know Nothings, and did circulate them.

This is a portion of Mr. Ligon's record. Is it such a one as even a Know Nothing can stand? We know many of the Know Nothings in the Red Land District, and unless we are mistaken, they will scorn to vote for so late a convert. Mr. Ligon has been false to Mr. Wise. What assurance have they that he will not be false to Mr. Flournoy? He has betrayed Democracy. Where is the guarantee that he will not betray Know Nothingism? We shall have more to say on this subject.—*Lynchburg Republican.*

From the Charlottesville Jeffersonian.

DR. LIGON VERSUS THE KNOW NOTHINGS.

The following certificates of gentlemen of unimpeachable standing in Nelson county, one of whom is an old line Whig, will speak for themselves. Dr. Ligon has certainly placed himself in a very unenviable position before the people of the district. In the face of the facts revealed by these certificates, we cannot perceive how any man who values political honesty in a candidate can give his support to Dr. Ligon:

I hereby certify, that in repeated conversations with Dr. Littleberry N. Ligon, about the Know Nothing party, the last of which was on the fourth Sunday in March last, he repeated to me, in substance, as follows: That his son, Joseph Ligon, had been accused of belonging to this Know Nothing party, and that he (Dr. L. N. Ligon) said he would as soon be accused of being a horse-thief, as to be accused of belonging to this Know Nothing party.

JAMES H. BRENT.

Nelson County, April 24th, 1855.

This is to certify, that in half dozen or more conversations with Dr. L. N. Ligon, respecting the objects of the Know Nothing party, he remarked, that he believed that party to be composed of Whigs principally, and that their principal object was to break down the Democratic party; he also stated that he would sooner be a horse-thief than belong to such a party. I mentioned several Democrats that I believed belonged to the Know Nothing party; his son Joseph was one of the number, to which the Doctor replied that he did not think his son belonged to that party, for he had observed that he had rather be a horse-thief than to belong to such a party, and that he saw no change in his son's countenance, when he, the Doctor made that remark.

WM. N. BRYANT.

Nelson County, April 24th, 1855.

I hereby certify, that in a conversation, with Dr. L. N. Ligon, he spoke in very bitter terms of the Know Nothings; one remark which I distinctly recollect, was, that he did not consider them any better than a pack of damed horse thieves.

NATHAN BRYANT.

Nelson County, April 24th, 1855.

I certify that in frequent conversations with Dr. L. N. Ligon, he, in every conversation, denounced the Know Nothing party in the harshest terms, and in our conversation, I told him that it was suspected that his son Joseph belonged to the Know Nothing Order; he, the Doctor, said he had heard the same thing—did not know that it was so—but that he had said in his son's presence, that he had rather see a son of his a horse thief than a Know Nothing.

Dr. Ligon was an open advocate of Mr. Wise's election, up to Saturday before Nelson March Court last.

FLOYD L. WHITEHEAD.

Nelson County, April 24th, 1855.

I certify that in a conversation with Dr. L. N. Ligon, at Nelson February Court last, that I asked him if his son Joseph belonged to the Know Nothing party; he replied that he did not know, but that he had as soon his son was caught in a pack of horse thieves as among the Know Nothings; that he believed it was a plot to take in Democrats, who did not understand the meaning of it.

WM. GILES.

Nelson County, April 24th, 1855.

I do hereby certify, that on my return home from February Court, I fell in with Dr. L. N. Ligon. I asked him what he thought of the Know Nothings, and how he liked their platform. He replied that he did not like them; that if they should get a majority, the country would be ruined; that it was a scheme of the Northern Abolitionists to deceive the South; that if they could obtain a majority in both houses of Congress, and obtain a President, they would dissolve this Union, and involve the country in all the horrors and calamities of a civil war; that to prevent such a state of things, he thought all the Whigs who were Whigs from principle, and the Democrats, ought to unite, and use all the means in their power to put down that abominable party. He also advocated the election of Mr. Wise, and said that the foreigners and the Catholics were only a hobby to take in and deceive the ignorant.

Given under my hand this 25th of April, 1855.

OBADIAH HENDERSON.

In this district, Mr. Wm. J. Robertson was appointed elector; but resigning in consequence of the pressure of professional engagements. Mr. William F. Gordon, Jr. of Albemarle was substituted, and greatly distinguished himself by his speeches against the secret foe.

VII. In the seventh district, Hon. William Smith was an independent candidate for re-election. He was elected by a large majority, although his advocacy of several of the doctrines of the Know Nothing party alienated many of his oldest party friends, and induced many to regard him as the candidate of the Know Nothing rather than of the Democratic party. Messrs. Lee of Orange, Funsten of Alexandria, and Marye of Fredericksburg, openly opposed his re-election, and opposed him on the stump. Many Democratic votes were given for gentlemen who were not candidates for Congress, in consequence of Gov. Smith's course. During the present session of Congress, however, Gov. Smith has voted with the Democratic party, and appears anxious to return to its bosom.

Mr. B. H. Berry, of the town of Alexandria, was the elector in this district, and addressed the people of nearly every county in the district.

VIII. In the eighth district, Hon. Charles James Faulkner was the Democratic candidate for Congress. He was opposed by Mr. Alexander Bote-

LER, a member of the Know Nothing party, and a gentleman of considerable ability as a popular speaker. The district was canvassed with great energy by the candidates. In this district the Know Nothings relied confidently upon the success of their candidate, but the sleepless industry and ability displayed by Mr. FAULKNER secured his election by a respectable majority. Personal difficulties between the candidates, it was feared, would at one time result in a hostile meeting between Messrs. Faulkner and Boteler, but an honorable and satisfactory adjustment was accomplished by the friends of the parties.

Mr. THOMAS M. ISBELL, of Jefferson, at one time a distinguished member of the State Senate from the Appomattox district, was the elector in this district, and delivered several very able and eloquent addresses during the canvass.

IX. Hon. JOHN LETCHER, of Lexington, was a candidate for re-election in the ninth district, and met with no opposition. Mr. LETCHER is everywhere regarded as one of the most laborious and useful public men in the State, and his course as a member of Congress had won for him the esteem of his political adversaries, and the admiration of his own party. He is the representative of that famous "Tenth Legion," which, since the days of Jefferson, has never failed to present an unbroken front to the enemies of Democracy. Again and again, in times of extreme peril, have Rockingham and Shenandoah saved the State from the curse of federal misrule. In the last election, the patriotic voters of those two famous counties rolled up a majority so overwhelming as to leave doubts respecting the existence of Know Nothingism in that section of the State.

GEO. E. DENEALE, Esq., for many years the representative of Rockingham in the Senate, was the elector.

Mr. WM. H. HARMAN, of Augusta, one of the most talented and promising lawyers in the Valley of Virginia, was the senatorial elector for Augusta, and contributed as much as any man in the State, by his frequent and powerful speeches, to the success of our party. This gentleman received a very large vote at the Staunton Convention for the office of Lieutenant Governor.

X. Hon. Z. KIDWELL was the Democratic candidate for Congress in the tenth district, and was opposed by the Rev. Mr. PENDLETON of Bethany College, the nominee of the Know Nothing party. In this district the Know Nothings resorted to every conceivable expedient to defeat the Democratic candidate. Secret instructions and circulars were brought to light which revealed a system of fraud and trickery unworthy of respectable men, and which effectually destroyed the prospects of the Know Nothing party in that district. Mr. Kidwell was re-elected by a very large majority.

Hon. SHERRARD CLEMENS, an ex-member of Congress, and the author of an excellent campaign document published elsewhere in this volume, was the elector for the eighth district.

XI. In the eleventh district, Mr. CHARLES S. LEWIS was the Democratic candidate for Congress. He was opposed and defeated by Mr. CARLISLE, the Know Nothing candidate, who was some years ago a Democratic member of the Senate of Virginia.

BENJAMIN W. JACKSON, Esq. of Wood County, a young and talented Democrat was the elector. Mr. Jackson was a few years ago a prominent member of the house of delegates.

XII. In the twelfth district, Hon. HENRY A. EDMONDSON was the Democratic nominee for Congress. Mr. Edmondson has been for many years in Congress and has the entire confidence of his constituents. He was opposed by Mr. WALLER STAPLES, of Montgomery, a former member of the Legislature of Virginia, and a leading member of his party in that district. The candidates canvassed the district most actively, and Mr. Edmondson's speeches were marked by great force and eloquence. He was elected by a large majority.

Hon. A. A. CHAPMAN, for many years a member of Congress, and one of our most distinguished men, was the elector in this district.

XIII. Hon. FAYETTE MCMULLIN, for several years past a member of Congress, was a candidate for re-election in the thirteenth district. He was elected by an overwhelming majority. Mr. CONNELLY F. TRIGG was the Know Nothing candidate.

This district was the theatre of the most animated and exciting canvass in Virginia. In the early part of the campaign the secret order foretold that they would sweep the ABINGDON district by an overwhelming majority. The reiterated declarations of the secret order of their certain and easy victory aroused to activity the most distinguished Democrats of that section of the State. Yielding to the solicitations of his friends, EX-GOVERNOR FLOYD of Washington County, the elector for that district declared himself a candidate for the Legislature. He was bitterly opposed by the most eloquent and popular Know Nothing in that section of the State. A fierce and relentless war was waged upon the Know Nothing party by such men as EX-GOVERNOR FLOYD, THOMAS L. PRESTON, BENJAMIN RUSH FLOYD and WILLIAM H. COOK. The Know Nothings upon their side spared nothing to win that victory of which they had so frequently and so confidently boasted. But from the accounts which have reached us there never were delivered in Virginia more eloquent and able speeches than were those of the champions of our party in Little Tennessee. Addressing themselves to the good sense and patriotism of the intelligent yeomanry of that section of the State, they crushed an organization which at one time threatened the overthrow of our party. The overwhelming majority given by our party for the Democratic ticket in southwest Virginia, was the result of the indefatigable exertions of those eloquent champions to whom we have referred. Contrary to the expectations of both parties, in other portions of the State, Governor Floyd and Mr. Thomas L. Preston were elected to the Legislature by large majorities.

THE SIGNAL GUN FROM THE RICHMOND EXAMINER.

At the Staunton Gubernatorial Convention, the two leading Democratic journals of the State differed as to which was the most suitable man to receive the nomination, Mr. Wise or Mr. Leake. The *Enquirer* took sides with the former, the *Examiner* with the latter. The Enquirer went immediately into the fight, but the Examiner, although declaring promptly after the convention, as we have seen, its purpose, to support Mr. Wise, yet from certain local reasons did not choose to open its battery until about the first of February. After this time no journal could have rendered more effective service to any party. We have drawn freely from that able and independent journal in this compilation, and in doing so we thought we could do nothing to answer our purpose better. On the eve of the election the following editorial, which we designate as the Signal Gun, appeared in the Examiner:

TO THE INVINCIBLE DEMOCRACY OF VIRGINIA.

This is the last time our words can reach the great body of our readers before the election. We are glad that these last words are words of encouragement, confidence and assurance. We use no electioneering artifice—we express no hesitating opinion, when we tell the Democracy of Virginia, that, if they do their duty, the victory is theirs. On no former occasion in the history of their battles and victories have the party been so universally aroused and fiercely indignant as now. Hesitating somewhat in the early part of the canvass—doubtful for a moment as to the true line of duty—they have been thoroughly aroused during the latter months of the contest, and—outraged, disgusted and incensed at the intrusion of so foul a thing as Know Nothingism in a Southern community, and in virtuous Virginia—they have risen up as one man to break its head and cast its loathsome carcass from the presence of decency and virtue.

The frogs and locusts and vermin which infested Egypt, did not produce a more profound antipathy or universal loathing and retching among her people, than our honest Democracy of Virginia feel towards the polluting filth and nauseating slime which is denoted by the vulgarism—Sam. And they mean to deal with the intrusion in a summary way. They have a herculean task before them more formidable than the cleansing of the Augean stables; but, considering that great emergencies require great exertions, every man is resolved to make thorough work of his task, and to do it with an energy and completeness which will leave nothing to be done over again hereafter. The spirit of the Democracy everywhere—in every grand division and section, as well as in every county and precinct in the State,—is the same. One instinctive resolve and one common purpose actuates the whole mass. It is not any artificial organization, the result of political machinery and thorough party drill, that has produced this intense unity of sentiment and of resolve; but it is the intuitive loathing of what is mean, low, and vile, which actuates the heart of Virginia, and bands her democracy together in serried phalanx. The old party lines fade and vanish in this contest. The impure ingredients that before had an accidental place in the Democratic mass fall off under the attraction of the foreign substance that is brought in contact, leaving the pure lump of genuine Democracy cleansed and refined. The old opposing party also falls to pieces, giving up its dross and impurity to the newly imported foreignism, and leaving the pure Virginianism to seek its natural affinity in the mother element of unadulterated Virginia Democracy.

No, this is no contest about men that our Democracy are waging now. It is not that we want to elect this man or to beat that man. It is not that our attachments to these candidates as men, or hostilities to those candidates as men, lead us to vote so and so. But the sentiment of the Virginia Democracy is: *This is a foul, demoralizing, debasing, filthy thing, that has got into Virginia pastures from the Northern pig-sty, and is turning our land of honesty, truthfulness, good manners, and manly frankness, into a very Yankee's slough of falsehood, slander, deceit, cunning, detraction, meanness and vileness. For the love we bear our Commonwealth, and for the hatred she inspires in her sons for all that is mean, grovelling and despicable, we must beat down this foul beast and smite it unto death.*

Who so craven and false of heart as to believe we shall fail in the righteous, noble work? Who can divest hims lf so far of the generous confidence that a brave man feels in the triumph of the right, as to entertain one thought of failure? The man deserves to be pilloried who allows the belief to possess him, that SAM, the bastard of a Five Points jail-bird, is going to triumph in Virginia. He is no Democrat—no Virginian—no man, that can harbor the thought.

It cannot be, and will not be. Virginia Democracy will carry Virginia as sure as the rising and setting of the sun. Angered, aroused, indignant and ferocious beyond all former precedent, our glorious, invincible Democracy long for the onset and thirst for the battle. As the hind pants for the water brooks, so they pant for the day of vengeance.

And woe, woe unto those who have provoked their holy wrath. Woe unto the men who have brought deceit, cunning, duplicity, midnight and dark lantern plottings into Virginia. The day of retribution is at hand. The vengeance of the Lord is upon the heels of the false Egyptians, Phillistines, Moabites, Edomites, Ishmaelites. The Lord has brought sharp swords upon them, to make them food for the fowls of heaven and the beasts of the field. See how the clouds roll and mutter and the fire flashes before them. The anger of the righteous cometh fast upon them with the noise and fury of the storm, which shall surely overtake them.

Well is it for that man of Virginia, this day, who shall barter his house for an helmet, and sell his garment for a sword, and cast in his lot with the children of Democracy. But woe, woe, unto him who, for carnal ends and self seeking, has withheld himself from the great work, and joined his hand with the enemy—for the curse shall abide upon him—even the bitter curse of MEROZ—forever and ever more.

THE CONCLUSION OF THE CANVASS. MR. WISE'S LETTER.

Mr. Wise concluded the campaign at Leesburg, the county seat of Loudon, in one of his masterly efforts. He had been regularly in the field from the first of January to the seventh of May. In that time he had traveled more than three thousand miles, had been upon the stump fifty times, and had consumed two hundred hours in public speaking. When he concluded, he was much enfeebled and exhausted from the excessive labors he had undergone. In all probability, nothing saved his life but his indomitable and patriotic spirit. He went from Leesburg to Washington city, and there awaited the decision of the people of Virginia. He wrote the following letter on his arrival in that city. In this letter can be seen the true and fervid patriotism beaming and flashing in every sentence.

TO THE PEOPLE OF VIRGINIA.

Fellow Citizens:—I have now finished the canvass of the State. On the 7th inst., at Leesburg, I met my last appointment. Incessant and excessive labors, for 127 days, have so impaired my health and strength, that I must desist from further effort and seek rest. I retire from the "stump" the less reluctantly' because I may now justly claim that I have faithfully tried to do my part, and I can confidently leave the rest to the unsubdued and unterrified Democracy and its loyal hosts.

Never were the sound, conservative, conscientious, and stake-holding Republicans in Virginia, better organized and more aroused than they are at the present time. It has been deserted by a few who left their party for its good; but, in turn, the very flower of the old opposition of Whiggery, respectable in times past for its profession of conservatism and its love of law and order have chosen to elect Democracy with all the ills they complain of it, rather than to fly to those they *"know not of."*

The *personnel* of the party was never more purified, and the numerical majority was never larger than it promises to be at the coming election. As in 1801, the Democracy stood "like a wall," and rolled back the tide of federalism, so now it stands and will roll back the tide of fanaticism! It will prove itself to be the *visible invincible!* It is roused, and will rally to the polls 10,000 voters more than ever gave the *viva voce* before! And the *viva voce* will rend the veil from the *"invisible,"* and defend the freedom and independence of the elective franchise and the Constitution and the laws, against the conspiracy of the dark lantern.

It will forbid any power in Virginia to interpose between our conscience and our God.

It will save the Protestant Churches from the pollution of party politics, and conserve its powers of truth for the pulling down of strongholds, free from the taint and violence of persecution. It will trust in God, and defend the Christian faith from Intolerance, and allow poor humanity to indulge in the virtues of charity and peace on earth, and good will to all men.

It will only oppose any "legislative enactment" to interfere with the rights of the members of any Church as citizens; but it will deny the power of the Legislature to annul the new Constitution, which has made the act of religious freedom irrepealable. That act is now organic law. And the Democratic conservatism will allow no party nor power to set up a higher law, and say that a man *shall* be burthened, when the Constitution says he shall *not* be burthened, for reason of his religious opinion, by being excluded from eligibility to office, or by removal from office because of his religion or the place of his birth.

It will prevent the repudiation of the right of Naturalization, for which the nation poured out its blood and treasure, for three years in the second war of Independence with Great Britain.

It will defend the State right to regulate citizenship.

It will not deny to the oppressed a home, nor prevent the population "of these States" still requiring hundreds of millions of immigrants, who bring with them hundreds of millions of money.

It will allow the poor, as well as the rich, to come and "drink of the waters" of liberty freely. And it will remember that all are not criminals whom European despots call such, and send away from troubling their dominion. It will take by the hands other criminals besides John Mitchell, and feel for others in the prison-houses and dungeons of the Old World besides him who once was tenant of Olmutz!

It will jealously guard against the Foreign influence which is insidiously sent from Exeter Hall in Old England to Williams' Hall in New England, to invade America in the name of an "American" party; and it will watch the oppressor, not the oppressed, abroad, as did "Washington, Jefferson, Madison and Jackson!"

It will defend the freedom and independence of the elective franchise against the conspiracy which would bind voters by test oaths to reject men of a particular religious faith, marked for proscription; and which would not leave suffrage as free to elect as to reject those whom the constitution and the laws have made eligible to office.

It will especially guard the office of Governor from the avowed intent to wield the appointing power so as not to obey the limitations of qualification for office, fixed by the constitution, but to obey rules of appointment established by an irresponsible and unauthorized Secret Oligarchy, formed to set up the *Higher Law* of its own proscription for its own exclusive and selfish ends.

It will see that the oath itself of the Governor's office is not prevented by sectarian bigotry to set up a religious test as a qualification for office.

It will defend the General Government from the consolidation which would establish itself on what is called the *independence* of Congress.

It will defend public policy from the faith of the American system, Harbors, Rivers, and Pacific Railroads, and Protective Tariffs, and Internal Improvements by the General Government, now again advanced by a Winchester Council of the American party.

It will defend the State against agrarianism, freesoilism and abolitionism, now threatening to invade the South from Northern and non-slaveholding Councils of Know Nothingism. It will defend society against the demoralization of a cabal sworn to practice dissimulation and perfidy between man and man. And it will defend religion against the demons of anti-Christ!

With perfect and abiding confidence in the power of Truth and Democracy—of a purified, exalted and triumphant majority for these impregnable positions, I go home to Accomac, and await the polls of the people. I cannot do so without thanking thousands, of the sections of the State through which I have passed, for their uniform hospitality, kindness and respect, and without saying that the chief gratification with which I part from a daily intercourse with the masses of the people is that I have endeavored to sow the seeds of truth only in the popular mind, and I trust that they will be fruitful of blessings to individuals, to the State and to the country.

I am, very truly and respectfully,

Your fellow-citizen,

HENRY A. WISE.

WASHINGTON CITY, May 10th, 1855.

OFFICIAL VOTE OF VIRGINIA.

Below we give the official vote of the election in Virginia on the 24th of May 1855, for Governor, Lieutenant Governor and Attorney General. The returns we derive from the office of the Secretary of State; therefore, they may be relied on as nearly correct. The vote of the State for Governor, is 83,424 for Mr. Wise; 73,244 for Mr. Flournoy—total, 156,668—majority for Mr. Wise, 10,180. This result vindicates the correctness of our estimate, calculated from the unofficial returns. Our table always exhibited Mr. Wise's majority a little over 10,000, while estimates from other sources made the majority fall considerably below that amount. The average Democratic majority in the State, exhibited by this election, is 11,225—Mr. Bocock having received the highest, and Mr. Patton the lowest vote:—*Enquirer*.

	Governor.		Lt. Governor.		Att. General.	
	H. A. Wise,	T. S. Flournoy,	E. W. McComas,	J. M. H. Beale,	W. P. Bocock,	J. M. Patton,
Accomac,	816	932	748	926	737	924
Albemarle,	1069	1220	1096	1197	1095	1202
Alexandria,	399	820	395	818	397	818
Alleghany,	337	206	338	205	340	203
Amelia,	309	234	321	203	331	214
Amherst,	688	680	692	666	698	678
Appomattox,	513	247	528	231	559	216
Augusta,	1336	2426	1361	2404	1360	2409
Barbour,	753	331	746	328	747	329
Bath,	222	276	220	274	220	273
Bedford,	1067	1328	1105	1310	1107	1308
Berkeley,	923	905	920	905	923	904
Boone,	280	138	298	113	229	119
Botetourt,	960	537	968	530	971	527
Braxton,	119	571	107	581	107	579
Brooke,	333	432	332	429	328	440
Brunswick,	556	224	556	206	554	214
Buckingham,	496	551	505	536	526	521
Cabell,	501	383	578	296	471	360
Campbell,	979	1535	1000	1517	1018	1510
Caroline,	643	615	664	608	664	612
Carroll,	657	311	639	299	646	304
Charles City,	124	175	116	149	116	158
Charlotte,	443	398	429	384	444	381
Chesterfield,	975	503	1003	506	999	507
Clarke,	361	320	359	309	358	313
Craig,	304	120	305	116	304	113
Culpeper,	443	528	438	514	425	543
Cumberland,	277	306	281	295	286	296
Dinwiddie,	421	234	415	225	429	227
Doddridge,	349	226	345	219	352	218
Elizabeth City,	187	175	181	172	181	172
Essex,	266	316	272	305	275	308
Fairfax,	512	631	500	612	500	608
Fauquier,	920	1040	922	1032	920	1035
Fayette,	271	301	245	299	235	297
Floyd,	566	447	569	437	565	436
Fluvanna,	443	458	472	436	465	452
Franklin,	1253	906	1265	893	1268	890
Frederick,	1335	1203	1343	1196	1344	1199
Giles,	418	405	426	391	417	393
Gilmer,	411	242	407	248	407	256
Gloucester,	381	317	301	224	401	316
Goochland,	385	262	409	250	409	253
Grayson,	553	266	547	262	547	262
Greenbrier,	533	870	511	873	522	864
Greene,	532	42	528	41	528	43
Greenesville,	206	73	210	67	213	70

Halifax,	1163	587	1183	550	1191	550
Hampshire,	1118	845	1126	835	1121	841
Hanover,	706	553	718	548	722	541
Hancock,	221	291	220	290	218	282
Hardy,	651	708	649	693	648	692
Harrison,	1017	921	1014	916	1011	917
Henrico,	765	983	781	963	780	974
Henry,	507	430	519	399	527	403
Highland,	444	342	447	343	445	344
Isle of Wight,	669	173	670	165	675	162
Jackson,	592	637	595	634	593	635
James City,	44	126	39	130	39	129
Jefferson,	862	934	865	923	859	924
Kanawha,	571	1537	579	1517	570	1529
King George,	189	191	197	189	197	190
King William,	333	111	344	104	336	110
King & Queen,	397	307	318	308	399	301
Lancaster,	143	175	149	154	152	168
Lee,	1113	377	1073	375	1073	374
Lewis,	572	426	578	422	572	424
Logan,	366	76	389	68	352	76
Loudoun,	690	2015	672	1997	671	1994
Louisa,	613	461	630	446	632	455
Lunenburg,	465	201	475	195	483	191
Madison,	672	109	657	104	647	117
Marion,	1135	459	1134	438	1132	440
Marshall,	608	984	612	981	613	982
Mason,	348	737	343	723	*732	*336
Matthews,	273	221	267	215	265	216
Mecklenburg,	874	480	763	463	765	462
Mercer,	417	350	390	343	375	344
Middlesex,	231	180	234	175	234	176
Monongalia,	1325	662	1325	657	1322	658
Monroe,	577	891	577	884	576	877
Montgomery,	660	592	657	580	655	580
Morgan,	266	415	266	411	267	411
Nansemond,	340	556	333	550	331	551
Nelson,	436	740	446	729	447	728
New Kent,	175	201	175	195	175	196
Nicholas,	114	460	114	458	116	456
Norfolk County,	1068	1263	1075	1254	1081	1258
Northampton,	235	288	222	281	222	282
Northumberland,	296	316	304	309	303	312
Nottoway,	228	187	229	152	230	160
Ohio,	1110	1741	1133	1702	1105	1733
Orange,	395	349	394	239	393	346
Page,	1033	72	1022	69	1022	69
Patrick,	722	496	723	468	731	467
Pendleton,	558	408	560	402	560	404
Pittsylvania,	1335	1352	1364	1313	1385	1312
Pleasants,	228	206	226	207	227	205
Pocahontas,	457	107	448	105	449	109
Powhatan,	287	152	293	144	292	149
Preston,	798	737	803	730	805	729
Princess Anne,	307	325	313	319	312	321

	Governor.		Lt. Governor.		Att. General.	
	H. A. Wise,	T. S. Flournoy,	E. W. McComas,	J. M. H. Beale,	W. P. Bocock,	J. M. Patton,
Prince Edward,	427	355	428	337	435	334
Prince George,	369	131	378	128	391	128
Prince William,	659	249	665	246	664	244
Pulaski,	305	272	306	269	306	269
Putnam,	393	387	390	380	392	384
Raleigh,	80	259	78	258	75	258
Randolph,	438	308	430	289	413	296
Rappahannock,	490	485	493	477	491	481
Richmond,	164	364	166	364	167	364
Ritchie,	488	353	492	349	485	348
Roanoke,	600	307	605	304	605	301
Rockbridge,	1147	1206	1161	1184	1163	1190
Rockingham,	2700	610	2681	584	2681	609
Russell,	989	580	983	575	982	574
Scott,	797	509	792	503	794	494
Shenandoah,	2031	185	2032	171	2032	176
Smyth,	654	571	649	564	648	566
Southampton,	568	486	580	488	582	487
Spotsylvania,	619	604	630	598	626	503
Stafford,	474	359	470	359	470	359
Surry,	230	141	220	136	230	137
Sussex,	381	100	376	96	379	98
Taylor,	487	465	484	461	485	460
Tazewell,	1102	189	1049	176	1053	172
Tyler,	430	360	434	355	437	348
Upshur,	496	286	498	281	495	284
Warren,	500	271	438	265	499	265
Warwick,	21	57	19	53	19	53
Washington,	1284	948	1281	949	1281	947
Wayne,	347	319	410	238	252	221
Westmoreland,	83	395	88	395	91	393
Wetzel,	549	80	532	79	532	79
Wirt,	259	217	263	213	261	210
Wood,	747	839	642	885	635	902
Wyoming,	82	116	83	112	80	113
Wythe,	829	724	838	704	830	710
York,	109	169	93	157	94	158
Norfolk City,	552	922	517	901	478	887
Petersburg,	783	747	790	733	787	743
Richmond City,	1166	2144	1180	2117	1189	2126
Williamsburg,	51	66	47	65	48	66
	83,424	73,244	83,068	71,689	83,731	71,613

RECAPITULATION.

Wise,		83,424
Flournoy,		73,244
	Majority,	10,180
McComas,		83,068
Beale,		71,689
	Majority,	11,379
Bocock,		83,731
Patton,		71,613
	Majority,	12,118

It is proper to add here, however, that the count of this vote which was subsequently made by the Legislature, under the requirement of the constitution, did not result precisely as exhibited by the foregoing table. The Legislative computation exhibited the following results :

STATE SENATORS ELECTED IN 1855.

From Rockingham and Pendleton—Geo. E. Deneale, D.
From Sussex, Southampton and Greensville—W. W. Cobb, D.
From Dinwiddie, Amelia and Brunswick—Wm. F. Thompson, D.
From Lunenburg, Nottoway, and Prince Edward—Thos. H. Campbell, D.
From Pittsylvania—W. H. Wooding, D.
From Henry, Patrick, and Franklin—Archibald Stuart, D.
From Hanover and Henrico—Chastain White, D.
From Gloucester, Matthews, and Middlesex—John W. Catlett, D.
From King and Queen, King William, and Essex—Beverly B. Douglass, D.
From Stafford, King George, and Prince William—J. M. Taliaferro, D.
From Madison, Culpeper, Orange, and Greene—Thomas N. Welch, D.
From Louisa, Goochland, and Fluvanna—Wm. M. Ambler, D.
From Jefferson and Berkeley—Francis Yates, D.
From Frederick, Clarke, and Warren—Oliver R. Funsten, D.
From Bath, Highland, and Rockbridge—James H. Paxton, D.
From Carroll, Floyd, Grayson, Montgomery, and Pulaski—Harvey Deskins, D.
From Smythe, Wythe, and Washington—Thomas M. Tate, D.
From Mason, Jackson, Cabell, Wayne, and Wirt—Fleet W. Smith, K. N.
From Wetzel, Marshall, Marion, and Tyler—James G. West, D.
From Monongalia, Preston, and Taylor—J. B. Huddleson, D.
From Accomac and Northampton—O. B. Finney, K. N.
From Norfolk and Princess Anne—P. H. Daughtrey, K. N.
From Campbell and Appomattox—Thomas H. Flood, K. N.
From Loudoun—Noble S. Braden, K. N.
From Boone, Logan, Kanawha, Putnam, and Wyoming—Andrew S. Parks, K. N.

SENATORS ELECTED IN 1853.

From Norfolk City—W. N. McKenney, K. N.
From Isle of Wight, Nansemond and Surry—W. J. Arthur, D.
From Petersburg and Prince George—J. A. Jones, D.
From Powhatan, Cumberland and Chesterfield—Wm. Old, Jr. D.
From Mecklenburg and Charlotte—L. W. Tazewell, K. N.
From Halifax—R. Logan, D.
From Bedford—J. F. Johnson, K. N.
From Williamsburg, James City, Charles City, New Kent, York, Elizabeth City and Warwick—Robert Saunders, K. N.
From Richmond City—O. P. Baldwin, K. N.
From Richmond, Lancaster, Northumberland and Westmoreland—Elliott M. Braxton, D.
From Caroline and Spottsylvania—Wm. A Moncure, D.
From Fairfax and Alexandria—Henry W. Thomas, K. N.
From Fauquier and Rappahannock—J. K. Marshall, K. N.
From Albemarle—B. F. Randolph, D.
From Amherst, Nelson and Buckingham—R. K. Irving, K. N.
From Hampshire, Hardy and Morgan—J. C. B. Mullen, K. N.
From Shenandoah and Page—T. Buswell, D.
From Augusta—C. R. Harris, D.
From Botetourt, Alleghany, Roanoke and Craig—Douglas B. Layne, D.
From Mercer, Monroe, Giles and Tazewell—Manlius Chapman, D.
From Scott, Lee and Russell—J. F. McElhany, K. N.
From Nicholas, Fayette, Pocahontas, Raleigh, Braxton and Greenbrier—T. Creigh, K. N.
From Ritchie, Doddridge, Harrison, Pleasants and Wood—U. M. Turner, K. N.
From Upsher, Barbour, Lewis, Gilmer and Randolph—Albert G. Reger, D.
From Brooke, Hancock and Ohio—L. Steenrod, D.

MEMBERS OF THE HOUSE OF DELEGATES OF VIRGINIA ELECTED MAY, 1855.

Accomac—Arthur Watson, K. N.
Albemarle—Thomas Wood, K. N., and Wm. T. Early, K. N.
Alexandria—Lawrence B. Taylor, K. N.
Alleghany and Bath—Samuel Carpenter, D.
Amelia and Nottoway—W. F. C. Gregory, D.
Amherst—Dudley Davies, K. N.
Appomattox—C. H. Jones, D.
Augusta—Adam McChesney, K. N.; A. Bolivar Christian, K. N.; John D. Imboden, K. N.
Barbour—Joseph Daniels, D.
Bedford—W. M. Burwell, K. N.; Samuel P. R. Moorman, K. N.
Berkeley—J. B. Hoge, D.; R. D. Seaman, D.
Botetourt and Craig—F. H. Mays, D.; Robert M. Wiley, D.
Braxton and Nicholas—Marshall Triplett, K. N.
Brooke and Hancock—O. W. Langfitt, K. N.
Brunswick—Edward Dromgoole, D.
Buckingham—Thos. M. Bondurant, K. N.
Cabell—H. J. Samuels, D.
Campbell—F. B. Deane, K. N.; M. B. Nowlin, K. N.
Caroline—Daniel C. Dejarnette, D.
Carroll—John Carroll, D.
Charles City, James City and New Kent—Wm. Bush, K. N.

Charlotte—Jos. H. Roberts, D.
Chesterfield—Jeremiah Hobbs, D.
Clarke—Buckner Ashby, D.
Culpeper—Perry J. Eggborn, K. N.
Cumberland and Powhatan—W. P. Dabney, D.
Dinwiddie—John J. Crawford, D.
Doddridge and Tyler—Absy George, D.
Elizabeth City, Warwick, York and Williamsburg—Joseph Segar, K. N.
Essex and King and Queen—M. R. H. Garnett, D.
Fairfax—James Thrift, K. N.
Fauquier—Bailey Shumate, K. N.; Richard H. Carter, K. N.
Fayette and Raleigh—Wm. Tyree, K. N.
Floyd—Pleasant Howell, D.
Fluvanna—Geo. P. Holman, D.
Franklin—Wm. H. Edwards, D.; Peter Hancock, D.
Frederick—R. C. Bywaters, D.; G. P. Baker, D.
Giles—A. G. Pendleton, D.
Gilmer and Wirt—P. Hays, D.
Gloucester—Warner T. Jones, D.
Goochland—John C. Rutherfoord, D.
Grayson—John Dickinson, D.
Greenbrier—A. G. Davis, K. N.
Greene and Orange—John H. Lee, D.
Greensville and Sussex—Wm. T. Lundy, D.
Halifax—J. H. Edmunds, D.; Chas. Craddock, D.
Hampshire—Asa Hiett, D.; Isaac Parsons, D.
Hanover—Wm. Nelson, D.
Hardy—F. B. Welton, D.
Harrison—Robert Johnson, D.; A. S. Holden, D.
Henrico—Henry Cox, K. N.
Henry—A. Hughes Dillard, D.
Highland—A. H. Byrd, D.
Isle of Wight—Jas. F. Crocker, D.
Jackson—W. P. Frost, K. N.
Jefferson—Wells J. Hawks, D.; T. Harris Towner, K. N.
Kanawha—John Thompson, K. N., (dead) B. H. Smith, K. N.
King George and Stafford—John Seddon, D.
King William—Harrison B. Tomlin, D.
Lancaster and Northumberland—W. H. Harding, K. N.
Lee—Job B. Crabtree, D.; Dr. H. Riggs, D.
Lewis—John Brannon, D.
Logan, Boone and Wyoming—J. H. Anderson, D.
Louisa—Jos. K. Pendleton, D.
Loudoun—H. B. Powell, K. N.; R. L. Wright, K. N.
Lunenburg—George W. Hardy, D.
Madison—James L. Kemper, D.
Marion—John S. Barnes, D.; Ulysses N. Arnett, D.
Marshall—R. C. Hollady, K. N.
Mason—G. B. Thomas, K. N.
Matthews and Middlesex—Geo. L. Nicholson, D.
Mecklenburg—Wm. E. Dodson, D.
Mercer—N. French, K. N.
Monongalia—J. Lantz, D.; R. W. Caruthers, D.
Monroe—Alexander Clark, K. N.; Alexander D. Haynes, K. N.
Montgomery—C. A. Ronald, D.
Morgan—Lemuel Vanorsdall, K. N.

Nansemond—Nathl. Riddick, K. N.
Nelson—W. M. Cabell, K. N.
Norfolk City—W. D. Roberts, K. N.
Norfolk County—C. W. Murdaugh, K. N.; Max. Herbert, K. N.
Northampton—E. J. Spady, K. N.
Ohio—Jas. Paul, K. N.; John Brady, K. N.; G. L. Cranmer, K. N.
Page—Mann Spitler, D.
Patrick—Wm. A. Burwell, D.
Pendleton—Jas. B. Kee, D.
Petersburg—J. H. Claiborne, D.
Pittsylvania—Richard M. Kirby, D.; Thomas W. Walton, D.
Pleasants and Ritchie—John Collins, D.
Pocahontas—Adam Nottingham, D.
Preston—J. A. F. Martin, D.; E. T. Brandon, D.
Prince Edward—Thomas T. Tredway, D.
Prince George and Surry—Benj. C. Drew, D.
Princess Anne—John Woodhouse, K. N.
Prince William—Chas. E. Sinclair, D.
Pulaski—John S. Draper, D.
Putnam—Ro. N. B. Thompson, D.
Randolph—S. Bosworth, K. N.
Rappahannock—Edward T. Jones, D.
Richmond City—H. K. Ellyson, K. N.; H. B. Dickinson, K. N.; R. C. Stanard, K. N.
Richmond County and Westmoreland—L. C. Berkeley, K. N.
Roanoke—Colin Bass, D.
Rockbridge—R. L. Doyle, K. N.; A. Patterson, K. N.
Rockingham—J. M. R. Sprinkle, D.; J. G. Brown, D.; Wm. B. Yancey, D.
Russell—G. W. Chandler, D.; —— Kelley, D.
Scott—J. T. McIver, D.
Shenandoah—J. S. Calvert, D.; P. Pitman, D.
Smyth—Thos. L. Preston, D.
Southampton—J. W. Gurley, D.
Spottsylvania—Oscar M. Crutchfield, D.
Taylor—Chas. W. Newlon, D.
Tazewell—Wm. M. Gillespie, D.
Upshur— —— Carper, D.
Warren—Samuel W. Thomas, D.
Washington—Wm. K. Heiskell, D.; John B. Floyd, D.
Wayne—Jeremiah Wellman, D.
Wetzel—David West, D.
Wood—A. J. Bowman, K. N.
Wythe—David Graham, D.

THE 24TH DAY OF MAY IN VIRGINIA, IN 1855.

On the 24th day of May 1855, the great battle between the North and the South was fought on the soil of Virginia. Virginia was the battle ground upon which that fell-destroyer, abolition Know Nothing fanaticism, was "crushed out" in pushing its direful inroads upon the sunny South. It was here in Virginia that the British lion crouched in servile obedience beneath the golden wings of Washington's eagle. And it was here in Virginia, that the foul and loathsome cockatrice, Know Nothingism, crouched (spaniel like) beneath the patriotic tread of the sturdy husbandman, the stigmatising lash, the burning invective and withering satire of that champion of States Rights, and defender of the constitution and of civil and religious liberty—Henry A. Wise. And it is here in Virginia, that we intend to keep spotless that rich legacy of political policy, bequeathed to us by Thomas Jefferson and James Madison. The Democracy of Virginia will, at all times, and under all circumstances, fly their colors. Our platform is now, as it has ever been, a strict observance of the tenets of States Rights. We know no section, no clique, no party, no platform, no man,—but only the States Rights flag left us by Jefferson and Madison, which we expect to live under, fight under, and die under. We bid defiance to the wooden horse. Our banner in envied grandeur still floats over the impregnable ramparts of Truth, Right and Justice, and will continue to flaunt its ægis folds until the bird of liberty, with the stars and stripes around its neck, shall wing itself from the western continent.

The 4th of July commemorates the day on which the American people repudiated the British yoke; the 24th of May commemorates the day on which the PEOPLE, THE DEMOCRACY OF VIRGINIA, REPUDIATED THAT WHICH WAS WORSE THAN BRITISH BONDAGE—Know Nothingism. The 24th day of May 1855 is a second declaration of the citizens of Virginia, TO BE FREE AND INDEPENDENT. May the day ever live as one of our proudest epochs, in the hearts of all true lovers of Civil and Religious Liberty.

From the Richmond Examiner, May 29th, 1855.

THE DEMOCRATIC TRIUMPH.

The election returns which fill our columns this morning will give to our readers the details of that crushing and utterly annihilating victory which the Democracy have won over their boastful, exultant and secret adversary. We have swept the State like a mountain torrent, deluging every culvert, and drowning Know Nothing candidates of every rank and degree, from Flournoy down to Sam's candidates for the stray coroner's and constable's places of the State. The Democratic legions are triumphant from the mountains to the seashore, and the Democratic shouts of victory are heard in every valley and mountain of the State. Our candidate for Governor is probably elected by a splendid majority of at least twelve thousand, we have returned our unbroken phalanx of Democratic Congressmen, and we shall have a larger Democratic majority than usual in both branches of the Legislature.

There remains not one peg for Sam to hang a hope upon. The deluge has left no dry place for the weary feet of the conquered; and the few Know Nothings who have been elected to the Legislature already feel their laurels withering upon their brows, and burning them like a hot iron. The boasting, blustering, menacing, confident foe, who but yesterday proclaimed the speedy destruction of the Democratic party of Virginia, has been routed at the ballot-box by that noble old party which, in this State, has never known defeat. The great highway along which we have marched to greatness and renown is paved with the bones of just such political monstrosities as that which we slew on Thursday. It is as much the duty and the mission of the Virginia Democracy to slay parties like Sam, as it was that of Hercules to kill giants, dragons hydras and other monsters. We have done our duty, and freed the republic from the consequences of sectional strife and a fearful war of races.

We care not how Sam, like a huge decapitated serpent, may squirm, twist and struggle in the free States. He may lash his huge tail in New England, and jerk and wriggle his headless trunk in Pennsylvania, but all the world knows that on Thursday last his head was taken off with a dexterity and scientific precision which the Virginia Democracy have only acquired by long practice. A few months ago the late Samuel entered this State, took possession of our culverts, and hissed forth various and sundry decrees for the overthrow of Democracy, Catholicism, and the annoyance of the quiet, inoffensive foreigners of this State. But in performing a tilt against the Democracy, he ran against a snag, and expired on Thursday last, having lived just long enough to bury one small grave-digger, and extinguish an humble gas-man. The election has demonstrated that Know Nothingism, in its best days in this State, was nothing but a mild, small beer type of that poor, collapsed old Whig party, which we have beaten with commendable regularity for many years past. The mysteries and secrecy of Know Nothingism concealed not its strength, but its weakness in numbers and resources.

We notice the election and re-election of many of the ablest men of our party to the Legislature. In such men as Floyd, Crutchfield, Edmunds, Rutherfoord, Garnett, and many others whom we might name, our readers will recognize men well suited for the important duties of legislation next winter.

We have but one regret as far as the result in this State is concerned, and that is the defeat of that estimable gentleman and distinguished and indefatigable Democrat, Robert A. Mayo, of Henrico. To that gentleman's energy and sleepless activity, we are indebted for a reduction of hundreds in what was at one time the Know Nothing strength in Henrico. His services will be long remembered by his party.

We commend the gentlemanly good humor and philosophy of our neighbor of the *Whig* to the subordinate journals of the Know Nothings. The Democrats are not to be provoked or annoyed by the impotent exhibitions of childish rage and frenzy of the minor organs of that party to which they have just administered a well-deserved spanking. We tender to our chivalrous neighbor of the *Whig* our sincere condolences, and venture to express the hope that its trip to Salt River may be both pleasant and instructive. The season is a delightful one for going to the country, and the thousand beauties of Spring, with its flowers and balmy breezes, will soon assuage the grief of our friend and neighbor. We have learnt also, from a most reliable source, that our venerable *protege*, Botts, bears the defeat of Mr. Scott with a degree of fortitude worthy of a christian and a philosopher. He is, we learn, busily qualifying himself for the ministry, having announced at the African Church on Tuesday last, the scope and character of his recent theological studies.

APPENDIX.

SPEECH OF HON. S. A. DOUGLAS, OF ILLINOIS.

IN THE UNITED STATES SENATE, MARCH 3, 1854, ON NEBRASKA AND KANSAS.

Mr. Houston. It is now half-past eleven o'clock. I cannot see any particular necessity for going on to-night, and therefore we might as well adjourn.

Several Senators. No, no.

Mr. Houston. Then I give notice that I shall take the floor after the senator from Illinois gets through.

Mr. Sumner. Before the debate closes, I hope to be heard on some points.

Mr. Douglas. We shall hear the senator from Massachusetts, of course, upon whatever points he may desire to speak. I would gladly have agreed to an arrangement by which it should have been understood that the vote would be taken at any fixed time; but we found it impossible to come to an agreement to fix any day or any hour on which the vote should, by common consent, be taken. Consequently we have thought it was better to insist upon proceeding to a vote to-night. I will not occupy the attention of the Senate longer than I can possibly help in doing justice to myself.

Mr. Houston. Objection has been made to my course it seems, because I evinced a disinclination to consent to fix any particular day for the closing of the debate. I did not see any necessity for doing so, and therefore I could not consent to it. I do not care how soon the debate closes; I hope it will be concluded speedily; but I do not wish to have it done informally, nor in the hurried manner in which it has been pressed on the Senate. I claim all the privileges of a senator; but I am perfectly willing to consent to an adjournment, or any other arrangement which the Senate may make. I am in a minority, but I shall yield to the will of the Senate.

Mr. Douglas. I think there seems to be a pretty good disposition manifested now, and we shall be able to close the debate and proceed to the vote in a very short time.

Mr. President, before I proceed to the general argument upon the most important branch of this question, I must say a few words in reply to the senator from Tennessee, [Mr. Bell,] who has spoken upon the bill to-day. He approves of the principles of the bill; he thinks they have great merit; but he does not see his way entirely clear to vote for the bill, because of the objections which he has stated, most of which relate to the Indians.

Upon that point, I desire to say that it has never been the custom in territorial bills to make regulations concerning the Indians within the limits of the proposed Territories. All matters relating to them it has been thought wise to leave to subsequent legislation, to be brought forward by the Committee on Indian Affairs. I did venture originally in this bill to put in one or two provisions upon that subject; but, at the suggestion of many senators on both sides of the chamber, they were stricken out, in order to allow the appropriate committee of the Senate to take charge of that subject. I think, therefore, since we have stricken from the bill all those provisions which pertain to the Indians, and reserved the whole subject for the consideration and action of the appropriate committee, we have obviated every possible objection which could reasonably be urged upon that score. We have every reason to hope and trust that the Committee on Indian Affairs will propose such measures as will do entire justice to the Indians, without contravening the objects of Congress in organizing these Territories.

But, sir, allusion has been made to certain Indian treaties, and it has been intimated, if not charged in direct terms, that we were violating the stipulations of those treaties in respect to the rights and lands of the Indians. The senator from Texas [Mr. Houston] made a very long and interesting speech on that subject; but it so happened, that most of the treaties to which he referred were with Indians not included within the limits of this bill. We have been informed, in the course of the debate to-day, by the chairman of the Committee on Indian Affairs, [Mr. Sebastian,] that there is but one treaty in existence relating to lands or Indians within the limits of either of the proposed Territories, and that is the treaty with the Ottawa Indians, about two hundred persons in number, owning about thirty-four thousand acres of land. Thus it appears, that the whole argument of injustice to the red man, which in the course of this debate has called forth so much sympathy and indignation, is confined to two hundred Indians, owning less than two townships of land. Now, sir, is it possible that a country, said to be five hundred thousand square miles in extent, and large enough to make twelve such States as Ohio, is to be consigned to perpetual barbarism merely on account of that small number of Indians, when the bill itself expressly provides that those Indians and their lands are not to be included within the limits of the proposed Territories, nor to be subject to their laws or jurisdiction? I would not allow this measure to invade the rights of even one Indian, and hence I inserted in the first section of the bill that none of the tribes with whom we have treaty stipulations should be embraced within either of the Territories, unless such Indians shall voluntarily consent to be included therein by treaties hereafter to be made. If any senator can furnish me with language more explicit, or which would prove more effectual in securing the rights of the Indians, I will cheerfully adopt it.

Well, sir, the Senator from Tennessee, in a very kind spirit, here raises the objection for me to answer, that this bill includes Indians within the limits of these Territories with whom we have no treaties; and he desires to know what we are to do with them. I will say to him, that that is not a matter of inquiry which necessarily or properly arises upon the passage of this bill; that is not a proper inquiry to come before the Committee on Territories. You have in all your territorial bills included Indians within the boundaries of the Territories. When you erected the Territory of Minnesota, you had not extinguished the Indian title to one foot of land in that Territory west of the Mississippi river, and to the major part of that Territory the Indian title remains unextinguished to this day. In addition to those wild tribes, you removed Indians from Wisconsin and located them within Minnesota since the Territory was organized. It will be a question for the consideration of the Committee on Indian Affairs, and for the action of Congress, when, in settlement and civilization, it shall become necessary to change the present policy in respect to the Indians. When you erected the territorial government of Oregon, a few years ago, you embraced within it all the Indians living in the Territory without their consent, and without any such reservations in their behalf as are contained in this bill. You had not at that time made a treaty with those Indians, nor extinguished their title to an acre of land in that Territory, nor indeed have you done so to this day. So it is in the organization of Washington Territory. You ran the lines around the country which you thought ought to be within the limits of the Territory, and you embraced all the Indians within those lines; but you made no provision in respect to their rights or lands; you left that matter to the Committee on Indian Affairs, to the Indian laws, and to the proper department, to be arranged afterwards as the public interests might require. The same is true in reference to Utah and New Mexico.

In fact, the policy provided for in this bill, in respect to the Indians, is that which is now in force in every one of the Territories. Therefore, any senator who objects to this bill on that score should have objected to and voted against every territorial bill which you have now in existence. Yet my friend from Texas has taken occasion to remind the Senate several times that it was a matter of pride—and it ought to be a matter of patriotic pride with him—that he voted for every measure of the compromise of 1850, including the Utah and New Mexico territorial bills, embracing all the Indians within their limits. My friend from Tennessee, too, has been very liberal in voting for most of the territorial bills; and I therefore trust that the same patriotic and worthy motives which induced him to vote for the territorial act of 1850 will enable him to give his support to the present bill, especially as he approves of the great principle of popular sovereignty upon which it rests.

The senator from Tennessee remarked further, that the proposed limits of these two Territories were too extensive, that they were large enough to be erected into eight different States; and why, he asked, the necessity of including such a vast amount of country within the limits of these two Territories? I must remind the senator that it has always been the practice to include a large extent of country within one territory, and then to subdivide it from time to time as the public interest might require. Such was the case with the old Northwest Territory. It was all originally included within one territorial government. Afterwards Ohio was cut off; and then Indiana, Michigan, Illinois, and Wisconsin, were successively erected into separate territorial governments, and subsequently admitted into the Union as States.

At one period, it will be remembered, the Territory of Wisconsin included the country embraced within the limits of the States of Wisconsin and Iowa, and a part of the State of Michigan, and the Territory of Minnesota. There is country enough within the Territory of Minnesota to make two or three States of the size of New York. Washington Territory embraces about the same area. Oregon is large enough to make three or four States as extensive as Pennsylvania, Utah two or three, and New Mexico four or five of like dimensions. Indeed, the whole country embraced within the proposed Territories of Nebraska and Kansas, together with the States of Arkansas, Missouri, and Iowa, and the larger part of Minnesota, and the whole of the Indian country west of Arkansas, once constituted a territorial government, under the name of the Missouri Territory. In view of this course of legislation upon the subject of territorial organization, commencing before the adoption of the Constitution of the United States and coming down to the last session of Congress, it surely cannot be said that there is anything unusual or extraordiaary in the size of the proposed Territory, which should compel a senator to vote against the bill, while he approves of the principles involved in the measure.

It has also been urged in debate that there is no necessity for these territorial organizations; and I have been called upon to point out any public and national considerations which require action at this time. Senators seem to forget that our immense and valuable possessions on the Pacific are separated from the States and organized Territories, on this side of the Rocky mountains by a vast wilderness, filled by hostile savages; that nearly a hundred thousand emigrants pass through this barbarous wilderness every year, on their way to California and Oregon; that these emigrants are American citizens, our own constituents, who are entitled to the protection of law and government; and that they are left to make their way, as best they may, without the protection or aid of law or government.

The United States mails for New Mexico and Utah, and all official communications between this government and the authorities of those Territories, are required to be carried over these wild plains, and through the gorges of the mountains, where you have made no provision for roads, bridges, or ferries to facilitate travel, or forts or other means of safety to protect life. As often as I have brought forward and urged the adoption of measures to remedy these evils, and afford security against the dangers to which our people are constantly exposed, they have been promptly voted down as not being of sufficient importance to command the favorable consideration of Congress. Now, when I propose to organize the Territories, and allow the people to do for themselves what you have so often refused to do for them, I am told that there are not white inhabitants enough permanently settled in the country to require and sustain a government. True there is not a very large population there, for the very good reason that your Indian code and intercourse laws exclude the settlers, and forbid their remaining there to cultivate the soil. You refuse to throw the country open to settlers, and then object to the organization of the Territories upon the ground that there is not a sufficient number of inhabitants.

The senator from Connecticut [Mr. SMITH] has made a long argument to prove that there are no inhabitants in the proposed Territories, because nearly all of those who have gone and settled there have done so in violation of certain old acts of Congress which forbid the people to take possession of and settle upon the public lands until after they should be surveyed and brought into market.

I do not propose to discuss the question whether these settlers are technically legal inhabitants or not. It is enough for me that they are a part of our own people; that they are settled on the public domain; that the public interests would be promoted by throwing that public domain open to settlement; and that there is no good reason why the protection of law and the blessings of government should not be extended to them. I must be permitted to remind the senator that the same objection existed in its full force to Minnesota, to Oregon and to Washington, when each of those Territories were organized; and that I have no recollection that he deemed it his duty to call the attention of Congress to the objection, or considered it of sufficient importance to justify him in recording his own vote against the organization of either of those Territories.

Mr. President, I do not feel called upon to make any reply to the argument which the senator from Connecticut has urged against the passage of this bill upon the score of expense in sustaining these territorial governments, for the reason that, if the public interests require the enactment of the law, it follows as a natural consequence that all the expenses necessary to carry it into effect are wise and proper.

I will now proceed to the consideration of the great principles involved in the bill, without omitting, however, to notice some of those extraneous matters which have been brought into this discussion with the view of producing another anti-slavery agitation. We have been told by nearly every senator who has spoken in opposition to this bill, that at the time of its introduction the people were in a state of profound quiet and repose; that the anti-slavery agitation had entirely ceased; and that the whole country was acquiescing cheerfully and cordially in the compromise measures of 1850 as a final adjustment of this vexed question.

Sir, it is truly refreshing to hear senators, who contested every inch of ground in opposition to those measures when they were under discussion, who predicted all manner of evils and calamities from their adoption, and who raised the cry of repeal, and even resistence, to their execution, after they had become the laws of the land—I say it is really refreshing to hear these same senators now bear their united testimony to the wisdom of those measures, and to the patriotic motives which induced us to pass them in defiance of their threats and resistance, and to their beneficial effects in restoring peace, harmony, and fraternity to a distracted country. These are precious confessions from the lips of those who stand pledged never to assent to the propriety of those measures, and to make war upon them so long as they shall remain upon the statute-book. I well understand that these confessions are now made, not with the view of yielding their assent to the propriety of carrying those enactments into faithful execution, but for the purpose of having a pretext for charging upon me, as the author of this bill, the responsibility of an agitation which they are striving to produce. They say that I, and not they, have revived the agitation. What have I done to render me obnoxious to this charge? They say I wrote and introduced this Nebraska bill. That is true; but I was not a volunteer in the transaction. The Senate, by a unanimous vote, appointed me chairman of the territorial committee, and associated five intelligent and patriotic senators with me, and thus made it our duty to take charge of all territorial business. In like manner, and with the concurrence of these complaining senators, the Senate referred to us a distinct proposition to organize this Nebraska Territory, and required us to report specifically upon the question. I repeat, then, we were not volunteers in this business. The duty was imposed upon us by the Senate. We were not unmindful of the delicacy and responsibility of the position. We were aware that from 1820 to 1850 the abolition doctrine of congressional interference with slavery in the Territories and new States had so far prevailed as to keep up an incessant slavery agitation in Congress, and throughout the country, whenever any new Territory was to be acquired or organized. We were also aware that, in 1850, the right of the people to decide this question for themselves, subject only to the Constitution, was substituted for the doctrine of congressional intervention. The first question, therefore, which the committee were called upon to decide, and indeed the only question of any material importance, in framing this bill, was this: Shall we adhere to and carry out the principle recognized by the compromise measures of 1850, or shall we go back to the old exploded doctrine of congressional interference, as established in 1820, in a large portion of the country, and which it was the object of the Wilmot proviso to give a universal application, not only to all the territory which we then possessed, but all which we might hereafter acquire? There were no other alternatives. We were compelled to frame the bill upon the one or the other of these two principles. The doctrine of 1820 or the doctrine of 1850 must prevail. In the discharge of the duty imposed upon us by the Senate, the committee could not hesitate upon this point, whether we consulted our individual opinions and principles or those which were known to be entertained and boldly avowed by a large majority of the Senate. The two great political parties of the country stood solemnly pledged before the world to adhere to the compromise measures of 1850, "in principle and substance." A large majority of the Senate, indeed every member of the body, I believe, except the two avowed abolitionists, [Mr. Chase and Mr. Sumner] profess to belong to the one or the other of these parties, and hence was supposed to be under a high moral obligation to carry out the "principle and substance" of those measures in all new territorial organizations. The report of the committee was in accordance with this obligation. I am arraigned, therefore, for having endeavored to represent the opinions and principles of the Senate truly; for having performed my duty in conformity with the parliamentary law; for having been faithful to the trust reposed in me by the Senate. Let the vote this night determine whether I have thus faithfully represented your opinions. When a majority of the Senate shall have passed the bill; when a majority of the

24

States shall have endorsed it through their representatives upon this floor; when a majority of the South and a majority of the North shall have sanctioned it; when a majority of the Whig party and a majority of the Democratic party shall have voted for it, when each of these propositions shall be demonstrated by the vote this night on the final passage of the bill, I shall be willing to submit the question to the country, whether, as the organ of the committee, I performed my duty in the report and bill which have called down upon my head so much denunciation and abuse.

Mr. President, the opponents of this measure have had much to say about the mutations and modifications which this bill has undergone since it was first introduced by myself, and about the alleged departure of the bill, in its present form, from the principle laid down in the original report of the committee as a rule of action in all future territorial organizations. Fortunately there is no necessity, even if your patience would tolerate such a course of argument at this late hour of the night, for me to examine these speeches in detail, and to reply to each charge separately. Each speaker seems to have followed faithfully in the footsteps of his leader—in the path marked out by the abolition confederates in their manifesto, which I exposed on a former occasion. You have seen them on their winding way, meandering the narrow and crooked path in Indian file, each treading close upon the heels of the other, and neither venturing to take a step to the right or left, or to occupy one inch of ground which did not bear the foot-print of the abolition champion. To answer one, therefore, is to answer the whole. The statement to which they seem to attach the most importance, and which they have repeated oftener perhaps than any other, is, that, pending the compromise measures of 1850, no man in or out of Congress, ever dreamed of abrogating the Missouri compromise; that from that period down to the present session nobody supposed that its validity had been impaired, or anything done which rendered it obligatory upon us to make it inoperative hereafter; that at the time of submitting the report and bill to the Senate, on the 4th of January last, neither I nor any member of the committee ever thought of such a thing; and that we could never be brought up to the point of abrogating the eighth section of the Missouri act until after the senator from Kentucky introduced his amendment to my bill.

Mr. President, before I proceed to expose the many misrepresentations contained in this complicated charge, I must call the attention of the Senate to the false issue which these gentlemen are endeavoring to impose upon the country, for the purpose of diverting public attention from the real issue contained in the bill. They wish to have the people believe that the abrogation of what they call the Missouri compromise was the main object and aim of the bill, and that the only question involved is, whether the prohibition of slavery north of 36° 30′ shall be repealed or not? That which is a mere incident they choose to consider the principal. They make war on the means by which we propose to accomplish an object, instead of openly resisting the object itself. The principle which we propose to carry into effect by the bill is this: That *Congress shall neither legislate slavery into any Territories or State, nor out of the same; but the people shall be left free to regulate their domestic concerns in their own way, subject only to the Constitution of the United States.*

In order to carry this principle into practical operation, it becomes necessary to remove whatever legal obstacles might be found in the way of its free exercise. It is only for the purpose of carrying out this great fundamental principle of self-government that the bill renders the eighth section of the Missouri act inoperative and void.

Now, let me ask, will these senators who have arraigned me, or any one of them, have the assurance to rise in his place and declare that this great principle was never thought of or advocated as applicable to territorial bills, in 1850; that, from that session until the present, nobody ever thought of incorporating this principle in all new territorial organizations; that the Committee on Territories did not recommend it in their report; and that it required the amendment of the senator from Kentucky to bring us up to that point? Will any one of my accusers dare to make this issue, and let it be tried by the record? I will begin with the compromises of 1850. Any senator who will take the trouble to examine our journals will find that on the 25th of March of that year, I reported from the Committee on Territories two bills including the following measures: the admission of California, a territorial government for Utah, a territorial government for New Mexico, and the adjustment of the Texas boundary. These bills proposed to leave the people of Utah and New Mexico free to decide the slavery question for themselves, in the precise language of the Nebraska bill now under discussion. A few weeks afterwards, the Committee of Thirteen took those two bills and put a wafer between them, and reported them back to the Senate as one bill, with some slight amendments. One of those amendments was, that the territorial legislatures should not legislate upon the subject of African slavery. I objected to that provision upon the ground that it subverted the great principle of self-government upon which the bill had been originally framed by the Territorial Committee. On the first trial, the Senate refused to strike it out, but subsequently did so, after full debate, in order to establish that principle as the rule of action in territorial organizations.

Mr. Dodge, of Iowa. It was done on your own motion.

Mr. Douglas. Upon this point I trust I will be excused for reading one or two sentences from some remarks I made in the Senate on the 3rd of June, 1850:

"The position that I have ever taken has been that this the slavery question, and all other questions relating to the domestic affairs and domestic policy of the Territories, ought to be left to the decision of the people themselves, and that we ought to be content with whatever way they would decide the question, because they have a much deeper interest in these matters than we have, and know much better what institutions will suit them, than we, who have never been there, can decide for them."

Again, in the same debate, I said:

"I do not see how those of us who have taken the position which we have taken, (that of non-interference,) and have argued in favor of the right of the people to legislate for themselves on this question, can support such a provision without abandoning all the arguments which we urged in the presidential campaign in the year 1848, and the principles set forth by the honorable senator from Michigan in that letter which is known as the 'Nicholson letter.' We are required to abandon that platform; we are required to abandon those principles, and to stultify ourselves, and to adopt the opposite doctrine; and for what? In order to say that the people of the Territories shall not have such institutions as they shall deem adapted to their condition and their wants. I do not see, sir, how such a provision as that can be acceptable either to the people of the north or the south."

Mr. President, I could go on and multiply extract after extract from my speeches in 1850, and prior to that date to show that this doctrine of leaving the people to decide these questions for themselves is not an "after-thought" with me, seized upon this session for the first time, as my calumniators have so frequently and boldly charged in their speeches during this debate, and in their manifesto to the public. I refused to support the celebrated omnibus bill in 1850 until the obnoxious provision was stricken out, and the principle of self-government restored, as it existed in my original bill. No sooner were the compromise measures of 1850 passed, than the abolition confederates, who lead the opposition to this bill now, raised the cry of repeal in some sections of the country, and in others forcible resistance to the execution of the law. In order to arrest and suppress the treasonable purposes of these abolition confederates, and avert the horrors of civil war, it became my duty, on the 23d of October, 1850, to address an excited and frenzied multitude at Chicago, in defence of each and all of the compromise measures of that year. I will read one or two sentences from that speech, to show how those measures were then understood and explained by their advocates:

" *These measures are predicated on the great fundamental principle that every people ought to possess the right of forming and regulating their own internal concerns and domestic institutions in their own way.*"

Again:

"These things are all confided by the Constitution to each State to decide for itself, and I KNOW OF NO REASON WHY THE *same principle should not be confided to the Territories.*"

In this speech it will be seen that I lay down a general principle of universal application, and make no distinction between territories north or south of 30° 30′.

I am aware that some of the abolition confederates have perpetrated a monstrous forgery on that speech, and are now circulating through the abolition newspapers the statement that I said that I would "cling with the tenacity of life to the compromise of 1820." This statement, false as it is—a deliberate act of forgery, as it is known to be by all who have ever seen or read the speech referred to—constitutes the staple article out of which most of the abolition orators at the small anti-Nebraska meetings manufacture the greater part of their speeches. I now declare that there is not a sentence, a line, nor even a word in that speech, which imposes the slightest limitation on the application of the great principle embraced in this bill in all new territorial organizations, without the least reference to the line of 36° 30′.

At the session of 1850–'51, a few weeks after this speech was made at Chicago, and when it had been published in pamphlet form and circulated extensively over the States, the legislature of Illinois proceeded to revise its action upon the slavery question, and define its position on the compromise of 1850. After rescinding the resolutions adopted at a previous session, instructing my colleague and myself to vote for a proposition prohibiting slavery in the Territories, resolutions were adopted approving the compromise measures of 1850. I will read one of the resolutions, which was adopted in the House of Representatives, by a vote of 61 yeas to 4 nays:

"Resolved, That our liberty and independence are based upon the right of the people to form for themselves such a government as they may choose; that this great privilege—the birthright of freemen, the gift of Heaven, secured to us by the blood of our ancestors—ought to be extended to future generations; and no limitation ought to be applied to this power, in the organization of any Territory of the United States, of either a Territorial government or a State Constitution: *Provided,* The government so established shall be republican, and in conformity with the Constitution."

Another series of resolutions having passed the Senate almost unanimously, embracing the same principle in different language, they were concurred in by the House. Thus was the position of Illinois, upon the slavery question, defined at the first session of the legislature after the adoption of the compromise of 1850.

Now, sir, what becomes of the declaration which has been made by nearly every opponent of this bill, that nobody in this whole Union ever dreamed that the principle of the Utah and New Mexican bill was to be incorporated into all future territorial organizations? I have shown that my own State so understood and declared it at the time in the most implicit and solemn manner. Illinois declared that our "liberty and independence" rest upon this "principle;" that the principle "ought to be extended to future generations;" and that "no limitation ought to be applied to this power in the organization of any Territory of the United States." No exception is made in regard to Nebraska. No Missouri compromise lines; no reservations of the country north of 36° 30′. The principle is declared to be the "birthright of freemen;" the "gift of Heaven," to be applied without limitation, in Nebraska as well as Utah, north as well as south of 36° 30′.

It may not be out of place here to remark that the legislature of Illinois, at its recent session, has passed resolutions approving the Nebraska bill; and among the resolutions is one in the precise language of the resolution of 1851, which I have just read to the Senate.

Thus I have shown, Mr. President, that the legislature and people of Illinois have always understood the compromise measures of 1850 as establishing certain principles as rules of action in the organization of all new Territories, and that no limitation was to be made on either side of the geographical line of 36° 30′.

Neither my time nor your patience will allow me to take up the resolutions of the different States in detail, and show what has been the common understanding of the whole country upon this point. I am now vindicating myself and my own action against the assaults of my calumniators; and, for that purpose, it is sufficient to show that, in the report and bill which I have presented to the Senate, I have only carried out the known principles and solemnly declared will of the State whose representative I am. I will now invite the attention of the Senate to the report of the committee, in order that it may be known how much, or rather how little, truth there is for the allegation which has been so often made and repeated on this floor, that the idea of allowing the people in Nebraska to decide the slavery question for themselves was a "sheer after thought," conceived since the report was made, and not until the senator from Kentucky proposed his amendment to the bill.

I read from that portion of the report in which the committee lay down the principle by which they proposed to be governed:

"In the judgment of your committee, those measures (compromise of 1850) were intended to have a far more comprehensive and enduring effect than the mere adjustment of the difficulties arising out of the recent acquisition of Mexican territory. They were designed to establish certain great principles, which would not only furnish adequate remedies for existing evils, but *in all time to come* avoid the perils of a similar agitation, *by withdrawing the question of slavery from the halls of Congress and the political arena, and committing it to the arbitrament of those who were immediately interested in and alone responsible for its consequences.*"

After making a brief argument in defence of this principle, the report proceeds, as follows:

"From these provisions, it is apparent that the compromise measures of 1850 affirm and rest upon the following propositions:

"First. That all questions pertaining to slavery in the Territories, and in the new States to be formed therefrom, are to be left to the decision of the people residing therein, by their appropriate representatives, to be chosen by them for that purpose."

And, in conclusion, the report proposes a substitute for the bill introduced by the senator from Iowa, and concludes as follows:

"The substitute for the bill which your committee have prepared, and which is commended to the favorable action of the Senate, proposes to carry these propositions and principles into practical operation, in the precise language of the compromise measures of 1850."

Mr. President, as there has been so much misrepresentation upon this point, I must be permitted to repeat that the doctrine of the report of the committee, as has been conclusively proved by these extracts, is—

First. That the whole question of slavery should be withdrawn from the Halls of Congress, and the political arena, and committed to the abitrament of those who are immediately interested in and alone responsible for its existence.

Second. The applying this principle to the Territories and the new States to be formed therefrom, all questions pertaining to slavery were to be referred to the people residing therein.

Third. That the committee proposed to carry these propositions and principles into effect in the precise language of the compromise measures of 1850.

Are not these propositions identical with the principles and provisions of the bill on your table? If there is a hair's breadth of discrepancy between the two, I ask any senator to rise in his place and point it out. Both rest upon the great principle, which forms the basis of all our institutions, that the people are to decide the question for themselves, subject only to the Constitution.

But my accusers attempt to raise up a false issue, and thereby divert public attention from the real one, by the cry that the Missouri compromise is to be repealed or violated by the passage of this bill. Well, if the eighth section of the Missouri act, which attempted to fix the destinies of future generations in those Territories for all time to come, in utter disregard of the rights and wishes of the people when they should be received into the Union as States, be inconsistent with the great principle of self-government and the Constitution of the United States, it ought to be abrogated. The legislation of 1850 abrogated the Missouri compromise, so far as the country embraced within the limits of Utah and New Mexico was covered by the slavery restriction. It is true, that those acts did not in terms and by name repeal the act of 1820, as originally adopted, or as extended by the resolutions annexing Texas in 1845, any more than the report of the Committee on Territories proposes to repeal the same acts this session. But the acts of 1850 did authorize the people of those Territories to exercise "all rightful powers of legislation consistent with the Constitution," not excepting the question of slavery; and did provide that, when those Territories should be admitted into the Union, they should be received with or without slavery as the people thereof might determine at the date of their admission. These provisions were in direct conflict with a clause in a former enactment, declaring that slavery should be forever prohibited in any portion of said Territories, and hence rendered such clause inoperative and void to the extent of such conflict. This was an inevitable consequence, resulting from the provisions in those acts which gave the people the right to decide the slavery question for themselves, in conformity with the Constitution. It was not necessary to go further and declare that certain previous enactments, which were incompatible with the exercise of the powers conferred in the bills, "are hereby repealed." The very act of granting those powers and rights have the legal effect of removing all obstructions to the exercise of them by the people, as prescribed in those territorial bills. Following that example, the Committee on Territories did not consider it necessary to declare the eighth section of the Missouri act repealed. We were content to organize Nebraska in the precise language of the Utah and New Mexican bills. Our object was to leave the people entirely free to form and regulate their domestic institutions and internal concerns in their own way, under the Constitution; and we deemed it wise to accomplish that object in the exact terms in which the same thing had been done in Utah and New Mexico by the acts of 1850. This was the principle upon which the committee reported; and our bill was supposed, and is now believed, to have been in accordance with it. When doubts were raised whether the bill did fully carry out the principle laid down in the report, amendments were made, from time to time, in order to avoid all misconstruction, and make the true intent of the act more explicit. The last of these amendments was adopted yesterday, on the motion of the distingushed senator from North Carolina, (Mr. Badger,) in regard to the revival of any laws or regulations which may have existed prior to 1820. That amendment was not intended to change the legal effect of the bill. Its object was to repel the slander which had been propagated by the enemies of the measure in the north, that the southern supporters of the bill desired to legislate slavery into these Territories. The south denies the right of Congress either to legislate slavery into any Territory or State, or out of any Territory or State. Non-interventoin by Congress with slavery in the States or Territories is the doctrine of the bill, and all the amendments which have been agreed to have been made with the view of removing all doubt and cavil as to the true meaning and object of the measure.

Mr. President, I think I have succeeded in vindicating myself and the action of the committee from the assaults which have been made upon us in consequence of these amendments. It seems to be the tactics of our opponents to direct their arguments against the unimportant points and incidental questions which are to be affected by carrying out the principle, with the hope of relieving themselves from the necessity of controverting the principle itself. The senator from Ohio [Mr. CHASE] led off gallantly in the charge that the committee, in the report and bill first submitted, did not contemplate the repeal of the Missouri compromise, and could not be brought to that point until after the senator from Kentucky offered his amendment. The senator from Connecticut [Mr. SMITH] followed his lead, and repeated the same statement. Then came the other senator from Ohio, [Mr. WADE,] and the senator from New York, [Mr. SEWARD,] and the senator from Massachusetts, [Mr. SUMNER,] all singing the same song, only varying the tune.

Let me ask these senators what they mean by this statement? Do they wish to be understood as saying that the report and first form of the bill did not provide for leaving the slavery question to the decision of the people in the terms of the Utah bill? Surely they will not dare to say that, for I have already shown that the two measures were identical in principle and enactment. Do they mean to say that the adoption of our first bill would not have had the legal effect to have rendered the eighth section of the Missouri act "inoperative and void," to use the language of the present bill? If this be not their meaning, will they rise in their places and inform the Senate what their meaning was? They must have had some object in giving so much prominence to this statement, and in repeating it so often. I address the question to the senators from Ohio and Massachusetts, [Mr. CHASE and Mr. SUMNER.] I despair in extorting a response from them; for, no matter in what way they may answer upon this point, I have in my hand the evidence over their own signatures, to disprove the truth of their answer. I allude to their appeal or manifesto to the people of the United States, in which they arraign the bill and report, in coarse and savage terms, as a proposition to repeal the Missouri compromise, to violate plighted faith, to abrogate a solemn compact, &c., &c. This document was signed by these two senators in their official capacity, and published to the world before any amendments had been offered to the bill. It was directed against the committee's first bill and report, and against them alone. If the statements in this document be true, that the first bill did repeal the eighth section of the Missouri act, what are we to think of the statements in their speeches since, that such was not the intention of the committee, was not the recommendation of the report, and was not the legal effect of the bill? On the contrary, if the statements in their subsequent speeches are true, what apology do those senators propose to make to the Senate and country for having falsified the action of the committee in a document over their own signatures, and thus spread a false alarm among the people, and misled the public mind in respect to our proceedings? These senators cannot avoid the one or the other of these alternatives. Let them seize upon either, and they stand condemned and self-convicted; in the one case by their manifesto, and in the other by their speeches.

In fact, it is clear that they have understood the bill to mean the same thing, and to have the same legal effect in whatever phase it has been presented. When first introduced, they denounced it as a proposition to abrogate the Missouri restriction. When amended, they repeated the same denunciation, and so on each successive amendment. They now object to the passage of the bill for the same reason, thus proving conclusively that they have not the least faith in the correctness of their own statements in respect to the mutation and changes in the bill.

They seem very unwilling to meet the real issue. They do not like to discuss the principle. There seems to be something which strikes them with terror when you invite their attention to that great fundamental principle of popular sovereignty. Hence you find that all the memorials they have presented are against repealing the Missouri compromise, and in favor of the sanctity of compacts—in favor of preserving plighted faith. The senator from Ohio is cautious to dedicate his speech with some such heading as "Maintain Plighted Faith." The object is to keep the attention of the people as far as possible from this principle of self-government and constitutional rights.

Well, sir, what is this Missouri compromise, of which we have heard so much of late? It has been read so often that it is not necessary to occupy the time of the Senate in reading it again. It was an act of Congress, passed on the 6th of March, 1820, to authorize the people of Missouri to form a constitution and a State government, preparatory to the admission of such State into the Union. The first section provided that Missouri should be received into the Union "on an equal footing with the original States in all respects whatsoever." The last and eighth section provided that slavery should be "forever prohibited" in all the territory which had been acquired from France north of 36° 30′, and not included within the limits of the State of Missouri. There is nothing in the terms of the law that purports to be a compact, or indicates that it was anything more than an ordinary act of legislation. To prove that it was more than it purports to be on its face, gentlemen must produce other evidence, and prove that there was such an understanding as to create a moral obligation in the nature of a compact. Have they shown it?

I have heard but one item of evidence produced during this whole debate, and that was a short paragraph from Niles's Register, published a few days after the passage of the act. But gentlemen aver that it was a solemn compact, which could not be violated or abrogated without dishonor. According to their understanding, the contract was that, in consideration of the admission of Missouri into the Union, on an equal footing with the original States in all respects whatsoever, slavery should be prohibited forever in the Territories north of 36° 30′. Now, who were the parties to this alleged compact? They tell us that it was a stipulation between the north and the south. Sir, I know of no such parties under the Constitution. I am unwilling that there shall be any such parties known in our legislation. If there is such a geographical line, it ought to be obliterated forever, and there should be no other parties than those provided for in the Constitution, viz: the States of this Union. These are the only parties capable of contracting under the Constitution of the United States.

Now, if this was a compact, let us see how it was entered into. The bill originated in the House of Representatives, and passed that body without a southern vote in its favor. It is proper to remark, however, that it did not at that time contain the eighth section, prohibiting slavery in the Territories; but in lieu of it, contained a provision prohibiting slavery in the proposed State of Missouri. In the Senate, the clause prohibiting slavery in the State was stricken out, and the eighth section added to the end of the bill, by the terms of which slavery was to be forever prohibited in the territory not embraced in the State of Missouri north of 36° 30′. The vote on adding this section stood, in the Senate, 34 in the affirmative, and 10 in the negative. Of the northern senators, 20 voted for it and 2 against it. On the question of ordering the bill to a third reading as amended, which was the test vote on its passage, the vote stood 24 yeas, 20 nays. Of the northern senators, 4 only voted in the affirmative, and 18 in the negative. Thus it will be seen that, if it was intended to be a compact, the north never agreed to it. The northern senators voted to insert the prohibition of slavery in the Territories; and then, in the proportion of more than four to one, voted against the passage of the bill. The north, therefore, never signed the compact, never consented to it, never agreed to be bound by it. This fact becomes very important in vindicating the character of the north for repudiating this alleged compromise a few months afterwards. The act was approved and became a law on the 6th of March, 1820. In the summer of that year, the people of Missouri formed a constitution and State government preparatory to admission into the Union, in conformity with the act. At the next session of Congress, the Senate passed a joint resolution declaring Missouri to be one of the States of the Union, on an equal footing with the original States. This resolution was sent to the House of Representatives, where it was rejected by northern votes, and thus Missouri was voted out of the Union, instead of being received into the Union under the act of the 6th of March, 1820, now known as the Missouri compromise. Now, sir, what becomes of our plighted faith, if the act of the 6th of March, 1820, was a solemn compact, as we are now told? They have all rung the changes upon it, that it was a sacred and irrevocable compact, binding in honor, in conscience, and morals, which could not be violated or repudiated without perfidy and dishonor! The two senators from Ohio, (Mr. Chase and Mr. Wade,) the senator from Massachusetts, [Mr. Sumner,] the senator from Connecticut, [Mr. Smith,] the senator from New York, [Mr. Seward,] and perhaps others, have all assumed this position.

Mr. Seward. Will the senator excuse me for a moment?

Mr. Douglas. Certainly.

Mr. Seward. Mr. President, I have foreseen that it would be probable that the honorable senator from Illinois would have occasion to reply to many arguments which have been made by the opponents of this measure; and it would seem, therefore, to create a necessity, on the part of the opponents of the bill, to answer his arguments afterwards. Yet, at the same time, meaning to be fair and desiring to have no such advantage as the last word, but to leave it to him, to whom it rightly belongs, I had proposed, if agreeable to him, when he should state anything which controverted my own position, to make the answer during his speech, instead of deferring it until afterwards. To me the last word is never of any advantage; but I know that it is to him, and ought to be so regarded by him. I have a word to say here, and I propose to say another word at another time; but if it be at all uncomfortable to the senator, I will reserve what I have to say until after he concludes.

Mr. Douglas. If it will take but a minute, I will yield now; but if the senator is to take considerable time, I prefer to go on myself.

Mr. Seward. No, sir, I make no long speeches anywhere; I never make a long speech, and therefore I would prefer saying what I have to submit now, if the honorable senator prefers it.

Mr. Douglas. Very well.

Mr. Seward. I thought he would. In the first place, I find that the honorable senator is coming upon my own ground in regard to compromises.

Mr. Douglas. That is not a vindication of any point which I have attacked. I hope the honorable senator will state his point.

Mr. Seward. I am going to state the point, or I will state nothing. Whoever will refer to my antecedents, will find that in the year 1850 I expressed opinions on the subject of legislative compromises between the north and south, which, at that day, were rejected and repudiated.

Mr. Douglas. If the object of the senator is to go back, and go through all his opinions, I cannot yield the floor to him; but if his object is now to show that the north did not violate the Missouri compromise, I will yield.

Mr. Seward. If the honorable senator will allow me just one minute and a half, without dictating what I shall say within that minute and a half, I shall be satisfied.

Mr. Douglas. Certainly, I will consent to that.

Mr. Seward. I find that the honorable senator from Illinois is standing upon the ground upon which I stood in 1850. I have nothing to say now, in favor of that ground. On this occasion, I stand upon the ground, in regard to compromises, which has been adopted by the country. Then, when the senator tells me that the north did not altogether, willingly and unanimously, consent to the compromise of 1820, I agree to it; but I have been overborne in the country, on the ground that if one northern man carried with him a majority of Congress he bound the whole north. And so I hold in regard to the compromise of 1820, that it was carried by a vote which has been held by the south and by the honorable senator from Illinois to bind the north. The south having received their consideration and equivalent, I only hold him, upon his own doctrine and the doctrine of the south, bound to stand to it. That is all I have to say upon that point.

A few words more will cover all that I have to say about what the honorable senator may say hereafter as to the north repudiating this contract. When I was absent, I understood the senator alluded to the fact that my name appeared upon an appeal which was issued by the honorable senator from Ohio, and some other members of Congress, to the people, on the subject of this bill. Upon that point it has been my intention throughout to leave to the honorable senator from Illinois, and those who act with him, whatever there is of merit, and whatever there is of responsibility for the present measure, and for all the agitation and discussion upon it. Therefore as soon as I found, when I returned to the Capitol, that my name was on that paper, I caused it to to be made known and published, as fully and extensively as I could, that I had never been consulted in regard to it; that I know nothing about it; and that the merit of the measure, as well as the responsibility, belonged to the honorable senator from Ohio, and those who co-operated with him; and that I had never seen the paper on which he commented; nor have I in any way addressed the public upon the subject.

Mr. Douglas. I wish to ask the senator from New York a question. If I understood his remarks when he spoke, and if I understand his speech as published, he averred that the Missouri compromise was a compact between the north and the south; that the north performed it on its part; that it had done so faithfully for thirty years; that the south had received all its benefits, and the moment these benefits had been fully realized, the south disavowed the obligations under which it had received them. Is not that his position?

Mr. Seward. I am not accustomed to answer questions put to me, unless they are entirely categorical, and placed in such a shape that I may know exactly, and have time to consider, their whole extent. The honorable senator from Illinois has put a very broad question. What I mean to say, however, and that will answer his purpose, is, that his position, and that the position of the south is, that this was a compromise; and I say that the north has never repudiated that compromise. Indeed, it has never had the power to do so. Missouri came into the Union, and Arkansas came into the Union, under that compromise; and whatever individuals may have said, whatever individuals, more or less humble than myself, may have contended, the practical effect is, that the south has had all that she could get by that compromise, and that the north is now in the predicament of being obliged to defend what was left to her. I believe that answers the question.

Mr. Douglas. Now, Mr. President, I choose to bring men directly up to this point. The senator from New York has labored in his whole speech to make it appear that this was a compact; that the north had been faithful; and that the south acquiesced until she got all its advantages, and then disavowed and sought to annul it. This he pronounced to be bad faith; and he made appeals about dishonor. The senator from Connecticut [Mr. Smith] did the same thing, and so did the senator from Massachusetts, [Mr. Sumner,] and the senator from Ohio, [Mr. Chase.] That is the great point to which the whole abolition party are now directing all their artillery in this battle. Now, I propose to bring them to the point. If this was a compact, and if what they have said is fair, or just, or true, who was it that repudiated the compact?

Mr. Sumner. Mr. President, the senator from Illinois, I know, does not intend to misstate my position. That position as announced in the language of the speech which I addressed to the Senate, and which I now hold in my hand, is, "this is an infraction of solemn obligations, assumed beyond recall by the south, on the admission of Missouri into the Union as a slave State; which was one year after the act of 1820.

Mr. Douglas. Mr. President, I shall come to that; and I wish to see whether this was an obligation which was assumed "beyond recall." If it was a compact between the two parties, and one party has been faithful, it is beyond recall by the other. If, however, one party has been faithless, what shall we think of them, if, while faithless, they ask a performance?

Mr. Seward. Show it.

Mr. Douglas. That is what I am coming to. I have already stated that, at the next session of Congress, Missouri presented a constitution in conformity with the act of 1820; that the senate passed a joint resolution to admit her; and that the House refused to admit Missouri in conformity with the alleged compact, and, I think, on three distinct votes rejecting her.

Mr. Seward. I beg my honorable friend, for I desire to call him so, to answer me frankly whether he would rather I should say what I have to say in this desultory way, or whether he would prefer that I should answer him afterwards; because it is with me a rule in the Senate never to interrupt a gentleman, except to help him in his argument.

Mr. Douglas. I would rather hear the senator now.

Mr. Seward. What I have to say now, and I acknowledge the magnanimity of the senator from Illinois in allowing me to say it, is, that the north stood by that compact until Missouri came in with a constitution, one article of which denied to colored citizens of other States the equality of privileges which were allowed to all other citizens of the United States, and then the North insisted on the right of colored men to be regarded as citizens, and entitled to the privileges and immunities of citizens. Upon that a new compromise was necessary. I hope I am candid.

Mr. Douglas. The senator is candid, I have no doubt, as he understands the facts; but I undertake to maintain that the North objected to Missouri because she allowed slavery, and not because of the free-negro clause alone.

Mr. Seward. No, sir.

Mr. Douglas. Now I will proceed to prove that the North did not object, solely on account of the free-negro clause; but that in the House of Representatives at that time, the North objected as well because of slavery in regard to free negroes. Here is the evidence. In the House of Representatives, on the 12th of February, 1821, Mr. Mallory, of Vermont, moved to amend the Senate joint resolution for the admission of Missouri, as follows:

"To amend the said amendment, by striking out all thereof after the word *respects*, and inserting the following: 'Whenever the people of the said State, by a convention, appointed according to the manner provided by the act to authorize the people of Missouri to form a constitution and State government, and for the admission of such State into the Union on an equal footing with the original States, and to prohibit slavery in certain territories, approved March 6, 1820, adopt a constitution conformably to the provisions of said act, and shall IN ADDITION *to said provision, further provide, in and by said constitution, that neither slavery nor involuntary servitude shall ever be allowed in said State of Missouri*, unless inflicted as a punishment for crimes committed against the laws of said State, whereof the party accused shall be duly convicted: *Provided*, That the civil condition of those persons who now are held to service in Missouri shall not be affected by this last provision.'"

Here I show, then, that the proposition was made that Missouri should not come in unless, in addition to complying with the Missouri compromise, so called, she would go further, and prohibit slavery within the limits of the State.

Mr. Seward. Now, then, for the vote.

Mr. Douglas. The vote was taken by yeas and nays. I hold it in my hand. Sixty-one northern men voted for that amendment, and thirty-three against it. Thus the North, by a vote of nearly two to one, expressly repudiated a solemn compact upon the very matter in controversy, to wit: that slavery should not be prohibited in the State of Missouri.

Mr. Weller. Let the senator from New York answer that.

Mr. Douglas. I should like to hear his answer.

Mr. Seward. I desire, if I shall be obtrusive by speaking in this way, that senators will at once signify, or that any senator will signify that I am obtrusive. But I make these explantions in this way, for the reason that I desire to give the honorable senator from Illinois the privilege of hearing my answer to him as he goes along. It is simply this: That this doctrine of compromises is, as it has been held, that if so many northern men shall go with so many southern men as to fix the law, then it binds the north and south alike. I therefore have but one answer to make: that the vote for the restriction was less than the northern vote which was given against the whole compromise.

Mr. Douglas. Well, now, we come to this point: We have been told, during this debate, that you must not judge of the north by the minority, but by her majority. You have been told that the minority, who stood by the Constitution and the rights of the south, were dough-faces.

Mr. Seward. I have not said so. I will not say so.

Mr. Douglas. You have all said so in your speeches, and you have asked us to take the majority of the north.

Mr. Seward. I spoke of the practical fact. I never said anything about dough-faces.

Mr. Douglas. You have asked us to take the majority instead of the minority.

Mr. Seward. The majority of the country.

Mr. Douglas. I am talking of the majority of the northern vote.

Mr. Seward. No, sir.

Mr. Douglas. I hope the senator will hear me. I wish to call him to the issue. I stated that the north in the House of Representatives voted against admitting Missouri into the Union under the act of 1820, and caused the defeat of that measure; and he said that they voted against it on the ground of the free-negro clause in her constitution, and not upon the ground of slavery. Now, I have shown by the evidence that it was upon the ground of Slavery, as well as upon the other ground; and that a majority of the north required not only that Missouri should comply with the compact of 1820, so called, but that she should go further, and give up the whole consideration which the senator says the south received from the north for the Missouri compromise. The compact, he says, was that in consideration of slavery being permitted in Missouri, it should be prohibited in the Territories. After having procured the prohibition in the Territories, the north, by a majority of her votes, refused to admit Missouri as a slaveholding State, and, in violation of the alleged compact, required her to prohibit slavery as a further condition of her admission. This repudiation of the alleged compact by the north is recorded by yeas and nays, sixty-one to thirty-three, and entered upon the Journal, as an imperishable evidence of the fact. With this evidence before us, against whom should the charge of perfidy be preferred?

Sir, if this was a compact, what must be thought of those who violated it almost immediately after it was formed? I say it was a calumny upon the north to say that it was a compact. I should feel a flush of shame upon my cheek, as a northern man, if I were to say that it was a compact, and that the section of the country to which I belong received the consideration, and then repudiated the obligation in eleven months after it was entered into. I deny that it was a compact in any sense of the term. But if it was, the record proves that faith was not observed; that the contract was never carried into effect; that after the north had procured the passage of the act prohibiting slavery in the Territories, with a majority in the House large enough to prevent its repeal, Missouri was refused admission into the Union as a slaveholding State, in conformity with the act of March 6, 1820. If the proposition be correct, as contended for by the opponents of this bill, that there was a solemn compact between the north and south that, in consideration of the prohibition of slavery in the Territories, Missouri was to be admitted into the Union in conformity with the act of 1820, that compact was repudiated by the north and rescinded by the joint action of the two parties within twelve months from its date. Missouri was never admitted under the act of the 6th of March, 1820. She was refused admission under that act. She was voted out of the Union by northern votes, notwithstanding the stipulation that she should be received; and, in consequence of these facts, a new compromise was rendered necessary, by the terms of which Missouri was to be admitted into the Union conditionally—admitted on a condition not embraced in the act of 1820, and, in addition, to a full compliance with all the provisions of said act. If, then, the act of 1820, by the eighth section of which slavery was prohibited in the Territories, was a compact, it is clear to the comprehension of every fair-minded man that the refusal of the north to admit Missouri, in compliance with its stipulations, and without further conditions, imposes upon us a high moral obligation to remove the prohibition of slavery in the Territories, since it has been shown to have been procured upon a condition never performed.

Mr. President, inasmuch as the senator from New York has taken great pains to impress upon the public mind of the north the conviction that the act of 1820 was a solemn compact, the violation or repudiation of which by either party involves perfidy and dishonour, I wish to call the attention of that senator [Mr. SEWARD] to the fact, that his own State was the first to repudiate the compact and to instruct her senators in Congress not to admit Missouri into the Union in compliance with it, nor unless slavery should be prohibited in the State of Missouri.

Mr. Seward. That is so.

Mr. Douglas. I have the resolutions before me, in the printed Journal of the Senate. The senator from New York is familiar with the fact, and frankly admits it:

STATE OF NEW YORK,
IN ASSEMBLY, *November*, 13, 1820.

"Whereas the legislature of this State, at the last session, did instruct their senators and request their representatives in Congress to oppose the admission, as a State, into the Union, of any territory not comprised within the original boundaries of the United States, without making the prohibition of slavery therein an indispensable condition of admission; and whereas this legislature is impressed with the correctness of the sentiments so communicated to our senators and representatives: Therefore—

"*Resolved*, (if the honorable the Senate concur herein,) That this legislature does approve of the principles contained in the resolutions of the last session; and further, if the provisions contained in any proposed constitution of a new State deny to any citizens of the existing States the privileges and immunities of citizens of such new State, that such proposed constitution should not be accepted or confirmed; the same, in the opinion of this legislature, being void by the Constitution of the United States. And that our senators be instructed, and our representatives in Congress be requested, to use their utmost exertions to prevent the acceptance and confirmation of any such constitution."

It will be seen by these resolutions, that at the previous session the New York legislature had "instructed" the senators from that State "TO OPPOSE THE ADMISSION, AS A STATE, INTO THE UNION OF ANY TERRITORY not comprised within the original boundaries of the United States, WITHOUT MAKING THE PROHIBITION OF SLAVERY THEREIN AN INDISPENSABLE CONDITION OF ADMISSION."

These instructions are not confined to territory north of 36° 30′. They apply, and were intended to apply, to the whole country west of the Mississippi, and to all territory which might hereafter be acquired. They deny the right of Arkansas to admission as a slaveholding State, as well as Missouri. They lay down a general principle to be applied and insisted upon everywhere, and in all cases, and under all circumstances. These resolutions were first adopted prior to the passage of the act of March 6, 1820, which the senator now chooses to call a compact. But they were renewed and repeated on the 13th of November 1820, a little more than eight months after the adoption of the Missouri compromise, as instructions to the New York senators to resist the admission of Missouri as a slaveholding State, notwithstanding the stipulations in the alleged compact. Now, let me ask the senator from New York by what authority he declared and published in his speech that the act of 1820, was a compact which could not be violated or repudiated without a sacrifice of honour, justice, and good faith. Perhaps he will shelter himself behind the resolutions of his State, which he presented this session, branding this bill as a violation of plighted faith.

Mr. Seward. Will the senator allow me a word of explanation?

Mr. Douglas. Certainly, with a great deal of pleasure.

Mr. Seward. I wish simply to say that the State of New York, for now thirty years, has refused to make any compact on any terms by which a concession should be made for the extension of slavery. But, by the practical action of the Congress of the United States, compromises have been made, which, it is held by the honorable senator from Illinois and by the south, bind her against her consent and approval. And therefore she stands throughout this whole matter upon the same ground—always refusing to enter into a compromise, always insisting upon the prohibition of slavery within the Territories of the United States. But, on this occasion, we stand here with a contract which has stood for thirty years, notwithstanding our protest and dissent, and in which there is nothing left to be fulfilled except that part which is to be beneficial to us. All the rest has been fulfilled, and we stand here with our old opinions on the whole subject of compromises, demanding fulfillment on the part the south, which the honorable senator from Illinois on the present occasion represents.

Mr. Douglas. Mr. President, the senator undoubtedly speaks for himself very frankly and very candidly.

Mr. Seward. Certainly I do.

Mr. Douglas. But I deny that on this point he speaks for the State of New York.

Mr. Seward. We shall see.

Mr. Douglas. I will state the reason why I say so. He has presented here resolutions of the State of New York which have been adopted this year, declaring the act of March 6, 1820, to be a "solemn compact."

I read from the second resolution:

"But at the same time duty to themselves and to the other States of the Union demands that when an effort is making to violate a solemn compact, whereby the political power of the State and the privileges as well as the honest sentiments of its citizens will be jeoparded and invaded, they should raise their voice in protest against the threatened infraction of their rights, and declare that the negation or repeal by Congress of the Missouri compromise will be regarded by them as a violation of right and of faith, and destructive of that confidence and regard which should attach to the enactments of the federal legislature."

Mr. President, I cannot let the senator off on the plea that I, for the sake of the argument, in reply to him and other opponents of this bill, have called it a compact; or that the south have called it a compact; or that other friends of Nebraska have called it a compact which has been violated and rendered invalid. He and his abolition confederates have arraigned me for a violation of a compact, which, they say, is binding in morals, in conscience and honor. I have shown that the legislature of New York, at its present session, has declared it to be "a solemn compact," and that its repudiation would "be regarded by them as a violation of right, and of faith, and destructive of confidence, and regard." I have also shown, that if it be such a compact, the State of New York stands self-condemned and self-convicted as the first to repudiate and violate it.

But since the senator has chosen to make an issue with me in respect to the action of New York, with the view of condemning my conduct here, I will invite the attention of the senator to another portion of these resolutions. Referring to the fourteenth section of the Nebraska bill, the legislature of New York says:

"That the adoption of this provision would be in derogation of the truth, a gross violation of plighted faith, and an outrage and indignity upon the free States of the Union, whose assent has been yielded to the admission into the Union of Missouri and Arkansas, with slavery, in reliance upon the faithful observance of the provision now sought to be abrogated known as the Missouri compromise, whereby slavery was declared to be 'forever prohibited in all that territory ceded by France to the United States, under the name of Lousiana, which lies north of 36° 30′ north latitude, not included within the limits of the State of Missouri."

I have no comments to make upon the courtesy, and propriety exhibited in this legislative declaration, that a provision in a bill, reported by a regular committee of the Senate of the United States, and known to be approved by three-fourths of the body, and which has since received the sanction of their votes, is "in derogation of truth, a gross violation of plighted faith, and an outrage and indignity," &c. The opponents of this measure claim a monopoly of all the courtesies and amenities, which should be observed among gentlemen, and especially in the performance of official duties; and I am free to say that this is one of the mildest and most respectful forms of expression in which they have indulged. But there is a declaration in this resolution to which I wish to invite the particular attention of the Senate and the country. It is the distinct allegation that "the free States of the Union," including New York, yielded their "assent to the admission into the Union of Missouri and Arkansas, with slavery, in reliance upon the faithful observance of the provision known as the Missouri compromise."

Now, sir, since the legislature of New York has gone out of its way to arraign the State on matters of truth, I will demonstrate that this paragraph contains two material statements in direct "derogation of truth." I have already shown, beyond controversy, by the records of the legislature, and by the journals of the Senate, that New York never did give her assent to the admission of Missouri with slavery! Hence, I must be permitted to say, in the polite language of her own resolutions, that the statement that New York yielded her assent to the admission of Missouri with slavery is in "derogation of truth!" and, secondly, the statement that such assent was given "in reliance upon the faithful observance of the Missouri compromise" is equally "in derogation of truth." New York never assented to the admission of Missouri as a slave State, never assented to what she now calls the Missouri compromise, never observed its stipulations as a compact, never has been willing to carry it out; but on the contrary has always resisted it, as I have demonstrated by her own records.

Mr. President, I have before me other journals, records, and instructions, which prove that New York was not the only free State that repudiated the Missouri compromise of 1820 within twelve months from its date. I will not occupy the time of the Senate at this late hour of the night by referring to them, unless some opponent of the bill renders it necessary. In that event, I may be able to place other senators and their States in the same unenviable position in which the senator from New York has found himself and his State.

I think I have shown, that to call the act of the 6th of March 1820 a compact, binding in honor, is to charge the northern States of this Union with an act of perfidy unparalleled in the history of legislation or of civilization. I have already adverted to the facts, that in the summer of 1820 Missouri formed her constitution, in conformity with the act of the 6th of March; that it was presented to Congress at the next session; that the senate passed a joint resolution declaring her to be one of the States of the Union, on an equal footing with the original States; and that the house of representatives rejected it, and refused to allow her to come into the Union, because her constitution did not prohibit slavery.

These facts created the necessity for a new compromise, the old one having failed of its object, which was to bring Missouri into the Union. At this period in the order of events—in February 1821—when the excitement was almost beyond restraint, and a great fundamental principle, involving the right of the people of the new States to regulate their own domestic institutions, was dividing the Union into two great hostile parties—Henry Clay, of Kentucky, came forward with a new compromise, which had the effect to change the issue and make the result of the controversy turn upon a different point. He brought in a resolution for the admission of Missouri into the Union, not in pursuance of the act of 1820, not in obedience to the understanding when it was adopted, and not with her constitution as it had been formed in conformity with that act, but he proposed to admit Missouri into the Union upon a "fundamental condition," which condition was to be in the nature of a solemn compact between the United States on the one part and the State of Missouri on the other part, and to which "fundamental condition" the State of Missouri was required to declare her assent in the form of a "solemn public act." This joint resolution passed, and was approved March 2, 1821, and is known as Mr. Clay's Missouri compromise, in contradiction to that of 1820, which was introduced into the Senate by Mr. Thomas, of Illinois. In the month of June, 1821, the legislature of Missouri assembled and passed the "solemn public act," and furnished an authenticated copy thereof to the President of the United States, in compliance with Mr. Clay's compromise, or joint resolution. On August 10, 1821, James Monroe, President of the United States, issued his proclamation, in which, after reciting the fact that on the 2d of March, 1821, Congress had passed a joint resolution "providing for the admission of the State of Missouri into the Union, on a certain condition;" and that the general assembly of Missouri, on the 26th of June, having, "by a solemn public act, declared the assent of said State of Missouri to the fundamental condition contained in said joint resolution," and having furnished him with an authentic copy thereof, he, "in pursuance of the resolution of Congress aforesaid," declared the admission of Missouri to be complete.

I do not deem it necessary to discuss the question whether the conditions upon which Missouri was admitted were wise or unwise. It is sufficient for my present purpose to remark, that the "fundamental condition" of her admission related to certain clauses in the constitution of Missouri in respect to the migration of free negroes into that State; clauses similar to those now in force in the constitutions of Illinois and Indiana, and perhaps other States; clauses similar to the provisions of law in force at that time in many of the old States of the Union; and, I will add, clauses which, in my opinion, Missouri had a right to adopt under the Constitution of the United States. It is no answer to this position to say, that those clauses in the constitution of Missouri were in violation of the Constitution. If they did not conflict with the Constitution of the United States, they were void; if they were not in conflict, Missouri had a right to put them there, and to pass all laws necessary to carry them into effect. Whether such conflict did exist is a question which, by the Constitution, can only be determined authoritatively by the Supreme Court of the United States. Congress is not the appropriate and competent tribunal to adjudicate and determine questions of conflict between the constitution of a State and that of the United States. Had Missouri been admitted without any condition or restriction, she would have had an opportunity of vindicating her constitution and rights in the Supreme Court—the tribunal created by the Constitution for that purpose.

By the condition imposed on Missouri, Congress not only deprived that State of a right which she believed she possessed under the Constitution of the United States, but denied her the privilege of vindicating that right in the appropriate and constitutional tribunals, by compelling her, "by a solemn public act," to give an irrevocable pledge never to exercise or claim the right. Therefore Missouri came in under a humiliating condition—a condition not imposed by the Constitution of the United States, and which destroys the principle of equality which should exist, and by the Constitution does exist, between all the States of this Union This inequality resulted from Mr. Clay's compromise of 1821, and is the principle upon which that compromise was constructed." I own that the act is couched in general terms and vague phrases and therefore may possibly be so construed as not to deprive the State of any right she might possess under the Constitution. Upon that point I wish only to say, that such a construction makes the "fundamental condition" void, while the opposite construction would demonstrate it to be unconstitutional. I have before me the "solemn public act" of Missouri to this fundamental condition. Whoever will take the trouble to read it will find it the richest specimen of irony and sarcasm that has ever been incorporated into a solemn public act.

Sir, in view of these facts I desire to call the attention of the senator from New York to a statement in his speech, upon which the greater part of his argument rested. His statement was, and it is now being published in every abolition paper, and repeated by the whole tribe of abolition orators and lecturers, that Missouri was admitted as a slaveholding State, under the act of 1820; while I have shown, by the President's proclamation of August 10, 1821, that she was admitted in pursuance of the resolution of March 2, 1821. Thus it is shown that the material point of his speech is contradicted by the highest evidence—the record in the case. The same statement, I believe, was made by the senator from Connecticut [Mr. Smith] and the senators from Ohio [Mr. Chase and Mr. Wade] and the senator from Massachusetts [Mr. Sumner.] Each of these senators made and repeated this statement, and upon the strength of this erroneous assertion called upon us to carry into effect the eighth section of the same act. The material fact upon which their arguments rested being overthrown, of course their conclusions are erroneous and deceptive.

Mr. Seward. I hope the Senator will yield for a moment, because I have never had so much respect for him as I have to-night.

Mr. Douglas. I see what course I have to pursue in order to command the Senator's respect. I know now how to get it. [Laughter.]

Mr. Seward. Any man who meets meets me boldly commands my respect. I say that Missouri would not have been admitted at all into the Union by the United States except upon the compromise of 1820. When that point was settled about the restriction of slavery, it was settled in this way; that she should come in with slavery, and that all the rest of the Louisiana purchase, which is now known as Nebraska, should be forever free from slavery. Missouri adopted a constitution, which was thought by the northern States to infringe upon the right of citizenship guarantied by the Constitution of the United States, which was a new point altogether; and upon that point debâte was held and upon it a new compromise was made, and Missouri came into the Union upon the agreement that, in regard to that question, she submitted to the Constitution of the United States, and so she was admitted into the Union.

Mr. Douglas. Mr. President, I must remind the senator again that I have already proven that he was in error in stating that the north objected to the admission of Missouri merely on account of the free negro clause in her constitution. I have proven by the vote that the north objected to her admission because she tolerated slavery; this objection was sustained by the north by a vote of nearly two to one. He cannot shelter himself, therefore, under the free negro dodge, so long as there is a distinct vote of the north objecting to her admission; because, in addition to complying with the act of 1820, she did not also prohibit slavery, which was the only consideration that the south was to have for agreeing to the prohibition of slavery in the Territories. Then, having deprived the senator, by conclusive evidence from the records, of that pretext, what do I drive him to? I compel him to acknowledge that a new compromise was made.

Mr. Seward. Certainly there was.

Mr. Douglas. Then, I ask, why was it made? Because the north would not carry out the first one. And the best evidence that the north did not carry out the first one is the senator's admission that the south was compelled to submit to a new one. Then, if there was a new compromise made, did Missouri come in under the new one or the old one.

Mr. Seward. Under both.

Mr. Douglas. This is the first time, in this debate, it has been intimated that Missouri came in under two acts of Congress. The senator did not allude to the resolution of 1821 in his speech; none of the opponents of this bill have said it. But it is now admitted that she did not come into the Union under the act of 1820 alone. She had been voted out under the first compromise, and this vote compelled her to make a new one, and she came in under the new one; and yet the senator from New York, in his speech, declared to the world that she came in under the first one. This is not an immaterial question. His whole speech rests upon that misapprehension or misstatement of the record.

Mr. Seward. You had better say misapprehension.

Mr. Douglas. Very well. We will call it by that name. His whole argument depends upon that misapprehension. After stating that the act of 1820 was a compact, and that the north performed its part of it in good faith, he arraigns the friends of this bill for proposing to annul the eighth section of the act of 1820 without first turning Missouri out of the Union, in order that slavery may be abolished therein by the act of Congress. He says to us, in substance: "Gentlemen, if you are going to rescind the compact, have respect for that great law of morals, of honesty, and of conscience, which compels you first to surrender the consideration which you have received 'under the compact.'" I concur with him in regard to the obligation to restore consideration when a contract is rescinded. And, inasmuch as the prohibition in the Territories north of 36° 30′ was obtained, according to his own statement, by an agreement to admit Missouri as a slaveholding State on an equal footing with the original States, "in all respects whatsoever," as specified in the first section of the act of 1820; and, inasmuch as Missouri was refused admission under said act, and was compelled to submit to a new compromise in 1821, and was then received into the Union on a fundamental condition of inequality, I call on him and his abolition confederates to restore the consideration which they have received, in the shape of a prohibition of slavery north of 36° 30′, under a compromise which they repudiated, and refused to carry into effect. I call on them to correct the erroneous statement in respect to the admission of Missouri, and to make a restitution of the consideration by voting for this bill. I repeat, that this is not an immaterial statement. It is the point upon which the abolitionists rest their whole argument. They could not get up a show of pretext against the great principle of self-government involved in this bill, if they could not repeat all the time, as the senator from New York did in his speech, that Missouri came into the Union with slavery, in conformity to the compact which was made by the act of 1820, and that the south, having received the consideration, is now trying to cheat the north out of her part of the benefits. I have proven that, after abolitionism had gained its point so far as the eighth section of the act prohibited slavery in the Territory, Missouri was denied admission by northern votes until she entered into a compact by which she was understood to surrender an important right now exercised by several States of the Union.

Mr. President, I did not wish to refer to these things. I did not understand them fully in all their bearings at the time I made my first speech on this subject; and, so far as I was familiar with them, I made as little reference to them as was consistent with my duty; because it was a mortifying reflection to me, as a Northern man, that we had not been able, in consequence of the abolition excitement at the time, to avoid the appearance of bad faith in the observance of legislation, which has been denominated a compromise. There were a few men then, as there are now, who had the moral courage to perform their duty to the country and the Constitution, regardless of consequences personal to themselves. There were ten Northern men who dared to perform their duty by voting to admit Missouri into the Union on an equal footing with the original States, and with no other restriction than that imposed by the Constitution. I am aware that they were abused and denounced as we are now; that they were branded as dough-faces, traitors to freedom, and to the section of the country whence they come.

Mr. Geyer. They honored Mr. Lanman, of Connecticut, by burning him in effigy.

Mr. Douglas. Yes, sir; these Abolitionists honored Mr. Lanman in Connecticut just as they are honoring me in Boston, and other places, by burning me in effigy.

Mr. Cass. It will do you no harm.

Mr. Douglas. Well, sir, I know it will not; but why this burning in effigy? It is the legitimate consequences of the address which was sent forth to the world by certain Senators whom I denominated, on a former occasion, as the Abolition confederates. The Senator from Ohio presented here the other day a resolution—he says unintentionally, and I take it so—declaring that every Senator who advocated this bill was a traitor to his country, to humanity, and to God; and even he seemed to be shocked at the results of his own advice when it was exposed. Yet he did not seem to know that it was, in substance, what he had advised in his address, over his own signature, when he called upon the people to assemble in public meetings and thunder forth their indignation at the criminal betrayal of precious rights; when he appealed to ministers of the gospel to desecrate their holy calling, and attempted to inflame passions, and fanaticism, and prejudice against Senators who would not consider themselves very highly complimented by being called his equals? And yet, when the natural consequences of his own action and advice come back upon him, and he presents them here, and is called to an account for the indecency of the act, he professes his profound regret and surprise that anything should have occurred which could possibly be deemed unkind or disrespectful to any member of this body!

Mr. Sumner. I rise merely to correct the Senator in a statement in regard to myself, to the effect that I had said that Missouri came into the Union under the act of 1820, instead of the act of 1821. I forebore to designate any particular act under which Missouri came into the Union, but simply asserted, as the result of the long controversy with regard to her admission, and as the end of the whole transaction, that she was received as a slave State; and that on being so received, whether sooner or later, whether under the act of 1820 or 1821, the obligations of the compact were fixed—irrevocably fixed—so far as the South is concerned.

Mr. Douglas. The Senator's explanation does not help him at all. He says he did not state under what act Missouri came in; but he did say, as I understood him, that the act of 1820 was a compact, and that, according to that compact, Missouri was to come in with slavery, provided slavery should be prohibited in certain territories, and did come in in pursuance of the compact. He now uses the word "compact." To what compact does he allude? Is it not to the act of 1820? If he did not, what becomes of his conclusion that the 8th section of that act is irrepealable? He will not venture to deny that his reference was to the act of 1820. Did he refer to the joint resolution of 1821, under which Missouri was admitted? If so, we do not propose to repeal it. We admit that it was a compact, and that its obligations are irrevocably fixed. But that joint resolution does not prohibit slavery in the territories. The Nebraska bill does not propose to repeal it, or impair its obligations in any way. Then, sir, why not take back your correction, and admit that you did mean the act of 1820, when you spoke of irrevocable obligations and compacts? Assuming, then, that the Senator meant what he is now unwilling either to admit or deny, even while professing to correct me, that Missouri came in under the act of 1820, I aver that I have proven that she did not come into the Union under that act. I have proven that she was refused admission under that alleged compact. I have, therefore, proven incontestibly that the material statement upon which his argument rests is wholly without foundation, and unequivocally contradicted by the record.

Sir, I believe I may say the same of every speech which has been made against the bill, upon the ground that it impaired the obligation of compacts. There has not been an argument against the measure, every word of which in regard to the faith of compacts is not contradicted by the public records. What I complain of is this: The people may think that a Senator, having the laws and journals before him, to which he could refer, would not make a statement in contravention of those records. They make the people believe these things, and cause them to do great injustice to others, under the delusion that they have been wronged, and their feelings outraged. Sir, this address did for a time mislead the whole country. It made the Legislature of New York believe that the act of 1820 was a compact which it would be disgraceful to violate; and, acting under that delusion, they framed a series of resolutions, which, if true and just, convict that State of an act of perfidy and treachery unparalled in the history of free governments. You see, therefore, the consequences of these misstatements. You degrade your own State, and induce the peeple, under the impression that they have been injured, to get up a violent crusade against those whose fidelity and truthfulness will in the end command their respect and admiration. In consequence of arousing passions and prejudices, I am now to be found in effigy, hanging by the neck, in all the towns where you have the influence to produce such a result. In all these excesses, the people are yielding to an honest impulse, under the impression that a grievous wrong has been perpetrated. You have had your day of triumph. You have succeeded in directing upon the heads of others a torrent of insult and calumny from which even you shrink with horror, when the fact is exposed that you have become the conduits for conveying it into this hall. In your State, sir, (addressing himself to Mr. Chase,) I find that I am burnt in effigy in your abolition towns. All this is done because I have proposed, as it is said, to violate a compact! Now, what will those people think of you when they find out that you have stimulated them to these acts, which are disgraceful to your State, disgraceful to your party, and disgraceful to your cause, under a misrepresentation of the facts, which misrepresentation you ought to have been aware of, and should never have been made?

Mr. Chase. Will the Senator from Illinois permit me to say a few words?

Mr. Douglas. Certainly.

Mr. Chase. Mr. President, I certainly regret that anything has occurred in my State which should be otherwise than in accordance with the disposition which I trust I have ever manifested to treat the Senator from Illinois with entire courtesy. I do not wish, however, to be understood, here or elsewhere, as retracting any statement which I have made, or being unwilling to reassert that statement when it is directly impeached. I regard the admission of Missouri, and the facts of the transaction connected with it, as constituting a compact between the two sections of the country; a part of which was fulfilled in the admission of Missouri, another part in the admission of Arkansas, and other parts of which have been fulfilled in the admission of Iowa, and the organization of Minnesota, but which yet remains to be fulfilled in respect to the Territory of Nebraska, and which, in my judgment, will be violated by the repeal of the Missouri prohibition. That is my judgment. I have no quarrel with Senators who differ with me; but upon the whole facts of the transaction, however, I have not changed my opinion at all, in consequence of what has been said by the honorable Senator from Illinois. I say that the facts of the transaction, taken together, and as understood by the country for more than thirty years, constitute a compact binding in moral force; though, as I have always said, being embodied in a legislative act, it may be repealed by Congress, if Congress see fit.

Mr. Douglas. Mr. President, I am sorry that the Senator from Ohio has repeated the statement that Missouri came in under the compact which he says was made by the act of 1820. How many times have I to disprove the statement? Does not the vote to which I have referred show that such was not the case? Does not the fact that there was a necessity for a new compromise show it? Have I not proved it three times over? and is it possible that the Senator from Ohio will repeat it in the face of the record, with the vote staring him in the face, and with the evidence which I have produced? Does he suppose that he can make his own people believe that his statement ought to be credited in opposition to the solemn record? I am amazed that the Senator should repeat the statement again unsustained by the fact, by the record, and by the evidence, and overwhelmed by the whole current and weight of the testimony which I have produced.

The Senator says, also, that he never intended to do me injustice, and he is sorry that the people of his State have acted in the manner to which I have referred. Sir, did he not say, in the same document to which I have already alluded, that I was engaged, with others, in "a criminal betrayal of precious rights," in an "atrocious plot?" Did he not say that I and others were guilty of meditated bad faith?" Are not these his exact words? Did he not say that "servile demagogues" might make the people believe certain things, or attempt to do so? Did he not say everything calculated to produce and bring upon my head all the insults to which I have been subjected publicly and privately—not even excepting the insulting letters which I have received from his constituents, rejoicing at my domestic bereavements, and praying that other and similar calamities may befal me? All these have resulted from that address. I expected such consequences when I first saw it. In it he called upon the preachers of the Gospel to prostitute the sacred desk in stimulating excesses; and then, for fear that the people would not know who it was that was to be insulted and calumniated, he told them, in a postcript, that Mr. Douglas was the author of all this iniquity, and that they ought not to allow their rights to be made the hazard of a presidential game! After having used such language, he says he meant no disrespect—he meant nothing unkind! He was amazed that I said in my opening speech that there was anything offensive in this address; and he could not suffer himself to use harsh epithets, or to impugn a gentleman's motives! No! not he! After having deliberately written all these insults, impugning motive and character, and calling upon our holy religion to sanctify the calumny, he could not think of losing his dignity by bandying epithets, or using harsh and disrespectful terms!

Mr. President, I expected all that has occurred, and more than has come, as the legitimate result of that address. The things to which I referred are the natural consequences of it. The only revenge I seek is to expose the authors, and leave them to bear, as best they may, the just indignation of an honest community, when the people discover how their sympathies and feelings have been outraged, by making them the instruments in performing such desperate acts.

Sir, even in Boston I have been hung in effigy. I may say that I expected it to occur even there, for the Senator from Massachusetts lives there. He signed his name to that address; and for fear the Boston Abolitionists would not know that it was he, he signed it "Charles Sumner, Senator from Massachusetts." The first outrage was in Ohio, where the address was circulated under the signature of "Salmon P. Chase, Senator from Ohio." The next came from Boston—the same Boston, sir, which, under the direction of the same leaders, closed Fanueil Hall to the immortal Webster in 1850, because of his support of the compromise measures of that year, which all now confess have restored peace and harmony to a distracted country. Yes, sir, even Boston, so glorious in her early history—Boston, around whose name so many historical associations cling, to gratify the heart and exalt the pride of every American—could be led astray by Abolition misrepresentations so far as to deny a hearing to her own great man, who had shed so much glory upon Massachusetts and her metropolis! I know that Boston now feels humiliated and degraded by the act. And, sir, (addressing himself to Mr. Sumner,) you will remember that when you came into the Senate, and sought an opportunity to put forth your Abolition incendiarism, you appealed to our sense of justice by the sentiment, "Strike, but hear me first." But when Mr. Webster went back in 1850 to speak to his constituents in his own self-defence, to tell the truth, and to expose his slanderers, you would not hear him, but *you struck first!*

Again, sir, even Boston, with her Fanueil Hall consecrated to liberty, was so far led astray by abolitionism, that when one of her gallant sons, gallant by his own glorious deeds, inheriting a heroic revolutionary name, had given his life to his country upon the bloody field of Buena Vista, and when his remains were brought home, even that Boston, under abolition guidance and abolition preaching, denied him a decent burial, because he lost his life in vindicating his country's honor upon the southern frontier! Even the name of Lincoln, and the deeds of Lincoln, could not secure for him a decent interment, because abolitionism follows a patriot beyond the grave. [Applause in the galleries.]

The presiding officer, Mr. Mason, in the chair. Order must be preserved.

Mr. Douglas. Mr. President, with these facts before me, how could I hope to escape the fate which had followed these great and good men? While I had no right to hope that I might be honored as they had been under abolition auspices, have I not a right to be proud of the distinction and the association? Mr. President, I regret these digressions. I have not been able to follow the line of argument which I had marked out for myself, because of the many interruptions. I do not complain of them. It is fair that gentlemen should make them, inasmuch as they have not the opportunity of replying; hence I have yielded the floor, and propose to do so cheerfully whenever any senator intimates that justice to him or his position requires him to say anything in reply.

Returning to the point from which I was diverted.

I think I have shown that, if the act of 1826, called the Missouri compromise, was a compact, it was violated and repudiated by a solemn vote of the House of Representatives in 1821, within eleven months after it was adopted. It was repudiated by the north by a majority vote, and that repudiation was so complete and successful as to compel Missouri to make a new compromise, and she was brought into the Union under the new compromise of 1821, and not under the act of 1820. This reminds me of another point made in nearly all the speeches against this bill, and, if I recollect right, was alluded to in the abolition manifesto; to which, I regret to say, I had occasion to refer so often. I refer to the significant hint that Mr. Clay was dead before any one dared to bring forward a proposition to undo the greatest work of his hands. The senator from New York [Mr. Seward] has seized upon this insinuation, and elaborated, perhaps, more fully than his compeers; and now the abolition press suddenly, and as if by miraculous conversion, teems with eulogies upon Mr. Clay and his Missouri compromise of 1820.

Now, Mr. President, does not each of these senators know that Mr. Clay was not the author of the act of 1820? Do they not know that he disclaimed it in 1850 in this body? Do they not know that the Missouri restriction did not originate in the House of which he was a member? Do they not know that Mr. Clay never came into the Missouri controversy as a compromiser until after the compromise of 1820 was repudiated, and it became necessary to make another? I dislike to be compelled to repeat what I have conclusively proven, that the compromise which Mr. Clay effected was the act of 1821, under which Missouri came into the Union, and not the act of 1820. Mr. Clay made that compromise after you had repudiated the first one. How, then, dare you call upon the spirit of that great and gallant statesman to sanction your charge of bad faith against the south on this question?

Mr. Seward. Will the senator allow me a moment?

Mr. Douglas. Certainly.

Mr. Seward. In the year 1851 or 1852, I think 1851, a medal was struck in honor of Henry Clay, of gold, which cost a large sum of money, which contained eleven acts of the life of Henry Clay. It was presented to him by a committee of citizens of New York, by whom it had been made. One of the eleven acts of his life which was celebrated on that medal, which he accepted, was the Missouri compromise of 1820. This is my answer.

Mr. Douglas. Are the words "of 1820" upon it?

Mr. Seward. It commemorates the Missouri compromise.

Mr. Douglas. Exactly. I have seen that medal; and my recollection is that it does not contain the words "of 1820." One of the great acts of Mr. Clay was the Missouri compromise, but what Missouri compromise? Of course the one which Henry Clay made, the one which he negotiated, the one which brought Missouri into the Union, and which settled the controversy. That was the act of 1821, and not the act of 1820. It tends to confirm the statement which I have made. History is misread and misquoted, and these statements have been circulated and disseminated broadcast through the country, concealing the truth. Does not the senator know that Henry Clay, when occupying that seat in 1850, [pointing to Mr. Clay's chair,] in his speech of the 6th of February of that year, said that nothing had struck him with so much surprise as the fact that historical circumstances soon passed out of recollection; and he instanced, as a case in point, the error of attributing to him the act of 1820. [Mr. Seward nodded assent.] The senator from New York says that he does remember that Mr. Clay did say so. If so, how is it, then, that he presumes now to rise and quote that medal as evidence that Henry Clay was the author of the act of 1820?

Mr. Seward. I answer the senator in this way: that Henry Clay, while he said he did not disavow or disapprove of that compromise, transferred the merit of it to others who were more active in procuring it than he, while he had enjoyed the praise and the glory which were due from it.

Mr. Douglas. To that I have only to say that it cannot be the reason; for Henry Clay, in that same speech, did take to himself the merit of the compromise of 1821, and hence it could not have been modesty which made him disavow the other. He said that he did not know whether he had voted for the act of 1820 or not; but he supposed that he had done so. He furthermore said that it did not originate in the House of which he was a member, and that he never did approve of its principles; but that he may have voted, and probably did vote for it, under the pressure of the circumstances.

Now, Mr. President, as I have been doing justice to Mr. Clay on this question, perhaps I may as well do justice to another great man, who was associated with him in carrying through the great measures of 1850, which mortified the Senator from New York so much, because they defeated his purpose of carrying on the agitation. I allude to Mr. Webster. The authority of his great name has been quoted for the purpose of proving that he regarded the Missouri act as a compact—an irrepealable compact. Evidently the distinguished Senator from Massachusetts (Mr. Everett) supposed he was doing Mr. Webster entire justice when he quoted the passage which he read from Mr. Webster's speech of the 7th of March 1850, when he said that he stood upon the position that every part of the American continent was fixed for freedom or for slavery by irrepealable law.

The Senator says that, by the expression "irrepealable law," Mr. Webster meant to include the compromise of 1820. Now, I will show that that was not Mr. Webster's meaning—that he was never guilty of the mistake of saying that the Missouri act of 1820 was an irrepealable law. Mr. Webster said in that speech, that every foot of territory in the United States was fixed as to its character for freedom or slavery by an irrepealable law. He then enquired if it was not so in regard to Texas? He went on to prove that it was; because, he said, there was a compact in express terms between Texas and the United States. He said the parties were capable of contracting, and that there was a valuable consideration; and hence, he contended, that in that case there was a contract binding in honor, and morals, and law: and that it was irrepealable without a breach of faith.

He went on to say:

"Now, as to California and New Mexico, I hold slavery to be excluded from those Territories by a law even superior to that which admits and sanctions it in Texas—I mean the law of nature, of physical geography, the law of the formation of the earth."

That was the irrepealable law which he said prohibited slavery in the Territories of Utah and New Mexico. He next went on to speak of the prohibition of slavery in Oregon, and he said it was an "entirely useless, and, in that connexion, senseless proviso."

He went further, and said:

"That the whole territory of the States in the United States, or in the newly-acquired territory of the United States, has a fixed and settled character, now fixed and settled by law, which cannot be repealed in the case of Texas without a violation of public faith and cannot be repealed by any human power in regard to California or New Mexico; that, *under one or other of these laws*, every foot of territory in the States, or in the Territories, has now received a fixed and decided character."

What irrepealable laws? "One or the other" of those which he had stated. One was the Texas compact, the other the law of nature and physical geography; and he contended that one or the other fixed the character of the whole American continent for freedom or for slavery. He never alluded to the Missouri compromise, unless it was by the allusion to the Wilmot proviso in the Oregon bill, and there he said it was a useless, and, in that connexion, senseless thing. Why was it a useless and a senseless thing? Because it was re-enacting the law of God; because slavery had already been prohibited by physical geography. Sir, that was the meaning of Mr. Webster's speech. My distinguished friend from Massachusetts, (Mr. Everett,) when he reads the speech again, will be utterly amazed to see how he fell into such an egregious error as to suppose that Mr. Webster had so far fallen from his high position as to say that the Missouri act of 1820 was an irrepealable law.

Mr. Everett. Will the gentleman give way for a moment?

Mr. Douglas. With great pleasure.

Mr. Everett. What I said on that subject was, that Mr. Webster, in my opinion, considered the Missouri compromise as of the nature of a compact. It is true, as the Senator from Illinois has just stated, that Mr. Webster made no allusion, in express terms, to the subject of the Missouri restriction. But I thought then, and I think now, that he referred in general terms to that as a final settlement of the question, in the region to which it applied. It was not drawn in question then on either side of the House. Nobody suggested that it was at stake. Nobody intimated that there was a question before the Senate whether that restriction should be repealed or should remain in force. It was not distinctly, and in terms, alluded to, as the gentleman correctly says, by Mr. Webster, or anybody else. What he said in reference to Texas, applied to Texas alone. What he said in reference to Utah and New Mexico, applied to them alone; and what he said with regard to Oregon, to that Territory alone. But he stated in general terms, and four or five times, in the speech of the 7th of March 1850, that there was not a foot of land in the United States or its Territories the character of which, for freedom or slavery, was not fixed by some irrepealable law; and I did think then, and I think now, that by the "irrepealable law," as far as concerned the territory north of 36° 30′, and included in the Louisiana purchase, Mr. Webster had reference to the Missouri restriction, as regarded as of the nature of a compact. That restriction was copied from one of the provisions of the ordinance of 1787, which are declared in that instrument itself to be articles of compact. The Missouri restriction is the article of the ordinance of 1787 applied to the Louisiana purchase. That this is the correct interpretation of Mr. Webster's language, is confirmed by the fact that he said, more than once, and over again, that all the North lost by the arrangement of 1850, was the non-imposition of the Wilmot proviso upon Utah and New Mexico. If, in addition to that, the North had lost the Missouri restriction over the whole of the Louisiana purchase, could he have used language of that kind, and would he not have attempted, in some way or other, to reconcile such a momentous fact with his repeated statements that the measures of 1850 applied only to the territories newly acquired from Mexico?

Mr. Douglas. Mr. President, I will explain that matter very quickly. Mr. Webster's speech was made on the 7th of March 1850, and the territorial bills and the Texas boundary bill were first reported to the Senate by myself on the 25th of the same month. Mr. Webster's speech was made upon Mr. Clay's resolution, when there was no bill pending. Then the omnibus bill was formed about the 1st of May subsequently; and hence this explains the reason why Mr. Webster did not refer to the principle involved in these acts, and to the necessary effect of carrying out the principle.

Mr. Everett. The expression of Mr. Webster, which I quoted in my remarks on the 8th of February, was from a speech on Mr. Soule's amendment, offered, I think, in June. In addition to this, I have before me an extract from a still later speech of Mr. Webster, made quite late in the session, on the 17th of July 1850, in which he reiterated that statement. In it he said:

"And now, sir, what do Massachusetts and the north, the anti-slavery States, lose by this adjustment. What is it they lose? I put that question to every gentleman here, and to every gentleman in the country. They lose the application of what is called the 'Wilmot proviso' to these territories, and that is all. There is nothing else, I suppose, that the whole North are not ready to do. They wish to get California into the Union; they wish to quiet New Mexico; they desire to terminate the dispute about the Texan boundary in any reasonable manner, cost what it reasonably may. They make no sacrifice in all that. What they do sacrifice is exactly this: The application of the Wilmot proviso to the Territory of New Mexico and the Territory of Utah, *and that is all.*"

Could Mr. Webster have used language like this if he had understood that, at the same time, the non-slaveholding States were losing the Missouri restriction, as applied to the whole vast territory included in the bills now before the Senate?

Mr. Douglas. Of course that was all, and if he regarded the Missouri prohibition in the same light that he did the Oregon prohibition, it was a useless, and, in that connexion, a senseless proviso; and hence the north lost nothing by not having that same senseless, useless proviso applied to Utah and New Mexico. Now, to show the senator that he must be mistaken as to Mr. Webster's authority, let me call his attention back to this passage in his 7th of March speech:

"Under *one or other* of these laws, every foot of territory in the States or Territories has now received a fixed and decided character."

What laws did he refer to when he spoke of "one or other of these laws?" He had named but two, the Texas compact and the law of nature, of climate, and physical geography, which excluded slavery. He had mentioned none other; and yet he says "one or other" prohibited slavery in all the States or Territories—thus including Nebraska, as well as Utah and New Mexico.

Mr. Everett. That was not drawn in question at all.

Mr. Douglas. Then if it was not drawn in question, the speech should not have been quoted in support of the Missouri compromise. It is just what I complain of, that, if it was not thus drawn in question, that use ought not to have been made of it. Now, Mr. President, it is well known that Mr. Webster supported the compromise measures of 1850, and the principle involved in them, of leaving the people to do as they pleased upon this subject. I think, therefore, that I have shown that these gentlemen are not authorized to quote the name either of Mr. Webster or Mr. Clay in support of the position which they take, that this bill violates the faith of compacts. Sir, it was because Mr. Webster went for giving the people in the Territories the right to do as they pleased upon the subject of slavery, and because he was in favor of carrying out the Constitution in regard to fugitive slaves, that he was not allowed to speak in Faneuil Hall.

Mr. Everett. That was not my fault.

Mr. Douglas. I know it was not; but I say it was because he took that position; it was because he did not go for a prohibitory policy; it was because he advocated the same principles which I now advocate, because he went for the same provisions in the Utah bill which I now sustain in this bill, that Boston abolitionists turned their back upon him, just as they burnt me in effigy. Sir, if identity of principle, if identity of support as friends, if identity of enemies fix Mr. Webster's position, his authority is certainly with us, and not with the abolitionists. I have a right, therefore, to have the sympathies of his Boston friends with me, as I sympathized with him when the same principle was involved.

Mr. President, I am sorry that I have taken up so much time; but I must notice one or two points more. So much has been said about the Missouri compromise act, and about a faithful compliance with it by the north, that I must follow that matter a little further. The senator from Ohio [Mr. WADE] has referred, to-night, to the fact that I went for carrying out the Missouri compromise in the Texas resolutions of 1845, and in 1848, on several occasions; and he actually proved that I never abandoned it until 1850. He need not have taken the pains to prove that fact; for he got all his information on the subject from my opening speech upon this bill. I told you then that I was willing, as a northern man, in 1845, when the Texas question arose, to carry the Missouri compromise line through that State, and in 1848 I offered it as an amendment to the Oregon bill. Although I did not like the principle involved in that act, yet I was willing, for the sake of harmony, to extend to the Pacific, and abide by it in good faith, in order to avoid the slavery agitation. The Missouri compromise was defeated then by the same class of politicians who are now combined in opposition to the Nebraska bill. It was because we were unable to carry out that compromise, that a necessity existed for making a new one in 1850. And then we established this great principle of self-government which lies at the foundation of all our institutions. What does his charge amount to? He charges it, as a matter of offence, that I struggled in 1845 and in 1848 to observe good faith; and he and his associates defeated my purpose, and deprived me of the ability to carry out what he now says is the plighted faith of the nation.

Mr. Wade. I did not charge the senator with anything except with making a very excellent argument on my side of the question, and I wished he would make it again to-night. That was all.

Mr. Douglas. What was the argument which I made? A southern senator had complained that the Missouri compromise was a matter of injustice to the south. I told him he ought not to complain of that when his southern friends were here proposing to accept it; and if we could carry it out, he had no right to make such a complaint. I was anxious to carry it out. It would not have done for a northern man who was opposed to the measure, and unwilling to abide it, to take that position. It would not have become the senator from Ohio, who then denounced the very measure which he now calls a sacred compact, to take that position. But, as one who had always been in favor of carrying it out, it was legitimate and proper that I should make that argument in reply.

Sir, as I have said, the south were willing to agree to the Missouri compromise in 1848. When it was proposed by me to the Oregon bill, as an amendment, to extend that line to the Pacific, the south agreed to it. The senate adopted that proposition, and the House voted it down. In 1850, after the omnibus bill had broken down, and we proceeded to pass the compromise measures separately, I proposed, when the Utah bill was under discussion, to make a slight variation of the boundary of that Territory, so as to include the Mormon settlements, and not with reference to any other question; and it was suggested that we should take the line of 36° 30′. That would have accomplished the local objects of the amendment very well. But when I proposed it, what did these free-soilers say? What did the senator from New Hampshire, [Mr. Hale,] who was then their leader in this body, say? Here are his words:

"Mr. Hale. I wish to say a word as a reason why I shall vote against the amendment. I shall vote against 36° 30′, *because I think there is an implication in it.* [Laughter.] I will vote for 37° or 36° either, just as it is convenient; but it is idle to shut our eyes to the fact that here is an attempt in this bill—I will not say it is the intention of the mover—to pledge this Senate and Congress to the imaginary line of 36° 30′, because there are some *historical recollections connected with it in regard to this controversy about slavery.* I will content myself with saying that *I never will, by vote or speech, admit or submit to anything that may bind the action of our legislation here to make the parallel of 36° 30′ the boundary line between slave and free territory.* And when I say that, I explain the reason why I go against the amendment."

These remarks of Mr. Hale were not made on a proposition to extend the Missouri compromise line to the Pacific, but on a proposition to fix 36° 30′ as the southern boundary line of Utah, for local reasons. He was against it because there might be, as he said, an implication growing out of historical recollections in favor of the imaginary line between slavery and freedom. Does that look as if his object was to get an implication in favor of preserving sacred this line, in regard to which gentlemen now say there was a solemn compact? That proposition may illustrate what I wish to say in this connexion upon a point which has been made by the opponents of this bill as to the effect of an amendment inserted on the motion of the senator from Virginia, [Mr. Mason,] into the Texas boundary bill. The opponents of this measure rely upon that amendment to show that the Texas compact was preserved by the acts of 1850. I have already shown, in my former speech, that the object of the amendment was to guaranty to the State of Texas, with her circumscribed boundaries, the same number of States which she would have had under her larger boundaries, and with the same right to come in with or without slavery, as they please.

We have been told over and over again that there was no such thing intimated in debate as that the country cut off from Texas was to be relieved from the stipulation of that compromise. This has been asserted boldly and unconditionally, as if there could be no doubt about it. The senator from Georgia [Mr. Toombs] in his speech, showed that, in his address to his constituents of that State, he had proclaimed to the world that the object was to establish a principle which would allow the people to decide the question of slavery for themselves, north as well as south of 36° 30′. The line of 36° 30′ was voted down as the boundary of Utah, so that there should not be even an implication in favor of an imaginary line to divide freedom and slavery. Subsequently, when the Texas boundary bill was under consideration, on the next day after the amendment of the senator from Virginia had been adopted, the record says:

"Mr. Sebastian moved to add to the second article the following:

"'On the condition that the territory hereby ceded may be, at the proper time, formed into a State, and admitted into the Union, with a constitution with or without the prohibition of slavery therein, as the people of the said Territory may at the time determine.'"

Then the senator from Arkansas did propose that the territory cut off should be relieved from that restriction in express terms, and allowed to come in according to the principles of this bill. What was done? The debate continued:

"Mr. Foote. Will my friend allow me to appeal to him to move this amendment when the territorial bill for New Mexico shall be up for consideration? It will certainly be a part of that bill, and I shall then vote for it with pleasure. Now it will only embarrass our action."

Let it be remarked, that no one denied the propriety of the provision. All seemed to acquiesce in the principle; but it was thought better to insert it in the territorial bills, as we are now doing, instead of adding it to the Texas boundary bill. The debate proceeded:

"Mr. Sebastian. My only object in offering the amendment is to secure the assertion of this principle beyond a doubt. The principle was acquiesced in without difficulty in regard to the territorial government established for Utah, a part of this acquired territory, and, it is proper, in my opinion, that it should be incorporated in this bill.

"Messrs. Cass, Foote, and others. Oh, withdraw it.

"Mr. Sebastian. I think this is the proper place for it. It is uncertain whether it will be incorporated in the other bill referred to, and the bill itself may not pass."

It will be seen that the debate goes upon the supposition that the effect was to release the country north of 36° 30′ from the obligation of the prohibition; and the only question, was whether the declaration that it should be received into the Union "with or without slavery" should be inserted in the Texas bill, or the territorial bill.

The debate was continued, and I will read one or two other passages:

"Mr. Foote. I wish to state to the senator a fact of which, I think, he is not observant at this moment; and that is, that the senator from Virginia has introduced an amendment, which is now a part of the bill, which recognises the Texas compact of annexation in every respect.

"Mr. Sebastian. I was aware of the effect of the amendment of the senator from Virginia. It is in regard to the number of States to be formed out of Texas, and is referred to only in general terms."

Thus it will be seen that the senator from Arkansas, then explained the amendment of the senator from Virginia, which had been adopted, in precisely the same way in which I explained it in my opening speech. The senator from Arkansas continued :

"If this amendment be the same as that offered by the senator from Virginia there can certainly be no harm in reaffirming it in this bill, to which I think it properly belongs."

Thus it will be seen that nobody disputed that the restriction was to be removed ; and the only question was, as to the bill in which that declaration would be put. It seems, from the record, that I took part in the debate, and said :

"Mr. Douglas. This boundary as now fixed, would leave New Mexico bounded on the east by the 103° of longitude up to 36° 30′, and then east to the 100° ; and it leaves a narrow neck of land between 36° 30′ and the old boundary of Texas, that would not naturally and properly go to New Mexico when it should become a State. This amendment would compel us to include it in New Mexico, or to form it into another State. When the principle shall come up in the bill for the organization of a territorial government for New Mexico, no doubt the same vote which inserted it in the omnibus bill, and the Utah bill will insert it there.

"Several Senators. No doubt of it."

Upon that debate the amendment of the senator from Arkansas was voted down, because it was avowed and distinctly understood that the amendment of the senator from Virginia, taken in connexion with the remainder of the bill, did release the country ceded by Texas, north of 36° 30′ from the restriction ; and it was agreed that if we did not put it into the Texas boundary bill, it should go into the territorial bill. I stated, as a reason why it should not go into the Texas boundary bill, that if it did it would be a compact, and would compel us to put the whole ceded country into one State, when it might be more convenient and natural to make a different boundary. I pledged myself then that it should be put into the territorial bill ; and when we considered the territorial bill for New Mexico we put in the same clause, so far as the country ceded by Texas was embraced within that territory, and it passed in that shape. When it went into the House, they united the two bills together, and thus this clause passed in the same bill, as the senator from Arkansas desired.

Now, sir, have I not shown conclusively that it was the understanding in that debate that the effect was to release the country north of 36° 30′, which formerly belonged to Texas, from the operation of that restriction, and to provide that it should come into the Union with or without slavery, as its people should see proper?

That being the case, I ask the senator from Ohio [Mr. Chase] if he ought not to have been cautious when he charged over and over again that there was not a word or a syllable uttered in debate to that effect? Should he not have been cautious when he said that it was a mere after-thought on my part? Should he not have been cautious when he said that even I never dreamed of it up to the 4th of January of this year? Whereas the record shows that I made a speech to that effect during the pendency of the bills of 1850. The same statement was repeated by nearly every senator who followed him in debate in opposition to this bill ; and it is now being circulated over the country, published in every abolition paper, and read on every stump by every abolition orator, in order to get up a prejudice against me and the measure I have introduced. Those gentlemen should not have dared to utter the statement without knowing whether it was correct or not. These records are troublesome things sometimes. It is not proper for a man to charge another with a mere after-thought because he did not know that he had advocated the same principles before. Because he did not know it he should not take it for granted that nobody else did. Let me tell the senators that it is a very unsafe rule for them to rely upon. They ought to have had sufficient respect for a brother senator to have believed, when he came forward with an important proposition, that he had investigated it. They ought to have had sufficient respect for a committee of this body to have assumed that they meant what they said.

When I see such a system of misinterpretation, and misrepresentation of views, of laws, of records, of debates, all tending to mislead the public, to excite prejudice, and to propagate error, have I not a right to expose it in very plain terms, without being arraigned for violating the courtesies of the Senate?

Mr. President, frequent reference has been made in debate to the admission of Arkansas as a slave-holding State, as furnishing evidence that the abolitionists and freesoilers, who have recently become so much enamored with the Missouri compromise, have always been faithful to its stipulations and implications. I will show that the reference is unfortunate for them. When Arkansas applied for admission in 1836, objection was made in consequence of the provisions of her constitution in respect to slavery. When the abolitionists and fresoilers of that day were arraigned for making that objection, upon the ground that Arkansas was south of 36° 30′, they replied that the act of 1820 was never a compromise, much less a compact, imposing any obligation upon the successors of those who passed the act to pay any more respect to its provisions than to any other enactment of ordinary legislation. I have the debates before me, but will occupy the attention of the Senate only to read one or two paragraphs. Mr. Hand of New York, in opposition to the admission of Arkansas as a slave-holding State, said:

"I am aware it will be, as it has been already contended, that by the Missouri compromise, as it has been preposterously termed, Congress has parted with its right to prohibit the introduction of slavery into the territory south of 36° 30′ north latitude."

He acknowledged that by the Missouri compromise, as he said it was preposterously termed, the north was estopped from denying the right to hold slaves south of that line; but, he added:

"There are, to my mind, insuperable objections to the soundness of that proposition."

Here they are:

"In the first place, there was no compromise or compact whereby Congress surrendered any power, or yielded any jurisdiction; and, in the second place, if it had done so, it was a mere legislative act, that could not bind their successors, it would be subject to a repeal at the will of any succeeding Congress."

I give these passages as specimens of the various speeches made in opposition to the admission of Arkansas by the same class of politicians who now oppose the Nebraska bill upon the ground that it violates a solemn compact. So much for the speeches. Now for the vote. The Journal which I hold in my hand, shows that forty-nine northern votes were recorded against the admission of Arkansas.

Yet, sirs, in utter disregard—and charity leads me to hope, in profound ignorance—of all these facts, gentlemen are boasting that the north always observed the contract, never denied its validity, never wished to violate it; and they have even referred to the cases of the admission of Missouri and Arkansas as instances of their good faith.

Now, is it possible that gentlemen could suppose these things could be said and distributed in their speeches without exposure? Did they presume that, inasmuch as their lives were devoted to slavery agitation, whatever they did not know about the history of that question did not exist? I am willing to believe, I hope it may be the fact, that they were profoundly ignorant, of all these records, all these debates, all these facts, which overthrow every position they have assumed. I wish the senator from Maine, [Mr. Fessenden,] who delivered his maiden speech here to-night, and who made a great many sly stabs at me, had informed himself upon the subject before he repeated all these groundless assertions. I can excuse him for the reason that he has been here but a few days, and, having enlisted under the banner of the abolition confederates, was unwise and simple enough to believe that what they had published could be relied upon as stubborn facts. He may be an innocent victim. I hope he can have the excuse of not having investigated the subject. I am willing to excuse him on the ground that he did not know what he was talking about, and it is the only excuse which I can make for him. I will say, however, that I do not think he was required by his loyalty to the abolitionists to repeat every disreputable insinuation which they made. Why did he throw into his speech that foul inuendo about a "northern man with southern principles," and then quote the senator from Massachusetts [Mr. Sumner] as his authority? Ay, sir, I say that foul insinuation. Did not the senator from Massachusetts, who first dragged it into this debate, wish to have the public understand that I was known as a northern man with southern principles? Was not that the allusion? If it was, he availed himself of a cant phrase in the public mind, in violation of the truth of history. I know of but one man in this country who ever made it a boast that he was "a northern man with southern principles," and *he* [turning to Mr. Sumner] was *your* candidate for the Presidency in 1848. [Applause in the galleries.]

The Presiding Officer, [Mr. Mason.] Order, order.

Mr. Douglas. If his sarcasm was intended for Martin Van Buren, it involves a family quarrel, with which I have no disposition to interfere. I will only add that I have been able to discover nothing in the present position or recent history of that distinguished statesman, which would lead me to covet the *sobriquet* by which he is known—"a northern man with southern principles."

Mr. President, the senators from Ohio and Massachusetts, [Mr. Chase and Mr. Sumner,] have taken the liberty to impeach my motives in bringing forward this measure. I desire to know by what right they arraign me, or by what authority they impute to me other and different motives than those which I have assigned. I have shown from the record that I advocated and voted for the same principles and provisions in the compromise acts of 1850, which are embraced in this bill. I have proven that I put the same construction upon those measures immediately after their adoption that is given in the report which I submitted this session from the Committee on Territories. I have shown that the legislature of Illinois at its first session, after those measures were enacted, passed resolutions approving them, and declaring that the same great principles of self-government should be incorporated into all territorial organizations. Yet, sir, in the face of these facts, these senators have the hardihood to declare that this was all an "afterthought" on my part, conceived for the first time during the present session; and that the measure is offered as a bid for presidential votes! Are they incapable of conceiving that an honest man can do a right thing from worthy motives? I must be permitted to tell those senators that their experience in seeking political preferment does not furnish a safe rule by which to judge the character and principles of other senators!

I must be permitted to tell the Senator from Ohio that I did not obtain my seat in this body, either by a corrupt bargain or a dishonorable coalition! I must be permitted to remind the Senator from Massachusetts that I did not enter into any combinations or arrangements by which my character, my principles, and my honor, were set up at public auction or private sale in order to procure a seat in the Senate of the United States! I did not come into the Senate by any such means.

Mr. Weller. But there are some men whom I know that did.

Mr. Chase, (to Mr. Weller.) Do you say that I came here by a bargain?

The Presiding Officer, [Mr. Mason.] Order must be preserved in the Senate.

Mr. Weller. I will explain what I mean.

The Presiding Officer. The Senator from Illinois is entitled to the floor.

Mr. Dodge of Iowa. I call both the Senator from California and the Senator from Ohio to order.

Mr. Douglas. I cannot yield the floor until I get through. I say, then, there is nothing which authorized that Senator to impugn my motives.

Mr. Chase. Will the Senator from Illinois allow me? Does he say that I came into the Senate by a corrupt bargain?

Mr. Douglas. I cannot permit the Senator to change the issue. He has arraigned me on the charge of seeking high political station by unworthy means. I tell him there is nothing in my history which would create the suspicion that I come into the Senate by a corrupt bargain or a disgraceful coalition.

Mr. Chase. Whoever says that I came here by a corrupt bargain states what is false.

Mr. Weller. Mr. President. ———

Mr. Douglas. My friend from California will wait till I get through, if he pleases.

The Presiding Officer. The Senator from Illinois is entitled to the floor.

Mr. Douglas. It will not do for the Senator from Ohio to return offensive expressions after what I have said and proven. Nor can I permit him to change the issue, and thereby divert public attention from the enormity of his offence, in charging me with unworthy motives; while performing a high public duty, in obedience to the expressed wish and known principles of my State. I choose to maintain my own position, and leave the public to ascertain, if they do not understand, how and by what means he was elected to the Senate.

Mr. Chase. If the Senator will allow me, I will say, in reply to the remarks which the Senator has just made, that I did not understand him as calling upon me for any explanation of the statement which he said was made in regard to a presidential bid. The exact statement in the address was this—it was a question addressed to the people: "Would they allow their dearest rights to be made the hazards of a presidential game?" That was the exact expression. Now, sir, it is well known that all these great measures in the country are influenced, more or less, by reference to the great public canvasses which are going on from time to time. I certainly did not intend to impute to the Senator from Illinois—and I desire always to do justice—in that any improper motive. I do not think it is an unworthy ambition to desire to be a President of the United States. I do not think that the bringing forward of a measure with reference to that object would be an improper thing, if the measure be proper in itself. I differ from the Senator in my judgment of the measure. I do not think the measure is a right one. In that I express the judgment which I honestly entertain. I do not condemn his judgment; I do not make, and I do not desire to make, any personal imputations upon him in reference to a great public question.

Mr. Weller. Mr. President—

Mr. Douglas. I cannot allow my friend from California to come into the ring at this time, for this is my peculiar business. I may let him in after awhile. I wish to examine the explanation of the senator from Ohio, and see whether I ought to accept it as satisfactory. He has quoted the language of the address. It is undeniable that that language clearly imputed to me the design of bringing forward this bill with a view of securing my own election to the presidency. Then, by way of excusing himself for imputing to me such a purpose, the senator says that he does not consider it "an unworthy ambition;" and hence he says that, in making the charge, he does not impugn my motives. I must remind him that, in addition to that insinuation, he only said, in the same address, that my bill was a "criminal betrayal of precious rights;" he only said it was "an atrocious plot against freedom and humanity;" he only said that it was "meditated bad faith;" he only spoke significantly of "servile demagogues;" he only called upon the preachers of the Gospel and the people at their public meetings to denounce and resist such a monstrous iniquity. In saying all this, and much of the same sort, he now assures me, in the presence of the Senate, that he did not mean the charge to imply an "unworthy ambition;" that it was not intended as a "personal imputation" upon my motives or character; and that he meant "no personal disrespect" to me as the author of the measure. In reply, I will content myself with the remark, that there is a very wide difference of opinion between the senator from Ohio and myself in respect to the meaning of words, and especially in regard to the line of conduct which, in a public man, does not constitute an unworthy ambition.

Mr. Weller. Now, I ask my friend from Illinois to give way to me for a few moments.

Mr. Douglas. I yield the floor.

Mr. Weller. I made a remark which no doubt gave cause to this digression in the argument of the senator from Illinois. I presume that I know the circumstances under which the senator from Ohio was elected to this body. I intimated them in the expression of opinion which I gave a few moments ago. I do not know that the senator was elected here under a compromise, or an agreement, or an express bargain. I entertain no personal feeling of ill-will against the senator, however little respect I may have for his political opinions. I propose to state some facts, however, connected with his election, and leave others to decide how far they constituted a bargain. Soon after the admission of Ohio into the Union, a law had been passed prohibiting negroes and their descendants from testifying in a court of justice when a white man was a party—the same law required a negro, upon coming within the limits of the State, to give bond and security that he would not become a pauper. This law was particularly odious to the abolitionists, and the democrats had uniformly opposed its repeal, upon the ground that such an act would encourage and invite emigrants of that class to the State. Such persons, they held, would add nothing to the real strength of the State. Certain judges of the supreme and other courts were to be elected by the legislature. Some members of the board of public works were to be appointed. For these places there were, as is usually the case, a multitude of applicants. The political power between the two great parties in the legislature was so equally divided that a few (three or four, I believe) abolitionists held the balance between them. An effort was made to compromise with the whigs and elect an abolitionist in the other branch of Congress to the Senate. This failed. Propositions were then made to the democrats, which resulted in the repeal of the "black-laws," the appointment of certain democrats to judgeships, &c., and the election of Mr. Chase to the Senate. These facts transpired about the time I left the State for California, and I know gave great dissatisfaction to a large portion of the people.

Mr. Chase. I know that the senator from California means to state the facts correctly; but I think justice to myself, and justice to my State, requires me to say that he is not correctly informed in regard to the material facts. The truth is, and I owe it to my State to say it, that in the legislature, at the time of my election, there were three parties, one of them known as the independent democrats, or sometimes as free-soilers, another known as the old-line democrats, and another known as whigs. It was impossible for either of these three parties to elect its candidate of itself, and that happened which I believe has happened in very many of the States north and south.

Mr. Weller. How many votes had the third party?

Mr. Chase. Ten or twelve. There were ten or twelve gentlemen elected as freesoilers; but it is true the whig portion of them did not vote for me. I got none but democratic votes. I received the democratic portion of the freesoil vote, and I received the whole of the old-line democratic vote, without a single exception. On the other hand, some gentlemen, generally concurring with me in political views in most respects, and also in respect to slavery, but belonging to the old-line organization, were elected as members of the supreme court. That is the whole of it.

So far as the repeal of the black laws is concerned; those laws which, I think, the senator from South Carolina [Mr. Butler] once mentioned as a subject of reproach against the people of Ohio, by which bonds were required for the good behavior of every colored person coming into the State, and by which every colored person was excluded as a witness upon the trial of a white man, that whole matter of repeal occurred prior to the election, and had no connexion with it as far I know.

Mr. Weller. Was not that part of the agreement which resulted in your election? I know these laws were repealed at the same session, and I always understood it was a part of the bargain.

Mr. Chase. It had no connexion with it, so far as I know. I have no doubt that the Senator thinks it had, but he is mistaken. Now, I take occasion to say that the repeal of these inhuman and oppressive laws was a measure demanded by the people. I rejoiced at their repeal. I believe that everybody who has investigated the subject thinks that that repeal was a humane measure—a wise, fit, and a proper measure. Everybody who knows anything about the population of my State since that, knows, that, far from having been productive of any injury, it has resulted in great good. That is all I have to say.

Mr. Sumner. Will the Senator from Illinois yield the floor to me for a moment?

Mr. Douglas. As I presume it is on the same point, I will hear the testimony.

Mr. Sumner. Mr. President, I shrink always instinctively from any effort to repel a personal assault. I do not recognize the jurisdiction of this body to try my election to the Senate; but I do state, in reply to the Senator from Illinois, that if he means to suggest that I came into the body by any waiver of principles; by any abandonment of my principles of any kind; by any effort or activity of my own, in any degree, he states that which cannot be sustained by the facts. I never sought, in any way, the office which I now hold; nor was I a party, in any way, directly or indirectly, to those efforts which placed me here.

Mr. Weller. My only excuse for intermeddling with this matter was, that I am, I believe, the only member of the Senate who is a native of Ohio. I took occasion to say, some days ago, that I was very much mortified that my native State should be represented in the manner she is on this floor. I happened to be familiar, as I have stated, with the circumstances under which the Senator on my right (Mr. Chase) was elected. He was elected to the Senate the very year that I left the State of Ohio, and I was very glad to have an opportunity of changing my residence on that remarkable occasion. [Laughter.] That is the only apology which I have to offer for intermeddling with what is otherwise a personal matter between the Senator from Ohio and the Senator from Illinois. Usually, I have as much as I can do to attend to my own affairs—I am rarely a volunteer in the controversies of others.

Mr. Douglas. I do not complain of my friend from California for interposing in the manner he has; for I see that it was very appropriate in him to do so.

But, sir, the Senator from Massachusetts comes up with a very bold front, and denies the right of any man to put him on defence for the manner of his election. He says it is contrary to his principles to engage in personal assaults. If he expects to avail himself of the benefit of such a plea, he should act in accordance with his professed principles, and refrain from assaulting the character and impugning the motives of better men than himself. Everybody knows that he came here by a coalition or combination between political parties holding opposite and hostile opinions. But it is not my purpose to go into the morality of the matters involved in his election. The public know the history of that notorious coalition, and have formed its judgment upon it. It will not do for the Senator to say that he was not a party to it, for he thereby betrays a consciousness of the immorality of the transaction, without acquitting himself of the responsibilities which justly attach to him. As well might the receiver of stolen goods deny any responsibility for the larceny, while luxuriating in the proceeds of the crime, as the senator to avoid the consequences resulting from the mode of his election, while he clings to the office. I must be permitted to remind him of what he certainly can never forget, that when he arrived here, to take his seat for the first time, so firmly were senators impressed with the conviction that he had been elected by dishonorable and corrupt means, there were very few who, for a long time, could deem it consistent with personal honor to hold private intercourse with him. So general was that impression, that for a long time he was avoided and shunned as a person unworthy of the association of gentlemen. Gradually, however, these injurious impressions were worn away by his bland manners and amiable deportment; and I regret that the senator should now, by a violation of all the rules of courtesy and propriety, compel me to refresh his mind upon these unwelcome reminiscences.

Mr. Chase. If the senator refers to me, he is stating a fact of which I have no knowledge at all. I came here——

Mr. Douglas. I was not speaking of the senator from Ohio, but of his confederate in slander, the senator from Massachusetts, [Mr. SUMNER.] I have a word now to say to the other senator from Ohio, [Mr. WADE.] On the day when I exposed this abolition address, so full of slanders and calumnies, he rose and stated that, although his name was signed to it, he had never read it; and so willing was he to endorse an abolition document, that he signed it in blank, without knowing what it contained.

Mr. Wade. I have always found them true.

Mr. Douglas. He stated that from what I had exposed of its contents he did not hesitate to endorse every word. In the same speech he said, that in Ohio a negro was as good as a white man; with the avowal that he did not consider himself any better than a free negro. I have only to say that I should not have noticed it if none but free negroes had signed it!

The senator from New York, [Mr. SEWARD,] when I was about to call him to account for this slanderous production, promptly denied that he ever signed the document. Now, I say, it has been circulated with his named attached to it; then I want to know of the senators who sent out the document, who forged the name of the senator from New York?

Mr. Chase. I am glad that the senator has asked that question. I have only to say, in reference to that matter, that I have not the slightest knowledge in regard to the manner in which various names were appended to that document. It was prepared to be signed, and was signed, by the gentlemen here who are known as independent democrats, and how any other names came to be added to it is more than I can tell.

Mr. Douglas. It is not a satisfactory answer, for those who confess to the preparation and publication of a document filled with insult and calumny, with forged names attached to it for the purpose of imparting to it respectability, to interpose a technical denial that they committed the crime. Somebody did forge other people's names to that document. The senators from Ohio and Massachusetts [Mr. CHASE and Mr. SUMNER] plead guilty to the authorship and publication; upon them rests the responsibility of showing who committed the forgery.

Mr. President, I have done with these personal matters. I regret the necessity which compelled me to devote so much time to them. All I have done and said has been in the way of self-defence, as the Senate can bear me witness.

Mr. President, I have also occupied a good deal of time in exposing the cant of these gentlemen about the sanctity of the Missouri compromise, and the dishonour attached to the violation of plighted faith. I have exposed these matters in order to show that the object of these men is to withdraw from public attention the real principle involved in the bill. They well know that the abrogation of the Missouri compromise is the incident and not the principal of the bill. They well understand that the report of the committee and the bill propose to establish the principle in all territorial organizations, that the question of slavery shall be referred to the people to regulate for themselves, and that such legislation should be had as was necessary to remove all legal obstructions to the free exercise of this right by the people.

The eighth section of the Missouri act standing in the way of this great principle must be rendered inoperative and void, whether expressly repealed or not, in order to give the people the power of regulating their own domestic institutions in their own way, subject only to the Constitution.

Now, sir, if these gentlemen have entire confidence in the correctness of their own position, why do they not meet the issue boldly and fairly, and controvert the soundness of this great principle of popular sovereignty in obedience to the Constitution? They know full well that this was the principle upon which the colonies separated from the crown of Great Britian, the principle upon which the battles of the revolution were fought, and the principle upon which our republican system was founded. They cannot be ignorant of the fact that the revolution grew out of the assertion of the right on the part of the imperial government to interfere with the internal affairs and domestic concerns of the colonies. In this connexion I will invite attention to a few extracts from the instructions of the different colonies to their delegates in the Continental Congress, with a view of forming such a union as would enable them to make successful resistance to the efforts of the crown to destroy the fundamental principle of all free government by interfering with the domestic affairs of the colonies.

I will begin with Pennsylvania, whose devotion to the principles of human liberty, and the obligations of the Constitution, has acquired for her the proud title of the Key-stone in the arch of republican States. In her instructions is contained the following reservation:

"Reserving to the people of this colony the sole and exclusive right of regulating the internal government and police of the same."

And, in a subsequent instruction, in reference to suppressing the British authority in the colonies, Pennsylvania uses the following emphatic language:

"Unanimously declare our willingness to concur in a vote of the Congress declaring the United Colonies free and independent States, provided the forming the government and the regulation of the internal police of this colony be always reserved to the people of the said colony."

Connecticut, in authorizing her delegates to vote for the Declaration of Independence, attached to it the following condition:

"Saving that the administration of government, and the power of forming governments for, and the regulation of the internal concerns and police of each colony, ought to be left and remain to the respective colonial legislatures."

New Hampshire annexed this proviso to her instructions to her delegates to vote for independence:

"Provided the regulation of our internal police be under the direction of our own assembly."

New Jersey imposed the following condition:

"Always observing that, whatever plan of confederacy you enter into, the regulating of the internal police of this province is to be reserved to the colonial legislature."

Maryland gave her consent to the Declaration of Independence upon the condition contained in this proviso:

"And that said colony will hold itself bound by the resolutions of a majority of the United Colonies in the premises, provided the sole and exclusive right of regulating the internal government and police of that colony be reserved to the people thereof."

Virginia annexed the following condition to her instructions to vote for the Declaration of Independence:

"Provided that the power of forming government for, and the regulations of the internal concerns of the colony, be left to respective colonial legislatures."

I will not weary the senate in multiplying evidence upon this point. It is apparent that the Declaration of Independence had its origin in the violation of that great fundamental principle which secured to the people of the colonies the right to regulate their own domestic affairs in their own way; and that the revolution resulted in the triumph of that principle, and the recognition of the right asserted by it. Abolitionism proposes to destroy the right, and extinguish the principle for which our forefathers waged a seven years' bloody war, and upon which our whole system of free government is founded. They not only deny the application of this principle to the Territories, but insist upon fastening the prohibition upon all the States to be formed out of those Territories. Therefore, the doctrine of the abolitionists—the doctrine of the opponents of the Nebraska and Kansas bill, and of the advocates of the Missouri restriction—demand congressional interference with slavery, not only in the Territories, but in all the new States to be formed therefrom. It is the same doctrine when applied to the Territories and new States of this Union, which the British government attempted to enforce by the sword upon the American colonies. It is this fundamental principle of self-government which constitutes the distinguishing feature of the Nebraska bill. The opponents of the principle are consistent in opposing the bill. I do not blame them for their opposition. I only ask them to meet the issue fairly and openly, by acknowledging that they are opposed to the principle which it is the object of the bill to carry into operation. It seems that there is no power on earth, no intellectual power, no mechanical power that can bring them to a fair discussion of the true issue. If they hope to delude the people, and escape detection for any considerable length of time under the catch-word "Missouri compromise," and "faith of compacts," they will find that the people of this country have more penetration and intelligence than they have given them credit for.

Mr. President, there is an important fact connected with this slavery resolution, which should never be lost sight of. It has always arisen from one and the same cause. Whenever that cause has been removed, the agitation has ceased; and whenever the cause has been renewed, the agitation has sprung into existence. That cause is, and ever has been, the attempt on the part of Congress to interfere with the question of slavery in the Territories and new

States formed therefrom. Is it not wise, then, to confine our action within the sphere of our legitimate duties, and leave this vexed question to take care of itself in each State and Territory, according to the wishes of the people thereoof, in conformity to the forms and in subjection to the provisions of the Constitution?

The opponents of the bill tell us that agitation is no part of their policy, that their great desire is peace and harmony; and they complain bitterly that I should have disturbed the repose of the country by the introduction of this measure. Let me ask these professed friends of peace and avowed enemies of agitation, how the issue could have been avoided? They tell me that I should have let the question alone—that is, that I should have left Nebraska unorganized, the people unprotected, and the Indian barrier in existence, until the swelling tide of emigration should burst through, and accomplish by violence what it is the part of wisdom and statesmanship to direct and regulate by law. How long could you have postponed action with safety? How long could you maintain that Indian barrier, and restrain the onward march of civilization, Christianity, and free government by a barbarian wall? Do you suppose that you could keep that vast country a howling wilderness in all time to come, roamed over by hostile savages, cutting off all safe communication between our Atlantic and Pacific possessions? I tell you that the time for action has come, and cannot be postponed. It is a case in which the "let alone" policy would precipitate a crisis which must inevitably result in violence, anarchy, and strife.

You cannot fix bounds to the onward march of this great and growing country. You cannot fetter the limbs of the young giant. He will burst all your chains. He will expand, and grow, and increase, and extend civilization, Christianity, and liberal principles. Then, sir, if you cannot check the growth of the country in that direction, is it not the part of wisdom to look the danger in the face, and provide for an event which you cannot avoid? I tell you, sir, you must provide for continuous lines of settlement from the Mississippi valley to the Pacific ocean. And in making this provision, you must decide upon what principles the Territories shall be organized; in other words, whether the people shall be allowed to regulate their domestic institutions in their own way, according to the provisions of this bill, or whether the opposite doctrine of congressional interference is to prevail. Postpone it, if you will; but whenever you do act, this question must be met and decided.

The Missouri compromise was interference; the compromise of 1850 was non interference, leaving the people to exercise their rights under the Constitution. The Committee on Territories were compelled to act on this subject. I, as their chairman, was bound to meet the question. I chose to take the responsibility, regardless of consequences personal to myself. I should have done the same thing last year, if there had been time; but we know, considering the late period at which the bill then reached us from the House, that there was not sufficient time to consider the question fully, and to prepare a report upon the subject. I was, therefore, persuaded by friends to allow the bill to be reported to the Senate, in order that such action might be taken as should be deemed wise and proper.

The bill was never taken up for action; the last night of the session having been exhausted in debate on the motion to take up the bill. This session, the measure was introduced by my friend from Iowa, [Mr. Dodge,] and referred to the Territorial Committee during the first week of the session. We have abundance of time to consider the subject; it was a matter of pressing necessity, and there was no excuse for not meeting it directly and fairly. We were compelled to take our position upon the doctrine either of intervention or non-intervention. We chose the latter, for two reasons: first, because we believed that the principle was right; and, second, because it was the principle adopted in 1850, to which the two great political parties of the country were solemnly pledged.

There is another reason why I desire to see this principle recognised as a rule of action in all time to come. It will have the effect to destroy all sectional parties and sectional agitations. If, in the language of the report of the committee, you withdraw the slavery question from the halls of Congress and the political arena, and commit it to the abitrament of those who are immediately interested in and alone responsible for its consequences, there is nothing left out of which sectional parties can be organized. It never was done, and never can be done on the bank, tariff, distribution, or any other party issue which has existed, or may exist, after this slavery question is withdrawn from politics. On every other political question these have always supporters and opponents in every portion of the Union—in each State, county, village, and neighborhood—residing together in harmony and good-fellowship, and combating each other's opinions and correcting each other's errors in a spirit of kindness and friendship. These differences of opinion between neighbors and friends, and the discussions that grow out of them, and the sympathy which each feels with the advocates of his own opinions in every other portion of this wide-spread republic, adds an overwhelming and irresistible moral weight to the strength of the confederacy.

Affection for the Union can never be alienated or diminished by any other party issues than those which are joined upon sectional or geographical lines. When the people of the North shall all be rallied under one banner, and the whole South marshalled under another banner, and each section excited to frenzy and madness by hostility to the institutions of the other, then the patriot may well tremble for the perpetuity of the Union. Withdraw the slavery question from the political arena, and remove it to the States and Territories, each to decide for itself, such a catastrophe can never happen. Then you will never be able to tell, by any senator's vote for or against any measure, from what State or section of the Union he comes.

Why, then, can we not withdraw this vexed question from politics? Why can we not adopt the principle of this bill as a rule of action in all new territorial organizations? Why can we not deprive these agitators of their vocation, and render it impossible for senators to come here upon bargains on the slavery question? I believe that the peace, the harmony, and perpetuity of the Union require us to go back to the doctrines of the Revolution, to the principles of the Constitution, to the principles of the compromise of 1850, and leave the people, under the Constitution, to do as they may see proper in respect to their own internal affairs.

Mr. President, I have not brought this question forward as a northern man or as a southern man. I am unwilling to recognise such divisions and distinctions. I have brought it forward as an American senator, representing a State which is true to this principle, and which has approved of my action in respect to the Nebraska bill. I have brought it forward not as an act of justice to the south more than to the north. I have presented it especially as an act of justice to the people of those Territories, and of the States to be formed therefrom, now and in all time to come.

I have nothing to say about northern rights or southern rights. I know of no such divisions or distinctions under the Constitution. The bill does equal and exact justice to the whole Union, and every part of it; it violates the rights of no State or Territory, but places each on a perfect equality, and leaves the people thereof to the free enjoyment of all their rights under the Constitution.

Now, sir, I wish to say to our southern friends, that if they desire to see this great principle carried out, now is their time to rally around it, to cherish it, preserve it, make it the rule of action in all future time. If they fail to do it now, and thereby allow the doctrine of interference to prevail, upon their heads the consequence of that interference must rest. To our northern friends, on the other hand, I desire to say, that from this day henceforward, they must rebuke the slander which has been uttered against the south, that they desire to legislate slavery into the Territories. The south has vindicated her sincerity, her honor on that point, by bringing forward a provision, negativing, in express terms, any such effect as a result of this bill. I am rejoiced to know that, while the proposition to abrogate the eighth section of the Missouri act comes from a free State, the proposition to negative the conclusion that slavery is thereby introduced comes from a slaveholding State. Thus, both sides furnish conclusive evidence that they go for the principle, and the principle only, and desire to take no advantage of any possible misconstruction.

Mr. President, I feel that I owe an apology to the Senate for having occupied their attention so long, and a still greater apology for having discussed the question in such an incoherent and desultory manner. But I could not forbear to claim the right of closing this debate. I thought gentlemen would recognise its propriety when they saw the manner in which I was assailed and misrepresented in the course of this discussion, and especially by assaults still more disreputable in some portions of the country. These assaults have had no other effect upon me than to give me courage and energy for a still more resolute discharge of duty. I say frankly that in my opinion, this measure will be as popular at the north as at the south, when its provisions and principles shall have been fully developed and become well understood. The people at the north are attached to the principles of self-government; and you cannot convince them that that is self-government which deprives a people of the right of legislating for themselves, and compels them to receive laws which are forced upon them by a legislature in which they are not represented. We are willing to stand upon this great principle of self-government everywhere; and it is to us a proud reflection that, in this whole discussion, no friend of the bill has urged an argument in its favor which could not be used with the same propriety in a free State as in a slave State, and *vice versa*. But no enemy of the bill has used an argument which would bear repetition one mile across Mason and Dixon's line. Our opponents have dealt entirely in sectional appeals. The friends of the bill have discussed a great principle of universal application, which can be sustained by the same reasons, and the same arguments, in every time and in every corner of the Union.

MR. WISE IN WASHINGTON CITY AFTER THE RESULT WAS KNOWN.

After it was fully ascertained that Mr. Wise was certainly Governor elect of Virginia, his friends and admirers of the City of Washington concluded to call him out, being then in their midst. Arrangements being made, Mr. Wise was to address in a brief manner the citizens irrespectively of party, from the balcony in front of Brown's Hotel. Early in the evening the crowd commenced assembling, and when the hour for speaking arrived, we are told by persons who were present, that such an assemblage of human beings had scarcely if ever been seen in that city on any similar occasion. Mr. Wise appeared, calm and serene, and made a few remarks—when the infuriated Know Nothings set up, and kept up, the most unearthly and demoniac yell that was ever heard on this side of or in all probability even in the infernal regions. Mr. Wise made several attempts to go on; but his voice was incontinently stifled by the yells of this midnight banditti and culvert swarm of debauched ruffians and rowdies. Finally his friends withdrew him from the presence of the rabble. They still continued to bawl and vociferate in this manner until, to carry out a simile of Spanish barbarity, they erected in the centre of the street a *garote*, when some victimised babbler mounted the sunless scaffold, with the iron collar already adjusted, and commenced a Know Nothing harangue. This dissipated orator, with much gravity of manner and air of superiority, ranted about the "*insidious* encroachments of the Pope of Rome, the Holy Bible," &c. Now and then at the top of his voice, with a countenance frantic with fear, and nervous with fanaticism, he exclaimed "Americans must rule America." Here was a genuine specimen of a Know Nothing harangue. When you have heard this Shibboleth about seventy-five times in a discourse of eighty minutes, you may set it down that you have had what was known about the middle of the nineteenth century as a Know Nothing harangue. After several of the leaders had harangued thus to their satisfaction, this disgraceful mob dispersed to their several dens. Such was the courtesy shown to a stranger and a distinguished Virginian in the Federal City! Such was Know Nothing politeness in the middle of the nineteenth century!

From the Enquirer.

THE WAY THE MONEY WAS LOST.

I have compiled a few extracts from Know Nothing papers printed before the election, to show "the way the money was lost." They may serve as a caution for the future. They fully show that the Know Nothings are eminently entitled to the name they have assumed. Such statements and estimates as are to be found in the extracts below, were never made by Wise-men. The game of "brag" was "the order of the day" with Sam's family, and many a poor fellow was duped out of his money by it. I particularly commend the perusal of these extracts to sick persons and those who are in low spirits. They cannot be read without creating a laugh:

THE PROSPECT STILL BRIGHTENING.—We subjoin additional letters of the most encouraging character from the Southwest. *Sam* is evidently making tremendous progress all over the State. *Wise* is a used up man. After next Thursday, he will be heard of no more. A thousand cheers for the victorious Flournoy.—[*Whig, May* 19.

"The Junto without even the honor of a decent burial."

The political sky is clear and unclouded. A few shadows at first obscured the brilliancy of the sun—but they have been dissipated into thin air, and are no longer visible. The great American army, moving steadily and harmoniously under these auspicious circumstances, will, beyond a doubt, achieve a most brilliant victory. The *disjecta membra* of Juntoism, after the election, will be scattered far and wide, without even the honor of a decent burial.—[*Richmond Whig, May* 7.

Fifteen hundred Know Nothing majority in Richmond.

Richmond achieved a glorious and startling victory in her charter elections; but that triumph is as nothing compared with that which is shortly to crown her afresh. The great American party of this city is firmly, and enthusiastically resolved to give Flournoy, Beale and Patton, a majority of not less than 1500! This is no vain boasting, but the State will soon see the prediction converted into sober reality.—[*Richmond Whig, May* 11.

[Richmond gave 977 Know Nothing majority.]

Wise will be defeated by 20,000.

The following is extracted from a letter from a Virginian, now a merchant in Baltimore:—"I received the other day a letter on business from an extensive merchant in Richmond, Va., who said, 'Business is good, and I really believe Wise will be defeated by 20,000.'"—[*Norfolk Beacon, May* 2.

Flournoy's majority 34,000.

There are known to be 72,000 members of the American party in Virginia. This force, together with the 15,000 Whig votes, which the Chronicle concedes to Mr. Flournoy, would make an aggregate of 87,000 votes, leaving Mr. Wise but 53,000, and electing Flournoy by 34,000 majority. That will do for today.—[*American Organ of Washington City.*

Wise not more than 30,000 *votes in the State.*

ELECTIONS.—For the information of our readers we have compiled the vote of the last Presidential contest in the cities where municipal elections have been held, and have compared the result, in order that they may see how fast the Democracy is tottering to its fall:

American gain (in Richmond, Portsmouth, Alexandria, Lynchburg and Fredericksburg) 1496 in a vote of a little over 6000.

A corresponding gain in the different counties would not leave Wise with more than 30,000 votes after the election. We hope, therefore, that "Sam" will respect the misfortunes of the poor deluded traveller of "Onancock" and only beat him by about twenty thousand majority.—[*Floyd Intelligencer.*

600 *Majority for Flournoy in Preston County.*

PRESTON.—A correspondent says, "Sam is here in every neighborhood, and Wiseocracy is so weak it dare not show its face. Flournoy will carry the county by 600 majority, and it usually gives a majority the other way of about 150. We intend too to elect an American Congressman in spite of Wise and all other demagogues."—[*Penny Post, May* 7.

[Preston gave Wise 57 majority.]

SOUTH-WESTERN VIRGINIA.

Wise cannot get 10 *votes where Johnson got* 100.

LEE COUNTY.—"Sam" has been all around here, and will sweep South-western Virginia, such as no country was ever swept before. The people have become sick of demagogueism, and their only desire appears now to be, to retrieve the past. Wise cannot possibly get 10 votes where Johnson received 100, and this is not particularly confined to any particular locality, but will characterize the election throughout the entire South-west. This you may state as an unalterable certainty. I have always been a Democrat, but have been so completely disgusted with the action of the party, in forcing upon us a broken down, false, hacknied, renegade ticket, that I determined to be off forever. I consider this the very time to break down the severity of party, and give the country good and true men in the State and National offices. "Let Americans rule America," is my motto.—[*Penny Post.*

[Lee county gave Wise 736 majority. It gave Johnson 234. South-western Virginia (McMullen's district) gave Johnson 450 majority. It gives Wise 3,500 majority. Yet it was an "unalterable certainty" that Wise would not get "10 votes where Johnson got 100."

Boteler's Majority over Faulkner, 600.

We received the most favorable reports from the Loudoun district. Mr. Boteler is gaining friends wherever he appears, and will beat Faulkner from 200 to 300 votes.

Other estimates make Boteler's majority as high as 600.—[*American Organ.*

A Great Political "Ground Swell" on the South-Side.

HENRY COUNTY.—The Lynchburg Virginian assures us that late advices from this county are exceedingly encouraging. The American cause is daily gaining ground, while Wise stock is rapidly declining. It is the same case in Floyd, Patrick, Carroll and Franklin—indeed, in all the counties south of the river. The American party will sweep the south-side country, after the manner of a tornado. It will leave nothing standing which dares to oppose it. Verily, the great political ground-swell of 1840 is nothing compared with that of 1855.—[*Richmond Whig, before the election.*

[Henry gave Wise 99 majority; Floyd, 125 majority; Patrick, 192 majority; Carroll, 359 majority; and Franklin, 347 majority. Such was the way in which the "American party" swept the south-side country, "after the manner of a tornado."

Tazewell County—Wise's Defeat an Absolute Certainty.

TAZEWELL COUNTY.—A letter from a gentleman of this county informs us that the prospects for the American cause are most encouraging. The people there, he says, will resent, with manly indignation, the abusive epithets which Mr. Wise applies to the Know Nothings. The same spirit prevails throughout that whole section, and Wise's defeat is regarded as an absolute certainty.—[*Richmond Whig*, May 7.

[Tazewell gave Mr. Wise 915 majority!—and the same spirit prevailed throughout that whole section."]

Paulus Powell, the Worst Beaten Man in Virginia.

HON. PAULUS POWELL.—Is there a faithful Democrat in Virginia who will rejoice with us, when we announce that intelligence from all portions of the Red Land district assures us of the certainty of this gallant, tried public servant's re-election?—[*Richmond Examiner.*

Our information is exactly the reverse of this, and living upon the border of the district, familiarly acquainted with most of the counties composing it, we have better opportunities than the Examiner of knowing the true state of things. We will wager the Examiner "a ducat to a denier" that Mr. Powell is one of the worst beaten candidates in Eastern Virginia?[—*Lynchburg Virginian, before the election.*

[Powell's majority in the District is 793.]

"Official" from the North-west—15,000 *Majority against Wise.*

From the North-west, that is the portion of Virginia north and west of the Alleghany mountains, we are permitted to give the following extract of a letter from official sources :

"We now number 201 councils, and about 25,000 members, and increasing rapidly. As to withdrawals, there has not been 100 withdrawals outside of Harper's Ferry.

"I think that when the vote is counted from the West, that Mr. Wise will find at least 15,000 against him."

The reader will bear in mind that this is *official*, and we respectfully call upon the Junto, if they deny the statement as to withdrawals, to give us the names. We don't want so many indefinite localities and mythical "defectors." Our butterfly chasing days were over years ago.—[*Penny Post,* May 5.

[The "15,000 against Wise in the North-west" turned out to be about 1500 in his favor.]

Eight Know Nothing Congressmen Elected, and a Majority of the Legislature.

THE CAMPAIGN.—Notwithstanding the ridiculous statements of the anti-American press in regard to the defections and a host of other dire calamities said by them to have overtaken the American party, we still continue to receive the most encouraging accounts from every section. Our prospects certainly indicate the election of the whole State ticket—eight out of thirteen Congressmen, and a majority at least of the Legislature. The American ticket will sweep the West like a tornado.—[*Penny Post.*

[There is a Democratic majority of 54 in the Legislature.]

The "Ground-Swell"—Greenbrier the Banner County in the "Great American Revolution."

GREENBRIER.—From this county, we have the intelligence that "Flournoy, Beale and Patton will roll up a tremendous majority on the 24th of May. Everything is harmonious and determined. Greenbrier. will be the banner county in this great American Revolution. Nothing can stay the ground-swell."—*Penny Post, May* 5.

[Greenbrier gave Flournoy 336 majority. It gave Sumners 622 majority.]

A most Overwhelming Defeat to the Enemies of Sam.

"SAM."—Our country exchanges bring us most cheering accounts of the prospects of this invincible gentleman. The progress which he has made, and is now making in Virginia, is unparaleled in the history of political parties, and we predict as the result of his operations the most overwhelming defeat to his enemies, ever sustained by any party in the Old Dominion. We append a few extracts from correspondents of the True American, from different counties, as to his doings.—*Lynchburg Virginian, before the election.*

[Here followed a number of letters, the reading of which at this time would make a dying man laugh.]

Col. Roane Elected Triumphantly.

Essex and King and Queen.—From these counties we have the most flattering accounts. Col. Roane, the candidate in opposition to Mr. Garnett, will be elected triumphantly. The State ticket will also be strongly supported. A friend writes us that the Know-Nothings are as thick as "grasshoppers" in that section.—*Penny Post, April* 30.

[Col. Roane, Know-Nothing, was defeated "triumphantly."

Ligon's Majority so very Large, that we fear to name it.

Ligon's majority in Nelson and Amherst will be so very large, that we fear to name it. It will exceed the most sanguine anticipations of Sam's friends.—[*Charlottesville Advocate, before the election.*

[Ligon's majority in the two counties named was 162. Is the Advocate still "afraid to name it?"

Wise beaten by 40,000.

A great and overwhelming revolution is sweeping over the whole country. "Revolutions," it is said, "never go backward." In Virginia, it has almost entirely obliterated old party lines. The wave has reached the mountains, and washed the sand out of the eyes of the people. With the opposition Mr. Wise has, it is utterly impossible for him to succeed. He cannot stand up against opposition within and without his own party. He cannot win the race with Gen. Bayly tripping him up at this corner, Bowden knocking him down at that, Extra Billy hedging up his way at a third, Nat. Claiborne digging a pit-fall for him at a fourth, all the time sweating and panting with his associate "renegades" lashed to his back. The indications are that he will be beaten 20,000—some say 40,000.—[*Abingdon Virginian, before the election.*

Four to Five Hundred Majority in Hardy.

We are assured that Hardy will roll up a majority of from four to five hundred for the American ticket, and that there are not four Whigs in the county who will vote for Wise.—[*Romney Intelligencer, May* 4.

[Hardy gave 57 majority for the "American" ticket. It gave 388 majority for Summers.]

W. K. Pendleton "Elected with Ease."

We have cheering accounts from all parts of this Congressional District. W. K. Pendleton, American, will, I think be elected with ease, over Dr. Kidwell. Mr. P. is a popular speaker, and has canvassed the district thoroughly. He will make his mark in Congress if elected.—[*Correspondence of the Penny Post, May* 11.

[Dr. Kidwell's majority is 1336.]

"Our Nat" Certainly Elected, "and no Mistake."

FRANKLIN DISTRICT.—The news from this district is cheering. Claiborne is gaining every day, and will, we are informed by letters from some of the Knowing ones, most certainly be elected. Bocock is awfully frightened and no mistake. Old Pittsylvania and Patrick will give him a terrible lashing, and one from the effects of which he will not be able to recover in time to take his seat in the next Congress. Our "Nat" will however be in Washington about that time to attend to the interest of the people of the Franklin Congressional District. Mark our prediction and don't forget.—[*Floyd Intelligencer, May* 12.

"Especially in Pittsylvania."

CAMPBELL, BEDFORD, HENRY, PITTSYLVANIA AND HALIFAX.—We saw an intelligent Democrat, yesterday, who has recently travelled over the above counties. He is a member of the Order, knows what he speaks, and is reliable in everything. He represents the prospects of our ticket as being in all respects most brilliant. He visited many councils, knew the people, and found large numbers of Democrats in the Order in all these counties. The unjust and false charges against Mr. Flournoy are recoiling with tremendous effect upon the miscreants who make them. Very, very few have left the Order, and most of them who have done so will vote the American ticket, while numbers are coming in daily. The greatest enthusiasm prevailed, especially in Pittsylvania.—[*Penny Post, May* 9.

[Pittsylvania gave Flournoy 20—It gave Summers 166 majority.]

"Heavy Gains in the Valley."

"The Valley will certainly do remarkably well, and will show heavy gains." [*Correspondence of the Post, May* 9.

[A correspondent of the Enquirer, a few days ago, showed the side on which the gains were in the Valley. Wise's majority in the Valley is about 10,000.]

"No disposition to Manufacture Public Opinion."

We have no disposition to enter into the manufacture of public opinion, as do the Wise organs, or crow, until after the election; but there never was a more apparent and manifest fact than that Thomas S. Flournoy will be Governor by more than 20,000 majority. Every indication from all quarters is to that effect.—[*Wheeling Times* (*Abolition*) *May* 5.

Millson defeated by 600 *to* 1,000 *Majority.*

"This (Millson's) Congressional District will give the American ticket from 600 to 1,000 majority, and it may even exceed that number. Great enthusiasm prevails throughout the entire district. The reported withdrawals in this section are base fabrications."—[*Correspondent of the Richmond Whig, May* 22.

[Millson's majority is about 568.]

Sam's Majority in Floyd 225 *to* 375.

FLOYD COUNTY.—"The majority in this county will not be less than 225, and we are making every effort to carry it up to 375. Scott's majority was only 83."—[*Correspondent of the Richmond Whig, May* 22.

[Floyd county gave Wise 125 majority.]

Sam's Majority in Patrick 350.

Patrick County.—"Place no reliance on the statement in the Enquirer in regard to this county. You may safely put down the majority for the American ticket in Patrick at 350, and I surely believe it will exceed that. From Henry, Franklin and Floyd, I have the most cheering account of the progress of the great American movement."—*Correspondent of the Richmond Whig, May* 22.

[Wise's majority in Patrick is 192.]

"Saw but one man in 5 *months against Sam."*

Frederick and Page Counties.—"I rejoice to inform you that the cause of our country is progressing so well in this (Frederick) county. I have traveled very considerably for the last 5 months in the upper end of this and the lower end of Hampshire county, and in all that time *I have met with but one man that was against us*, and I feel assured that I am warranted in saying that old Frederick will give a majority of 150 for our nominees.

"I have also been informed that there are upwards of 400 members in Page.

"Having belonged to the Democratic party, I am utterly astonished at the course they pursue in regard to this great national movement. They seem to be blinded not only to the best interests of society, but of the country."—[*Correspondent of the Richmond Whig, May* 22.

[Frederick gave 130 for Wise—and the official vote of Page is 1033 for Wise, 72 (!) for Flournoy. If the gentleman will travel "five months" through Page, he will probably be able to find rather more than "one man" against Sam.]

A Handsome Majority for Sam in Pulaski County.

Pulaski County.—"We shall elect our county delegate, Thomas Poage, and give the Winchester ticket a handsome majority."—*Correspondent of the Richmond Whig, May* 22.

[Pulaski gave Mr. Wise "a handsome majority," and didn't elect Mr. Poage.]

Sam's Majority 1500 *in Kidwell's District—and* 2000 *In Lewis's District.*

"As to the report of withdrawals in the North-West, it is false. We have but few, and we take in five to one that withdraws. We will carry this district by 1500 majority, and we have 2000 to overcome. We will elect Pendleto Congress. The adjoining district will do better than what we do. There is 1600 majority against them, and they will carry it by 2000.—[*Correspondent of the Richmond Whig, May* 22.

[Kidwell's majority upwards of 1300—and Sam's majority in Lewis's district 391, instead of "2000."]

An overwhelming Majority for Sam's candidates.

Hanover County.—Dear Post: We are augmenting our forces daily and nightly. We will give Reins, Flournoy and Scott a tremendous vote. Thompson, American candidate for the House of Delegates, will certainly be elected by an overwhelming majority.—[*Correspondent of the Post, May* 17.

Nearly Every Man in favor of the Know Nothing. Ticket!

HANOVER AND NEW KENT.—Dear Post:—I happened a few days since to be among the people of New Kent and Hanover, when, greatly to my surprise, men whom a few years ago, were the strongest advocates of Democracy are now seizing every chance to let their friends know that Flournoy is the man of their choice and not Henry A. Wise, the slanderer of all parties. So far, Mr. Editor, as I was able to learn, there are few members of the American Order in the above counties, but so well are the people convinced of its republican and national principles that nearly every man I saw will go for the whole ticket. You can rest assured that both counties will give a larger majority than has ever been given for any other party. I am yours, &c.—[*Correspondent of the Penny Post.*

[Hanover gave the Democratic ticket about 200 majority.]

George W. Palmore Elected in Cumberland and Powhatan.

CUMBERLAND.—We have very cheering news from this (Cumberland) county. George W. Palmore will be elected from Powhatan and Cumberland, and the American ticket will get one hundred majority in the latter county.—[*Penny Post, before the election.*

[The "American" ticket got 25 majority in "the latter county"—and Mr. Palmore was defeated by about 100 majority. Powhatan gave Wise a majority of 137.]

Louisa—"Statements Utterly Unfounded."

LOUISA.—Various exaggerated calculations have been made by the Anti-American party in regard to their anticipated majorities in this county—claiming as high as 200 for Judge Caskie, &c. These statements we have the best reason for knowing are utterly unfounded. With the gallant Clayton G. Coleman as our standard bearer for the State Senate, and the other excellent candidates in the field, we confidently anticipate a glorious triumph in Louisa.—[*Penny Post, May* 17.

[The majority for Caskie in Louisa was precisely 200—644 to 444.]

"Sam" in Mecklenburg.

In this county (Mecklenburg) our information is that Hutcherson, the American candidate for the Legislature, will certainly be elected. At the last election the whole vote of the country was 1167, and the Democratic majority was about 340. Flournoy is certain to get, next Thursday, at least 600 votes. Pretty good progress in one county. There are seven councils in the county, and the Presidents of four of them are Old Line Democrats. We learn also that there was a free barbecue at Williamson's store last Saturday, after which thirty-eight joined the order, twenty-two of whom were Democrats.—[*Penny Post, May* 17.

[Mecklenburg gives Mr. Wise and the whole Democratic ticket about 400 majority. Johnson's majority over Summers was 317.]

Botetourt 175 *or* 225 *Majority for Flournoy.*

BOTETOURT COUNTY.—"**From the statistics I send, you will perceive that the American party have a clear majority of the votes in this county, besides** scores of outsiders to be sympathizing with us and will vote our ticket. Pierce's majority was 317. We shall change this into at least 175 and very likely to 225, for Flournoy, Beale and Patton."—[*Richmond Whig, May* 15.

[Botetourt gave Wise 430 majority.]

"Sam" Dividing Marion County.

"We shall poll 900 votes in Marion, which is half of the whole."—[*Correspondent of the Richmond Whig, May* 22.

[The vote of Marion stands, for Wise 1127, Flournoy 450.]

20,000 *and Probably* 40,000 *Majority for Flournoy.*

We shall not be satisfied with less than 20,000 majority for Flournoy. We are disposed to think we shall double that figure. "Press on the column," therefore, we say, and look not to the right or left until after the election. We wish to have as large a majority as possible. Already certain of success, we wish something more than mere victory. We desire to secure a triumph!—[*Penny Post, May* 7.

What a "Fall," my Countrymen!

"PRESS ON THE COLUMN."—As the day of election approaches, the confidence of the American party rises. Already 72,000 strong, their numbers are daily increasing. So certain are they of success, that we fear they may be induced to relax their exertions. We trust that may not be the case. Let us keep up the fire until we exterminate the enemy. We shall give Mr. Wise such a fall that he will stand no more chance of rising than Lucifer.—[*Penny Post, May* 7.

Mr. Wise Ruminating in Accomac.

"Revolutions never go backward. The grand political revolution of the Know Nothings is the spontaneous uprising of the people against political trickery and party corruptions. It were as vain to attempt to check its progress as to stop the tornado in its course. It has the *imprimatur* of popular approval, and Mr. Wise ought by this time to be convinced of the futility of attempting to arrest it. Beneath the classic shades of "Only, near Onancock," he may ruminate on the result—and from the instructive teachings of the past may gather some valuable lessons for the future."—*Richmond Whig, May* 8.

Know Nothing Sympathy for the Dead Wise Men.

We can assure our anti-American friends here that we feel no little sympathy for them in the present condition of political affairs—the certain, overwhelming defeat that awaits them at the coming election staring them in the face. We know they feel bad—the forebodings of their approaching doom haunt them day and night. Now, we must say we have not the least objection that they should, to the last, show true pluck and grit—indeed, these qualities will always challenge our admiration; but we are solicitous that they should be preparing to fold their togas about them and die with the grace and dignity that become the remaining few of a once powerful and honorable party—that they will so deport themselves in this last death-struggle, that the future faithful historian will be unable to find the least spot upon their fairness, truth or honor. We do really hope that we shall have it in our power, after the election, with a clear con-

science, to comply with the old maxim—"to say nothing but good of the dead."
—[*Kanawha Republican, May* 2.

"Sam Doing Wonders in Brunswick."

We learn that "Sam" is doing wonders in the Democratic county of Brunswick. Two councils have been started in that county, and they are working finely. Brunswick is the last county in the State in which "Sam" was introduced. Nevertheless he will give a good account of himself and family even there on election day.—[*Penny Post, May* 17.

[Sure enough, Sam "did wonders in Brunswick." Wise's majority is 332. Johnson's majority over Summers was 154.]

A Large majority for Sam in Smyth County.

We learn that there are seven councils in Smyth county, all in full blast, and working finely. The order numbers some of the best men in the county, and will give a large majority for the Winchester ticket.—[*Penny Post, May* 17.

[Smyth gave Wise 83 majority.]

Our "Nat" Elected by 800 *to* 1,000 *Majority.*

THE HALIFAX CONGRESSIONAL DISTRICT.—"Information received from every county in this district renders certain the election of Claiborne by a majority from 800 to 1,000, while Flournoy will not fall short of 1500, and the best informed gentlemen say it will go beyond 2,000."—*Richmond Whig, May* 15.

["Our Nat" was defeated by 1,700 majority.]

Tazewell County Safe for Trigg—Trigg Elected.

WYTHEVILLE.—"Dear Whig:—Rejoice! rejoice! for truly have the friends of American and haters of foreign policy, cause to do so here. The determined progeny of Sam now number in this county 800 good and true. It is now universally conceded that Trigg will get a majority over both Martin and McMullen, not only in this county, but in the whole district. Tazewell is thought safe for Trigg; Smyth will give a very large majority; Preston's fate is sealed, and Sheffey's majority may be safely put down at 100."—[*Richmond Whig, May* 15.

[Tazewell gave the whole Democratic ticket more than 900 majority—and Trigg was defeated by McMullen, by a majority of about 3,500.]

Sam in Rockingham.

Sam introduced himself to the good people of Rockingham in September last, in the persons of an old Rockingham Democrat, who now resides in Albemarle, and an Alexandria Democrat. Endorsed thus by two "old liners," he was most cordially received, and we have never for a moment felt any disposition to cut his acquaintance. His family is now large and respectable, having daily additions of pure old Jackson Democrats, who can never forget how Henry A. Wise used to abuse them and their party. You may rest assured, that the Winchester ticket will receive at least 1500 votes in this county.—[*Richmond Whig, May* 15.

[The vote of Rockingham was: Wise 2,702, Flournoy 612.]

The Penny Post Entitling Itself to the Gratitude of Betters.

A Chance.—The love of money is the besetting sin of the people of this world. We scarcely ever meet a man who does'nt want more than he has. *We are very sure then that we should entitle ourselves to the gratitude of many if we direct them to a plan by which money can be made.* Well, listen, all ye lucre-loving sinners, and we will tell you how $ 5,000 can be made as clear as grit in a little more than a month. Here it is :

Just get $ 2,500 and come to this office, and we will direct you to a gentleman who has $ 5,000, and who is particularly green. He is anxious to bet that amount to $ 2,500, that Flournoy will be elected. Well, of course, you have seen accounts of so many withdrawals, and of course you *know* that the Know Nothing house is fast tumbling to pieces. So bring us your $ 2,500 and stake it as we direct, deposit it in Bank, and on the 4th Thursday in May, you'll be $ 5,000 richer than you are now—*if Wise is elected.*—[*Richmond Penny Post.*

From the Richmond Enquirer.

OBITUARY OF SAM.

It has fallen to our lot to perform the melancholy task of announcing to his friends and the public, the death of the lamented "Sam." He departed this life on the 24th day of May, 1855, at a place in Virginia, called the Polls, after a short illness of extreme mental and bodily suffering. In the morning of the 24th, on which the sad catastrophe occurred, he was, apparently, in fine health and spirits, and manifested, it was observed by everybody, unusual activity in his business. But, alas ! before night he was numbered with those that have been. Indeed, the writer saw him the very day he died ; he said he never felt better, and promised himself a long, happy, and prosperous life. What shadows we are ! Sam's days were swifter than a weaver's shuttle, and spent without "Hope." His days were few and evil. As for "Sam," his days are as grass ; as a flower of the field he flourisheth, the breeze of public opinion passed over him, he is gone, and the places in Virginia, that knew him once, will know him no more for ever. Because, "Sam" goeth to his long home, and the mourners go about the streets. As the particulars of his death may be gratifying to his friends at a distance, we give them, as we received them, from the most authentic sources.

About one o'clock, in the afternoon of the 24th, "Sam" became dejected, and was soon after taken with a nausea at the stomach, and vomiting up of a quantity of crude indigestible matter, supposed to be green fruit, with which he had overloaded his stomach, brought from Massachusetts ; this was soon followed by a violent purging at the Polls ; when great debility ensued, terminating in death.

The friends of the deceased, both North and South, may be assured that no pains or expense was wanting here to save the life of this estimable man. Steam and electricity were taxed to the highest power—servants were going day and night after the doctors, and the most skillful "knowing" ones, North and South, were employed—Councils were held in every corner, and groups of the most eminent practitioners, were seen here and there in solemn conclave—consulting physicians were called in to confer with family doctors—the prayers of the church and the advice of the most eminent divines, in other States, was earnestly solicited—the elders of the church were called for, to anoint him with oil; but all in vain—"Sam's" time had come—the decree had gone forth—a portion of the members of the Whig church which had long been in a cold and dead state, but had began to "strengthen the things that remain, and were ready to perish," and to pray and hope for a revival, saying, all our help must come from "Sam," now sunk in deep despair; and a universal gloom, as still as the grave, hung over the vestals of the "Dim Lantern." The patient was in an awful state of collapse, and every expedient was tried to produce a re-action in the system. Blisters or Sinapisms, composed of different ingredients, and spread on *blue*. paper, were constantly applied to the extremities, at the polls; but they failed to draw. American "Gnats" instead of Spanish flies, were applied to the back, and "Clay" poultices to the abdomen; and the celebrated "Patent" gruel, (said to be a specific in every disease,) given as an injection; but there was no "Hope." "*Sic transit gloria mundi!*"

After the physicians had despaired of "Sam's" body, the Doctors of Divinity were sent for to take care of his soul. An eminent Divine (from Kentucky) who visited him in his last moments, conversed freely with him on the subject of religion. His remarks were published in the Presbyterian Critic. He assured "Sam" that he need not be under any apprehensions about his "future destiny;" that his conduct and principles were in perfect accordance with the Word of God, and he was perfectly orthodox. "Sam" had no fears upon that score; he had endeavoured to obey the will of the "Grand Master," and what he had committed to him, he had kept to the day of his death. But, turning from the Doctor to one of the family—a gentleman from Lunenburg, a Mr. T., (who, it is thought, will never forget the remark and the impression it made on him,) he observed, he was conscious of his approaching dissolution, and he would die perfectly "*contented*," if he only knew *what* killed him. The Doctor gravely remarked, he believed that it was that "intense Democracy" of Virginia that was the immediate cause of his death. Mr. T., it will be remembered, retired from "Sam" "with a bird in the hand;" and that "Goode" gentleman, whose death he predicted, is still alive. The above mentioned is the Kentucky Doctor that prophesied of "Sam," before his death, in Virginia, said the coming of "Sam" would be as the coming of the Kingdom of Heaven, "in silence, (secretly,) without *observation*." "That is the way," said he, "in which all 'grand' movements come." (Mark the expression, "grand movement," "Grand Master," "Grand Council,"—everything grand about "Sam;" "Sam is one of the grandees.) Said that "Sam" would swallow Democracy and live forever; that "Sam's" family would swallow up every other family in America, and there would be left but one national, native-born, American family—"Sam's!!!" But if "Sam" swallowed a small dose of Democracy, and he died instantly, what would become of him if he should take a full dose? The Democratic Medical Faculty has just prescribed the following dose for "Sam" in Virginia: Take—

Of Wise, 9 or 10,000 drops.
" Congress 13 do.
" Legislature 48 do.

Given in pure Democracy, in broken doses, at the polls, in the day time—"Sam" will be dead by next morning. If "Sam" should revive, give the same in larger doses. For a "National" dose, see Democratic Dispensatory. See, also, "Rush" on Sam at the polls.

We had predicted that poor "Sam" had been deceived—that he had not examined the ground of his hope. The Doctors have led him to rely on secrecy for salvation, and faith alone in the "Grand Master;" preaching to him that "every grand movement must be secret," when they ought to have urged him to come out, and make an open, bold profession of his religion before the world, that it might be seen whether his practice accorded with his principles. Not to be "ashamed of 'Sam' before men;" "let his light so shine"—"not to put it under a bushel"—that we are "children of the day, not of the night." And, above all, to have referred him to his "Bible in hand"—particularly that passage in John xviii: 19; (if he wished to come as the kingdom of heaven): "The High Priest then asked Jesus of his doctrine." 20: "Jesus answered him, I spake openly to the world: I even taught in the Synagogue and in the Temple, where the Jews always resort, and in secret have I said nothing." And, again: "This thing was not done in a corner" (or a culvert.) "Sam" ought to have been taught that the kingdom of heaven came openly, (though it came not with "observation," that is, with great outward pomp, and a particular locality, as a temporal kingdom,) and not secretly, like the Jesuits; that it had a visible organization, and that publicity was its grand characteristic. The 70 disciples were sent out by the Ruler, himself, of the Kingdom, to preach before the world, that "the Kingdom of Heaven was at hand." So "Sam" ought to have sent out his "72,000" disciples to preach his doctrines, and to announce his coming; and, verily, (according to Mr. Botts and other prophets,) they would not have gone over Virginia, before "Sam" would be in all his power and glory. But, on the contrary, whenever the Know Nothings were asked by the Democrats when the kingdom of "Sam" should come, and what its doctrines, they answered and said, "Sam cometh not with observation." Neither shall they say, Lo! here, or, lo! there, for, behold, "Sam" is within you. For as the lightning that lighteneth out of the one part under Heaven, shineth unto the other part under Heaven, so shall "Sam" be in his day. Here the analogy of the Know Nothing commentators, between the kingdom of "Sam" and the kingdom of Heaven, fails. "Sam" goes, it is true, by the telegraph, but is unseen. The lightning is seen under the whole Heavens. Not so with the great "Invisible and Invincible." And as it was in the days of Noah, (continue these same doctors, in the same chapter,) so shall it be also in the days of "Sam." The Democrats were carousing, say they, until the day that the Know Nothings were taken into the ark and the flood of Know Nothingism came and destroyed them all. Likewise, also, it was in the days of Lot: "They did eat and drink," &c. But the same day that "Sam" went out of Sodom, it rained fire and brimstone from "Sam" on the Democrats, and destroyed them all. Even so shall it be in the days of "Sam;" so saith the prophet. The delayed retribution is impending, and like every other great retribution, it takes those it falls on by surprise—(The "Critic.") On whose head, tell me, did the fire and brimstone fall, at the polls in Virginia? Who was taken by surprise? "Sam" was taken in his own net. Who is feasting and reveling now, till the flood comes again, walking in political lasciviousness, lusts of power, excess of wine, revelings, banquetings, and abominable idolatries, wherein they think it strange that ye run not with them to the same excess of not speaking evil of you? It is "Sam" in Philadelphia, like Belshazzar in Babylon, giving a great feast to a thousand of his lords, his wives and concubines. But, a finger has written over against the dim "lantern," on the plaster of the wall; and (the magicians, astrologers, chaldeans, and soothsayers, are failing,) Daniel, as before, will be sent for to interpret it. Daniel will teach Sam that the Most High ruleth in the kingdom of men—that Sam had not humbled himself since his fall in Virginia. And, therefore, for the thought of his heart, this is the interpretation of the thing: Mene—Thy kingdom is numbered. Tekel—Thou art weighed. Peres—Thy kingdom is divided. In vain will "Sam" sing "he brought me into the 'banqueting house,' and his banner over me was love." Sam has prepared this great feast in imitation of Queen Esther's emancipation of the Jews, to liberate the slaves of the south; and "Sam," like Haman, boasts that no man is permitted to come to the "banquet" prepared by the Queen, but himself. Yet all this (honor) avails me nothing, says he, so long as I see Democrats in office. But, mark! Haman will hang himself on the very gallows he is preparing for Mordecai; and Esther will be celebrated by the Democrats. The Kentucky doctors also said, that the poor Democrats, (like the Demoniacs, when they saw Christ approach them,) would "scream at the bare mention of Sam" !!! Who screamed at the polls? "Sam"—the "invincible Sam." And it turns out to be, that it was the Know Nothings, (whose name they say was legion,) that besought the Democracy that they might go into the herd of swine, (Northern abolitionists,) and, behold, the whole herd of swine rushed headlong down a precipice and were drowned in the sea, and the herdsmen, (the Northern Whigs,) that attended them fled into the city, (of Philadelphia,) and the whole city came out and besought the Democracy to depart out of their course. The Doctors mistook Democracy for Demoniacy! If "Sam" is so expert in casting out devils, it is a wonder he has not dispossessed himself, long ago. This, indeed, would be Belzebub, casting out the Devil—"Sam's" kingdom divided against itself—the harlot of Massachusetts complaining of the "whore of Babylon!"

As to the disease with which "Sam" died, there are various conjectures. Some think he died of Flux, or "Fusion," (as it is termed in modern nomenclature,) from the appearance of his stools or "platforms"—that is, a running together of Northern Abolitionists with Northern Whigs, against the Catholics for power and office. The purging which Sam got at the polls did not indicate that his bowels were *open*, for physicians know, that, in dysentery, the purging is a secretion from the bowels themselves, while the food, or natural passages, are retained; so, that, although he disgorged (by the mouth) a good deal of what he had swallowed, and lost flesh, he was still bound in the bowels to the last. "Sam" had been subject to costiveness from his birth, both at the mouth, by oath, and in the belly. But a few weeks before his death, being alarmed at his situation, he was wont to go out very badly from his lodging, and take an aperient, but the physicians forbid it. Said that a sudden evacuation would produce such debility, it would certainly carry him off—to confine himself closely to his room and keep quiet. There is a great anxiety now to know, I am told, that of the different kinds of isms "Sam" eat, which it was that disagreed with him, so that they might diet him hereafter, for dysentery (running from the lodges) and obstinate costiveness of the bowels—secresy is hereditary in the family. They are still bound, as before, and now under the care of the Philadelphia doctors, who advise them to touch nothing but what agrees with them. But a Philadelphia doctor can't cure "Sam"—he is too far gone. There are others of opinion that "Sam" died from sheer debility, (or "civil disability") from being overheated in the crusades. Some contend he had the Scrofula or King's Evil—hatred to free institutions—(as freedom of opinion, alien, &c., can never be mentioned in his presence without producing nausea at the stomach) which he inherited from old federal Sam and which broke out, now and then, in various branches of the Whig family, there being a predisposition to the disease. Others again, presume that he was killed by swallowing too many different kinds of isms at once, as appears from a post mortem examination, there having been found about forty in his belly, in an indigestible state. The last one which he swallowed just before he died—American or Know Nothingism—lodged in his throat, and produced Bronchitis at the polls. Some conjectured, and not without reason, that "Sam" had Hydrophobia, from his dread of "Holy Water," as he had been bitten by a canine fanatic at the North, during dog-days there. Others supposed he took cold travelling in Missouri and the territories of Kansas and Nebraska; while many think that he was wounded in a rencounter with the "Fugitive Slave Bill." Others think he died from emaciation—that he pined away from pure love for the Negroes, the Union and Native Americans, and envy at the prosperity of the South. Some think that he was literally consumed with lust for power and office, and they gave him the balsam of Know Nothingism. Many, again, suppose that he died from refusing to take stimulus, from his conscientious scruples about "Maine Liquour," and from substituting sour butter-milk in the Sacrament, in the place of wine. While not a few are persuaded he suffered from religious melancholy, or derangement from discarding the Bible from his heart, and substituting Know Nothingism. But the most probable opinion is that the immediate cause of his death, was the shock from the Democratic battery, when the positive and negative poles were brought together, to cure him of the Rheumatism, which he got by going out *too late at night!* All these, no doubt, contributed to "Sam's" sufferings. Never did a poor man groan under a greater complication of maladies, than did "Sam" in Virginia; and it was, no doubt, best for him and the community, that he was taken away in his youth, for his disease was a contagious one, whatever might have been its nature in other respects. The Democratic Faculty, as soon as he died, recommended that the room (Virginia) should be *constantly* fumigated with vinegar, (Democratic principles,) and well ventilated. The clothing, as well as the bedding, ought to be often removed and all offensive odors (particularly the fæces) should be removed as speedily as possible.

As to the *character* of "Sam" he was perfectly consistent in his "Platform" and practice. He stood broad in public estimation. No man doubted his veracity, purity or piety. His Bible was always in hand, if not in heart. He loved (like the good Samaritan) his neighbor as himself. His charity covered a multitude of sins in others, and extended to all without exception. He was particularly noted for entertaining *strangers*, for he thought that thereby he might entertain angels unawares. In creed, Sam was a Unitarian, and required his followers to swear by and believe in one God, and he propagated this doctrine under the cover of political principle.

If Sam's conscious scruples about slavery, wine, &c., in the Bible, did lead him to reject the New Testament and its authors, yet he very piously believed, like Mahomet, in the unity of God, and received a small portion of the Old Testament. "Sam" was a good author; he wrote pamphlets, in which he "denied that Christ made an intoxicating wine, and if he did, he was no Saviour for him." And he had the charity to believe, that "if Christ had known the misery he brought on the world by making an intoxicating liquor, he never would have made it." Sam's doctrines in the Church in which he was first brought up, had prepared him for any emergency in the State. But no man was more tolerant or more opposed to retaliation. He was perfectly willing that every man should think for himself in matters of religion. That all religious sects and denominations of professing christains, should have their own ways of thinking and modes of worship; that "every one should be fully persuaded in his own mind," was "Sam's" motto written on his forehead—a living epistle to be read of all men, whatever he might have kept behind. He read with horror, and tears in his eyes, how they used to fry men, for thinking, on gridirons, and drive them out of the country just for opinion sake. Sam, although not a Presbyterian, Baptist, Methodist, Episcopalian, or Roman Catholic, but of the Know Nothing persuasion, yet he loved all, and was all things to all men, peradventure, he might win some. He held that when in Rome, (where he often went,) we must do as Rome does. He had lately joined the Know Nothing church, and was a consistent member to the day of his death. He possessed a zeal for God, exactly according to Know Nothingism. He was a great Protestant. He protested against all party spirit and sectarianism in Church and State, but his own "American party." He "set aside all parties for the time at least," (Pres. Critic) except the Know-Nothing party. How beautifully consistent was "Sam!" Sam was a great Patriot. He so loved his country, that he called himself "American," "National Republican," "Star Spangled Banner," &c.; following the example of the good old Roman fathers who called themselves the opposite of what they were—Pius, Clement, (mild) Innocent, Felix, (happy) Celestine, (Heavenly,) &c. "Sam" was not only exceedingly exemplary in his own conduct and conversation, but he brought up his children in the way they should go, and they never lived to be old enough to depart from it. "Sam kept a family Record in his Bible where he recorded all the births of his children. It is true he omitted the deaths, but this is excusable, as his feelings were so tender, he couldn't think on the subject. At his death, "Sam" had 72,000 children in Virginia, besides grand children.—They were as the stars of Heaven in multitude. He had been promised a numerous seed. It was said in "Sam" "all the nations of the earth should be blessed," and he should live forever. "*The American party involves the overthrow of every other party*," "*Democracy has lived* 100 *years; 'Sam' will swallow Democracy and live forever*," is the language of the prophet of Kentucky.

"Sam was born in Massachusetts, of royal parentage, and was descended in a direct line from a British Whig family. His ancestors emigrated from England to America before the revolutionary war. After the war, "British Whig" Sam, died, and left an only son, "Federal" Sam—a respectable honest man, but of bad principles—he became odious by his connection with the Adams family in Massachusetts. Federal Sam died, and left an only son, Whig Sam. He died and left an only son, National Republican Sam. He died, and left an only son, Whig "Sam" or "Sam Pure" again, named after his grand father, Whig Sam. This family separated from the Whig family South, and "Sam" married an abolition lady in Massachusetts, a relation of Adams, Greeley, Seward, Wilson, &c.

The fruit of this connection, was Know-Nothing or American "Sam." So that Know Nothing Sam was an abolitionist on the maternal side, and on the paternal a Whig. Now this is the genealogy of "Sam." British Whig Sam begat Federal Sam. Federal Sam begat Whig Sam again. Whig Sam begat National Republican Sam. National Republican Sam begat Know Nothing Sam. And all the generations of Sam, from British Whig Sam to Know Nothing Sam, are five generations. And the days of the years of Sam are about three-score years and ten; and if by reason of strength they be four-score years, yet is their strength, labor and sorrow; for it is soon cut off and we fly away. So teach us to number our days, that we may apply our hearts unto wisdom—may all the Know Nothings pray.

Sam having heard through the Board of Domestic Missions, (the Grand Council,) of the ignorance and superstitious devotion of the Heathen in Virginia to the Constitution, his soul was stirred within him; for he saw they were wholly given to idolatry. He determined to visit that destitute region, on a missionary tour, and preach to them the gospel of Know Nothingism—to declare unto them the "unknown (or Know-Nothing) God" whom they ignorantly worshipped; but the climate proving unfavorable to his health, he died in Virginia, May 24th, 1855.

While on this mission South, American Sam married a Miss Know-Nothing, his first cousin, for he had relations in Virginia, both on the mother's and father's side, who had settled in that State before, and in other States. This marriage united the Know Nothing family North, with the Know Nothing family South. But this match was opposed by the most respectable portion of the Whig family South, who, about the time of "Sam's" death, married into the Democratic family. We may observe here, that although Sam claims kin with the Washington, Jefferson, Madison and Jackson family, they are not blood relations. He tries to trace his pedigree to those families, (to get office.) Although he dogs Virginia for her family pride.—Sam's amiable consort, is now in desolate widowhood. She is advised to marry again, as soon as it is decent, as Sam left his matters in a bad condition and she needs funds. She is already beginning to wax wanton and will marry. They say that the Know Nothing church ought not to be burthened with the support of such. But the younger widows refuse; (that is to take on the charity of the Church) for when they have begun to wax wanton, they will marry; having condemnation because they have cast off their first faith. And with all this they learn to be idle, wandering about from North to South, and not only idle, but tattlers also, and busy-bodies in other men's matters, speaking things which they ought not. I will, therefore, (says the Grand Council) that the young women marry and bear children." Sam's widow needs not the slightest encouragement on this score, for it is reported that she was discovered recently ogling a young Democratic gentleman of the Know Nothing family at the funeral who owned negroes!!!

Sam and his wife, it is well known, married each other for money, at first, or for "quills," as they say. But, alas! they were both deceived, "deceiving and being deceived;" and when they came together, they found each other perfectly featherless!!! Love had jumped out of the window, and they had commenced quarreling, and if Death had not parted them, they would have soon parted themselves. As a Had Nothing had married a Know Nothing, the public thought it was a first rate match at first, and the conjugal knot for brevity was written thus, "00."

The widow Know Nothing declares now, that she is determined never to marry a man for office again; it is too perishable a property—she means to marry next time for "darkeys." This will please the public and all parties south. She will never be caught running off secretly again with a man, but means to stand boldly before the parson and be married publicly in the Church, in the day time, and will be choice and exclusive in nothing but inviting persons to the wedding, or the banquet. She is said to be gone North now, looking out, a remarkable gay widow—it is thought that she puts out the idea, however, of marrying for negroes, merely to marry, and really dislikes negro property, (as she is a Northern lady,) and as soon as she is married, will go North and settle in a free State. We understand that such a match is about being made up now, by some of the family in Philadelphia. In the mean time, the widow Know Nothing is putting on the most coquetish airs imaginable, even in the church, which she enters with a lofty head and a most significant waddle. But the Democracy, because the widow of Sam is haughty and walks with a stretched-forth neck and wanton eyes, walking and mincing as she goes, and making a tinkling with her feet; therefore, the Democracy will smite with a scar the crown (the Grand Council) of her head and discover her secrets; in that day, will take away the bravery of her tinkling ornaments about her feet, and her curls and her round ties like the moon; the chains, and the bracelets, and the muffles; the bonnets and the ornaments of the legs, and the headbands and the tabets and the ear rings; the rings and nose jewels; the changeable suits of apparel, and the mantles, and the crimples and the crisping-pins, the glasses and the fine linen, and the hoods and the veils. And it shall come to pass that instead of a sweet smell, there shall be a stink; and instead of a girdle, a rent; and instead of well-set hair, baldness; and instead of a stomacher, a girding of sackcloth; and burning instead of beauty. Wherefore, let us Democrats walk honestly as in the day, not in rioting and drunkenness, not in chambering and wantonness, not in strife and envying. Let us, therefore, cast off the works of darkness. For when they speak great swelling words of vanity ("American Nationality," Protestant civilization," "National Union," "National Republican," "Grand President," "Grand Council," "American Platform,") they allure through the lusts of flesh (for office) through much wantonness, those that were clean escaped from them, who live in error; while they promise (the slaves) liberty, they themselves are the servants of corruption. But we warn the Democratic family of the mouth of this "strange woman," which is as a "deep pit," or a "culvert." Listen to the counsel of the

"Wise man :" "My son attend unto my wisdom and bow thine ear to mine understanding; 2. That thou mayest regard discretion, and that thy lips may keep knowledge; 3. For the lips of a strange woman drop as honey-comb, and her mouth is smoother than oil; but her end is bitter as wormwood and sharp as a two-edged sword; her feet go down to death; her steps take hold on Hell; lest thou should ponder the path of life, her ways are movable that thou canst not know them. Hear me now, O ye children, depart not from the word of my mouth; remove thy way far from her, come not nigh the door of her Lodge." Her ways are moveable ! ! !

Sam was decently interred, at the Polls in Virginia, where he died; and many of the Democratic family attended the funeral and assisted at the burial. His obsequies were conducted with all the honor and solemnity due to his character and station. The funeral sermon was preached by a minister of the Know Nothing denomination; and the text was taken from Job 3, 3. Let the day perish wherein I was born, and the night it is said there is a man child conceived, (with the following inclusive:) 11. Why died I not from my mother's womb? 13. For now should I have lain still and be quiet, I should have slept; then had I been at rest. 14. With Kings and Counsellors of the earth, which have built destitute places for themselves. 16. Or, as a hidden untimely birth, I had not been; as infants which never saw light. 6, 5. Doth the wild ass bray when he hath grass? or loweth the ox over his fodder? My brethren have dealt deceitfully as a brook, and as a stream of brooks they pass away. 17. What time they wax warm they vanish. 18. The paths of their way are turned aside; they go to "nothing" and perish.

17.5. But as you for all, do ye return and come now; for I cannot find one "Wise man" among you. 19.15. They that dwell in my house count me for a stranger: I am an outcast in their sight. 19. All my inward friends abhor me; and they whom I love have turned against me. 20.4. Knowest not thou this of old, since man was placed upon the earth? 5. That the triumphing of the wicked is short, and the joy of the hypocrite but for a moment. 15. He hath swallowed riches, and he shall vomit them up again. God shall cast them out of his belly; 19. Because he hath oppressed and hath forsaken the poor; 20. Surely, she shall not be quiet in his belly. 21. There shall none of his meats be left. 23. When he is about to fill his belly, God shall cast the fury of his wrath upon him, and shall rain it upon him while he is eating. 27. This is the portion of a wicked man and the heritage of oppressors. 15. Those that remain of him shall be buried in death, and his widow shall not weep. 29.2. O that I were as in months passed; 30.9. But now I am their song; yea, I am a by-word ("Sam") to them: They abhor me, they flee from me.

With many words did the preacher exhort the residue of "Sam" to work out their salvation with fears and trembling, knowing that the Grand Council "worked" in them to will and to do of his own good pleasure; to make their calling and election sure in 1856. He encouraged the family with the hope of the resurrection of Sam. Our "Gnat," said he, was Clay born, and the Democratic decree had gone forth, to dust he should return, yet he shall resurrect. As to brother Flournoy, there was Stan-Hope in his name, and there should be "hope" in his death, that it was needful that Sam should put off this vile body, that he might come forth with a more glorious body and name. He predicted a millennium in 1856, when "all parties," and the Devil of Democracy should be chained a thousand years, and Know Nothingism have free scope and be glorified." "Sam should swallow Democracy and live forever." These services were introduced by singing, "Hark from the tombs," which was chanted with awful solemnity; the whole congregation of Know Nothings were in tears. The second hymn, was the Resurrection Hymn, and raised by "our brother Nat Claiborne:"

And must this body die,
  This feeble frame decay,
And must these active limbs of mine
  Lie mouldering in the "Clay?"
Arrayed in glorious grace,
  Shall these vile bodies shine,
And every shape and every face
  Look heavenly and divine.

Then came the third hymn, raised by father Beale:

On Jordan's stormy banks I stand,
  And cast a *wishful eye*,
To Canaan's fair and happy land,
  Where *my possessions* lie.

Services closed by singing S. M. Doxology, and the benediction was pronounced:

Give *Federal* "Sam" the praise,
  Give glory to his son,
And to the *children* of his grace
  Be equal honor done.

The congregation was then dismissed.

What rendered the services peculiarly interesting, was, Brother Tazewell, who had arrived to a state of assurance and had not doubted of his election for some time, struck up in some distant corner of the church:

When I can read my title clear,
  To *mansions* in the skies,
I'll bid farewell to every fear,
  And wipe my weeping eyes.

The whole congregation chimed in and sung with great animation at the prospect of the revival of Sam.

The deceased left a will, in which, after distributing offices among all his children, he left the residue of his estate to his widow Know Nothing dowager.

This will was made before his death, (as he was in bad health) and never altered. In a codicil to the will, he expressed a wish, that if his widow had a child, (which was expected) that after her death, her property should go to it, and if it died under age, it should revert to the Whig family. Messrs. Flournoy, Beale, Patton, Claiborne, Tazewell and Watkins were appointed executors in Virginia, by the "Grand" court. They have just wound up Sam's matters, and find that he has nothing to give, and a great many of his children have been taken into the Democratic family for support.

In the meantime the widow Know Nothing is in Philadelphia, expecting every day to have a *little one*: and speculation is rife what sort of a thing it will be. Some think it will prove an abortion, others premature and it won't live. Some think it will be black, others think it will be mulatto. Some think it will be white on one side of its face, and black on the other: and that it will turn one side or the other North, or South, as it suits. Some think she will have twins differing in some particulars, but alike in the main, enough to show that they are old Sam's children. They are now disputing about the name. They are trying to pick out a very popular name, as the old lady says, they mean to make him President after a while, if he lives to be grown. They say he must not have any double name; but "National" Sam, "American" Sam, "Protestant Republican" Sam, or some "Grand" general name, that will give Sam a free pass throughout the United States. I think they will call him after his grand-father, "National" Republican Sam. Sam will beget a son in his own likeness.

ROANOKE.

[From the Petersburg South Side Democrat.]

LETTER FROM MR. WISE.

We publish the following interesting correspondence between Mr. Wise and the committee appointed at a late meeting of the Petersburg democracy, to invite him to a barbecue to be given in this city at such day as he might designate.

[CORRESPONDENCE.]

PETERSBURG, Virginia, May 31st, 1855.

Sir:—At a meeting of the Democracy of Petersburg on the 30th inst., we were appointed a committee to invite you to an old fashioned Virginia barbecue, to be given on such day as you may appoint. It is with the greatest satisfaction that we now perform the duty. Your inappreciable services in the recent canvass have inspired the democracy of this city, and the adjoining country, with an earnest desire to see you, and to extend to you their thanks for your eminent services and gallant bearing during the contest, and their earnest congratulations at the signal success that has attended them.

The importance to free government of the principles involved in the late election, and their triumphant assertion, demands something more than an ordinary celebration of the event.

The Democracy of the Cockade City, the only Democratic city in the Commonwealth, are proud of their right to be the first to entertain as their guest their distinguished and gallant leader.

Permit us to conclude by expressing to you, as individuals, our high admiration of, and regard for your private as well as your public virtues, and the hope that you will find it compatible, not merely with your feelings and wishes, but with your convenience also, to comply with the request of a portion of your friends and constituents.

Very respectfully,

R. K. MEADE,
F. E. RIVES,
J. J. THWEATT,
THOMAS WALLACE,
B. B. VAUGHAN,

Committee.

[REPLY.]

ONANCOCK, Virginia, June 9th, 1855.

Gentlemen:—In reply to yours of the 31st ult., I beg you to present to the Democracy of Petersburg my most grateful thanks. May Heaven forever bless the Cockade City and the South Side counties around her, for doing their full part in defending the faith and the altars of Virginia. There is no section whose people I would be prouder to greet, none whose good opinions I am more desirous to deserve. Petersburg is with the country and the country is with her. Her name, her honor, her interests, shall be enshrined by the Democracy —that steadfast, homestead Democracy of Virginia, which is too intelligent, too conscientious, and has too much at stake not to be conservative. But, gentlemen, however grateful I feel to you, you must allow me the indulgence of remaining quietly at home. I would have sacrificed much more than I did in the late canvass to prevent defeat under my lead, but I assure you the labors I underwent nearly cost me my life. I was absent nearly five months from my children and Mrs. Wise, whose health now requires my constant nursing. My domestic affairs too, need every every moment of my time until I must leave for Richmond. I therefore decline no less than three such invitations as yours by this mail. If I accept one, I must all, and I cannot accept any without great inconvenience. But let me say to you, that I hope our friends will seize the moment to strengthen the Democratic cause. Events are coming, you may rely on it, for which we ought to be prepared. How? As early as is prudent reorganize, by having a conference of our friends throught the State.

I am, faithfully yours,

HENRY A. WISE.

To R. K. Meade, Thomas Wallace, Francis E. Rives, B. B. Vaughan, J. J. Thweatt, Esqrs.

From the Enquirer.

LETTER FROM HENRY A. WISE.

We copy from the last Elizabeth City (N. C.) Democratic Poineer, the following eloquent letter, addressed by the Hon. Henry A. Wise to the Committees of Gates and other counties, who had invited him to address the people at Gatesville during the late campaign. The Pioneer says: "We publish in another column a letter from the Hon. Henry A. Wise, in reply to an invitation to attend the late Democratic Mass Meeting near Gatesville. We regret exceedingly that the gentleman who received it failed to place it in our hands at an earlier day. But, though the occasion is past, which called it forth it loses none of its interest thereby. It is characteristic of its author—bold, able and withering. It gives a passing notice to those Know Nothing emissaries who went to Virginia to electioneer during the recent canvass there, and expresses the earnest wish of the author for an opportunity to scourge them at their own doors in return. But the whole letter is full of interest. Read it, and if any regret is felt after rising from its perusal, it will be that you did not have an opportunity of hearing its distinguished author "scourge" Know Nothingism on the stump."

ONLY, (Near Onancock,) VA.,
July 1st, 1855.

James C. Skinner, Esq.:

Dear Sir:—I have delayed a reply to yours of the 18th ult., in order to try to make arrangements to accept the kind and pressing invitation of the Committees of Gates, Perquimans, Pasquotank, Chowan, and Currituck, in North Carolina, to participate with them in a Democratic Mass Meeting to be held in the county of Gates, sometime between the 10th of July and the 1st of August next, the precise day to be fixed by my appointment. I have the strongest desire to meet your Democracy. It holds the brighter than golden links which bind the two elder sister States of the South, North Carolina and Virginia together. Those links are of our earliest history, of our revolution for independence, of our past political struggles for republican freedom, of common sacrifices and co-operation in the past and of common hopes for the future. The Federal party of old and the Fanatical party of the present day (the last is worse than the first,) never tried and never tended to unite themselves with the Southern States, or parties or men, but rather with Northern. Whenever Democracy has been dominant in North Carolina, that State has always been united with Virginia, which has always been Democratic; and whenever either Federalism or Fanaticism has prevailed there, Virginia and North Carolina have been divided from each other, both in councils and in action. I would gladly see them inseparable—inseparable as Macon was from Jefferson and Madison. Our fathers were as Jonathans and Davids to each other, and I would have their children so united as to preserve the union of all, North and South, by their inseparable union with each other! No, not for selfish, or sectional ends would I bind them together, but for national, constitutional, State rights, Union abiding ends, I would have them so solid a phalanx of freedom standing side by side and sustained by all their sisters of the conservative school, that no influence, no "*ism*," shall be able to assail or destroy the institutions of our confederacy. Those institutions, State and Federal, have been sorely and insidiously invaded of late. The invaders were daring enough to touch the sacred soil of this blessed mother Commonwealth. They mustered emissaries from every quarter—from abroad, from Exeter Hall in old England, from Canada, from New England, from New York, Pennsylvania, Ohio, Tennessee; and I regret especially to be compelled to admit that some of the most venomous, desperate, most unscrupulous and audacious came here from the South of us—from North Carolina—to corrupt the popular mind, to instil poison and sow Dragon's teeth among us. They dared not intermeddle in our canvass publicly, on the "stump," in debate, before the people, but they skulked to secret conclaves, and by the light of "dark lanterns" which "burnt a gloom," they implored our voters to save them and their plots of mischief from exposure and explosion. They urged in their agony of midnight harangues that the battle was with them for life or death—that if they did not succeed they would sink down to lower depths of infamy—that if victory did not crown their conspiracy they would be dishonored and disgraced, would be a by-word and a reproach, politically forever! They cowered before the lance of Democracy in Virginia, and the monstrous treason was here hurled to its despair. A Pandemonium has lately been held in Philadelphia, and there it was plainly proved that not the worst enemies of the South were from the North. The Sams of Virginia and North Carolina were no less traitorous to our Constitution and laws, Federal Union and State Rights, and homes and altars than were the *priestcraft* party of the North, who would not seemingly keep them company or abide their councils. To expose these Southern emissaries in your midst, I would like, at their own doors, to scourge them for their nightly prowling about our doors in the late Virginia canvass. But these would be the least of my aims in attending your District Mass Meeting. I would be glad to implore you in person to be true to the faith of the Fathers of this Republic; to protect the fames of our Protestant churches; to forbid the bans between Church and State, which a subtle and wily priestcraft is contriving under the false cry of proscribing popery; to fight on and fight ever to have this land continue forever to be the "land of the free and the home of the brave;" to contend for Constitutions and Bills of Rights, and Statutes to reign over us, and not to subject us to the higher law of a secret oligarchy, worse than that of any German Gehime Gericht!—to free us from the "dagger and the cord" of political assassination!—to preserve the dignity and individuality and independence of voters at the polls!—to save the laws from a conspiracy against their operation!—to save the South from an Old England and New England combination, which would shave the American Samson of his strength, knowing that cotton is his hair, and that cotton cannot be cultivated but by African slave labor in the land of the lagoon and the alligator, and which is, therefore, now striving to abolish African slavery in the South, or to dissolve the blessed union of these United States, now so strong, *by their power to pull the cotton string*, that they need no standing army, no navy, no tax for either, whilst all the world besides is necessarily armed and taxed for the cost of war! This is not half, this is not a beginning of what I would discourse you and all, North and South, about in these strange times, when old things seem to be passing away and all things seem to be coming new. I would go back to the old. I would "recur to fundamental principles," to the teachings of the Revolution, to the faith of the fathers, to the religion of the simpler and purer times of the Republic. But I can't by pen or by word, or in public meeting any where, for a long time to come, I fear, indulge the wish to enlarge upon and illustrate and inculcate these themes. I wish you would rise to their full height. Organize, assemble, be watchful and be prepared to meet the enemy whenever and however he approaches. I regret I cannot venture to accept your invitation, but I will always be found doing what I can, wherever I may be placed, to further the patriotic ends—the country's ends you aim at with me.

I beg you to assure your committee of my profoundest acknowledgment, and to accept for them and yourself individually my sincere thanks, and believe me.

Yours in the bonds and brotherhood of a sound and conservative Democracy.

HENRY A. WISE.

MR. WISE AND THE NEW YORK HARDS AND SOFTS.

The following letter, addressed by Mr. Wise to a friend, has been handed to us for publication. As it is an explanation, by Mr. Wise, of the letter which he addressed to "The Young Men's Democratic Union Club of the City of New York," and which has been the subject of very extensive criticism by journals in and out of Virginia, we cannot in justice to him refuse the request that it be laid before our readers. It will be perceived that the sentiments contained in this letter very nearly correspond with those in an editorial upon the same subject which appeared in the Enquirer some days since:

ONLY, NEAR ONANCOCK, VIRGINIA,
July 30th, 1855.

My Dear Sir:—Yours of the 24th inst., calling my attention to an editorial of the Richmond Examiner of that day, headed "*The New York Herald and ourselves again—Gov. Wise and the Van Buren Democracy*," was not received until yesterday. It was *missent* to Old Point Comfort, and I can't account for such negligence in the mails. Fortunately, this morning, for the first time since it was written, I saw my letter in print, to which this editorial refers. I inclose it to you, and ask for its republication in the Enquirer, in order that every fair-minded person may judge of the justice of the Examiner to me.

I was addressed by neither *Hards* nor *Softs* from New York. A most patriotic letter came to me from "The Young Men's Democratic Union Club," of the City of New York, congratulating the Democracy of Virginia upon their recent triumph over a common enemy, and breathing nothing but a greeting sympathy with our success. Was I to doubt or distrust any portion of our fellow countrymen who thus openly committed themselves *to the same cause with ourselves?* Was I to stop and enquire:—Tell me first, gentlemen, are you Hards or Softs? I must distinguish between you in my reply.—Certainly, such a course of response would have been unbecoming and ungracious. And, if they had avowed themselves either Hard or Soft, was it not enough that they cordially congratulated the result of the Virginia election? Would not that of itself show the current and direction of their sentiments and sympathies; and would not both be such as *we* could approve most heartily? But when you see that they were a Young Men's Club, and a Democratic Union Club, aiming to preserve the Union of the States, and to restore the union of the factions of the party in their own State, I ask, was it for me to meddle in any local and personal divisions of our friends in a sister State? No. I addressed them, as you see, hurriedly and hastily, but warmly and cordially as I would address them again. And by reading the letter all may see *what* it was and *what it is* in which I "cordially, then, with all my heart and all my head" united, and *with whom* I united. Again, I repeat, that my "heart and soul are with the '*Young Men's Democratic Union Club*'" of New York, in their patriotic efforts to unite the Democracy in their State and everywhere, again on the National platform of '51 and '52. I will know no *Hards* and no *Softs* in Democracy. All are Democrats, or they are not. *If Democrats*, they will not repudiate the sentiments of my letter; and if Democrats, they will not foment dissensions in the Democratic camp, in the very face of Democracy's most formidable foe.

I have not a word of comment to make on the Examiner's article. If divisions must come amongst us in Virginia, they shall not come through me; and I say: "Woe unto him through whom they shall come!" The public is witness of what I have borne in silence and patience, before and during the late canvass. I mean to forbear to the last extremity, to promote the harmony and to unite the whole strength of our party in Virginia, and everywhere, for the defence of the rights of the States and of the Union of the States; for the maintainance of the Constitution and laws of the Federal Government; for the muniments of individual inalienable rights of the citizens of the States, and to prevent the Samson of America from being shorn of a single hair of his strength by the treason and madness which would "abolish African slavery or dissolve the Union," under the lead of the minions and money of a "Foreign Influence." Certainly the Examiner will unite in these ends. You are welcome to publish this.

Yours, hastily but truly,

HENRY A. WISE.

We submit the following correspondence to our readers without comment, feeling assured that they will come to right conclusions in the premises, without any aid or explanation from us :

CORRESPONDENCE.

Hon. Henry A. Wise:

Sir :—The strictures of the Richmond Examiner upon your letter of reply to the invitation of the "Young Men's Democratic Union Club," of this city, to address them upon the occasion of their last anniversary, and the false position in which it labors to place you, make it my duty, as the presiding officer of that association, to convey to you in a few plain, but earnest and heartfelt words, the feelings which prompted our invitation, and the sentiments awakened by your reply.

The great purpose of our association, and chief article of its constitution, is the union of the Democratic party. To this end—as essential to the permanent and happy union of the States; to the preservation of all their rights as separate and distinct sovereignties, co-ordinate in authority and dignity; and to the just limitation of both State and Federal powers within the boundaries of a strict construction of the Constitution—all our efforts are directed. On that old Democratic basis we united as a political association in 1852, and upon that basis we stand, and expect always to stand. You can conceive, therefore, sir, the regret with which we saw the division in the Democratic party of this State, and the painful solicitude with which we have watched its development in sectional organization and divided effort. But this strange and novel antagonism between brethren of our own household excited in us no other feelings than mingled shame and sorrow at their suicidal folly, and a patient determination to stand steadily upon the high vantage ground of principles preferred by both, and await the moment when better councils and kinder influences should re-unite them against the common enemy.

Your triumph in Virginia, which was in fact the triumph of our own old faith over the Proteus of Whig Abolitionism, in alliance with the new and pernicious heresy of Know Nothingism, appeared to us to offer the very point and occasion of re-union. Every Democrat, of every faction, professed to rejoice in it. Our joy was unfeigned; and we were glad to believe the sentiment as honest as it appeared to be universal. Why, then, we asked ourselves, should not all, claiming to be Democrats, join in the exhibition of their satisfaction at a result so honorable to our arms; and, forgetting the mere personal and sectional quarrels, notoriously engendered by low ambition and the lust of office, seize the auspicious moment and heartily co-operate for a common good? Had they done so, your victory in Virginia would have been but the initiative in a series of brilliant triumphs, and the whole field of the Union, swept by the irresistible columns of the conservative Democracy, would have ceased to be insulted by the presence either of an open or covert foe to that Union which we cherish as our best inheritance, or the principles which ensure its perpetuity. It was not the fault of the Young Men's Democratic Union Club if that golden opportunity was neglected. But our object is Union, not war. We desire to reflect upon no man. We are willing to believe it rather an unfortunate mistake than a wilful error.

You, sir, however, understood us. You appreciated our motives, and shared our hopes. You answered our invitation to assist us in the undertaking promptly, warmly—right from the heart. You replied rather with the generous impulsiveness of friendship than the calculating coldness of the politician. And, sir, give us leave to say, however old-fashioned the notion may appear to the trading politicians of the times, even in politics, the heart is often wiser than the head. The sentiment which came warm and glowing from your heart, found and kindled an answering spark in ours. We thanked you, then, with a spontaneous and irresistible impulse, a true Democratic confidence, for your hearty and comfortable words. We thank you again for their frank and manly repetition;—and we tell you that in every purpose which animates you or any other Democrat, the end of which is peace, union, the conservation of the rights of the States, the integrity of the constitution and the federal power, the defeat of sectionalism, fanaticism, and every pretended principle which would elevate itself above the Constitution, and usurp the rights of State, territory or citizen—which would, in short, disturb the nice adjustment and harmonious proportions of our social and political structure—the Young Men's Democratic Union Club of New York are with you, and with them, cordially—with all their heart and all their head.

You say well, therefore, "that all may see what it was and what it is in which you cordially unite." It is something "tangible to feeling as to sight;" at once the ethical and material good of this great Republican Confederation of thirty-one sovereign States, distinct yet blended; obeying, like the planets, the law which ordains them forever to revolve around a common centre, yet never centralizing; gravitating to each other in the magnificent harmony of Republican order and unity, but never blending into the portentous consolidation precursive of despotic power.

It is Democracy—the Democracy of Jefferson and Jackson—with which you unite. It was the union of that Democracy we aimed at, and will never cease to aim at. It was to an occasion dedicated to the purposes of that Union we invited you. And if the apparent egotism of the illustration may be pardoned for its truth's sake, I think my election as presiding officer of the Association, on the very anniversary to which you were invited, afforded a very plain and unanswerable argument for its entire freedom from sectional prejudice or passion. A Virginian by birth, although for many years identified with the Empire State in interest and affection, I can never forget to love the Old Dominion, nor adopt any part of a political creed not catholic enough to embrace both North and South. Neither my birth-place nor my sentiments were a secret from any member of the Association, and they did me the honor to elect me with a full knowledge that I recognized neither sectionalism nor fanticism as elements of the faith or the Constitution of the Democratic party.

Let me assure you, as well as the "Examiner," in conclusion of a letter already trespassing too much upon your patience, that the Young Men's Democratic Union Club of New York acknowledge no higher law than the Constitution of the United States; no holier bond than the union of the States; no worthier purposes than the consolidation and success of that party upon whose well-tested principles they believe the whole glorious edifice can alone securely rest. In the letter of the Constitution they find the only rule of political faith and practice which can bind their country in a golden band and brotherhood of justice; and, whether the suicidal knife, which aims to sever it, be raised by mad fanaticism, or hell-engendered ambition; whether it be levelled at one portion of the Union or the other—before the bosom which it threatens—before the rights it would destroy—before the sovereignty or the citizen it would immolate upon the altar of its insanity—they trust always to see the Democratic party throw the shield of its principles and the protection of its power; and their highest aim and ambition is to be instrumental, however humbly, in uniting every true-hearted Democrat behind that invulnerable defence.

I have the honor to be, sir,

Most truly and respectfully,

Your obedient servant,

S. WALLACE CONE,
President of the Young Men's
Democratic Union Club, N. Y.

P. S.—You are at liberty to make whatever use you may think proper of the above.

S. W. C.

ONLY, NEAR ONANCOCK, VA.,
AUGUST 23, 1855.

To S. WALLACE CONE,
President of the Young Men's Democratic Union Club, New York:

Dear Sir:—Yours of the 14th instant reached me most opportunely. Before this you will have seen that the Richmond Examiner has handsomely acknowledged its mistake. It is well, perhaps, that it mistook your meaning and mine.

Attention has been drawn to your noble and patriotic purposes, and they will be approved and be assisted by the entire Democracy of the South. Those who love and would abide by the wise federal Constitution and the sacred Union of our States, in the South, know and feel that we have "a host of freedom, which is the host of God," for our friends in the North. We will not tolerate the idea of a separation from you for an instant, and we will depend upon your faith and your devotion to co-operate with us in defending the good work of our fathers against internal as well as external foes. We will, North and South, defend the Rights of the States, and the most precious of these: the Rights of each State to the Blessed Union of the States. We will defend the Constitution of the Union as the only standard of State Rights. And we will defend the individual and inalienable rights of man:—his rights of property and his person, all his finite rights which pertain to poor mortality, and above all his infinite right, the only one "not of the earth earthy," his heaven reaching right, which pertains to immortality—his right of religious liberty—his freedom of conscience—his right to easement in the way to God!

Thus I understood you, thus I took your greeting, and thus I greeted you back. Carp who will, I will grasp your hands as a brother upon the pledges to these rights, for which I am willing to stake "life, fortune and sacred honor." But no one will object. Petty jealousies will be laid aside, manly patriots will summon sober reason to their sides, and we will triumph in the right. God grant our country and its friends His guidance and His rule? Yours, devotedly, with all my head and heart.

HENRY A. WISE.

THE DOWDELL FESTIVAL IN ALABAMA.

[From the Montgomery Advertiser and Gazette.]

In a brief notice of the Dowdell festival, written for our last issue, we presented an abstract of the speech of our distinguished townsman, Mr. Yancey, which the reader has doubtless perused with interest. We should like also to present a sketch of the speeches delivered by the other orators of the occasion; but we are unable to do so, for the reason that no notes were taken of them.

One of the most intelligent and patriotic of Alabama's sons, (not a public man, however,) in a private letter, says: "Our gifted and noble friend, Yancey, is right in theory, as far as he goes, except that he has *not quite faith enough* in the National Democracy. I want Southern *union* and *self-reliance*, in order, first, to strengthen and build up the conservative national Democracy; and, secondly, in the 'last resort,' to enable us to sustain ourselves against the world; but let us live in the Union *if we may*. *All* the Northern Democratic leaders are with us on practical issues."

We concur with our correspondent in the opinion that Mr. Yancey underestimates the assistance the South is likely to derive from the National Democracy of the North. Mr. Yancey thinks that our gallant friends in the North are already rendered powerless by the predominance of Abolition sentiments in that quarter. We, on the contrary, have strong hopes that a reaction has commenced in several of the free States in favor of the true principles of the government. From the tone of the press, and other indications, we think that Mr. Bright will be sustained in Indiana, and Mr. Douglas in Illinois. We have strong hopes, also, of Pennsylvania, New Jersey, New Hampshire, and Michigan, through the influence of their conservative statesmen and the "sober, second thought" of their people. We may be too sanguine, but we cannot withhold the expression of our opinion that the South has much to expect from the National Democracy of the North.

But Mr. Yancey is right in impressing upon the minds of the Southern people the idea of self-reliance. "Forewarned," let us be "forearmed and well prepared" for future emergencies.

In connection with the proceedings at the Oak Bowery Dinner, we would call attention to the letters of Gov. Wise, Gov. Winston, Mr. Bullock, and Mr. Gwin, in reply to the Committee of Invitation. They were not received in time to be read at the dinner, but they will be perused with pleasure by the republicans who were present, as well as by many who were not.

The letter of Mr. Wise will attract particular attention. The opening sentence of his letter is in response to a complimentary passage in the note of invitation. The whole letter is eloquent and spirit-stirring. We understand that one of the regular toasts prepared for the occasion was in these words:

"HENRY A. WISE: The Knight *sans peur sans reproche*—who met 'Sam'—the redoubtable Sam—Sam the Sampson on the plains of Virginia, and sent him, like Caius Marius, 'to a marsh in Italy'—a son of whom the grand old 'mother of States and statesmen' might well have been proud in her best days; when the national coronal was lustrous with her jewels—a Tribune of the people! He deserves the highest office in the nation, and if he lives will attain it."

[LETTER FROM MR. WISE.]

Only, near Onancock, Va.,
August 23, 1825.

Gentlemen:—Yours of the 13th inst. came to hand yesterday.

I stand on the shore of my "Ocean home," and meet Alabama, coming greeting, with arms and bosom open, with expanding chest and dilating nostril, as I have often met Heaven's sweet airs and Ocean's waves as they came with inspiring and re-invigorating freshness. The blessed child State seems to rush to the arms of the mother State, and Virginia takes Alabama close home to her bosom, and embraces her with motherly pride and affectionate joy. I did not for a moment doubt or distrust her. She is too Southern, too conservative, too Constitution-loving, too true to State Rights, and too fondly cherishes the most precious of State Rights—the Union of the States—and prizes too inestimably the inalienable rights of individual man—his finite rights of property and rights of person, and above all his infinite right—the only one not "of the earth, earthy"—the only right of poor humanity pertaining to immortality—the Heaven-high right of Religious Liberty—the soul-saving right of Freedom of Conscience. She is too true to the American Revolution, and to the memories and faith of the Fathers of the Republic, ever to have betrayed the great cause, the holy mission of America upon Earth! She was too intelligent to be duped by a worse than veiled prophet; she had too much integrity to countenance political imposture; she was too Protestant and too Christian to allow the ways to God to be barred and bolted by sectarian bigotry and intolerance; she loved the Churches of her faith too well to allow them to be corrupted by a touch of party political power, and by leaving the spiritual for the carnal kingdom; and she was too patriotic to permit the liberties of the State to be destroyed by an union of Church and State, brought about by a Priestcraft Power ambitiously aspiring to lay its hands on temporal things, and to control conscience, and will and reason, and to make laws, and to debate "what we shall eat and what we shall drink, and wherewith we shall be clothed!" The hypocrites who skulked in the shades between "midnight and one hour before day-break," with "dark-lantern" in hand, making night hideous with howls of "down with the Pope!" were dragging the robes of Christ's righteousness through the mire of party politics to set up a Protestant Popery here, in America, instead of leaving Catholic Popery to die of itself in Italy! The impostors who exultingly boast that "Americans shall rule America"—as if, from Washington's days down to these days of "isms," America has not been all the time ruled by Americans—exclaim against "Foreign influence," and are letting in that European, that British-born intruder, whom they call "Sam"—the most insidious foreign foe who has ever entered the back door of our country, like a thief in the night!

The Old World is ravaged by war, and yet we need no standing armies, no navy, and to pay taxes for none. Why? It is, in three words, because—"Cotton is King!" *Uncle* Sam, not Sam, holds the British Lion, and the Gallic Cock and Russian Black Eagle by cotton strings, which he may pull at any time. Cotton is Power, Cotton is Peace-Maker; Cotton is the hair of the Sampson of the United States of North America, and Cotton can be planted, and hoed, and gathered, and ginned, and packed and sent to market, in the land of the Southern sun, by African slave labor alone. Hence the cry, that "African slavery shall be abolished, or the American Union shall be dissolved." Exeter Hall has so whispered to Williams Hall, of Boston, and New England Preachers of Christian Politics have joined the British, the Old England policy and party cry, that the Nebraska Bill shall be repealed—no slave territory shall be admitted as a State—slavery shall be abolished, or the Union shall be dissolved! Either alternative would shave our Sampson of his strength.

The Kansas and Nebraska Bill repealed the Missouri Compromise, which was the first act to violate Washington's injunction not to recognize geographical lines—which was the first to make a border between the North and the South—which was the first to begin a separation of the States! Now, the Kansas and Nebraska Bill simply restores us to *statu quo ante* 1819, '20, where Washington and Hancock, Adams and Jefferson, Virginia and Massachusetts, and the old Thirteen, stood. It brought us back to the Constitution. The question is, shall it be repealed, and a heart-burning statute be restored to the place of the Constitution? Virginia votes no, North Carolina no, Georgia, glorious Georgia, no, Alabama no. The entire slaveholding states will, notwithstanding the hesitancy of gallant but blood-stained Kentucky, all unite in shouting, as a host of Freedom, as friends of America—

"African slavery shall not be abolished!
"The American Union of States shall not be dissolved!"

Then let us abide, under the Ægis of the Constitution and the Laws. To defend these, I will stake "life, fortune and sacred honor," against internal as well as external foes.

The South is full of emissaries from abroad, and they must be guarded against. We have a host of patriotic friends in the North, and they must be cherished as well-beloved brothers. There are patriots there who will rally to rescue and restore the sacred things which are in danger, and I implore you, for their sakes, for our own, to favor no sectional war, to countenance no alienation of feeling from the North, but to rely on reason and argument, and a moral sense of right, and to adhere ourselves to the Constitutional compact. This will save us and save all, if anything will; and if nothing will, we will be innocent. We will not bear the world's curse of aiding to destroy the only hopes of mankind for the light, and love and charity of human freedom. And if the worst comes to the worst, "God will speed the right."

I cannot leave home before January next, and could not be in time for your feast to your gallant Representative, the Hon. J. F. Dowdell. Feast him well, and let him roll the people's good cheer like a sweet morsel under his tongue, and let that tongue ever speak the sentiments of Truth and Justice to the People, and let them ever repay him with their "sweet voices."

I cordially greet you back, and am

Yours, devotedly,

HENRY A. WISE.

To WM. F. SANFORD, JNO. H. THOMAS, CHRISTOPHER DAVIS, and others, Committee.

HENRY A. WISE TO THE BOSTON NEGRO STEALERS.

ONLY, NEAR ONANCOCK,
Accomac County, Va., Oct. 5, 1855.

Gentlemen:—On my return home, after an absence of some days, I found yours of the 19th ult., "respectfully inviting me to deliver one of the lectures of the course on slavery, at Tremont Temple, in the city of Boston, on Thursday evening, January 10th, 1856; or, if that time will not suit my engagements, you request that I will mention at once what Thursday evening, between the middle of December and the middle of March next, will best accommodate me."

Now, gentlemen, I desire to pay you due respect, yet you compel me to be very plain with you, and to say that your request, in every sense, is insulting and offensive to me. What subject of slavery have you "initiated" lectures upon? I cannot conceal it from myself that you have undertaken, in Boston, to discuss and decide whether my property, in Virginia, ought to remain mine or not, and whether it shall be allowed the protection of laws, federal and State, wherever it may be carried or may escape in the United States; or, whether it shall be destroyed by a higher law than the constitutions and statutes!

Who are you, to assume thus such a jurisdiction over a subject so delicate and already fixed in its relation by a solemn compact between the States, and by States which are sovereign? I will not obey your summons nor recognize your jurisdiction. You have no authority and no justification for thus calling me to account at the bar of your tribunal, and for thus arraigning an institution established by laws which do not reach you and which you cannot reach, by calling on me to defend it.

You send me a card, to indicate the character of the lecturers. It reads:

"Admit the bearer and lady to the Independent Lectures on Slavery. Lecture committee, S. G. Howe, T. Gilbert, George F. Williams, Henry T. Parker, W. Washburn, B. B. Mussey, W. B. Spooner, James W. Stone."

It is endorsed:

"Lectures at the Tremont Temple, Boston, 1854–'5. November 23, Hon. Charles Sumner, Rev. John Pierpont, poet. December 7, Hon. Salmon P. Chase, of Ohio. December 14th, Hon. Anson Burlingame. December 21, Wendell Phillips, Esq. December 28, Cassius M. Clay, Esq., of Kentucky. January 4, Hon. Horace Greeley. January 11, Rev. Henry Ward Beecher. January 18, Hon. John P. Hale. January 25, Ralph Waldo Emmerson, Esq. February 8, Hon. Nathaniel P. Banks, Jr. February 15, Hon. Lewis D. Campbell, of Ohio. February 22, Hon. Sam. Houston, of Texas. March 1, Hon. David Wilmot, of Pennsylvania. March 8th, Hon. Charles W. Upham."

All *Honorables* and *Squires*, except those who are *Reverends!* The card does verily indicate their characters by simply naming them. And your letter, gentlemen, is franked by "C. Sumner, U. S. S." With these characteristics, I am at no loss to understand you and your purposes.

You say, "during the next season, a large number of gentlemen from the South will be invited," &c., &c. I regret it, if any others can be found in the slaveholding States to accept your invitation. You plead the example of Gen. Houston. It is the last I would follow. I have no doubt that you accorded very respectful attention to him last winter, and were very grateful for his services in your cause.

You offer "one hundred and fifty dollars to be paid to the lecturer, he bearing his own expenses." Let me tell you that Tremont Temple cannot hold wealth enough to purchase one word of discussion from me, there, whether mine, here, shall be mine or not; but I am ready to volunteer, without money and without price, to suppress any insurrection, and repel any invasion which threatens or endangers the State Rights of Virginia, or my individual rights under the laws and constitutions of my country, or the sacred Union, which binds Slave States and Free States together in one bond of National Confederacy, and in separate bonds of Independent Sovereignties!

In short, gentlemen, I will not deliver one of the lectures of the course on Slavery, at the Tremont Temple, in Boston, on Thursday evening, January 10th, 1856; and there will be no Thursday evening between the middle of December and the middle of March next, or between that and doomsday, which will best accommodate me for that purpose.

I give you an immediate answer, and at my earliest convenience, indicate to you that "the particular phase of the subject" that I will present is, deliberately: TO FIGHT IF WE MUST.

Your obedient servant,

HENRY A. WISE.

To S. G. Home, Phys. and Sup't Blind Inst.
Jno. M. Clark, High Sheriff.
Sam'l May, Merchant.
Philo Sanford, Ex-Treasurer State.
N. B. Shurtlett, Phys. and Antiquarian.
Jos. Story, Pres't Com. Council.
Thos. Russell, Judge.
Jas. W. Stone, Phys.

From the Boston Advertiser, (Whig.)

LETTER FROM MR. WISE.

We take pleasure in laying before our readers the subjoined letter from Hon. Henry A. Wise, the Governor elect of the ancient Commonwealth of Virginia, addressed to the Lecture Committee of the Mercantile Library Association, in answer to an invitation to lecture in this city before that association during the coming winter. The truly national tone of this letter must renew in the mind of the reader the patriotic feelings which of old knit together the colonies of Massachusetts and Virginia in times of darkness and trouble; and will cause a regret that Mr. Wise's preparations for the duties of the important office on which he is about to enter, will prevent his accepting the invitation, and will deprive us of the pleasure of welcoming to Boston so distinguished a guest, who (as he informs us in the letter) has never yet visited any part of New England.

This letter is the more significant, because another committee in behalf of the "lectures on slavery," in their indiscreet zeal, by calling upon Mr. Wise to lecture upon slavery in Boston, succeeded in pestering him into writing a letter, which we are free to say we regretted to see in print, though we can easily understand the feeling of annoyance that gave rise to its sharpness of expression. Whatever ill feeling (if any) the former letter may have engendered in the minds of our right-thinking citizens, will be dispelled on the perusal of that which we publish below:

ONLY, NEAR ONANCOCK, VA., Nov. 11, 1855.

Gentlemen:—Yours of the 2d inst. was awaiting my arrival at home yesterday, from a temporary absence at Washington City.

I gratefully acknowledge the compliment of your invitation to deliver one of a course of lectures, during the present winter, before the Mercantile Library Association of Bosston.

I am well assured of the highly respectable character, and of the laudable objects of your *literary* association, and no body of the kind could have been more honored than you have been by the illustrious orators and statesmen who have shed upon your lectures the lights of their great minds. I have no doubt too of the "cordial welcome" I would receive from "very many" of your hospitable citizens; but it is not in my power, gentlemen, to accept your invitation. The situation of my private affairs, and the duty of preparing for months to come for new scenes of public service, will engross all my time and attention the whole of the coming winter. I have been compelled to decline every call of the same kind from many quarters in my own State, and other States besides yours.

I sincerely regret this the more, because I have *never yet set my foot* on the beloved soil of that portion of my country called New England. This has not been owing to any antagonism on my part towards that favored section. Massachusetts especially, I have been taught to venerate and cherish as the elder sister of Virginia. When I reflect upon their attitudes and relations in the darkness and gloom of the night of revolution—when I listen to their hails, sister to sister—Virginia to Massachusetts, Massachusetts to Virginia—in the "times which tried men's souls"—when I watch the fires kindling on the heights of Boston, and see Virginia going forth across the rivers and over the land, by the sea, leading her best beloved son by the hand, dripping blood and tears at every step there and back, leaving *him* there on post to guard your very city, and to make the oppressors evacuate it!—and when I contrast this picture with the present state of things in our confederacy, which makes you assure me "that the feelings of the people of Massachusetts towards my State are not those of antagonism," I gush forth in anguish and ask—Why a necessity for such assurance? Why any antagonism between these, the devoted States of Hancock and Washington? May God in his mercy and in love guide them, as of yore! May they ever be cemented in union by the blood of the revolution! And whenever another night of gloom and trial shall come, may they hail and cheer each other on again to victory, for civil and religious liberty.

Yours truly,

HENRY A. WISE.

To CHARLES G. CHASE and others, committee, &c.

POWERFUL LETTER FROM THE HON. H. A. WISE TO THE NATIONAL DEMOCRATIC MEETING IN NEW YORK.

ONLY, NEAR ONANCOCK,
Thursday, October 18, 1855.

GENTLEMEN :—I gratefully acknowledge yours of the 10th, post-marked the 13th, and regret that it is not in my power to accept your invitation to attend and address a mass meeting of the National Democratic party of the City and County of New York, at the Metropolitan Theatre, on Monday, the 22d inst. The situation of my family is such that I cannot leave home before some time after the 22d instant, and I could not, from the date of receiving your letter, reach New York by that day in person ; but I give you a fervent, and I would gladly make it an effectual response.

I have carefully examined the platform which you inclosed of your late Convention, held at Weiting Hall in the City of Syracuse, August 23, 1855, and I hail the National Democracy of New York as brethren worthy to be accredited in faith and accepted in fellowship by every patriot in the land. You are national, not in the sense of consolidation, but in the constitutional sense ; you are national, as opposed to exclusive and sectional ; and you are national, not like the party of "ebony and topaz," not like the "light-houses in the skies" of the younger Adams in 1828, nor like the "fusion of confusion" party in these days of later "isms ;" not "National Republican," but you are "National Democratic." You assert your devotion to the Constitution ; reindorse, in theory and practice, the resolutions of the Democratic National Conventions of 1848 and 1849, and you obey the lesson of the fathers by recurring to frugality and economy, and to all "the fundamental principles of free government" in the administration of public affairs. In all these I heartily concur, and unite still further with you upon the doctrine of State Rights and strict construction of the Constitution as applied to all questions, and particularly to domestic State questions, and the principle of non-intervention by Congress, so as not to deprive States of their sovereign rights, individuals of their private rights, and the people of the Territories of their just and natural political powers.

The Constitution, and not any temporary and temporizing compromise statute, is the true and only standard of national right. The Constitution, in its strict sense, and not according to the latitudinarian construction of a loose federal majority ; the Constitution, which leaves all powers not expressly granted where it found them, the reserved rights of the sovereign States ; the Constitution, which created certain federal relations and rights of private citizens, among the most important of which is perfect equality between citizens of the respective States on the common grounds of federal jurisdiction ; perfect comity between the citizens of State and States, and common property between them in the national domain and dominion ; the Constitution is the law of our Confederacy. It is no respecter of persons ; it holds all alike, and equally under its protecting guardianship wherever it applies. It pries not into your private possession, nor into mine. It knows not whether you own one species of property or I another. It recognizes us only as citizens of co-equal State sovereignties, who are confederated under its shield, and it provides protection for whatever right belongs to either of us on ground which belongs to both. The mere municipal authority, the Congress cannot deprive States and their citizens of this equality, this comity, and this common property of the Confederacy.

If you may go to the common Territory with what is rightfully yours in New York, I may meet you there with whatever is lawfully mine in Virginia. Congress may not say that I shall not migrate with slave property and hold it there ; for if they may say that, they may, in like manner, say that you shall not go there with horses and household goods, and hold them ; and if they may declare against the right of either, they may invade inalienable rights, and enact laws not within the competency of legislation.

The sovereign act of defining what shall and what shall not be tenable property by the citizen, can be determined only by the conventional power of the people, forming organic law—a Constitution changing a Territory into a State. Until the new State comes into being, no power upon earth can lawfully deprive you of your horses and household goods, or me of my slave in Kansas, unless the private property be taken for public use with just compensation. And, gentlemen, you say truly "that the peace and quiet of the country demand that it should be left to the people of the Territories to determine for themselves," what their Constitution of Government shall be, not only in respect to slavery, but every other local question. The public peace is endangered by this "disturbing subject." It is a practical question of right, and threatens to be one of force. Force has already been exerted "on the border," and in the face of this danger there is an organized "Fusion" which must, if persisted in, compel a resort to arms in order to resist evil spirits, combined to repeal the "Kansas Nebraska bill, and to re-establish the Missouri Prohibition."

Prior to 1819-20, the Constitution reigned supreme on this subject. It was then invaded by a repealable, partial, sectional statute, called the Missouri Compromise. It was the first separation of the States—it first sectioned the country like a survey of the public lands—it first said to the people the dividing language of Lot and Abraham—to some "go North" to some "go South" —it was the first line which divided North from South, more in feeling than in fact. Did it not make a geographical demarcation—a line of latitude, the boundary of legal limitations, and determine that what was constitutional on one side of it, should be unconstitutional on the other side of it? No, said its friends at the time of its passage, it leaves slavery to be governed by the law of climate. It is a climatory not a territorial or sectional line. It means to "follow nature," to let Jack Frost be king of the subject; as slavery was profitable South, and as frost pinched negroe's toes and fingers too sharp north of 36.30 for it to be profitable there, the question never should be raised con-slavery south, nor pro-slavery north of that line of latitude. Well admitting this to be a more consistent and rational construction of the "agreement to disagree," did the "fanatics of fusion" so abide it? Never! In every phase of the Compromise, first and last, they have broken its letter and spirit. Incessantly they have raised the question con-slavery South and North, East and West everywhere. In the States and Territories and District, in the Indian country on the trade in transitu between States, Districts and Territories, on the acquisition of territory, on the organization and admission of States into the Union, on questions of peace and war, ever, everywhere, always, in season and out of season, they have raised the question against slavery, until they have, on various occasions, nearly raised the very demon of civil war and disunion! They have harbored English emissaries; raised foreign funds; wielded associated influence and capital; wearied Congress with petitions; fatigued the public mind with compromises; filled it with reviling and abuse; pensioned press, pulpit, preacher, teacher; run underground railroads; spirited away runaways; have scattered broadcast tales of holy horrors; painted on the stage, scenes; written log-cabin novels; lectured, ranted, rioted, until they have made us a divided people, until they have cut the continent in two by a line of border feuds; until they have separated our churches; set us apart socially, at the watering and other places, and until they have engendered a sectional antagonism more becoming enemies in hostile array, than tolerant neighbors even, much less "united brethren"—children of one father—children of a common country, the only children the Father of that country ever had, whose farewell is still our warning!

Within the year I have stood on the rock of Point Pleasant overlooking the grave of Cornstalk, the battle ground between the Indian and the Long Knife, fattened by the blood of the conquest, whereby Virginia secured the eminent domain of the whole Northwest Territory. There before me spread out that vast domain, now a giant group of civilized sovereignties, empires of power, a compact tier of free States! Who made them free States? Their mother slave State. Virginia, by her deed of cession, on her own conditions, with a liberality large as a love of continental country, made Ohio and her sisters of the Northwest Territory free States. Her's was no Wilmot Proviso. It was a whole and entire grant to freedom, the first ever made upon earth like it, and made before the Constitution of the United States was formed. After "a more perfect Union" was formed, a permanent, uniform, universal, organic law began to reign. It left the domestic institutions with the States. It defines the only cases where the Federal authority can intervene. One of the cases is that of a slave flying from one State to another, he shall be restored to his master. By a double tier of laws, Federal and State, by constitutional and by statute laws, the master may reclaim him. And yet, gentlemen, though thus fortified by laws, organic and legislative, State and Federal, I might as well have a thousand dollars floating on a chip in the Ohio river, as to own a slave worth that sum on the Virginia shores of that river! What then? The laws do not reign! The very free soil which Virginia first consecrated on the continent is made the underground for the railroads of her runaways!

Gentlemen, Mr. Webster once asked a group of Southern members of Congress, of whom I was one, with an effect I can never forget: "Shall your children be aliens to my children—shall my children be aliens to your children?" And now whilst Fusionists are "ding-donging" us about aliens and foreign influence, I ask, in the language of Scripture: "Who is our brother?" Shall Ohio be alien and enemy to Virginia?—shall Virginia be alien and enemy to Ohio?—Should Ohio be thus a land of refuge from her mother State?—Was it for this that the North West was ceded?—that Ohio was made perpetually free by Virginia? Bitter, bitter reflections for a Virginia son, proud of what his mother State has done for liberty and union! I looked up and down the Ohio and Kanawha river valleys, and saw the richest soil and minerals—the most beautiful lands I have ever known God's sun to shine upon, or heaven's dews to water; lands more valuable for slave labor than any others to be found in our limits. And yet no slave can safely be carried there to labor. And what the State of Ohio is to the frontier tier of counties on those rivers, they soon must become to the counties behind them in the interior of Virginia, because no tie, no interest, no association of slavery can exist there. Thus, like the cancer, "Freesoil and Fusion" are eating into our very vitals. Thus are we constricted in our rights of property, in our peace and personal safety! With this example, can you wonder that the State of Missouri should be deeply excited and interested by the attempt of associated wealth and influence—perhaps foreign influence in part—to constrict her border in like manner by a cordon of "Fusion and Freesoil?" Tell me, gentlemen, would any foreign power be allowed to insult and endanger the whole nation as the slave-holding States and their citizens are outraged in every offensive form by the Fusionists of the North? Tell me not they are weak and harmless when they can send so many Senators and Representatives to Congress—when they can form the most formidable political parties—so long as they can seize and hold such States as the venerable mother State of Hancock and desecrate Faneuil Hall—so long as they can carry Ohio—so long as they can distract and divide and dwarf in the Union the very Empire State of New York! What, then, is to be done? The "envy, hatred, malice and all uncharitableness" which this engenders cannot continue to smoulder much longer without bursting out into a general and devouring flame. The Kansas-Nebraska bill repealed the odious mark whence malice and mischief hurled incendiary torches across the border line. It removed a heart-burning statute of sectionalism and attempted to restore peace under the ægis of the Constitution. But the cry is now: "Repeal of the Kansas-Nebraska bill and restoration of the Missouri Compromise!" This raises the issue: "Shall the Constitution reign as it did reign from the year 1789 to the years 1819-20?" With head and heart, might and soul, I unite with you for the reign of the Constitution over all compromises! No higher, no lower law than the Constitution.

Are the Fusionists, indeed, fatally bent on dissolution of the Union, or a civil, sectional war? I tell you solemnly, that depends upon the strength, nerve, virtue and wisdom of the sound, conscientious, conservative patriots in the North. If you can come to the aid of the Constitution, at this crisis, big with the fate of the Union, it may be saved. God Almighty grant it! The Union, I say to you, as I have said to the South, as I have said first and said last and delight to repeat—the Union is one of the most precious rights of the States. I never meant thereby to express the sentiment implied by the platform of the Pandemoniums at Philadelphia—that, *per se*, it is the most precious of rights, and must be preserved at every sacrifice. I never uttered such error as that; but I do say that the Union is the sacred palladium of our highest and holiest rights. It is, if you please, not of itself liberty, it is not equality, it is not sovereignty, it is not independence—it is not especially, the end of our government, but it is the means by which all the ends we ought to aim at are secured, and it is the means which Washington relied on as indispensable to our existence as a people. It is the "E Pluribus Unum" by which one is made thirty-one in strength, by which Virginia's sovereignty is fortified thirty-fold. Measured by what it is capable of attaining, by what it binds and holds fast, by what it has done and may do yet for this people and all men, it is inestimable. It achieved the American Revolution, the Declaration of Independence, the Constitution, settlement of the public lands, the land system, the peace policy, the second war for "free trade and sailor's rights," the principles of neutral rights, the long line of measures for development and progress of the human species, the acquisitions from Mexico, and is the bulwark of freedom and the hope of the oppressed throughout the world. It does not consist in the mere confederacy or joining of States. It consists in the Constitution, in the love and affection and brotherhood of our people throughout the country. If these links be broken it is dissolved. If broken and it binds at all, it will bind as a chain and it will gall as a chain, and it will cease to bind when fetters find foes who will not be bound by them. I for one had rather see the continent shaken by earthquakes than to see the Union of these States dissolved, but it is simply the means of innumerable and inestimable ends of good; and if it ceases to subserve them, to secure liberty, equality, sovereignty, independence, peace, power, and pre-eminence among the nations of the earth, let it meet its fate! Why make a sacrifice to save it? We will not count its cost—no mere material interest could weigh it down in the scales; but it is with the political union of the States as it is with the matrimonial union of persons; the oath of the altar, love, truth, constancy, fidelity require devotion, devotion to the last extremity—to bear and forbear—to make any and every honorable sacrifice—to count mere interest nothing; but if honor be touched, then on the instant, to dissolve the bands which bind to infamy, though it break the bands which bind to life! And, I ask, will not the slave States be dishonored if they allow themselves to be provincialized by being excluded from equality in the Union! The Fusionists intend that they shall be so dishonored. Their intent shall never be executed! We will cling to the Constitution, and when that is assailed, we will defend it with all the means which God and nature have put into our hands; and when these fail, the Union, the eagle, the flag, will be but emblems of a past Republic, destroyed by a weakness and wickedness unparalleled in the folly and crime of mankind! We demand nothing else but good faith in keeping the covenants of the Constitution. We demand not that any other people should be slaveholders. We will certainly not force a slave upon their service. But we do demand to be "let alone"—to be left undisturbed in our rights, and unmolested to enjoy the property protected by our laws. If we are not allowed to be and remain at peace, we must prepare for war. The hypocrites and knaves who are trading on the pious attachment of our people to the Union will find, when it is too late, that slaveholders can be driven to self-defence, and that they can trust—but I forbear! We will unite to prevent horrors which it is painful to imagine in the worst, even, of contingencies to come.

As to the secret "Americans"—the Know Nothings—day has broke upon them. And it is amusing to see Sam's bats and owls of midnight, flitting and flapping, blind, about in the sunlight. They are seeking sorrily to skulk from light and sight—here some flap back to poor, deserted Whiggery, and there some escape to the "Republican" fusion. The day has dissolved the charm. The true bird of America, Jove's own eagle, is on a wing that never tires, in the lambent light of the mid-heavens. Uncle Sam has roused himself and shaken off the slumber and stupor of the night dreams, and is at his active work in broad day.

The devil baited the hooks of some preachers with the politics of the Pope's big toe; and the hooks of some politicians with the unco-righteousness of a knavish priestcraft, and set them bobbing together for the souls of dupes, for the corruption of the Church, and for the destruction of the State. No heat but one could have ever welded such a fusion. In the Shades they were taught their parts by the gloom light of the Dark Lantern! But—

"The sun is in the heavens, and life on earth!"

Day has caught them in their incantations, and light is dispelling their mysteries. The next you will see of Sam, he will be on his knees praying against slavery and John Barleycorn. He has dropped Pope Pius Nonus, and has just discovered, after all he has said about his Holiness' supremacy, that every naturalized Catholic takes an oath expressly to renounce all allegiance to any and every prince, power, potentate, king, sovereign or state, and particularly to the prince, power, potentate, king, sovereign or state, of which he was before a subject. And he begins to admit that if an extra-judicial oath may bind a Know-Nothing to passive obedience and non-resistance to an unseen, intangible, irresponsible, secret oligarchy, that perchance, we may rely on the judicial oaths of naturalized citizens to renounce allegiance to all supremacy whatever except the sovereignty of the United States of North America.

I give you the right hand of fellowship in opposition to the sumptuary laws which have of late years disgraced the codes of some of our States. Why, some Legislatures seem to have lost the horn-books of personal liberty! They are for free soil and free negroes, but war upon the liberties of free white men! They seem to have never known that there were such things, first invented in North America, as bills of rights, defining those which are inalienable and fixing the limits of legislation! Where was the principle of Liquor laws to stop? No where short of invading every inalienable right of individual man. If municipal law cannot touch vested rights, much less can it invade the natural rights of the individual person. In such a dominion as that of England, they may hardly dare to confine the rights of the person to "air, to light and to flowing water," at this day; but here there never was a moment, since colonial times, when the rights of persons were not infinitely extended beyond these out of the reach of legislation. Oh! but they say that such laws are sanitary, not sumptuary. And who made them Hospitalers of Hygeia, health nurses for the people? Health is about as private a possession, about as "*intus et in cute*," personal as any man can be endowed with. Who created a government to turn Quack and proscribe physic? "Physic to the dogs!" There are other things which destroy health besides alcohol. Eating as well as drinking, gluttony as well as drunkenness hurts health. Will any one say that legislation may take charge of my table, and my diet and appetite, and say what I shall eat? If they may prohibit a man from buying and selling whiskey, may they not prohibit his planting and sowing on his own fee-simple soil, of his buying and selling the corn and rye from which the whiskey is distilled? Again, French corsets have hurt more the health of whole generations, have crippled for their own lives and for their posterity too, more women and children than ever John Barleycorn slew of men! Shall a Hiss committee be allowed by law to inspect Madame's and Miss's chambers, and see whether whalebone and hard cord encompass ladies' waists too tight? The idea would be ridiculous, if it was not so insufferably tyrannous. You cannot legislate men to morality; you must educate them to liberty and virtue. Manners and morals must begin at the mother's knee; must be trained in the schools, and home and domestic teaching must give to the country pupils fit for the schools, and the schools must give to the country a people who will require no such despotic laws. They don't suit a people fit to be free; they corrupt and demoralize a people already fit to be slaves. The last source I would appeal to, for temperance in eating and drinking, is a Legislature, Federal or State. O! ye Metropolitan high livers! what tales Champagne and London Dock, and canvas backs, and terrapins, and oysters could tell upon your example of abstemiousness and self-denial! How your temperance tells upon your livers! and your legislation, too, at times! The truth is, all these "isms" come from the same nidus of the same cocatrix. They come from the Scribes and Pharisees, who would take care of others' consciences; they are inventions of ambitious priestcraft—or men who have a little religion to help their secular affairs, and who are a little worldly to help their religious affairs—of "preachers of Christian politics," who are subtlely aspiring to civil, secular and political power—of men who don't "render unto Cæsar the things which are Cæsar's," nor "unto God the things which are God's"—of hypocrites who would superserviceably cut off an ear for their Master with the sword, without his orders and against his law, and who would deny Him thrice before the cock crew once. And these are aided by cowardly and knavish politicians, who either fear or fawn upon their secret and sinister influences. We have only to drive out all such from the temple, as the dove-sellers were driven out by the Master whose "pure and undefiled religion before God and the Father is, to visit the widow and the fatherless, and to keep one's self unspotted from the world!"

Finally, gentlemen, according with you, as I do, in the leading principles of your platform, I cordially accept your invitation to unite with you in engrafting them upon the policy of the country. And I especially concur with you in the sentiment that it is upon principle alone we ought to unite; and that all coalitions between those who essentially differ on cardinal points, are unprincipled and demoralizing. And here I might pause; but, long as this letter is, I have a word more to say. I hope I have answered your kind compliment in its own spirit, without enquiring whether your have any alias—any other name under Heaven by which you are known among men than that of National Democrats. I have purposely omitted to do so.

Like yourselves, another body of Democrats of New York, lately, approached me fairly and openly, and I responded gratefully to them as I do to you. I was soon upbraided with having given "aid and comfort" to a certain party called "Softs." Now, some one may say that I have likewise given in adhesion to the Hards of New York. Well, all I can say for myself is, that I don't mean to know any Hard or Soft names for my friends who will unite with me in "the mission of the Democracy to proclaim and maintain the great doctrine of civil and religious liberty, and to uphold and enforce the constitution in its sublime principles of justice and equality."

You must not wonder that your Democratic friends in Virginia are often confused by names and things in New York. We wish to see a united Democracy there on the old grounds of Jefferson and Jackson. We hear of Hard, and Soft, and Half Shells, and the ideas we form of them can be best illustrated by a subject of natural history. We have in our waters gentlemen, a crustaceous animal called a crab—a sea fish, with fins and claws at both ends, and it can run either end foremost. Poke at him this way and he runs that—that way and he runs this! He is remarkable, gentlemen, for his transformations. At one time catch him and crack his claw and his shell is hard, very hard, hard enough for barnacles to grow upon his back, and it will not separate or be detached from the inner cuticle. In that state he is the Hard Crab proper. At another time, catch him and crack his claw—when he is hard, be sure to crack his claw, gentlemen, and you will find that, though his outer shell is still very hard, yet it will separate and can be detached from the inner cuticle or film over the muscles. He is then called the "Peeler," his shell will peal off from, without breaking, the inner shell. Later, catch him and you need not crack his claw to see what he is, for his outer shell is then opening at every suture, and the crab is swelling out of its Hard and taking upon itself its Soft shell. In that state he is called a "Buster," bursting his shell. And as "Peeler" or "Buster" he is very fat, and a bait fit to catch the very "monarchs of the deep" with! Later still, he has slipped out of his hard shell, by a sort of peristaltic motion, and left it along the strand, and has become wholly a soft crab. In that state he is good bait too, and is preyed upon by hard crabs and other fishes, and he is inert and can hardly crawl out of harm's way. Then, again, this same crab, gentlemen, begins to harden from soft to hard again, as he had before softened from hard to soft. Found in this, his second intermediate state, he has become poor but more active, is not so good for bait, and he is called a "Buckram," for that he is so like the fabric of that name, and his shell is then flexible like vellum. So that you see we have an idea of some Hards who are "Peelers," tending to Soft, and of some Softs who are "Buckrams," tending to Hards. And there is such a Hardening to Soft, and such a Softening to Hard, that we cannot distinguish the politicians of New York as we do crabs—sometimes by sight, sometimes by touch, and sometimes by cracking their claws. But this I do say, that I think I can see you are Democrats; that I can distinguish you, unmistakably, by the platform of principle you have put forth, and I am anxious and ready to stand by and with and for any portion of the Democracy of New York who will unite on the platform of civil and religious liberty, as defined by the constitution and bills of rights of our State and Federal governments, and as defended by our State sovereignties and our Federal Union. I cannot and will not unite with any Wilmot Proviso, with any dark lantern, or with any sumptuary law party!

And how is it that New York is divided against herself in this great cause, "which, down the tide of time, unborn ages yet will honor and admire?" She, the Empire State—she, the centre of commerce—she, the city set upon a hill, to waste her strength, to expend her substance, to dwarf her influence, to lower her dignity, to eclipse the light of her own fame and glory by distracting divisions, by disastrous discord, by confusion of her friends and fusion of her foes! Rally and rescue! Shall the spoils separate us from each other and from our country? No! nor principalities, nor powers, nor things present, nor things to come. We will strike together, and strike home for our God, our Country and our Constitution!

Yours, in the faith,

HENRY A. WISE.

To *Alex'r C. Morton*, Chairman, &c. &c.

THE KNOW NOTHING PHILADELPHIA PLATFOM.

NOTES AND COMMENTS.

On the 14th June, 1855, an Astrologer announced in the papers that there was to be a grand conjunction of the sun, moon, and the planet Saturn, which portended, among other things, fires, diseases, accidents, and loss of reputation to the vulgar. This dire conjunction brought forth, also, the platform of the Know Nothing Convention. Who, after this, shall doubt the influence of the stars! Saturn is of course the planet that presides over the destinies of Sam, their initials being the same. But Saturn alone could do nothing; he was compelled to call in the assistance of the sun and moon, and then, with "a long pull, a strong pull, and a pull altogether," Sam was delivered of a Platform. But the operation broke him in two:

Parturient montes; nascitur ridiculus mus.

From all parts of the country came the picked men of the party. There was assembled the very flower of Know Nothingism, the quintessence, the *adar gul* of that inimitable Order. The convention was the mirror of Sambodum. But this was not enough: the cream of this incomparable galaxy was skimmed off and set apart to elaborate a scheme of principles wherewith to butter the brains of the people. And now, with the aid of the sun, moon and Saturn, to say nothing of his rings and his moons, here it is.

On looking it over, however, the first impression that is felt, is a doubt as to its authenticity. In all fairness, the opinion of the public gave the Know Nothings credit for that common degree of ability that is found in the ordinary proceedings of the most unpretending meetings of citizens, everywhere in our country. There are some very respectable truisms, trite and hackneyed by frequent repetition, indeed, in the platform. But they are out of place, vaguely expressed, and utterly insignificant where they stand. They do not save the rest of the document, they infuse no life into the inert pile. Yet, since there is every appearance of its official character, and meetings of Know Nothings have endorsed it, let us regard it as authentic.

I. The first Article is decidedly misplaced in a declaration of political principles. Any one in the least imbued with religious feeling, must be shocked to see the Deity called down, as it were, to preside over a deliberation such as this Know Nothing Convention must have presented. For, in reading this article, the mind recalls a certain other platform of more ancient date and higher sanction, having as a clause of its first article: "Thou shalt not take the name of the Lord thy God in vain; for the Lord will not hold him guiltless that taketh his name in vain." What right had the Convention to disregard the commonest decencies which even the irreligious observe before the sober eye of the public? Besides, did it not occur to any one of that assembly that it ill became the state of mortality to assume that tone of patronizing superiority towards the Supreme Being, which would be offensive and impertinent, towards a mere man whose dignity of character, age or station entitled him to particular respect?

But what, in the name of all the darkness of Egypt, is to be understood by "every step by which we have advanced to the *character* of an independent nation?" or, again, by "some token of providential *agency*." It is scarcely possible even to speak of this first article without the appearance of profaneness. But surely the observation may be made that there would have been, at least, some meaning in a "token of providential *favor*." There is no Know Nothing but must have had an opportunity of hearing that not only our career as a nation is conducted by providential agency, but the very least occurrence that takes place is the result of that agency. Not a sparrow can fall to the ground without it.

Whatever reason can be supposed to have led to this "acknowledgment," by that same reason the doctrine of the Trinity, the immortality of the soul, and a state of future reward and punishment, or eternal responsibility, ought to have been inserted in the Platform. And their non-appearance is, in view of the first article, a fair and irresistible presumption that the Know Nothing leaders knew they could not obtain a concurrence of the majority of the body to these points; or, that they themselves were not willing to profess them.

II. The second Article of their creed is composed of as much froth and fustian, and as many long words of three, four and five syllables, about patriotism, the revolution, &c., &c., as could be packed into the space assigned. "Sentiments of profoundly intense American feeling!" (Quotha!) This is piling up the agony to some purpose: not content with a feeling, or the sentiment of a feeling, they must have a profoundly intense feeling to have a sentiment of, to be put under development and cultivation, like a tender exotic under a glass bell, to be put into the second article of the Platform—and no where else. For out of this article there is mighty little account made of "emulation and veneration," or "patriotism and heroism," or "institutions and constitutions." Their passionate attachment is to the emoluments of the offices they are longing for, and most of them would and will, in time to come, be seen kicking the National Platform from Dan to Beersheba, if a five, three or two thousand dollar office is danced before their eyes, as no small portion of them are even now kicking and trampling upon the Constitution and laws of the United States.

III. The third Article is, "The maintenance of the Union of these United States." Well done! Is it really possible that Sam, in his High-mightiness will condescend to let us preserve the Union? We ought to be thankful. But not too fast—there is a qualification: "as the paramount political good." This spoils all. The beginning was excellent and complete in itself. Sam was not willing, however, to leave us the Union simply and unconditionally. The existence of the clique of political agitators, who are endeavoring to create a new party, alone is a danger to our Union. The prominence they assign to this question of the maintenance of the Union, is most inauspicious. And their evident determination to agitate the subject, is an imminent peril to that Union, which it behooves every good citizen of the republic to watch with the utmost solicitude. Fortunately, the party has at every turn added something to the public indignation, that its first rumored existence created. And this attitude will only serve to increase it. Their attack is very insidious; for thus they proceed. The Union, they say, is in danger, it must be maintained, *we* must maintain it. Then, as it becomes necessary to make the people believe all this, they magnify whatever they can force into an opposition to the Union, or whatever they can bring forward as a source of disunion, thereby creating and extending the very peril they pretend to put down. Sly Sam, he is quite a Nic Macchiavelli on a small scale. It was in this manner the Convention at Philadelphia gave that importance to the fanatics of the North which otherwise they could not have attained. It enabled them to assume the appearance of a dignified minority retiring undismayed, from the injustice of force and numbers. By such tricks the Know Nothings would justify all this outcry about Union. They are endeavoring to get up something like an opposition to it that they may appear to have something to battle with on that ground.

IV. More fine speeches. Obedience to the Constitution! "A habit of reverential obedience to the laws!" When the Know Nothings recognise that it is necessary for them solemnly to assure the people that they will obey the Constitution and laws, it is a case for the merry to laugh at, and the grave to pity. But mark the difference! There is no devotion or loyalty to the Constitution expressed here; nothing but a cold obedience, very much as when men obey and submit to laws that condemn them. But they have a tender and sacred regard for certain acts of statesmanship, &c. What is meant by this? Whatever particular act may be referred to, it is plain the Know Nothings set above the laws, the compact of Union, and the Constitution in their political devotions, certain acts of statesmanship, as a fixed and settled national policy. There is a lurking peril here, skillfully concealed, it is true, and which, to develope, would require more space than we can give to the whole platform.

V. Here they show what they mean by reverence for the laws. They only require that the laws be radically revised. Not so bad for Sam! When he is about to declare himself in opposition to anything, he first displays any amount of respect and veneration for it.

VI. In Article sixth, the Know Nothings continue to show their regard for the laws by repealing, modifying, &c., another whole class of them. Most excellent Sam! While the people are growing more jealous of Federal tendencies, here is a Convention sending out its decrees to the State Legislatures.

Those who framed our Constitution never intended that a body called the National Council, should assume the part of dictator, pronounce upon the details of legislative enactments in the States; the action of Congress; the regulation of the Executive; the Constitution and the Union; a national system of education; the limitation of the religious rights or opinions of the people; and set forth a peculiar sectarian definition of the Supreme Being. It is fortunate that this body, insignificant in itself, should have been rendered still more so, by a violent disruption and secession; fortunate that its members are such political ciphers that their ukase possesses no shade of authority.

Our American form of government recognizes no such thing as a National Council. Let the Know Nothings disguise themselves as they will, they never hit upon the true American feeling, tone, look and bearing. Least of all can they do so by reviving the old Whig attempts to "palsy the will of the constituent," such as is this of a National Council.

VII. If the reader has any inclination to risibility, it will be almost impossible to read the 7th Article without a smile or even a genuine, frank, hearty laugh. This article is specially adapted to assist digestion. "Corrupt means of forcing upon people political creeds!" Was ever a creed forced upon people before in this land with such violence as Know Nothingism? Some curious experiments were once made by a naturalist in forcing turkies to swallow iron balls covered with strong and sharp prickles. The operations of Sam are very similar to those experiments; and his platform to those iron balls. When the turkies were killed, it was found that the action of their internal organs had completely worn down the iron spikes, so that no sign of them remained. Most of the principles of this platform appear to be, in the same way, worn down by the individual moral gizzards of those who assume to belong to that party. Sam further professes admiration for the maxim that "Office should seek the man, and not man the office." Is not this an exquisitely touching specimen of Arcadian simplicity and verdant innocence? What high esteem Sam has shown for this sentiment and the will of the people in the case of Franklin Pierce and Henry A. Wise!

VIII. If in the 8th Article the National Council had commenced by saying, "Blue is yellow: to conclude, therefore, blue is red," they would have been quite as logical as they are in what they do say. But if Sam will be absurd, he is unfortunate in always being so when on the subject of religion. He may rest assured that Americans intend to govern America without requiring his permission. And the proof is, that no share of administration will be entrusted to the Grand Mogul or his adherents, for we Americans have a natural antipathy for despotism.

IX. This is one of the prickles which Know Nothing gizzards will soonest wear down.

X. Here is the first and only principle in the platform that properly belongs to an exposition of political views by a party. It is, moreover, expressed in a sensible, straightforward manner. It is fairly opening a plain issue for public opinion, which the people will settle to their satisfaction. Sam would do well to press this matter vigorously.

XI. The first two lines here are excellent in themselves. But the principle they contain is not altogether proper for a party platform. However, the thing is so good in itself, that this would matter little. But Sam, with his usual propensity for spoiling his own work when not already bad, immediately proceeds to overlay it with a mass of verbiage that completely alters its first significance. The question of the Bible in schools is, in particular, misplaced in a platform of party principles.

But on behalf of the good people of these United States, one request is to be made of the Know Nothings. Let them think, act and speak as they will; let them rage on to their satisfaction about Catholic and Foreigner; but let them not meddle with education. Their party is going to pieces before it is fairly built up, but a threat like this would cut short the slender chances of popularity they have remaining. A rush of fanatics from Boston and New York would be let loose to propagate Abolitionism, Bloomerism, Fourierism, and every pestilent device of the denizens of those menageries of monomaniacs, throughout all our borders. The newspaper is the whole, or almost the whole education of numbers; and a noble system of morals, religion, politics, historical, philosophical and social science, and taste in literature and art, might be diffused by a well-conducted press. The newspaper is a school, without seeming so, which may disseminate throughout the community a spirit of high refinement and cultivation, maintaining that due balance between different important subjects which it is so difficult to adjust; rendering rightful honor to rare examples of morality and piety, and so spreading the emulation of these qualities; keeping alive among the people a correct understanding of the political principles upon which our constitution, laws and social characteristics are founded, in which lie the sources of our independence and happiness as men and as a nation; and reflecting an image of the progress of the useful and finer arts which belong to true civilization and enlightenment. The career of Benjamin Franklin, which commenced with a newspaper, to end with the Declaration of Independence, may be referred to here as an illustration of this subject. But rake up New England, New York and Pennsylvania—rake up the Know Nothing press everywhere, and it will appear what Sam is likely to do in this matter, to say nothing of the stupendous system of deception he has saved from the ruins of the Whig party.

XII. Another pretended defence of the Union. Sam, however, has so little of our national character in his composition, that he is incapable of barely understanding what union means. His essential instincts are against union. From the first it was necessary to bind his adherents by oath to keep them united together, and to veil their proceedings in secrecy to hide their dissensions. No sooner do the Know Nothings attempt to come out as a national party, than they divide in two. Is not this a fine sample of union? They have sown dissension between Protestant and Catholic. Is this their idea of union? They have arrayed native against foreigner, parent against son. Is this union? They have even formed a plan of dividing American from American by secret organization. They have built a wall between North and South, where there was only a narrow ditch before. They have introduced a quarrel between the people and the executive, where before, it was understood and agreed, that the executive was the people, that it stood for and represented them. They have carried the harsh and bitter spirit of division into the matter of education. But to pursue the enumeration no farther, we ask again, are not these fine samples of Sam's conception of union?

Are the Know Nothings entitled to prate about maintaining the Union? As well might a man born blind attempt to paint the rainbow, the finest natural emblem of the covenant of union, as Sam to persuade the people to entrust this Union of sovereign States to his care.

Sam makes the following astounding announcement: "There can be no dishonour in submitting to the laws". Now this looks so like a very commonplace truism, every citizen should respect the laws, that at first it appears to be mere filling up. But wishing to do Sam justice, a closer examination leads to the question: why did he give it this peculiar form of expression? Then, looking to see what laws in particular are referred to, it appears that existing laws on the subject of slavery are meant. This lets in a flash of light. And now we fully conceive this brilliant sentiment: "There can be no dishonor in *submitting* to the laws"—oh, no; the dishonor lies upon the head of those who *made* the laws. This is what Sam intends by his, at first, unaccountable mention of dishonor.

And now, how is Sam going to *submit* to these laws? His platform, Articles IV., V., VI., the reader has not forgotten, shows that his way of submitting to the laws is to set about a "radical and essential" "revision," "modification" and "repeal" of the laws. A word to the wise.

There is little doubt that in the National Council the words Union, Constitution, and some others were incessantly repeated, but still less that the word by far most frequently uttered, and most vehemently by every fragment of that disunited body, was Treason. If every part pronounced this of the rest, is it too much to make a unanimous vote of the council of it, to be applied to the whole body?

XIII. Is a very pretty sentiment.

XIV. Here Sam fulfils a prediction we made long ago. His self importance made him altogether too talkative to refrain from letting out his secret on the least occasion. He now gives up the attempt. And, like Samson of old, the Delilah of hope having fondled the mystery out of him, will cut off his locks; and he will lose the only source of his strength. No more tying together of foxes by the tail; no more slaughters with the jawbone of an ass! Alas, poor Sammy!

From the Union.

FOREIGN-BORN CITIZENS IN THE AMERICAN REVOLUTION.

The writer of this communication is a native citizen of the United States, and his ancestors, for not less than six generations, were also natives of this country. This circumstance will tend to show that he can have no natural bias or prejudice in favor of foreigners. In common with other native citizens, he has sometimes heard with regret of newly-arrived foreigners interfering with or assuming an undue importance in our elections, and lacking that modest deference to intelligent native-born citizens that common sense urges as due to them, and which is also due, to a certain extent, to the intelligent foreign-born citizens of long residence among us. But is it prudent or just for this cause to join in a general and indiscriminate crusade against all foreigners? As regards the prudence of such a course, are we not suffering now, in the high prices of all kinds of edible products, for the want of thousands of brawny arms to subdue our almost countless acres of uncultivated land? And, as regards its justice, are we not morally bound to look to our history, and to reflect that this is a country which, with the exception of a few Indian tribes, is made up of emigration—of Penn and his peaceful colonists, to Pennsylvania; of the Pilgrim Fathers, driven to Plymouth Rock; of Calvert and his followers, seeking religious liberty on the shores of Maryland; of the Huguenots, taking refuge in South Carolina; and of innumerable companies of colonists ever since, fleeing from religious and political persecutions, and finding an asylum in this hitherto happy country? In the language of Hezekiah Niles' patriotic song—

> "'Tis my now native land, happy land of the free;
> 'Tis the last hope of all men—of sweet liberty!"

Yes! the liberty of conscience, the liberty of speech, and the liberty of participating in "the pursuit of happiness," so long as there is no trenching on the rights of a neighbor.

But I do not propose to enter into an argument on the propriety of a general disfranchisement of foreigners—a subject which has already been so ably argued as to leave those who favored extreme disqualification with hardly any ground to stand upon—but simply to show how large a debt we had contracted towards persons of foreign birth for the liberty we now enjoy—liberties achieved by those gallant spirits, mostly native, but many of them foreign, who in our revolutionary war battled for American independence, and the rights of civil and religious freedom.

I have no immediate means of determining what number of valiant men born out of the country drew the sword and shouldered the musket in our revolutionary contest; but no man can read any history of that important period of our national existence without being satisfied that there were thousands so engaged. We have, however, abundant evidence to show that many of those persons rendered themselves illustrious by their heroic deeds, and that the record of "the times that tried men's souls" has woven for them an imperishable chaplet. I will cite the names of a few:

Commodore John Barry, born in the county of Wexford, Ireland, commanded the ship Black Prince, that was converted into a vessel of war, and subsequently he was appointed by Congress to command the brig Lexington, of 16 guns; then the Raleigh, of 32 guns; then the frigates Alliance and the United States; and in a number of actions shed lustre on the young flag of America.

Judge George Bryan, born in Dublin, Ireland. His father having given him a sufficiency to establish him in mercantile business, at the age of 21 he embarked for Philadelphia, where he remained until his death. He was a delegate to Congress in 1775, in which he became known for his advocacy of petitions and remonstrances against the arbitrary measures of Great Britain. Soon after the Declaration of Independence he was elected Lieutenant Governor of Pennsylvania, and afterwards Governor of that State. Subsequently he was a member of the Legislature, and then Judge of the Supreme Court of Pennsylvania—such was then the gratitude of the American people for the services of foreign-born citizens.

Captain James Chrystie, born in Edinburg, Scotland, in 1777 was promoted to the command of a company, which he held until the end of the war. On the discovery of Arnold's plot at West Point, Gen. Washington selected Captain Chrystie for an important service, and said to him: "Captain Chrystie, you are to receive no written orders from me. The business is that you proceed with all possible expedition to West Point, and examine particularly the state of that garrison in every respect; and to visit all the intermediate posts for the same purpose. Make this known to no one but the commanding officer at each post; and you are to enjoin on them the secrecy of the grave; commit nothing to writing." Here the General paused. "Has your excellency any further orders?" enquired Captain Chrystie. "Yes," replied the General, "one, and a very sorious one; that is, Captain Chrystie, that on this occasion you are not to let me hear of your being taken prisoner. Do you understand me?" "Perfectly well," replied Captain Chrystie, "you shall not hear of that event." Captain Chrystie proceeded alone, and executed this commission in a satisfactory manner, and made such a report as set the mind of General Washington perfectly at ease.

Charles Clinton, born in Ireland, (father of George Clinton, afterwards Vice-President of the United States,) died in 1773, in the 83d year of his age, conjuring his sons in his last moments to stand by the liberties of their country.

Major Willian Croghan, born in Ireland, was engaged in the battles of Brandywine, Germantown and Monmouth. He was the father of Col. George Croghan, the gallant defender of Fort Sandusky in our second war with Great Britain.

Colonel William Richardson Davie, born in White Haven, England, commanded a battalion of dragoons with much credit during the revolutionary war; and subsequently rose to great eminence at the bar in North Carolina, and was sent as ambassador to France by the elder President Adams.

Major General Horatio Gates, born in England, was called from his retirement in Virginia, and recommended to Congress by General Washington. His great services, especially at Saratoga, have made his name a household word.

Major William Gwinn, born in Ireland, joined the revolutionary army in 1776, and served with credit. He died in Baltimore county in 1819, in the 70th year of his age.

Alexander Hamilton, born in the island of St. Croix, in the West Indies, was distinguished through the revolutionary war for his high qualifications in military science—especially at Yorktown—and was our first Secretary of the Treasury.

General William Irvine, born in Ireland, joined the revolutionary army in 1774; and was an active member of a public meeting recommending Congress to assemble, denouncing the Boston port bill, expressing a sympathy with the sufferers, and declaring their willingness and determination to make any sacrifices necessary for the support of American rights. He was appointed a colonel of a regiment, in command of which he was captured in an attempt to surprise a vanguard of the British army. After his release he became the commanding General of the second Pennsylvania brigade.

Andrew Irvine, a brother to the foregoing, was a lieutenant in the revolutionary war.

Colonel (afterwards General) James Jackson, born in Devon, England, was distinguished for his military services in the South during the revolutionary war. He died in the city of Washington on the 19th of January, 1806, while attending to his duties as a Senator of the United States.

Major John James, born in Ireland, was distinguished for his military services in the South.

Commodore John Paul Jones, born in Galway county, Scotland. His matchless naval prowess and courage told with terrible effect on the mother country.

Major General Baron De Kalb, born in Germany, received eleven wounds in the battle of Camden. To a British officer, who condoled with him, he said: "I thank you for your generous sympathy, but I die the death I always prayed for—the death of a soldier fighting for the rights of man." He survived but a few days. Congress resolved that a monument should be erected to his memory in the town of Annapolis, State of Maryland.

Thaddeus Kosciusko, born in Poland—his fame classic in two hemispheres.

General Hugh Mercer, born in Aberdeen, Scotland, distinguished himself in the battles of Trenton and Princeton.

Major General Richard Montgomery, born in Ireland, fell in the attack on Quebec, December 31, 1775, aged 38. In a debate in the British Parliament, the death of this gallant general was lamented in strains of the most pathetic eloquence that ever were heard in the House of Commons. Three of the principal orators, Mr. Burke, Mr. Fox, and Colonel Barre, vied with each other in the panegyric of that hero. General Burgoyne, though he expressed a strong zeal against the American cause, in a very handsome manner did justice to his merits, and said that all his virtues were abundantly rewarded when they were thus "praised, wept and honored by the muse he loved." Lord North, the prime minister, censured the unqualified liberality of the praises bestowed on General Montgomery by the gentlemen of the opposition, because they were bestowed on a *rebel;* and said he could not join in lamenting his death as a public loss. He admitted that he was brave; that he was able; that he was humane; that he was generous; but still he was only a brave, able, humane and generous rebel; and said that the verse of the tragedy of Cato might be applied to him:

"Curse on his virtues, they've undone his country."

Robert Morris, born in Liverpool, England, was the superintendent of our finances during the revolutionary war, and his credit supplied the country when the military chest had been drained of its last dollar.

Major General William Moultrie, born in England, was distinguished for his heroic services in the revolutionary war, and especially for his defence of the city of Charleston. He was afterwards Governor of South Carolina.

Thomas Paine, born in England, was the author of "Common Sense," "The Crisis," "Rights of Man," &c. Whatever his faults, he rendered powerful aid by his pen to the revolutionary cause.

Count Pulaski, born in Poland, was mortally wounded in defence of the city of Savannah, where Congress has erected a monument to his memory.

Major General Frederick William Steuben, born in Prussia, was a volunteer in the action at Monmouth, and commanded in the trenches at Yorktown on the day which terminated our revolutionary struggle with Great Britain.

Major General Gilbert Lafayette, born in France. In "Dunlap's Pennsylvania Packet," printed in Philadelphia, of August 19, 1777, I find, in a letter from an American in Paris to a gentleman in Pennsylvania, dated April 10, 1777, the following announcement:

"This letter will be put into your hands by the Marquis de Lafayette, of a noble and ancient family in France, connected by birth and marriage with the first in the kingdom, and in possession of an estate of upwards of fourteen thousand pounds sterling per annum, beloved and almost adored by his numerous acquaintance; but preferring glory to every enjoyment which these in the arms of a young and beautiful wife and young family, could give him, he courts danger in defence of our cause, which is here universally celebrated as the cause of mankind."

He came and lent us his powerful aid, shedding his blood in defence of our liberties. From Brandywine to Yorktown his name shines conspicuous in our annals.

Fellow-citizens, in the Representatives' Hall of yonder capitol there are two portraits—one of GEORGE WASHINGTON, the Father of his Country, the other of GILBERT LAFAYETTE, who crossed the ocean to strike for freedom. Will you, with sacrilegious hand and base ingratitude, tear down the latter from those walls in obedience to a senseless fanaticism against foreigners? I trust not.

F. J.

Washington, D. C., May 8, 1855.

From the Richmond Enquirer.

KNOW NOTHINGISM UNVEILED.

We comply with the request of patriotic Democrats in North Carolina and, to-day publish at length the Constitution of the "National Council of the United States of North America," and the State Council of North Carolina, with the Ritual, Degrees and all the other paraphernalia of the most mischievous and dangerous oligarchy that ever conspired against civil and religious liberty. The election in the old North State is rapidly approaching, and our friends are making a gallant fight. They feel confident that the people of North Carolina cannot hesitate as to their duty, when they shall be enlightened as to the trickery and monstrous purposes of a Secret Order, whose inevitable tendency is to destroy all individual freedom of action, and to make Americans the blind and servile instruments of an irresponsible, Jesuitical, proscriptive and tyrannical oligarchy. In North Carolina the Democracy are waging uncompromising war upon Know Nothingism, exposing its dark movements and purposes, and appealing to the intelligence, honesty and patriotism of the people. By such a course the Democracy of Virginia laid "Sam" low—a similar result will be seen in North Carolina. All that the people want is light —and a flood of it is shed upon the subject by the following publication of official Know Nothing documents. They explain themselves, and require no comment:

Constitution of the National Council of the United States of North America.

Article First.

This organization shall be known by the name and title of THE NATIONAL COUNCIL OF THE UNITED STATES OF NORTH AMERICA, and its jurisdiction and power shall extend to all the States, Districts and Territories of the United States of North America.

Article Second.

The object of this organization shall be to protect every American citizen in the legal and proper exercise of all his civil and religious rights and privileges; to resist the insidious policy of the Church of Rome, and all other foreign influence against our republican institutions in all lawful ways; to place in all offices of honor, trust, or profit, in the gift of the people, or by appointment, none but native born Protestant citizens, and to protect, preserve and uphold the union of these States and the Constitution of the same.

Article Third.

Sec. 1.—A person to become a member of any Subordinate Council must be twenty-one years of age; he must believe in the existence of a Supreme Being as the Creator and Preserver of the Universe. He must be a native born citizen; a Protestant, either born of Protestant parents, or reared under Protestant influence; and not united in marrriage with a Roman Catholic; *provided, nevertheless*, that in this last respect, the State, District or Territorial Councils shall be authorized to so construct their respective Constitutions as shall best promote the interests of the American cause in their several jurisdictions; and *provided, moreover*, that no member who may have a Roman Catholic wife shall be eligible to office in this Order; and *provided, further*, should any State, District or Territorial Council prefer the words "Roman Catholic" as a disqualification to membership, in place of "Protestant" as a qualification, they may so consider this Constitution and govern their action accordingly.

Sec. 2.—There shall be an interval of three weeks between the conferring of the First and Second Degrees; and of three months between the conferring of the Second and Third Degrees—*provided*, that this restriction shall not apply to those who may have received the Second Degree previous to the first day of December next; and *provided, further*, that the Presidents of State, District, and Territorial Councils may grant dispensations for initiating in all the Degrees, officers of new Councils.

Sec. 3.—The National Council shall hold its Annual meetings on the first Tuesday in the month of June, at such place as may be designated by the National Council at the previous Annual meeting, and it may adjourn from time to time. Special meetings may be called by the President, on the written request of five delegations representing five State Councils; *provided*, that sixty day's notice shall be given to the State Councils previous to said meeting.

Sec. 4.—The National Council shall be composed of seven delegates from each State, to be chosen by the State Councils; and each District or Territory where a District or Territorial Council shall exist, shall be entitled to send two delegates, to be chosen from said Council—*provided*, that in the nomination of candidates for President and Vice President of the United States, each State shall be entitled to cast the same number of votes as they shall have members in both Houses of Congress. In all sessions of the National Council, thirty-two delegates, representing thirteen States, Territories or Districts, shall constitute a quorum for the transaction of business.

Sec. 5.—The National Council shall be vested with the following powers and privileges:

It shall be the head of the Organization for the United States of North America, and shall fix and establish all signs, grips, passwords, and such other secret work, as may seem to it necessary.

It shall have the power to decide all matters appertaining to National Politics.

It shall have the power to exact from the State Councils, quarterly or annual statements as to the number of members under their jurisdictions, and in relation to all other matters necessary for its information.

It shall have the power to form State, Territorial or District Councils, and to grant dispensations for the formation of such bodies, when five Subordinate Councils shall have been put in operation in any State, Territory, or District, and application made.

It shall have the power to determine upon a mode of punishment in case of any dereliction of duty on the part of its members or officers.

It shall have the power to adopt cabalistic characters for the purpose of writing or telegraphing. Said characters to be communicated to the Presidents of the State Councils, and by them to the Presidents of the Subordinate Councils.

It shall have the power to adopt any and every measure it may deem necessary to secure the success of the Organization; provided, that nothing shall be done by the said National Council in violation of the Constitution; and provided further, that in all political matters, its members may be instructed by the State Councils, and if so instructed, shall carry out such instructions of the State Councils which they represent until overruled by a majority of the National Council.

Article Fourth.

The President shall always preside over the National Council when present, and in his absence the Vice President shall preside, and in the absence of both the National Council shall appoint a President *pro tempore;* and the presiding officers may at all times call a member to the chair, but such appointment shall not extend beyond one sitting of the National Council.

Article Fifth.

Sec. 1.—The officers of the National Council shall be a President, Vice President, Chaplain, Corresponding Secretary, Recording Secretary, Treasurer, and two Sentinels; with such other officers as the National Council may see fit to appoint from time to time; and the Secretaries and Sentinels may receive such compensation as the National Council shall determine.

Sec. 2.—The duties of the several officers created by this Constitution shall be such as the work of this Organization prescribes.

Article Sixth.

Sec. 1.—All officers provided for by this Constitution, except the Sentinels, shall be elected annually by ballot. The President may appoint Sentinels from time to time.

Sec. 2.—A majority of all the votes cast shall be requisite to an election for an office.

Sec. 3.—All officers and delegates of this Council, and of all State, District, Territorial and Subordinate Councils, must be invested with all the Degrees of this Order.

Sec. 4.—All vacancies in the elective offices shall be filled by a vote of the National Council, and only for the unexpired term of the said vacancy.

Article Seventh.

Sec. 1.—The National Council shall entertain and decide all cases of appeal and it shall establish a form of appeal.

Sec. 2.—The National Council shall levy a tax upon the State, District, or Territorial Councils, for the support of the National Council, to be paid in such manner and at such times as the National Council shall determine.

Article Eighth.

This National Council may alter and amend this Constitution at its regular Annual meeting in June next, by a vote of the majority of the whole number of the members present. (Cincinnati, Nov. 24, 1854.)

RULES AND REGULATIONS.

Rule one.—Each State, District or Territory, in which there may exist five or more Subordinate Councils working under dispensations from the National Council of the United States of North America, or under regular dispensations from some State, District or Territory, are duly empowered to establish themselves into a State, District or Territorial Council, and when so established, to form for themselves Constitutions and By-Laws for their government, in pursuance of, and in consonance with, the Constitution of the National Council of the United States; provided, however, that all District, or Territorial Constitutions shall be subject to the approval of the National Council of the United States. (June, 1854.)

Rule two.—All State, District or Territorial Councils, when established, shall have full power and authority to establish all Subordinate Councils within their respective limits; and the Constitutions and By-Laws of all such Subordinate Councils, must be approved by their respective State, District or Territorial Councils. (June, 1854.)

Rule three.—All State, District or Territoral Councils, when established and until the formation of Constitutions, shall work under the Constitution of the National Council of the United States. (June, 1854.)

Rule four.—In all cases where, for the convenience of the Organization, two State or Territorial Councils may be established, the two Councils together shall be entitled to but thirteen delegates* in the National Council of the United States —the proportioned number of delegates to depend on the number of members in the Organizations; *provided*, that no State shall be allowed to have more than one State Council, without the consent of the National Council of the United States. (June, 1854.)

Rule five.—In any State, District or Territory, where there may be more than one Organization working on the same basis (to wit, the Lodges' and "Councils") the same shall be required to combine; the officers of each Organization shall resign, and new officers be elected; and thereafter these bodies shall be known as State Councils, and Subordinate Councils, and new Charters shall be granted to them by the National Council. (June, 1854.)

Rule six.—It shall be considered a penal offence for any brother not an officer of a Subordinate Council, to make use of the sign or summons adopted for public notification, except by direction of the President; or for officers of a Council to post the same at any other time than from midnight to one hour before daybreak, and this rule shall be incorporated into the By-laws of the State, District and Territorial Councils. (June, 1854.)

Rule seven.—The determination of the necessity and mode of issuing the posters for public notification shall be entrusted to the State, District or Territorial Councils. (June, 1854.)

Rule eight.—The respective State, District or Territorial Councils shall be required to make statements of the number of members within their respective limits, at the next meeting of this National Council, and annually thereafter, at the regular annual meeting. (June, 1854.)

Rule nine.—The delegates to the National Council of the United States of North America, shall be entitled to three dollars per day for their attendance upon the National Council, and for each day that may be necessary in going and returning from the same; and five cents per mile for every mile they may necessarily travel in going to, and returning from, the place of meeting of the National Council; to be computed by the nearest mail route: which shall be paid out of the Treasury of the National Council. (November, 1854.)

Rule ten.—Each State, District or Territorial Council, shall be taxed four cents per annum, for every member in good standing belonging to each Subordinate Council under its jurisdiction on the first day of April, which shall be reported to the National Council, and paid into the National Treasury, on or before the first day of the annual session, to be held in June; and on the same day in each succeeding year. And the first fiscal year shall be considered as commencing on the first day of December, 1854, and ending on the fifteenth day of May, 1855. (November, 1854.)

Rule eleven.—The following shall be the Key to determine and ascertain the purport of any communication that may be addressed to the President of a

* **Note.—See Constitution, Art. 3, Sec. 4, p. 5.**

State, District or Territorial Council by the President of the National Council, who is hereby instructed to communicate a knowledge of the same to said officers :

A	B	C	D	E	F	G	H	I	J	K	L	M
1	7	13	19	25	2	8	14	20	26	3	9	15
N	O	P	Q	R	S	T	U	V	W	X	Y	Z
21	4	10	16	22	5	11	17	23	6	12	18	24

Rule twelve.—The clause of the article of the Constitution relative to belief in the Supreme Being is obligatory upon every State and Subordinate Council, as well as upon each individual member. (June, 1854.)

Rule thirteenth.—The following shall be the compensation of the officers of this Council :

1st. The Corresponding Secretary shall be paid two thousand dollars per annum, from the 17th day of June, 1854.

2d. The Treasurer shall be paid five hundred dollars per annum, from the 17th day of June, 1854.

3d. The Sentinels shall be paid five dollars for every day they may be in attendance on the sittings of the National Council.

4th. The Chaplain shall be paid one hundred dollars per annum, from the 17th day of June, 1854.

5th. The Recording Secretary shall be paid five hundred dollars per annum, from the 17th day of June, 1854.

6th. The Assistant Secretary shall be paid five dollars per day, for every day he may be in attendance on the sitting of the National Council. All of which is to be paid out of the National Treasury, on the draft of the President. (November, 1854.)

SPECIAL VOTING.

Vote first.—This National Council hereby grants to the State of Virginia two State Councils, the one to be located in Eastern and the other in Western Virginia, the Blue Ridge Mountains being the geographical line between the two jurisdictions. (June, 1854.)

Vote second.—The President shall have power, till the next session of the National Council, to grant dispensations for the formation of State, District, or Territorial Councils, in form most agreeable to his own discretion, upon proper application being made. (June, 1854.)

Vote third.—The seats of all delegates to and members of the present National Council shall be vacated on the first Tuesday in June, 1855, at the hour of six o'clock in the forenoon; and the National Council convening in annual session upon that day, shall be composed exclusively of delegates elected under and in accordance with the provisions of the Constitution, as amended at the present session of this National Council : *provided*, that this resolution shall not apply to the officers of the National Council. (November, 1854.)

Vote fourth.—The Corresponding Secretary of this Council is authorized to have printed the names of the delegates to this National Council; also, those of the Presidents of the several State, District, and Territorial Councils, together with their address, and to forward a copy of the same to each person named; and further, the Corresponding Secretaries of each State, District, and Territory, are requested to forward a copy of their several Constitutions to each other. (November, 1854.)

Vote fifth.—In the publication of the Constitution and the Ritual, under the direction of the Committee—brother Deshler, Damrell and Stephens—the name, Signs, Grips, and Passwords of the Order, shall be indicated by [* * *,] and a copy of the same shall be furnished to each State, District and Territorial Council, and to each member of that body. (November, 1854.)

Vote sixth.—A copy of the Constitution of each State, District, and Territorial Council, shall be submitted to this Council for examination. (November, 1854.)

Vote seventh.—It shall be the duty of the Treasurer, at each annual meeting of this body, to make a report of all monies received or expended in the interval. (November, 1854.)

Vote eighth.—Messrs. Gifford, of Pa.; Barker, of N. Y.; Deshler, of N. J.; Williamson, of Va.; and Stephens, of Md., are appointed a committee to confer with similar committees that have been appointed for the purpose of consolidating the various American Orders, with power to make the necessary arrangements for such consolidation—subject to the approval of this National Council, at its next session. (November, 1854.)

Vote ninth.—On the receipt of the new Ritual by the members of this National Council who have received the third degree, they or any of them may, and they are hereby empowered to confer the third degree upon members of this body in their respective States, Districts and Territories, and upon the Presidents and other officers of their State, District, and Territorial Councils. And further, the Presidents of the State, District, and Territorial Councils shall in the first instance confer the third degree upon as many of the Presidents and officers of their Subordinate Councils, as can be assembled together in their respective localities, and afterwards the same may be conferred upon officers of other subordinate Councils, by any presiding officer of a Council, who shall have previously received it under the provisions of the Constitution. (November, 1854.)

Vote tenth.—To entitle any delegate to a seat in this National Council, at its annual session in June next, he must present a properly authenticated certificate that he was duly elected as a delegate to the same; or appointed a substitute in accordance with the requirements of the Constitutions of State, Territorial, or District Councils. And no delegate shall be received from any State, District or Territorial Council, which has not adopted the Constitution and Ritual of this National Council. (November, 1854.)

Vote eleventh.—The committee on printing the Constitution and Ritual is authorized to have a sufficient number of the same printed for the use of the Order. And no State, District, or Territorial Council, shall be allowed to reprint the same. (November, 1854.)

Vote twelfth.—The right to establish all Subordinate Councils in any of the States, Districts, and Territories represented in this National Council, shall be confined to the State, District, and Territorial Councils, which they represent. (November, 1854.)

Constitution for the Government of Subordinate Councils.

Article I.

Sec. 1.—Each Subordinate Council shall be composed of not less than thirteen members, all of whom shall have received all the degrees of the Order, and shall be known and recognized as ——— Council, No. ——— of the ——— of the county of———, and State of North Carolina.

Sec. 2.—No person shall be a member of any Subordinate Council in this State, unless he possesses all the qualifications, and comes up to all the requirements laid down in the Constitution of the National Council, and whose wife, (if he has one,) is not a Roman Catholic.

Sec. 3.—No application for membership shall be received and acted on from a person residing out of the State, or resides in a county where there is a Council in existence, unless upon special cause to be stated to the Council, to be judged of by the same; and such person, if the reasons be considered sufficient, may be initiated the same night he is proposed, provided he resides five miles or more from the place where the Council is located. But no person can vote in any Council, except the one of which he is a member.

Sec. 4.—Every person applying for membership, shall be voted for by ballot, in open Council, if a ballot is requested by a single member. If one third of the votes cast be against the applicant, he shall be rejected. If any applicant be rejected, he shall not be again proposed within six months thereafter. Nothing herein contained shall be construed to prevent the initiation of applicants privately, by those empowered to do so, in localities where there are no Councils within a convenient distance.

Sec. 5.—Any member of one Subordinate Council wishing to change his membership to another Council, shall apply to the Council to which he belongs, either in writing or orally through another member, and the question shall be decided by the Council. If a majority are in favor of granting him an honorable dismission, he shall receive the same in writing, to be signed by the President and countersigned by the Secretary. But until a member thus receiving an honorable dismission has actually been admitted to membership in another Council, he shall be held subject to the discipline of the Council from which he has received the dismission, to be dealt with by the same, for any violation of the requirements of the Order. Before being received in the Council, to which he wishes to transfer his membership, he shall present said certificate of honorable dismission, and shall be received as new members are.

Sec. 6.—Applications for the Second Degree shall not be received except in Second Degree Councils, and voted on by Second and Third Degree members only, and applications for the Third Degree shall be received in Third Degree Councils, and voted on by Third Degree members only.

Article II.

Each Subordinate Council shall fix on its own time and place for meeting: and shall meet at least once a month, but where nct very inconvenient, it is recommended that they meet once a week. Thirteen members shall form a quorum for the transaction of business. Special meetings may be called by the President, at any time, at the request of four members of the Order.

Article III.

Sec. 1.—The members of each Subordinate Council shall consist of a President, Vice President, Instructor, Secretary, Treasurer, Marshal, Inside and Outside Sentinel, and shall hold their offices for the term of six months, or until their successors are elected and installed.

Sec. 2.—The officers of each Subordinate Council, (except the sentinels, who shall be appointed by the President,) shall be elected at the first regular meetings in January and July, separately, and by ballot; and each shall receive a majority of all the votes cast to entitle him to an election. No member shall be elected to any office, unless he be present and signify his assent thereto at the time of his election. Any vacancy which may occur by death, resignation, or otherwise, shall be filled at the next meeting thereafter, in the manner and form above described.

Sec. 3.—*The President.*—It shall be the duty of the President of each Subordinate Council, to preside in the Council, and enforce a due observance of the Constitution and rules of the Order, and a proper respect for the State Council and the National Council—to have sole and exclusive charge of the Charter and the Constitution and Ritual of the Order, which he must always have with him when his Council is in session, to see that all officers perform their respective duties—to announce all ballotings to the Council—to decide all questions of order—to give the casting vote in all cases of a tie—to convene special meetings when deemed expedient—to draw warrants on the Treasurer for all sums, the payment of which is ordered by the Council—and to perform such other duties as are demanded of him by the Constitutions and Ritual of the Order.

Sec. 4.—The Vice President of each Subordinate Council shall assist the President in the discharge of his duties, whilst his Council is in session; and in his absence, shall perform all the duties of the President.

Sec. 5.—The Instructor shall perform the duties of the President, in the absence of the President and Vice President, and shall, under the direction of the President, perform such duties as may be assigned to him by the Ritual.

Sec. 6.—The Secretary shall keep an accurate record of the proceedings of the Council. He shall write all communications, fill all notices, attest all warrants drawn by the President for the payment of money; he shall keep a correct roll of all the members of the Council, together with their age, residence and occupation, in the order in which they have been admitted; he shall, at the expiration of every three months, make out a report of all work done during that time, which report he shall forward to the Secretary of the State Council; and when superseded in his office, shall deliver all books, papers, &c., in his hands, to his successor.

Sec. 7.—The Treasurer shall hold all monies raised exclusively for the use of the State Council, which he shall pay over to the Secretary of the State Council at its regular sessions, or whenever called upon by the President of the State Council. He shall receive all monies for the use of the Subordinate Council and pay all amounts drawn for on him, by the President of the Subordinate Council, if attested by the Secretary.

Sec. 8.—The Marshal shall perform such duties, under the direction of the President, as may be required of him by the Ritual.

Sec. 9.—The Inside Sentinel shall have charge of the inner door, and act under the directions of the President. He shall admit no person, unless he can prove himself a member of this order, and of the same Degree in which the Council is opened, or by order of the President, or is satisfactorily vouched for.

Sec. 10.—The Outside Sentinel shall have charge of the outer door, and act in accordance with the orders of the President. He shall permit no person to enter the outer door unless he give the password of the Degree in which the Council is at work, or is properly vouched for.

Sec. 11.—The Secretary, Treasurer, and Sentinels, shall recive such compensation as the Subordinate Councils may each conclude to allow.

Sec. 12.—Each Subordinate Council may levy its own fees for initiation, to raise a fund to pay its dues to the State Council, and to defray its own expenses. Each Council may, also, at its discretion, initiate without charging the usual fee, those it considers unable to pay the same.

Sec. 13.—The President shall keep in his possession the Constitution and Ritual of the Order. He shall not suffer the same to go out of his possession under any pretence whatever, unless in case of absence, when he may put them in the hands of the Vice President or Instructor, or whilst the Council is in session, for the information of a member wishing to see it, for the purpose of initiation, or conferring of Degrees.

Article IV.

Each Subordinate Council shall have power to adopt such By-Laws, Rules, and Regulations, for its own government, as it may think proper, not inconsistent with the Constitutions of the National and State Councils.

FORM OF APPLICATION

For a Charter to organize a new Council.

Post Office ——— county,
Date ———.

To ———
President of the State Council of North Carolina :

We, the undersigned, members of the Third Degree, being desirous of extending the influence and usefulness of our organization, do hereby ask for a Warrant of Dispensation, instituting and organizing us as a subordinate branch of the Order, under the jurisdiction of the State Council of the State of North Carolina, to be known and hailed as Council No. ———, and to be located at ———, in the county of ———, State of North Carolina.

And we do hereby pledge ourselves to be governed by the Constitution of the State Council of the State of North Carolina, and of the Grand Council of the U. S., N. A., and that we will, in all things, conform to the rules and usages of the Order.

Names. Residences.

FORM OF DISMISSION

From one Council to another.

This is to certify that Brother ———, a member of ——— Council, No. ———, having made an application to change his membership from this Council to that of ——— Council, No. ——, at ———, in the county of ———, I do hereby declare, that said brother has received an honorable dismission from this Council, and is hereby recommended for membership in ——— Council, No. ———, in the county of ———, N. C.; provided, however, that until Brother ——— has been admitted to membership in said Council, he is to be considered subject to the discipline of this Council, to be dealt with by the same for any violation of the requirements of the Order. This the ——— day of ———, 185—, and the ——— year of American Independence.

——— President ——— Council,
No. ———.

——— Secretary.

FORM OF CERTIFICATE

For Delegates to the State Council.

——— Council, No. ———,
——— county of ———, N. C.

This is to certify that ——— and ——— were, at the regular meeting of this Council, held on the ———, 185—, duly elected delegates to represent this Council in the next annual meeting of the State Council, to be held in ———, on the 3d Monday in November next. And by virtue of the authority in me reposed, I do hereby declare the said ——— and ——— to be invested with all the rights, powers and privileges of the delegates as aforesaid. This being the ——— day of ———, 185—, and the —— year of our National Independence.

——— ——— President of
——— Council, No. ——

——— ——— Secretary.

FORM OF NOTICE.

From the Subordinate Councils to the State Council, whenever any member of a Subordinate Council is expelled.

—— Council, No. ——,
—— county of ——, N. C.

To the President of the State Council of North Carolina:

Sir:—This is to inform you that at a meeting of this Council, held on the —— day of ——, 185—, —— —— was duly expelled from membership in said Council, and thus deprived of all the privileges, rights and benefits of this Organization.

In accordance with the provision of the Constitution of the State Council, you are hereby duly notified of the same, that you may officially notify all the Subordinate Councils of the State to be upon their guard against the said ——, as one unworthy to associate with patriotic and good men, and (*if expelled for violating his obligation*) as a perjurer to God and his country. The said —— is about —— years of age, and is by livelihood, a ——.

Duly certified, this the —— day of ——185—, and in the year of our National Independence.

—— —— President of
—— Council, No. ——.

—— Secretary.

FIRST DEGREE COUNCIL.

To be admitted to membership in this order, the applicant shall be—

1st. Proposed and found acceptable.
2nd. Introduced and examined under the guarantee of secrecy.
3d. Placed under the obligation which the order imposes.
4th. Required to enroll his name and place of residence.
5th. Instructed in the forms and usages and ceremonies of the order.
6th. Solemnly charged as to the objects to be obtained, and his duties.

[A recommendation of a candidate to this order, shall be received only from a brother of approved integrity. It shall be accompanied by minute particulars as to name, age, calling, and residence, and by an explicit voucher for his qualifications, and a personal pledge for his fidelity. These particulars shall be recorded by the secretary in a book kept for that purpose. The recommendation may be referred, and the ballot taken at such time, and in such a manner as the State Council may prescribe; but no communication shall be made to the candidate until the ballot has been declared in his favor. Candidates shall be received in the ante-room by the Marshal and the Secretary.]

OUTSIDE.

Marshal.—Do you believe in a supreme Being, the Creator and Preserver of the universe.

Ans.—I do.

Marshal.—Before proceeding further, we require a solemn obligation of secrecy and truth. If you will take such an obligation, you will lay your right hand upon the Holy Bible and Cross.

(When it is known that the applicant is a Protestant, the cross may be omitted, or affirmation may be allowed.)

OBLIGATION.

You do solemnly swear (or affirm) that you will never reveal anything said or done in this room, the names of any persons present, nor the existence of this society, whether found worthy to proceed or not, and that all your declarations shall be true, so help you God?

Ans.—"I do."

Marshal.—Where were you born?

Marshal.—Where is your permanent residence?

(If born out of the jurisdiction of the United States, the answer shall be written, the candidate dismissed with an admonition of secrecy, and the brother vouching for him suspended from all the privileges of the order, unless upon satisfactory proof that he has been misinformed.)

Marshal.—Are you twenty-one years of age?

Ans.—"I am."

Marshal.—Were you born of Protestant parents or were you reared under Protestant influence?

Ans.—"Yes."

Marshal.—If married, is your wife a Roman Catholic?

("No" or "Yes"—the answer to be valued as the Constitution of the State Council shall provide.)

Marshal.—Are you willing to use your influence and vote only for native-born American citizens for all offices of honor, trust or profit in the gift of the people, to the exclusion of all foreigners and aliens, and Roman Catholics in particular, and without regard to party predilections?

Ans.—"I am."

INSIDE.

(The Marshal shall then repair to the council in session, and present the written list of names, vouchers and answers to the President, who shall cause them to be read aloud, and a vote of the council to be taken on each name, in such manner as prescribed by its bye-laws. If doubts arise in the ante-room, they shall be referred to the council. If a candidate be dismissed, he shall be admonished to secrecy. The candidates declared elected shall be conducted to seats within the council, apart from the brethren. When all are present the President by one blow of the gavil, shall call to order and say:)

President.—Brother Marshal, introduce the candidates to the Vice-President.

Marshal.—Worthy Vice-President, I present to you these candidates, who have duly answered all questions.

Vice-President, rising in his place.—Gentlemen, it is my office to welcome you as friends. When you shall have assumed the patriotic vow by which we are all bound, we will embrace you as brothers. I am authorized to declare that our obligations enjoin nothing which is inconsistent with the duty which every good man owes to his Creator, his country, his family or himself. We do not compel you, against your convictions, to act with us in our good work; but should you at any time wish to withdraw, it will be our duty to grant you a dismissal in good faith. If satisfied with this assurance, you will rise upon your feet, *(pausing till they do so,)* place the left hand upon the breast, and raise the right hand towards heaven.

(The brethren to remain seated till called up.)

OBLIGATION.

In the presence of Almighty God and these witnesses, you do solemnly promise and swear that you will never betray any of the secrects of this society, nor communicate them even to proper candidates, except within a lawful council of the order; that you never will permit any of the secrets of this society to be written, or in any other manner made legible, except for the purpose of official instruction; that you will not vote, nor give your influence for any man, for any office in the gift of the people, unless he be an American born citizen, in favor of Americans ruling America, nor if he be a Roman Catholic; that you will in all political matters, so far as this order is concerned, comply with the will of the majority, though it may conflict with your personal preference, so long as it does not conflict with the Constitution of the United States of America or that of the State in which you reside; that you will not, under any circumstances whatever, knowingly recommend an unworthy person for initiation, nor suffer it to be done if in your power to prevent it; that you will not, under any circumstances, expose the name of any member of this order, nor reveal the existence of such an association; that you will answer an *imperative notice* issued by the proper authority; obey the command of the State Council, President, or his deputy, while assembled by such notice, and respond to the claim of a *sign* or a *cry* of the order, unless it be physically impossible; and that you will acknowledge the State Council of ——— as the legislative head, the ruling authority, and the supreme tribunal of the order in the State of ———, acting under the jurisdiction of the National Council of the United States of North America.

Binding yourself in the penalty of excommunication from the order, the forfeiture of all intercourse with its members, and being denounced in all the societies of the same, as a wilful traitor to your God and your country.

(The President shall call up every person present by three blows of the gavil, when the candidates shall all repeat after the Vice-President in concert:)

All this I voluntarily and sincerely promise, with a full understanding of the solemn sanctions and penalties.

Vice-President.—You have now taken solemn oaths, and made as sacred promises as man can make, that you will keep all our secrets inviolate; and we wish you distinctly to understand that he that takes these oaths and makes these promises, and then violates them, leaves the foul, the deep and blighting stain of perjury resting on his soul.

President.—(Having seated all by one blow of the gavil.)—Brother Instructor, these new brothers having complied with the demands of the order, are entitled to the secrets and privileges of the same. You will, therefore, invest them with everything appertaining to the first degree.

Instructor.—Brothers: the practices and proceedings in our order are as follows:

We have pass-words necessary to be used to obtain admission to our councils; forms for our conduct while there; means of recognizing each other when abroad; means of mutual protection; and methods for giving notices to members.

At the outer door you will* (*make any ordinary alarm* to attract the notice of the outside sentinel.)

When the wicket is opened you will pronounce the (*words—what's the pass,*) in a whisper. The outside sentinel will reply (*Give it*), when you will give the term pass-word and be admitted to the ante-room. You will then proceed to

* In the Ritual the words in parenthesis are omitted. In the key to the Ritual, they are written in figures—the alphabet used being the same as printed below. So throughout.

Key to Unlock Know Nothing Communications.

A	B	C	D	E	F	G	H	I	J	K	L	M
1	7	13	19	25	2	8	14	20	26	3	9	15
N	O	P	Q	R	S	T	U	V	W	X	Y	Z
21	4	10	16	22	5	11	17	23	6	12	18	24

the inner door and give (*one rap*). When the wicket is opened, give your name, the number of, and location of your council, the explanation of the term pass, and the degree pass-word.

If these be found correct, you will be admitted; if not, your name will be reported to the Vice-President, and must be properly vouched for before you can gain admission to the council. You will then proceed to the centre of the room and address the (*President*) with the countersign, which is performed thus, (*placing the right hand diagonally across the mouth.*) When this salutation is recognized, you will quietly take your seat.

This sign is peculiar to this degree, and is never to be used outside of the council room, nor during the conferring of this degree. When retiring, you will address the (*Vice-President*) in the same manner, and also give the degree pass-word to the inside sentinel.

The "term pass-word" is (*We are.*)

(The pass-word and explanation is to be established by each State Council for its respective subordinates.)

The "explanation" of the "term-pass," to be used at the inner door, is (*our country's hope.*)

The "degree pass-word" is (*Native.*)

The "travelling pass-word" is (*The memory of our pilgrim fathers.*)

(This word is changed annually by the President of the National Council of the United States, and is to be made and used only when the brother is traveling beyond the jurisdiction of his own State, District or Territory. It and all other pass-words must be communicated in a whisper, and no brother is entitled to communicate them to another, without authority from the presiding officer.)

The "sign of recognition" is (*grasping the right lappel of the coat with the right hand, the fore finger being extended inwards.*)

The "answer" is given by (*a similar action with the left hand.*)

The "grip" is given by (*an ordinary shake of the hand.*)

The person challenging shall (*then draw the fore finger along the palm of the hand.*) The answer will be given by (*a similar action forming a link by hooking together the ends of the fore finger;*) when the following conversation ensues—the challenging party first saying (*is that yours?*) The answer, (*it is.*) Then the response (*how did you get it?*), followed by the rejoinder (*it is my birth-right.*)

Public notice for a meeting is given by means of a (*piece of white paper the shape of a heart.*)

(In cities† the *** of the *** where the meeting is to be held, will be written legibly upon the notice; and upon the election day said *** will denote the *** where your presence is needed. This notice will never be passed, but will be *** or thrown upon the sidewalk with a *** in the centre.)

If information is wanting of the object of the gathering, or of the place, &c., the inquirer will ask of an undoubted brother (*where's when?*) The brother will give the information if possessed of it; if not, it will be yours and his duty to continue the inquiry, and thus disseminate the call throughout the brotherhood.

If the color of (*the paper*) be (*red,*) it will denote actual trouble, which requires that you come prepared to meet it.

The "cry of distress"—to be used only in time of danger, or where the American interests requires an immediate assemblage of the brethren—is (*oh, oh, oh.*) The response is (*hio, hio, h-i-o.*)

The "sign of caution"—to be given when a brother is speaking unguardedly before a stranger—is (*drawing the fore-finger and thumb together across the eyes, the rest of the hand being closed,*) which signifies "keep dark."

† Concerning what is said of cities, the key to the Ritual says; "Considered unnecessary to decipher what is said in regard to cities."

Brothers, you are now initiated into and made acquainted with the work and organization of a council of this degree of the order; and the Marshal will present you to the worthy President for admonition.

President.—It has, no doubt, been long apparent to you, brothers, that foreign influence and Roman Catholicism have been making steady and alarming progress in our country. You cannot have failed to observe the significant transition of the foreigner and Romanist from a character quiet, retiring, and even abject, to one bold, threatening, turbulent and despotic in its appearance and assumptions. You must have become alarmed at the systematic and rapidly augmenting power of these dangerous and unnatural elements of our national condition. So is it, brothers, with others beside yourselves in every State of the Union. A sense of danger has struck the great heart of the nation. In every city, town and hamlet, the danger has been seen and the alarm sounded. And hence true men have devised this order as a means of disseminating patriotic principles, of keeping alive the fire of national virtue, of fostering the national intelligence, and of advancing America and the American interest on the one side, and on the other of checking the strides of the foreigner or alien, or thwarting the machinations and subverting the deadly plans of the Papist and Jesuit.

NOTE.—The President shall impress upon the initiates the importance of secrecy, the manner of proceeding in recommending candidates for initiation, and the responsibility of the duties which they have assumed.

SECOND DEGREE COUNCIL.

Marshal.—Worthy President: These brothers have been duly elected to the second degree of this order. I present them to you for obligation.

President.—Brothers: You will place your left hand upon your right breast, and extend your right hand towards the flag of our country, preparatory to obligation. (Each council room should have a neat American flag festooned over the platform of the President.)

OBLIGATION.

You, and each of you, of your own free will and accord, in the presence of Almighty God and these witnesses, your left hand resting upon your right breast, and your right hand extended to the flag of your country, do solemnly and sincerely swear, that you will not under any circumstances disclose in any manner, nor suffer it to be done by others, if in your power to prevent it, the name, signs, passwords, or other secrets of this degree, except in open council for the purpose of instruction; that you will in all things conform to all the rules and regulations of this Order, and to the constitution and by-laws of this or any other council to which you may be attached, so long as they do not conflict with the Constitution of the United States, nor that of the State in which you reside; that you will under all circumstances, if in your power so to do, attend to all regular signs or summons that may be thrown or sent to you by a brother of this or any other degree of this order; that you will support in all political matters, for all political offices, members of this order in preference to other persons; that if it may be done legally, you will, when elected or appointed to any official station conferring on you the power to do so, remove all foreigners, aliens, or Roman Catholics from office or place, and that you will in no case appoint such to any office or place in your gift. You do also promise and swear that this and all other obligations which you have previously taken in this order, shall ever be kept through life sacred and inviolate. All this you promise and declare, as Americans, to sustain and abide by, without any hesitation or mental reservation whatever. So help you God and keep you steadfast.

(Each will answer "I do.")

President.—Brother Marshal, you will now present the brothers to the Instructor for instructions in the second degree of the order.

Marshal.—Brother Instructor, by direction of our worthy President, I present these brothers before you that you may instruct them in the secrets and mysteries of the second degree of the order.

Instructor.—Brothers, in this degree we have an entering sign and a countersign. At the outer door proceed (*as in the first degree.*) At the inner door you will make (*two raps,*) and proceed as in the first degree, giving the second degree pass-word, which is (*American,*) instead of that of the first degree. If found to be correct, you will then be admitted, and proceed (*to the centre of the room,*) giving the countersign, which is made thus (*extending the right arm to the national flag over the President, the palm of the hand being upwards.*)

The sign of recognition in this degree is the same as in the first degree, with the addition of (*the middle finger,*) and the response to be made in a (*similar manner.*)

Marshal, you will now present the brothers to the worthy President for admonition.

Marshal.—Worthy President, I now present these candidates to you for admonition.

President.—Brothers, you are now duly initiated into the second degree of this order. Renewing the congratulations which we extended to you upon your admission to the first degree, we admonish you by every tie that may nerve patriots, to aid us in our efforts to restore the political institutions of our country to their original purity. Begin with the youth of our land. Instil into their minds the lessons of our country's history—the glorious battles and the brilliant deeds of patriotism of our fathers, through which we received the inestimable blessings of civil and religious liberty. Point them to the example of the sages and the statesmen who founded our government. Implant in their bosoms an ardent love for the Union. Above all else, keep alive in their bosoms the memory, the maxims, and the deathless example of our illustrious WASHINGTON.

Brothers, recalling to your minds the solemn obligations which you have severally taken in this and the first degree, I now pronounce you entitled to all the privileges of membership in this the second degree of our Order.

THIRD DEGREE COUNCIL.

Marshal.—Worthy President, these brothers having been duly elected to the third degree of this order, I present them before you for obligation.

President.—Brothers, you will place yourselves in a circle around me, each one crossing your arms upon your breasts, and grasping firmly each other's hands, holding the right hand of the brother on the right, and the left hand of the brother on the left, so as to form a circle, symbolical of the links of an unbroken chain, and of a ring which has no end.

Note.—This degree is to be conferred with the national flag elevated in the centre of the circle, by the side of the President or Instructor, and not on less than five at any one time, in order to give it solemnity, and also for the formation of the circle—except in the first instance of conferring it on the officers of the State and subordinate councils, that they may be empowered to progress with the work.

The obligation and charge in this degree may be given by the President or Instructor, as the President may prefer.

OBLIGATION.

You and each of you, of your own free will and accord, in the presence of Almighty God and these witnesses, with your hands joined in token of that fraternal affection which should ever bind together the States of this Union—forming a ring, in token of your determination that, so far as your efforts can avail, this Union shall have no end—do solemnly and sincerely swear [or affirm] that you will not under any circumstances disclose in any manner, nor suffer it to be done by others if in your power to prevent it, the name, signs, pass-words or other secrets of this degree, except to those to whom you may prove on trial to be brothers of the same degree, or in open council, for the purpose of instruction; that you do hereby solemnly declare your devotion to the Union of these States; that in the discharge of your duties as American citizens, you will uphold, maintain and defend it; that you will discourage and discountenance any and every attempt, coming from any and every quarter, which you believe to be designed or calculated to destroy or subvert it, or to weaken its bonds; and that you will use your influence, so far as in your power, in endeavoring to procure an amicable and equitable adjustment of all political discontents or differences, which may threaten its injury or overthrow. You further promise and swear [or affirm,] that you will not vote for any one to fill any office of honor, profit or trust of a political character, whom you know or believe to be in favor of a dissolution of the Union of these States, or who is endeavoring to produce that result; that you will vote for and support for all political offices, third or Union degree members of this Order in preference to all others; that if it may be done consistently with the constitution and laws of the land, you will, when elected or appointed to any official station which may confer on you the power to do so, remove from office or place all persons whom you know or believe to be in favor of a dissolution of the Union, or who are endeavoring to produce that result; and that you will in no case appoint such persons to any political office or place whatever. All this you promise and swear [or affirm] upon your honor as American citizens and friends of the American Union, to sustain and abide by without any hesitation or mental reservation whatever. You also promise and swear [or affirm] that this and all other obligations which you have previously taken in this order, shall ever be kept sacred and inviolate. To all this you pledge your lives, your fortunes, and your sacred honors. So help you God and keep you steadfast.

(Each one shall answer, "I do.")

President.—Brother Marshal, you will now present the brothers to the Instructor for final instruction in this the third degree of the Order.

Marshal.—Instructor, by direction of our worthy President, I present these brothers before you that you may instruct them in the secrets and mysteries of this the third degree of our Order.

Instructor.—Brothers, in this degree as in the second, we have an entering pass-word, a degree pass-word and a token of salutation. At the outer door (*make any ordinary alarm.* The outside sentinel will *say U; you say ni;* the sentinel will rejoin *on.*) This will admit you to the inner door. At the inner door you will make (*three*) distinct (*raps.*) Then announce your name, with the number (or name) and location of the council to which you belong, giving the explanation to the pass-word, which is (*safe.*) If found correct, you will then be admitted, when you will proceed to the centre of the room, and placing the (*hands on the breast with the fingers interlocked,*) give the token of salutation which is (*by bowing to the President.*) You will then quietly take your seat.

The sign of recognition is made by the same action as in the second degree, with the addition of (*the third finger,*) and the response is made by (a smilar action with *the left hand.*)

(The grip is given by taking hold of the *hand in the usual way*, and then by *slipping the fingers around on the top of the thumb;* then extending the *litttle finger and pressing the inside* of the *wrist*. The person challenging shall say, *do you know what that is?* The answer is, *yes*. The challenging party shall say, further, *what is it?* The answer is, *Union*.)

[The Instructor will here give the grip of this degree, with explanations, and also the true password of this degree, which is (*Union*.)]

CHARGE.

To be given by the President.

Brothers, it is with great pleasure that I congratulate you upon your advancement to the third degree of our Order. The responsibilities you have now assumed, are more serious and weighty than those which preceded, and are committed to such only as have been tried and found worthy. Our obligations are intended as solemn avowals of our duty to the land that gave us birth; to the memories of our fathers; and to the happiness and welfare of our children. Consecrating to your country a spirit unselfish and a fidelity like that which distinguished the patriots of the Revolution, you have pledged your aid in cementing the bonds of a Union which we trust will endure forever. Your deportment since your initiation has attested your devotion to the principles we desire to establish, and has inspired a confidence in your patriotism, of which we can give no higher proof than your reception here.

The dangers which threaten American Liberty arise from foes without and from enemies within. The first degree pointed out the source and nature of our most imminent peril, and indicated the first measure of safety. The second degree defined the next means by which, in coming time, such assaults may be rendered harmless. The third degree, which you have just received, not only reiterates the lessons of the other two, but it is intended to avoid and provide for a more remote, but no less terrible danger, from domestic enemies to our free institutions.

Our object is briefly this:—to perfect an organization modelled after that of the Constitution of the United States, and co-extensive with the confederacy. Its object and principles, in all matters of national concern, to be uniform and identical, whilst in all local matters the component parts shall remain independent and sovereign within their respective limits.

The great result to be attained—the only one which can secure a perfect guaranty as to our future—is UNION; permanent, enduring, fraternal UNION! Allow me, then, to impress upon your minds and memories the touching sentiments of the Father of his Country, in his farewell address:

"The unity of government which constitutes you one people," says Washington, "is justly dear to you, for it is the main pillar in the edifice of your real independence, the support of your tranquility at home, of your peace abroad, of your safety, your prosperity—even that liberty you so justly prize. " * * It is of infinite moment that you should properly estimate the immense value of your *National Union*, to your collective and individual happiness. You should cherish a cordial, habitual and immovable attachment to it; accustoming yourselves to think and speak of it, as the palladium of your political safety and prosperity; watching for its preservation with jealous anxiety; discountenancing whatever may suggest even a suspicion that it can in any event be abandoned; and indignantly frowning upon the dawning of every attempt to alienate any portion of our country from the rest, or to enfeeble the sacred ties which now bind together the various parts."

Let these words of paternal advice and warning, from the greatest man that ever lived, sink deep into your hearts. Cherish them, and teach your children to reverence them, as you cherish and reverence the memory of Washington himself. The Union of these States is the great conservator of that liberty so dear to the American heart. Without it, our greatness as a nation would disappear, and our boasted self-government prove a signal failure. The very name of Liberty, and the hopes of struggling Freedom throughout the world, must perish in the wreck of this Union. Devote yourselves, then, to its maintenance, as our fathers did to the cause of independence; consecrating to its support, as you have sworn to do, your lives, your fortunes, and your sacred honors.

Brothers: Recalling to your minds the solemn obligations which you have severally taken in this and the preceding degrees, I now pronounce you entitled to all the privileges of membership in this organization, and take pleasure in informing you that you are now members of the Order of (*the American Union.*)

OFFICERS OF THE NATIONAL COUNCIL.

President, James W. Barker, of New York, N. Y.
Vice President, W. W. Williamson, of Alexandria, Va.
Corresponding Secretary, C. D. Deshler, of New Brunswick, N. J.
Recording Secretary, James M. Stephens, of Baltimore, Md.
Treasurer, Henry Crane, of Cincinnati, Ohio.
Inside Sentinel, John P. Hilton, of Washington, D. C.

CONSTITUTION OF THE

NORTH CAROLINA STATE COUNCIL.

Adopted January 18th, 1855.

Article I.

Sec. 1.—This body shall be known by the name of the NORTH CAROLINA STATE COUNCIL; and shall be composed of delegates appointed by the Subordinate Councils, as hereinafter provided.

Sec. 2.—A person to become a member of any Subordinate Council in this State, must be twenty-one years of age; he must believe in the existence of a Supreme Being as the Creator and Preserver of the Universe; he must be a native-born citizen, a Protestant, either born of Protestant parents, or reared under Protestant influence; and not united in marriage with a Roman Catholic.

Sec. 3.—The State Council shall be composed of two delegates from each Subordinate Council in the State, to be appointed at the first regular meeting of the same, that shall be held after the first day of October in each and every year, whose term of appointment shall continue for one year; provided, that this section shall not affect the tenure of office, until the first day of October, 1855, of any member of the present Council; and provided further, that an appointment may be made at any regular meeting of said Subordinate Councils to fill vacancies.

Sec 4.—The State Council shall be vested with the following powers, viz:

It shall be the chief head and authority of the Order in the State of North Carolina, subject to the requirements of the National Council. It shall have power to establish term and explanation passwords for the State, and Subordinate Councils in the State, and such other secret work as to it may seem necessary. It shall have power to exact from the Subordinate Councils, annual or quarterly statements as to the number of members under their respective jurisdictions, and also as to all other matters it may deem essential for full and necessary information. It shall have the sole power of forming and establishing Subordinate Councils in the State, and of granting dispensations or charters for the same—provided, however, that when the State Council is not in session, the President thereof may grant such dispensations—and provided, further, that no dispensation or charter shall be issued hereafter for the formation of a Subordinate Council, unless the application therefor be signed by at least thirteen full degree members of this Order, who are in good and regular standing. It shall have the power to decide on a mode of punishment in case of a dereliction of duty on the part of its officers or members.

Sec. 5.—The State Council shall hold its regular annual meeting on the third Monday in November of each and every year, at such place in the State as may be agreed on by the same at the preceding regular annual session—provided, however, that the President of the State Council may convene the same in the city of Raleigh, at any time he may think the interests of the Order imperiously require it.

Article II.

Sec. 1.—The officers of the State Council shall be a President, Vice President, Secretary, Treasurer, Marshal, Chaplain, Inside Sentinel, Outside Sentinel, and such other officers as the State Council may see fit to appoint from time to time; and the Secretary, Treasurer, and Sentinels shall receive such compensation for their services, as the Council may determine.

Article III.

Sec. 1.—The President shall preside when present, and in his absence the Vice President shall preside; and in the absence of both, the Council shall elect a President *pro tem.*, and the presiding officer may at all times call a member to the chair, but such appointment shall never extend beyond one day.

Sec. 2.—The President shall preserve order, and cause the Constitution and the laws to be strictly observed by all the members. His decisions upon all points of order shall be obeyed, unless reversed upon appeal. He shall have the casting vote in all cases. He shall sign all orders on the State Treasurer for the payment of money, and all other documents requiring his signature. He shall fill all vacancies in the State offices, until the next regular annual meeting of the Council. He shall transmit the ritual passwords, or other secret matters of the Order, to the proper officers of the Subordinate Councils—and exercise general supervision over the Order throughout the State, according to its Constitution, Laws, and usages.

Sec. 3.—The Secretary shall keep a record of the proceedings of the State Council; file all documents connected therewith; preserve all books and papers belonging to the same; and have the custody of the seal of the same. He shall receive all monies due to the State Council, and pay over the same to the Treasurer; attest all orders drawn on the Treasurer for monies appropriated by the State Council, and keep the accounts of the State Council with the Subordinate Councils. He shall attest all dispensations and orders of the State Council, and when directed, summon all members to attend its special meetings. He shall transmit an annual report of the state of the Order, in North Carolina, to the President of the National Council. He shall conduct the necessary correspondence of the State Council, and attend to such other clerical business as the State Council may direct. He shall be entitled to receive for his services such compensation as the State Council may, from time to time, determine upon, not exceeding the sum of $500 per year, and shall give such bond and security as the State Council may require.

Sec. 4.—The Treasurer shall have the custody of the funds of the State Council; keep accurate accounts of all monies received by him from the Secretary, and pay all orders drawn on him by the President, and attested by the Secretary. He shall keep all his accounts regularly posted up in a book, to be kept for the purpose, at every regular session of the State Council, and submit them to the same, or to any committee appointed for that purpose, together with a written report setting forth in detail the affairs and condition of the Treasury. He shall give such bond and security as the State Council may from time to time require, and in a sum not less than double the amount he will probably at any one time have in his hands; and he shall receive such compensation for his services as the State Council may agree upon, not exceeding the sum of $100 per annum.

Sec. 5.—The Marshal shall obey the orders of the President in the government and proceedings of the State Council; shall present officers elect for installation; receive and introduce delegates and visitors, and perform such other appropriate duties as the State Council may direct.

Sec. 6.—The Chaplain's duty will be to open the sessions of the State Council with prayer, and to lecture before the Subordinate Councils, as may be convenient.

Article IV.

Sec. 1.—All officers of the State Council, provided for in this Constitution (except the Sentinels, who shall be appointed by the President,) shall be elected by ballot, at the regular annual meeting of the Council; and shall, on the last day of the session of the same, be installed in such manner and form as the National Council, or the President thereof, may establish.

Sec. 2.—A majority of the votes cast shall be necessary to an election to any office.

Sec. 3.—In all sessions of the State Council, forty members shall constitute a quorum, for the transaction of business.

Article V.

Sec. 1.—The State Council shall hear and decide all questions of appeal from the decisions of Subordinate Councils, and may establish a form of appeal.

Sec. 2.—The State Council shall have power to levy a tax upon the Subordinate Councils, for the support of the National Council, to be paid in such manner and at such times as the National Council shall determine. It shall also have power to levy a tax for the support of the State Council, to be paid at such time and in such manner as the State Council shall determine.

Article VI.

The delegates to the National Council shall be elected by ballot at the regular annual meeting of the State Council, in November.

Article VII.

The State Council shall have power to adopt all such by-laws, rules and regulations for its own government, and also for the government of the Subordinate Councils, as it may deem necessary for uniformity and the general good of the Order, not inconsistent with this Constitution, or the Constitution of the National Council.

Article VIII.

Sec. 1.—The political powers of the State Council shall be limited to the selection of candidates for State officers, to be supported by the members of this Order—which selections may be by ballot, or *viva voce*, as the Council may decide; provided, however, that in the selection of a candidate for Governor of the State, the State Council may, at its regular annual meeting next before the election for such offices, either make the nominations itself, or call a convention of the order in the State, at such time and place as the State Council may decide for the purpose of making such nominations—and in case of the calling of such convention, the Subordinate Councils shall be represented in such convention, as according to the provisions of this Constitution they are to be represented in the State Council, and subject to the same manner and proportionate strength in casting the vote.

Sec. 2.—In the selection of candidates for all offices to be filled by the General Assembly, the following method shall be preserved, viz:

For United States Senators, Secretary of State, Treasurer, Comptroller, Superintendent of Common Schools, Judges of the Supreme and Superior Courts, Attorney General, and Solicitors, and all other offices now provided, or hereafter created by law, whose appointment devolve on the General Assembly, a majority of the State Council shall decide upon the candidate to be supported by the Order.

Sec. 3.—In the selection of candidates for Congress, the Subordinate Councils in each Congressional District, shall each select three delegates, who shall meet on the second Monday in May, of each year in which the Congressional elections take place, at the places fixed by law for comparing the votes in the said District, and proceed to select the candidate for that District. A majority of all the delegates from all the Subordinate Councils in each and every county, shall cast the same number of votes the said county is entitled to members in the House of Commons in the State Legislature—a majority of the whole number of votes cast being necessary to a selection; provided, however, that in those Congressional Districts in which the law provides that the returns shall be compared at some place other than a county town, in such Districts the delegates shall meet at the county town in such county instead of the place designated by law.

Sec. 4.—The selection of candidates for members of the General Assembly shall be by the Subordinate Councils in the following manner, viz: For members of the House of Commons, for Sheriff, Clerks of the County and Superior Courts, County Solicitors, and all other officers elected by the people or the County Courts, if there be but one Council in the county, the Council shall make the selection by the vote of the majority—if there be more than one Council in the county, then each Council shall select one delegate for every thirteen members, not counting fractions, in the same, and when delegates from the several Councils shall have met at such time and place as may be agreed upon, the majority shall make the selection; provided, however, that where there is more than one Council in a county, the Council at the county seat shall have the power to appoint the time and place for the assembling county conventions for the nomination of candidates, and calling general meetings of the Order in said county for the good of the same. In the selection of candidates for State Senators, the same rule shall prevail, except that the delegates from the Councils in the Districts where the District is composed of more counties than one, shall meet at such time and place as may be agreed on by them, and then and there make the nomination.

Sec. 5.—In the election of candidates for Mayor, or Intendant of towns, and of Commissioners for the same, the Subordinate Council in such town shall make the nominations by ballot; and in those towns where the several wards vote separately for Commissioners in the same, the candidates shall be nominated for one ward at a time, instead of nominating the whole Board by general ticket; a majority of the whole number of ballots cast being necessary to a choice.

Sec. 6.—In the selection of candidates for Electors of President and Vice-President, the Subordinate Councils in each Electoral District, shall each select three delegates, who shall meet at such time as the good of the Order may require the ticket to be formed, at the places fixed by law for comparing the votes in such Electoral District, and proceed to select the candidate for Elector in that Electoral District. The same rules, regulations and provisions shall be observed, as to the place and manner of making the selections, as are provided for the selections of candidates for Congress.

Sec. 7.—In all nominations herein provided for, whether by the State or Subordinate Councils, the vote shall be by ballot.

Sec. 8.—Members of this Order who shall fail to sustain the nominations of the same for office, shall be dealt with in the following manner, viz:—A member of the Order who shall merely fail to vote for the candidate of the Order, without voting for any one else, shall, for the first offence, be reprimanded by the President, in the presence of his Council; and for the second offence, shall be expelled. Those voting against the candidates of the Order, or who allow themselves to be run as opposition candidates against the same, shall be expelled. Members of the Legislature who shall refuse to support the nominees of the State Council, for offices to be filled by the General Assembly, shall be reported by the President of the State Council to the Subordinate Council to which such member may belong, to be dealt with; provided, however, that in all these cases here provided for, every such recusant member shall, before being dealt with, be duly notified to appear before the Council, and be heard in defence—and if three-fourths of the Council then present, shall suppose that the recusant member has acted ignorantly, or from a want of a full appreciation of his obligation, the Council may, by a vote of three-fourths, excuse him, upon the promise that he will not so offend again.

Sec. 9.—When a member is expelled by any one of the Subordinate Councils, the same shall be notified to the President of the State Council, with the name, age, and occupation of the person expelled—and the President of the State Council shall immediately notify every Subordinate Council in the State. The person so expelled to be thus published as a perjurer and traitor, unworthy the notice or regard of good men: and the President of the State Council shall keep on hand blank notices printed, for immediate use.

Article IX.

In the decision of all disputed questions that may arise in the State Council, the vote shall be taken *per capita*, unless a call for a division by counties is seconded by one-fourth of the members present—in which case the vote shall be taken by counties, a majority of the delegates from the Subordinate Council or Councils in each county represented, casting as many votes as the said county is entitled to members in the House of Commons of the State Legislature. In the decision of all questions, the vote of the majority shall prevail. This method of voting shall equally apply in the election of officers of the State Council, and to nominations for political office or place.

Article X.

Sec. 1.—For the entire work of the Order, including Ritual, the Constitution of the National Council, the Constitution of the State Council, and the Constitutions for Subordinate Councils, each Subordinate Council shall pay the sum of five dollars; and for every dispensation and charter for opening Councils, the applicants therefor shall pay the sum of three dollars.

Sec. 2.—Each Subordinate Council shall pay an annual contribution of 25 cents for each member under its jurisdiction, one half to be paid into the Treasury of the State Council semi-annually, to be paid over by the Secretary to the Treasurer of the State Council; provided, however, that the Subordinate Councils may exempt from the payment of this contribution, such of its members as they may suppose it would bear heavily upon.

Article XI.

No alteration or amendment of this Constitution shall be made, unless proposed in writing and signed by at least seven members of the State Council, submitted at least one day before its adoption, and afterwards concurred in by two-thirds of the members present.

OFFICERS OF THE NORTH CAROLINA STATE COUNCIL.

President, P. F. Pescud, Raleigh.
Vice-President, John M. Mathews, Elizabeth City.
Secretary, W. H. Harrison, Raleigh.
Treasurer, E. L. Harding, Raleigh.
Marshal, S. E. Phillips, Raleigh.
Chaplain, Rev. James Reid, Louisburg.

LYNCHBURG KNOW NOTHING CONVENTION.

The Lynchburg Convention, as it was termed, to distinguish it from a secret authoritative *council* of the Order, was held on the 19th day of October 1855, in commemoration of the crouching of the British lion before the American eagle upon the plains of Yorktown. The 19th of October, 22d of February, and the 4th day of July, are favorite days with Know Nothings for political assemblies. We would suggest, (should they ever have an occasion to convene and deliberate again,) the 24th day of May, as a day in every sense of the word suitable.

This Lynchburg Convention, after several attempts at organization, finally appointed as president Capt. Richard G. Morris, of Richmond city. The president on taking the chair, as usual, (even amongst Know Nothings,) returned thanks for the honor conferred upon him. After the election of other officers, &c., the Convention proceeded to business.

The secretary, Mr. Gilman, of Wheeling, then called over the names of the counties; the delegates present answering for their respective counties. When the list was concluded, the counties, towns and cities of the State represented were *forty-two;*—Dr. Caldwell, a travelling dentist, representing ten counties. A committee was appointed by the president to report resolutions for the adoption of the body; Mr. A. Judson Crane, of Richmond, being chairman. After the committee had retired and concocted their resolutions, they were brought before the Convention for adoption. These resolutions embodied a complete and final surrender of the main issues this party had made in the State of Virginia, but five months previous. The resolutions passed by this Convention counseled the abandonment of the ceremonies of initiation, the oaths, signs, secrets and passwords. And, finally, Mr. Samuel G. Staples, from near the Ball mountains of Patrick, introduced a resolution, which was carried, inviting all good and true men into their fold who professed to owe no temporal allegiance to any foreign power. This was certainly a virtual surrender of the Catholic test. The Catholic, as well as all other foreigners, cannot become citizens of this nation until they do renounce all allegiance to all foreign powers, potentates, kings, deys, sultans, popes, czars and emperors. But before the 24th day of May 1855, in Virginia, no member of the Catholic church, or who had Catholic parents, or worse than all, who had a Catholic wife, could be entitled to any of the privileges of the native born. There was only one dissenting voice to the resolutions adopted; and that was the "Lone Star," Mr. Woodfin, of the county of Buckingham. He considered the resolutions a complete surrender of the principles of the "*American Party.*" But the Convention paid but little attention to the gentleman from Buckingham, he being unfortunately a renegade democrat.

After the deliberations of the day were over, the Convention adjourned to Friends' warehouse to listen to the patriotic appeals of distinguished orators. Mr. Thomas Stanhope Flournoy discoursed the audience for about three hours upon the so-called principles of the "*American Party.*" Mr. A. Judson Crane, of the *Richmond congressional district,* was then loudly called for, but excused himself on account of indisposition. Then came Mr. John D. Imboden, of Augusta. Mr. Nathaniel C. Claiborne, of Franklin, was then called for. He appeared, and in his peculiar way amused the audience for a little while. Then appeared the *eloquent* but *totally unprepared* and *off-hand orator*, Mr. Waller Staples, of Montgomery. We have read the Hon. Jere. Clemens's eulogy upon Henry Clay, likewise the eulogy of the Hon. John C. Breckenridge, and also William Wirt's upon Thomas Jefferson and John Adams, but Mr. Staples' *off-hand speech* before that Convention surpassed and totally eclipsed anything that we, in the most extravagant mood of imagination, could possibly conceive of. If the Know Nothing party had not just abolished their ceremonies of initiation, &c., we should have looked out for a council as soon as the oration was over. It is said that John Hampden Pleasants attempted to take down in short hand the speech of John Randolph, of Roanoke, in the delivery of his eloquent Philippic against the administration of John Q. Adams, but the eloquence, pathos and satire of the orator completely entranced him. It was so on this occasion. A reporter from the New York Herald was present, but after hearing a few sentences from the gentleman of Montgomery, and seeing his anatomical mien, he threw himself back and appeared (as did the whole audience) perfectly enraptured and bewildered. Virginia has had her Henrys, her Randolphs, her Morrisses, and gave birth to a Clay, but still she has her Staples. The last orator upon the stand was Dr. Withers, of Campbell. He, in his remarks, was very timely and sensible, and finally wound up the ball by telling his fellow orators that he was fearful that all their speaking was like a gentleman he once heard of, who was very much engaged at breakfast one morning, eating some boiled eggs and reading the morning's paper; when his mind was abstracted from his plate to his paper, still continuing to devour the eggs, to his great surprise, just as he swallowed, he heard a chicken chirp. He very cosily continued to read, but at the same time carelessly remarked to the unfortunate chicken, that *he chirped a little too late!* He feared that all their speaking was a little too late. The doctor is decidedly a man of observation, forecast and good sense.

Thus concluded this grand but futile rally of the remnants, fragments, defeated candidates for the Board of Public Works, Congress, Senates, Legislature, &c. &c. These were the last funeral obsequies performed by the followers and admirers of poor Sam since the 24*th of May.* "The way of the trangressor is hard."—Proverbs. We will here insert the proceedings and resolutions of this Convention, as they appeared in the Richmond Whig.

[Correspondence of the Dispatch.]

KNOW NOTHING CONVENTION.

ATFERNOON SESSION—FIRST DAY.

Lynchburg, Oct. 19.

The Convention met in the afternoon, and Mr. Staples, of Patrick, from the Committee to report Permanent officers for the Convention, reported the following names:

President—Capt. Richard G. Morris, of Richmond.

Vice Presidents—J. D. Imboden, of Augusta; Wm. Collins, of Halifax; John T. Anderson, Botetourt; Dr. Patterson, Amherst; Maurice Langhorne, Lynchburg; A. J. Crane, Richmond; Dr. Caldwell, Greenbrier.

Secretaries—Wm. Semple, Richmond; W. Gilman, Wheeling; Robt. Ridgway, Richmond; J. McDonald, Lynchburg; S. T. Peters, Lynchburg; Mr. Duke, Floyd; J. C. Shields, Lynchburg.

Mr. R. G. Morris rose and returned thanks for the honor conferred on him. It had been so long since he had been connected with a legislative body, that he would ask the Convention to bear with him in the discharge of the duties of the chair. They had assembled upon the discharge of an important duty, and it was important that they should exercise forbearance and a compromising spirit. He thought the American party the only hope for saving the Union. All that remained of the old parties at the North, save the Hard Shells and Silver Greys, had become abolitionized, and declared that no more Slave States should enter the Union. If they succeed, disunion will be the result. A dark cloud hovered over the Union, and the thunder of abolitionism can be heard roaring around us. It was time for true patriots to rally around our beloved Union, and save it from the ruin consequent on the efforts of fanaticism.

Mr. Imboden moved that the Secretary call over the counties of the State, and that the names of the delegates from them should be recorded.

The Secretary called over the list, and the following counties were shown to be represented: Albemarle, Alleghany, Amherst, Appomattox, Augusta, Bedford, Botetourt, Braxton, Buckingham, Campbell, Caroline, Charlotte, Cumberland, Elizabeth City, Floyd, Franklin, Fayette, Fluvanna, Gloucester, Greenbrier, Giles, Halifax, Henrico, Kanawha, Lewis, Monroe, Montgomery, Nicholas, Nelson, Nottoway, Ohio, Pocahontas, Pulaski, Patrick, Pittsylvania, Prince Edward, Randolph, Roanoke, Rockbridge, Wythe, Richmond City, Lynchburg, Wheeling.

On motion of Mr. Ridgway, all persons who belonged to or sympathized with the American party, were invited to record their names as delegates from the counties from which they came.

Mr. Imboden moved the appointment of a committee of thirteen to prepare business for the action of the convention; and nominated Mr. A. J. Crane as chairman of the same.

The President appointed the following gentlemen to constitute the committee: A. J. Crane, Richmond; J. D. Imboden, Augusta; Wm. Burwell, Bedford; Dr. Payne, Lynchburg; Walter Staples, Montgomery; John Mosby, Elizabeth City; P. Bolling, Prince Edward; Dr. Charles Cocke, Albemarle; Col. J. D. Davis, Amherst; A. D. Mitchell, Henrico; John Gilmer, Pittsylvania; R. C. McClure, Rockbridge.

On motion of Mr. Ridgway, the convention then adjourned until 7 o'clock, P. M.

Night Session.—The convention re-opened to-night, at 7, P. M.

Mr. Crane, chairman of the committee to report business for the convention, made the following partial report:

Resolved, That this convention adopt the Philadelphia Platform, with the following exposition of the 8th section:

Resolved, That the 8th Section of the Philadelphia platform is not intended, in the opinion of this convention, to exclude any citizen from public station, on account of his religious faith, but only such as may have reserved a paramount allegiance to a foreign potentate.

The convention then adjourned until next day, 9 A. M.

PROCEEDINGS OF THE SECOND DAY.

Lynchburg, Oct. 20th, 12 M.

The convention re-assembled this morning, and proceeded to the business before them.

On motion of Mr. J. T. Anderson, the two resolutions in the partial report of the committee submitted last night, were separated and made to read as follows:

Resolved, That this convention adopt the Philadelphia platform.

Resolved, That the 8th section of the Philadelphia platform is not intended, in the opinion of this Convention, to exclude any citizen from political station on account of his religious faith, but only such as may have reserved paramount allegiance to a foreign potentate.

Mr. Crane, from the Committee to prepare Resolutions, reported in full, as follows:

Resolved, That in the 12th section of the Philadelphia platform we recognize a true national and constitutional adjustment of the vexed question of slavery, and we pledge the American party of Virginia to an unyielding resistance to any change or modification, in substance or spirit, of that section.

Resolved, That the wholesale proscription recommended by the organs of the Democratic party of this State, of more than half of the native citizens of Virginia, deserves the most decided reprobation of every honest and patriotic citizen; that the hypocritical reason assigned for this proscription, viz: the false charge of proscription against the American party, is an insult to an intelligent people; that such a charge comes with a bad grace from a party who have always proscribed their political opponents, and who disfranchised nearly one half of the freemen of this State by a fraudulent system of legislative gerrymandering unparalleled in party legislation.

Resolved, That the open interference of the Federal Government in the recent elections of Virginia deserves the indignant reprobation of every good citizen.

Resolved, That in vindication of public morality and of the necessity for the formation of a new party, we hereby recommend a rigid investigation of the manner in which official trusts have been discharged by the Federal and State Governments, and a publication of all facts developed thereby.

Resolved, That in the opinion of this Convention, the nominations of the American party, for President and Vice President of the United States, should be postponed to a period not later than the 1st of June.

Resolved, That this committee recommend to the convention, the appointment of a committee of three, whose duty it shall be to prepare and publish an address to the people of Virginia, setting forth the principles of the American party, in accordance with the principles of the platform and the resolutions adopted by the Convention at their present session.

(Under this resolution the President appointed Messrs. Wm. M. Burwell, A. J. Crane and Robert Ridgway. On motion the President was added to the committee.)

Resolved, That, in the judgment of this convention, all ceremonies of initiation into the American party be discontinued, and all obligations of secrecy removed—that its meeting should be open and public, and its proceedings conducted in accordance with the usages of political bodies—and we invite the co-operation of all good men who approve the principles and objects of the party.

All of the resolutions reported by the committee were adopted without discussion save the last one, which was strongly opposed by Mr. D. J. Woodfin of Buckingham, who contended that the party had already yielded too much to outside influence. Should the ban of secrecy be removed, the cry would go forth that the order had changed into an open Whig organization—a cry which had been often sounded during the last canvass. He said that in the last election there were no withdrawals until the party commenced yielding to outside influence, and relaxing their strict secrecy. Then it was that their adversaries found out who were members of the organization, and commenced operating upon them. From that time withdrawals commenced.

The resolution was supported by Messrs. Wm. M. Burwell, of Bedford; J. T. Anderson, of Botetourt; S. G. Staples, of Patrick; W. R. Staples, of Montgomery; and J. D. Imboden, of Augusta. The principal arguments advanced were the utter uselessness of secrecy and the great efforts made by the Democracy in the last campaign to bring the order into discredit on account of it. The principles of the party had not been attacked, and instead, the enemy had ridiculed and condemned the ceremonies, secrecy, &c., of the order.

Mr. W. T. Sutherlin, of Danville, offered the following resolution as a substitute for that of the committee:

Resolved, That this Convention recommend to the American party of Virginia an open, thorough and complete organization in each county in the State.

Mr. S. afterwards withdrew the resolution as an amendment to that of the committee, and offered it as a distinct resolution, in which form it was adopted.

The vote was then taken on the committee's resolution, and it was adopted without a dissenting voice.

Mr. Imboden, of Augusta, offered the following resolution:

Resolved, That this Convention recommend to the American Party of Virginia to hold a Convention in the city of Richmond on the 14th of January next.

As a substitute for the above, which met with some opposition, Mr. Imboden offered a resolution calling an American Mass Meeting in the city of Richmond, on the 31st inst., which was adopted.

Mr. Staples of Patrick, offered the following resolution, which was adopted:

Resolved, That this Convention recommend the holding of Conventions in each Congressional District, for the purpose of sending delegates to the National Convention, and that three delegates be sent from said Congressional Districts with power to cast such vote only as may be prescribed by the National Convention.

Dr. Patterson of Amherst, offered a resolution admitting to public office any citizen who shall openly disclaim allegiance to a foreign potentate.

As the Convention was rapidly breaking up and members leaving, the resolution was withdrawn.

After the usual vote of thanks to the officers of the Convention, and to the citizens of Lynchburg, for their hospitality, the Convention adjourned *sine die.*

THE NATIONALITY OF THE DEMOCRATIC PARTY.

In the States of OHIO and CONNECTICUT, the Whig and Know Nothing parties have been thoroughly abolitionized, and their elections and declarations, their acts and their words, render the fact unquestionable. They are waging a war of extermination on slavery, in and out of Congress at this time.

In those two States, where the hostility to slavery is stronger than in any other, either of the western or New England States, the Democracy are not merely conservative on that question, they are more—they are the defenders of the South and her peculiar institution, as the following resolutions will prove.

We copy *in extenso* the following resolutions of the late Democratic State Convention of Connecticut:

DEMOCRATIC STATE CONVENTION OF CONNECTICUT.

The Hartford Times, of the 15th instant, contains a full report of the proceedings of the Democratic State Convention of Connecticut, which was held at New Haven on the preceding day. It was one of the largest delegated conventions ever held in Connecticut. Our readers have already been advised of the of the nominations of State officers by this convention. The following resolutions, which were unanimously adopted, are worthy of extensive circulation. They breathe the right spirit, and admirably meet all the issues raised by the enemies of the Democratic party:

"*Resolved,* That the strict adherence of the President of the United States to those great principles of constitutional government which have received the entire sanction of the democracy of the Union, and the checks which he has interposed upon legislation at war with those principles by his vetoes of the insane land bill, and the river and harbor bill, assure us that, under his administration, the country will be secure from any inroads upon that constitution which is the written bond uniting thirty-one sovereign States, and on the strict construction of which depends the harmonious existence of our confederated system.

Resolved, That the power of Congress over the Territories of the U. States should be only employed to such an extent as the necessities of the case may require, and for the equal benefit of all the parties to the federal compact, and that when any Territory, having the requisite number of inhabitants, applies for admission into the Union as a sovereign State, she must, to be received as a co-equal member of the family of States, be admitted with such constitution as her people may ordain, provided said constitution does not conflict with the organic law of the confederacy.

Resolved, That those just and equitable laws providing for the naturalization of those born in other lands, established in accordance with the principles of the signers of the Declaration of Independence, and continued to this day without any interruption, save that caused by the bigoted federalists under the administration of John Adams, have contributed to the growth of this republic and the fraternization of its inhabitants; and that these laws are essentially the part of that wise American policy which, founded on a comprehensive and philanthropic basis, has signalized our beloved country as the home of the exile and oppressed, and will make her as renowned for her power and greatness as she is distinguished for her freedom and enterprise.

Resolved, That, in order to recognise in the most solemn form the principles of religious freedom, the constitution of the United States doth ordain that 'Congress shall make no law respecting an establishment of religion, or prohibiting the free exercise thereof,' and that the various States have, almost without exception, incorporated some distinct acknowledgment of religious liberty into their several constitutions, and that thus religious freedom has become, by the action of the sovereign States and of the general government, whose powers are derived from those States, a great American principle.

Resolved, That political parties organized with the view of shutting out from all posts of political trust the members of any religious denomination, do virtually condemn that system of religious liberty which is American in its character, beneficent in its conception, and which has greatly promoted the harmony and happiness of the people; and that all political organizations founded on hatred of religious creed or prejudice of birth are alien to the great ideas of American liberty and American progress, and deserve the condemnation of American freemen."

At a convention of the Democratic party in Ohio, held at Dayton, Oct. 29th, 1855, after eloquent addresses from several prominent Democrats in favor of the Kansas Nebraska act:

"Capt. E. A. King, from the committee on resolutions, reported the following, which were received severally with loud applause, and adopted without a dissenting voice.

"*Whereas:* The formal reorganization and consolidation of the old Abolition party of the North, under the name of "Republican party," into an avowed northern faction bounded by a geographical line, and pledged to an unrelenting warfare, even to the destruction of the Constitution and the sundering of the Union, upon the domestic institutions of the people of all the States lying south of that line, demands of the only National party now in existence, the Democracy of the United States, but especially of that of the North, that laying aside old issues and controversies, they should come up as one man to the full measure of the exigencies which press upon us, and boldly meet the new and living questions of the day:

"Therefore, we a portion of the Democracy of Ohio and the North, in public meeting assembled, do resolve and declare:—

"*Resolved,* That we congratulate the people of the United States, on the final inauguration of the grand scheme of domestic policy for which the Democratic party of the Union so many years contended, and the consequent prosperity, which, under the auspices of that party, has distinguished every section of the country, vindicating at once the sound doctrine and policy of that party, and the intelligence, patriotism, and discriminating justice of the American people.

Resolved, That the powers of the Federal Government, are derived solely from the constitutional compact to which the several States are parties: that these are limited by the plain sense and intention of the instrument consitituting that compact; that the grants of power made in that instrument, ought to be strictly construed by all the departments and agents of the government: that all powers not expressly granted or necessarily implied, are expressly reserved to the States respectively, or to the people: that it is inexpedient and dangerous to exercise powers of doubtful constitutionality.

Resolved, That in delegating a portion of their powers to be exercised by the Federal government, the States retained, severally, the exclusive and sole right over their own domestic institutions and police, and are alone responsible for them; and that any intermeddling of any one or more States, or of a combination of their citizens, with the domestic institutions and police of the others on any ground or under any pretext whatever, political, moral, or religious, with a view to their alteration or subversion, is an assumption of superiority, not warranted by the Constitution, insulting to the States interfered with, tending to endanger their domestic peace and tranquility, subversive of the objects for which the Constitution was framed, and by necessary consequence, tending to weaken and destroy the Union itself.

Resolved, That domestic slavery as it exists in the southern States of this Union, comprises an important part of their domestic institutions inherited from their ancestors, and existing at the adoption of the Constitution, by which it is recognized as constituting an essential element in the distribution of its powers among the States; and that no change of opinion or feeling on the part of the other States of the Union in relation to it, can justify them or their citizens in open and systematic attacks thereon with a view to its overthrow; and that all such attacks are in manifest violation of the mutual and solemn pledge to protect and defend each other, given by the States respectively on entering into the constitutional compact which formed the Union, and as such is a manifest breach of faith and a violation of the most solemn obligations, moral and religious.

Resolved, That Congress has no power, under the Constitution, to interfere with or control the domestic institutions of the several States; and that such States are the sole and proper judges of everything appertaining to their own affairs, not prohibited by the Constitution; and that all efforts of Abolitionists, or others, by whatever name known, made to induce Congress to interfere with questions of slavery, or to take incipient steps in relation thereto, whether for the abolition of slavery in the District of Columbia, or the Territories, or its prohibition therein, or for the interdiction of the coastwise or inter-state slave trade, or the repeal of the Fugitive Slave Law, or of the Kansas Nebraska act, are calculated to lead to the most alarming and dangerous consequences; and that all such efforts have an inevitable tendency to diminish the happiness of the people and endanger the stability and permanency of the Union, and ought not to be countenanced by any friend of our political institutions.

Resolved, That regarding these compromises of the Constitution, solemnly entered into by its founders, as wise and necessary provisions, and such as ought neither to be disregarded nor tampered with, we are for the Constitution as it is, and the Union as it is; and that we will preserve, maintain and defend both at every hazard, observing with scrupulous and uncalculating fidelity, every article, requirement and compromise of the constitutional compact between these States, to the letter and in its utmost spirit, and recognizing no "higher law" between which and the constitution we know of any conflict.

Resolved, That the Constitution was "the result of a spirit of amity, and of that mutual deference and concession which the peculiarities of our political situation rendered indispensable;" and that by amity, conciliation and compromise alone can it and the Union which it established, be preserved: and that it is the duty of all good citizens to frown indignantly upon every attempt wheresoever and by whomsoever made, to array one section of the Union against the other, to foment jealousies or heart burnings between them by systematic and organized misrepresentation, denunciation and calumny, and thereby to render alien in feeling and affection the inheritors of so noble a common patrimony, purchased by our fathers at so great expense of blood of treasure.

Resolved, That the Constitution confers no power upon Congress to establish or prohibit slavery in the Territories of the United States: that these Territories are the common property of the States in their federal capacity, purchased by the common blood and treasure of all the States: and that the people of each and every State, have the right to an equal participation in every respect, in the use of these Territories in common, without interference by Congress.

Resolved, That the right of the people of each particular State and Territory to establish their own constitution or form of government; to choose and regulate their own domestic institutions of every kind, and to legislate for themselves' is a fundamental principle of all free government; that it is the self same right to secure which our ancestors waged the war of the revolution; a right lying at the very foundation of all our free institutions, recognized in the Declaration of Independence, and established and secured by the Constitution of the United States; and we hereby endorse and reaffirm this *now* disputed principle, as it is embodied in the Acts for the organization of Utah and New Mexico in 1850, and of Kansas and Nebraska in 1854.

Resolved further, That the foregoing right is no otherwise limited or restricted by the Constitution of the United States, except so far as the constitution of a State applying for admission into the Union is required to be "republican," or representative in form; a limitation in no wise affected by the domestic institution of slavery; and that therefore all efforts to exclude a State from such admission, on the ground that her constitution or laws sanction slaveholding, are violations alike of sound democratic principles and of the Constitution of the Union.

Resolved, That the introduction of moral or religious questions into the political controversies and issues of the day, is a wide departure from the ancient principles and sound policy of the country; at war with the true interests of the people, corrupting alike to morals, religion and politics, and of most pernicious and dangerous tendency; and that therefore we are uncompromisingly opposed to the provisions of the "Maine Liquor Law," so called, the principles of the "Order of Know Nothings," and the fanaticisms and wicked and traitorous purposes of Abolitionism."

A SPEAKER ELECTED.

The protracted struggle for the speakership was brought to a close last evening by the election of Hon. N. P. Banks. Nine full weeks were consumed before this result was attained, and it was finally brought about by the adoption of the plurality rule. Although it is absolutely certain that there is a majority of the representatives in the House who agree with Mr. Banks on the sectional questions which now agitate the country, yet it has been demonstrated, again and again, that a portion of his own political friends would never agree to vote for him for Speaker, and hence that he could never be elected by a majority vote.

As we have remarked, the contest was finally terminated under the operation of the plurality rule. The votes taken during several days past had indicated that a Speaker could only be chosen by resorting to that rule. There was a strong repugnance amongst the national members to its adoption, more especially after the revolting declaration of Mr. Banks as to the test of superiority in the races. The southern Know Nothings manifested a determination against casting their votes for the democratic nominees not less persistent than their refusal to vote for Mr. Banks. On Friday, however, propositions were made by Democrats to which the southern Know Nothings indicated a disposition to accede—the one proposing Mr. Oliver, an old-line Whig, and the other Mr. Aiken, a National Democrat, for Speaker. The votes on these propositions, compared with that given on the same day on a resolution declaring Mr. Banks the Speaker, showed so little difference that it was exceedingly doubtful what would be the result upon the adoption of the plurality rule. At this point Mr. Smith, of Tennessee, believing that the chances of Mr. Aiken were at least equal to those of Mr. Banks, brought forward a resolution for the plurality rule. Mr. Orr immediately withdrew unconditionally his name as the democratic nominee, and the resolution was adopted. The result was, as we have stated, the election of Mr. Banks by a plurality of three votes—Mr. Banks receiving 103 votes, and Mr. Aiken 100—six national Americans throwing their votes on Mr. Fuller, and four Republicans throwing theirs on Mr. L. D. Campbell. It is apparent that a perfect union of the national members (the four Republicans voting for Mr. Campbell) would have elected Mr. Aiken by a plurality of three. Thus has ended the most extraordinary struggle that has ever occurred. Although the result is one which every national man will regret, yet, as the Republicans have a known majority in the House, and therefore were entitled to the Speaker, there is reason for acquiescing, inasmuch as it enables the machinery of government once more to move on.

Saturday, February 2, 1856.

HOUSE OF REPRESENTATIVES.

The House met at 12, m.

Prayer by the Rev. Mr. Cummins.

The journal of yesterday was read and approved.

The Clerk stated that the first business in order was the resolution submitted by the gentleman from Kentucky, [Mr. Talbott,] as follows:

Resolved, That the Hon. Alexander H. Stephens be, and he is hereby declared Speaker of the House of Representatives for the 34th Congress.

Mr. Talbott had offered the resolution without having any conference with the honorable gentleman whose name was contained in it. He had hoped that it would reconcile all the discordant elements of the House, and bring about an organization. He rose for the purpose of withdrawing the resolution at the request of the gentleman from Georgia.

Mr. Smith, of Tennessee, stated that he had heretofore voted against the plurality rule; but the vote of yesterday indicating that there was at least the chance of the election of a man of sound national principles under its operation, he therefore offered the following resolution, and called for the previous question:

Resolved, That the House will proceed immediately to the election of a Speaker *viva voce;* and if, after the roll shall have been called three times, no member shall have received a majority of the whole number of votes, the roll shall again be called, and the member who shall then receive the largest number of votes, provided it be a majority of a quorum, shall be duly declared Speaker of the House of Representatives of the Thirty-fourth Congress.

Mr. Goode, of Virginia, moved to lay the resolution on the table; which motion was not agreed to—yeas 104, nays 114.

The previous question was seconded, and the main question was ordered to be now put.

The question was taken, and the resolution was adopted—yeas 113, nays 104—as follows:

YEAS—Messrs. Albright, Allison, Ball, Banks, Barbour, Barclay, Henry Bennett, Benson, Billinghurst, Bingham, Bishop, Bliss, Bradshaw, Brenton, Buffington, Burlingame, James H. Campbell, Chaffee, Bayard Clark, Ezra Clark, Clawson, Clingman, Colfax, Comins, Covoke, Cragin, Cumback, Damrell, Timothy Davis, Day, Dean, De Witt, Dick, Dickson, Dodd, Durfee, Edie, Flagler, Galloway, Giddings, Gilbert, Granger, Grow, Robert B. Hall, Harlan, Herbert, Hickman, Holloway, Thomas R. Horton, Howard, Jewett, Kelley, Kelsey, King, Knapp, Knight, Knowlton, Knox, Kunkel, Leiter, Mace, Matteson, McCarty, Meacham, Killian Miller, Morgan, Morrill, Mott, Murray, Nichols, Norton, Andrew Oliver, Parker, Pearce, Pelton, Pennington, Perry, Pettit, Pike, Pringle, Purviance, Ritchie, Robbins, Roberts, Robison, Sabin, Sage, Sapp, Sherman, Simmons, Samuel A. Smith, Spinner, Stanton, Stranahan, Tappan, Thorington, Thurston, Todd, Trafton, Tyson, Wade, Walbridge, Waldron, C. C. Washburne, E. B. Washburne, Israel Washburn, Watson, Welch, Wells, Williams, Wood, Woodruff, and Woodworth—113.

NAYS—Messrs. Aiken, Allen, Barksdale, Bell, Hendley S. Bennett, Bocock, Bowie, Boyce, Branch, Brooks, Broom, Burnett, Cadwalader, John P. Campbell, Lewis D. Campbell, Carlile, Caruthers, Caskie, Howell Cobb, W. R. W. Cobb, Cox, Crawford, Davidson, H. Winter Davis, Denver, Dowdell, Dunn, Edmundson, Elliott, English, Etheridge, Eustis, Evans, Faulkner, Florence, Foster, H. M. Fuller, T. J. D. Fuller, Goode, Greenwood, Augustus Hall, J. M. Harris, S. W. Harris, T. L. Harris, Harrison, Hoffman, Houston, George W. Jones, J. Glancy Jones, Keitt, Kennett, Kidwell, Lake, Letcher, Lindley, Lumpkin, A. K. Marshall, Humphrey Marshall, S. S. Marshall, Maxwell, McMullen, McQueen, Smith Miller, Millson, Millward, Moore, Mordecai Oliver, Orr, Paine, Peck, Phelps, Porter, Powell, Puryear, Quitman, Ready, Ricaud, Rivers, Ruffin, Rust, Sandidge, Savage, Scott, Shorter, William Smith, William R. Smith, Sneed, Stephens, Stewart, Swope, Talbott, Trippe, Underwood, Vail, Valk, Walker, Warner, Watkins, Wheeler, Whitney, Winslow, D. B. Wright, J. V. Wright, and Zollicoffer—104.

[The announcement was applauded in the galleries.]

Mr. Orr, of South Carolina, said that his name had been put in nomination some two weeks ago by the Democratic party for the speakership, and though very many ballots had taken place since that time, and although the members of that party supposed that by changing their nominee they might increase and strengthen them, yet the result had shown that they were mistaken in the conclusion to which they arrived. The complimentary vote given yesterday to his colleague [Mr. Aiken] rendered it very evident to his mind that that gentleman would be able to concentrate a greater strength than himself, and as he desired to see the House organized upon national principles, and in opposition to sectionalism, he took occasion, after returning his thanks to his party friends for their fidelity and confidence in nominating and sustaining him, to withdraw unconditionally his name from the contest.

Mr. Boyce, of South Carolina, moved to rescind the resolution just adopted.

Mr. Smith, of Tennessee, moved to lay that motion on the table; which was agreed to—yeas 117, nays 101.

[Applause in the galleries.]

Cries of "Call the roll."

Mr. Jones, of Tennessee, moved an adjournment of the House, in order to give members an opportunity to confer, that they might cast their votes understandingly in the great crisis which they were now approaching. The motion was not agreed to—yeas 84, nays 133.

[Applause in the galleries.]

Cries of "Call the roll."

Mr. Walker, of Alabama, moved to rescind the plurality resolution.

Mr. Clingman raised the point that the motion was not in order, it having been decided once already during the day.

The Clerk thought that the motion was in order, but submitted the question to the House, and it was decided that it was not in order—yeas 83, nays 128.

Mr. Paine, of North Carolina, moved that the House do now adjourn; which motion was not agreed to.

[Applause in the galleries.]

Mr. Orr said that if the House was to be annoyed by continued applause he would have to move that the galleries be cleared. He did not allude to the ladies' gallery. [Laughter.]

[Cries of "Call the roll."]

VOTE FOR SPEAKER.

The House then proceeded to vote for Speaker, it being the first under the plurality rule.

The Clerk called the roll the one hundred and thirtieth time, with the following result:

Whole number of votes, 215; necessary to a choice, 108: of these—

Mr. Banks received,	102
Aiken,	93
H. M. Fuller,	14
L. D. Campbell,	4
Wells,	2

Mr. Richardson, of Illinois, gave notice that he had paired off with Mr. Emrie, otherwise he would have voted for Mr. Aiken.

There being no choice, the House proceeded to the one hundred and thirty-first vote, being the second under the plurality rule, with the following result:

Whole number of votes, 214; necessary to a choice, 108: of these—

Mr. Banks received	102
Aiken,	93
H. M. Fuller,	13
L. D. Campbell,	4
Wells,	2

So there was no choice.

Mr. Kennett, of Missouri, moved that the House do now adjourn; which motion was not agreed to. [Applause.]

The House then proceeded to the one hundred and thirty-second vote, being the third under the plurality rule, with the following result:

Whole number of votes, 213; necessary to a choice, 107: of these—

Mr. Banks received	102
Aiken,	93
H. M. Fuller,	13
L. D. Campbell,	4
Wells,	2

So there was no choice.

Mr. Rust, of Arkansas, moved that the House do now adjourn; which motion was not agreed to—yeas 52, nays 162.

[Shouts of "Call the roll."]

Mr. Fuller, of Pennsylvania, desired to repeat what he had said upon two former occasions, that he was not, and did not desire to be, a candidate. [Applause.] One hundred and thirty ballots would have satisfied him that he was not the choice of a majority of the body, and upon no other terms, upon no other conditions, would he consent to take that position. He again returned his acknowledgments to the genlemen who had honored him with their support, and he requested them to cast their suffrages for a better and abler man.

During the call of the roll on the last ballot the following explanations were made.

Mr. Barclay, of Pennsylvania, said that his votes stood on the record, and he saw no reason why he should change them. He had been adverse, from the first to the last, to anything that looked like a coalition with know nothingism, he did not care whether it came from the North or the South. He had on three votes this morning cast his votes away, and before he again cast a vote he wished to ask the gentleman from South Carolina [Mr. Aiken] whether he had written a letter to the honorable gentleman from Kentucky [Mr. H. Marshall], and whether he had made any pledges satisfactory to the Southern wing of the National American party?

Mr. Rust objected to the gentleman proceeding further.

Mr. Aiken said that he was not a candidate for the office of Speaker. If his friends saw fit to elect him to that position, he would serve them to the best of his ability. [Great applause.]

Mr. A. K. Marshall, of Kentucky, said that he and those with whom he acted had discharged their duty to their party, and it now remained for them to discharge it to their country. He voted for Aiken.

Several other gentlemen made explanations before voting for Aiken.

The House then proceeded to the one hundred and thirty-third vote for Speaker, and the last vote under the plurality rule, with the following result: whole number of votes, 214: of these—

Mr. Banks received,	103
Aiken,	100
H. M. Fuller,	6
L. D. Campbell,	4
Wells,	1

The following is the vote in detail:

For Mr. Banks.—Messrs. Albright, Allison, Ball, Barbour, Henry Bennett, Benson, Billinghurst, Bingham, Bishop, Bliss, Bradshaw, Brenton, Buffington, Burlingame, James H. Campbell, Lewis D. Campbell, Chaffee, Ezra Clark, Clawson, Colfax, Comins, Covode, Cragin, Cumback, Damrell, Timothy Davis, Day, Dean, De Witt, Dick, Dickson, Dodd, Durlee, Edie, Flagler, Galloway, Giddings, Gilbert, Granger, Grow, Robert B. Hall, Harlan, Holloway, Thomas R. Horton, Howard, Kelsey, King, Knapp, Knight, Knowlton, Knox, Kunkel, Leiter, Mace, Matteson, McCarty, Meacham, Killian Miller, Morgan, Morrill, Mott, Murray, Nichols, Norton, Andrew Oliver, Parker, Pearce, Pelton, Pennington, Perry, Pettit, Pike, Pringle, Purviance, Ritchie, Robbins, Roberts, Robison, Sabin, Sage, Sapp, Sherman, Simmons, Spinner, Stanton, Stranahan, Tappan, Thorington, Thurston, Todd, Trafton, Tyson, Wade, Walbridge, Waldron, Cadwalader C. Washburne, Ellihu B. Washburne, Israel Washburn, Watson, Welch, Wood, Woodruff, and Woodworth—103.

For Mr. Aiken.—Messrs. Allen, Barksdalle, Bell, Hendley S. Bennett, Bocock, Bowie, Boyce, Branch, Brooks, Burnett, Cadwalader, John P. Campbell, Carlile, Caruthers, Caskie, Clingman, Howell Cobb, Williamson R. W. Cobb, Cox, Crawford, Davidson, Denver, Dowdell, Edmundson, Elliott, English, Etheridge, Eustis, Evans, Faulkner, Florence, Foster, Thomas J. D. Fuller, Goode, Greenwood, Augustus Hall, J. Morrison Harris, Sampson W. Harris, Thomas L. Harris, Herbert, Hoffman, Houston, Jewitt, George W. Jones, J. Glancy Jones, Keitt, Kelly, Kennett, Kidwell, Lake, Letcher, Lindley, Lumpkin, Alexander K. Marshall, Humphrey Marshall, Samuel S. Marshall, Maxwell, McMullen, McQueen, Smith Miller, Milson, Mordecai Oliver, Orr, Paine, Peck, Phelps, Porter, Powell, Puryear, Quitman, Reade, Ready, Ricaud, Rivers, Ruffin, Rust, Sandidge, Savage, Shorter, Samuel A. Smith, William Smith, Wm. R. Smith, Sneed, Stephens, Stewart, Swope, Talbott, Trippe, Underwood, Vail, Walker, Warner, Watkins, Wells, Wheeler, Williams, Winslow, Daniel B. Wright, John V. Wright, and Zollicoffer—100.

For Mr. Fuller.—Messrs. Broom, Clark of New York, Cullen, Davis of Maryland, Millward, and Whitney—6.

For Mr. Campbell.—Messrs. Dunn, Harrison, Moore, and Scott—4.

For Mr. Wells.—Mr. Hickman.

Mr. Benson, of Maine, one of the tellers, announced that Nathaniel P. Banks, jr., of Massachusetts, was duly elected Speaker.

Mr. A. K. Marshall raised the question that the House itself must declare the result, and that the Clerk could neither do so himself nor delegate any one to do so. He should be very sorry to see the Clerk depart from that course which had hitherto secured him so many friends.

After some debate on this point, in which Messrs. Rust, Clingman, Cobb, of Georgia, Smith of Alabama, Paine of North Carolina, H. Marshall, Campbell of Ohio, Herbert, and Stewart participated, and during which Mr. Aiken asked permission of the House to conduct the gentleman from Massachusetts [Mr. Banks] to the chair, as the duly elected Speaker of the House.

Mr. Clingman offered the following resolution:

"Resolved, That, by reason of the adoption of the proposition known as the plurality resolution, and the votes taken under it, the Hon. N. P. Banks, jr., of Massachusetts, has been duly chosen Speaker, and is hereby so declared."

After some debate, the previous question was called on the resolution, and seconded, and ordered to be now put.

The question was taken, and the resolution was adopted—yeas 156, nays 40—as follows:

Yeas—Messrs. Aiken, Albright, Allen, Allison, Ball, Barbour, Barclay, Bell, Henry Bennett, Benson, Billinghurst, Bingham, Bishop, Bliss, Bowie, Bradshaw, Branch, Brenton, Broom, Buffington, Burlingame, Cadwalader, James H. Campbell, Lewis D. Campbell, Chaffee, Bayard Clarke, Ezra Clark, Clawson, Clingman, Howell Cobb, Colfax, Comins, Covode, Cox, Cragin, Cullen, Cumback, Damrell, Timothy Davis, Day, Dean, De Witt, Dick, Dickson, Dodd, Dunn, Durfee, Edie, English, Etheridge, Evans, Flagler, Florence, Thomas J. D. Fuller, Galloway, Giddings, Gilbert, Granger, Grow, Robert B. Hall, Harlan, J. Morrison Harris, Sampson W. Harris, Harrison, Herbert, Hickman, Hoffman, Holloway, Thomas R. Horton, Howard, Jewitt, George W. Jones, J. Glancy Jones, Kelley, Kelsey, Kennett, King, Knapp, Knight, Knowlton, Knox, Kunkel, Leiter, Lumpkin, Mace, Matteson, McCarty, Meacham, Killian Miller, Millward, Moore, Morgan, Morrill, Mott, Murray, Nichols, Norton, Andrew Oliver, Parker, Pearce, Pelton, Pennington, Perry, Pettit, Pike, Porter,

Pringle, Purviance, Puryear, Reade, Ready, Ritchie, Rivers, Robbins, Roberts, Robison, Sabin, Sage, Sapp, Scott, Sherman, Simmons, Samuel A. Smith, William R. Smith, Spinner, Stanton, Stephens, Stewart, Stranahan, Talbott, Tappan, Thorington, Thurston, Todd, Trafton, Tyson, Underwood, Vail, Wade, Walbridge, Waldron, Warner, Cadwalader, C. Washburne, Ellihu B. Washburne, Israel Washburn, Watkins, Watson, Welch, Wells, Wheeler, Whitney, Williams, Winslow, Wood, Woodruff, and Woodworth—156.

NAYS—Messrs. Barksdale, Hendley S. Bennett, Boyce, Burnett, John P. Campbell, Carlile, Caskie, Crawford, Davidson, H. Winter Davis, Dowdell, Edmundson, Elliott, Foster, Goode, Greenwood, Thomas L. Harris, Houston, Keitt, Kidwell, Lake, Letcher, Alexander K. Marshall, Maxwell, McMullen, McQueen, Mordecai Oliver, Orr, Phelps, Powell, Ruffin, Rust, Sandidge, Savage, Shorter, Sneed, Trippe, Walker, Daniel B. Wright, and John V. Wright —40.

The Clerk appointed Messrs. H. M. Fuller, Aiken, and L. D. Campbell to conduct Mr. Banks to the chair.

Mr. Banks, on taking the chair acknowledged the honor done him in a brief and neat speech.

The usual oath of office was then administered to him by Mr. Giddings.

On motion of Mr. Stanton, of Ohio, the following resolution was unanimously adopted :

"Resolved, That the thanks of this House are eminently due, and are hereby tendered, to John W. Forney, Esq., for the distinguished ability, fidelity and impartiality with which he has presided over the deliberations of the House of Representatives during the arduous and protracted contest for Speaker which has just closed."

On motion of Mr. Cobb, of Georgia, the House, at 7 o'clock, adjourned.

From *Luzerne Union*, Jan. 30, 1856.

HON. HENRY M. FULLER.—HIS SOMERSET.

In order to make an answer to the very many letters we have received as to the antecedents of Henry M. Fuller, we have collected together to-day, some facts connected with that honorable gentleman's antecedents. The gentlemen who have written us on this subject, will please take this for an answer, as it embodies the facts which we have at hand. Here, in this district, no man will be found, can be found, who has any regard for truth, that will pretend to say that the gentleman was ever anything else than an Abolitionist, and as such, received the hearty support of the rankest of them. A Whig, a Free Soiler, an Abolitionist, a Wilmot Proviso man, a Know Nothing—this is the history of the gentleman's political career. He never pretended that he was anything else, till he bid for the Speakership. To gain this, he did not merely repudiate his old faith, and turn his back on his old friends and old principles, but he denied that he was one of them, and was elected on their platform. Not only a change of faith, which might under some circumstances be justified, but a denial that he ever advocated such a faith as his friends always claimed for him.

A correspondent of the New York Times, of the 19th of January, instant, holds this language :

"*Anti-Nebraska did not Elect him.*—Mr. Fuller, of Pennsylvania, became restive in the debate to-day, and distinctly denied that he was elected by the Anti-Nebraska sentiment of his district. Mark this enunciation, Anti-Nebraska men of Pennsylvania, and take care that when you nominate again, you make the fetters of principle at least strong enough to be understood by the candidate."

"He denied that he was elected by the Anti-Nebraska sentiment of his district!!!!" Can this be possible? Can it be, that a man in his senses could utter such a palpable, open, and bare-faced falsehood? He "not elected by the Anti-Nebraska sentiment!" When his friends justified him on the ground that he had a right to change his views, we thought they went far in the deed of character, particularly as they elected him on a pledge to vote to repeal the "infamous Nebraska act—to restore the Missouri line;" but what will they say now, when their man denies that he was the exponent of their views? What can they say? Nothing—absolutely nothing. With their fingers in their mouths, they are silent! But it is a silence that is ominous. It is a silence that precedes the storm and the whirlwind, and so the honorable gentleman will find it, if he ever enters the political track again. We spoke of his friends justifying him for "a change of opinion"—we mean his personal political friends. The masses of the old line who gave him their support, whisper "treason," and call to mind a worthy old gentleman who betrayed his master.

But let us see what the issue was before the canvass, which resulted in the gentleman's election. The *Record of the Times*, of this place, the organ of Mr. Fuller, knows full well what the issue was, and that we may not be mistaken, we will quote from that paper, and see how this matter was understood at the time. But in the first place, what was the Democratic issue? We will see the affirmative first.

On the 12th of September, 1854, the Democratic conferees of the counties composing the district, met and put in nomination Col. Wright, for Congress. To show the platform they made for him, we copy from this paper of the 13th September, 1854. The resolutions were drawn by the vigorous pen of the late Samuel P. Collings, Esq., who recently died in Tangiers, at the time a United States Consul.

"*Resolved,* That in the large intelligence, generous impulses, and frank and cordial character of their nominee for Congress, the Democracy have a guarantee that he will represent their interests and maintain the character of this District honorably and faithfully in Congress; that the only rational objection heretofore urged for withholding any portion of Democratic support, was fairly removed by his upright and honorable course during the late session of Congress; and that any present opposition, from the same quarter, to his triumphant election, under the fair and honorable nomination enjoyed by him, would be an act of unjustifiable persecution, an exhibition of personal spite and malignity with which no honest Democrat can sympathize, and calculated to clothe with dark suspicion the former motives avowed by its authors.

"*Resolved,* That the patriots of the Revolution in achieving and establishing the freedom and independence of these States, vindicated and asserted the great principle of popular sovereignty and equal rights as affirmed and declared in the late acts of Congress, organizing the territories of Nebraska and Kansas; that nature, and nature's God, appeal to the virtue, the integrity and intelligence of the people, to guard this precious principle as the ark of the covenant of their safety: and that the sufferings, the perils and the blood of the Revolution, will have been wasted in vain, and the dearest hopes of man on earth yielded up, when this great principle is sacrificed.

"*Resolved,* That the Missouri Compromise was an act of usurpation by Congress, and a fraud upon the people of these States: that Congress is sworn to uphold the Constitution and not to interpolate or destroy it: that any acquiescence in, or submission to, changes of the fundamental law by Congress, would be in the last degree dangerous to the liberties of the people: and that the repeal of the Missouri Compromise was a wise and necessary measure to efface from the statute books a precedent violation of the great charter of our independence and to arrest further insidious encroachments upon the great principle of popular sovereignty and equal rights."

Here is the Democratic platform—and we copy extracts from the letter of acceptance of Col. Wright—it is too long for publication entire. Also the letter announcing his nomination. It may be found in the files of this paper of the 20th of September, 1854.

STEELE'S HOTEL, Wilkes-Barre,
September 12, 1854.

HON. HENDRICK B. WRIGHT—

Dear Sir:—The Democratic Congressional Conference this day assembled and have placed you in nomination before the people of this District for Congress. The undersigned are a committee appointed by said Conference to communicate to you the fact and request your acceptance. In making this communication pleasure combines with duty. Your course upon the various measures which came before Congress, at the late session, has justly confirmed you in their confidence and regard. We refer especially to the great measure establishing the principle of popular sovereignty in the Territories of this Union—a principle vital to the security of every freeman: dear to his heart, and upon which is based his enjoyments of civil and religious freedom. We especially refer to this measure as first in importance. Your votes against squandering the public money in misnamed improvements being in accordance with the one settled policy of this District, is also gratifying to know. In your publicly expressed views upon religious toleration, we heartily accord. Your votes upon the Homestead bill, and in favor of old soldiers' rights, are true indexes of a hearty, sound and consistent Democrat. And it is our hearty prayer that the people appreciating their true interests may return you to Congress by a triumphant majority.

Your friends and fellow citizens,

JOHN DEEN, JR.,
HUDSON OWEN,
JOHN V. SMITH.

WILKES-BARRE, Sept. 14th, 1854.

* * * * *

"In the acceptance of the nomination which you have tendered me, and which was stamped with so much unanimity in the primary meetings of the people, I have no policy as to my future course to conceal. The journal of the last Congress will exhibit my course as to the past. No voter of this District shall have occasion to say I have deceived him. He who casts his vote for me, does it with full knowledge of my political faith. I assume that he who solicits the suffrage of the people for so high a place as a seat in the councils of this nation, should frankly and honestly avow his opinions. There should be no concealment—there should be no falsehood, as it is a post of honor, he who seeks to attain it, should be a man of honor, and resort to no low device;—no huckstering pretext to obtain it. You say, Gentlemen, that as to my course among "the various measures which came before Congress at the late session," and which elicits your "confidence and regard," you refer "especially to the great measure establishing the principle of popular sovereignty in the Territories of this Union—a principle vital to the security of every freeman—dear to his heart, and upon which is based his enjoyment of civil and religious freedom." Your allusion is to the bill establishing Territorial Government in Kansas and Nebraska. I spoke in favor of that bill. I voted for that bill—and as I then said, on the floor of Congress—I now repeat—that "I would rather be stricken down as the advocate of popular freedom, than be returned to the House in opposition to the great principle." Before taking my seat, I swore to support the Constitution of my country. Among its wise provisions, I found that, "The powers not delegated to the United States, by the constitution, nor prohibited by it to the States, are reserved to the States respectfully, or to the people." That power which was not conceded, to the general government, but reserved in the people, I resolved, so far as I was concerned, should remain there. Wisdom dictated the reservation and fanaticism should never change it. Congress had no power, even by implication, (an abhorrent doctrine at best) to interfere with law-making power of States or Territories. On the 6th of March, 1820, the 16th Congress passed an act establishing a territorial government for Missouri, in which was incorporated a provision that "slavery should be prohibited, north of thirty-six degrees and thirty minutes north latitude" in the territory ceded by France, under the name of Louisiana; thus implying that slavery should not be prohibited south of that line. In favor of the repeal of the law establishing this line, I cast my vote. I did so under the conviction that the power to make laws for the territories was, under the constitution, in "the people," and not in Congress. I had good reason to believe that the hardy pioneers who subdued the forests and broke up the prairies—who were exposed to the toils and privations of a frontier life—whose battles were with the wild beast and the savage, should not be deprived of making their own laws, as their situation and condition might warrant. That they were better judges of this than I; and to deprive them of this privilege would be an act of usurpation and tyranny. I desire that the people, who went to these new Territories, might go there as freemen, and not as slaves; and if in their good judgment, they pleased to make a slave Territory of it, it was no business of mine. However much I may condemn slavery as an abstract question, I had nothing to do with the act of the freemen of Kansas and Nebraska. My allegiance was to the Constitution. Had I been guilty of usurping that power which the people had expressly reserved to themselves, I should have committed a wrong; and done an act of gross injustice to the people of those Territories; to the people of my own State; to the people of this Union—and to liberal principles throughout the world—nay, I should have violated my solemn oath. To please fanaticism, I could not do this; nor could a reasonable man expect it of me."

* * * * * * * *

"I have been charged with treason for my vote on the Kansas and Nebraska bill! This is the kind of treason that rankled in the heart of Jefferson, when he had the temerity to assert the doctrine that the people were intelligent enough to govern themselves—and opposed to the idea of consolidated power. It was the treason of Jackson when he threw himself between the encroachments of the Federal government, and the sovereign rights of the States; in his vetoes of the Bank and the Maysville Road bill.

"**And the man who votes for sovereign power to remain with the enlightened freemen of this land; in the place of robbing them of it:—is the Traitor to whom I will cling—and to whom I will do reverence. The indefatigable and persevering pioneer, who settles these new territories as his home—and that of his children—who reclaims the wilderness and makes it blossom as the rose—**

who builds churches and school-houses;—and above all, who defends his country and supports her treasury, shall not by my act, or vote, be robbed of his civil rights—and denied the privilege of participating in making his own laws. I am not numbered among those philanthropists of these latter days—who yield the privilege of labor; of taxation—of battle,—to the citizens of Kansas and Nebraska, and deny him the right of making his own laws. If this be treason, then I am a traitor!—and along with me in this catalogue of treason—is Franklin Pierce, Lewis Cass, Stephen A. Douglas, R. M. T. Hunter—and one hundred and twelve members of the House of Representatives of the United States."

The foregoing extracts will show the plain and unmistakable platform of Col. Wright—and on the stump, from one end of the District to the other, he carried it out—dissembling nothing—publicly, everywhere, proclaiming the doctrine of his address.

What was Mr. Fuller and his friends at, about these times?

On the 12th of September 1854, (See *Record of the Times*, of the 13th of Sept.,) the Whig County Convention met. They nominated Mr. Fuller—and laid down for him, the following platform:

"*Resolved*, That while we question not the right to alter or amend any act of Congress by subsequent legislation, we view the passage of the act of the last session commonly called the 'Kansas Nebraska Bill,' as a wanton, unprovoked, and cruel violation of plighted faith between the Northern and Southern portions of this confederacy—wanton, because unrequired by the circumstances of that portion of the public domain—unprovoked, because to the extent of their ability the Northern States had fully executed the compromise measures of 1850—cruel, because destined to shackle with slavery a Territory larger than the old thirteen States.

"*Resolved*, That while we recognize and will carry out in good faith all our constitutional obligations, we are opposed to the extension of slavery beyond existing limits, and to any further increase of its power in the National Councils.

"*Resolved*, That sincerely holding these views, we do hereby mark the authors, aiders and abetters of that act as men unworthy the support of enlightened freemen for any office in their gift.

"*Resolved*, That we have undiminished confidence in Hon. H. M. Fuller, and that our conferees are instructed to use all honorable means to secure his re-nomination."

Then while they had "undimished confidence in Mr. Fuller," they "marked the aiders and abetters and authors of that act as men unworthy the support of enlightened freemen!!" As Mr. Fuller was not an "aider nor supporter" of the infamous act—he had the "confidence" of the party—Nay, the "undiminished confidence."

His conferees met—they nominated him—and soon after he and Judge Pollock started canvassing the District—as none of these speeches are reported we cannot give extracts. In the one at Tunkhannock, Mr. Fuller went further on the Abolition question than Gov. Pollock—they both denounced the Nebraska Kansas bill—and both pledged a repeal as far as was in their power.

They came to Wilkes-Barre—they both made speeches here—and both denounced the Kansas bill, and preached Know Nothingism. The Times of Oct. 4, 1854, says:

"After the Judge the Hon. H. M. Fuller spoke in his happiest style, and explained his position on the question of Slavery to the satisfaction of every freeman present."

That "exposition" was the repeal of Nebraska and the restoration of the Missouri line, and we can prove it by 100 witnesses on the ground!

From the paper of the same date we copy the following editorial:

"☞ Freemen bear in mind that the issue is not merely about men. Neither Wright nor Fuller—Pollock nor Bigler, has any claim personally thus to upheave the popular Masses, like ocean into mountain billows. In voting (a most sacred right) you express your opinions of the great question at issue. Pollock and Fuller stand before you as the representatives of Freedom, opposed to the extension of Slavery into Nebraska, Ohio, Pennsylvania, everywhere throughout the Union. Their opponents, Bigler and Co., justify the principle that would so extend Slavery. Which do you approve? A solemn question. Your votes will record your opinions."

This is the language of the Fuller organ? Does he call this Anti-Nebraska sentiments? Does he change his opinion? "Anti-Nebraska did not elect him." Out, out upon such hypocrisy! Neither Wright nor Fuller was the question? It was Freedon and Slavery.

We now copy from the Whig press—when it was said Mr. Fuller had changed his principles—the County press. The *Pittston Gazette*, a Whig paper, which warmly supported Mr. Fuller—in the issue of the 28th of Dec., 1855, holds this language:

"For one, we most heartily regret that our representative had not adhered to the position which was generally understood he occupied—namely that of an out and out anti-Nebraska man—opposed to the admission of Kansas upon any other terms than that slavery should not be tolerated there—and upon the subject of the Missouri compromise; that it should as an act of simple justice to the free States, be restored."

The *Scranton Herald*, another Whig county paper, and which also supported Mr. Fuller—in its columns of the 20th of December, 1855, discourses in this wise—and Mr. Fuller will not make an issue with either of these editors—nor will he say they have stated falsehoods:

"On the Nebraska question, the popular will is decidedly opposed to every motive and principle which was developed in its passage; whether it was designed to extend the curse of slavery, or to promote the aggrandizement of the demagogues who urged and accomplished its success. Mr. Fuller was understood to be the exponent of the will of the people in this question: to be as warmly devoted to the cause of freedom as any one among his constituents. In his speeches he openly and unreservedly avowed his principles to be in accordance with the known sentiments of the great mass of the people. His opponent was an ultra Nebraska man, and supposed to be the very antipodes of Mr. Fuller, in respect to all his political principles. If the latter has published on the floor of Congress any sentiment in conflict with these, he has proved false to the platform upon which he was sustained and elected."

"In his speeches, he openly and unreservedly avowed his principles." Not so, Mr. Lathrop! Mr. Fuller said in Congress, in the first place, that he would let Kansas and Nebraska alone, and now that "he was not elected by the Anti-Nebraska sentiment of his district." In your language, then, (and you were his political friend,) "he has proved false to the platfoım on which he was elected," and who doubts it?

We have thus copied from the three Whig journals in this county, all of which gave him an honest support, to show his platform, and we leave it to others to say whether his has been the conduct of an honorable man!

In Mr. Fuller's speech, in answer to Mr. Zollikoffer's question, he said, "my political existence commenced since that flood,"—the Wilmot Proviso. He should have said in it. We will show his Hyde Park letter hereafter; when he was running for Canal Commissioner, he wrote the celebrated Hyde Park letter, in which he fully endorses the Wilmot Proviso. We have not room for it now. And yet this man is applauded by Southern men when he tells them that "his political existence commenced since that flood." Southern men will be very careful what importance they give to Mr. Fuller's declarations. We will give the Hyde Park letter soon, and in the meantime let Southern men ask Mr. Fuller if he is not now a member of the committee appointed by the Black Republican convention, which met in Pittsburg, in this State, in September, 1855, and which nominated Passmore Williamson as their candidate for Canal Commissioner. He will hardly be bold enough to deny this, too. But judging from what he has said, no human power can tell what he may say hereafter.

Having denied that he was elected by the Anti-Nebraska sentiment of his district, when he gave pledge upon pledge to the Anti-Nebraska men, that if they would elect him, he would vote for the repeal of the law, and the restoration of the Missouri line, we cannot say what he will do next.

His own friends accuse him of having "falsified his platform"—it is his duty now either to acknowledge publicly that he has wantonly deceived them, or resign his seat, and go to some other district than this. He is little aware of the state of things with an injured and outraged constituency. He will know.

LIST OF MEMBERS

Of the House of Representatives of the United States. Thirty-fourth Congress—First Session. Commencing Monday, December 3, 1855.

Maine.

John M Wood, K. N.
John J. Perry, K. N.
Ebenezer Knowlton, K. N.
Samuel P. Benson,
Israel Washburn, Jr.
Thomas J. D. Fuller, D.—6.

New Hampshire.

James Pike, K. N.
Mason W. Tappan, K. N.
Aaron H. Cragin, K. N.—3.

Vermont.

James Meacham,
Justin S. Morrill, K. N.
Alvah Sabin.—3.

Massachusetts.

Robert B. Hall, K. N.
James Buffington, K. N.
William S. Damrell, K. N.
Linus B. Comins, K. N.
Anson Burlingame, K. N.
Timothy Davis, K. N.
Nath'l P. Banks, Jr., K. N.
Chauncey L. Knapp, K. N.
Alexander De Witt, K. N.
Calvin C. Chaffee, K. N.
Mark Trafton, K. N.—11.

Rhode Island.

Nathaniel B. Durfee, K. N.
Benj. B. Thurston, K. N.—2.

CONNECTICUT.

Ezra Clarke, Jr., K. N.
John Woodruff, K. N.
Sidney Dean, K. N.
Wm. W. Welch, K. N.—4.

NEW YORK.

William W. Valk, K. N.
James S. T. Stranahan, K. N.
Guy R. Pelton, K. N.
John Kelly, D.
Thomas R. Whitney, K. N.
John Wheeler, K. N.
Thomas Childs, Jr., K. N.
Abram Wakeman, K. N.
Bayard Clark, K. N.
Ambrose S. Murray,
Rufus H. King, K. N.
Killian Miller, K. N.
Russell Sage, K. N.
Samuel Dickson,
Edward Dodd, K. N.
George A. Simmons,
Francis E. Spinner,
Thomas R. Horton,
Jonas A. Hughston,
Orsamus B. Matteson, K. N.
Henry Bennett, K. N.
Andrew Z. McCarty, K. N.
William A. Gilbert,
Amos P. Granger,
Edwin B. Morgan,
Andrew Oliver,
John M. Parker,
William H. Kelsey,
John Williams,†
Benjamin Pringle, K. N.
Thomas T. Flagler, K. N.
Solomon G. Haven, K. N.
Fran. S. Edwards, K. N.—33.

NEW JERSEY.

Isaiah D. Clawson, K. N.
George R. Robbins, K. N.
James Bishop, K. N.
George Vail, D.
A. C. M. Pennington, K. N.—5.

PENNSYLVANIA.

Thomas B. Florence, D.
Job R. Tyson, K. N.
William Millward, K. N.
Jacob Broom, K. N.
John Cadwalader, D.
John Hickman, D.
Samuel C. Bradshaw, K. N.
J. Glancy Jones, D.
Anthony E. Roberts, K. N.
John C. Kunkel, K. N.
James H. Campbell, K. N.
Henry M. Fuller, K. N.
Asa Packer, D.
Galusha A. Grow,
John J. Pearce, K. N.
Lemuel Todd, K. N.
David F. Robison, K. N.
John R. Edie, K. N.
John Covode, K. N.
Jonathan Knight, K. N.
David Ritchie, K. N.
Samuel A. Purviance, K. N.
John Allison, K. N.
David Barclay, D.
John Dick, K. N.—25.

DELAWARE.

Elisha D. Cullen, K. N.—1.

MARYLAND.

James A. Stewart, D.
James B. Ricaud, K. N.
J. Morrison Harris, K. N.
H. Winter Davis, K. N.
Henry W. Hoffman, K. N.
Thomas F. Bowie,* D.—6.

VIRGINIA.

Thomas H. Bayly, D.
John S. Millson, D.
John S. Caskie, D.
William O. Goode, D.
Thomas S. Bocock, D.
Paulus Powell, D.
William Smith, D.
Charles J. Faulkner, D.
John Letcher, D.
Zedekiah Kidwell, D.
John S. Carlile, K. N.
Henry A. Edmundson, D.
Fayette McMullin, D.—13.

NORTH CAROLINA.

Robert T. Paine, K. N.
Thomas Ruffin, D.
Warren Winslow, D.
Lawrence O'B. Branch, D.
Edwin G. Reade, K. N.
Richard C. Puryear, K. N.
Burton Craige, D.
Thos. L. Clingman,* D.—8.

SOUTH CAROLINA.

John McQueen, D.
William Aiken, D.
Lawrence M. Keitt, D.
Preston S. Brooks, D.
James L. Orr, D.
William W. Boyce, D.—6.

GEORGIA.

James L. Seward, D.
Martin J. Crawford, D.
Robert P. Trippe, K. N.
Hiram Warner, D.
John H. Lumpkin, D.
Howell Cobb, D.
Nathaniel G Foster, K. N.
Alex. H. Stephens,* D.—8.

ALABAMA.

Percy Walker, K. N.
Eli S. Shorter, D.
James F. Dowdell, D.
William R. Smith, K. N.
George S. Houston, D.
Williamson R. W. Cobb, D.
Sampson W. Harris, D.—7.

MISSISSIPPI.

Daniel B. Wright, D.
Hendley S. Bennett, D.
William Barksdale, D.
William A. Lake, K. N.
John A. Quitman, D.—5.

LOUISIANA.

George Eustis, Jr., K. N.
Miles Taylor, D.
Thomas G. Davidson, D.
John M. Sandidge, D.—4.

OHIO.

Timothy C. Day,
John Scott Harrison, K. N.
Lewis D. Campbell, K. N.
Matthias H. Nichols,
Richard Mott,
J. Reece Emrie, K. N.
Samuel Galloway, K. N.
John Sherman, K. N.
Philemon Bliss,
William R. Sapp, K. N.
Edward Ball, K. N.
Charles J. Albright, K. N.

OHIO—(*Continued.*)

Aaron Harlan, K. N.
Benjamin Stanton, K. N.
Cooper K. Watson, K. N.
Oscar F. Moore, K. N.
Valentine B. Horton, K. N.
Benjamin F. Leiter, K. N.
Edward Wade,
Joshua R. Giddings,
John A. Bingham, K. N.—21.

KENTUCKY.

Henry C. Burnett, D.
John P. Campbell, K. N.
Warner L. Underwood, K. N.
Albert G. Talbott, D.
Joshua H. Jewett, D.
John M. Elliott, D.
Humphrey Marshall, K. N.
Alexander K. Marshall, K. N.
Leander M. Cox, K. N.
Samuel F. Swope, K. N.—10.

TENNESSEE.

Albert G. Watkins,* D.
William H. Sneed, K. N.
Samuel A. Smith, D.
John H. Savage, D.
Charles Ready, K. N.
George W. Jones, D.
John V. Wright, D.
Felix K. Zollicoffer, K. N.
Emerson Etheridge, K. N.
Thomas Rivers, K. N.—10.

INDIANA.

Smith Miller, D.
William H. English, D.
George G. Dunn,‡
William Cumback, K. N.
David P. Holloway, K. N.
Lucian Barbour, K. N.
Harvey D. Scott,‡
Daniel Mace, K. N.
Schuyler Colfax, K. N.
Samuel Brenton, K. N.
John U. Pettit.—11.

ILLINOIS.

Elihu B. Washburn,
James H. Woodworth,
Jesse O. Norton, K. N.
James Knox, K. N.
William A. Richardson, D.
Thomas L. Harris, D.
James C. Allen, D.
——— ———,
Samuel S. Marshall, D.—9.

MISSOURI.

Luther M. Kennet, K. N.
Gilchrist Porter,§
James J. Lindley, K. N.
Mordecai Oliver,* D.
John G. Miller,
John S. Phelps, D.
Samuel Caruthers,* D.—7.

ARKANSAS.

Alfred B. Greenwood, D.
Albert Rust, D.—2.

MICHIGAN.

William A. Howard, K. N.
Henry Waldron, K. N.
David S. Walbridge, K. N.
George W. Peck, D.—4.

FLORIDA.

Augustus E. Maxwell, D.—1.

TEXAS.

Lemuel D. Evans, K. N.
P. H. Bell, D.—2.

IOWA.

Augustus Hall, D.
James Thorington, K. N.—2.

WISCONSIN.

Daniel Wells, Jr., D.
Cadwalader C. Washburne,
Charles Billinghurst.—3.

CALIFORNIA.

James W. Denver, D.
Philip T. Herbert, D.—2.

Delegate from the Territory of Minnesota.

Henry M. Rice.—1.

Delegate from the Territory of Oregon.

Joseph Lane.—1.

Delegate from the Territory of New Mexico.

José Manuel Gallegos.—1.

Delegate from the Territory of Utah.

John M. Bernhisel.—1.

Delegate from the Territory of Washington.

J. Patton Anderson.—1.

Delegate from the Territory of Kansas.

John W. Whitfield.—1.

Delegate from the Territory of Nebraska.

Bird B. Chapman.—1.

K. N.—Know Nothings. D.—Democrats. Those in *italics* voting for Banks.
*—Formerly Whigs. †—Voting for J. L. Orr. ‡—Whigs voting for Pennington.
§—Whig voting for Fuller.

THE PHILADELPHIA HETEROGENEOUS "PSEUDO-*AMERICAN* KILKENNY CONVENTION, FEBRUARY THE 22D, 1856.

The Know Nothing party, from every locality, met in the city of Philadelphia on the 22d day of February, 1856, pursuant to orders, and put forth the following ticket:

For President, MILLARD FILLMORE, of New York.
For Vice President, ANDREW JACKSON donelson, of Tennessee.

Mr. Fillmore, Gen. Sam Houston, of Texas, and John M. Clayton, of Delaware, are the triumvirate that is said to have first organized the Know Nothing party in the United States; consequently, one of the *three* had to receive the nomination for President; and as Mr. Fillmore had absented himself from the scenes of political broils, on a tour to Europe, he was thought to be the most available to catch the votes of old line Whigs, anti-Cuba and fishy Democrats. We shall not pretend to raise the hackneyed cry of abolition against Mr. Fillmore; but suffice it to say, that a recurrence to his votes whilst a member of Congress, his Erie letter, his reprieve of two negro-stealers whilst President, and his nomination without a platform—with nothing to bind him—without a pledge to carry out; all go to show that, if elected, he will adopt a programme most suited to his taste, and to the tastes of the innumerable isms that will evidently rally to his support.

To show that Andrew Jackson donelson, the candidate upon this Kilkenny ticket for the Vice Presidency, regarded Mr. Fillmore unsound upon the subject of slavery, as late as the spring of 1851, we have only to introduce what Andrew Jackson donelson says upon that subject whilst editor of the Union.

We copy from the Washington Union, May the 17th, 1851.

MR. FILLMORE AND ABOLITION.

The special organ complains of our allusion to the part which Mr. Fillmore acted on the abolition question, alleging that in the last election, "*it was the staple of stump speeches and party resolutions, and the American people elected Mr. Fillmore to the Vice Presidency in spite of it.*" According to the logic of the special organ, the statute of limitations exculpates entirely the agency of the Whig party in giving birth and dignity to political Anti-Slavery in order to secure the election of General Taylor and Mr. Fillmore, but must be interpreted in the very opposite sense when it suits its convenience to assert that the Democratic party is responsible for the Buffalo platform, and for the combination which elected Mr. Sumner to the Senate of the United States. This kind of logic will not do, and is so contrary to the rules of common sense, that we are inclined to think it is only a way the special organ has of manifesting its ill-will that two such distinguished members of the cabinet as Messrs. Webster and Corwin should have left us some records on the subject which make *the true logic* one of the qualities that must ever be excluded from the *Republic.* Did not Mr. Corwin implore the Abolitionists to vote for Mr. Fillmore, saying, *they are my children—my Whig children? Did not Mr. Webster say the same thing, in substance, when he reproached the Buffalo plat-*

form as a theft—an illicit taking of Whig property? But the special organ, admitting all this, says, in substance, *Did not the people elect Mr. Fillmore in spite of it? And can it be supposed that anything which Mr. Fillmore did before the last election is to have any weight in determining his claims as the present candidate of the Whig party for the Presidency?*

This is the point which we wished to see distinctly put by the special organ, in order that our readers may not mistake the lame and impotent defence which it sets up for the *invincibility* of the present administration. Instead of making the manly declaration which the truth demands, that the combination by which Gen. Taylor was elected implicated the Whig party, both as the author of political anti-slavery and the beneficiary of all the results of the power it bestowed—instead, we say, of admitting what is as clear as daylight on this subject, and founding the desire of Mr. Fillmore to be elected to the Presidency on the magnanimity of his countrymen, who might forgive such a fault in the presence of the credit which is due to him for his conduct as the present head of the administration—the special organ prefers to persevere in charging unjustly the Democratic party, which has nobly defied the incendiary spirit of abolition in all the stages of its encroachment on the peace and harmony of the land.

But if in this respect the special organ is unfortunate, it is not less so in maintaining that the election of Mr. Fillmore to the presidency precludes an inquiry into the objections which were made to him during that canvass. This is indeed strange logic, whether applied to morals, laws, or politics. The wrong done by individuals or parties is often not really understood until the authors have been long in possession of the advantage which tempted them to commit the wrong. If such logic were recognised by the people—if the objections made to the election of an individual to the presidency are to be considered as invalidated by his success—one of the highest safeguards against the dangers of party spirit would be withdrawn. Such logic would have kept John Quincy Adams in power; for all the faults of his administration were anticipated, as the natural result of his unsound political principles, by those who opposed his election. Yet it did not avail him to say to the American people that the objections made to his re-election had been disposed of by his first election, and to plead that, if they were true, the constituted authorities ought never to have trusted him with the highest office in the gift of the republic.

We assure the special organ that we have no desire to profit by the very bad defence it makes for Mr. Fillmore, when it tells us that we ought not to go back to the circumstances which connect him with the abolition societies; but we insist upon it that common justice claims for the democratic party the merit of not being responsible for the sins of those societies, by whose influence, we feel authorized in saying, the whig ticket succeeded at the last election. It will not do to answer this demand for justice by saying that the Erie letter "*was printed and reprinted ten thousand times*" during the last election, nor that Gen. Campbell asserts that he "*knew Mr. Fillmore to be as free from abolition sentiments as any man in the North.* Gen. Campbell cannot be presumed to know Mr. Fillmore as well as Messrs. Webster and Corwin, whose testimony is before the whole country, proving, beyond all doubt or dispute, that abolition and free-soil were the property of whiggery, relied upon for a political purpose, and never abondoned until it was seen that a political power thus organized could not exist without destroying our Constitution and Union.

But it is not alone on this question of the responsibility of the administration for the evils of political anti-slavery, that we think the defence of the special organ will be, and ought to be, unsatisfactory to the country. When we stated facts proving the inadequate protection of our interests on our Mexican frontier, the reply set up was that we seemed disposed to take the side of the Mexican government; or that at best, all that could be made out of that fact was, that a democratic Congress had left the War Department without means for the next fiscal year, *which does not commence until the first of July next.* All the means were granted that were asked for during the past two years; and yet the frontier was not defended during that time, and the singular excuse is given that the appropriations for the estimates of the next year were not what the heads of bureaus had desired. What relation could there be between such appropriations and the depredations of Indians that had occurred a year before, and to prevent which there had been the most ample means provided by Congress?

Who is ANDREW JACKSON donelson? The adopted son of President Jackson? No! Far from it. ANDREW JACKSON donelson is the nephew, if we are correctly informed, of the wife of President Jackson, and was named for the express purpose of inheriting the estate of General Jackson; but Old Hickory not fancying the gentleman, adopted Andrew Donelson, also a nephew of his wife, and had his name changed from Andrew Donelson to Andrew Jackson, Jr. Therefore Andrew Jackson, Jr., inherited the whole of the Old Hero's estate, and is now quietly residing at the Hermitage. ANDREW JACKSON donelson (of Tulip Hill) is no more the adopted son of President Jackson than a man unborn, but on the other hand, is a pompous renegade of great pretensions, with the faculty of presumption developed at the expense of all the rest of the bumps.

CONCLUDING REMARKS.

In the foregoing compilation of political matter, we have thought it unnecessary in the majority of instances, to make any prefatory remarks, as the whole object has been to present and preserve such articles, letters and speeches as were elicited during, antecedent and subsequent to the great fight of the South against Know Nothingism. Some portions of the work will show the consequences and disorganized state of things resulting from the influence of Know Nothingism; whilst other parts are designed for reference in the approaching Presidential election; and to show that the Democratic party is the only palladium of this great Republic.

INDEX.

WYTHE'S VIRGINIA REPORTS.

Decisions of Cases in Virginia, by the High Court of Chancery, with remarks upon decrees by the Court of Appeals reversing some of those decisions, by George Wythe, Chancellor of said court. Second and only complete edition. With a Memoir of the Author, Analysis of the Cases, and an Index, by B. B. Minor, L.B. And with an Appendix, containing references to cases in Pari Materia, an Essay on Lapse, Joint Tenants and Tenants in Common, &c., &c., by Wm. Green, Esq. 8vo. sheep, $4.

All of the old editions of this work are imperfect, and yet copies have been sold at auction as high as $ 10, such has been the demand for it.

New and only complete edition.

Published by

J. W. RANDOLPH.

MATHEWS' GUIDE.

A Guide to Commissioners in Chancery, with practical forms for the discharge of their duties; adapted to the new Code of Virginia, by James M. Mathews, Attorney at Law, author of "Digest of the Laws of Virginia." 8vo. sheep, $ 2 50. Every Commissioner should have a copy of the work.

Published by

J. W. RANDOLPH.

HENING AND MUNFORD'S VIRGINIA REPORTS.

New edition. 4 vols. 8vo. sheep, $ 20.

Reports of Cases argued and determined in the Supreme Court of Appeals of Virginia, with select cases, relating chiefly to points of practice decided by the Superior Chancery for the Richmond district; by Wm. W. Hening and Wm. Munford. A new edition, with memoirs of the judges whose decisions are reported; the present rules of the Court of Appeals, and of the Chancery Court in Richmond; references to the subsequent decisions of the Court of Appeals, and to existing statutes in pari materia, with the points herein reported, and a list of the cases over-ruled, edited by B. B. Minor, L.B.

Published by

J. W. RANDOLPH.

RULES OF THE COURTS.

Rules of the Court of Appeals from its establishment to the present time. Also, Rules of the District Courts of Fredericksburg and Williamsburg. 8vo. paper, 12c. The only complete edition.

Published by

J. W. RANDOLPH.

NORTH CAROLINA AND VIRGINIA.

The Westover Manuscripts, containing a History of the Dividing Line betwixt Virginia and North Carolina; a Journey to the Land of Eden; A. D. 1733; a Progress to the Mines; written from 1728 to 1736, and now first published; by William Byrd, of Westover. 8vo. boards, $ 1 25.

For sale by

J. W. RANDOLPH.

PLANTATION BOOK.

Plantation and Farm Instruction, Regulation, Record, Inventory and Account Book, for the use of Managers of Estates and for the better ordering and management of plantation and farm business in every particular. By a Southern Planter. "Order is heaven's first law." 4to., hf. roan, $ 2.

This Book is by one of the best and most systematic farmers in Virginia, and experienced farmers have expressed the opinion that those who use it will save hundreds of dollars.

Published by J. W. RANDOLPH.

RUFFIN ON MANURES.

An Essay on Calcareous Manures, by Edmund Ruffin, a practical Farmer of Virginia from 1812: Founder and sole Editor of the Farmers' Register; Member and secretary of the former State Board of Agriculture; formerly Agricultural Surveyor of the State of South Carolina; and president of the Virginia State Agricultural Society. Fifth edition, amended and enlarged. Fine edition, 8vo., printed on good paper, and strongly bound, library style, $ 2; cheap edition, 12mo., muslin, $ 1 25.

Published by J. W. RANDOLPH,
Richmond, Va.

JEFFERSON'S NOTES.

Notes on the State of Virginia. By Thomas Jefferson. Illustrated with a map of Virginia, Maryland, Delaware and Pennsylvania. A New Edition, prepared by the Author, containing many Notes and Plates never before published. 8vo. muslin, $ 2 50.

Published by J. W. RANDOLPH.

CAMPBELL'S VIRGINIA.

Introduction to the History of the Colony and Ancient Dominion of Virginia, by Charles Campbell. 8vo. muslin, $ 1 50.

"Mr. Campbell's History of Virginia is presented to the public in a very unpretending form, and is written in a clear, agreeable and manly style, without affectation, with new and elaborate conceits of expression, and defaced by no ambitious and deliberate flights of rhetoric. The subject is a good one, and it is treated as if the author felt assured of its intrinsic attractions. He has evidently scrutinized the appropriate evidences in their sources, and the reader may repose with confidence in his statements."—*North Amer. Review.*

Published by

J. W. RANDOLPH.

VIRGINIA DEBATES OF 1798.

The Virginia Report of 1799-1800, touching the Alien and Sedition Laws, together with the Virginia Resolutions of December 21, 1798, the debate and proceedings thereon in the House of Delegates of Virginia, and several other documents illustrative of the Report and Resolutions. New edition. 8vo. half calf, $ 1 50.

Published by

J. W. RANDOLPH.

www.ingramcontent.com/pod-product-compliance
Lightning Source LLC
LaVergne TN
LVHW021244110826
845150LV00002B/403